Windows® Communication Foundation 4 Step by Step

John Sharp

Published with the authorization of Microsoft Corporation by:
O'Reilly Media, Inc.
1005 Gravenstein Highway North
Sebastopol, California 95472

Printed and bound in the United States of America.

1 2 3 4 5 6 7 8 9 M 5 4 3 2 1 0

Microsoft Press titles may be purchased for educational, business or sales promotional use. Online editions are also available for most titles (*http://my.safaribooksonline.com*). For more information, contact our corporate/institutional sales department: (800) 998-9938 or *corporate@oreilly.com*. Visit our website at *microsoftpress.oreilly.com*. Send comments to *mspinput@microsoft.com*.

Acquisitions and Development Editor: Russell Jones
Production Editor: Kristen Borg
Production Services: Octal Publishing, Inc.
Technical Reviewer: Ashish Ghoda and Kenn Scribner
Indexing: Potomac Indexing, LLC
Cover: Karen Montgomery
Illustrator: Robert Romano

978-0-735-64556-1

Contents at a Glance

Table of Contents

What do you think of this book? We want to hear from you!

Microsoft is interested in hearing your feedback so we can continually improve our books and learning
resources for you. To participate in a brief online survey, please visit:

www.microsoft.com/learning/booksurvey/

Acknowledgments

On the back cover of his book, "Dirk Gently's Holistic Detective Agency," Douglas Adams depicts an invoice presented by Mr. Gently to his client for attempting to find her missing cat. It contains the following items:

Item	Charge
Finding cat (deceased)	£50.00
Detecting and triangulating vectors of interconnectedness of all things	£150.00
Tracing same to beach on Bahamas, fare and accommodation	£1500.00
Struggling on in face of draining skepticism from client, drinks	£327.00
Saving the human race from total extinction	No charge

Douglas Adams's book was published in 1987, but 23 years later I find myself empathizing with Dirk Gently. Happily, my own beloved feline, Ginger, is still very much with us, but in common with many service-oriented developers these days, I spend more and more time searching for solutions that enable me to connect all things together. Clearly, my home office is not quite a beach on the Bahamas, but I do admit to enjoying a decent amount of time sunning myself in the stands at Edgbaston (the home of Warwickshire County Cricket Club) watching batsmen attempting to endanger workmen building the new pavilion with lofted drives over the boundary, while I contemplate how to configure pieces of software to get them to interoperate and communicate correctly. My wife is always a little skeptical of how our jaunts to see how Warwickshire fares against other county cricket teams amounts to "work," but she enjoys the cricket as much as I do, so she does not complain.

In the world of connected solutions, Microsoft Windows Communication Foundation has proved an absolute boon, and although I am yet to be convinced that it has saved the human race from extinction, I have authored papers and even produced a video on how using WCF can help to save your organization (this may be hyperbole, but you know what we technophiles are like when we desperately want to convince management of the need to invest in new software and machinery!). To this end, I always count it an absolute privilege whenever I get the chance to write in depth about fun, new technology; as I mentioned in the previous edition of this book, I thank all at Content Master for allowing me to spend a significant amount of my time doing it.

It would also be very remiss of me not to thank Russell Jones at O'Reilly Media, who badgered me and patiently waited while I found the time to get started on this project as well as for all his support and help in editing and correcting my grammar during the initial drafts of each chapter, and to Bob Russell at Octal Publishing, who had the unrewarding job of having to wade through every chapter seeking out any remaining "British-isms." Additionally, sincere thanks are due to Ashish Ghoda and Kenn Scribner who took on the daunting task of checking the technical accuracy of my work and who provided valuable advice, guidance, and corrections whenever I was wrong (any remaining technical errors in the book are my own, of course). Also, thanks to Lin Joyner at Content Master, who expended a significant effort at great personal risk to her own sanity, for agreeing to test many of the exercises for me.

Finally, I must pay the greatest tribute to my long-suffering family: to Diana, my wife and fellow cricket-watcher, who is never short of advice when seeing a batsman struggle against a short-pitched delivery ("Just hit the ball!"); to James who grew up and left home to go to university while I was writing Chapter 17; and to Francesca who has learned from my wife what it takes to make a truly excellent cup of tea.

And to Ginger—please stop trying to walk across my keyboard as I type.

—John Sharp

Introduction

Microsoft Windows Communication Foundation (WCF), alongside Windows Workflow Foundation (WF) and Windows Presentation Foundation (WPF), has become part of the primary framework for building the next wave of business applications for the Microsoft Windows operating system. WCF provides the underpinning technology driving distributed solutions based on the Microsoft platform; with it, you can build powerful service-oriented systems designed to address connected services and applications. WCF is also an integral technology for building and accessing services running in the cloud under Windows Azure.

You can use WCF to create new services as well as augment and interoperate with many existing services created by using other technologies. When designing distributed applications in the past, you frequently had to choose a specific technology, such as Web services, COM+, Microsoft Message Queue, or .NET Framework Remoting. That choice often had a fundamental impact on the architecture of your solutions. In contrast, WCF provides a consistent model for implementing scalable and extensible systems that employ a variety of technologies with which you can design and architect your solutions without being restricted by a specific connectivity mechanism.

In short, if you are building professional, service-oriented solutions for Windows, you need to learn about WCF.

Who This Book Is For

This book will show you how to build connected applications and services using WCF. If you are involved in designing, building, or deploying applications for the Microsoft Windows operating system, sooner or later you are going to need to become familiar with WCF. This book will give you the initial boost you need to quickly learn many of the techniques required to create systems based on WCF. The book takes a pragmatic approach, covering the concepts and details necessary to enable you to build connected solutions.

Assumptions

To get the most from this book, you should meet the following profile:

- You should be an architect, designer, or developer who will be creating solutions for the Microsoft Windows family of operating systems.

- You should have experience developing applications using Visual Studio and C#.

- You should have a basic understanding of concepts such as transactions, Web services, security, and message queuing.

Finding Your Best Starting Point in This Book

This book is designed to help you build skills in a number of essential areas. It assumes that you are new to WCF and takes you step by step through the fundamental concepts of WCF, feature by feature. The techniques and ideas that you see in one chapter are extended by those in subsequent chapters; therefore, most readers should follow the chapters in sequence and perform each of the exercises. However, if you have specific requirements or are only interested in certain aspects of WCF, you can use the table below to find your best route through this book.

If you are	Follow these steps
New to Web services and distributed applications and need to gain a basic understanding of WCF.	1. Install the code samples as described in the "Code Samples" section of this Introduction. 2. Work through Chapters 1 to 5 sequentially and perform the exercises. 3. Complete Chapters 6 to 18 as your level of experience and interest dictates.
New to Web services and distributed applications and need to learn how to use WCF to implement solutions using common Web services features such as sessions, transactions, and reliable messaging.	1. Install the code samples as described in the "Code Samples" section of this Introduction. 2. Work through Chapters 1 to 10 sequentially and perform the exercises. 3. Complete Chapters 11 to 18 as your level of experience and interest dictates.
Familiar with Web services and distributed applications, and need to learn about WCF quickly, including its advanced features.	1. Install the code samples as described in the "Code Samples" section of this Introduction. 2. Skim the first chapter for an overview of WCF, but perform the exercises. 3. Read Chapter 2 and perform the exercises. 4. Skim Chapter 3. 5. Read Chapters 4 and 5 and complete the exercises. 6. Skim Chapters 6 to 10, performing the exercises that interest you. 7. Complete the remaining chapters and exercises.
Familiar with security concepts but need to understand how to use the security features that WCF provides.	1. Install the code samples as described in the "Code Samples" section of this Introduction. 2. Skim the first three chapters. 3. Read Chapters 4 and 5 and perform the exercises. 4. Skim Chapters 6 to 15. 5. Read Chapter 17 and complete the exercises. 6. Skim Chapter 18.

If you are	Follow these steps
Referencing the book after working through the exercises.	1. Use the index or the Table of Contents to find information about particular subjects. 2. Read the Summary sections at the end of each chapter to find a brief review of the concepts and techniques presented in the chapter.

Conventions and Features in This Book

This book presents information using conventions designed to make the information readable and easy to follow. Before you start, read the following list, which explains conventions you'll see throughout the book and points out helpful features that you might want to use:

- Each exercise is a series of tasks. Each task is presented as a series of numbered steps (1, 2, 3, and so on). A bullet (■) indicates an exercise that has only one step.

- Reader aids labeled "Note" and "Tip" provide additional information or alternative methods for completing a step successfully.

- Reader aids labeled "Important" alert you to information you need to check before continuing.

- Text that you type appears in **bold**.

- A plus sign (+) between two key names means that you must press those keys at the same time. For example, "Press Alt+Tab" means that you hold down the Alt key *while* you press the Tab key.

System Requirements

You'll need the following hardware and software to complete the practice exercises in this book:

- Microsoft Windows 7 Professional, Enterprise, or Ultimate editions.

> **Note** Some of the exercises require you to create local users and security groups. This feature is not available with Windows 7 Home Basic or Home Premium editions.

- Microsoft Visual Studio 2010 Professional, Premium, Ultimate, or Test Professional editions, including SQL Server 2008 Express.

Note The exercises in this book are not intended to work with Visual Studio 2010 Express edition.

- 1.6 GHz or faster 32-bit (x86) or 64-bit (x64) processor.

- 1 GB RAM (32-bit) or 2 GB RAM (64-bit).

- 20 GB available hard disk space (32-bit) or 25 GB (64-bit).

- DirectX 9 graphics device with WDDM 1.0 or higher driver.

- Microsoft mouse (or compatible) pointing device.

Some of the exercises require that you have installed Internet Information Services (IIS) and Message Queuing (MSMQ). You will also need the *AdventureWorks* database provided with the code samples for this book. Download and installation instructions are provided later in this introduction.

 Important If you have other tools or services that establish network connections, you may need to temporarily halt them if they use the same ports required by the exercises in this book (alternatively, you can replace the port numbers referenced by the exercises with others of your own choice). For example, some of the exercises reference port 8080. If you have the Apache Web server running on your development computer, it defaults to using port 8080, so you may need to halt or reconfigure this service.

Code Samples

Follow these steps to download and install the code samples and other companion content on your computer so that you can use them with the exercises:

1. Navigate to *http://oreilly.com/catalog/9780735645561/*.

2. Click the Companion Content link.

   You'll see instructions for downloading the .zip archive containing the companion content files.

3. Unpack the .zip archive into your Documents folder. This action creates the following folder containing the exercise and solution files for each chapter:

   Microsoft Press\WCF Step By Step

Installing and Configuring Internet Information Services and Microsoft Message Queue

Many of the exercises in this book require you to build WCF services hosted by using Internet Information Services (IIS). You must make sure that you have installed and configured IIS on your computer, and you must have installed ASP.NET version 4.0 with IIS. Additionally, some exercises use Microsoft Message Queue (MSMQ) as the transport for connecting client applications to services, so you must also install the MSMQ Server Core. The following instructions describe how to do this. Note that you require administrative access to your computer to install and configure IIS and MSMQ.

1. Log on to Windows as an account that has Administrator access.

2. On the Windows Start menu, click Control Panel, and then click Programs. In the Programs pane, under Programs And Features, click Turn Windows Features On Or Off.

3. In the Windows Features dialog box, expand Internet Information Services, and then select the following features:

   ❑ Web Management Tools | IIS Management Console

   ❑ Web Management Tools | IIS 6 Management Compatibility | IIS 6 Metabase and IIS 6 Configuration Compatibility

   ❑ World Wide Web Services | Application Development Features | ASP.NET (this will also select .NET Extensibility, ISAPI Extensions, and ISAPI Filters)

   ❑ World Wide Web Services | Common Http Features | Directory Browsing (Default Document should already be selected)

   ❑ World Wide Web Services | Security | Basic Authentication and World Wide Web Services | Security | Windows Authentication (Request Filtering should already be selected)

4. Expand Microsoft Message Queue (MSMQ) Server, and then select Microsoft Message Queue (MSMQ) Server Core (do not select the individual items in the Microsoft Message Queue (MSMQ) Server Core folder).

5. Click OK, and then wait for the features to be installed and configured.

Installing ASP.NET Version 4.0

The exercises in this book rely on ASP.NET Version 4.0 being installed and configured with IIS. To do this, perform the following tasks:

1. On the Windows Start menu, click All Programs, click Microsoft Visual Studio 2010, click Visual Studio Tools, right-click Visual Studio Command Prompt (2010), and then click Run As Administrator. In the User Account Control dialog box, click Yes.

2. In the Visual Studio Command Prompt window, type the following command:

    ```
    aspnet_regiis -iru
    ```

3. When the command has completed, leave the Visual Studio Command Prompt window open; you will use it again after installing the *AdventureWorks* database.

Installing and Configuring the *AdventureWorks* Database

The exercises and examples in this book make use of the *AdventureWorks* sample database. If you don't already have this database installed on your computer, a copy of the database installation program is supplied with the companion content for this book. Follow these steps to install and configure the database:

1. Log on to Windows as an account that has administrator access if you have not already done so.

2. Verify that the SQL Server (SQLEXPRESS) service is running.

> **Tip** Start the SQL Configuration Manager utility in the Configuration Tools folder, located in the Microsoft SQL Server 2008 program group. In the left pane, click SQL Server Services. In the right pane, examine the status of the SQL Server (SQLEXPRESS) service. If the status is Stopped, right-click the service, and then click Start. Wait for the status to change to Running, and then close SQL Configuration Manager.

3. Using Windows Explorer, move to the Microsoft Press\WCF Step By Step\Setup folder located within your Documents folder.

4. Double-click the file AdventureWorks2008_SR4.exe. If the User Account Control dialog box appears, click Yes.

5. Wait while the WinZip Self-Extractor tool unzips the installation program.

6. When the SQL Server 2008R2 Database Installer dialog box appears, read the license agreement. If you agree with the license terms, select the I Accept The License Terms check box, and then click Next.

7. On the AdventureWorks 2008 Community Sample Database SR4 page, set the Installation Instance to SQLEXPRESS, select the *AdventureWorks OLTP* database, deselect all other databases, and then click Install.

> **Note** Make sure that you select the AdventureWorks OLTP database and *not* Adventure-Works OLTP 2008. Depending on how you have configured SQL Server, not all databases will be available anyway, and you may see a warning icon against some of these databases. You can ignore these warnings because these databases are not required.

8. On the Installation Execution page, wait while the database is installed and configured, and then click Finish.

8. Return to the Visual Studio Command Prompt window running as Administrator in the Microsoft Press\WCF Step By Step\Setup folder.

9. Type the following command:

```
osql -E -S .\SQLEXPRESS -i aspnet.sql
```

This command should complete without any errors (it will display a series of prompts, "1> 2> 1> 1> 2> 1> 1> 2> 1> 2> 1>").

> **Note** The script aspnet.sql creates user accounts for the DefaultAppPool and ASP.NET v4.0 applications pools used by IIS and grants these accounts access to the *AdventureWorks* database.

10. Close the Visual Studio Command Prompt window.

Using the Code Samples

Each chapter in this book explains when and how to use any code samples for that chapter. When it's time to use a code sample, the book will list the instructions for how to open the files. The chapters are built around scenarios that simulate real programming projects, so you can easily apply the skills you learn to your own work.

For those of you who like to know all the details, following is a list of the code sample, Visual Studio projects, and solutions, grouped by the folders where you can find them.

> **Important** Many of the exercises require administrative access to your computer. Make sure you perform the exercises using an account that has this level of access.

Solution Folder	Description
Chapter 1	
Completed\ProductsService	This solution gets you started. Creating the ProductsService project leads you through the process of building a simple WCF service hosted by IIS. You can use the service to query and update product information in the *AdventureWorks* database.
	The ProductsClient project is a console-based WCF client application that connects to the *ProductsService* service. You use this project for testing the WCF service.
Chapter 2	
ProductsClient	This solution is the starting point for the exercises in this chapter. It contains a copy of the completed client application from Chapter 1.
Completed\ProductsClient	This solution contains a version of the client application that connects to the *ProductsService* service by using a TCP connection.
Completed\HostedProducts ServiceHost	This solution contains Windows Presentation Foundation application that provides a host environment for the *ProductsService* service. You use this application to manually start and stop the service.
	You configure the ProductsClient application to connect to the service hosted by this application by using an HTTP endpoint.
Completed\WindowsProduct Service	This solution contains a Windows Service that hosts the *Products Service* service. You can start and stop the service from the Services applet in the Windows Control Panel.
	You reconfigure the ProductsClient application to connect to this service by using an endpoint based on the Named Pipe transport.
Chapter 3	
ProductsServiceFault	This solution contains a copy of the ProductsServiceLibrary, Products ServiceHost, and ProductsClient applications from Chapter 2. It is used as a starting point for the exercises in this chapter.
Completed\UntypedProducts ServiceFault	The *ProductsService* service in this solution traps exceptions and reports them back to the client application as untyped SOAP faults, which are caught and handled by the ProductsClient application.
Completed\StronglyTyped ProductsServiceFault	The *ProductsService* service in this solution reports exceptions as typed SOAP faults, defined by using fault contracts. The Products Client application catches these strongly typed SOAP faults as exceptions.
Chapter 4	
ProductsService	This solution contains three projects: the *ProductsService* service, the ProductsServiceHost application, and the ProductsClient. These projects are configured to catch and handle SOAP faults, as described in Chapter 3. This solution forms the starting point for the exercises in this chapter.

Solution Folder	Description
Chapter 4 (continued)	
Completed\NetTcpProducts ServiceWithMessageLevelSecurity	This solution contains an implementation of the *ProductsService* service, the ProductsServiceHost application, and the Products Client applications that applies message-level security over a TCP binding.
Completed\BasicHttpProducts ServiceWithTransportLevel Security	This solution shows how to implement transport-level security over an HTTP binding.
Completed\WS2007Http ProductsServiceWithMessage LevelSecurity	This version of the solution contains a host that implements message-level security over an HTTP binding.
Completed\ProductsService WithBasicAuthentication	This solution contains a version of the *ProductsService* service that implements basic authentication and displays the name of the user calling the *ListProducts* operations. The client application explicitly provides the name and password of the user connecting to the service.
Completed\ProductsService WithWindowsAuthentication	This solution is similar to the previous one, except that the *Products Service* service implements Windows authentication. The credentials for the client application are picked up from the user's login session.
Completed\ProductsService WithAuthorization	The *ProductsService* service in this solution authorizes users according to the Windows security group to which they belong. Users that do not belong to a specified security group are denied access when they attempt to invoke operations.
Chapter 5	
ProductsClient	This folder contains a copy of the client application that is used for testing the various configurations of the *InternetProductsService* service in this chapter.
Completed\ASPNETMembership	This solution contains the *InternetProductsService* service that is deployed to IIS and authenticates users by using the ASP.NET Role Provider rather than Windows security groups.
Completed\ASPNETMemberShip UsingCertificates	The *InternetProductsService* service in this solution uses the ASP. NET Role Provider in conjunction with certificates to authenticate users.
Completed\MutualAuthentication UsingCertificates	The *InternetProductsService* service in this solution uses a certificate to authenticate itself to the client application.
Chapter 6	
ProductsService	This solution contains an amended copy of the ProductsClient, ProductsServiceLibray, and ProductsServiceHost projects from Chapter 4. The service implements message-level security and authenticates users by using Windows tokens. This solution is used as the starting point for the exercises in this chapter.

Solution Folder	Description
Chapter 6 (continued)	
ProductsServiceWithVersioned ServiceContract	This solution contains an implementation of the *ProductsService* service and a client application that provides these two versions of the service contract. It is used by some of the exercises in the second part of the chapter.
Completed\ProductsService WithProtectedOperations	This solution contains a version of the *ProductsService* service in which client applications are required to encrypt and sign request messages for some operations, but only sign requests for others. The proxy class in the ProductsClient application has been updated to encrypt and sign, or just sign messages, as appropriate. The purpose of this solution is to show how changing security requirements for operations can break a service contract.
Completed\ProductsService WithAdditionalBusinessLogic	The *ProductsService* service in this solution contains additional methods. However, because these methods implement internal logic for the service and are not exposed as part of the service contract, they do not require that existing client applications are updated.
Completed\ProductsService WithModifiedServiceContract	This solution contains a version of the *ProductsService* service with an additional operation and a modified service contract. The client application has not been updated, but it still works although it cannot invoke the new operation.
Completed\ProductsService WithVersionedServiceContract	The *ProductsService* service in this solution exposes two versions of the service contract, enabling existing client applications to use the old contract while exposing the additional operation to new client applications.
Completed\ProductsServiceWith AdditionalFieldsInDataContract	This solution shows the effects that modifying a data contract can have on client applications and how you can implement a data contract that supports clients expecting different versions of a data contract.
Chapter 7	
Completed\ShoppingCart	This solution contains a completed version of the initial *Shopping CartService* service that implements shopping cart functionality and a client application that exercises this functionality. This solution is used as the basis for subsequent exercises in this chapter.
Completed\ ShoppingCartContextModes	The *ShoppingCartService* service in this solution demonstrates the use of the Single instance context mode.
Completed\ShoppingCartWith State	The *ShoppingCartService* service in this solution uses the *PerCall* instance context mode and contains code that saves the instance state to XML files.
Completed\ShoppingCart WIthSequencedOperations	This solution shows how to control the sequence in which a client application can invoke operations and control the lifetime of a session.

Solution Folder	Description
Chapter 7 (continued)	
DurableShoppingCart	This solution contains a version of the *ShoppingCartService* service that implements the *PerSession* instance context mode. The solution also contains a GUI client application called Shopping CartGUIClient. This solution is used by exercises that convert the *ShoppingCartService* service into a durable service.
Completed\DurableShoppingCart	This solution contains a completed implementation of the durable version of *ShoppingCartService* service.
Chapter 8	
Completed\ProductsWorkflow	This solution contains a workflow service called *ProductsWork flowService* that retrieves the details of a specified product. The solution also includes a basic console client application to test the service.
Completed\ProductsWorkflow WithFaultHandling	The *ProductsWorkflowService* service in this solution shows how to catch exceptions in a service and send SOAP faults to a client application.
ProductsClient	This version of the client application for the *ProductsWorkflow Service* service that generates SOAP faults.
Completed\ProductsWorkflow WithIISDeployment	This solution shows how to deploy the *ProductsWorkflowService* service to IIS.
Completed\ProductsWorkflow WithCustomHost	This solution demonstrates how to create a custom host application for a workflow service.
Completed\ShoppingCartService	This solution contains a completed version of the *ShoppingCart Service* service implemented as a workflow service.
ShoppingCartGUIClient	This is a copy of the ShoppingCartGUIClient developed in Chapter 7. It is used to test the workflow version of the *ShoppingCartService* service.
Completed\ShoppingCartWith HostAndClient	This solution contains a complete version of the workflow version of the *ShoppingCartService* service, hosted in a custom host application and accessed from the ShoppingCartGUIClient application.
Completed\DurableShopping CartWithHostAndClient	This solution demonstrates how to implement a workflow service as a durable service.
Chapter 9	
ShoppingCartService	This solution contains a copy of the non-durable ShoppingCart Service, ShoppingCartServiceHost, and ShoppingCartClient projects from Chapter 7. It is used as the starting point for the exercises in this chapter.

Solution Folder	Description
Chapter 9 (continued)	
Completed\ShoppingCartService	This solution contains a version of the *ShoppingCartService* service that uses transactions to maintain database integrity. The client application initiates the transactions.
ProductsWorkflow	This solution shows how to implement transactions in a workflow service. It is based on the *ProductsWorkflowService* from Chapter 8. The client application is also based on a workflow.
Chapter 10	
ShoppingCartService	This solution contains a completed version of the Shopping CartService, ShoppingCartHost, and ShoppingCartClient applications from Chapter 9. It is used as the starting point for the exercises in this chapter.
Completed\ShoppingCartService	This solution shows how to configure the *ShoppingCartService* service and ShoppingCartClient application to implement reliable sessions. You run the client application and use the WCF Service Trace Viewer utility to examine the messages passing between the client application and service.
Completed\ShoppingCart ServiceWithReplayDetection	This solution implements a custom binding for the *Shopping CartService* service and ShoppingCartClient applications to support the secure conversation protocol and provide automatic message replay detection.
Chapter 11	
ShoppingCartService	This solution contains a copy of the completed ShoppingCart Service and ShoppingCartClient projects from Chapter 10. The binding and endpoint configuration has been removed from the ShoppingCartHost project. In the exercises in this chapter, you implement these items in code rather than by providing them in a configuration file.
Completed\ShoppingCartService	This solution contains an implementation of the ShoppingCartHost application that programmatically creates a custom binding rather than using one of the WCF predefined bindings.
Completed\ShoppingCart ServiceWithMessageInspector	This solution shows how to create a custom service behavior with which you can inspect request messages sent to the service and response messages that it sends back to client applications.
ProductsService	This solution contains a copy of the *ProductsService* service from Chapter 6. The code and configuration information in the client that connects to the service and sends request messages has been removed. You add code that performs these tasks programmatically in the exercises in this chapter.
Completed\ProductsService	This solution contains a completed version of the ProductsClient application. The client application connects to the service by creating a binding and a channel programmatically rather than using a generated proxy class.

Solution Folder	Description
Chapter 11 (continued)	
ProductsServiceWithManualProxy	This solution shows how to inherit from the *ClientBase* generic abstract class to implement a proxy class that enables a client application to authenticate itself to the service.
SimpleProductsService	This solution contains a stripped down version of the *Products Service* service and client application. You add code to the client application to connect to the service by creating a binding and a channel and then manually create and send a SOAP message to the service.
Completed\SimpleProducts Service	This solution contains a completed version of the client application that manually creates and sends a SOAP message to the service. It receives the response also as a SOAP message.
Chapter 12	
Completed\OneWay	This solution contains a new service called *AdventureWorksAdmin*. The *AdventureWorksAdmin* service exposes an operation that can take significant time to run. It demonstrates how to implement this operation as a one-way operation. You also use this solution to understand the circumstances under which a one-way operation call can block a client application and how to resolve this blocking.
Completed\Async	This solution contains a version of the *AdventureWorksAdmin* service that implements an operation that can execute asynchronously.
MSMQ	This solution contains a copy of the *AdventureWorksAdmin* service that acts as the starting point for the exercises that demonstrate how to use MSMQ as the transport for a WCF service.
Completed\MSMQ	This version of the solution contains a completed implementation of the *AdventureWorksAdmin* service that uses a message queue to receive messages from client applications. You run the client application and service at different times and verify that messages sent by the client application are queued and received when the service runs.
Chapter 13	
Throttling	This solution contains a simplified, non-transactional version of the *ShoppingCartService* service and an extended version of the client application that simulates multiple users connecting to the service. This solution provides the starting point for the exercises showing how to implement throttling.
Completed\Throttling	This solution contains the completed version of the *Shopping CartService* service. You use this service to test the way in which you can configure WCF to conserve resources during periods of heavy load.

Solution Folder	Description
Chapter 13 (continued)	
MTOM	This solution contains a service called *ShoppingCartPhotoService* that retrieves photographic images of products from the *Adventure Works* database. The solution also contains a basic WPF client application that displays images sent by the server. You use this solution to examine how a WCF service transmits messages containing large amounts of binary data.
Completed\MTOM	This version of the service encodes the binary data constituting the image by using the Message Transmission Optimization Mechanism (MTOM). You use this solution to generate message traces that you examine so you can see how the messages are encoded.
Streaming	This solution contains a version of the *ShoppingCartPhotoService* that uses streaming to send the image data to the client application rather than MTOM.
Chapter 14	
ProductsService	This solution contains a copy of the *ProductsService* service hosted by the ASP.NET Development Web Server, and client application that connects to this service. This solution is used as the starting point for the exercises that show how to implement service discovery.
Completed\ProductsServiceWith AdHocDiscovery	The *ProductsService* service in this solution implements ad hoc discovery. It is deployed to IIS. The client application is modified to broadcast a discovery request and retrieve the address of the *ProductsService* service.
Completed\ProductsServiceWith Announcements	In this version of the solution, the *ProductsService* service sends announcement messages when it starts up and shuts down. The client application listens for service announcements and caches the URLs of services as they come on-line. When the client application sends a request, it looks up the URL of the service in this cache.
Completed\ProductsServiceWith ManagedDiscovery	This solution shows how to implement a discovery proxy. The *ProductsService* service sends announcement messages, and the discovery proxy listens for these messages and caches the URLs of services as they come on-line. The client application is modified to retrieve the address of the *ProductsService* from the discovery proxy.
LoadBalancingRouter	This solution contains an amended copy of the durable Shopping CartService, ShoppingCartServiceHost, and ShoppingCartGUIClient from Chapter 7. It is used as the basis for the exercises that show how to implement routing inside a WCF service.
Completed\LoadBalancing Router	This solution contains a WCF service called *ShoppingCartService Router* that acts as a load-balancing router for two instances of the *ShoppingCartService* service. The client application connects to the router, which transparently redirects requests to one instance or the other of the *ShoppingCartService* service.

Solution Folder	Description
Chapter 14 (continued)	
ShoppingCartServiceWithRouter	This solution contains another copy of the durable Shopping CartService, ShoppingCartServiceHost, and ShoppingCartGUI Client from Chapter 7, except that the host application is precon-figured with two HTTP endpoints. This solution provides the start-ing point for the exercises that show how to implement a WCF routing service.
Completed\ShoppingCartService WithRouter	This solution contains a completed implementation of the WCF routing service
MessageInspector	This solution contains a version of the *MessageInspector* behavior created in Chapter 11. It is used to test the routing service in the ShoppingCartServiceWithRouter project by displaying the details of messages as they are received by the ShoppingCartHost project.
Chapter 15	
Completed\ProductsSales	This solution contains a REST Web service called *ProductsSales Service*, host, and client application that provides access to sales information. The client application tests the *ProductsSalesService* service by sending requests that query the details of orders and customers.
Completed\ProductsSales WithUpdates	This solution contains an updated version of the *ProductsSales Service* service that supports insert, update, and delete operations. The client application is extended to test this functionality.
Completed\SalesData	This solution contains a REST Web service called *SalesData* that also provides access to customer and order information. This ser-vice is implemented by using the WCF Data Services template. The SalesDataClient application in this solution uses the client library for the service to connect and send requests to the service.
Chapter 16	
ProductsServiceV3	This solution contains another version of the *ProductsService* ser-vice that provides an additional operation that updates the price of a product. The solution also contains a host application, and a client application for testing the service.
Completed\ProductsServiceV3	In this solution, the *ProductsService* service implements a callback contract. The operation that changes the price of a product is reconfigured as a one way operation, and the callback contract enables the service to asynchronously notify the client application of the result of the operation when it has completed.
Completed\ProductsServiceV3 WithEvents	This version of the *ProductsService* service implements an event-ing mechanism. Instances of the client applications subscribe to an event, and the service uses a callback contract to notify each sub-scribing client when the event occurs.

Solution Folder	Description
Chapter 17	
ShoppingCartService	This solution contains a completed version of the *ShoppingCart Service* service, host, and client applications from Chapter 10. It is used as the starting point for the exercises in this chapter.
Completed\ShoppingCartService	The *ShoppingCartService* service in this solution implements claims-based security. The client application uses Windows CardSpace to manage user credentials and send claims information to the service. The service uses verified claims to authorize access to users.
Chapter 18	
ASPNETService	This solution contains a legacy ASP.NET Web site called ASPNET ProductsService. This Web site provides an ASP.NET Web service. The solution also contains a client application that connects to this Web service. Both applications were developed by using the .NET Framework 2.0. The service is used as the basis for exercises that show how to migrate an ASP.NET Web service to WCF and the .NET Framework 4.0.
ProductsServiceHost	This project contains the host application for the WCF service that implements the functionality migrated from the *ASPNETService* Web service.
Completed\ASPNETService	This solution is a version of the *ASPNETProductsService* service that has been migrated to WCF, together with the host and client applications. The code in the client application has not changed, and connects to WCF service in exactly the same way as it did to the original ASP.NET Web service.
Products	This solution contains a legacy COM+ application that you configure to appear to client applications as a WCF service.
ProductsClient	This solution contains an incomplete copy of the ProductsClient application for testing the Products COM+ application by connecting to it as though it was a WCF service. You finish this application during the exercises in this chapter.
Completed\ProductsClient	This solution contains the completed version of the ProductsClient application.

Uninstalling the Code Samples

To remove the code samples from your computer, delete the folder Microsoft Press\WCF Step By Step from your Documents folder by using Windows Explorer.

Errata and Book Support

We've made every effort to ensure the accuracy of this book and its companion content. If you do find an error, please report it on our Microsoft Press site at *oreilly.com*:

1. Go to *http://microsoftpress.oreilly.com*.

2. In the Search box, enter the book's ISBN or title.

3. Select your book from the search results.

4. On your book's catalog page, under the cover image, you'll see a list of links. Click View/Submit Errata.

You'll find additional information and services for your book on its catalog page. If you need additional support, please e-mail Microsoft Press Book Support at *mspinput@microsoft.com*.

Please note that product support for Microsoft software is not offered through the addresses above.

We Want to Hear from You

At Microsoft Press, your satisfaction is our top priority, and your feedback our most valuable asset. Please tell us what you think of this book at:

http://www.microsoft.com/learning/booksurvey

The survey is short, and we read *every one* of your comments and ideas. Thanks in advance for your input!

Stay in Touch

Let's keep the conversation going! We're on Twitter: *http://twitter.com/MicrosoftPress*.

Chapter 1
Introducing Windows Communication Foundation

After completing this chapter, you will be able to:

- Explain the purpose of Windows Communication Foundation.

- Use the .NET Framework 4.0 and Visual Studio 2010 to build a WCF service.

- Deploy a WCF service to Microsoft Internet Information Services (IIS).

- Build a client console application to test the WCF service.

- Describe the principles underpinning a Service-Oriented Architecture (SOA) and how WCF facilitates building applications and services for an SOA.

This chapter provides you with an introduction to Windows Communication Foundation (WCF) and shows you how to create, deploy, and access a simple WCF service. This is very much a "scene-setting" chapter. During its course, you will meet many of the features of WCF. In subsequent chapters, you will expand your knowledge of the various topics presented here.

What Is Windows Communication Foundation?

I assume that you are reading this book because you want to know how to build distributed applications and services by using WCF. But what is WCF, and why should you use it, anyway? To answer these questions, it is helpful to take a few steps back into the past.

The Early Days of Personal Computer Applications

In the early days of the personal computer, most business solutions comprised integrated suites of applications, which typically consisted of word processing software, a spreadsheet program, and a database package (much like Microsoft Office does these days). A skilled user could store business data in the database, analyze this data using the spreadsheet program, and maybe create reports and other documents integrating the data and the analyses by using the word processor. More often than not, these applications would all be located on the same computer, and the data and file formats they used would be proprietary to the application suite. This was the classic desktop business platform; it was single-user and usually with very limited scope for multitasking.

As personal computers became cheaper and more widely adopted as business tools, the next challenge was to enable multiple users to share the business data stored on them. This was not actually a new challenge; multi-user databases had been available for some time, but they ran predominantly on mainframe computers rather than PCs. However, networking solutions and network operating systems (NOS) soon started to appear for the PC platform, enabling departments in an organization to connect their PCs together and share resources. Database management system vendors produced versions of their software for the networked PC environment, adapted from the mainframe environment, which allowed networked PC solutions to share their business data more easily.

Inter-Process Communications Technologies

A networked platform is actually only part of the story. Although networking solutions permitted PCs to communicate with each other and share resources such as printers and disks, applications needed to be able to send and receive data and coordinate their actions with other applications running at the same time on other computers. Many common inter-process communications mechanisms were available, such as named pipes and sockets. These mechanisms were very low-level; using them required a good understanding of how networks function. The same is true today. For example, building applications that use sockets to send and receive data can be a challenging occupation; ostensibly the process is quite simple, but factors such as coordinating access (you don't want two applications trying to read from the same socket at the same time) can complicate matters. As computers and networks evolved, so did the variety and capabilities of the inter-process communications mechanisms. For example, Microsoft developed the Component Object Model, or COM, as the mechanism for communicating between applications and components running on the Windows platform. Developers can use COM to create reusable software components, link components together to build applications, and take advantage of Windows services. Microsoft itself uses COM to make elements of its own applications available as services for integration into custom solutions.

Microsoft originally designed COM to enable communications between components and applications running on the same computer. COM was followed by DCOM (distributed COM), which allowed applications to access components running on other computers over a network. DCOM was itself followed by COM+. COM+ incorporated features such as integration with Microsoft Transaction Server so applications could group operations on components together into transactions. The results of these operations could either be made permanent (committed) if they were all successful or automatically undone (rolled back) if some sort of error occurred. COM+ provided additional capabilities such as automatic resource management (for example, if a component connects to a database, you can ensure that the connection is closed when the application finishes using the component) and asynchronous operations (useful if an application makes a request to a component that can take a long time to fulfill; the application can continue processing, and the component can alert the application by sending it a message when the operation has completed). COM+ was followed in turn by the .NET Framework, which further extended the features available. Microsoft renamed the technology yet again to Enterprise Services. The .NET Framework also provided several new technologies for building networked components. One example was Remoting, with which a client application could access a remote object hosted by a remote server application as though it were running locally, inside the client application.

The Web and Web Services

Technologies such as COM, DCOM, COM+, Enterprise Services, and .NET Framework Remoting all work well when applications and components are running within the same local area network inside an organization. They are also specific to the Microsoft Windows family of operating systems.

While Microsoft was developing COM and DCOM, the World Wide Web appeared. The World Wide Web is based on the Internet, which has been around for several decades. The World Wide Web provides an infrastructure with which developers can build applications that can combine components and other elements located almost anywhere in the world, running on computers of varying architectures, and that execute on a bewildering array of operating systems (not just Windows). The first generation of "Web applications" was quite simple and consisted of static Web pages that users could download and view using a Web browser running on their local computer. The second generation provided elements of programmability, initially through the use of components, or applets, that could be downloaded from Web sites and executed locally in the user's Web browser. These have been followed by the third generation—Web services. A Web service is an application or component that executes on the computer hosting the Web site rather than the user's computer. A Web service can receive requests from applications running on the user's computer, perform operations on the computer hosting the Web service, and send a response back to the application running on the user's computer. A Web service can also invoke operations in other Web services, hosted elsewhere on the Internet. These are global, distributed applications.

You can build Web services that execute on Windows by using Visual Studio and the .NET Framework. You can create Web services for other platforms by using other technologies, such as Java and the Java Web Services Developers Pack. However, Web services are not specific to any particular language or operating system. To establish Web services as a global mechanism for building distributed applications, developers had to agree on several points, including a common format for data, a protocol for sending and receiving requests, and handling security. All of these features had to be independent of the platform being used to create and host Web services.

Using XML as a Common Data Format

Different types of computers can store the same values by using different internal representations—for example, computers based on a "big-endian" 32-bit processor use a different format for numeric data than a computer based on a "small-endian" 32-bit processor. So, to share data successfully between applications running on different computers, developers had to agree on a common format for that data that was independent of the architecture of the computer they were using. To cut a long story short, the currently accepted universal data format is eXtensible Markup Language, or XML. XML is text based and human readable (just), and lets you define a grammar for describing just about any type of data that you need to handle. In case you have not seen XML data before, here is an example:

```
<Person>
  <Forename>John</Forename>
  <Surname>Sharp</Surname>
  <Age>46</Age>
</Person>
```

> **More Info** For detailed information about XML and how you can use it, visit the XML.org Web site at *http://www.xml.org*.

Without trying too hard, you can probably guess what this data actually means. An application that needs to send information about a person to another application could format the data in this way, and the receiving application should be able to parse the data and make sense of it. However, there is more than one way to represent this information by using XML. You could also structure it like this:

```
<Person Forename="John" Surname="Sharp" Age="46" />
```

There are many other variations that are possible as well. How does an application know how to format data so that another application can read it correctly? The answer is that both applications have to agree on a layout. This layout is referred to as the XML schema for the data. Now this is neither the time nor the place to become embroiled in a discussion of how XML schemas work. Just accept that an application can use an XML schema to convey information about how the data it is emitting is structured, and the application receiving the data can use this schema to help parse the data and make sense of it.

So, by adopting XML and schemas as a common data format, applications running on different computers can at least understand the data that they are using.

> **More Info** If you want to know more about XML schemas and how they work, visit the World Wide Web Consortium (W3C) Web site at *http://www.w3.org/XML/Schema*.

Sending and Receiving Web Service Requests

By using XML and XML schemas to format data, Web services and users' (or client) applications can pass data back and forth in an unambiguous manner. However, client applications and Web services still need to agree on a protocol when sending and receiving requests. Additionally, a client application needs to be able to know what messages it can send to a Web service and what responses it can expect to receive.

To curtail another long story, Web services and client applications communicate with each other using SOAP (formerly known as the Simple Object Access Protocol). The SOAP specification defines a number of aspects, of which the most important are:

- The format of a SOAP message
- How data should be encoded
- How to send messages
- How to handle replies to these messages

A Web service can publish a Web Services Description Language (WSDL) document, which is a piece of XML (conforming to a standard XML schema) that describes the messages the Web service can accept and the structure of the responses it will send back. A client application can use this information to determine how to communicate with the Web service.

> **More Info** If you want detailed information about SOAP, visit the World Wide Web Consortium page at *http://www.w3.org/TR/soap*. If you want further information about WSDL, visit the page at *http://www.w3.org/TR/wsdl20*.

JavaScript Object Notation and Rich Internet Applications

The XML/SOAP model for defining and transmitting messages in an interchangeable format is well understood but might be too cumbersome in some situations. These technologies can generate a lot of overhead if the data in the messages that they are transmitting or receiving is small, as is typically the case in modern Rich Internet Applications (RIAs).

A RIA is an application that usually runs remotely by using a Web browser but provides many of the characteristics associated with desktop applications. To provide the rich interactive desktop style typically involves the use of Web scripting languages such as JavaScript as well as technologies such as those encompassed by AJAX (Asynchronous JavaScript and XML). Many vendors provide frameworks, such as Microsoft SilverLight, that developers can use to implement RIAs quickly and easily, based on these technologies.

Although XML forms part of the AJAX technology set, a more lightweight approach is to use the native format defined by JavaScript for representing objects and serializing them for transmission across the network. This format has been standardized as the JavaScript Object Notation, or JSON. Despite its name, JSON is a completely language-independent format that is based on conventions that most programmers will find familiar. It organizes data into name/value pairs, or collections of values, depending on whether you are handing a simple data item or a more complex structure such as an array.

JSON data is transmitted as text. The JSON equivalent of the XML structure that describes a Person, shown earlier, looks like this:

```
{ "forename": "John". "surname": "Sharp", "age": 46 }
```

You can read and write JSON data by writing code directly, but many developers prefer to use JSON parsers to convert their data into JSON format automatically, especially for structures that are more complex than this simple example. JSON parsers are available for most modern development languages and environments that are used for building distributed applications, such as WCF.

> **More Info** For further information about JSON, go to the JSON Web site as *http://json.org*.

Handling Security and Privacy in a Global Environment

Security is concerned with identifying users and services and then authorizing their access to resources. In a distributed environment, maintaining security is vitally important. In an isolated, non-networked, desktop environment, you could physically secure a PC to prevent an unauthorized user from typing on its keyboard or viewing its screen; however, when you connect computers together over a network, physical security is no longer sufficient. You now need to ensure that users accessing shared resources, data, and components running on a computer over a network have the appropriate access rights. Companies developing operating systems, such as Microsoft with Windows, incorporate many security features into their own platforms. Typically, these features include maintaining a list of users and the credentials that they use to identify these users, such as their passwords. These solutions can work well in an environment where it is possible to maintain such a list (for instance, within a single organization), but if you wish to make your services available outside of your enterprise, clearly it is not feasible to record identity and credential information for all computers and users accessing your services across the World Wide Web.

A lot of research has been performed to investigate and understand the challenges of maintaining security in a global environment, and many solutions have been proposed. To communicate in a secure manner, Web services and client applications need to agree on the form of security that they will use and how they will identify and verify each other. The Organization for the Advancement of Structured Information Standards (OASIS) is a consortium of organizations that has proposed a number of standard mechanisms for implementing security, such as using username/password pairs, X509 certificates, and Kerberos tokens. If you are creating Web services that provide access to privileged information, you should consider using one of these mechanisms to authenticate users.

> **More Info** For detailed information about the OASIS security standards, visit the OASIS Web Service Security site at *http://www.oasis-open.org/committees/tc_home.php?wg_abbrev=wss*.

Privacy is closely related to security and is equally important—especially when you start to communicate with services on the World Wide Web. You don't want other users to be able to intercept and read the messages flowing between your applications and Web services. To this end, Web services and client applications must also agree on a mechanism to ensure the privacy of their conversations. Typically, this means encrypting the messages that they exchange. As with security, there are several mechanisms available for encrypting messages, the most common of which rely on using public and private keys.

> **More Info** For a good overview and introduction to public key cryptography, visit the Wikipedia Web site at *http://en.wikipedia.org/wiki/Public-key_cryptography*.

Incorporating security and privacy into a Web service and client application can be a nontrivial task. To make life easier for developers building Web services using the Microsoft .NET Framework, Microsoft introduced the Web Services Enhancements (WSE) package. WSE was an add-on for earlier versions of Visual Studio. It was designed to help create Web services that retain compatibility with the evolving Web service standards of the time. WSE provided wizards and other tools for generating much of the code necessary to help protect Web services and client applications and to simplify the configuration and deployment of Web services.

Service-Oriented Architectures and Windows Communication Foundation

Software developers soon appreciated that the principles of Web services could be applied in a more generalized manner, leading to the concept of "Software as a Service" and the trend toward implementing a Service-Oriented Architecture, or SOA. The driving force behind SOA is the realization that to remain competitive and profitable, the business solutions of an organization must be able to adapt quickly to the changing business environment. The key architectural principles behind SOA are the ability to reuse existing software assets wherever possible and expose the functionality of these assets as a set of services.

A service provides a well-defined set of operations that support the business logic of the organization. A developer can implement these operations by invoking new and existing software assets, and composing these items in whatever way is necessary to satisfy the requirements of the organization. A service hides the details of its implementation, and service creators can compose new functionality by transparently combining calls to other applications and other services. The keys to implementing a successful service are:

- Providing a reusable and extensible interface based on well-defined standards to maximize interoperability

- Providing a scalable hosting environment within which a service can respond quickly to user requests, even under an extreme load

This is where the Microsoft Windows operating system and WCF come into their own.

WCF provides a model with which you can implement services that conform to many commonly-accepted styles and standards, including SOAP, XML, and JSON. Additionally, WCF supports many Microsoft-specific technologies for building components, such as Enterprise Services and Microsoft Message Queue (MSMQ), and supports a unified programming model for many of these technologies. This allows you to build solutions that are as independent as possible from the underlying mechanism being used to connect services and applications together. By using WCF, you can combine these technologies and make them accessible to non-Microsoft applications and services.

It is difficult, if not impossible, to completely divorce the programmatic structure of an application or service from its communications infrastructure, but WCF lets you come very close to achieving this goal much of the time. Additionally, by using WCF, you can maintain backward compatibility with many of the preceding technologies. For example, a WCF client application can easily communicate with a Web service that you created by using WSE.

The Windows operating system can implement a scalable, secure, and robust platform for an SOA. Windows Server 2008 is highly optimized for this environment, and you can build extensible clusters of Windows Server computers by making use of inexpensive commodity hardware. On the other hand, if you do not wish to maintain the hardware required to host an SOA solution yourself, you can subscribe to Windows Azure.

Windows Azure is a cloud computing platform. It supplies on-demand compute and storage facilities located in data centers managed by Microsoft. You can build and test your services locally and then upload them to a data center where they will run on one or more virtual machines on computers managed and maintained by Microsoft staff. You can specify parameters that cause the service to scale out onto multiple computers as demand increases and to scale back as and when demand drops. Windows Azure provides a highly-connectable architecture that enables client applications to locate and invoke your services. This connectivity makes use of features provided with WCF.

More Info For further information about cloud computing and Windows Azure, visit the "Windows Azure Platform" page on the Microsoft Web site at *http://www.microsoft.com/windowsazure*.

To summarize, if you are considering building scalable distributed applications and services, and implementing an SOA running on the Windows platform, you should use WCF.

Building a WCF Service

Visual Studio 2010 provides the ideal environment for building WCF services and applications. Visual Studio includes several project templates that you can use to build WCF services. You will use the WCF Service template to create a simple WCF service that exposes methods for querying and maintaining information stored in a database. The database used by the exercises in this book is the sample *AdventureWorks* OLTP database.

Note The script for creating the *AdventureWorks* OLTP database is provided with the downloadable samples for this book. The Introduction contains instructions on how to install and configure this database for use with the exercises in this book. You can also download the database from the CodePlex site; search for *Sample Databases for Microsoft SQL Server 2008 (December 2009) Samples Refresh 4* and download the file *AdventureWorks2008_SR4.exe*. Note that there might be later versions of this database available, but the examples in this book have only been tested against the December 2009 release.

The AdventureWorks company manufactures bicycles and accessories. The database contains details of the products that the company sells, sales information, details of customers, and employee data. In the exercises in this chapter, you will build a WCF service that provides these operations:

- List the products sold by AdventureWorks
- Obtain the details of a specific product
- Query the current stock level for a product
- Modify the stock level of a product

The data required by these exercises is stored in the *Product* and *ProductInventory* tables in the *AdventureWorks* database. Figure 1-1 shows these tables. There is a one-to-many relationship between them; one *Product* record can be related to many *ProductInventory* records. This is because products are stored in one or more numbered bins in the warehouse, and each bin is on a named shelf. The tables are joined across the ProductID column.

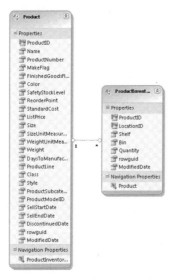

FIGURE 1-1 Tables holding product information in the *AdventureWorks* database.

To simplify the code that you need to write to access the database, but also to ensure that the exercises are as realistic as possible, you will make use of the ADO.NET Entity Framework. This is part of the .NET Framework 4.0 and is provided with Visual Studio 2010. The purpose of the Entity Framework is to provide an object mapping between tables in a database and a set of objects that you can use in your applications and services. Using the Entity Framework, you can build an entity model that specifies the database and tables that you want to use and generate an object model that you can use to query these tables, as well as insert, update, and delete data. A major advantage of using the Entity Framework is that you can build applications that are independent of the underlying database management system, and you can access data without having to understand how the database management system works (you do not need to know SQL).

> **More Info**   The exercises in this book only scratch the surface of the Entity Framework. If you want more information about the Entity Framework, please visit the ADO.NET Entity Framework page at *http://msdn.microsoft.com/en-us/data/aa937723.aspx*.

Build the Entity Model for the WCF Service

1. Start Visual Studio 2010 and create a new project using the Class Library template in the Visual C# folder in the Installed Templates pane. Specify the following properties for the solution:

Property	Value
Name	ProductsEntityModel
Location	C:\Users*YourName*\Documents\Microsoft Press\WCF Step By Step\Chapter 1 (Replace *YourName* with your Windows user name.)
Solution name	ProductsService

> **Note** To save space throughout the rest of this book, I will simply refer to the path C:\Users\<*YourName*>\Documents\ as your Documents folder.

2. In Solution Explorer, in the ProductsEntityModel project, delete the Class1.cs file by using the following procedure:

   a. Right-click the Class1.cs file, and then click Delete.

   b. In the dialog box, click OK to confirm the deletion.

3. Add a new item to the ProductsEntityModel project:

   ❑ In Solution Explorer, right-click the ProductsEntityModel project, point to Add, and then click New Item.

4. In the Add New Item—ProductsEntityModel dialog box, in the Installed Templates pane click the Data folder under Visual C# Items. In the middle pane, click the ADO.NET Entity Data Model template. In the *Name* field, type **ProductsModel.edmx**, and then click Add.

   The Entity Data Model Wizard appears.

5. In the Entity Data Model Wizard, on the Choose Model Contents page, click Generate From Database, and then click Next.

6. On the Choose Your Data Connection page, click New Connection.

   The Choose Data Source dialog box appears.

> **Note** If you have previously created database connections, the Choose Data Source dialog box might not appear, and the Connection Properties dialog box might be displayed instead. If this happens, click Change, and the Choose Data Source dialog box will appear.

7. In the Choose Data Source dialog box, click Microsoft SQL Server, and then click Continue or OK.

   The Connection Properties dialog box appears.

8. In the Connection Properties dialog box, in the *Server name* field, type **.\SQLExpress**. In the *Select or enter a database name* field, type **AdventureWorks**, and then click OK.

   The Entity Data Model Wizard resumes.

Note Specifying the server name as *.\SQLExpress* causes Visual Studio to connect to the local instance of SQL Server Express running on your computer.

9. On the Choose Your Data Connection page, verify that the Save Entity Connection Settings In App.Config As: check box is selected. Change the name to **AdventureWorks Entities** if necessary.

 The connection settings used by the entity model will be stored in the application configuration file using this name as the key.

10. Click Next.

 The Choose Your Database Objects page appears.

11. On the Choose Your Database Objects page, expand Tables and select (check) the *Product (Production)* and *ProductInventory (Production)* tables. Verify or specify the following values for the other items on this page, and then click Finish.

Item	Value
Pluralize or singularize generated object names	*Selected*
Include foreign key columns in the model	*Selected*
Model Namespace	AdventureWorksModel

Visual Studio generates the entity model and it is displayed. It should contain the two entities, *Product* and *ProductInventory*, and it should resemble the model shown earlier in Figure 1-1.

The Entity Framework generates classes for each entity defined by the entity model. In this case, the classes are called *Product* and *ProductInventory*. The classes contain properties for each field in the corresponding tables in the database.

The Entity Framework also generates a class called *AdventureWorksEntities* that provides methods that you can use to connect to the *AdventureWorks* database and populate a pair of collection properties called *Products* and *ProductInventories* with instances of the *Product* and *ProductInventory* classes. To retrieve data from the *AdventureWorks* database, you simply create an instance of the *AdventureWorksEntities* class and access the data through the *Products* and *ProductInventories* collection properties.

Notice that the ProductsEntityModel project contains an application configuration file. This file was generated by the Entity Data Model Wizard; it contains the information that the *AdventureWorksEntities* class requires to connect to the *AdventureWorks* database.

12. Build the project:

 ❑ In Solution Explorer, right-click the ProductsEntityModel project, and then click Build.

Now that you have built the entity model, you can start to build the WCF service that provides operations that access the *AdventureWorks* database by using this model.

Create the *ProductsService* WCF Service

1. Add a new Web site project to the ProductsService solution:

   ❏ In Solution Explorer, right-click the ProductsService solution, point to Add, and then click New Web Site.

   > **Note** From now on, I will assume that you understand how to create new solutions and projects by using Visual Studio 2010. I will simply ask you to create a new solution or project, although I will specify the template and any specific project names that you should use.

2. In the Add New Web Site dialog box, in middle pane, click the WCF Service template. Verify that the *Web location* field is set to *File System*, type **C:\Users*YourName*\ Documents\Microsoft Press\WCF Step By Step\Chapter 1\ProductsService\ ProductsService** (as shown in the following image), and then click OK.

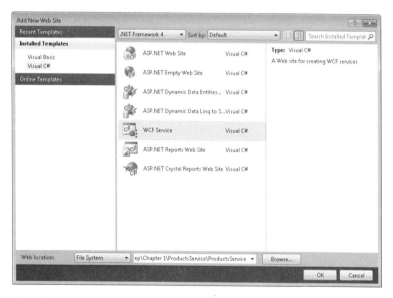

Visual Studio 2010 actually provides several templates for creating a WCF service; the WCF Service template that you are using here creates a WCF service as part of a Web application. You will see in later chapters how you can implement a WCF service in a library, as part of a standalone application, or as part of a Workflow Foundation service application.

The WCF Service template generates code for a default service, and it is worth examining this code briefly. At the top of the Service.cs file, you will find the usual *using* statements referencing the *System*, *System.Collections.Generic*, *System.Linq*, and *System.Text* namespaces, but you will also see additional statements that reference the *System.ServiceModel*, *System.Service Model.Web*, and *System.Runtime.Serialization* namespaces, as shown in Figure 1-2.

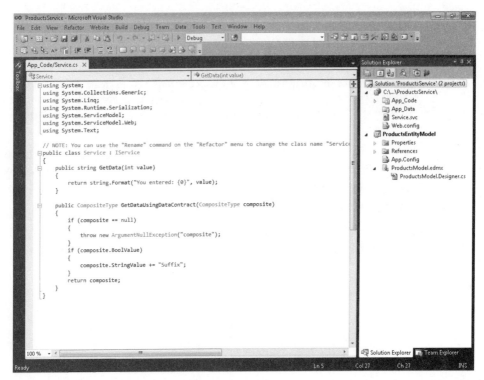

FIGURE 1-2 The default code generated for a WCF service.

The *System.ServiceModel* namespace contains the classes that WCF uses to define services and their operations. You will see many of the classes and types in this namespace as you progress through this book. WCF uses the classes in the *System.Runtime.Serialization* namespace to convert objects into a stream of data suitable for transmitting over the network (a process known as serialization). It also uses them to convert a stream of data received from the network back into objects (deserialization). You will learn a little about how WCF serializes and deserializes objects later in this chapter, and you will look at serialization and deserialization in more depth as you progress through this book. The *System.ServiceModel.Web* namespace contains types that you can use to build WCF services that follow the Representational State Transfer model, commonly known as REST. This is an approach to representing services as a set of resources and entities; you will learn more about this architectural style in Chapter 15, "Building REST Web Services."

The code shown in the *Service* class in the Service.cs file shows an example of a simple WCF service. This service provides two methods called *GetData* and *GetDataUsingDataContract*. The details of these two methods are unimportant at the moment; it's sufficient to say that they show examples of how to implement operations. In a WCF service, an operation is simply a method that takes zero or more parameters and can return a value. When a client application sends a message to a WCF service, the WCF runtime converts the message into a method call and passes the data contained in the message as parameters to the method. Similarly, when the method returns, any return value is packaged into a message and transmitted back to the client application.

You should notice that the *Service* class implements an interface called *IService*. If you expand the App_Code folder for the C:\...\ProductsService\ Web site in Solution Explorer, you will see a file called IService.cs. If you examine this file, you will see that it contains the following code:

```
using System.Collections.Generic;
using System.Linq;
using System.Runtime.Serialization;
using System.ServiceModel;
using System.ServiceModel.Web;
using System.Text;

// NOTE: You can use the "Rename" command on the "Refactor" menu to change the interface
name "IService" in both code and config file together.
[ServiceContract]
public interface IService
{

        [OperationContract]
        string GetData(int value);

        [OperationContract]
        CompositeType GetDataUsingDataContract(CompositeType composite);

        // TODO: Add your service operations here
}

// Use a data contract as illustrated in the sample below to add composite types to service
operations.
[DataContract]
public class CompositeType
{
        bool boolValue = true;
        string stringValue = "Hello ";

        [DataMember]
        public bool BoolValue
        {
                get { return boolValue; }
                set { boolValue = value; }
        }
```

```
[DataMember]
public string StringValue
{
        get { return stringValue; }
        set { stringValue = value; }
}
}
```

The *IService* interface simply defines the *GetData* and *GetDataUsingDataContract* methods implemented by the *Service* class. This is known as the service contract, and it makes use of the *ServiceContract* and *OperationContract* attributes, which you will learn about in the next section. The IService.cs file also contains a class called *CompositeType* (this is the type returned by the *GetDataUsingDataContract* method) that references the *DataContract* and *DataMember* attributes. This is an example of a data contract, and you will learn about this shortly, as well.

Defining the Contracts

The structure of a WCF service enables you to adopt a "contract-first" approach to development. When performing contract-first development, you define the interfaces, or contracts, that the service will implement and then build a service that conforms to these contracts. This is not a new technique; COM developers have been using a very similar strategy for the last decade or so. The point behind using contract-first development is that you can initially concentrate on the design of your service. If necessary, it can quickly be reviewed to ensure that it does not introduce any dependencies on specific hardware or software before you perform too much development. Remember that in many cases client applications might not be built using WCF, or even be running on Windows.

In the following exercises, you will define the data and service contracts for the *ProductsService* WCF service. The data contract specifies the details of products that the WCF service can pass to operations. The service contract defines the operations that the WCF service will implement.

Define the Data Contract for the WCF Service

1. In the IService.cs file, delete the code and comments for the *IService* interface and the *CompositeType* class, leaving just the *using* statements at the top of the file.

2. In Solution Explorer, change the name of the IService.cs file to IProductsService.cs:

   ❏ Right-click the IService.cs file, click Rename, and then type **IProductsService.cs**.

> **Best Practice** It is good practice to change the name of the file containing the service contract from IService.cs to a name that more closely reflects the name or purpose of the service.

3. Add the following namespace to the IProductsService.cs file:

```
namespace Products
{
}
```

4. Add the following *ProductData* class to the *Products* namespace:

```
// Data contract describing the details of a product passed to client applications
[DataContract]
public class ProductData
{
    [DataMember]
    public string Name;

    [DataMember]
    public string ProductNumber;

    [DataMember]
    public string Color;

    [DataMember]
    public decimal ListPrice;
}
```

This class defines the data that the WCF service will pass back to client applications. It is a subset of the data defined by the entity model that you created earlier.

The *DataContract* attribute identifies the class as defining a type that can be serialized and deserialized as an XML stream by WCF. All types that you pass to WCF operations or return from WCF operations must be serializable by WCF. You can apply the *Data Contract* attribute to classes, structures, and enumerations.

You mark each member of the type with the *DataMember* attribute; any members not tagged in this way will not be serialized.

> **Note** You can use any other types that already have a data contract defined for them as the types of data members inside a data contract. You can also use any serializable type. This includes types such as string, int, and decimal, as well as many of the more complex types such as the Collection classes.

Define the service contract for the WCF service

1. Add the *IProductsService* interface shown in the following to the *Products* namespace, after the *Product* class:

```
// Service contract describing the operations provided by the WCF service
[ServiceContract]
public interface IProductsService
{
    // Get the product number of every product
    [OperationContract]
    List<string> ListProducts();

    // Get the details of a single product
    [OperationContract]
    ProductData GetProduct(string productNumber);

    // Get the current stock level for a product
    [OperationContract]
    int CurrentStockLevel(string productNumber);

    // Change the stock level for a product
    [OperationContract]
    bool ChangeStockLevel(string productNumber, short newStockLevel, string shelf,
        int bin);
}
```

Defining a service contract as an interface in this way lets you separate the definition of the contract from its implementation. You use the *ServiceContract* attribute to mark the interface as a service contract (the WCF runtime relics on the interface being tagged with this attribute when it is generating metadata for client applications that wish to use this service). Each method that you want to expose should be tagged with the *Operation Contract* attribute. It is also worth noting that you can use generic types (such as *List< >*) as the types of parameters or return values in a WCF service contract as long as the types you specify are serializable by WCF. You will learn much more about the details of service contracts as you proceed through this book.

Implementing the Service

Now that you have specified the structure of the data passed to the WCF service by using a data contract and defined the shape of the WCF service by using a service contract, the next step is to write the code that actually implements the service contract. As with any interface, you must implement every method defined by the service contract in the WCF service. Note that if you define additional methods in the WCF service that are not in the service contract, those methods will not be visible to client applications using the service.

Implement the WCF Service

1. Add a reference to the ProductsEntityModel project to the WCF service.

    a. In Solution Explorer, right-click the C:\...\ProductsService\ Web site, and then click Add Reference.

    b. In the Add Reference dialog box, click the Projects tab.

    c. Click the ProductsEntityModel project, and then click OK.

2. Add a reference to the *System.Data.Entity* assembly to the WCF service.

    a. In Solution Explorer, right-click the C:\...\ProductsService\ Web site, and then click Add Reference.

    b. In the Add Reference dialog box, click the .NET tab.

    c. Click *System.Data.Entity* (make sure that you select the version 4.0.0.0 assembly if more than one version is shown), and then click OK.

    The *System.Data.Entity* assembly contains the system types required to fetch data by using the entity model in the ProductsEntityModel project.

3. In Solution Explorer, rename the Service.cs file in the *App_Code* folder as ProductsService.cs.

4. Double-click the newly-renamed ProductsService.cs file to display it in the Code And Text Editor window, and then remove the *Service* class and its associated comment, leaving only the *using* statements in the file.

5. Add the following *using* statement to the list at the top of the file:

    ```
    using ProductsEntityModel;
    ```

    The *ProductsEntityModel* namespace contains the types that define the entity model in the ProductsEntityModel project.

6. Add the *Products* namespace to the ProductsService.cs file, as follows:

    ```
    namespace Products
    {
    }
    ```

7. Add the following class to the *Products* namespace:

    ```
    // WCF service that implements the service contract
    // This implementation performs minimal error checking and exception handling

    public class ProductsServiceImpl : IProductsService
    {
    }
    ```

Notice that a class that provides a WCF service should indicate that it implements a service contract—in this case, *IProductsService*—by using standard C# inheritance notation.

8. Add the *ListProducts* method to the *ProductsServiceImpl* class, as shown in bold in the following code example:

```
public class ProductsServiceImpl : IProductsService
{
    public List<string> ListProducts()
    {
        // Create a list for holding product numbers
        List<string> productsList = new List<string>();

        try
        {
            // Connect to the AdventureWorks database by using the Entity Framework
            using (AdventureWorksEntities database = new AdventureWorksEntities())
            {
                // Fetch the product number of every product in the database
                var products = from product in database.Products
                                select product.ProductNumber;

                productsList = products.ToList();
            }
        }
        catch
        {
            // Ignore exceptions in this implementation
        }

        // Return the list of product numbers
        return productsList;
    }
}
```

 Important For the sake of clarity, this method does not include any significant exception handling. In the real world, you should check for exceptions in a more comprehensive manner and handle them accordingly. You will learn how to do this in Chapter 3, "Making Applications and Services Robust."

This method uses the classes generated by the Entity Framework to connect to the *AdventureWorks* database and retrieve the product number of every product as a list of strings. The statement

```
using (AdventureWorksEntities database = new AdventureWorksEntities())
```

creates an instance of the *AdventureWorksEntities* class called *database* and connects to the *AdventureWorks* database. The LINQ query finds the product number of all products in the database and creates an *IQueryable* collection. The *ToList()* method fetches all products and stores them in a *List* collection object which is assigned to the *productsList* variable.

Notice that you can access the products in the database by using the *Products* property of the *AdventureWorksEntity* object. Remember that this is a collection property that contains *Product* objects.

> **Note** The Entity Framework fetches data on demand. When you create an instance of the *AdventureWorksEntities* class, no data is retrieved until you fetch it by calling the *ToList* method of the *products* collection.
>
> You might also be curious why the *productsList* variable is initialized as new list of strings at the start of the method, only for it to be overwritten by the code in the *try* block. This is a defensive mechanism that ensures that the *productsList* variable is always set to a meaningful value should the code in the *try* block fail for some reason. You will see an example of how such a failure might occur in Chapter 3.

9. Add the *GetProduct* method (shown in bold in the following) to the *ProductsServiceImpl* class.

```
public class ProductsServiceImpl : IProductsService
{
    ...
    public ProductData GetProduct(string productNumber)
    {
        // Create a reference to a ProductData object
        // This object will be instantiated if a matching product is found
        ProductData productData = null;

        try
        {
            // Connect to the AdventureWorks database by using the Entity Framework
            using (AdventureWorksEntities database = new AdventureWorksEntities())
            {
                // Find the first product that matches the specified product number
                Product matchingProduct = database.Products.First(
                    p => String.Compare(p.ProductNumber, productNumber) == 0);

                productData = new ProductData()
                {
                    Name = matchingProduct.Name,
                    ProductNumber = matchingProduct.ProductNumber,
                    Color = matchingProduct.Color,
                    ListPrice = matchingProduct.ListPrice
                };
            }
        }
        catch
        {
            // Ignore exceptions in this implementation
        }

        // Return the product
        return productData;
    }
}
```

The *GetProduct* method connects to the *AdventureWorks* database by using an *Adventure WorksEntities* object; it uses the *First* extension method of the *Products* collection to fetch the details of the first product it finds in the database that has a product number that matches the parameter passed in to the *GetProduct* method. The data from the matching *Product* object are used to populate a *ProductData* object, which is returned by the *GetProduct* method.

Note that if the specified product number is not found in the database, the *First* method throws an exception. This exception is caught by the *GetProduct* method, which ignores it. If this happens, the *GetProduct* method returns a null *ProductData* object.

10. Add the *CurrentStockLevel* method to the *ProductsServiceImpl* class, as shown in bold in the following:

```
public class ProductsServiceImpl : IProductsService
{
    ...
    public int CurrentStockLevel(string productNumber)
    {
        // Obtain the total stock level for the specified product.
        // The stock level is calculated by summing the quantity of the product
        // available in all the bins in the ProductInventory table.

        // The Product and ProductInventory tables are joined over the
        // ProductID column.

        int stockLevel = 0;

        try
        {
            // Connect to the AdventureWorks database by using the Entity Framework
            using (AdventureWorksEntities database = new AdventureWorksEntities())
            {
                // Calculate the sum of all quantities for the specified product
                stockLevel = (from pi in database.ProductInventories
                              join p in database.Products
                              on pi.ProductID equals p.ProductID
                              where String.Compare(p.ProductNumber,productNumber) == 0
                              select (int)pi.Quantity).Sum();
            }
        }
        catch
        {
            // Ignore exceptions in this implementation
        }

        // Return the stock level
        return stockLevel;
    }
}
```

The *CurrentStockLevel* method takes a product number as a parameter and calculates the volume of this product that is currently in stock. Remember that products are stored in one or more bins on various shelves in the warehouse. This method uses a LINQ query to find all items in the *ProductsInventories* collection that have a product ID that matches the specified product number. It then sums the quantities in each matching *ProductsInventory* object.

> **Important** Ideally, you should also perform some validation checking on the *product-Number* parameter to verify that it does not contain strings that could be indicative of an attempted SQL Injection attack. However, such input validation has been omitted in this example, for clarity.

11. Add the *ChangeStockLevel* method (shown in bold in the following) to the *Products-ServiceImpl* class:

```
public class ProductsServiceImpl : IProductsService
{
    ...
    public bool ChangeStockLevel(string productNumber, short newStockLevel,
                                 string shelf, int bin)
    {
        // Modify the current stock level of the selected product
        // in the ProductInventory table.
        // If the update is successful then return true, otherwise return false.

        // The Product and ProductInventory tables are joined over the
        // ProductID column.

        try
        {
            // Connect to the AdventureWorks database by using the Entity Framework
            using (AdventureWorksEntities database = new AdventureWorksEntities())
            {
                // Find the ProductID for the specified product
                int productID =
                    (from p in database.Products
                     where String.Compare(p.ProductNumber, productNumber) == 0
                     select p.ProductID).First();

                // Find the ProductInventory object that matches the parameters passed
                // in to the operation
                ProductInventory productInventory = database.ProductInventories.First(
                    pi => String.Compare(pi.Shelf, shelf) == 0 &&
                        pi.Bin == bin &&
                        pi.ProductID == productID);

                // Update the stock level for the ProductInventory object
                productInventory.Quantity += newStockLevel;

                // Save the change back to the database
                database.SaveChanges();
            }
        }
    }
```

```
        catch
        {
            // If an exception occurs, return false to indicate failure
            return false;
        }

        // Return true to indicate success
        return true;
    }
}
```

This method updates the quantity in stock for the specified product, in the specified bin, on the specified shelf. If this product is not actually located in this bin, on this shelf, the *First* extension method on the second LINQ query throws an exception and the method returns false to indicate that no update occurred. If a matching *ProductInventory* object is found, the *ChangeStockLevel* method sets the *Quantity* property to the value of the *newStockLevel* parameter, saves the changes back to the database, and returns true to indicate that the update was successful.

Notice that the *SaveChanges* method of the *AdventureWorksEntity* class performs the database update. The *SaveChanges* method generates SQL *UPDATE* statements for each object in the *Products* and *ProductInventories* collections that has been modified; SQL *DELETE* statements for each object in these collections that has been removed; and SQL *INSERT* statements for each object added to these collections.

12. Build the C:\...\ProductsService\ Web site, and correct any errors if necessary.

Configuring and Testing the Service

The WCF service that you have built runs the same way as a regular Web application and is hosted by a Web server. In this case, when you created the WCF service, you set the location to a folder in the file system, so when you run the service it will execute by using the ASP.NET Development Server provided with Visual Studio. You will see later in this chapter how you can package and deploy the service to run in Internet Information Services (IIS). You can also host a WCF service in a variety of other environments, including a stand-alone application, a Windows service application, and Windows Server Azure. You will learn more about hosting services in some of these environments in Chapter 2, "Hosting a WCF Service."

You need to provide the host environment with service configuration information so it knows which class contains the WCF service and how it should listen for requests from client applications. WCF provides default options for much of this configuration information, but you can override these defaults with values that meet your specific requirements. You will learn about many of these configuration options as you progress through this book.

In the following exercises you will perform a minimal configuration and test the WCF service using Internet Explorer. Later in this chapter, you will test the service by building a client application that connects to the service and invokes its operations.

Configure the WCF Service

1. In the C:\...\ProductsService\ Web site, double-click the Service.svc file to display it in the Code And Text Editor window. The contents of the file look like this:

```
<%@ ServiceHost Language="C#" Debug="true" Service="Service"
    CodeBehind="~/App_Code/Service.cs" %>
```

The Service.svc file specifies the name and location of the class that implements the WCF service. Visual Studio generated that file when you first created the WCF service, but it is now out of date because you changed both the name of the WCF service class and the name of the file that contains the class.

2. In the Service.svc file, change the value of the *Service* attribute to *Products.Products ServiceImpl*, and the value of the *CodeBehind* attribute to reference the ProductsService.cs file, as shown in bold in the following:

```
<%@ ServiceHost Language="C#" Debug="true" Service="Products.ProductsServiceImpl"
    CodeBehind="~/App_Code/ProductsService.cs" %>
```

> **Note** The name of the WCF service class must be fully qualified with the namespace that contains the service.

3. In the C:\...\ProductsService\ Web site, open the Web.config file. This is the configuration file for the WCF service; it looks like this (the layout has been changed slightly to make it more readable in this book):

```
<?xml version="1.0"?>
<configuration>
  <system.web>
    <compilation debug="false" targetFramework="4.0">
      <assemblies>
        <add assembly="System.Data.Entity, Version=4.0.0.0, Culture=neutral,
          PublicKeyToken=B77A5C561934E089"/>
      </assemblies>
    </compilation>
  </system.web>
  <system.serviceModel>
    <behaviors>
      <serviceBehaviors>
        <behavior>
```

```
                <!-- To avoid disclosing metadata information, set the
                   value below to false and remove the metadata endpoint
                   above before deployment -->
                <serviceMetadata httpGetEnabled="true"/>
                <!-- To receive exception details in faults for debugging purposes,
                   set the value below to true.  Set to false before deployment to
                   avoid disclosing exception information -->
                <serviceDebug includeExceptionDetailInFaults="false"/>
              </behavior>
            </serviceBehaviors>
          </behaviors>
          <serviceHostingEnvironment multipleSiteBindingsEnabled="true"/>
        </system.serviceModel>
        <system.webServer>
          <modules runAllManagedModulesForAllRequests="true"/>
        </system.webServer>
      </configuration>
```

The key part to notice in this configuration file is the *<system.serviceModel>* section. You can use this section to specify the endpoints to which the service listens for client requests, to configure the security requirements of the service, and to specify the policy requirements and behavior of the service. The configuration file generated by the WCF Service template simply modifies the behavior to enable the WCF service to publish its metadata (client applications can use this metadata to discover the operations that the service implements) and to turn off debugging details. Most of the remaining configuration elements are left at their default values; the service will listen for client requests by using the HTTP protocol on the default port used by the Web server hosting the WCF service.

You will learn a lot more about the configuration elements available in the *<system. serviceModel>* section as you perform the exercises in this book.

4. In Solution Explorer, in the ProductsEntityModel project, open the App.config file.

   This configuration file contains the connection string generated by the Entity Data Model Wizard for connecting to the *AdventureWorks* database (highlighted in bold in the example that follows):

```
<?xml version="1.0" encoding="utf-8"?>
<configuration>
  <connectionStrings>
    <add name="AdventureWorksEntities"
connectionString="metadata=res://*/ProductsModel.csdl|res://*/ProductsModel.ssdl|res:/
/*/ProductsModel.msl;provider=System.Data.SqlClient;provider connection
string=&quot;Data Source=.\SQLExpress;Initial Catalog=AdventureWorks;Integrated
Security=True;MultipleActiveResultSets=True&quot;"
providerName="System.Data.EntityClient" />
  </connectionStrings>
</configuration>
```

5. Copy the *<connectionStrings>* element and the *AdventureWorksEntities* connection string to the Web.config file for the WCF service. Insert this element in the *<configuration>* section, before the *<system.Web>* section, as shown in bold in the following:

```
<?xml version="1.0"?>
<configuration>
  <connectionStrings>
    <add name="AdventureWorksEntities"
connectionString="metadata=res://*/ProductsModel.csdl|res://*/ProductsModel.ssdl|res:/
/*/ProductsModel.msl;provider=System.Data.SqlClient;provider connection
string=&quot;Data Source=.\SQLExpress;Initial Catalog=AdventureWorks;Integrated
Security=True;MultipleActiveResultSets=True&quot;"
providerName="System.Data.EntityClient" />
  </connectionStrings>
  <system.web>
    ...
  </system.web>
  ...
</configuration>
```

 Note The *connectionString* element should be entered on a single line, without breaks.

6. Save the Web.config file.

Test the WCF Service by Using Internet Explorer

1. In Solution Explorer, in the C:\...\ProductsService\ Web site, right-click the Service.svc file, and then click View in Browser.

   The ASP.NET Development Server starts, and Internet Explorer runs, displaying the page shown in the following image (the port number shown in the URL might be different for your service):

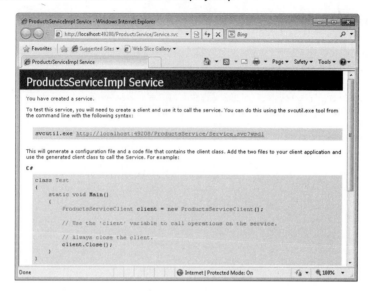

This is the help page for the WCF service. It verifies that the WCF service has been configured correctly (you will see error messages if the WCF service cannot start) and provides information showing how you can build a client application that can connect to the WCF service.

2. Click the URL displayed in Internet Explorer.

   Another page appears, as shown in the following image:

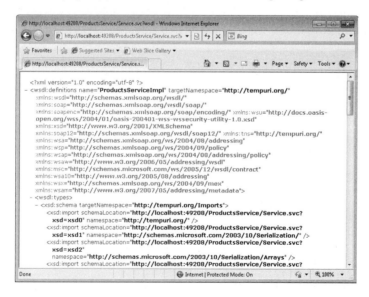

This page shows the metadata that describes the service. You can see that this is an XML document that uses the WSDL schema. The elements in this document describe the operations that the WCF service exposes and the messages that it can receive and send. The operations are derived from the methods you implemented, and the messages are based on the parameters that each method takes and the return values that each method passes back.

Developers familiar with WSDL can take this description and use it to build client applications that can connect to your service. This sounds like an imposing task, but fortunately many development environments, including Visual Studio, provide tools that can convert a WSDL description of a service and generate code for a proxy class that client applications can use to access the service. This is the approach that you will take in the next section.

3. Close Internet Explorer and return to Visual Studio.

Deploying a WCF Service in IIS Without an .svc File

The .svc file is a special content file that IIS uses to recognize a WCF service. It provides the information that the hosting environment in IIS uses to activate the WCF runtime and start the service. The .svc file always forms part of the address of a WCF service hosted by using IIS (this is not the case with other hosting environments, as you will see in Chapter 2).

WCF 4.0 provides a feature called *Configuration-Based Activation*, with which you can combine the information normally included in the .svc file directly into the Web.config file for a WCF service hosted by IIS. To do this, you add a *<serviceActivations>* section to the *<serviceHostingEnvironment>* part of the configuration file and provide values for the *relativeAddress* and *service* elements. The *relativeAddress* element should be a string that looks like a filename with the .svc extension, and the *service* element should specify the fully qualified type that implements the WCF service. The following code fragment shows an example that configures the *ProductsService* WCF service:

```xml
<?xml version="1.0"?>
<configuration>
  ...
  <system.serviceModel>
    ...
    <serviceHostingEnvironment multipleSiteBindingsEnabled="true">
      <serviceActivations>
        <add relativeAddress="NoServiceFile.svc"
            service="Products.ProductsServiceImpl" />
      </servicaActivations>
    </serviceHostingEnvironment>
  </system.serviceModel>
  ...
</configuration>
```

> With this configuration, you can remove the Service.svc file from the Web site and access the *ProductsService* WCF service by using the URL *http://localhost:49208/ProductsService/NoServiceFile.svc* (your port number might vary).

Building a WCF Client Application

You have seen that you can view the metadata for a WCF service by using a Web browser such as Internet Explorer and querying the metadata endpoint for the service; in a WCF service, the metadata endpoint is the URL of the service with the extension *?wsdl*. Visual Studio can use the metadata published by a WCF service to generate a proxy class that a client application can use to connect to the service. The proxy class provides the same operations and messages as the WCF service, but it makes them available as methods, parameters, and return values. The code in the proxy class converts the method calls into request messages and converts the response messages received from a service back into method calls. Thus, the client application is not exposed to the internal details of building messages and can access the WCF service in a manner very similar to calling methods in ordinary local objects.

In the following exercise, you will build a console client application to test the *ProductsService* WCF service.

Build the Console Client Application

1. In Visual Studio, add a new project to the ProductsService solution using the information in the following table:

Item	Value
Template	Console Application
Name	ProductsClient
Location	Microsoft Press\WCF Step By Step\Chapter 1\ProductsService (within your Documents folder [this is the default location])

2. In Solution Explorer, add a reference to the *System.ServiceModel* assembly to the Products Client application. If you have more than one version installed on your computer, make sure that you add version 4.0.0.0 of this assembly.

3. Add a Service Reference for the *ProductsService* service to the ProductsClient application, as follows:

   a. In Solution Explorer, right-click the ProductsClient project, and then click Add Service Reference.

   The Add Service Reference dialog box appears.

b. In the Add Service Reference dialog box, click Discover.

The Address text box is populated with the address of the *ProductsService* service, and the service appears in the Services box.

> **Note** The Discover button is intended to find all WCF services that are part of the same solution as the client application. If you need to add a service reference for a WCF service that is located elsewhere, you can type the URL of the WCF service in the Address box and then click Go.

c. In the Services box, expand ProductsService/Service.svc, expand *ProductsServiceImpl*, and then click *IProductsService*. Verify that the four operations, *ChangeStockLevel*, *CurrentStockLevel*, *GetProduct*, and *ListProducts* appear in the Operations box, as shown in the following image:

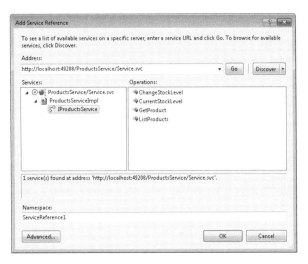

d. In the Namespace text box, type **ProductsService**, and then click OK.

You should notice that the Service References folder appears in Solution Explorer, under the ProductsClient project. If you expand the Service References folder, you will see an entry called ProductsService. This service reference contains the proxy class. You can view the code for the proxy class if you click the Show All Files button in the Solution Explorer toolbar, expand the ProductsService entry, expand Reference.svcmap, and then double-click Reference.cs. Be careful not to change any of this code.

> **Hint** If you do accidentally modify the code for the proxy class, you can regenerate it quite easily; in Solution Explorer, right-click the *ProductsService* service reference and then click Update Service Reference.

4. In Solution Explorer, double-click the App.config file for the ProductsClient project to display this file in the code view window. This is the WCF client configuration file that's generated at the same time as the proxy class. It contains the settings the client application uses to connect to the WCF service. It looks similar to this:

```
<?xml version="1.0" encoding="utf-8" ?>
<configuration>
  <system.serviceModel>
    <bindings>
      <basicHttpBinding>
        <binding name="BasicHttpBinding_IProductsService" closeTimeout="00:01:00"
            openTimeout="00:01:00" receiveTimeout="00:10:00" sendTimeout="00:01:00"
            allowCookies="false" bypassProxyOnLocal="false"
            hostNameComparisonMode="StrongWildcard"
            maxBufferSize="65536" maxBufferPoolSize="524288"
            maxReceivedMessageSize="65536"
            messageEncoding="Text" textEncoding="utf-8" transferMode="Buffered"
            useDefaultWebProxy="true">
          <readerQuotas maxDepth="32" maxStringContentLength="8192"
              maxArrayLength="16384" maxBytesPerRead="4096"
              maxNameTableCharCount="16384" />
          <security mode="None">
            <transport clientCredentialType="None" proxyCredentialType="None"
                realm="" />
            <message clientCredentialType="UserName" algorithmSuite="Default" />
          </security>
        </binding>
      </basicHttpBinding>
    </bindings>
    <client>
      <endpoint address="http://localhost:49208/ProductsService/Service.svc"
          binding="basicHttpBinding"
          bindingConfiguration="BasicHttpBinding_IProductsService"
          contract="ProductsService.IProductsService"
          name="BasicHttpBinding_IProductsService" />
    </client>
  </system.serviceModel>
</configuration>
```

WCF client applications do not have the same degree of default configuration options as WCF services. Consequently, you must specify this information explicitly, so the configuration file for a client application might contain a lot more information than the corresponding service configuration file.

The *<client>* section toward the end of the file specifies how the client connects to the service. The *<endpoint>* element provides the details of the service that the client application requires to communicate with it. An endpoint contains three key pieces of information: an address, a binding, and a contract. An endpoint can also have an optional name that you can reference in the code of your client application; this is useful if you connect to multiple services because each service can have its own named endpoint in the client configuration file.

The address is the URL of the service (in this case, *http://localhost:49208/ProductsService/ Service.svc*).

The binding element specifies items such as the transport mechanism used to access the Web service and the protocol to use, among other items. A service can use one of a number of standard bindings built into WCF. When you configured the service, you did not specify any binding information, so the default *basicHttpBinding* binding was used. This binding is based on the HTTP protocol and is compatible with many existing Web services and client applications built with technologies other than WCF. In addition, you can modify the properties of a binding to specify additional information, such as time-out values, message encodings, and security requirements.

The example generated for the client application creates a binding configuration called *BasicHttpBinding_IProductsService*. This configuration is referenced from the definition of the client endpoint. A client application must use the same binding configuration as the service in order to communicate with it successfully. If you modify the configuration for a WCF service, you must make the corresponding changes to the configuration files for each client. Fortunately, the binding configuration is exposed by a service as part of its metadata, so if you modify the configuration for a service, you can regenerate the binding configuration for a client by using the *Update Service Reference* feature described earlier. You will learn much more about bindings and binding configurations in Chapter 2.

Finally, the contract element indicates the contract that the service implements, which in turn dictates the messages that a client application can send and expect to receive when communicating with the service. Again, you will learn a lot more about service contracts throughout the exercises in this book.

5. Open the Program.cs file for the ProductsClient project in the Code And Text Editor window. Add the *using* statements (shown in bold in the following) to the list at the top of the file:

```
using System;
using System.Collections.Generic;
using System.Linq;
using System.Text;
using System.ServiceModel;
using ProductsClient.ProductsService;

namespace ProductsClient
{
    class Program
    {
        static void Main(string[] args)
        {
        }
    }
}
```

You should always add a reference to the *System.ServiceModel* assembly and namespace to a WCF client application because they provide the methods needed to communicate with a WCF service. The *ProductsClient.ProductsService* namespace contains the proxy class for the *ProductsService* WCF service.

6. In the *Main* method, add the statements, shown in bold in the following:

```
static void Main(string[] args)
{
    // Create a proxy object and connect to the service
    ProductsServiceClient proxy = new ProductsServiceClient();
}
```

The *ProductsServiceClient* class is the name of the proxy type generated earlier. This code creates a new instance of the proxy and connects to the *ProductsService* service.

> **Note** The constructor for the *ProductsServiceClient* class is overloaded. The default con-
> structor is useful if the client configuration defines a single endpoint for connecting to a
> service. If there is a choice of endpoints with different configurations, you can specify the
> name of the endpoint to use, like this:
>
> ```
> ProductsServiceClient proxy =
>     new ProductsServiceClient("BasicHttpBinding_IProductsService");
> ```
>
> Other overloads enable you to explicitly specify the address of the service and the binding
> to use if you wish to override the settings in the configuration file.

7. Add the following code (shown in bold) to the *Main* method, just below the code added in the previous step:

```
static void Main(string[] args)
{
    // Create a proxy object and connect to the service
    ProductsServiceClient proxy = new ProductsServiceClient();

    // Test the operations in the service

    // Obtain a list of all products
    Console.WriteLine("Test 1: List all products");
    string[] productNumbers = proxy.ListProducts();
    foreach (string productNumber in productNumbers)
    {
        Console.WriteLine("Number: {0}", productNumber);
    }
    Console.WriteLine();

}
```

This block of code tests the *ListProducts* method. This method should return an array of strings containing the product number of every product in the database. The *foreach* statement iterates through the list and displays them.

8. Add the following code (shown in bold) to the *Main* method, after the previous statements:

```
static void Main(string[] args)
{
    ...
    Console.WriteLine("Test 2: Display the details of a product");
    ProductData product = proxy.GetProduct("WB-H098");
    Console.WriteLine("Number: {0}", product.ProductNumber);
    Console.WriteLine("Name: {0}", product.Name);
    Console.WriteLine("Color: {0}", product.Color);
    Console.WriteLine("Price: {0}", product.ListPrice);
    Console.WriteLine();
}
```

This section of code tests the *GetProduct* method. The *GetProduct* method returns the details for the specified product (in this case, product WB-H098) as a *ProductData* object. Remember that the definition of the *ProductData* type was specified in the data contract for the WCF service. The code defining this type in the client application was generated from the metadata for the service and can be found in the Reference.cs file, in the ProductsService.svcmap folder, under the *ProductsService* service reference in Solution Explorer.

9. Add the following code (shown in bold) to the end of the *Main* method:

```
static void Main(string[] args)
{
    ...
    // Query the stock level of this product
    Console.WriteLine("Test 3: Display the stock level of a product");
    int numInStock = proxy.CurrentStockLevel("WB-H098");
    Console.WriteLine("Current stock level: {0}", numInStock);
    Console.WriteLine();
}
```

This block of code tests the *CurrentStockLevel* method. The value returned should be the total number of product WB-H098 held in the warehouse.

10. Add the following code (shown in bold) to the *Main* method:

```
static void Main(string[] args)
{
    ...
    // Modify the stock level of this product
    Console.WriteLine("Test 4: Modify the stock level of a product");
    if (proxy.ChangeStockLevel("WB-H098", 100, "N/A", 0))
    {
        numInStock = proxy.CurrentStockLevel("WB-H098");
        Console.WriteLine("Stock changed. Current stock level: {0}", numInStock);
    }
```

```
        else
        {
            Console.WriteLine("Stock level update failed");
        }
        Console.WriteLine();
    }
```

This code tests the *ChangeStockLevel* method. Product WB-H098 is located on shelf "N/A," in bin 0, and this code adds another 100 to the volume in stock. The code then calls the *CurrentStockLevel* method again, which should return the new stock level for this product.

11. Complete the *Main* method by adding the following code shown in bold:

```
static void Main(string[] args)
{
    . . .
    // Disconnect from the service
    proxy.Close();
    Console.WriteLine("Press ENTER to finish");
    Console.ReadLine();
}
```

You disconnect from a service by calling the *Close* method of the proxy. You should not attempt to call further methods by using the proxy without connecting again.

Note It is important that you close the *proxy* object when you have finished with it, otherwise the connection might hold resources open on the server hosting the service. The *ProductsClientService* class actually implements the *IDisposable* interface, so you can employ a *using* construct, as shown below, to ensure that the proxy is closed appropriately; the *Close* method is called automatically when execution reaches the end of the block and the *proxy* object goes out of scope.

```
// Create a proxy object and connect to the service
using (ProductsServiceClient proxy = new ProductsServiceClient())
{
    // Use the proxy
    . . .

} // Disconnect and close the proxy automatically
```

12. Save the project and build the solution.

Configuring the Service Proxy

You might be wondering why the value returned by *ListProducts* is a string array when the WCF service implements this method as returning a *List<string>*. The answer lies in the way that the data is transmitted from the service to the client application.

When you build a WCF service, you define its operations in terms of types implemented by using the .NET Framework. As described earlier, the messages that you send and receive to and from a Web service are defined by using an XML schema. The WCF run-time converts the data in incoming messages for a service from this XML format into .NET Framework types and passes them as parameters to the methods that implement the service operations. Similarly, when a service returns a value from an operation, the WCF runtime converts the data back into XML and transmits it to the client application. If you have built the client application by using Visual Studio, the proxy converts the data from XML back into the native .NET Framework format before passing it to your code.

In many cases, the WCF runtime implements well-defined mappings for converting between XML and .NET Framework types; however, for collections there are several choices. The XML schema used by Web services defines its own representation for arrays, and the WCF runtime converts all collections into this XML format. When the proxy for a client application receives an XML array, it has no knowledge of the original .NET Framework type used by the service, and so by default it converts the XML array into a .NET Framework array.

If you want the data to be returned to your client application as a specific type of col-lection, you can configure the proxy to do so. In Solution Explorer, right-click the service reference for the proxy (ProductsService for the ProductsClient application) then click Configure Service Reference. You can specify the type that the proxy should use when it receives an XML array in the Collection type drop-down list, as shown in the following image. Note that this field defaults to System.Array.

The final step is to run the client application and verify that the service operates as expected.

Run the Client Application

1. Set the ProductsClient project and C:\...ProductsService\ Web site as the startup projects for the solution:

    a. In Solution Explorer, right-click the ProductsService solution, and then click Set StartUp Projects.

    b. In the Solution 'ProductsService' Property Pages window, click the Multiple Startup Projects radio button, and then set the Action property for the C:\...\Products Service\ and ProductsClient projects to **Start**. Leave the Action property for the ProductsEntityModel project set to *None*, and then click OK.

    c. In Solution Explorer, right-click the C:\...\ProductsService\ project, and then click Start Options.

    d. In the Property Pages window, select the Don't Open A Page. Wait For A Request From An External Application option, and then click OK.

 Note If you don't perform this final step, Visual Studio will start Internet Explorer running and browse to the Web site when you run the project.

2. Start the application without debugging:

    ❑ On the Debug menu, choose Start Without Debugging.

    A console window opens. A list of product numbers should appear first, followed by the details of product WB-H098 (a water bottle), the current stock level (252), and the stock level after adding another 100 (352):

```
C:\Windows\system32\cmd.exe
Number: TI-T723
Number: TO-2301
Number: TP-0923
Number: TI-M928
Number: TI-R982
Number: TI-T092
Number: UE-C304-L
Number: UE-C304-M
Number: UE-C304-S
Number: WB-H098

Test 2: Display the details of a product
Number: WB-H098
Name: Water Bottle - 30 oz.
Color:
Price: 4.9900

Test 3: Display the stock level of a product
Current stock level: 252

Test 4: Modify the stock level of a product
Stock changed. Current stock level: 352

Press ENTER to finish
```

3. Press Enter to terminate the program and return to Visual Studio.

Deploying a WCF Service to Internet Information Services

The *ProductsService* WCF service works well, but currently it runs within the confines of the ASP.NET Development Server. In the real world, you want to be able to access it from a location outside your development environment—which typically means deploying it to IIS. The various wizards and tools provided with Visual Studio and IIS make deploying a service a fairly simple operation. In the following exercises, you will deploy the *ProductsService* WCF service to IIS, reconfigure the client application to connect to the new address and then test it.

The exercises in this section require that you have administrator access to your computer and that you are running Visual Studio as an administrator. To do this, exit Visual Studio and restart it by using the following procedure:

1. On the Windows Start menu, click All Programs, click the Microsoft Visual Studio 2010 folder, right-click Microsoft Visual Studio 2010, and then click Run As Administrator.

2. In the User Account Control dialog box, either click Yes if you already have administrator access to your computer, or if you don't, enter the administrator password and then click Yes.

3. Open the ProductsService solution in the Microsoft Press\WCF Step By Step\Chapter 1\ ProductsService folder (within your Documents folder).

Deploy the WCF Service to IIS

1. In Solution Explorer, right-click the C:\...\ProductsService\ project, and then click Publish Web Site.

   The Publish Web Site dialog box appears.

2. Click the ellipsis button adjacent to the Target Location text box.

   Another dialog box appears (also called Publish Web Site) in which you specify the deployment location of your service. You can deploy the service to a local or remote installation of IIS (if you have the appropriate access rights), or to an FTP site.

3. Click Local IIS.

   The main window in the dialog box displays the Web sites on your local installation of IIS.

4. Click Default Web Site, and then in the upper-right corner or the dialog box, click the Create New Web Application button, as highlighted in the image that follows:

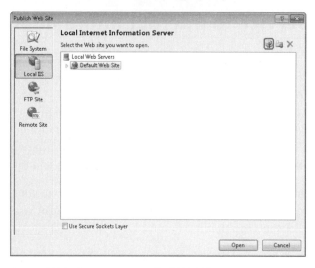

A new Web site appears, called *WebSite*.

5. Change the name of the new Web site to **ProductsService**, and then click Open.

6. In the Publish Web Site dialog box, click OK.

The files comprising your WCF service are compiled, and the compiled assemblies and configuration files are copied to the ProductsService virtual directory. You can verify that publication was successful by using Windows Explorer to examine the contents of the C:\inetpub\wwwroot\ProductsService folder which will have been created by this process. Note that—for security reasons—the source code for your service is not copied, only the compiled assemblies are copied. If you need to modify the code for your service, you should make the changes and test them locally by using the ASP.NET Development Server, and then use the Publish Web Site Wizard to publish the updated service.

Important By default, the WCF service will be deployed to run by using the IIS Default-AppPool. Unless you have reconfigured this application pool, it will attempt to run the service by using the .NET Framework Version 2.0, and will fail. In this case, you should therefore configure the ProductsService application in IIS to use something more appropriate, such as the ASP.NET v4.0 application pool. You can achieve this by performing the following steps:

1. Start Internet Information Services Manager as an administrator as follows.

   ❏ On the Windows Start menu, click Control Panel, click System And Security, click Administrative Tools, right-click Internet Information Services (IIS) Manager, and then click Run As Administrator. Enter the administrator password if you are prompted.

2. In Internet Information Services Manager, in the Connections pane, expand the connection that corresponds to your local computer, expand Sites, expand Default Web Site, and then click ProductsService.

3. In the Actions pane (on the right side), click Basic Settings.

4. In the Edit Application dialog box, click Select (adjacent to the Application pool box).

5. In the Select Application Pool dialog box, select ASP.NET v4.0, and then click OK.

6. In the Edit Application dialog box, click OK.

You should also note that when you host a WCF service in IIS, the service runs with the identity of the account specified by the application pool. You therefore need to ensure that the account for this identity has access to the resources used by the WCF service. In the case of the *ProductsService* service, you must provide the account used by the DefaultAppPool or the ASP.NET v4.0 application pool with access to the *AdventureWorks* database. The script aspnet.sql that you ran as part of the installation and configuration in the Introduction already adds the default accounts used by these application pools to SQL Server, but if you have reconfigured the application pools to use different accounts you must add them manually (to see the syntax, examine the aspnet.sql script in the Microsoft Press\WCF Step By Step\Setup folder, located within your Documents folder).

Reconfigure the Client Application and Test the Service

1. In Visual Studio, in the ProductsClient application, open the App.config file.

2. In the *<endpoint>* configuration section near the end of the file, change the address to **http://localhost/ProductsService/Service.svc**.

3. Save the file.

4. Start the ProductsClient application without debugging and verify that it runs success-fully. This time, however, it is connecting to the WCF service hosted by using IIS.

5. Close the application and return to Visual Studio.

Note If the client application fails with an exception, there are two common causes to look for. First, verify that you have not inserted any extraneous characters in the address in the application configuration file and that you have removed the port number and colon from the address. If the address is correct but the application still fails, the most likely cause is that the account used by the application pool hosting the service does not have appropriate access to the *AdventureWorks* database. The account must be a member of the *db_owner* role in the *AdventureWorks* database. For examples of how to add an account with this privilege to the database, see the aspnet.sql script in the Microsoft Press\WCF Step By Step\Setup folder.

WCF and the Principles of SOA

At the start of this chapter I mentioned that WCF is an ideal platform for implementing an SOA.

You have seen how you can quickly build services by using WCF that you can integrate into enterprise solutions. Apart from writing entirely new functionality, you can use WCF to implement services that wrap existing applications and connect them together in ways that were previously difficult to achieve. WCF can act as the "glue" for combining applications and components together. Additionally, WCF can make use of standard protocols, data formats, and communications mechanisms, enabling interoperability with services developed by using other technologies.

An SOA consists of a set of resources on a network that are made available as independent services and that can be accessed without requiring any knowledge of how they are implemented. You can combine the services in an SOA to create an enterprise application. I don't want to go into the full theory of SOA, but the main benefits are that you can create complex solutions that are independent of any specific platform and location. This means that you can quickly replace or upgrade a service or move a service to a different site (possibly running on faster hardware). As long as the service exposes the same interfaces as it did before the change, you can continue to use it without modifying any code. However, SOA is not a magic wand that will instantly solve all of your distributed application architecture problems. To successfully design and implement an SOA, you should be aware of what has become known as the "Four Tenets of Service Orientation." These are:

1. *Boundaries are explicit.*   Applications and services communicate by sending messages to each other. You should not make any assumptions about how a service processes a request or how a client application handles any response to a request. Following this principle can help remove dependencies between services and client applications. Additionally, sending and receiving messages has an associated cost in terms of communications. You should design the operations that services implement with this in mind and ensure that clients call services only when necessary.

2. *Services are autonomous.*   If you are building an application based on services, you might not have control over every service you are using, especially Web services hosted outside your organization. The location of a Web service might change, or a service might be temporarily taken offline for maintenance or other reasons. You should design your solutions to be loosely coupled so that they can tolerate these changes and continue running even if one or more services are unavailable.

3. *Services share schemas and contracts, not classes or types.*   Services publish information about the operations that they implement and the structure of the data that they expect to send and receive. Clients use this information when communicating with the service. You should design contracts and schemas to define the interfaces that your services expose. This can reduce the dependencies that clients have on a particular version of

your services. Services can change and evolve over time, and a new version of a service might appear that supercedes a previous version. If a service is updated, it should maintain compatibility with existing clients by continuing to implement existing contracts and send messages that conform to existing schemas. If you need to modify a service and provide additional functionality, you can add contracts and schemas that extend the original capabilities of the service while retaining the existing contracts and schemas. Older client applications should continue to work unchanged.

4. *Compatibility is based on policy.*   The schemas and contracts exposed by a service define the "shape" of the service but not the nonfunctional requirements that a client attempting to access the service must fulfill. For example, a service might have security requirements that state that clients must connect to it in a particular manner and send and receive messages by encrypting data in a specific way. This is an example of policy. The policy requirements of a service cannot be specified by using contracts and should not require additional coding on the part of the client or the service—these requirements might change over time, and so should be decoupled from the implementation of the service and clients. You should design services whose policy requirements are independent of any implementation, and you should force clients to abide by any policies required by the service. Additionally, all services and client applications must agree on how to specify this policy information (typically by using some sort of configuration file). This is the purpose of the WS-Policy framework, published by the World Wide Web Consortium and widely adopted by Web service developers.

> **More Info** For further information about the WS-Policy framework, visit the World Wide Web Consortium Web site at *http://www.w3.org/TR/2007/REC-ws-policy-20070904*.

This sounds like a lot to think about when creating services, but WCF has been designed with these principles in mind. As you progress through the rest of this book, you will encounter many of the features WCF provides to help you build services that conform to SOA best practices.

Summary

This chapter has introduced you to WCF. You should be familiar with the purpose of WCF and how to use it to create a simple Web service by adopting a contract-first approach to design. You have deployed a WCF Web service to IIS and seen how to create a client application that can access the service. Finally, you have learned the basic principles of SOA and should now understand that using WCF can help you to build services for an SOA, quickly and easily.

Chapter 2
Hosting a WCF Service

After completing this chapter, you will be able to:

- Describe how a WCF service runs.

- Explain the different ways you can host a WCF service.

- Build a Windows Presentation Foundation application and a Windows service that host a WCF service.

- Describe the different bindings available for communicating with a WCF service.

- Use multiple bindings with a WCF service.

In the previous chapter, you saw how to create a WCF service, how to deploy a WCF service to Internet Information Services (IIS), and how to access it from a client application. This chapter describes in more detail how a WCF service works and explains some of the other options you have for hosting a WCF service. In this chapter, you will build and configure host applications that process service requests and control the state of a WCF service. You will also learn more about how bindings work in WCF and how the WCF runtime uses bindings to implement the nonfunctional features of a service.

How Does a WCF Service Work?

Functionally, a WCF service is just an object that exposes a set of operations that client applications can invoke. When you build a service, you describe the operations for a service by using a service contract, and then create a class that implements that contract. To execute the service, you must provide a runtime environment for the service object and then make it available to client applications. The runtime environment for an object implementing a service is provided by a *host* application. You have already seen that you can use IIS to provide such a runtime environment. You can also create your own application to act as a host.

A host application must perform several tasks, which include:

- Starting and stopping the service

- Listening for requests from a client application and directing them to the service

- Sending any responses from the service back to the client applications

To understand more about how a host application works, it is helpful to look in detail at service endpoints and the way the WCF runtime uses the binding information specified in endpoints to enable client applications to connect to the service.

Service Endpoints

A host application makes a service available to client applications by providing one or more endpoints to which clients can send requests. An endpoint contains three pieces of information:

1. **The address of the service.** The form of a service address depends on several factors, including the transport protocol being used. Different transport mechanisms use different address spaces. For example, in Chapter 1, "Introducing Windows Communication Foundation," you deployed a service to IIS using the address *http://localhost/ ProductsService/ProductsService.svc*. This address specifies the virtual directory and the service definition (.svc) file. If you build your own custom host application, you can use a different transport mechanism, and you must specify an address that is appropriate to your chosen transport mechanism.

2. **The binding supported by the service.** The binding for a service describes how a client can connect to the service and the format of the data expected by the service. A binding can include the following information:

   ❑ The transport protocol. This must conform to the requirements of the service address. For example, if you are using IIS to host the service, you should specify the HTTP or HTTPS transport protocol. WCF also has built-in support for the TCP protocol, named-pipes, and message queues. You will see examples of addresses specified by using some of these transport schemes later in this chapter.

   ❑ The encoding format of messages. In many cases, request and response messages will be transmitted in XML format, encoded as ordinary text. However, in some cases you might need to transmit data using a binary encoding, especially if you are transmitting images or handling streams. You will learn more about using an appropriate encoding for messages in Chapter 13, "Implementing a WCF Service for Good Performance."

   ❑ The security requirements of the service. You can implement security at the transport level and at the message level, although different transport protocols have their own limitations and requirements. You will learn more about specifying the security requirements for a service in Chapter 4, "Protecting an Enterprise WCF Service," and in Chapter 5, "Protecting a WCF Service over the Internet."

   ❑ The transactional requirements of the service. A service typically provides access to one or more resources. Client applications update these resources by sending requests to the service. If a client makes multiple requests of a service that result in multiple updates, it can be important to ensure that *all* of these updates are made permanent. In the event of a failure, the service should undo *all* of these updates. This is the definition of a transaction. You will learn more about building WCF services that support transactions in Chapter 9, "Supporting Transactions."

❑   The reliability of communications with the service. Clients usually connect to services across a network. Networks are notoriously unreliable and can fail at any time. If a client application is performing a conversation (an ordered exchange of several messages) with a service, information about the reliability of the service is important. For example, the service should try to ensure that it receives *all* messages sent by the client—and receives them in the order that the client sent them. A service can ensure the integrity of conversations by implementing a reliable messaging protocol. You will learn more about reliable messaging in Chapter 10, "Implementing Reliable Sessions."

3.   The contract implemented by the service. A WCF service contract is an interface stored in a .NET Framework assembly and annotated with the *ServiceContract* attribute. The service contract describes the operations implemented by the service by tagging them with the *OperationContract* attribute. Any data passed to and from operations must be serializable. A service can define data contracts that describe the structure of complex data and how that data should be serialized. The service can publish the description of its service contract, which a client application can use to ascertain the operations that the service implements and to send messages that are correctly formatted.

Processing a Client Request

A service can respond to requests from multiple client applications simultaneously. To achieve this feat, the application hosting the service must be able to accept multiple incoming requests and direct service responses back to the appropriate client. Additionally, the host application must ensure that messages being sent between the client and service conform to the security, reliability, and transactional requirements of the binding being used. Fortunately, you don't need to write this functionality yourself. The WCF runtime environment for a client application and a service provides a collection of *channel* objects that can perform this processing for you.

A channel is responsible for handling one aspect of message processing, as specified by the bindings of a service. For example, a transport channel manages communications by using a specific transport protocol, and a transaction channel controls the transactional integrity of a conversation. The WCF runtime provides built-in channels for each of the supported transport protocols. The WCF runtime also provides channels that handle the different ways that WCF can encode data, manage security, implement reliability, and perform transactions. The WCF runtime composes channels into a channel stack. All messages passing between the client and the service go through each channel in the channel stack. Each channel in the channel stack transforms the message in some way, and the output from one channel is passed as input to the next. The channel stack operates in two directions: messages received from clients across the network proceed up the channel stack to the service, and response messages sent back from the service traverse the channel stack in the opposite direction back to the network and then to the client. If a channel cannot process a message, it reports an error, an error message is sent back to the client, and the message is not processed any further.

> **Note** There is an order to the channels in the channel stack. A transport channel always resides at the bottom of the stack and is the first channel to receive data from the network. On top of the transport channel will be an encoding channel. These two channels are mandatory; the remaining channels in a stack are optional.

When you start a service running, the WCF runtime uses the endpoint information specified as part of the service configuration and creates a *listener* object for each address specified for the service. When an incoming request is received, the WCF runtime constructs a channel stack by using the binding information specified for the address and routes the incoming data from the client through the stack. If a message successfully traverses all the channels in the channel stack, the transformed request is passed to an instance of the service for processing.

> **Note** The channel model used by WCF makes the WCF framework very flexible. If you need to add a new transport protocol or implement an additional piece of functionality, you can write your own channel to perform the processing required and link it into the channel stack by adding it to the binding description of the service. However, this task is beyond the scope of this book.

As mentioned earlier, a WCF service must be able to handle requests from multiple client applications simultaneously. To do this, the WCF runtime can create multiple concurrent instances of a service. The WCF runtime creates an *InstanceContext* object to control the interaction between the channel stack and a service instance. You can modify the way in which the WCF runtime instantiates a service instance through the *InstanceContext* object by specifying the *ServiceBehavior* attribute of the class that is implementing the service contract. The *ServiceBehavior* attribute has a property called *InstanceContextMode*, which can take the values shown in Table 2-1.

TABLE 2-1 *InstanceContextMode* **Values**

Value	Description
InstanceContextMode.PerCall	A new instance of the service will be created every time a client calls an operation. When the call completes, the service instance is recycled.
InstanceContextMode.PerSession	If the service implements sessions, a new instance of the service will be created at the start of the session and recycled when the session completes. A client can call the service several times during a session. However, the service instance cannot be used across more than one session. For more information about using sessions, see Chapter 7, "Maintaining State and Sequencing Operations."
InstanceContextMode.Single	Only one instance of the service is created, which is then shared by all clients and all sessions. The instance is created when the first client attempts to access it.

The default value for the *InstanceContextMode* property is *PerCall*. You can specify the *InstanceContextMode* property for a service like this:

```
[ServiceBehavior (InstanceContextMode=InstanceContextMode.PerSession)]
public class ProductsServiceImpl : IProductsService
{
    ...
}
```

A WCF client application can communicate with a WCF service by using a proxy class. You can generate this proxy class by using Visual Studio (as you did in Chapter 1) or by using the svcutil utility from the command line. This proxy class implements a channel stack on the client side. You configure this channel stack by using bindings in the same way that you do for a service. All responses received from a service pass through the channels in this stack. To communicate successfully, the client and the service should use an equivalent channel stack containing a compatible set of bindings.

> **Note** A client application can also communicate with a service by creating its own channel stack manually. This is useful if you need to add specific optimizations or customize the way in which the client application sends and receives messages. You will learn more about how to do this in Chapter 11, "Programmatically Controlling the Configuration and Communications."

Hosting a WCF Service by Using Windows Process Activation Service

In Chapter 1, you saw how to build and deploy a WCF service to IIS. IIS provides a comprehensive and scalable hosting environment for Web services; that is, services that client applications can connect to from the World Wide Web. Web services use the HTTP protocol to provide the communications transport. IIS listens for incoming HTTP requests, and when it receives one, it activates the appropriate service that handles that request. The HTTP protocol is a good choice to use as a transport for connecting to Web services across the Internet. However, if you are building client applications that access a service deployed within the same organization, other protocols can prove to be more efficient.

The Windows Process Activation Service (WAS) extends the functionality of IIS by removing the dependency on the HTTP protocol. Using WAS, you can host services that make use of other protocols, such as TCP, named pipes, and Microsoft Message Queues. WAS can listen for requests and activate a service that is waiting on an address that is based on any of these protocols. The important point to understand as far as a WCF service is concerned is that, for the most part, the protocol and the address are merely configuration details. The service contract, data contract, and service implementation are largely independent of the protocol and the host environment.

In the next exercise, you will configure WAS for the *ProductsService* service to enable it to receive requests over the TCP protocol. You will then update the ProductsClient application so it connects to the *ProductsService* service using the TCP protocol.

Installing and Configuring the Windows Process Activation Service

WAS is not installed and configured by default on Windows 7. To install WAS, perform the following steps as an administrator:

1. From the Windows Start menu, choose Control Panel, and then select Programs.

2. Under Programs and Features, click Turn Windows Features On And Off.

3. In the Windows Features dialog box, select Windows Process Activation Service and its sub-features, and then select Microsoft .NET Framework 3.51 and its sub-features, and then finally click OK.

> **Note** The Microsoft .NET Framework 3.51 feature contains the Windows Communication HTTP Activation and Windows Communication Foundation Non-HTTP Activation sub-features. You need these sub-features if you want to run WCF services using WAS.

Additionally, you should ensure that you have installed and registered the correct version of ASP.NET with IIS—installing and uninstalling WAS components can sometimes cause IIS to revert to an earlier version of ASP.NET. To do this, perform the following steps:

1. From the Windows Start menu, select All Programs | Microsoft Visual Studio 2010 | Visual Studio Tools, and then right-click Visual Studio Command Prompt (2010), and click Run As Administrator. Enter the administrator password if you are prompted.

2. In the Visual Studio Command Prompt window, run the following command to install ASP.NET for the .NET Framework 4.0:

```
aspnet_regiis -iru
```

3. Close the Visual Studio Command Prompt window.

Configure the Host Environment for the WCF Service to Support the TCP Protocol

1. Start Internet Information Services Manager as an administrator:

   ❑ From the Windows Start menu, open Control Panel. Select System and Security, click Administrative Tools, right-click Internet Information Services (IIS) Manager, and then click Run As Administrator. Enter the administrator password if you are prompted.

2. In Internet Information Services Manager, in the Connections pane, expand the connection that corresponds to your local computer, expand the Sites item, right-click Default Web Site, and then click Edit Bindings.

   The Site Bindings dialog box appears. If you have installed WAS correctly, it should list the default protocol bindings for the Web site, as shown in the following image:

   Notice that the binding information for the net.tcp protocol indicates that WAS is expecting TCP requests on port 808. You can modify this setting by selecting the Net. Tcp entry and clicking Edit. Alternatively, you can configure WAS to listen for TCP requests on multiple ports by clicking Add and adding an additional protocol binding. For this exercise, leave the net.tcp protocol binding with its default configuration.

3. In the Site Bindings dialog box, click Close.

4. In the Connections pane, expand the Default Web Site item, and then click the ProductsService application.

5. In the Actions pane (on the right-hand side), click Advanced Settings.

6. In the Advanced Settings dialog box, add a comma (**,**) and the text **net.tcp** to the Enabled Protocols box, as shown in the following image.

The Enabled Protocols configuration should contain a comma-separated list of network protocols. These are the protocols that WAS will use to listen for connection requests from client applications.

7. In the Advanced Settings dialog box, click OK.

The host environment for the *ProductsService* WCF service is now configured to listen for requests using the HTTP and TCP protocols. Client applications can connect through TCP by sending requests to port 808.

The next step is to configure the ProductsClient application with a binding that sends requests over TCP to this port.

Configure the Client Application to Connect by Using the TCP Protocol

1. Using Visual Studio, open the ProductsClient solution in the Microsoft Press\WCF Step By Step\Chapter 2\ProductsClient folder.

This solution contains a working copy of the ProductsClient application that you built in Chapter 1.

2. Build and run the ProductsClient application and verify that the ProductsService WCF service is still functioning correctly.

The ProductsClient application currently uses the HTTP protocol, and it should still be able to connect successfully to the service.

3. In Solution Explorer, open the app.config file for the ProductsClient project in the Code And Text Editor window.

4. In the *<client>* section towards the end of the file, add the following *<endpoint>* configuration, shown in bold in the following:

```
<client>
  <endpoint address="http://localhost/ProductsService/Service.svc"
      binding="basicHttpBinding"
      bindingConfiguration="BasicHttpBinding_IProductsService"
      contract="ProductsService.IProductsService"
      name="BasicHttpBinding_IProductsService" />
  <endpoint address="net.tcp://localhost/ProductsService/Service.svc"
      binding="netTcpBinding" contract="ProductsService.IProductsService"
      name="NetTcpBinding_IProductsService" />
</client>
```

   This endpoint specifies a TCP address (note that the protocol element of the URL is
   net tcp). The *netTcpBinding* binding specifies that the client should connect using
   the TCP protocol (*netTcpBinding* is a predefined binding provided with WCF, like
   basicHttpBinding—these predefined bindings are described in more detail later in this
   chapter.) The endpoint is also given a name, *NetTcpBinding_IProductsService*. You can
   actually identify endpoints by using whatever name you like, but this name follows
   the pattern generated by the Add Service Reference Wizard for the *basicHttpBinding*
   binding.

5. Open the Program.cs file for the ProductsClient project in the Code And Text Editor
   window.

6. In the *Main* method, locate the statement that creates the *proxy* object that the client
   application uses to connect to the WCF service. It looks like this:

```
ProductsServiceClient proxy = new ProductsServiceClient();
```

   If there is only a single endpoint defined in the client configuration, this statement connects to the service by using this endpoint. However, now that you have more than
   one endpoint available, you must specify which endpoint to use; if you try to run the
   ProductsClient application at this point it will fail with an *InvalidOperationException*
   exception and the message "An endpoint configuration for contract 'ProductsService.
   IProductsService' could not be loaded because more than one endpoint configuration
   for that contract was found. Please indicate the preferred endpoint configuration section by name."

7. Modify the statement that creates the proxy object and specify the name of the TCP
   endpoint configuration, as shown in bold in the following:

```
ProductsServiceClient proxy =
    new ProductsServiceClient("NetTcpBinding_IProductsService");
```

8. Build and run the ProductsClient application. It should function as before, except that
   this time it is using the TCP protocol to connect to the *ProductsService* WCF service.

Note You can verify that the ProductsClient application is not using HTTP if you stop the World Wide Web Publishing Service on your computer and run the client application again. WAS does not use this service, so the client should still be able to connect to the service. If the client was using an HTTP connection, the connection would fail with an *Endpoint NotFoundException* exception and the message "There was no endpoint listening at *http://localhost/ProductsService/Service.svc* that could accept the message."

If you do try this experiment, be sure to restart the World Wide Web Publishing Service again afterwards as you will need it for the exercises in the next chapters.

Hosting a Service in a User Application

Apart from using IIS or WAS, you have several other options available for hosting a WCF service:

- You can create an ordinary Windows application that a user runs to start and stop the WCF service.

- You can host the WCF service in a Windows Service so that it is available as long as Windows is running.

- You can host the WCF service in a Workflow Foundation Service application. This is really just a variation on using a Windows application, but the way in which you define and implement the service is different.

In the remainder of this chapter, you will see how to build a Windows application and a Windows Service that can host a WCF service. You will learn how to build and host a WCF service by using Workflow Foundation application, which is described in Chapter 8, "Implementing Services by Using Workflows." However, before beginning the practical exercises, you need to learn a little about the *ServiceHost* class.

Windows Server AppFabric

If you are hosting WCF services by using IIS or WAS in a production environment, you might want to consider implementing Windows Server AppFabric.

Windows Server AppFabric is a set of extensions to the Windows operating system aimed at making it easier for developers to build faster, scalable, and more-easily managed services. AppFabric provides a distributed in-memory caching service and replication technology that helps developers improve the speed and availability of ASP.NET Web applications and WCF services. AppFabric also includes hosting features that can simplify the deployment, monitoring, and management of services by making use of familiar tools such as PowerShell, Internet Information Services Manager, and Microsoft System Center.

The AppFabric Caching Service makes repeated access to the same data faster by caching this data in memory. It implements a distributed cluster model that can span many computers; to a client application or service, this cluster appears to be a single logical store, and the application or service is not concerned with which physical server holds an item of cached data. Applications and services can use APIs provided by AppFabric to store, query, modify, and remove data from the cache. The Caching Service implements configurable concurrency control to handle versioning of data that is accessed by multiple clients.

AppFabric Hosting Services provides a scalable and configurable environment for hosting WCF services. AppFabric Hosting Services can run on a set of load-balanced computers. You can use the templates provided with Visual Studio 2010 to build WCF services, and you can implement these services by using code or Workflow Foundation workflows. By using workflows, you can create business processes that can potentially be long-lived. AppFabric Hosting Services builds on the persistence services provided by Workflow Foundation to enable an administrator to specify that an instance of a service should be removed from memory and its state retained in a database if the service is inactive for any length of time. If a message is later received for this instance, AppFabric Hosting Services can resurrect it from the database and continue the instance running. An administrator configures the policy for persisting service instances by using the Manage WCF and WF Services feature added to Internet Information Services Manager by AppFabric.

The details of Windows Server AppFabric are beyond the scope of this book, but if you want more information see the "Windows Server AppFabric" page on the MSDN Web site at *http://msdn.microsoft.com/en-us/windowsserver/ee695849.aspx*.

Using the ServiceHost Class

So far in this chapter, the discussion has described the tasks that a host application for a WCF service must perform. If you are building your own host application rather than using IIS or WAS, you can achieve most of these tasks by using the *ServiceHost* class, available in the *System.ServiceModel* namespace. A *ServiceHost* object can instantiate a service object from an assembly holding the service class; configure the endpoints of the service by using bindings provided in a configuration file or in code; apply any security settings required by the service; and create listener objects for each address that you specify.

When you create a *ServiceHost* object, you specify the type of the class implementing the service. You can optionally specify the addresses that the *ServiceHost* object should listen to for requests, like this:

```
ServiceHost productsServiceHost = new ServiceHost(typeof(ProductsServiceImpl),
    new Uri("http://localhost:8000/ProductsService/ProductsService.svc"),
    new Uri("tcp.net://localhost:8080/TcpProductsService");
```

This example uses the ProductsService service that you created in Chapter 1; it uses two addresses: the first uses the HTTP transport, and the second uses TCP. Strictly speaking, the addresses that you specify in the *ServiceHost* constructor are *base addresses*. A base address is just the initial part of the address. If you provide an application configuration file that contains further address information, this information will be combined with the base addresses you specify here to generate the real addresses. For example, if you use the following code to instantiate the *ServiceHost* object:

```
ServiceHost productsServiceHost = new ServiceHost(typeof(ProductsServiceImpl),
    new Uri("http://localhost:8000/ProductsService"));
```

...and the application configuration contains an endpoint definition like this:

```
<endpoint address="ProductsService.svc" binding="basicHttpBinding"
name="ProductsServiceHttpEndpoint" contract="Products.IProductsService" />
```

...the WCF runtime will combine the two elements together to generate an address of *"http:// localhost:8000/ProductsService/ProductsService.svc"*. This is a very powerful feature with which an administrator can direct a service to use a particular address on a specified site. But it also provides the developer with full control over the selection of the site hosting the service.

If you omit the base address information in the *ServiceHost* constructor, like this:

```
ServiceHost productsServiceHost = new ServiceHost(typeof(ProductsServiceImpl));
```

...the WCF runtime will just use the address information specified in the application configuration file and automatically listen for requests on all configured endpoints. This gives the administrator complete control over the addresses and transports used by the service. For convenience, in the examples in this book, you will adopt this approach and specify the complete address information in the application configuration file wherever possible. However, when building your own enterprise applications, you might prefer to provide the base addresses for service endpoints programmatically.

> **Note** There is one minor side effect of specifying complete addresses in the application configuration file; if you are building a host application and you wish to enable metadata publishing, you must provide the URL for the service to use to publish its metadata in the *HttpGetUrl* or *HttpsGetUrl* properties of the *serviceMetadata* element of the service behavior. The convention is to specify the same address as the service, but with the suffix "/mex".

After you have created the *ServiceHost* object, you can start listening for requests by using the *Open* method, like this:

```
productsServiceHost.Open();
```

Opening a *ServiceHost* object causes the WCF runtime to examine the binding configuration for each endpoint of the service and start listening on each endpoint address. Opening a service can take some time. An overloaded version of the *Open* method is available that takes a *TimeSpan* object and throws an exception if the *Open* method does not complete within the specified time. Additionally, the *ServiceHost* class supports the .NET Framework asynchronous mode of operations through the *BeginOpen* and *EndOpen* methods implementing the *IAsyncResult* design pattern.

> **More Info**   The *IAsyncResult* design pattern is commonly used throughout the .NET Framework, and is not specific to WCF. For details, see the topic "Calling Asynchronous Methods Using IAsyncResult" in the .NET Framework Developer's guide, available in the Microsoft Visual Studio Documentation (also available online at *http://msdn.microsoft.com/en-us/library/ms228969.aspx*).

You stop a service by calling the *Close* method of the *ServiceHost* object. The *Close* method stops the WCF runtime from listening for more requests and gracefully shuts the service down; any work in progress is allowed to complete. As with the *Open* method, you can close a service asynchronously by using the *BeginClose* and *EndClose* methods.

The *ServiceHost* class also provides events that you can use to track the state of a *ServiceHost* object. Table 2-2 summarizes these events.

TABLE 2-2 *ServiceHost* **Events**

Event	Description
Opening	The *ServiceHost* object is opening the service and is processing the binding information for each endpoint so that it can start listening.
Opened	The *ServiceHost* object has successfully opened the service, which is now ready to accept client requests.
Closing	The *ServiceHost* is executing the close method and waiting for all current service requests to complete processing.
Closed	The service has shut down. No listeners are active, and clients cannot send requests.
Faulted	The service has encountered an unrecoverable error. You can examine the *ServiceHost* object to try to determine the cause of the fault, but clients can no longer use the service. You must close the service and open it again before clients can connect.
UnknownMessageReceived	The WCF runtime received a message that the service does not recognize. This can stem from a misconfigured client application or possibly as the result of an attack by a malicious client application.

Building a Windows Presentation Foundation Application to Host a WCF Service

Next, you'll see how to use the *ServiceHost* class to host a WCF service inside an ordinary Windows application. In the following exercise you will build a simple Windows Presentation Foundation (WPF) application to perform this task. Before getting into this application, however, you need to rebuild the WCF service in such a way that it can be more easily incorporated into the host application. You can do this by implementing the service in a WCF Service Library. A WCF service library is simply an assembly that contains one or more WCF services. Visual Studio provides a template you can use to build one.

Rebuild the *ProductsService* WCF Service as a WCF Service Library

1. In Visual Studio, create a new solution with a new project by using the WCF Service Library template. You can find this template in the WCF folder in the Installed Templates pane in the New Project dialog box, as shown in the following image:

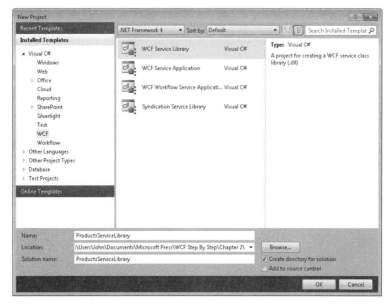

    Name the project **ProductsServiceLibrary** in a solution also called **ProductsService Library** and save it in the Microsoft Press\WCF Step By Step\Chapter 2 folder (within your Documents folder).

2. In Solution Explorer, delete the IService1.cs and Service1.cs files.

3. Add the IProductsService.cs and ProductsService files located in the Microsoft Press\ WCF Step By Step\Chapter 2 folder to the project as follows:

   a. In Solution Explorer, right-click the ProductsServiceLibrary project, point to Add, and then click Existing Item.

   b. In the Add Existing Item – ProductsServiceLibrary dialog box, browse to the Microsoft Press\WCF Step By Step\Chapter 2 folder, select the IProductsService.cs and ProductsService.cs files, and then click Add.

   These files contain a copy of the contracts and implementation for the ProductsService WCF service—the same code that you wrote during the exercises in Chapter 1.

4. Add a reference to the *ProductsEntityModel* assembly located in the Microsoft Press\ WCF Step By Step\Chapter 2 folder to the project, as follows:

   a. In Solution Explorer, right-click the ProductsServiceLibrary project, and then click Add Reference.

   b. In the Add Reference dialog box, click the Browse tab.

   c. Move to the Microsoft Press\WCF Step By Step\Chapter 2 folder, click the ProductsEntityModel.dll file, and then click OK.

   This assembly contains a copy of the entity data model for accessing the *AdventureWorks* database that you created in Chapter 1.

5. Add a reference to the *System.Data.Entity* assembly (use the .NET tab in the Add Reference dialog box).

6. Build the ProductsServiceLibrary project. It should compile without any warnings or errors.

Testing a WCF Service Library by Using the WcfTestClient Application

The WCF Service Library template provides a quick way for you to test a WCF service without building a host application or a client. If you run a WCF Service Library project, the project automatically starts a utility called WcfSvcHost. This utility hosts the service and configures it using the values specified in the application configuration file provided with the service. The WCF Service Library template also generates a default configuration file that you should edit to specify the name of the class that implements the name of your service, as well as the name of the contract that your service implements. Additionally, if your service accesses resources such as a database, you must add the appropriate connection strings to the configuration file. The following code shows an example of the application configuration file generated for the ProductsServiceLibrary project, with the connection string and modifications to the service name and the endpoint contract shown in bold:

```xml
<?xml version="1.0" encoding="utf-8" ?>
<configuration>
  <connectionStrings>
    <!-- Be sure the connection string forms a single line in the configuration
         file. The line is shown as multiple lines here for publishing purposes. -->
    <add name="AdventureWorksEntities"
connectionString="metadata=res://*/ProductsModel.csdl|res://*/ProductsModel.
ssdl|res://*/ProductsModel.msl;provider=System.Data.SqlClient;
provider connection string=&quot;Data Source=.\SQLExpress;Initial Catalog=AdventureWorks;
Integrated Security=True;MultipleActiveResultSets=True&quot;"
providerName="System.Data.EntityClient" />
  </connectionStrings>
  <system.web>
    <compilation debug="true" />
  </system.web>
  <!-- When deploying the service library project, the content of the config file must
       be added to the host's app.config file. System.Configuration does not support
       config files for libraries. -->
  <system.serviceModel>
    <services>
      <service name="Products.ProductsServiceImpl">
        <host>
          <baseAddresses>
            <add baseAddress =
        http://localhost:8732/Design_Time_Addresses/ProductsServiceLibrary/
          Service1/" />
          </baseAddresses>
        </host>
        <!-- Service Endpoints -->
        <!-- Unless fully qualified, address is relative to base address supplied
             above -->
        <endpoint address ="" binding="wsHttpBinding"
            contract="Products.IProductsService">
          <!--
              Upon deployment, the following identity element should be removed or
              replaced to reflect the identity under which the deployed service runs.
              If removed, WCF will infer an appropriate identity automatically.
          -->
          <identity>
            <dns value="localhost"/>
          </identity>
        </endpoint>
```

```
      <!-- Metadata Endpoints -->
      <!-- The Metadata Exchange endpoint is used by the service to describe itself
            to clients. -->
      <!-- This endpoint does not use a secure binding and should be secured or
            removed before deployment -->
      <endpoint address="mex" binding="mexHttpBinding" contract="IMetadataExchange"/>
    </service>
  </services>
  <behaviors>
    <serviceBehaviors>
      <behavior>
        <!-- To avoid disclosing metadata information,
        set the value below to false and remove the metadata endpoint above before
        deployment -->
        <serviceMetadata httpGetEnabled="True"/>
        <!-- To receive exception details in faults for debugging purposes,
        set the value below to true.  Set to false before deployment
        to avoid disclosing exception information -->
        <serviceDebug includeExceptionDetailInFaults="False" />
      </behavior>
    </serviceBehaviors>
  </behaviors>
 </system.serviceModel>
</configuration>
```

When the WcfSvcHost application starts, it runs minimized, but you can display it
by clicking the WCF Service Host icon that appears in the list of hidden icons in the
Windows Service task bar. If you display the application, it should look like the following
image:

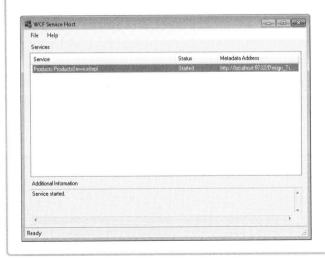

After the WcfSvcHost application has started, another application called WcfTestClient runs and displays the WCF Test Client window. This application connects to the WcfSvcHost application, queries the services that it hosts, obtains a description of the operations exposed by each service, and displays them as shown in the following image:

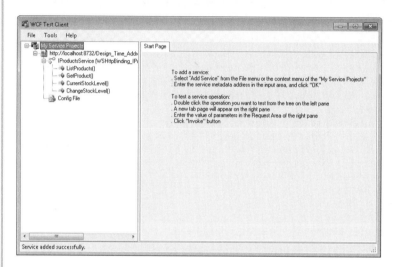

You can use the WCF Test Client window to test each operation and verify that they return the correct data. To do this, double-click an operation in the left pane, enter test values for each of the parameters displayed in the Request section in the right pane, and then click Invoke. The results generated by the service appear in the Response section. The following image shows the results of calling the *GetProduct* operation, passing the string WB-H098 as the value of the *productNumber* parameter:

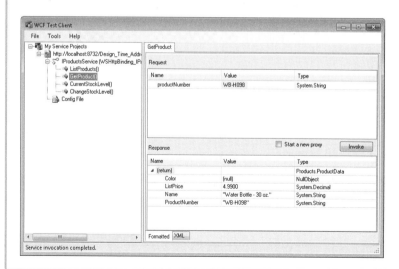

You now have the *ProductsService* WCF service in the form of an assembly that you can reference from the host application. The next step is to actually build the host application.

Create a Windows Application to Host the WCF Service

1. In Visual Studio, add a new project to the ProductsServiceLibrary solution using the information in the following table:

Item	Value
Template	WPF Application (in the Windows folder in the Installed Templates pane)
Name	ProductsServiceHost
Location	Microsoft Press\WCF Step By Step\Chapter 2\ProductsServiceLibrary

2. In Solution Explorer, rename the MainWindow.xaml file to HostController.xaml.

3. Open the App.xaml file in the Code And Text Editor window and change the *StartupUri* attribute of the *Application* element to **HostController.xaml**, as shown in bold in the following:

```
<Application x:Class="ProductsServiceHost.App"
    xmlns="http://schemas.microsoft.com/winfx/2006/xaml/presentation"
    xmlns:x="http://schemas.microsoft.com/winfx/2006/xaml"
    StartupUri="HostController.xaml"
    >
    <Application.Resources>

    </Application.Resources>
</Application>
```

4. Open the HostController.xaml file in the Code And Text Editor window. In the pane displaying the XAML description of the form, change the *Class* attribute to **Products ServiceHost.HostController**, change the *Title* attribute to **Products Service Host**, change the *Height* and *Width* of the window, and add the following code (shown in bold) to the form.

```
<Window x:Class="ProductsServiceHost.HostController"
        xmlns="http://schemas.microsoft.com/winfx/2006/xaml/presentation"
        xmlns:x="http://schemas.microsoft.com/winfx/2006/xaml"
        Title="Products Service Host" Height="300" Width="350">
    <Grid>
        <Button Height="23" HorizontalAlignment="Left" Margin="51,60,0,0"
            Name="start" VerticalAlignment="Top" Width="75"
            Click=" start_Click">Start</Button>
        <Button Height="23" HorizontalAlignment="Right" Margin="0,60,56,0"
            Name="stop" VerticalAlignment="Top" Width="75" IsEnabled="False"
            Click=" stop_Click">Stop</Button>
```

```
        <Label Height="23" HorizontalAlignment="Left" Margin="43,0,0,111"
          Name="label1" VerticalAlignment="Bottom" Width="88">Service Status:</Label>
        <TextBox IsReadOnly="True" Margin="133,0,59,107" Name="status"
          Text="Service Stopped" Height="26" VerticalAlignment="Bottom"></TextBox>
    </Grid>
</Window>
```

The code in the *<Window>* element changes the class reference to refer to the new name of the form.

The code in the *<Grid>* element adds two buttons, a label, and a text box to the form. The two buttons let users start and stop the WCF service, and the label and text box display messages indicating the current state of the WCF service (running or stopped). If you examine the *Click* attribute of the Start button, you can see that it invokes a method called *start_Click*. Similarly, the *Click* attribute of the Stop button invokes a method called *stop_Click*. You will write the code that implements these methods in the next exercise.

In the Design View window, verify that your form looks like the following image:

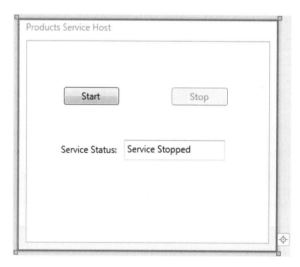

Notice that the Stop button is initially disabled. You will write code to enable it when the service has started.

5. In Solution Explorer, expand the HostController.xaml node and double-click the Host Controller.xaml.cs file to display it in the Code And Text Editor window. In this file, change all three occurrences of *MainWindow* to **HostController**, to match the class named in the XAML description of the form, as shown in bold in the following:

```
namespace ProductsServiceHost
{
    /// <summary>
    /// Interaction logic for HostController.xaml
    /// </summary>
```

```
public partial class HostController : Window
{
    public HostController()
    {
        InitializeComponent();
    }
}
}
```

You have created a simple form that will act as the user interface for the service host. Now you can add the code that actually starts and stops the service.

Add Logic to Start and Stop the WCF Service

1. In the ProductsServiceHost project, add a reference to the *System.ServiceModel* assembly.

2. Add a reference to the ProductsServiceLibrary project.

3. In the Code And Text Editor window displaying the C# code behind the *HostController* window, add the following *using* statements to the list at the top of the file:

```
using System.ServiceModel;
using Products;
```

4. Add the following *ServiceHost* variable shown in bold in the following to the *Host-Controller* class:

```
public partial class HostController : Window
{
    private ServiceHost productsServiceHost;

    public HostController()
    {
        InitializeComponent();
    }
}
```

You will use this variable to control the *ProductsService* service.

5. In the *HostController* class, add the *handleException* method shown in bold in the following immediately after the *HostController()* constructor:

```
public partial class HostController : Window
{
    ...
    public HostController()
    {
        InitializeComponent();
    }
```

```
    private void handleException(Exception ex)
    {
        MessageBox.Show(ex.Message, "Exception",
            MessageBoxButton.OK, MessageBoxImage.Error);
    }
}
```

This method simply displays the message for an exception in a message box. You will make use of this method to handle any exceptions when you start and stop the service.

6. After the *handleException* method, add the *start_Click* method shown in bold in the following to the *HostController* class:

```
public partial class HostController : Window
{
    ...
    private void handleException(Exception ex)
    {
        ...
    }

    private void start_Click(object sender, RoutedEventArgs e)
    {
        try
        {
            productsServiceHost = new ServiceHost(typeof(ProductsServiceImpl));
            productsServiceHost.Open();
            stop.IsEnabled = true;
            start.IsEnabled = false;
            status.Text = "Service Running";
        }
        catch (Exception ex)
        {
            handleException(ex);
        }
    }
}
```

This method runs when the user clicks the Start button. The first statement in this method creates a new *ServiceHost* object. The parameter to the *ServiceHost* constructor is the type that implements the data contract for the service. The *ServiceHost* object will retrieve the endpoint details with the binding information containing the address from the application configuration file, which you will add in the next exercise. The second statement starts the service host listening to this endpoint by calling the *Open* method. The remaining statements enable the Stop button on the form, disable the Start button, and modify the service status displayed in the window.

If an exception occurs while starting the service, the *handleException* method displays the reason for the exception.

7. Add the *stop_Click* method shown in bold in the following to the *HostController* class:

```
public partial class HostController : Window
{
    ...
    private void start_Click(object sender, RoutedEventArgs e)
    {
        ...
    }

    private void stop_Click(object sender, EventArgs e)
    {
        try
        {
            productsServiceHost.Close();
            stop.IsEnabled = false;
            start.IsEnabled = true;
            status.Text = "Service Stopped";
        }
        catch (Exception ex)
        {
            handleException(ex);
        }
    }
}
```

This method runs when the user clicks the Stop button. The *Close* method of the *ServiceHost* class stops it from listening for more requests. The other statements re-enable the Start button, disable the Stop button, and update the service status displayed in the window.

As before, the code calls the *handleException* method to report any exceptions that occur while stopping the service.

8. Build the solution.

The final step is to provide a configuration file and add the endpoint and binding information for the WCF service.

Configure the Windows Host Application

1. Add the App.config file located in the Microsoft Press\WCF Step By Step\Chapter 2 folder to the ProductsServiceHost project.

This file contains the connection string and the *<serviceModel>* configuration from the Web.config file used previously.

> **Note** The Add Existing Item – ProductsServiceLibrary dialog box does not display configu-ration files by default. To display them, click the drop-down list adjacent to the File Name text box and select All Files (*.*).

2. Open the App.config file in the Code And Text Editor window.

    Previously, when you hosted the service in IIS and WAS, you did not need to provide an endpoint definition in the configuration file. This was because the WCF runtime could deduce default values for each of the items that constituted the endpoint; the address was determined by concatenating the name of the .svc file to the virtual folder holding the service, the binding was assumed to be basic HTTP, and the service defined only a single service contract. When you build a custom host application, these assumptions are no longer valid, so you must specify them in the configuration file.

    Configuring a WCF service can be a complex task. However, Visual Studio provides a tool called the Service Configuration Editor as part of the Microsoft Windows SDK Tools, which you can use to configure a WCF service graphically.

3. Close the App.config file in the Code And Text Editor window, and then reopen it by using the Service Configuration Editor, as follows:

    ❑   In Solution Explorer, right-click the App.config file, and then click Edit WCF Configuration.

> **Note** If the Edit WCF Configuration command does not appear when you right-click the App.config file, select WCF Service Configuration Editor from the Tools menu. As soon as the Service Configuration Editor starts, close it immediately. If you right-click the App.config file, the Edit WCF Configuration command should now appear.

4. In the Service Configuration Editor, in the Configuration pane, click Services. In the Ser-vices pane, click Create A New Service.

    The New Service Element Wizard appears.

5. On the What Is The Service Type Of Your Service? page, click Browse.

    The Type Browser dialog box appears.

6. In the Type Browser dialog box, double-click the bin folder, double-click the Debug folder, click the *ProductsServiceLibrary* assembly, and then click Open.

    The Type Browser dialog box displays the type *Products.ProductsServiceImpl*. This is the type that implements the *ProductsService* service. If the assembly contained more than one WCF service, they would all be listed.

7. In the Type Browser dialog box, click **Products.ProductsServiceImpl**, and then click Open.

8. On the "What Is The Service Type Of Your Service?" page, click Next.

9. On the "What Service Contract Are You Using?" page, verify that the contract *Products.IProductsService* is selected, and then click Next.

10. On the "What Communications Mode Is Your Service Using?" page, select **TCP**, and then click Next.

11. On the "What Is The Address Of Your Endpoint*?*" page, in the Address box type **net. tcp://localhost:8080/TcpService**, and then click Next.

    This address indicates that the service will listen for TCP requests on port 8080. The identifier **TcpService** is just a logical name chosen for this exercise and does not correspond to a physical file or folder.

12. On the "The Wizard Is Ready To Create A Service Configuration Page," review the endpoint settings; if you are satisfied with them, click Finish.

    A service called *Products.ProductsServiceImpl* appears in the Configuration pane of the Service Configuration Editor.

13. Expand the Endpoints node under the *Products.ProductsServiceImpl* service.

    An anonymous endpoint appears (it is labeled *Empty Name*)

14. Click the anonymous endpoint.

    The right pane displays the configuration information for the service endpoint. You can use this pane to change the settings and modify the configuration if necessary.

15. In the Name field at the top of the Service Endpoint pane, type **NetTcpBinding_IProductsService**.

    This action gives the endpoint a name, following the conventions used by the Add Service Reference Wizard in Visual Studio.

16. From the File menu, choose Save to save the configuration file, and then close the Service Configuration Editor.

> **Note** When you return to Visual Studio, if you had the App.config file open in a code view window, Visual Studio will detect that the contents of the file have changed and alert you with a message box displaying "The file has been modified outside the source editor. Do you want to reload it?" If this happens, click Yes; otherwise, you risk losing the changes you have made by using the Service Configuration Editor.

17. In Visual Studio, open the App.config file in the ProductsServiceHost project to display it in the Code And Text Editor window. Examine the *<system.ServiceModel>* section. It should now contain a *<services>* section with the definition of a service called *Products. ProductsServiceImpl*, as shown in bold in the following:

```xml
<?xml version="1.0"?>
<configuration>
  <connectionStrings>
  ...
  </connectionStrings>
  <system.serviceModel>
    <services>
      <service name="Products.ProductsServiceImpl">
        <endpoint address="net.tcp://localhost:8080/TcpService"
         binding="netTcpBinding"
         bindingConfiguration="" name="NetTcpBinding_IProductsService"
         contract="Products.IProductsService" />
      </service>
    </services>
    <behaviors>
      ...
    </behaviors>
    ...
  </system.serviceModel>
</configuration>
```

18. In the *<serviceBehaviors>* section, change the value of the *httpGetEnabled* attribute or the *<serviceMetadata>* element to **false**.

    The service does not expose an endpoint that uses the HTTP protocol, so it cannot publish its metadata over an HTTP connection.

19. Build the solution.

When you execute the ProductsServiceHost application, it provides the host environment for your service. Your service is now running within the ProductsServiceHost application, and other client applications can access this service just as they could if it was hosted by using IIS or WAS. You can test the newly-hosted version of the ProductsService WCF service by using the same client application as before. All you need to do is configure it to connect to the new address.

Test the Windows Host Application

1. Add the ProductsClient project located in the Microsoft Press\WCF Step By Step\ Chapter 2\ProductsClient\ProductsClient folder to the ProductsServiceHost project.

2. Open the app.config file for the ProductsClient project in the Code And Text Editor window.

3. In the *<client>* section, change the address of the *NetTcpBinding_IProductsService* end-
    point to **net.tcp://localhost:8080/TcpService**, as shown in bold in the following:

```xml
<?xml version="1.0"?>
<configuration>
  <system.serviceModel>
    <bindings>
      ...
    </bindings>
    <client>
      <endpoint address="http://localhost/ProductsService/Service.svc"
                ... />
      <endpoint address="net.tcp://localhost:8080/TcpService"
                binding="netTcpBinding" contract="ProductsService.IProductsService"
                name="NetTcpBinding_IProductsService" />
    </client>
  </system.serviceModel>
</configuration>
```

    This is the address specified for the host application to which the *ProductsService* WCF
    service is set to listen.

 Note The address, binding, and contract of the client endpoint must match that of the ser-
    vice endpoint. However, the endpoint name can be different; this attribute is used only by
    the code in the client application to refer to the endpoint by name.

4. Open the Program.cs file for the ProductsClient project in the Code And Text Editor
    window. Add the statements shown in bold in the following to the start of the *Main*
    method.

```csharp
static void Main(string[] args)
{
    Console.WriteLine("Press ENTER when the service has started");
    Console.ReadLine();

    // Create a proxy object and connect to the service
    ProductsServiceClient proxy = new
        ProductsServiceClient("NetTcpBinding_IProductsService");
    ...
}
```

    This code waits for the user to press the Enter key before creating the proxy object that
    connects to the service. This will give you time to start the service running.

5. Build the solution.

6. In Solution Explorer, right-click the ProductsServiceLibrary solution, and then click Set
    StartUp Projects.

7. In the Solution 'ProductsServiceLibrary' Property Pages dialog box, click Multiple Startup Projects, set the Action for the ProductsClient and the ProductsServiceHost projects to **Start**, set the Action for the ProductsServiceLibrary project to **None**, and then click OK.

8. From the Debug menu, choose Start Without Debugging to start both projects running.

9. In the Products Service Host window, click Start, and wait for the Service Status text box to change to Service Running.

> **Note** If you are running Windows Firewall, a Windows Security Alert will appear. In the alert, click Allow Access to allow the service to open the TCP port.

10. In the console window that's running the ProductsClient application, press Enter. The application should run exactly as before, displaying a list of product numbers, displaying the details of product WB-H098, and then displaying and updating the stock level for this product.

11. Press Enter again to close the ProductsClient application.

12. In the Products Service Host window, click Stop, and then close the application.

Reconfiguring the Service to Support Multiple Endpoints

In the same way that a WCF service hosted by using WAS can support multiple protocols, so can a service that you host in an ordinary Windows application. While, as mentioned earlier, the TCP protocol is a good choice for connecting client applications and services that run within the same organization, on the same local area network, you might find that you also need to support client applications running on a remote network and that connect over the Internet. If you want to maintain connectivity and network performance inside and outside an organization, you should consider providing multiple endpoints: one for external clients accessing the service by using HTTP, and another for internal clients accessing the service by using TCP. This is what you will do in the next set of exercises.

Add an HTTP Endpoint to the WCF service

1. In Solution Explorer, in the ProductsServiceHost project, right-click the App.config file for the ProductsServiceHost project, and then click Edit WCF Configuration.

2. In the Service Configuration Editor, in the Configuration pane, expand the Services folder, expand *Products.ProductServiceImpl*, and then expand the Endpoints folder. The existing endpoint is listed, with the name *NetTcpBinding_IProductsService*.

3. In the Configuration pane, right-click the Endpoints folder, and then click New Service Endpoint.

4. In the Service Endpoint pane, set the properties of the endpoint using the values in the following table:

Property	Value
Name	BasicHttpBinding_IProductsService
Address	http://localhost:8000/ProductsService/Service.svc
Binding	basicHttpBinding
Contract	Products.IProductsService

> **Tip** If you click the ellipses button in the Contract field, you can search for the assembly containing the contract using the Contract Type Browser.

The address used here specifies port 8000. IIS uses the default port for the HTTP protocol (port 80). Attempting to create a new *ServiceHost* object that listens for an address on port 80 will result in an exception unless you stop IIS first.

Also notice that the address still appears to reference the *Service.svc* service definition file. However, you have not added this file to the service host application. In fact, a service definition file is used only by IIS and is optional if you are creating your own custom host application. This is because the information required to identify the assembly containing the class that implements the service is specified in the *ServiceHost* constructor. The address that you specify following the scheme, machine, and port ("ProductsService/Service.svc" in this example) is really just a logical identifier that the WCF service uses to advertise the service to clients, and to which clients can connect. As long as it has valid syntax for a Web URL, this part of the address can be almost anything. For consistency, when using the HTTP scheme, it is worthwhile retaining the service definition file element as part of the address—in case you want to revert to using IIS to host the service. However, this comment applies only to endpoints that use the HTTP and HTTPS transports. If you use a different mechanism, such as TCP, avoid referencing what looks like a filename in addresses.

5. Save the updated configuration, and then exit the Service Configuration Editor.

6. Examine the App.config file for the ProductsServiceHost project by opening it in the Code And Text Editor window. Notice that the new endpoint has been added to the *<service>* section, as shown in bold in the following:

```
...
<services>
  <endpoint address="net.tcp://localhost:8080/TcpService"
      bindingConfiguration="" name="NetTcpBinding_IProductsService"
      contract="Products.IProductsService" />
```

```
    <endpoint address="http://localhost:8000/ProductsService/Service.svc"
        binding="basicHttpBinding" name="BasicHttpBinding_IProductsService"
        contract="Products.IProductsService" />
    </service>
</services>
...
```

When the host application instantiates the *ServiceHost* object, it automatically creates an endpoint for each entry in the configuration file.

Reconfigure the Client Application to Connect to the HTTP Endpoint

1. In Solution Explorer, edit the app.config file for the ProductsClient project by using the Service Configuration Editor.

   Notice that you can use the Service Configuration Editor to configure WCF client applications as well as services. You do this by adding endpoint definitions to the Client folder.

2. In the Service Configuration Editor, in the Configuration pane, expand the Client folder, and then expand the Endpoints folder.

   You should see the definitions for two endpoints, called *BasicHttpBinding_IProducts Service* and *NetTcpBinding_IProductsService*. These are the endpoint definitions that you previously added to the app.config file.

3. Click the *BasicHttpBinding_IProductsService* endpoint. In the Client Endpoint pane, change the value of the Address field to **http://localhost:8000/ProductsService/ Service.svc**.

4. Save the client configuration file and exit the Service Configuration Editor.

5. Examine the app.config file for the ProductsClient application by opening it in the Code And Text Editor window. Notice that the new endpoint has been added to the client, as follows in bold:

```
<client>
    <endpoint address="http://localhost:8000/ProductsService/Service.svc"
        binding="basicHttpBinding"
        bindingConfiguration="BasicHttpBinding_IProductsService"
        contract="ProductsClient.ProductsService.IProductsService"
        name="BasicHttpBinding_IProductsService" />
    <endpoint address="net.tcp://localhost:8080/TcpProductsService"
        binding="netTcpBinding"
        contract="ProductsClient.ProductsService.IProductsService"
        name="NetTcpBinding_IProductsService" />
</client>
```

6. Edit the Program.cs file in the ProductsClient project. In the *Main* method, modify the statement that instantiates the proxy object to use the HTTP endpoint, as follows:

```
static void Main(string[] args)
{
    ...
    // Create a proxy object and connect to the service
    ProductsServiceClient proxy = new
        ProductsServiceClient("BasicHttpBinding_IProductsService");
    ...
}
```

7. Build the solution.

Unlike using TCP ports, if you wish to listen on a port by using the HTTP protocol, Windows insists that the account you are using to run a service has been granted access to the port specified by the HTTP address. This is for security purposes; starting a service that can accept requests from the outside world over an HTTP connection is a potential security risk, and the service listening for these requests and auctioning them must be trusted not to do horrible things to your computer.

Windows provides the *netsh* command that you can use to specify that an account should be granted access to a network resource, such as an HTTP port or URL, and reserve it for a named account. This account will have exclusive access to the resource. In the following procedure you will use the *netsh* command to reserve HTTP port 8000 for the account you are using to run the *ProductsServiceHost* application.

> **More Info** The *netsh* command provides an extensive set of features with which you can configure network communications components and privileges. This book makes use of various *netsh* commands from time to time, but the details of how these commands work is outside the scope of this volume. If you want more information about the *netsh* command, see the "Network Shell (Netsh)" page on the Microsoft TechNet Web site at *http://technet.microsoft.com/en-us/library/cc754753(WS.10).aspx*.

Reserve HTTP Port 8000

1. Open a command prompt window as Administrator, as follows:

a. On the Windows Start menu, in the Search Programs And Files box, type **cmd** (do not press Enter).

b. In the Programs list, right-click cmd, and then click Run As Administrator. Enter the administrator password if prompted.

2. In the command prompt window, type the following command (replace *UserName* with the name of your Windows account):

```
netsh http add urlacl url=http://+:8000/ user=UserName
```

Verify that the command responds with the message "URL reservation successfully added."

> **Tip** If you are unsure of the name of your account, run the command, *whoami*, in the command prompt window first.

> **Note** You can remove the port reservation when you have finished with it by using the following command:
>
> ```
> netsh http delete urlacl url=http://+:8000/
> ```

You are now in a position to start the ProductsService WCF service listening for HTTP requests.

Test the New Service Endpoint

1. From the Debug menu, select Start Without Debugging to start both projects running.

2. In the Products Service Host window, click Start and wait for the Service Status text box to change to "Service Running."

3. In the console window running the ProductsClient application, press Enter. The application should run exactly as before. This time, however, the client is connecting to the service by using the HTTP endpoint.

4. Press Enter again to close the ProductsClient application. Stop the service and close the Products Service Host window.

Understanding Endpoints and Bindings

By now, you should appreciate that endpoints and bindings are important parts of the framework provided by WCF. An endpoint specifies the point of contact for a service; it provides the address that the service listens to, the binding that the client must use to connect to the service, and the contract that defines the functionality exposed by the service. This is the information that a client application must specify to successfully connect to the service.

The binding itself is a curious beast because it can contain many pieces of crucial information. As described earlier, it helps to define the policy that client applications must respect if they wish to use the service. This policy includes items such as the transport mechanism (TCP, HTTP, named pipes, MSMQ, etc.), security requirements of the service (how does a client application identify itself, and how should messages be encrypted), the transactional specifications of the service, how the service supports reliable communications, and so on.

In technical terms, a WCF binding consists of one or more binding elements. A binding element handles one particular non-functional aspect of a service, such as whether it supports transactions or how the service implements security. You compose binding elements together in various combinations to create a binding. Every binding should have a single binding element describing the transport protocol, and a binding should also contain a binding element that handles message encoding. You can add further optional binding elements to provide or enforce further features in a service. A binding element corresponds to a channel. Remember that when a host opens a service, the WCF runtime uses each binding element in the binding configuration to create the channel stack. A client also creates a channel stack when it connects to the service by opening a proxy object. To ensure that a client application can communicate successfully with a service, it should use a binding configuration that provides binding elements that match those implemented by the service.

The WCF Predefined Bindings

The WCF library contains a number of classes in the *System.ServiceModel.Channels* namespace that implement binding elements. Examples include the *BinaryMessageEncodingBinaryElement* class that performs binary encoding and decoding for XML messages, the *AsymmetricSecurity BindingElement* class with which you can enforce security by performing asymmetric encryption, the *HttpsTransportBindingElement* that uses the HTTPS transport protocol for transmitting messages, and the *ReliableSessionBindingElement* that you can use to implement reliable messaging. Most binding elements also provide properties that you can use to modify the way in which the binding elements work. For example, the *AsymmetricSecurityBindingElement* class has a property called *DefaultAlgorithmSuite* with which you can specify the message encryption algorithm to use. WCF also lets you define custom binding elements if none of the predefined binding elements meets your requirements. (Creating custom binding elements is beyond the scope of this book.)

The composability of binding elements into bindings provides a great deal of flexibility, but clearly not all combinations of binding elements make sense. Additionally, if you are building solutions for a global environment, it is worth remembering that not all client applications and services in a distributed solution will necessarily have been developed using WCF; you should use bindings that are interoperable with services and applications developed using other technologies.

The WS-* Specifications and the WS-I Basic Profile

As described in Chapter 1, many specifications and protocols have been defined with the goal of ensuring interoperability between Web services. Examples include the WS-Security specification, which defines how Web services can communicate in a secure manner; WS-Transactions, which specify how to implement transactions across a disparate collection of Web services; and WS-ReliableMessaging, which describes a protocol that allows messages to be delivered reliably between distributed applications, even in the event of software component, system, or network failures. Collectively, these specifications are known as the WS-* specifications. To ensure interoperability, you should create Web services that conform to these specifications. Fortunately, the library of binding elements and preconfigured bindings provided with WCF abide by these specifications, but if you create your own custom binding elements you should be aware that you might be compromising interoperability.

Another point to bear in mind is that when you create a Web service, you make use of a number of technical standards, such as XML, WSDL, SOAP, and the various WS-* specifications. New versions of these standards are continually emerging and will inevitably become adopted in the future. This poses a challenge. For example, if you create a Web service that exposes its interface by using WSDL 2, and a client application is using WSDL 1.1, will the client application still work? If you factor in the possibility that various applications could potentially support different versions or subsets of the various standards then interoperability, which is one of the most important value propositions of Web services, becomes difficult to achieve. This is where the WS-I Basic Profile comes in.

WS-I—the Web Services Interoperability organization—defines a specific list of standards, versions, and additional rules that Web services and their clients should adopt to maintain interoperability. WS-I groups these items together into what is referred to as a *profile*. The current WS-I profile is called the WS-I Basic Profile 1.2 (although the WS-I Basic Profile 2.0 is currently being developed). Web services that conform to the WS-I Basic Profile 1.2 should automatically be compatible with client applications and other Web services that also conform to the WS-I Basic Profile 1.2, regardless of how the Web services and client applications are implemented or what technologies they use.

For a complete description of the WS-I Basic Profile 1.2, see the WS-I Basic Profile page at *http://ws-i.org/profiles/BasicProfile-1.2-WGD.html*.

The designers of WCF have provided a selection of predefined bindings in the WCF library, in the *System.ServiceModel* namespace. You have already used two of them: *BasicHttpBinding* and *NetTcpBinding*. Some of these bindings are aimed at clients and services primarily running on the Windows platform, but others (mainly the Web services bindings) are compatible with the WS-* specifications and the WS-I Basic Profile 1.1 and 1.2. Table 2-3 describes the bindings available in the WCF library:

TABLE 2-3 WCF Predefined Bindings

Binding	Description
BasicHttpBinding	This binding conforms to the WS-I Basic Profile 1.1 (for maximum backward compatibility with older Web services and client applications). It can use the HTTP and HTTPS transport protocols and encodes messages as XML text. Use this binding to build services that are compatible with client applications previously developed to access ASMX-based Web services.
BasicHttpContextBinding	This binding is similar to the *BasicHttpBinding* binding, except that it supports the use of HTTP cookies for storing and transmitting contextual information. This feature lets you build services that can transparently store state information with a client application and provide this state information whenever the client application sends messages to the service. It is useful for building conversational services, where the service needs to be able to correlate requests from different clients. This feature is described more in Chapter 7.
WS2007HttpBinding	This binding conforms to the WS-* specifications that support distributed transactions and secure, reliable sessions. It supports the HTTP and HTTPS transport protocols. Messages can be encoded as XML text or by using the Message Transmission Optimization Mechanism (MTOM). MTOM is an efficient encoding mechanism for transporting messages that contain binary data. You will learn more about MTOM in Chapter 13.
WSHttpBinding	This binding conforms to the pre-2007 draft of the WS-* specifications. It is provided so you can build client applications and services that are backward compatible with systems based on previous versions of WCF and the .NET Framework. You should use the *WS2007HttpBinding* binding for all new development.
WSHttpContextBinding	This binding extends the *WSHttpBinding* binding with support for transparently sending and receiving context information by using the headers in SOAP messages (not cookies). As with the *BasicHttp ContextBinding* binding, it is useful where the service needs to be able to correlate requests from different clients.
WSDualHttpBinding	This binding is similar to *WS2007HttpBinding*, but it is suitable for handling duplex communications. Duplex messaging allows a client and service to perform two-way communication without requiring any form of synchronization (the more common pattern of communication is the request/reply model where a client sends a request and waits for a reply from the service). You will learn more about using duplex messaging in Chapter 14, "Discovering Services and Routing Messages." Using this binding, messages can be encoded as XML Text or by using MTOM. However, this binding supports only the HTTP transport protocol, not HTTPS.

Binding	Description
WebHttpBinding	This binding supports Web services that implement the Representational State Transfer (REST) model and that expose data directly through HTTP requests and responses rather than by using SOAP messages. You will learn more about build REST Web services in Chapter 15, "Building REST Services."
WS2007FederationHttpBinding	This binding supports the WS-Federation specification. This specification enables Web services operating in different security realms to agree on a common mechanism for identifying users. A collection of cooperating Web services acting in this way is called a federation. An end-user that successfully connects any member of the federation has effectively logged into all of the members. WS-Federation defines several models for providing federated security, based on the WS-Trust, WS-Security, and WS-SecureConversation specifications. You will learn more about federation in Chapter 17, "Managing Identity with Windows CardSpace."
WSFederationHttpBinding	This binding supports the pre-2007 draft of the WS-Federation specification. Like the *WSHttpBinding* binding, it is provided so you can build solutions that are compatible with older WCF services.
NetTcpBinding	This binding uses the TCP transport protocol to transmit messages using a binary encoding. It offers higher performance than the bindings based on the HTTP protocols but less interoperability. It supports transactions, reliable sessions, and secure communications. This binding is ideally suited for use in a local area network and between computers using the Windows operating system.
NetTcpContextBinding	This binding extends the *NetTcpBinding* binding with the ability to transparently send and receive context data in SOAP headers.
NetPeerTcpBinding	This binding supports peer-to-peer communications between applications using the TCP protocol. It supports secure communications and reliable, ordered delivery of messages. Messages are transmitted by using a binary encoding. Using peer-to-peer communications is outside the scope of this book, but for more information, see the "Peer to Peer Networking" section in the Windows SDK Documentation.
NetNamedPipeBinding	This binding uses named pipes to implement high-performance communication between processes running on the same computer. It supports secure, reliable sessions and transactions. You cannot use this binding to connect to a service across a network.
NetMsmqBinding	This binding uses Microsoft Message Queue (MSMQ) as the transport to transmit messages between a client application and a service—both implemented by using WCF. It enables temporal isolation; messages are stored in a message queue, so the client and the service do not need to be running simultaneously. This binding supports secure, reliable sessions and transactions. Messages use a binary encoding.
MsmqIntegrationBinding	With this binding, you can build a WCF application that sends or receives messages from an MSMQ message queue. It is intended for use with existing applications that use MSMQ message queues (the *NetMsmqBinding* binding uses MSMQ as a transport between a WCF client and service).

Configuring Bindings

Later in this chapter, you will see that you can programmatically instantiate a binding and use it to create an endpoint for a service by using the *AddServiceEndpoint* method of the *Service Host* class. Similarly, you can write code to add a binding in a client application (you will see examples of these in Chapter 11, "Programmatically Controlling the Configuration and Communications"). However, as you have already seen, it is common to use a configuration file to specify the binding configuration information for a client and service. You can also set the binding properties either programmatically or using configuration. As an example, examine the app.config file for the ProductsClient application. It looks like this:

```xml
<?xml version="1.0"?>
<configuration>
  <system.serviceModel>
    <bindings>
      <basicHttpBinding>
        <binding name="BasicHttpBinding_IProductsService" closeTimeout="00:01:00"
            openTimeout="00:01:00" receiveTimeout="00:10:00" sendTimeout="00:01:00"
            allowCookies="false" bypassProxyOnLocal="false"
            hostNameComparisonMode="StrongWildcard"
            maxBufferSize="65536" maxBufferPoolSize="524288" maxReceivedMessageSize="65536"
            messageEncoding="Text" textEncoding="utf-8" transferMode="Buffered"
            useDefaultWebProxy="true">
          <readerQuotas maxDepth="32" maxStringContentLength="8192" maxArrayLength="16384"
              maxBytesPerRead="4096" maxNameTableCharCount="16384" />
          <security mode="None">
            <transport clientCredentialType="None" proxyCredentialType="None"
                realm="" />
            <message clientCredentialType="UserName" algorithmSuite="Default" />
          </security>
        </binding>
      </basicHttpBinding>
    </bindings>
    <client>
      <endpoint address="http://localhost:8000/ProductsService/Service.svc"
          binding="basicHttpBinding"
          bindingConfiguration="BasicHttpBinding_IProductsService"
          contract="ProductsService.IProductsService"
          name="BasicHttpBinding_IProductsService" />
      <endpoint address="net.tcp://localhost:8080/TcpService" binding="netTcpBinding"
          contract="ProductsService.IProductsService"
          name="NetTcpBinding_IProductsService" />
    </client>
  </system.serviceModel>
</configuration>
```

To recap from earlier, the *<client>* section specifies the endpoints for the client application. Each endpoint indicates the binding to use. Notice that the value specified in the *binding* attribute refers to the name of one of the predefined WCF bindings described earlier, although in the schema used by the configuration file they are specified by following the camelCase convention (with a lower-case initial letter.) The *<bindings>* section of the configuration file sets the properties of each binding—this section is optional if you are happy to use the default values for a binding. The previous example explicitly sets the values for some of the common properties of the *BasicHttpBinding* binding used by the client endpoint. You will learn a lot more about the properties of various bindings in subsequent chapters, and you can find a full list of the properties for each binding in the "<bindings>" section of the "Windows Communication Foundation Configuration Schema" topic in the Windows SDK Documentation provided with Visual Studio.

There is one additional feature that you should be aware of when configuring a binding; you can specify your own default binding configuration options. The following example adds a binding configuration for the *NetTcpBinding* binding that sets the *transferMode* property of the binding to *Streamed* (you will learn about how to implement streaming in a WCF service in Chapter 13). Notice that the binding is anonymous; it has no name attribute specified. The *StreamingService* service is configured to use the *NetTcpBinding* binding. It does not reference any particular binding configuration by name, so it will be configured with the system-defined default options. However, the anonymous binding configuration will then be applied and override the system-defined default setting for the *transferMode* property. Furthermore, this configuration will be applied to any other *NetTcpBinding* bindings implemented by the same service host unless they explicitly reference a named binding configuration, which would then be used instead.

```xml
<?xml version="1.0"?>
<configuration>
  <system.serviceModel>
    <bindings>
      <netTcpBinding>
        <binding transferMode="Streamed">
      </netTcpBinding>
    </bindings>
    <services>
      <service name="StreamingService">
        <endpoint address="net.tcp://localhost:8080/StreamedTcpService"
            binding="netTcpBinding"
            contract="ProductsService.IProductsService"
            name="NetTcpBinding_IProductsService" />
      </service>
    </services>
  </system.serviceModel>
</configuration>
```

Default Endpoints

When you created the first version of the *ProductsService* WCF service in Chapter 1, you did not specify any endpoint or binding information in the Web.config file. Instead, when the host environment (in this case IIS) started the service, it created a default endpoint definition based on the transport scheme implemented by the host (HTTP) and the URL defined by the logical address of the virtual folder holding the service. In fact, the host environment called the *AddDefaultEndpoints* method of the *ServiceHost* class to generate the details of this endpoint.

The *AddDefaultEndpoints* method adds an endpoint for all base addresses defined by the service for each service contract implemented by the service. So, for example, if the base address of a service is *http://localhost/ProductsService*, and the service implements a contract called *Products.IProductsService*, the *AddDefaultEndpoints* method generates an endpoint using the *BasicHttpBinding* binding, with an address generated from the base address of the service combined with the name of the .svc file provided with the service and the *Products.IProducts Service* contract. If a service implements two service contracts, the *AddDefaultEndpoints* method generates two endpoints, one for each contract. Similarly, if a service is configured with two base addresses and implements two contracts, the *AddDefaultEndpoints* method generates four endpoints (one endpoint for each combination of address and contract).

There is one small question that arises from this discussion; how does the *AddDefaultEndpoints* method actually know which binding to use. You have seen that the default binding for the HTTP transport is the *BasicHttpBinding* binding, which makes sense (for reasons of backward compatibility). But how does the *AddDefaultEndpoints* method come to this conclusion, rather than, for example, selecting the *WSHttpBinding* binding, which is also valid for the HTTP transport? The answer lies in the default protocol mapping specified in the machine.config file.

The machine.config file contains global configuration settings for the computer (not just WCF configuration settings). It is located in the C:\Windows\Microsoft.NET\Framework*vx.x.xxxx*\ Config folder on your computer, where *vx.x.xxxx* is the version of the .NET Framework that you have installed. This file contains a *<protocolMapping>* section that specifies the default mapping from network schemes to bindings, as follows:

```
<system.ServiceModel>
  ...
  <protocolMapping>
    <clear />
    <add scheme="http" binding="basicHttpBinding" bindingConfiguration="" />
    <add scheme="net.tcp" binding="netTcpBinding" bindingConfiguration="" />
    <add scheme="net.pipe" binding="netNamedPipeBinding" bindingConfiguration="" />
    <add scheme="net.msmq" binding="netMsmqBinding" bindingConfiguration="" />
  </protocolMapping>
  ...
</system.ServiceModel>
```

If you wish to change the default binding for a network scheme for a service, you can add a *<protocolMapping>* section to the Web.config or app.config file for the service and override the mapping in the machine.config file (do not change the machine.config file). For example, the following configuration changes the default binding for the HTTP scheme for a service to the *WSHttpBinding* binding.

```
<system.ServiceModel>
  ...
  <protocolMapping>
    <add scheme="http" binding="wsHttpBinding" bindingConfiguration="" />
  </protocolMapping>
  ...
</system.ServiceModel>
```

Also, notice that you can override the default configuration for a binding by providing a named binding configuration, and then referencing that configuration from the *binding Configuration* attribute, as described in the "Configuring Bindings" section on page 81.

Hosting a WCF Service in a Windows Service

To finish this chapter, you'll look at another option for hosting a WCF service and learn more about adding endpoints to a service programmatically. You'll also see another commonly used binding.

Hosting a WCF Service in a user application relies on the user starting and stopping the service—and not logging off. A better solution is to host a WCF service in a Windows service. This way, you can configure the Windows service to run automatically when Windows starts, but an administrator can still stop and restart the service if required.

In the exercises in this section, you will create a Windows service to act as a host for the *ProductsService* service. This service will limit requests to only client applications running on the same computer, so you will configure it to use the named pipe transport, listening to a fixed address.

> **More Info** The exercises in this section assume you are familiar with how Windows services function and that you understand how to use Windows Service Visual Studio template to create a new service. Windows services are distinct from WCF services, and a detailed discussion of how they work is outside the scope of this book. For further information about creating Windows services see the "Windows Service Applications" section in the Visual Studio 2010 Help documentation.

Create a New Windows Service to Host the WCF Service

1. Using Visual Studio, create a new solution using the information in the following table:

Item	Value
Template	Windows Service (in the Windows folder in the Installed Templates pane)
Name	WindowsProductsService
Location	Microsoft Press\WCF Step By Step\Chapter 2

2. In Solution Explorer, change the name of the Service1.cs file to **ServiceHostController.cs**. When prompted, click Yes to change all references to Service1 to **ServiceHostController** instead.

3. Add a reference to the *System.ServiceModel*, *System.Runtime.Serialization*, and *System. Data.Entity* assemblies.

4. Add a reference to the *ProductsEntityModel* assembly, located in the Microsoft Press\ WCF Step By Step\Chapter 2 folder.

5. Add the IProductsService.cs, ProductsService.cs, and app.config files located in the Microsoft Press\WCF Step By Step\Chapter 2 folder to the project.

6. Open the App.config file in the Code And Text Editor and set the value of the *httpGetEnabled* attribute of the *serviceMetadata* element in the *<serviceBehaviors>* section to **false**, as shown in bold in the following:

```xml
<?xml version="1.0"?>
<configuration>
  ...
  <system.ServiceModel>
    <behaviors>
      <serviceBehaviors>
        <behavior>
          ...
          <serviceMetadata httpGetEnabled="false" />
          ...
        </behavior>
      </serviceBehaviors>
    </behaviors>
  </system.ServiceModel>
</configuration>
```

7. Build the solution.

In the previous set of exercises, you saw that you had to specify an address when you used the *NetTcpBinding* binding with a service. You provided this information in the configuration file, together with binding information. In this set of exercises, you will bind the service to an endpoint by using code; the Windows service will use a named pipe for its endpoint because you want to restrict access to local client applications only.

Add Logic to Start and Stop the Windows Service

1. Open the ServiceHostController.cs file. In the Design View window, click the link to switch to the code view in the Code And Text Editor window.

2. In the Code And Text Editor window, add the following *using* statements to the list at the top of the file:

```
using System.ServiceModel;
using Products;
```

3. Add the variable shown in bold in the following to the *ServiceHostController* class:

```
public partial class ServiceHostController : ServiceBase
{
    private ServiceHost productsServiceHost;
```

```
public ServiceHostController()
{
    ...
}
...
}
```

You will use this variable to control the *ProductsService* service.

4. Add the following statements shown in bold in the following to the *ServiceHost Controller* constructor:

```
public partial class ServiceHostController : ServiceBase
{
    private ServiceHost productsServiceHost;

    public ServiceHostController()
    {
        InitializeComponent();

        // The name of the service that appears in the Registry
        this.ServiceName = "ProductsService";

        // Allow an administrator to stop (and restart) the service
        this.CanStop = true;

        // Report Start and Stop events to the Windows event log
        this.AutoLog = true;
    }
    ...
}
```

5. Add the statement shown in bold in the following to the *OnStart* method of the *Service HostController* class:

```
public partial class ServiceHostController : ServiceBase
{
    ...
    public ServiceHostController()
    {
        ...
    }

    protected override void OnStart(string[] args)
    {
        productsServiceHost = new ServiceHost(typeof(ProductsServiceImpl));
    }
    ...
}
```

This statement creates a new instance of the *ProductsService* service—but remember that the App.config file does not specify an address or binding. You will supply the endpoint information for the service in the next step.

6. Add the statements shown in bold in the following to the *OnStart* method:

```
protected override void OnStart(string[] args)
{
    productsServiceHost = new ServiceHost(typeof(ProductsServiceImpl));
    NetNamedPipeBinding binding = new NetNamedPipeBinding();
    productsServiceHost.AddServiceEndpoint(typeof(IProductsService),
        binding, "net.pipe://localhost/ProductsServicePipe");
    productsServiceHost.Open();
}
```

The first statement creates a *NetNamedPipeBinding* object. The second statement creates a new endpoint using this binding object. It associates the binding with the "//localhost/ProductsServicePipe" named pipe, and it specifies that the service listening to the pipe implements the *IProductsService* service contract. The code then opens the service and waits for clients to connect.

7. Add the code shown in bold in the following to the *OnStop* method of the *ServiceHost Controller* class:

```
public partial class ServiceHostController : ServiceBase
{
    ...
    protected override void OnStart(string[] args)
    {
        ...
    }

    protected override void OnStop()
    {
        productsServiceHost.Close();
    }
}
```

This statement closes the *ProductsService* service when the Windows service is shut down. Remember that WCF closes services gracefully, so the *Close* method can take some time to execute.

8. Build the solution.

In the next exercise, you will add an installer for the Windows service. You will configure the service to run using the *LocalSystem* account. If you want to select a different account, ensure that the account you specify has access to the tables in the *AdventureWorks* database.

Create the Service Installer

1. In Solution Explorer, double-click the ServiceHostController.cs file to display it in the Design View window.

2. Right-click anywhere in the Design View window, and then click Add Installer.

    The service installer is created and displays the *serviceProcessInstaller1* and *serviceInstaller1* components in the Design View window.

3. Click the *serviceInstaller1* component. In the Properties window, set the *ServiceName* property to **ProductsService**, and set the *StartType* property to **Automatic**.

> **Tip** If the Properties window is not visible, from the View menu, select Properties Window.

4. In the Design View window, click the *serviceProcessInstaller1* component. In the Properties window, set the *Account* property to **LocalSystem**.

5. Build the solution.

The next stage is to install the service and start it running.

Install the Windows Service

1. Open a Visual Studio Command Prompt window as Administrator.

    ❑ On the Windows Start menu, click All Programs, click Microsoft Visual Studio 2010, click Visual Studio Tools, right-click Visual Studio Command Prompt (2010), and then click Run as Administrator. Enter the administrator password if prompted.

2. In the Visual Studio Command Prompt window, move to the folder Microsoft Press\WCF Step By Step\Chapter 2\WindowsProductService\WindowsProductService\bin\Debug.

3. Run the following command to install the WindowsProductsService service:

    ```
    installutil WindowsProductsService.exe
    ```

    The *installutil* utility outputs a number of messages indicating the progress of the installation process. Verify that the service installed successfully, without reporting any errors.

4. Run the following command to start the Windows Services applet:

    ```
    services.msc
    ```

5. In the Services window, verify that the *ProductsService* service is present and configured using the property values specified by the service installer, as shown in the following image:

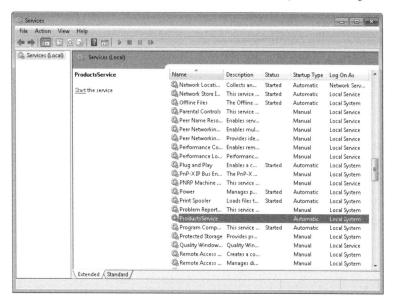

6. Start the service.

Tip If the service fails to start, check the Windows Application Event log. When a service fails, Windows reports exceptions and errors to this log.

In the final exercise of this chapter, you will use another copy of the ProductsClient application to test the Windows service. You will reconfigure the ProductsClient application to connect to the Windows service and verify that the service functions correctly.

Test the Windows Service

1. Return to Visual Studio. Add the ProductsClient project in the Microsoft Press\WCF Step By Step\Chapter 2\ProductsClient\ProductsClient folder to the WindowsProductsService solution.

2. Edit the app.config file for the ProductsClient project by using the Service Configuration Editor.

3. In the Client folder, right-click the *Endpoints* node, and then click New Client Endpoint. Add a new client endpoint using the following property values:

Property	Value
Name	NetNamedPipeBinding_IProductsService
Address	net.pipe://localhost/ProductsServicePipe
Binding	netNamedPipeBinding
Contract	ProductsService.IProductsService

4. Save the client configuration file and exit the Service Configuration Editor.

5. Edit the Program.cs file for the ProductsClient project. In the *Main* method, modify the statement that instantiates the proxy object to use the named pipe endpoint, as shown in bold in the following:

```
static void Main(string[] args)
{
    // Create a proxy object and connect to the service
    ProductsServiceClient proxy = new
        ProductsServiceClient("NetNamedPipeBinding_IProductsService");
```

6. Build the solution.

7. In Solution Explorer, right-click the ProductsClient project, and then click Set as StartUp Project.

8. From the Debug menu, select Start Without Debugging to start the client application running. Press Enter in the client console window.

    Again, the ProductsClient application should run exactly as before. This time, however, the client is communicating with the WCF service running in the Windows service by using a named pipe.

9. Press Enter to close the ProductsClient application.

10. Return to the Services applet and stop the *ProductsService* service.

    If you want to verify that the client application uses the Windows service and not some other instance of the *ProductsService* service that might be running (such as the Web service), try running the client after stopping the Windows service. It should fail with an *EndpointNotFoundException* exception stating that there is no endpoint listening at the address *net.pipe://localhost/ProductsServicePipe*.

> **Tip** You can uninstall the *WindowsProductsService* service by executing the command **installutil /u WindowsProductsService.exe** in a Visual Studio Command Prompt Window, in the bin\Debug folder for the WindowsProductsService project.

Summary

This chapter has shown you how to create an application that hosts a WCF service. You have seen the different types of applications that you can use for this purpose, and you have built a WPF application and a Windows service. You have also learned a lot more about how WCF uses bindings to specify the transport protocol, encoding mechanism, and other non-functional aspects of a service, such as reliability, security, and support for transactions. You have been introduced to the predefined bindings available in the WCF library. You have learned how to add multiple bindings to a service by using multiple endpoints. And finally, you have seen how to specify binding information by using a configuration file and how to specify a binding and endpoint for a service by using code.

Chapter 3
Making Applications and Services Robust

After completing this chapter, you will be able to:

- Explain how the WCF runtime can convert common language runtime exceptions into SOAP fault messages to transmit exception information from a WCF service.

- Use the *FaultContract* attribute in a service to define strongly typed exceptions as SOAP faults.

- Catch and handle SOAP faults in a client application.

- Describe how to configure a WCF service to propagate information about unanticipated exceptions to client applications for debugging purposes.

- Describe how to detect the *Faulted* state in a WCF service host application and how to recover from this state.

- Explain how to detect and log unrecognized messages sent to a service.

Detecting and handling exceptions is an important part of any professional application. In a complex desktop application, many different situations can raise an exception, ranging from programming errors or events such as unexpected or malformed user input, to failure of one or more hardware components in the computer running the application. In a distributed environment, the scope for exceptions is far greater. This is due to the nature of networks and the fact that, in some cases, neither the application nor the development or administrative staff has control over how the network functions or its maintenance (who is responsible for making sure that the Internet works?). If you factor in the possibility that your application might also access services written by some third party, who may modify or replace the service with a newer version (possibly untested!), or remove the service altogether, then you might begin to wonder whether your distributed applications will ever be able to work reliably.

This chapter shows you how to handle exceptions in client applications and services developed using WCF. You will see how to specify the exceptions that a WCF service can raise and how to propagate information about exceptions from a WCF service to a WCF client. You will also explore the states that a service can be in, how to determine when a host application switches from one state to another, and how to recover a service that has failed. Finally, you will see how to detect unrecognized messages sent to a service by client applications.

CLR Exceptions and SOAP Faults

A WCF service is a managed application that runs by using the .NET Framework common language runtime, or CLR. One important feature of the CLR is the protection that it provides when an error occurs; the CLR can detect many system-level errors and raise an exception if necessary. A managed application can endeavor to catch these exceptions and either attempt some form of recovery or at least fail in a graceful manner, reporting the reason for the exception and providing information that can help a developer to understand the cause of the exception in order to take steps to rectify the situation in the future.

CLR exceptions are specific to the .NET Framework. WCF is intended to build client applications and services that are interoperable with other environments. For example, a Java client application would not understand the format of a CLR exception raised by a WCF service or how to handle it. Part of the SOAP specification describes how to format and send errors in SOAP messages by using SOAP faults. The SOAP specification includes a schema for formatting SOAP faults as XML text and encapsulating them in a SOAP message. A SOAP fault must specify an error code and a text description of the fault (called the "reason"), and it can include other optional pieces of information. Interoperable services built using the WCF should convert .NET Framework exceptions into SOAP faults and follow the SOAP specification for reporting these faults to client applications.

> **More Info** For a detailed description of the format and contents of a SOAP fault, see the World Wide Web Consortium Web site *at http://www.w3.org/TR/soap12-part1/#soapfault.*

Throwing and Catching a SOAP Fault

The WCF library provides the *FaultException* class in the *System.ServiceModel* namespace. If a WCF service throws a *FaultException* object, the WCF runtime generates a SOAP fault message that is sent back to the client application.

In the first set of exercises in this chapter, you will add code to the WCF *ProductsService* service that detects selected problems when accessing the *AdventureWorks* database and uses the *FaultException* class to report these issues back to the client application.

Modify the WCF Service to Throw SOAP Faults

1. Using Visual Studio, open the ProductsServiceFault solution located in the Microsoft Press\WCF Step By Step\Chapter 3\ProductsServiceFault folder (within your Documents folder).

   This solution contains a copy of the ProductsServiceLibrary, ProductsServiceHost, and ProductsClient applications that you created in Chapter 2, "Hosting a WCF Service."

2. In the ProductsServiceLibrary project, open the ProductsService.cs file to display the code for the service in the Code And Text Editor window.

3. Locate the *ListProducts* method in the *ProductsServiceImpl* class.

   You should recall from Chapter 1, "Introducing Windows Communication Foundation," that this method uses the Entity Framework to connect to the *AdventureWorks* database and retrieve the product number of every product in the *Product* table. The product numbers are stored in a list which is returned to the client application. Notice that the exception handler for this method currently ignores all exceptions.

4. Modify the exception handler, as shown in bold in the following:

```
public List<string> ListProducts()
{
    ...
    try
    {
        ...
    }
    catch (Exception e)
    {
        // Edit the Initial Catalog in the connection string in app.config
        // to trigger this exception
        if (e.InnerException is System.Data.SqlClient.SqlException)
        {
            throw new FaultException(
                "Exception accessing database: " +
                e.InnerException.Message, new FaultCode("Connect to database"));
        }
        else
        {
            throw new FaultException(
                "Exception reading product numbers: " +
                e.Message, new FaultCode("Iterate through products"));
        }
    }

    // Return the list of product numbers
    return productsList;
}
```

If an exception occurs, this code examines the cause. If the *InnerException* property of the *Exception* object is a *SqlExecption*, then the exception was caused by the code that accesses the database in the Entity Framework. If the exception is some other type, then the problem must lie in the code that iterates through the list of products retrieved from the database. In both cases, this code creates a new *System.ServiceModel.FaultException* object with the details of the exception and throws it. The operation will stop running and will instead generate a SOAP fault containing a description of the fault and a fault code (which for the purposes in this example simply specifies a name for identification). This SOAP fault is sent back to the client.

Note If you don't create a *FaultCode* object, the WCF runtime will itself automatically generate a *FaultCode* object named "Client" and add it to the SOAP fault sent back to the client.

5. Build the solution.

Modify the WCF Client Application to Catch SOAP Faults

1. In the ProductsClient project, open the file Program.cs to display the code for the client application in the Code And Text Editor window.

2. In the *Main* method, add a *try/catch* block around the code that calls the operations in the WCF service, as shown in bold in the following:

```
static void Main(string[] args)
{
    ...
    // Test the operations in the service

    try
    {
        // Obtain a list of all products
        ...

        // Fetch the details for a specific product
        ...

        // Query the stock level of this product
        ...


        // Modify the stock level of this product
        ...

        // Disconnect from the service
        ...
    }
    catch (FaultException e)
    {
        Console.WriteLine("{0}: {1}", e.Code.Name, e.Reason);
    }

    Console.WriteLine("Press ENTER to finish");
    Console.ReadLine();
}
```

If any of the operations generate a SOAP fault, the WCF runtime on the client creates a *FaultException* object. The catch handler for the *FaultException* object displays the fault code and reason. The name of the fault code is the value specified by the *FaultCode* constructor in the service, and the *Reason* string is the text description of the fault provided by the service.

Test the FaultException Handler

 Important Before you perform this exercise, make sure that you still have port 8000 reserved for your application, as described in the exercise "Reserve HTTP Port 8000" in Chapter 2. To reserve this port, open a command prompt as Administrator, and run the following command (replace *UserName* with your Windows user name):

```
netsh http add urlacl url=http://+:8000/ user=UserName
```

1. In the ProductsServiceHost project, edit the App.config file. The *<connectionStrings>* section of this file contains the information used by the Entity Framework to connect to the *AdventureWorks* database.

2. In the *<add>* element of the *<connectionStrings>* section, change the *Initial Catalog* part of the *connectionString* attribute to refer to the **Junk** database, as follows (do not change any other parts of the *connectString* attribute):

```
<connectionStrings>
  <add ... connectionString="...;Initial Catalog=Junk;..." />
</connectionStrings>
```

3. Build and run the solution without debugging.

   The Products Service Host window and the ProductsClient console window should both start.

4. In the Products Service Host window, click Start.

   If a Windows Security Alert message box appears, click Allow Access.

5. When the service status in the Products Service Host window displays the message "Service Running," press Enter in the ProductsClient console window.

   After a short delay, the ProductsClient application reports an exception similar to the following when performing Test 1 (your message might vary if you are attempting to connect to the database as a different user):

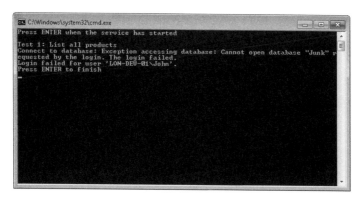

The ProductsService service failed when attempting to connect to the database—the SOAP fault code is "Connect to database."

6. Press Enter to close the ProductsClient console.

7. Click Stop in the Products Service Host window, and then close the application.

8. In the App.config file for the ProductsServiceHost application, change the database back to **AdventureWorks** in the *<connectionString>* attribute.

9. In the *ListProducts* method in the ProductsService.cs file, comment out the code that instantiates the *productsList* object and replace it with code that sets this object to **null**. In the body of the *try* block, add a statement that clears the *productsList* object before assigning it the data retrieved from the database, as shown in bold in the following:

```
public List<string> ListProducts()
{
    // Create a list for holding product numbers
    List<string> productsList = null; // new List<string>();

    try
    {
        // Fetch the product number of every product in the database
        var products = from product in database.Products
                    select product.ProductNumber;

        productsList.Clear();
        productsList = products.ToList();
    }
    catch (Exception e)
    {
        ...
    }
    ...
}
```

 Note The statement that calls *Clear* is actually redundant and is only used by this exercise to illustrate generating an exception that results in a SOAP fault.

10. Build and run the solution again, without debugging.

11. In the Products Service Host window, click Start.

12. When the service is running press Enter in the ProductsClient console window.

The ProductsClient application reports a different exception when performing Test 1:

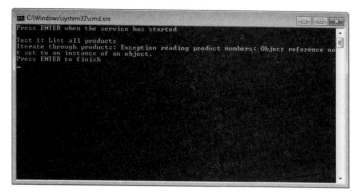

This time, the *ProductsService* service failed when clearing the list of products prior to iterating through the items retrieved from the database and adding them to the *productsList* collection (which is now set to *null*)—the SOAP fault code is "Iterate through products"; the reason explains that an object reference was not initialized correctly.

13. Press Enter to close the ProductsClient console window.

14. Click Stop in the Products Service Host form, and then close the application.

> **Note** Do not change the code in the *Listproducts* method back to the correct version just yet.

Using Strongly Typed Faults

Throwing a *FaultException* is very simple but is actually not as useful as it first appears. A client application must examine the *FaultException* object that it catches to determine the cause of the error, so it is not easy to predict what possible exceptions could occur when invoking a WCF service. In such situations, all developers can do is write generalized catch handlers with very limited scope for recovering from specific exceptions. You can think of this as analogous to using the *System.Exception* type to throw and handle exceptions in regular .NET Framework applications. A better solution is to use strongly typed SOAP faults.

In Chapter 1, you saw that a service contract for a WCF service contains a series of operation contracts defining the methods, or operations, that the service implements. A service contract can additionally include information about any faults that might occur when executing an operation. If an operation in a WCF service detects an exception, it can generate a specific SOAP fault message that it can send back to the client application. The SOAP fault message should contain sufficient detail so the user or an administrator can understand the reason for the exception and, if possible, take any necessary corrective action. A client application can use the fault information in the service contract to anticipate faults and provide specific handlers that can catch and process each different fault. These are strongly typed faults.

You specify the possible faults that can occur by using the *FaultContract* attribute in a service contract. This is what you will do in the next set of exercises.

Note You can only apply the *FaultContract* attribute to operations that return a response. You cannot use them with one-way operations. You will learn more about one-way operations in Chapter 12, "Implementing One-Way and Asynchronous Operations."

Use the *FaultContract* Attribute to Specify the SOAP Faults an Operation Can Throw

1. In the ProductsServiceFault solution, in the ProductsServiceLibrary project, open the IProductsService.cs file.

2. In the IProductsService.cs file, add the following classes shown in bold to the *Products Service* namespace:

```csharp
namespace ProductsService
{
    // Classes for passing fault information back to client applications
    [DataContract]
    public class SystemFault
    {
        [DataMember]
        public string SystemOperation { get; set; }

        [DataMember]
        public string SystemReason { get; set; }

        [DataMember]
        public string SystemMessage { get; set; }
    }

    [DataContract]
    public class DatabaseFault
    {
        [DataMember]
        public string DbOperation { get; set; }

        [DataMember]
        public string DbReason { get; set; }

        [DataMember]
        public string DbMessage { get; set; }
    }

    // Data contract describing the details of a product
    ...

    // Service contract describing the operations provided by the WCF service
    ...
}
```

These classes define types that you will use for passing the details of SOAP faults as exceptions from a service back to a client. Note that although both classes have a similar shape, you can pass almost any type of information in a SOAP fault; the key point is that the type and its members must be serializable. These two classes use the *Data Contract* and *DataMember* attributes to specify how they should be serialized.

3. Locate the *IProductsService* interface at the end of the IProductsService.cs file.

   Remember that this interface defines the service contract for the *ProductsService*.

4. In the *IProductsService* interface, modify the definition of the *ListProducts* operation, as shown in bold in the following code:

```
// Service contract describing the operations provided by the WCF service
[ServiceContract]
public interface IProductsService
{
    // Get the product number of every product
    [FaultContract(typeof(SystemFault))]
    [FaultContract(typeof(DatabaseFault))]
    [OperationContract]
    List<string> ListProducts();

    // Get the details of a single product
    ...

    // Get the current stock level for a product
    ...

    // Change the stock level for a product
    ...
}
```

The *FaultContract* attributes indicate that the *ListProducts* method can generate SOAP faults, which a client application should be prepared to handle. The parameter to the *FaultContract* attribute specifies the information that the SOAP fault will contain. In this case, the *ListProducts* operation can generate two types of SOAP faults: one based on the *SystemFault* type, and the other based on the *DatabaseFault* type.

Modify the WCF Service to Throw Strongly Typed Faults

1. In the ProductsService.cs file, locate the *ListProducts* method in the *ProductsServiceImpl* class.

2. Replace the code in the *catch* block that traps *SqlException* exceptions, as shown in bold in the following:

```
public List<string> ListProducts()
{
    ...
    try
    {
        ...
    }
    catch (Exception e)
    {
        // Edit the Initial Catalog in the connection string in app.config
        // to trigger this exception
        if (e.InnerException is System.Data.SqlClient.SqlException)
        {
            DatabaseFault dbf = new DatabaseFault
            {
                DbOperation = "Connect to database",
                DbReason = "Exception accessing database",
                DbMessage = e.InnerException.Message
            };

            throw new FaultException<DatabaseFault>(dbf);
        }
        else
        {
            ...
        }
    }
    ...
}
```

This block creates and populates a *DatabaseFault* object with the details of the exception. The *throw* statement creates a new *FaultException* object based on this *Database-
Fault* object. Note that in this case, the code makes use of the generic *FaultException*
class; the type parameter specifies a serializable type with the type-specific details of the
exception. At runtime, WCF uses the information in this object to create a SOAP fault
message. The *FaultException* constructor is overloaded, and you can optionally specify
a reason message and a fault code as well as the *DatabaseFault* object.

3. Replace the code in the *else* part of the *catch* block with that shown in bold, as follows:

```
public List<string> ListProducts()
{
    ...
    try
    {
        ...
    }
    catch (Exception e)
    {
        // Edit the Initial Catalog in the connection string in app.config
        // to trigger this exception
        if (e.InnerException is System.Data.SqlClient.SqlException)
```

```
    {
        ...
    }
    else
    {
        SystemFault sf = new SystemFault
        {
            SystemOperation = "Iterate through products",
            SystemReason = "Exception reading product numbers",
            SystemMessage = e.Message
        };

        throw new FaultException<SystemFault>(sf);
    }
}
    ...
}
```

This block of code is similar to the previous *catch* code, except that it creates a *System Fault* object and throws a *FaultException* based on this object. The rationale behind using a different type for the exception is that the kinds of exceptions that could arise when accessing a database are fundamentally different from the exceptions that could occur when reading configuration information. Although not shown in this example, the information returned by a database access exception could be quite different from the information returned by a system exception.

4. Build the solution.

You can now modify the client application to handle the exceptions thrown by the service. However, first you must regenerate the proxy class that the client uses to communicate with the service. The service is not currently running, so you cannot use the *Update Service Reference* feature of Visual Studio. Instead, you will use the *svcutil* utility to generate the proxy class from the assembly containing the *ProductsService* service.

Regenerate the Proxy Class for the WCF Client Application

1. Open a Visual Studio command prompt window and move to the folder \Microsoft Press\WCF Step By Step\Chapter 3\ProductsServiceFault\ProductsServiceLibrary\bin\ Debug folder.

2. Run the following command:

```
svcutil ProductsServiceLibrary.dll
```

This command runs the *svcutil* utility to extract the definition of the *ProductsService* service and the other types from the *ProductsServiceLibrary* assembly. It generates the following files:

❑ **Products.xsd**   This is an XML schema file that describe the structure of the, *DatabaseFault*, *SystemFault*, and *ProductData* types. The *svcutil* utility uses the information specified in the data contracts for these types to generate this file. Part of this file, displaying the *DatabaseFault* type, is shown in the following:

```xml
<?xml version="1.0" encoding="utf-8"?>
<xs:schema xmlns:tns="http://schemas.datacontract.org/2004/07/Products"
elementFormDefault="qualified"
targetNamespace="http://schemas.datacontract.org/2004/07/Products"
xmlns:xs="http://www.w3.org/2001/XMLSchema">
  <xs:complexType name="DatabaseFault">
    <xs:sequence>
      <xs:element minOccurs="0" name="DbMessage" nillable="true"
        type="xs:string" />
      <xs:element minOccurs="0" name="DbOperation" nillable="true"
        type="xs:string" />
      <xs:element minOccurs="0" name="DbReason" nillable="true"
        type="xs:string" />
    </xs:sequence>
  </xs:complexType>
  <xs:element name="DatabaseFault" nillable="true" type="tns:DatabaseFault" />
  ...
</xs:schema>
```

❑ **Tempuri.org.xsd**   This is another XML schema file. This schema describes the messages that a client can send to, or receive from, the *ProductsService* service. You will see later (in the WSDL file for the service) that each operation in the service is defined by a pair of messages; the first message in the pair specifies the message that the client must send to invoke the operation, and the second message specifies the response sent back by the service. This file references the data contract in the Products.xsd file to obtain the description of the *ProductData* type used by the response message of the *GetProduct* operation. The portion of this file that defines the messages for the *ListProducts* and *GetProduct* operations appears as follows:

```xml
<?xml version="1.0" encoding="utf-8"?>
  ...
  <xs:element name="ListProducts">
    <xs:complexType>
      <xs:sequence />
    </xs:complexType>
  </xs:element>
  <xs:element name="ListProductsResponse">
    <xs:complexType>
      <xs:sequence>
        <xs:element minOccurs="0" name="ListProductsResult" nillable="true"
          xmlns:q1="http://schemas.microsoft.com/2003/10/Serialization/Arrays"
          type="q1:ArrayOfstring" />
      </xs:sequence>
    </xs:complexType>
  </xs:element>
```

```
<xs:element name="GetProduct">
  <xs:complexType>
    <xs:sequence>
      <xs:element minOccurs="0" name="productNumber" nillable="true"
        type="xs:string" />
    </xs:sequence>
  </xs:complexType>
</xs:element>
<xs:element name="GetProductResponse">
  <xs:complexType>
    <xs:sequence>
      <xs:element minOccurs="0" name="GetProductResult" nillable="true"
        xmlns:q2="http://schemas.datacontract.org/2004/07/Products"
        type="q2:ProductData" />
    </xs:sequence>
  </xs:complexType>
</xs:element>
  ...
</xs:schema>
```

Note The name of this file and the namespace of the types in this file are dictated by the *ServiceContract* attribute of the interface implemented by the service. The name *Tempuri.org* is the default namespace. You can change it by specifying the *Namespace* parameter in the *ServiceContract* attribute, like this:

```
[ServiceContract (Namespace="Adventure-Works.com")]
```

❏ **Schemas.microsoft.com.2003.10.Serialization.Arrays.xsd**   This file is another XML schema that describes how to represent an array of strings in a SOAP message. The *ListProducts* operation references this information in the *ListProducts Response* message. The value returned by the *ListProducts* operation is a list of strings containing product numbers. As described in Chapter 1, the .NET Framework generic *List< >* type is serialized as an array when transmitted as part of a SOAP message.

❏ **Schemas.microsoft.com.2003.10.Serialization.xsd**   This XML schema file describes how to represent the primitive types (such as float, int, decimal, and string) in a SOAP message, as well as some other built-in types frequently used when sending SOAP messages.

❏ **Tempuri.org.wsdl**   This file contains the WSDL description of the service, describing how the messages and data contracts are used to implement the operations that a client application can invoke. It references the XML schema files to define the data and messages that implement operations. Notice that the definition of the *ListProducts* operation includes the two fault messages that you defined earlier:

```
. . .
<wsdl:operation name="ListProducts">
  <soap:operation soapAction="http://tempuri.org/IProductsService/ListProducts"
style="document" />
  <wsdl:input>
    <soap:body use="literal" />
  </wsdl:input>
  <wsdl:output>
    <soap:body use="literal" />
  </wsdl:output>
  <wsdl:fault name="DatabaseFaultFault">
    <soap:fault name="DatabaseFaultFault" use="literal" />
  </wsdl:fault>
  <wsdl:fault name="SystemFaultFault">
    <soap:fault name="SystemFaultFault" use="literal" />
  </wsdl:fault>
</wsdl:operation>
```

You can use the WSDL file and the XML schema files to generate the proxy class.

3. In the Visual Studio command prompt window, type the following command:

```
svcutil /namespace:*,ProductsClient.ProductsService tempuri.org.wsdl *.xsd
```

> **Note** The character between the asterisk (*) and the string *ProductsClient.ProductsService* is a comma (,).

This command runs the *svcutil* utility again, but this time it uses the information in the WSDL file and all the schema files (*.xsd) to generate a C# source file containing a class that can act as a proxy object for the service. The namespace parameter specifies the C# namespace generated for the class (the namespace shown here has been selected to be the same as that generated by Visual Studio in the exercises in Chapter 1, to minimize the changes required to the code in the client application; however, you will need to modify the client configuration file to match this namespace). The *svcutil* utility creates two files:

- **Products.cs**   This is the source code for the proxy class.

- **Output.config**   This is an example application configuration file that the client application could use to configure the proxy to communicate with the service. By default, the configuration file generates an endpoint definition with the *basicHttpBinding* binding.

> **Note** You can also use the *svcutil* utility to generate a proxy directly from a Web service endpoint rather than generating the metadata from an assembly. This is what Visual Studio does when you use the *Add Service Reference* feature. For more information about the *svcutil* utility, see the "ServiceModel Metadata Utility Tool" on the Microsoft Web site at *http://msdn.microsoft.com/en-us/library/aa347733.aspx*.

4. In Visual Studio, in the ProductsClient project, copy the app.config file and paste the copied file back into the ProductsClient project with the default name, Copy of app.config. This step is necessary because the next step will remove some important information from the app.config file that you will need later.

5. In the ProductsClient project, delete the *ProductsService* service from the Service References folder. As well as removing the service reference, this action also deletes the configuration information for accessing the service from the app.config file, which is why you made a copy of the original version of this file in the previous step.

6. Add the file Products.cs that you have just created to the ProductsClient project. This file is located in the Microsoft Press\WCF Step By Step\Chapter 3\ProductsServiceFault\ ProductsServiceLibrary\bin\Debug folder.

7. Delete the app.config file from the ProductsClient project and rename the file Copy of app.config as **app.config**.

8. Open the app.config file in the Code And Text Editor window. Change the contract for both client endpoints to **ProductsClient.ProductsService.IProductsService**, as shown in bold in the following.

```xml
<?xml version="1.0" encoding="utf-8" ?>
<configuration>
  <system.serviceModel>
    <bindings>
      ...
    </bindings>
    <client>
      <endpoint address="http://localhost:8000/ProductsService/Service.svc"
          binding="basicHttpBinding"
          bindingConfiguration="BasicHttpBinding_IProductsService"
          contract="ProductsClient.ProductsService.IProductsService"
          name="BasicHttpBinding_IProductsService" />
      <endpoint address="net.tcp://localhost:8080/TcpService" binding="netTcpBinding"
          contract="ProductsClient.ProductsService.IProductsService"
          name="NetTcpBinding_IProductsService" />
    </client>
  </system.serviceModel>

</configuration>
```

This change is necessary as you generated the types for the proxy in the *ProductsClient. ProductsService* namespace when you ran the *svcutil* utility.

Note You could have copied the output.config file generated by the *svcutil* utility to the ProductsClient project and renamed it as app.config rather than preserving and editing the original app.config file. However, although the output.config file specifies the correct type name for the contract attribute of the endpoint, it does include the address of the service, so you would have had to edit the file and add this information. Additionally, the output. config file only contains the definition of a single *BasicHttpBinding* endpoint, so you would also have needed to add the definition of the *NetTcpBinding* endpoint. It was simpler to modify the existing app.config file!

Modify the WCF Client Application to Catch Strongly Typed Faults

1. In the ProductsClient project, open the Program.cs file in the Code And Text Editor window.

2. Add the following *catch* handlers shown in bold after the *try* block in the *Main* method (leave the existing *FaultException* handler in place as well):

```
static void Main(string[] args)
{
    ...
    try
    {
        ...
    }
    catch (FaultException<SystemFault> sf)
    {
        Console.WriteLine("SystemFault {0}: {1}\n{2}",
            sf.Detail.SystemOperation, sf.Detail.SystemMessage,
            sf.Detail.SystemReason);
    }
    catch (FaultException<DatabaseFault> dbf)
    {
        Console.WriteLine("DatabaseFault {0}: {1}\n{2}",
            dbf.Detail.DbOperation, dbf.Detail.DbMessage,
            dbf.Detail.DbReason);
    }
    catch (FaultException e)
    {
        Console.WriteLine("{0}: {1}", e.Code.Name, e.Reason);
    }
    ...
}
```

These two handlers catch the *SystemFault* and *DatabaseFault* faults. Notice that the fields containing the exception information that are populated by the *ProductsService* (*SystemOperation*, *SystemMessage*, *SystemReason*, *DbOperation*, *DbMessage*, and *DbReason*) are located in the *Detail* field of the *FaultException* object.

 Important You must place these two exception handlers before the non-generic *FaultException* handler. The non-generic handler would attempt to catch these exceptions if it occurred first, and the compiler would not let you build the solution.

3. Build and run the solution without debugging.

4. When the Products Service Host window appears, click Start to run the service.

5. When the service has started, in the client application console window, press Enter.

The code in the *ListProducts* method in the *ProductsService* service still generates a null reference exception. The service throws a *FaultException*, containing a *SystemFault* object, which is serialized as a SOAP fault. The client application catches this fault and displays the details.

6. Press Enter to close the client application. Stop the service and close the Products Service Host window.

7. Edit the ProductsService.cs file in the *ProductsServiceHost* project. In the *ListProducts* method, restore the statement that initializes the *productsList* variable back to its original state and remove the code in the *try* block that calls the *Clear* method, as shown in the following:

```
public List<string> ListProducts()
{
    // Create a list for holding product numbers
    List<string> productsList = new List<string>();

    try
    {
        // Connect to the AdventureWorks database by using the Entity Framework
        using (AdventureWorksEntities database = new AdventureWorksEntities())
        {
            // Fetch the product number of every product in the database
            var products = from product in database.Products
                           select product.ProductNumber;

            productsList = products.ToList();
        }
    }
    catch (Exception e)
    {
        ...
    }
    ...
}
```

8. Edit the App.config file in the ProductsServiceHost project by using the Code And Text Editor window, and change the *Initial Catalog* part of the *connectionString* attribute to refer to the **Junk** database, as you did earlier:

```
<connectionStrings>
    <add ... connectionString="...;Initial Catalog=Junk;..." />
</connectionStrings>
```

9. Build and run the solution without debugging.

10. When the Products Service Host window appears, click Start to run the service.

11. When the service has started, in the client application console window, press Enter.

    The application configuration file for the service host application again refers to an invalid database. This "mistake" causes the service to generate a SOAP fault containing a *DatabaseFault* with details of the failure. The ProductsClient application catches this exception in the *FaultException<DatabaseFault>* handler.

12. Press Enter to close the client application. Stop the service and close the Products Service Host window.

13. Correct the *Initial Catalog* attribute in the app.config file for the ProductsServiceHost project and set it back to refer to the *AdventureWorks* database, as follows:

    ```
    <connectionStrings>
      <add ... connectionString="...;Initial Catalog=AdventureWorks;..." />
    </connectionStrings>
    ```

14. Build and run the solution without debugging.

15. In the Products Service Host window, start the service. Press Enter in the client application console window. Verify that the code now runs without any exceptions. Close the client console window, stop the service, and close the Products Service Host window when you have finished.

Reporting Unanticipated Exceptions

Specifying the possible exceptions that a service can throw when performing an operation is an important part of the contract for a service. If you use strongly-typed exceptions, you must specify every exception that an operation can throw in the service contract. If a service throws a strongly-typed exception that is not specified in the service contract, the details of the exception are not propagated to the client—the exception does not form part of the WSDL description of the operation used to generate the client proxy. There will inevitably be situations where it is difficult to anticipate the exceptions that an operation could throw. In these cases, you should catch the exception in the service, and if you need to send it to the client, raise an ordinary (non-generic) *FaultException* as you did in the first set of exercises in this chapter.

While you are developing a WCF service, it can be useful to send information about all exceptions that occur in the service—anticipated or not—to the client application for debugging purposes. You will see how you can achieve this in the next set of exercises.

Modify the WCF Service to Throw an Unanticipated Exception

1. In the ProductsServiceFault solution, in the ProductsServiceLibrary project, edit the ProductsService.cs file.

2. Add the following statement (shown in bold) as the first line of code in the *ListProducts* method in the *IProductsImpl* class:

```
public List<string> ListProducts()
{
    int i = 0, j = 0, k = i / j;
    ...
}
```

This statement will generate a *DivideByZeroException*. Note that the method does not trap this exception, and it is not mentioned in the service contract.

3. Build and run the solution without debugging.

4. In the Products Service Host window, click Start. In the client application console window, press Enter to connect to the service and invoke the *ListProducts* operation.

The service throws the *DivideByZero* exception. However, the details of the exception are not forwarded to the client application. Instead, the WCF runtime generates a very non-descript SOAP fault that is caught by the *DefaultException* handler in the client:

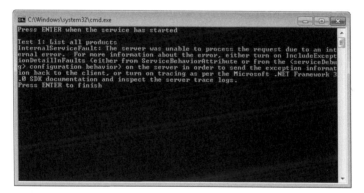

This lack of detail is actually a security feature. If the service provided a complete description of the exception to the client, then, depending on the information provided, a malicious user could glean potentially useful information about the structure of the service and its internal workings.

5. Close the client console window. Stop the service and close the Products Service Host window.

In the next exercise you will configure the host server to provide detailed information about unanticipated exceptions.

Configure the WCF Service to Send Details of Exceptions

1. In the ProductsServiceHost project, edit the App.config file by using the Code And Text Editor window.

2. In the *<serviceBehaviors>* section, edit the *<serviceDebug>* element in the *<behavior>* section and set the *includeExceptionDetailInFaults* attribute to true:

```
<?xml version="1.0"?>
<configuration>
  ...
  <system.serviceModel>
    ...
    <behaviors>
      <serviceBehaviors>
        <behavior>
          <!-- To avoid disclosing metadata information, set the value below to
               false and remove the metadata endpoint above before deployment -->
          <serviceMetadata httpGetEnabled="false"/>
          <!-- To receive exception details in faults for debugging purposes, set
               the value below to true.  Set to false before deployment to avoid
               disclosing exception information -->
          <serviceDebug includeExceptionDetailInFaults="true"/>
        </behavior>
      </serviceBehaviors>
    </behaviors>
    ...
  </system.serviceModel>
</configuration>
```

Setting the *includeExceptionDetailInFaults* attribute to *true* causes WCF to transmit the full details of exceptions when it generates SOAP faults for unanticipated errors.

3. Build and run the solution with debugging.

4. In the Products Service Host window, click Start. In the client application console window, press Enter.

The service throws the *DivideByZero* exception. This time, the client is sent specific information about the exception and reports it:

5. Close the client console window. Stop the service and close the Products Service Host window.

6. In the ProductsServiceLibrary project, edit the ProductsService.cs file.

7. In the *ListProducts* method, comment out the line of code that causes the *DivideBy ZeroException* exception.

8. In the App.config file for the ProductsServiceHost project, set the *includeException DetailInFaults* attribute of the *<serviceDebug>* element to false.

9. Build and run the solution without debugging.

10. In the Products Service Host window, start the service. Press Enter in the client application console window. Verify that the code runs without any exceptions. Close the client console window and the Products Service Host window when you have finished.

The previous exercise used the application configuration file to specify the *serviceDebug* behavior for the service. You can perform the same task by using the *ServiceBehavior* attribute of the class that implements the service, like this:

```
[ServiceBehavior(IncludeExceptionDetailInFaults=true)]
public class ProductsServiceImpl : IProductsService
{
    ...
}
```

However, it is recommended that you enable this behavior only by using the application configuration file. There are a couple of good reasons for this:

- You can turn the behavior on and off in the configuration file without rebuilding the application. You should not deploy an application to a production environment with this behavior enabled, and it is very easy to forget that you have enabled this behavior if you use the *ServiceBehavior* attribute in code.

- If you enable this behavior in code, you *cannot* disable it by altering the application configuration file. Rather more confusingly, if you *disable* this behavior in code, you *can* enable it in the application configuration file. The general rule is that if the *Include ExceptionDetailInFaults* behavior is enabled either in code or in the application configuration file, it will work. It must be disabled in *both* places to turn it off. Keep life simple by only specifying this behavior in one place—the application configuration file.

Managing Exceptions in Service Host Applications

In Chapter 2, you saw how to create a host application for a WCF service and use this application to control the lifecycle of the service. A service host application uses a *ServiceHost* object to instantiate and manage a WCF service. The *ServiceHost* class implements a finite-state machine. A *ServiceHost* object can be in one of a small number of states, and there are well-defined rules that determine how the WCF runtime transitions a *ServiceHost* object from one state to another. Some of these transitions occur as the result of specific method calls, while others are caused by exceptions in the service, in the communications infrastructure, or in the objects implementing the channel stack. A service host application should be prepared to handle these transitions and attempt recovery to ensure that the service is available whenever possible.

ServiceHost States and Transitions

When you instantiate a *ServiceHost* object, it starts in the *Created* state. In this state, you can configure the object; for example, you can use the *AddServiceEndpoint* method to cause the *ServiceHost* object to listen for requests on a particular endpoint. A *ServiceHost* object in this state is not ready to accept requests from client applications.

You start a *ServiceHost* object listening for requests by using the *Open* method (or the *Begin-Open* method if you are using the asynchronous programming model). The *ServiceHost* object moves to the *Opening* state while it creates the channel stacks specified by the bindings for each endpoint and starts the service. If an exception occurs at this point, the object transitions to the *Faulted* state. If the *ServiceHost* object successfully opens the communication channels for the service, it moves to the *Opened* state. Only in this state can the object accept requests from client applications and direct them to the service.

You stop a *ServiceHost* object from listening for client requests by using the *Close* (or *Begin-Close*) method. The *ServiceHost* object enters the *Closing* state. Currently running requests are allowed to complete, but clients can no longer send new requests to the service. When all outstanding requests have finished, the *ServiceHost* object moves to the *Closed* state. You can also stop a service by using the *Abort* method. This method closes the service immediately without waiting for the service to finish processing client requests. *Stopping* or aborting the service disposes the service object hosted by the *ServiceHost* object and reclaims any resources it was using. To start the service, you must recreate the *ServiceHost* object with a new instance of the service and then execute the *Open* method to reconstruct the channel stacks and start listening for requests again.

A *ServiceHost* object enters the *Faulted* state either when it fails to open correctly or if it detects an unrecoverable error in a channel used by the *ServiceHost* object to communicate with clients (for example, if some sort of protocol error occurs). When a *ServiceHost* object is in the *Faulted* state, you can examine the properties of the object to try and ascertain the cause of the failure, but you cannot send requests to the service. To recover the service, you should use the *Abort* method to close the service, recreate the *ServiceHost* object, and then execute the *Open* method again. Figure 3-1 summarizes the state transitions for a *ServiceHost* object along with the methods and conditions that cause the object to move between states.

> **Tip** You can determine the current state of a *ServiceHost* object by examining the value of the *State* property.

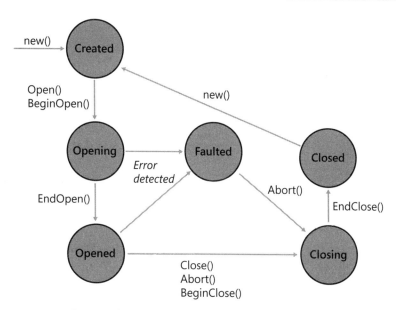

FIGURE 3-1 State transition diagram for the *ServiceHost* class.

Handling Faults in a Host Application

When a *ServiceHost* object moves from one state to another, it can trigger an event. These events were described in Table 2-2 in Chapter 2. From an error-handling perspective, the most important of these is the *Faulted* event, which occurs when a *ServiceHost* object enters the *Faulted* state. You should subscribe to this event, and provide a method that attempts to determine the cause, and then abort and restart the service, like this:

```
// ServiceHost object for hosting a WCF service
ServiceHost productsServiceHost;
productsServiceHost = new ServiceHost(...);
...
// Subscribe to the Faulted event of the productsServiceHost object
productsServiceHost.Faulted += (eventSender, eventArgs) =>
    {
        // FaultHandler method
        // Runs when productsServiceHost enters the Faulted state

        // Examine the properties of the productsServiceHost object
        // and log the reasons for the fault
        ...
        // Abort the service
        productsServiceHost.Abort();

        // Recreate the ServiceHost object
        productsServiceHost = new ServiceHost(...);

        // Start the service
        productsServiceHost.Open();
    };
...
```

Note You can use the *Close* method rather than *Abort* in the fault handler, but a service in the faulted state will not be able to continue processing current requests or receive new ones. Using the *Abort* method to close the service can reduce the time required in the *FaultHandler* method to restart the service.

Handling Unexpected Messages in a Host Application

One other exceptional circumstance that can arise in a host application is an unexpected message from a client. Client applications built by using the WCF library typically communicate with the service by using a proxy object, generated by using the *svcutil* utility. The proxy object provides a strongly-typed interface to the service that specifies the operations the client can request (and therefore the messages that the client sends). It is unlikely that a WCF client using a correctly generated proxy object will send an unexpected message. However, remember that a WCF service is simply a service that accepts SOAP messages, and developers building client applications can use whatever means they see fit for sending these messages. Developers building Java client applications will typically use Java-specific tools and libraries for constructing and sending SOAP messages. WCF also provides a low-level mechanism that allows developers to open a channel to a service, create SOAP messages, and then send them to the service, as shown in this fragment of code:

```
// Create a binding and endpoint to communicate with the ProductsService
BasicHttpBinding binding = new BasicHttpBinding();

EndpointAddress address = new EndpointAddress(
    "http://localhost:8000/ProductsService/Service.svc");

ChannelFactory<IRequestChannel> factory = new
    ChannelFactory<IRequestChannel>(binding, address);

// Connect to the ProductsService service
IRequestChannel channel = factory.CreateChannel();
channel.Open();

// Send a ListProducts request to the service
Message request = Message.CreateMessage(MessageVersion.Soap11,
    "http://tempuri.org/IProductsService/ListProducts");
Message reply = channel.Request(request);

// Process the reply
// (should be a SOAP message with a list of product numbers)
...
// Release resources and close the connection
reply.Close();
channel.Close();
factory.Close();
```

Don't worry too much about the details of this block of code—you will learn more about using Message and Channel objects in Chapter 11, "Programmatically Controlling the Configuration and Communications." The key statement is the line that creates the message sent to the ProductsService service:

```
Message request = Message.CreateMessage(MessageVersion.Soap11,
    "http://tempuri.org/IProductsService/ListProducts");
```

The second parameter to the *CreateMessage* method specifies the action that identifies the message sent to the service. If you recall the earlier discussion in this chapter describing the use of the *svcutil* utility to generate the client proxy, one of the files generated contained the WSDL description of the service. The WSDL description includes the definitions of each of the operations exposed by the service and the messages that an application sends to invoke these operations. Here is part of the WSDL describing the *ListProducts* operation:

```
<wsdl:operation name="ListProducts">
  <wsdl:input wsaw:Action="http://tempuri.org/IProductsService/ListProducts"
message="tns:IProductsService_ListProducts_InputMessage" />
  ...
</wsdl:operation>
```

When the service receives a message identified by the action *http://tempuri.org/IProducts Service/ListProducts*, it performs the *ListProducts* operation. If a client application sends a message specifying an action that the service does not recognize, the service host application raises the *UnknownMessageReceived* event. The host application can catch this event and record the unrecognized message, like this:

```
// ServiceHost object for hosting a WCF service
ServiceHost productsServiceHost;
productsServiceHost = new ServiceHost(...);
...
// Subscribe to the UnknownMessageReceived event of the
// productsServiceHost object
productsServiceHost.UnknownMessageReceived += (eventSender, eventArgs) =>
    {
        // UnknownMessageReceived event handler

        // Log the unknown message
        ...
        // Display a message to the administrator
        MessageBox.Show(string.Format(
            "A client attempted to send the message: {0} ",
            eventArgs.Message.Headers.Action));
    };
...
```

There could be a perfectly innocent explanation for a client sending a message such as this, or it could be part of a more concerted attack by a malicious user trying to probe a service and gather information about the operations it supports.

 Important The default value for the *httpGetEnabled* property of the *serviceMetadata* behavior is *false*, so unless you explicitly set it to *true*, WCF services do not publish their metadata. It is also worth noting that if you create a WCF service by using Visual Studio, the WCF Service template sets *httpGetEnabled* to *true*. Unless you explicitly need client applications to be able to access the metadata of a service, you should make sure that you reset this property to **false** when you deploy the service to a production environment.

One other possibility is that a WCF client application is using an out-of-date proxy object for sending messages to the service. If a developer modifies the service contract for a WCF service, she might change the messages that the service sends and receives. If any client applications that use the service are not updated, they might send messages that the service no longer understands. Therefore, if you update a service, you should ensure that you retain backward compatibility with existing clients. The same issues can arise with data contracts. You will learn more about how to update data contracts for a WCF service safely in Chapter 6, "Maintaining Service Contracts and Data Contracts."

Summary

In this chapter, you have seen how to use the *FaultException* class to send information about exceptions back to client applications as SOAP faults. You have seen how to use the *Fault Contract* attribute to specify the faults that a service can send and how to catch these faults in a client application. You have also seen how to propagate information about unanticipated exceptions from a service to a client for debugging purposes. You should understand how to make a service host application robust by tracking the states of a service, recovering from faults, and handling unexpected messages sent by client applications.

Chapter 4
Protecting an Enterprise WCF Service

After completing this chapter, you will be able to:

- Describe the different aspects of security that you should consider when implementing a WCF service.

- Explain how to provide privacy and integrity of messages at the message level and at the transport level when communicating between a client application and a WCF service.

- Explain how to configure a WCF service to authenticate users when running in a Windows environment and how a client application can provide a user's credentials to a WCF service for authentication.

- Describe how to define and use roles to authorize access to operations in a WCF service.

- Summarize how a WCF service can use impersonation to provide fine-grained access control over resources to authorized users.

Security is a fundamentally important aspect of any system, especially when a system comprises distributed applications and services. Security is also a very broad topic. For this reason, you are going to consider how to implement security in several different scenarios, spread across three chapters. This chapter concentrates on managing security within a single organization. In this environment, there is usually an inherent degree of trust between the computers running client applications and those hosting services. Users running applications are frequently members of the same, well-defined security domain. Services have access to the information in this security domain and can use it to authenticate users directly. In Chapter 5, "Protecting a WCF Service over the Internet," you will look at how to enforce security when client applications and services run in different security domains separated by an insecure network, where it is neither possible nor desirable to authenticate users directly. In Chapter 17, "Managing Identity with Windows CardSpace," you will see how to implement an identity meta-system to help authenticate users in a federated environment.

What Is Security?

Security is concerned with protecting users running client applications, services, and the messages that pass between them. Security encompasses a range of issues. The most common and familiar aspects of security include *authentication*—proof of identity—and *authorization*—access to resources based on identity. However, in a distributed environment, security has many other facets. These include:

- *Maintaining confidentiality of communications between a client application and a service.*   It is possible for applications to eavesdrop on the data being transmitted across the network. For example, take a look at the number of software and hardware network analyzers available—many administrators use them for tracking connectivity and bandwidth problems in a network, but an unscrupulous user could also track the packets passing over the network for malicious purposes. The information in these packets could include private financial data or confidential personal information that should not be common knowledge, even to other members of the same organization. Typically, you achieve confidentiality by encrypting messages.

- *Preventing tampering or corruption of messages.*   In an environment where message confidentiality is assured, it is still possible for a malicious user to intercept messages and corrupt them before sending them to their final destination. You can use techniques such as message hashing to generate a digital signature for the message, which a service can use to help detect corrupt or modified messages.

- *Ensuring verifiable delivery of messages.*   Even if a malicious user cannot decipher intercepted messages, the possibility of interception means that messages could either be diverted and not delivered at all or delivered repeatedly (known as a "replay attack"). Several schemes are available that can help detect replay attacks, including using a time stamp within a message (if the timestamp is outside reasonable limits when the service receives the message, it can discard the message) and assigning unique identifiers to messages (if the service receives two messages with the same identifier, it knows that there is a problem). Similarly, using a reliable message protocol can help to ensure that messages are either delivered to the destination within a reasonable time or that the sender will be alerted if they are not. You will learn more about reliable messaging in Chapter 10, "Implementing Reliable Sessions."

- *Preventing impersonation of services.*   Although not so common inside an enterprise as it is when using the Internet, it is possible for one service to impersonate another to obtain confidential data from a user. This phenomenon is sometimes known as "spoofing." The user running the client application believes they are communicating with the real service but are actually sending their details and other information to an entirely different service that happens to respond in a similar manner. This means that it can be as important for a client application to authenticate the service and verify that it is genuine as it is for a service to authenticate the user running the client application. in Chapter 5, you will look at how you can implement this form of two-way authentication by using certificates.

It is worth remembering that there is no such thing as absolute security. Hackers and fraudsters can invariably devise new and interesting ways to intercept, compromise, or otherwise disrupt the message flow. The important point is to be aware of the threats and have a plan for introducing countermeasures that can reduce their effects. Fortunately, WCF provides a highly extensible model that can adapt and evolve to meet many current security issues and (hopefully) counter new threats as they appear. The WCF implementation of security is also relatively unobtrusive. Through careful design and configuration, you can separate many of the security-related aspects of a client application and service from the business logic aspects, letting you modify or extend the security of your system without the need to rewrite large chunks of code.

Authentication and Authorization in a Windows Environment

To authenticate a user, a service must provide a means for a user to identify herself and then prove that identity. Many organizations maintain a single database of users and their means of identification. In a Windows environment, this typically means using Active Directory. In a single organization, it is not unreasonable to expect that all services and client applications have access to the same Active Directory database, so this database defines the security domain for the system. A service can be configured to use information held in the Active Directory database to authenticate users. When the user runs an application that accesses the service, the application can prompt the user for her user name and password and transmit this information to the service. The service can query Active Directory to verify that the user name is valid and the password is correct.

> **Note** Many of the discussions in this chapter that refer to Active Directory also apply to Windows computers that are not actually part of a domain but that maintain their own local users and groups database. The exercises in this chapter have been tested on a stand-alone computer running Microsoft Windows 7.
>
> In a Windows domain, a service can also identify users using the Kerberos protocol; a WCF client application can verify the identity of a service by using the same protocol. However, Kerberos is available only if you have access to a Windows Server domain controller. This chapter does not describe how to configure a WCF service and client application to perform Kerberos authentication. For a brief summary of how Kerberos authentication works, see the "How the Kerberos Version 5 Authentication Protocol Works" page at *http://technet.microsoft.com/en-us/library/cc772815(WS.10).aspx*. The article was originally written for Windows Server 2003, but it still applies to Windows Server 2008 and Windows 7.

This approach works regardless of where the user is actually running the client application; for example, it could be executing on a computer in the user's bedroom, connecting to the service across an Intranet link. However, a user located in the office might already have logged on to an organization's security domain, so prompting them for a user name and password again becomes cumbersome. Why should they need to keep on logging on? Fortunately, the Windows operating system provides support for this very common scenario. After a user successfully logs on to a security domain, Windows caches the details of the user's credentials in the user's logon process. When the user runs an application that requires authentication by a service, Windows can provide those details to the application, which can then forward them to the service. This mechanism is known as Windows Integrated Security.

> **Note** In a very large organization, the security domain might span several Active Directory data-bases that are managed independently by administrators in different parts of the organization. It is possible to configure trust relationships between these separate domains, effectively presenting them as a single security domain.

After a service has verified the identity of the user running the client application, it must then determine whether the user has the appropriate authority to invoke the specified operations. Typically, administrators assign users to *roles*, and the service developer can indicate which roles are allowed to access which operations. WCF can use .NET Framework declarative secu-rity to associate roles with operations and use a *role provider* to determine the roles to which a user belongs. The .NET Framework provides three role providers that you can use for storing role information:

- Windows Token Role Provider, which uses roles based on Active Directory groups.

- ASP.NET Role Provider, which uses roles stored in a SQL Server database.

- Authorization Store Role Provider, which uses roles defined by using the Microsoft Authorization Manager tool. This tool lets you store role information in either Active Directory or XML files.

> **More Info** For detailed information on using Microsoft Authorization Manager to define and implement roles, see the "Authorization Manager" page at *http://technet.microsoft.com/en-us/library/cc732077(WS.10).aspx*.

In this chapter, you will use the Windows Token Role Provider. This provider is ideal for use inside an enterprise that uses Windows Integrated Security for authentication. In Chapter 5, you will see how to use the ASP.NET Role Provider, which is better suited to Internet-based services.

Transport-Level and Message-Level Security

User identity information must be transported from a client application to a service. This information is sensitive, so it must be transmitted in as secure a manner as possible, which typically means encrypting these details. After a user has been authenticated, the contents of messages passing between the client application and service might also require some form of encryption, depending on the sensitivity of the information in these messages. There are many ways that client applications and services can achieve this goal, but the important point is that the client applications and the service must agree on the encryption mechanism that they use, and each must be able to decrypt messages sent by the other. Various standardization efforts have led to the use of public/private key cryptography to make the transfer secure.

> **More Info** For a good introduction to public key cryptography, visit the "Understanding Public Key Cryptography" page at *http://technet.microsoft.com/en-us/library/aa998077(EXCHG.65).aspx*. This page relates to Windows Exchange Server 2003, but the mechanism and principles apply to any system that implements public keys to protect messages and data.

When building Web services, you can perform authentication and encryption at two points when sending and receiving messages: at the transport level and at the message level.

Transport-Level Security

Transport-level authentication is typically implemented at the operating system level before the application or service receiving the message even knows that there is a message to receive. A service can specify the type of credentials it requires, but it is the operating system's responsibility to ensure that the correct credentials are provided and to validate them.

Many communications protocols can encrypt and decrypt data as it is sent and received. The most common example of such a protocol is HTTPS, which uses a technology called the Secure Sockets Layer (SSL) to encrypt and decrypt data by using keys provided in certificates. When a client application connects to a service using the HTTPS protocol, the underlying transport infrastructure for the client application and service negotiate the degree of encryption to perform. They then exchange a certificate containing keys that each can use to encrypt and decrypt messages. Because all this happens at the transport level, it is transparent to the client application and service; all they have to do is specify that they will communicate using the HTTPS protocol. However, an administrator must install and configure the appropriate certificates for the service host application.

> **More Info** In this chapter, you will configure HTTPS for use with a self-hosted WCF service. If you are hosting a WCF service in IIS, the configuration process is a little different. You will learn more about configuring HTTPS with IIS in Chapter 5.

Not surprisingly, you can also use transport-level security with the TCP protocol; the Windows operating system implements Transport Layer Security (TLS) over TCP. TLS is a successor to SSL and provides similar functionality. However, unlike using SSL with the HTTP bindings, the TCP bindings in WCF make use of TLS automatically.

Named pipes also support transport-level security but not message-level security.

Message-Level Security

Authentication at the message level is the responsibility of the service. The user credentials are included in messages sent to the service, and the service must verify that they are valid. Additionally, message-level privacy and integrity is also the responsibility of the client application and service—they encrypt and decrypt messages themselves using an agreed encryption algorithm and a negotiated set of encryption keys. Standards such as the WS-Security specification from OASIS describe the message-level security schemes that many Web services implementations have adopted. By following the WS-Security recommendations you can help to ensure the interoperability of your client applications and services with those developed by using technologies other than WCF.

Transport-level security has the advantage over message-level security in that it can often rely on hardware support and can be very efficient—encrypting and decrypting data can be a resource-intensive process, so anything that improves performance is very welcome. Additionally, transport-level authentication checks are enforced before the client application actually starts sending application-level messages, so performing authentication at this level detects authentication failures more quickly and with less network overhead.

The primary disadvantage of transport-level security is that it operates on a point-to-point basis; by the time the service receives a message, it has already been decrypted by the underlying transport mechanism. In a situation where a service should simply forward a message on to another service rather than process it, the intermediate service has full access to the message contents, meaning that the service could modify the message or extract confidential information before forwarding it. Using message-level encryption can help to mitigate this problem.

Message-level security provides end-to-end encryption. A client application and the service acting as the final destination can agree on an encryption key and an encryption algorithm to use for messages. When a message arrives at the intermediate service, it is still encrypted. If the intermediate service does not have access to the encryption key or it has no knowledge of the selected encryption algorithm, it cannot easily decrypt the message.

Implementing message-level security sounds like it could add quite a lot of work to the development effort required for building a service. However, WCF greatly simplifies matters and reduces the development effort required by incorporating much of the code required as part of the standard bindings that you can specify when configuring an endpoint for a service. All you need to do is set the properties of your selected binding appropriately (you will see several examples throughout this chapter).

Implementing Security in a Windows Domain

In the following exercises, you will see how to use transport-level and message-level security in some common scenarios that can arise within a single organization. Because it is easier to demonstrate and explain the concepts in this sequence, you will start by learning how to implement message confidentiality by encrypting messages. You will then see how to authenticate users running in a Windows environment, and finally, how to use the Windows Token Role provider to authorize access to operations.

Protecting a TCP Service at the Message Level

The *NetTcpBinding* binding automatically encrypts data at the transport level by using Transport Layer Security (TLS) over TCP. The *NetTcpBinding* binding also supports encryption at the message level, giving you a greater degree of control over the encryption algorithm used. You will use message-level security to implement message encryption in the first exercise.

Enable Message-Level Encryption for the *NetTcpBinding* Binding for the WCF Service

1. Using Visual Studio, open the solution file ProductsService.sln located in the Microsoft Press\WCF Step By Step\Chapter 4\ProductsService folder (within your Documents folder).

    This solution contains three projects: the *ProductsService* service, the ProductsServiceHost application, and the ProductsClient. These projects are configured to catch and handle SOAP faults, as described in Chapter 3, "Making Applications and Services Robust."

2. Expand the ProductsServiceHost project in Solution Explorer, right-click the App.config file, and then select Edit WCF Configuration from the context menu to open the configuration file in the Service Configuration Editor.

> **Tip** If the Edit WCF Configuration command does not appear, from the Visual Studio *Tools* menu, select WCF Service Configuration Editor, and then immediately close the Service Configuration Editor window. The Edit WCF Configuration command should now appear.

3. In the Service Configuration Editor, in the Configuration pane, right-click the Bindings folder, and then click New Binding Configuration.

4. In the Create A New Binding dialog box, select the *netTcpBinding* binding type, and then click OK.

    The WCF Service Configuration Editor generates a binding configuration with the default settings for the *NetTcpBinding* binding.

5. In the right pane of the Service Configuration Editor, change the *Name* property of the binding to **ProductsServiceTcpBindingConfig**.

Note This name does not conform to the pattern used for binding names generated by the Add Service Reference utility. This is because the Add Service Utility tends to generate bindings with the same names as endpoints. While this is perfectly legal, it can be confusing to an administrator for maintaining the configurations of a large number of services, endpoints, and bindings.

6. In the right pane, click the Security tab.

7. Change the *Mode* property to **Message**. Change the *AlgorithmSuite* property to **Basic128**. Leave the *MessageClientCredentialType* property set to *Windows*.

These settings cause the binding to use message-level security. Users will be expected to provide a valid Windows user name and password, and all messages will be encrypted by using the Advanced Encryption Standard (AES) 128-bit algorithm. This is a widely used algorithm that performs relatively quickly, but should provide sufficient privacy for messages inside an organization. However, if you are sending messages across a public wide area network such as the Internet, you might prefer to use Basic256, which is the default algorithm.

Note If you set the *Mode* property to **None**, the binding will not encrypt data and any settings you specify for transport-level or message-level security will be ignored. The *Transport* mode selects transport-level security (SSL) rather than message-level security, and the *TransportWithMessageCredential* mode implements message-level security to provide the identity of the user for authorization purposes, while performing encryption at the transport level. Transport-level encryption is usually more efficient than message-level encryption, although it requires more configuration on the part of the administrator, as you will see later in this chapter.

8. In the Configuration pane of the Service Configuration Editor, expand the *Products. ProductsServiceImpl* service in the Services folder, expand the Endpoints folder, and then click the *NetTcpBinding_IProductsService* endpoint.

9. In the Service Endpoint pane, set the *BindingConfiguration* property to **ProductsService TcpBindingConfig**.

This action associates the binding configuration with the binding. All messages sent by using the *ProductsServiceTcpBinding* binding will use message-level security and will be encrypted.

10. Save the configuration, and then exit the Service Configuration Editor.

11. In Visual Studio, open the file App.config in the ProductsServiceHost project. In the *<system.serviceModel>* section, you should see the new binding configuration and the reference to this configuration in the *ProductsServiceTcpBinding* endpoint, as follows:

```
...
<system.serviceModel>
  <bindings>
    <netTcpBinding>
      <binding name="ProductsServiceTcpBindingConfig">
        <security mode="Message">
          <message algorithmSuite="Basic128" />
        </security>
      </binding>
    </netTcpBinding>
  </bindings>
  <services>
    <service behaviorConfiguration="ProductsBehavior"
            name="Products.ProductsServiceImpl">
      <endpoint address="net.tcp://localhost:8080/TcpService" binding="netTcpBinding"
          bindingConfiguration="ProductsServiceTcpBindingConfig"
          name="NetTcpBinding_IProductsService" contract="Products.IProductsService" />
      ...
    </service>
  </services>
  ...
</system.serviceModel>
```

Be careful not to change anything in this file. Close the App.config file when you have finished examining it.

The service will expect clients that connect to the endpoint for this binding to use the same message-level security settings. You will configure the client next.

Enable Message-Level Encryption for the *NetTcpBinding* Binding in the WCF Client

1. In the ProductsClient project, edit the app.config file by using the Service Configuration Editor.

2. In the Service Configuration Editor, right-click the Bindings folder, and then click New Binding Configuration.

> **Note** The client configuration file already contains a binding configuration for the *basicHttpBinding* binding that was generated in Chapter 1, "Introducing Windows Communication Foundation." Be careful not to modify this binding configuration by mistake!

3. In the Create A New Binding dialog box, select the *netTcpBinding* binding type, and then click OK.

4. In the right pane of the Service Configuration Editor, change the Name property of the binding to **ProductsClientTcpBindingConfig**.

5. Click the Security tab.

6. Change the *Mode* property to **Message**. Change the *AlgorithmSuite* property to **Basic128**. Leave the *MessageClientCredentialType* property set to *Windows*.

> **Note** If you select a different algorithm suite for the client and server, they will not be able to decipher each other's communications. This will result in a runtime exception in the channel stack. If you are curious about this, try setting the AlgorithmSuite to TripleDes (for example) and examine the MessageSecurityException exception that occurs when you run the solution later.

7. In the Configuration pane, click the *NetTcpBinding_IProductsService* node in the End-points folder, under the Client folder.

8. In the right pane, set the *BindingConfiguration* property to **ProductsClientTcpBinding Config**.

9. Save the configuration, and then exit the Service Configuration Editor.

    If you examine the app.config file for the ProductsClient project, you will see that a binding configuration has been added to the *<bindings>* section. This configuration should be the same as that for the ProductsServiceHost project.

10. Edit the Program.cs file for the ProductsClient project in the Code And Text Editor window. In the *Main* method, change the statement that creates the proxy to connect to the service by using the *NetTcpBinding_IProductsService* endpoint, as shown in bold in the following:

```
static void Main(string[] args)
{
    Console.WriteLine("Press ENTER when the service has started");
    Console.ReadLine();

    // Create a proxy object and connect to the service
    ProductsServiceClient proxy = new
        ProductsServiceClient("NetTcpBinding_IProductsService");

    // Test the operations in the service
    ...
}
```

11. Start the solution without debugging.

12. In the Products Service Host window, click Start. If a Windows Security Alert dialog box appears, click Allow Access to allow the service to access the TCP port.

13. In the client console window, press Enter. Verify that the client application runs exactly as before.

14. Press Enter to close the client console window. Stop the service and close the Products Service Host window.

This exercise has shown you how easy it is to configure a WCF service and client application to secure messages by performing encryption, but how do you actually *know* that the messages have been encrypted? To answer this question, you can enable message tracing, and then examine the messages as they flow in and out of the service.

Configure Message Tracing for the WCF Service

1. In Visual Studio, edit the App.config file for the ProductsServiceHost project by using the Service Configuration Editor.

2. In the Configuration pane, expand the Diagnostics folder, and then click Message Logging.

3. In the Message Logging pane displaying the message logging settings, set the following properties to **True**:

    ❑ *LogEntireMessage*

    ❑ *LogMessagesAtServiceLevel*

    ❑ *LogMessagesAtTransportLevel*

    The *LogEntireMessage* property specifies whether the trace output should include the body of messages sent and received. Setting this property to *True* includes the body of the message. The default value, *False*, only traces the message header. Setting the *LogMessagesAtServiceLevel* property to *True* traces messages as they are presented to the service and as they are output from the service. If you are using message-level security, this trace will show the unencrypted messages after they have been received and decrypted at the message level (for incoming messages) or before they are encrypted (for outgoing messages). Setting the *LogMessagesAtTransportLevel* property to *True* traces messages as they are sent to or received from the transport level. If you are using message-level security, the messages traced at this point will be encrypted; although if you are using transport-level security, messages will already have been decrypted (for incoming messages) or not yet encrypted (for outgoing messages) at this point.

 Important   Tracing at the message level records messages in their unencrypted form. These messages could contain sensitive information. You should ensure that you protect the trace files that are generated and only let authorized users examine this data.

4. In the left pane, under the Diagnostics folder, right-click the Sources folder, and then click New Source.

    All tracing information for WCF is received from one or more trace sources. In this case, you will use the *MessageLogging* source provided with WCF, which traces messages. You can also use other sources. For example, the *ServiceModel* source traces events that occur in a service, such as tracking when a service starts listening, receives requests, and sends responses. You can even implement your own custom trace sources, although the details of how to do this are outside the scope of this book.

5. In the Trace Source pane, set the *Name* property to **System.ServiceModel.Message Logging**. Set the *Trace level* property to **Verbose**.

6. In the Configuration pane, under the Diagnostics folder, right-click the Listeners folder, and then click New Listener.

   A listener object is responsible for receiving data from the trace sources, formatting and filtering them, and then sending them to a destination.

7. In the Trace Listener pane, perform the following tasks:

   ❑ In the *Name* property, type **MessageLog**.

   ❑ In the *InitData* property, click the ellipses button. In the Save Log As dialog box, move to the Microsoft Press\WCF Step By Step\Chapter 4 folder. within your Documents folder. In the *File name* box, type **ProductsService.svclog**, and then click Save.

   ❑ The *InitData* property specifies the name of the file that the listener will use for saving trace data. When tracing starts, if this file does not exist, the listener will create it; otherwise, it will append trace information to the end of any existing data in the file.

   ❑ In the *TraceOutputOptions* property, click the drop-down arrow, and then clear all items in the list. The trace output options are useful if you are tracing messages for multiple client applications and you need to be able to correlate the different request and response messages. In this example, you will be running a single client application, so this additional information is not really necessary.

   ❑ Verify that the *TypeName* property is set to *System.Diagnostics.XmlWriterTrace Listener.* The listener can output data in several formats. However, you will be using another tool called the Service Trace Viewer to examine the trace output, and this tool expects the data to be in XML format.

   ❑ Click Add at the bottom of the Trace Listener pane. In the Add Tracing Source dialog box, select the **System.ServiceModel.MessageLogging** source, and then click OK.

8. Save the configuration, and then exit the Service Configuration Editor.

Run the WCF Client and Service to Examine the Trace Output

1. Start the solution without debugging.

2. In the Products Service Host window, click Start.

3. In the client console window, press Enter. Verify that the client application still runs correctly.

4. Press Enter to close the client console window. Stop the service and close the Products Service Host window.

5. On the Windows Start menu, click All Programs, click Microsoft Visual Studio 2010, click Microsoft Windows SDK Tools, and then click Service Trace Viewer.

6. In the Service Trace Viewer window, on the File menu, click Add.

7. In the Open dialog box, move to the Microsoft Press\WCF Step By Step\Chapter 4\ ProductsService folder within your Documents folder, select the file ProductsService. svclog, and then click Open.

8. In the Service Trace Viewer window, in the left pane, click the Message tab. You will see a list of messages sent and received by the service, identified by their *Action* values.

 Tip Expand the left pane and then expand the Action column in this pane to see more of the name for each action.

At the top of this list are a number of messages in the *http://schemas.xmlsoap.org/ ws/2005/02/trust* namespace. These messages are concerned with sending and verifying the user's identity and negotiating the encryption mechanism and encryption keys that the client application and WCF service will use for sending and receiving messages. These messages are followed by the application messages received and sent by the WCF service, identified by the *http://tempuri.org* namespace.

9. Click the first message with the action *http://tempuri.org/IProductsService/ListProducts*. Note that each action occurs twice. This is because you traced each message twice: once at the message level and once at the transport level.

10. In the lower-right pane, click the Message tab. The window will display the entire SOAP message. This is the version of the message passed from the transport level to the message level. The message has a rather lengthy SOAP header, which you can examine at your leisure. The interesting part is the SOAP body at the end of the message. This is the encrypted *ListProducts* request received from the client application. The *<e:CipherValue>* element contains the data for the request, as highlighted in the image that follows.

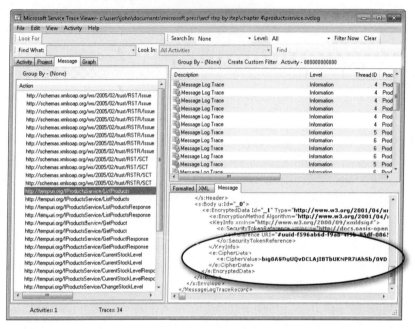

11. In the left pane, click the second message with the action *http://tempuri.org/ IProductsService/ListProducts*. In the right pane, scroll to the end of the Message pane. The *<body>* element contains is the unencrypted version of the message passed from the message level to the service, as shown in the following:

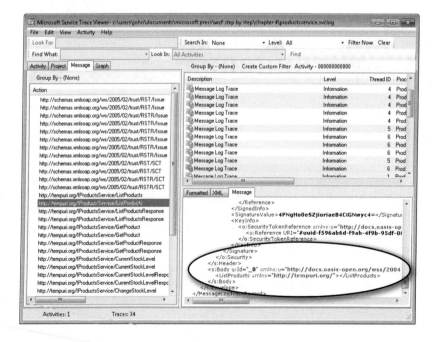

12. In the left pane, click the first message with the action *http://tempuri.org/IProductsService/ListProductsResponse*. In the lower-right pane, examine the message body in the Message pane. You can see that this is an unencrypted message containing the list of products returned in response to the *ListProducts* request. This message is the output from the service to the message level, and so it has not yet been encrypted.

13. In the left pane, click the second message with the action *http://tempuri.org/IProductsService/ListProductsResponse*. In the lower-right pane, scroll to the bottom of the Message pane and examine the message body. This time you can see that this is the encrypted response sent by the message level to the transport level for transmission back to the client.

14. Examine the other messages. When you have finished, close the Service Trace Viewer.

Protecting an HTTP Service at the Transport Level

If you recall, the ProductsServiceHost application exposes two endpoints to which clients connect: one based on the TCP protocol, and the other using HTTP. The HTTP endpoint is configured to use the *BasicHttpBinding* binding. The *BasicHttpBinding* binding conforms to the WS-BasicProfile 1.1 specification and is intended for use with existing legacy Web services and clients. It is fully interoperable with ASP.NET Web services. By default, this binding provides minimal security; for example, it does not support message-level encryption or authentication. To implement message confidentiality and remain interoperable with ASP.NET Web services, you should use transport-level security. This requires you to configure HTTPS. This is what you will do in the next set of exercises.

Note The *BasicHttpBinding* binding also supports message-level security. Ordinary ASP.NET Web services and client applications do not implement the WS-Security specification, and so they will not be able to communicate with a service that implements message-level security. However, Microsoft Web Services Enhancements (WSE) does support WS-Security, so Web services that you have created by using WSE can communicate with a WCF service through an endpoint based on the *BasicHttpBinding* binding by using message-level security.

Specify Transport-Level Security for the *BasicHttpBinding* Binding for the WCF Service

1. In Visual Studio, in the ProductsServiceHost project in Solution Explorer, edit the App.config file by using the Service Configuration Editor.

2. In the Service Configuration Editor, in the Configuration pane, right-click the Bindings folder, and then click New Binding Configuration.

3. In the Create A New Binding dialog box, select the *basicHttpBinding* binding type, and then click OK.

4. In the right pane of the Service Configuration Editor, change the *Name* property of the binding to **ProductsServiceBasicHttpBindingConfig**.

5. Click the Security tab.

6. Set the *Mode* property to **Transport**.

   In this mode, message security is provided by using HTTPS. You must configure SSL for the service by using a certificate. The client authenticates the service by using the service's SSL certificate. The service authenticates the client by using the mechanism specified by the *TransportClientCredentialType* property. The default value of None does not provide any authentication—you will examine some of the other values that you can specify for this property later in this chapter.

7. In the Configuration pane, expand the *ProductsServicesImpl* service in the Services folder, expand the Endpoints folder, and then click the *BasicHttpBinding_IProductsService* endpoint.

8. In the Service Endpoint pane, set the *BindingConfiguration* property to **ProductsServiceBasicHttpBindingConfig**.

9. HTTP Web services that implement transport-level security *must* specify the https scheme, so change the Address property, as shown in bold in the following:

   `https://localhost:8000/ProductsService/Service.svc`

10. Save the configuration, and then exit the Service Configuration Editor.

11. Rebuild the ProductsServiceHost project.

The next step is to reconfigure and modify the client to connect to the service by using the endpoint corresponding to the *BasicHttpBinding* binding.

Specify Transport-Level Security for the *BasicHttpBinding* Binding for the WCF Client

1. In the ProductsClient project, edit the app.config file by using the Service Configuration Editor.

2. In the Configuration pane, expand the Bindings folder, and then click the *BasicHttp Binding_IProductsService* binding.

3. In the right pane of the Service Configuration Editor, change the *Name* property of the binding to **ProductsClientBasicHttpBindingConfig**. (This is to make the name of the binding consistent with the other bindings you have created.)

4. Click the Security tab.

5. Change the *Mode* property to **Transport**.

6. In the Configuration pane, click the *BasicHttpBinding_IProductsService* endpoint in the Endpoints folder, within the Client folder.

7. In the Client Endpoint pane, change the *Address* property to use the https scheme, as shown below, and verify that the *BindingConfiguration* property has changed to refer to the *ProductsClientBasicHttpBindingConfig* binding configuration

   ```
   https://localhost:8000/ProductsService/Service.svc
   ```

8. Save the configuration, and then exit the Service Configuration Editor.

9. In Visual Studio, open the Program.cs file for the ProductsClient project in the Code And Text Editor window.

10. In the *Main* method, switch the statement that creates the proxy object to connect to the WCF service back to the endpoint named *BasicHttpBinding_IProductsService*, as shown in bold in the following code sample:

    ```
    static void Main(string[] args)
    {
        Console.WriteLine("Press ENTER when the service has started");
        Console.ReadLine();

        // Create a proxy object and connect to the service
        ProductsServiceClient proxy = new
            ProductsServiceClient("BasicHttpBinding_IProductsService");

        // Test the operations in the service
        ...
    }
    ```

11. Rebuild the ProductsClient project.

Although you have updated the WCF service and the client application, you have not yet configured transport security for the HTTPS protocol. If you try to run the service at this point, you will receive an error. In the next exercise, you will create a certificate for the WCF service and configure SSL for the service by using the *netsh* utility.

Configure the WCF HTTP Endpoint with an SSL Certificate

1. Open a Visual Studio Command Prompt window as an administrator, as follows:

   a. On the Windows Start menu, click All Programs, click Microsoft Visual Studio 2010, and then click Visual Studio Tools. Right-click Visual Studio Command Prompt (2010), and then click Run as administrator.

   b. Enter the administrator password if prompted.

2. In the Visual Studio Command Prompt window, type the following command:

   ```
   makecert -sr LocalMachine -ss My -n CN=HTTPS-Server -sky exchange -sk HTTPS-Key
   ```

   Verify that this command responds with the message "Succeeded."

The *makecert* utility is a useful tool for creating test certificates that you can use for development purposes. The command shown here creates a certificate that is stored in the *Personal* certificates store for the *LocalMachine* account. For detailed information about the options for the *makecert* utility, see the "Certificate Creation Tool" page on the Microsoft Web site at *http://msdn.microsoft.com/en-us/library/bfsktky3.aspx*.

> **Important** Certificates that you create by using the *makecert* utility should not be used in a production environment as they are not certified by a verifiable certification authority. Remember that the service uses this certificate to prove its identity. The client must be able to trust that this certificate was created by a reliable source that can verify the veracity of the service. When deploying a production service, you should obtain your certificates from a recognized certification authority, such as VeriSign or Thawte. Alternatively, you can use Active Directory Certificate Services, which enables an enterprise to generate its own certificates.

To use the *netsh* utility to configure SSL for the service, you need to find the thumbprint of the certificate. The thumbprint is a hexadecimal string that uniquely identifies the certificate. You can obtain this information by using the Certificates Microsoft Management Console snap-in.

3. In the command prompt window, type the following command:

   mmc

   This command starts the Microsoft Management Console, displaying the default Console Root window.

4. On the File menu, click Add/Remove Snap-In.

5. In the Add Or Remove Snap-Ins dialog box, in the Available Snap-Ins list, click Certificates, and then click Add.

6. In the Certificates Snap-In dialog box, select the **Computer** account, and then click Next.

7. In the Select Computer dialog box, select **Local computer**, and then click Finish.

8. In the Add Or Remove Snap-Ins dialog box, click OK.

9. In the Console Root window, expand the Certificates node, expand the Personal folder, and then click the Certificates folder.

   The HTTPS-Server certificate that you created by using the *makecert* utility should be displayed (you may have other certificates installed on your computer, as well):

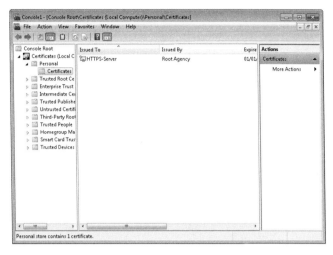

10. Double-click the HTTPS-Server certificate.

11. In the Certificate window, click the Details tab. Scroll to the bottom of the window displaying the details of the certificate. Click the *Thumbprint* property, and make a note of the hexadecimal string displayed in the lower window (your thumbprint will not be the same as that shown in the following image):

> **Tip** You might find it useful to simply select the text in the lower window and copy it to the Windows clipboard.

12. Click OK, close the Microsoft Management Console window without saving the console settings, and return to the Visual Studio Command Prompt window.

13. In the Visual Studio Command Prompt window, type the command shown below on a single line. Replace the hexadecimal string following the *certhash* parameter with the digits from the thumbprint of your certificate (remove all spaces from the thumbprint string):

```
netsh http add sslcert ipport=0.0.0.0:8000
    certhash=68969d3a7d1e1a843beec75fde266f5af4924c
    appid={00112233-4455-6677-8899-AABBCCDDEEFF}
```

If this command is successful, it should report the message "SSL Certificate successfully added."

> **Note** Be very careful to specify the correct thumbprint. If you receive the message "A specified logon session does not exist. It may already have been terminated," then you probably typed it incorrectly.

This command binds the certificate with the thumbprint indicated with the *certhash* parameter to the port indicated by the *ipport* parameter. The port is specified as the IP address of the computer followed by the port. Specifying an IP address of *0.0.0.0* denotes the local computer. The *appid* parameter is a GUID that identifies this binding of the certificate to the port; you can use any unique GUID.

14. You also need to re-reserve port 8000 for the *ProductsService* WCF service. Previously you registered this port for the HTTP endpoint for the service you created in Chapter 2, "Hosting a WCF Service." You must remove this reservation and create another for the HTTPS endpoint of the ProductsService WCF service.

In the Visual Studio Command Prompt window, type the following command to remove the existing HTTP reservation for port 8000:

```
netsh http delete urlacl url=http://+:8000/
```

This command should respond with the message "URL reservation successfully deleted." If you see the message "The parameter is incorrect," make sure that you added the trailing "/" character to the URL.

15. Type the following command to add a new HTTPS reservation for port 8000. Replace *UserName* with the name of your Windows account. Make sure that you specify **https** in the URL.

```
netsh http add urlacl url=https://+:8000/ user=UserName
```

Verify that the command responds with the message "URL reservation successfully added."

Leave the Visual Studio Command Prompt window open; you will use it again later in this chapter.

> **Warning** When a client application receives a certificate from a server, the WCF runtime attempts to ascertain that the certificate is valid and that the authority that issued it is trusted. The WCF runtime will fail this check when using the certificate that you have just installed. The following exercise shows how to force the WCF runtime to override this check and allow this certificate to be used. Note that you should *never* do this in a production environment! The code is provided as-is, and without further explanation (it is not the author's work—it was written by developers at Microsoft and is included in one of the WCF technology samples provided with Visual Studio). In the real world, you should go out and buy a valid certificate.

Add Code to the WCF Client to Override Certificate Validation Checking

1. In Visual Studio, edit the Program.cs file for the ProductsClient project.

2. Add the following *using* statements to the list at the top of the file:

```
using System.Security.Cryptography.X509Certificates;
using System.Net;
```

3. Add the following class to the *ProductsClient* namespace, just below the *Program* class:

> **Note** If you don't want to type the code in manually for this class, it is available in the PermissiveCertificatePolicy.cs file in the Chapter 4 folder.

```
// WARNING: This code is only needed for test certificates such as those
// created by makecert. It is not recommended for production code.
class PermissiveCertificatePolicy
{
    string subjectName;
    static PermissiveCertificatePolicy currentPolicy;
    PermissiveCertificatePolicy(string subjectName)
    {
        this.subjectName = subjectName;
        ServicePointManager.ServerCertificateValidationCallback +=
            new System.Net.Security.RemoteCertificateValidationCallback
            (RemoteCertValidate);
    }

    public static void Enact(string subjectName)
    {
        currentPolicy = new PermissiveCertificatePolicy(subjectName);
    }
```

```
    bool RemoteCertValidate(object sender, X509Certificate cert,
        X509Chain chain, System.Net.Security.SslPolicyErrors error)
    {
        if (cert.Subject == subjectName)
        {
            return true;
        }

        return false;
    }
}
```

4. Add the following statement (shown in bold) to the *Main* method of the *Program* class, immediately before creating the proxy object:

```
static void Main(string[] args)
{
    Console.WriteLine("Press ENTER when the service has started");
    Console.ReadLine();

    // Create a proxy object and connect to the service
    PermissiveCertificatePolicy.Enact("CN=HTTPS-Server");
    ProductsServiceClient proxy = new
        ProductsServiceClient("BasicHttpBinding_IProductsService");

    // Test the operations in the service
    ...
}
```

Run the WCF Client and Service

1. Start the solution without debugging.

2. In the Products Service Host window, click Start. The service should start successfully. If it fails, make sure that you have configured SSL correctly and reserved port 8000 on your computer with a URL that specified the HTTPS protocol.

3. In the client console window, press Enter. Verify that the client application runs correctly.

4. Press Enter to close the client console window. Stop the service and close the Products Service Host window.

Protecting an HTTP Service at the Message Level

You can configure the *BasicHttpBinding* binding to provide message-level security by selecting the Message security mode for the binding. In this mode, the service uses SOAP message-level security to encrypt the message. The service must have a certificate installed, and the client uses the public key from the service's certificate to perform the encryption. The service can send the certificate containing its public key at the start of the message exchange, or an administrator can install the service certificate on the client computer before the client application (in which case you must specify how to locate the service certificate in the client certificate store by adding a service behavior using the *<serviceCredentials>* element to the client configuration file). You will learn more about this in Chapter 5. Additionally, the only authentication mechanism supported by a WCF service that uses this mode requires that the client application identifies itself with a certificate—you cannot use authentication mechanisms such as Windows Integrated Security with this mode.

One other option is to use the *TransportWithMessageCredential* security mode. This is a hybrid combination of message-level and transport-level security. The service uses the HTTPS protocol and a certificate to provide message integrity and confidentiality at the transport level. Client authentication is handled at the message level by using SOAP message security, and the client application can provide a user name and password to identify the user. You will learn more about this security mode in Chapter 5.

If you really want to implement message-level security for a WCF service with the minimum of fuss and configuration, you can opt to use the *WS2007HttpBinding* binding. The *WS2007Http Binding* binding conforms to the current WS-* specifications and follows the WS-Security specification for encrypting messages and authenticating users by default. The following exercises demonstrate how to use the *WS2007HttpBinding* binding to implement message-level security over HTTP.

Configure the WCF Service with an Endpoint Based on the *WS2007HttpBinding* Binding

1. In Visual Studio, edit the App.config file for the ProductsServiceHost project by using the Service Configuration Editor.

2. In the Configuration pane, expand the *Products.ProductsServiceImpl* node under the Services folder, right-click Endpoints, and then click New Service Endpoint.

3. In the Service Endpoint pane, set the properties of the endpoint to the values in the following table. Leave all other properties with their default value:

Property	Value
Name	WS2007HttpBinding_IProductsService
Address	http://localhost:8010/ProductsService/Service.svc
Binding	ws2007HttpBinding
Contract	Products.IProductsService

Notice that the scheme used for the address of this endpoint is *http*, and not *https*.

4. Save the changes, and then exit the Service Configuration Editor.

5. Rebuild the ProductsServiceHost project.

6. Return to the Visual Studio Command Prompt window and type the following command to add an HTTP reservation for port 8010 (replace *UserName* with the name of your Windows account):

```
netsh http add urlacl url=http://+:8010/ user=UserName
```

Verify that the command responds with the message "Url Reservation Successfully Added."

Configure the WCF Client to Connect to the *WS2007HttpBinding* Endpoint

1. Edit the app.config file for the ProductsClient project by using the Service Configuration Editor.

2. In the Configuration pane, right-click Endpoints in the Client folder, and then click New Client Endpoint.

3. In the right pane, set the properties of the endpoint to the values in the following table:

Property	Value
Name	WS2007HttpBinding_IProductsService
Address	http://localhost:8010/ProductsService/Service.svc
Binding	ws2007HttpBinding
Contract	ProductsClient.ProductsService.IProductsService

4. Save the changes, and then exit the Service Configuration Editor.

5. In Visual Studio, open the Program.cs file in the ProductsClient project in the Code And Text Editor window. In the *Main* method, change the code that creates the proxy object to use the new binding, as follows:

```
static void Main(string[] args)
{
    ...
    ProductsServiceClient proxy = new
        ProductsServiceClient("WS2007HttpBinding_IProductsService");

    // Test the operations in the service
    ...
}
```

6. Rebuild the ProductsClient project.

Run the WCF Client and Service to Examine the Trace Output

1. Using Windows Explorer, delete the existing trace file ProductsService.svclog in the Microsoft Press\WCF Step By Step\Chapter 4\ProductsService folder.

2. In Visual Studio, start the solution without debugging.

3. In the Products Service Host window, click Start. In the client console window, press Enter. Verify that the client application still runs correctly. Press Enter to close the client console window. Stop the service and close the Products Service Host window.

4. Start the Service Trace Viewer utility and open the ProductsProducts.svclog file.

5. In the Service Trace Viewer window, in the left pane, click the Message tab.

6. Click the first message with the action *http://tempuri.org/IProductsService/ListProducts*. In the lower-right pane, click the Message tab, and then scroll down to the end of the message.

   You should see that the message has been encrypted—the body element of the message contains encrypted data in a *<e:CipherData>* section, as before. This is the message encrypted at the message level. Unlike using the *BasicHttpBinding* binding or *NetTcpBinding* binding, you did not need to specify any encryption settings when you created the binding because the *WS2007HttpBinding* binding automatically encrypts data at the message level.

7. In the left pane, click the second message with the action *http://tempuri.org/IProducts Service/ListProducts*. In the right pane, scroll to the end of the Message window. This is the unencrypted version of the message passed from the message level to the service.

8. Examine the two *ListProductsResponse* messages. As with the *NetTcpBinding* example earlier in this chapter, you can see the unencrypted version of the message being output by the service to the message level and the encrypted version of the message passing from the message level to the transport level.

9. Close the Service Trace Viewer.

The *WS2007HttpBinding* binding uses the 256-bit version of the AES encryption algorithm to encrypt data by default. You can select a different algorithm by creating a binding behavior and specifying the algorithm to use in the *AlgorithmSuite* property of the behavior, as you did when configuring message-level security for the *NetTcpBinding* binding earlier in this chapter.

Authenticating Windows Users

So far, you have seen how to configure the *NetTcpBinding*, *BasicHttpBinding*, and *WS2007HttpBinding* bindings to support confidentiality and privacy by encrypting messages. However, transporting messages securely is only useful if a service can verify the identity of the user running the client application. In the exercises that follow, you will look at how a service can authenticate a user when the client application and service are both running within the same Windows domain. In Chapter 5, you will see how to perform authentication when a client and service are located in different (possibly non-Windows) security domains.

You will start by adding code to the *ProductsService* WCF service that displays the name of the user calling the *ListProducts* operation. You will then be able to see the effect that the authentication options available in WCF have on the identity passed from a client application to a service.

> **Note** You can configure authentication to be largely transparent to the WCF service. You will see in the exercises in this section that most of the actual authentication process is performed by the WCF runtime executing the service. All the service needs to do is specify the type of authentication it requires.

Display the Name of the User Calling an Operation in the WCF Service

1. In Visual Studio, add a reference to the *PresentationFramework*, *PresentationCore*, *System.Xaml*, and *WindowsBase* assemblies to the ProductsServiceLibrary project.

2. Open the ProductsService.cs file.

   This file contains the code that implements the operations for the *ProductsService* service.

3. Add the following *using* statements to the list at the top of the file:

   ```
   using System.Threading;
   using System.Windows;
   ```

4. Locate the *ListProducts* method in the *ProductsServiceImpl* class. Add the following statements (shown in bold) as the first two lines of the method:

   ```
   public List<string> ListProducts()
   {
       string userName = Thread.CurrentPrincipal.Identity.Name;
       MessageBox.Show(string.Format("Username is {0}", userName),
           "ProductsService Authentication", MessageBoxButton.OK);
       ...
   }
   ```

   The first statement retrieves the name of the Windows user that the current thread is running on behalf of. The second statement displays the user name in a message box.

5. Edit the Program.cs file in the ProductsClient project. In the *Main* method, change the code that creates the proxy object to use the *BasicHttpBinding* binding, as follows:

```
static void Main(string[] args)
{
    ...
    ProductsServiceClient proxy = new
        ProductsServiceClient("BasicHttpBinding_IProductsService");

    // Test the operations in the service
    ...
}
```

6. Start the solution without debugging.

7. In the Products Service Host window, click Start. In the client console window, press Enter.

   A message box appears, displaying the user name sent by the client application. The user name will appear to be missing. This is not an error. By default, the *BasicHttpBinding* binding does not transmit identity information about users. All messages are sent as the anonymous user. This is not much use if you need to authenticate the user!

8. Click OK and verify that the client application still runs correctly.

9. Press Enter to close the client console window. Stop the service and close the Products Service Host window.

In the next set of exercises, you will revisit the *BasicHttpBinding* binding and implement user authentication. Many of the authentication options available for this binding apply to other bindings, as well.

Configure the *BasicHttpBinding* Binding for the WCF Service to Implement Basic Authentication

1. Edit the App.config file in the ProductsServiceHost project by using the Service Configuration Editor.

2. In the Configuration pane, expand the Bindings folder, and then click the *ProductsServiceBasicHttpBindingConfig* node.

3. In the right pane, click the Security tab.

   Notice that the *TransportClientCredentialType* property is currently set to *None*, so the service is not expecting client applications to provide authentication information about users, and anyone who can connect to the service can send it messages and invoke operations.

4. Set the *TransportClientCredentialType* property to **Basic**.

   When using Basic authentication, the client application must provide a user name and password, which is transmitted to the service. The WCF runtime executing the service can use this information to authenticate the user running the client application, and if the user is valid, it will provide the identity of the user to the service.

5. Save the configuration, and then close the Service Configuration Editor.

6. Start the solution without debugging.

7. In the Products Service Host window, click Start. In the client console window, press Enter.

   The client now fails with a *MessageSecurityException* exception, "The HTTP request is unauthorized with client authentication scheme 'Anonymous'... ." The WCF runtime for the service was expecting the client application to provide a user name and password, which it has not done. You will correct this in the next exercise.

8. Close the client console window, stop the service, and close the Products Service Host window.

Modify the WCF Client to Supply the User Credentials to the WCF Service

1. In Visual Studio, edit the app.config file in the ProductsClient project by using the Service Configuration Editor.

2. In the Configuration pane, expand the Bindings folder and click the *ProductsClientBasic HttpBindingConfig* node.

3. In the right pane, click the Security tab.

4. Set the *TransportClientCredentialType* property to **Basic**.

5. Save the configuration, and then close the Service Configuration Editor.

6. Open the Program.cs file in the ProductsClient project in the Code And Text Editor window.

7. In the *Main* method, add the following statements shown in bold immediately after the code that creates the proxy object (replace the text *Domain* with the name of your domain or computer [if you are not currently a member of a domain], replace *User-Name* with your user name, and replace *Password* with your password):

```
static void Main(string[] args)
{
    ...
    ProductsServiceClient proxy = new
        ProductsServiceClient("BasicHttpBinding_IProductsService");

    proxy.ClientCredentials.UserName.UserName = "Domain\\UserName";
    proxy.ClientCredentials.UserName.Password = "Password";

    // Test the operations in the service
    ...
}
```

The *ClientCredentials* property of a WCF proxy object presents a mechanism for a client application to provide the credentials to send to the service. The *UserName* property of the *ClientCredentials* property specifies the data for a *UserName* token, which can hold a user name and password. Other properties are available, such as *ClientCertificate*, with which you can supply different types of credentials information as required by the service configuration.

> **Warning** This code is for illustrative purposes in this exercise only. In a production application, you should prompt the user for their name and password. You should never hard-code these details into an application.

8. Start the solution without debugging.

9. In the Products Service Host window, click Start. In the client console window, press Enter.

   The client now successfully connects to the *ProductsService* WCF service. A message box appears, displaying the user name sent by the client application. This time, the user name appears as expected, verifying that the operation is executing with the credentials of the user (my user name is John, and my computer is called LON-DEV-01—your user name and computer are probably different).

10. Click OK and verify that the client application still runs correctly.

11. Press Enter to close the client console window. Stop the service and close the Products Service Host window.

By using Basic authentication, you can provide the user name and password of the user, and the WCF runtime executing the service will check that these credentials are valid. If you provide an invalid user name of password, the WCF runtime will reject the request and the client will receive another *MessageSecurityException* exception with the message "The HTTP request was forbidden... ."

> **Note** You can also configure the *NetTCPBinding* and *WS2007HttpBinding* bindings at the message level to require Username authentication. This is very similar to Basic authentication at the transport level as far as the client application is concerned, although somewhat different as far as the service is concerned because the service takes responsibility for authenticating the user itself (typically by using a custom database of user names and passwords). Additionally, if you are implementing Basic authentication, user names and passwords are not encrypted at the message level, so WCF insists that you configure the underlying transport to provide encryption to prevent the credential details from being transmitted across an open network as clear text.

Basic authentication is a good solution if the user running the client application is not currently logged in to the security domain used by the service. However, if the user is logged in to the domain, you can make use of Windows Integrated Security to provide the user's credentials automatically, rather than prompting the user for them again (or worse still, hardcoding them in your application!). You will do this in the next exercise.

Configure the *BasicHttpBinding* Binding for the WCF Service and Client to use Windows Authentication

1. Edit the App.config file in the ProductsServiceHost project by using the Service Configuration Editor.

2. In the Configuration pane, expand the Bindings folder, and then click the *Products ServiceBasicHttpBindingConfig* node.

3. In the right pane, click the Security tab.

4. Set the *TransportClientCredentialType* property to **Windows**.

5. Save the configuration, and then close the Service Configuration Editor.

6. In Visual Studio, edit the app.config file in the ProductsClient project by using the Service Configuration Editor.

7. Repeat the process in steps 2 through 5, above, and set the *TransportClientCredential Type* property of the *ProductsClientBasicHttpBindingConfig* binding configuration to **Windows**.

8. Save the configuration, and then close the Service Configuration Editor.

9. Edit the Program.cs file in the ProductsClient project.

10. In the *Main* method, comment out the two statements that add the user name and password to the *ClientCredentials* property of the *proxy* object.

11. Start the solution without debugging.

12. In the Products Service Host window, click Start. In the client console window, press Enter.

The message box appears displaying your Windows user name, which was sent by the client application. However, rather than requiring you to supply the user name and password, the WCF runtime executing the client application picked up this information from the user's process automatically.

> **Note** If you did not comment out the lines that populated the *ClientCredentials* object, the solution still works; the credentials provided are simply ignored. However, note the *Client-Credentials* property has a Windows property that you can use to provide a domain, user name, and password to the service if you want the service to run as a different Windows user. Any values that you specify in the *Windows* property override those retrieved from the user's login process. The usual warnings about hard-coding user names and password in your code still apply:
>
> ```
> proxy.ClientCredentials.Windows.ClientCredential.Domain = "Domain";
> proxy.ClientCredentials.Windows.ClientCredential.UserName = "UserName";
> proxy.ClientCredentials.Windows.ClientCredential.Password = "Password";
> ```

13. Click OK in the message box and verify that the client application still runs correctly.

14. Press Enter to close the client console window. Stop the service and close the Products Service Host window.

When you use Windows Integrated Security, user names and passwords are not transmitted as clear text. You can use Windows Integrated Security at the message level with the *NetTCPBinding* and *WS2007HttpBinding* bindings without the need to implement encryption at the transport level. The next exercise demonstrates this aspect of security for the *NetTcpBinding* binding.

Examine the Authentication Mechanism used by the *NetTcpBinding* Binding

1. Edit the App.config file in the ProductsServiceHost project by using the Service Configuration Editor.

2. In the Configuration pane, expand the Bindings folder, and then click the *ProductsService TcpBindingConfig* node.

3. In the right pane, click the Security tab.

4. Verify that the *MessageClientCredentialType* property is set to **Windows**.

You have been using Windows Integrated Security in earlier exercises without realizing it!

 Note The *WS2007HttpBinding* binding also defaults to using Windows Integrated Security.

5. Close the WCF Service Configuration Editor without saving changes.

6. Edit the Program.cs file for the ProductsClient project and modify the statement that creates the proxy object to use the *NetTcpBinding_IProductsService* endpoint, as follows:

```
static void Main(string[] args)
{
    ...
    ProductsServiceClient proxy = new
        ProductsServiceClient("NetTcpBinding_IProductsService");

    // proxy.ClientCredentials.UserName.UserName = "Domain\\UserName";
    // proxy.ClientCredentials.UserName.Password = "Password";

    // Test the operations in the service
    ...
}
```

7. Start the solution without debugging.

8. In the Products Service Host window, click Start. In the client console window, press Enter.

The familiar message box appears, displaying your Windows user name; this shows that the *NetTcpBinding* automatically picks up your identity from Windows.

9. Click OK and allow the client application to finish. Press Enter to close the client console window. Stop the service and close the Products Service Host window.

Authorizing Users

After a service has established the identity of the user, it can then determine whether the service should perform the requested operations for the user. Different operations in a service could be considered more privileged than others. For example, in the *ProductsService* WCF service, you might wish to let any staff that work in the warehouse query the product information in the *AdventureWorks* database but limit access to operations such as *ChangeStockLevel* (which modify data), to staff members who are stock controllers. WCF can use the features of the .NET

Framework so a developer can specify which users and roles have the authority to request operations. You can perform this task declaratively (by using attributes) or imperatively (by adding code to the operations).

The authorization mechanism implemented by WCF requires access to a database defining users and the roles that they can fulfill. If you are performing authentication by using Active Directory, it makes sense to use the *Active Directory* database to hold the roles for each user as well. Therefore, the first step is to ensure that the WCF service is configured to retrieve roles from Active Directory by using the Windows Token Role Provider.

> **Note** The following exercises require you to create new local users and groups on your computer. This feature is only available on Windows 7 Professional, Enterprise, and Ultimate editions. If you are running Windows 7 Home or Home Premium editions, you will need to skip over this exercise.

Configure the WCF Service to use the Windows Token Role Provider

1. Edit the App.config file in the ProductsServiceHost project by using the Service Configuration Editor.

2. In the Configuration pane, expand the Advanced folder, expand the Service Behaviors folder, and then click the *(Empty Name)* node.

   The behavior currently implemented by the service contains the *serviceMetadata* and *serviceDebug* elements that you saw in the previous chapters.

3. In the Behavior pane, click Add.

4. In the Adding Behavior Element Extension Sections dialog box, select *serviceAuthorization*, and then click Add.

   The *serviceAuthorization* behavior is added to the list of behaviors.

5. In the Configuration pane, click the *serviceAuthorization* element under the *Products Behavior* node.

6. In the serviceAuthorization pane, verify that the *PrincipalPermissionMode* property is set to *UseWindowsGroups*.

> **Note** By default, WCF uses the Windows Token Role Provider to authenticate users, so you don't actually need to perform these steps. However, you can configure the *serviceBehavior* element to specify a different role provider, such as the ASP.NET Role Provider or the Authorization Store Role Provider, mentioned earlier in this chapter, so it is instructional to see how you can configure authorization. (You will configure the service to use the ASP.NET Role Provider in Chapter 5.)

7. Save the configuration, and then close the Service Configuration Editor.

The next step is to define the roles that can request the operations in the WCF service. When using the Windows Token Role Provider, Active Directory groups correspond to roles, so you define groups in the Active Directory database and add users to these groups. In the next exercise you will also add two users called Fred and Bert who will be members of these groups.

> **Note** The following exercise assumes you do not have access to the Active Directory database for your organization, so it uses the Windows local users and groups database instead. The principles are the same, however.

Create Groups for Warehouse Staff and Stock Controller Staff

1. On the Windows Start menu, right-click Computer, and then click Manage. Enter the administrator password if you are prompted.

   The Computer Management console appears.

2. In the Computer Management console, under the System Tools node, expand the Local Users And Groups node, right-click the Groups folder, and then click New Group.

3. In the New Group dialog box, type **WarehouseStaff** for the *Group name*, and then click Create.

4. While still in the New Group dialog box, type **StockControllers** for the *Group name*, and then click Create again.

5. Click Close to close the New Group dialog box.

6. In the left pane of the Computer Management console, right-click the Users folder, and then click New User.

7. In the New User dialog box, use the values in the following table to set the properties of the user, and then click Create.

Property	Value
User name	Fred
Password	Pa$$w0rd
Confirm password	Pa$$w0rd
User must change password at next logon	*Unchecked*

8. Add another user by specifying the values in the following table, and then click Create again.

Property	Value
User name	Bert
Password	Pa$$w0rd
Confirm password	Pa$$w0rd
User must change password at next logon	*Unchecked*

9. Click Close, and then close the New User dialog box.

10. In the left pane of the Computer Management console, click the Users folder.

    The two new users should appear in the list in the right pane of the Computer Management console.

11. In the right pane of the Computer Management console, right-click Bert, and then click Properties.

12. In the Bert Properties dialog box, click the Member Of tab, and then click Add.

13. In the Select Groups dialog box, type **WarehouseStaff** in the text box, and then click OK.

    Bert is added to the *WarehouseStaff* group.

14. In the Bert Properties dialog box, click OK.

15. In the right pane of the Computer Management console, right-click Fred, and then click Properties.

16. In the Fred Properties dialog box, click the Member Of tab, and then click Add.

17. In the Select Groups dialog box, type **WarehouseStaff** in the text box, and then click OK.

18. Click Add again. In the Select Groups dialog box, type **StockControllers** in the text box, and then click OK.

    Fred is added to the *WarehouseStaff* and *StockControllers* groups—he has two roles.

19. In the Fred Properties dialog box, click OK.

20. Close the Computer Management console.

You can now use the groups you have just defined to specify the roles that can request each of the operations in the *ProductsService* service. To show how to specify authorization declaratively and imperatively, you will use attributes to specify the role for the operations that simply query the *AdventureWorks* database, but you will write code to specify the role that can modify the database.

Specify the Roles for the WCF Service Operations

1. In Visual Studio, open the ProductsService.cs file (in the ProductsServiceLibrary project) in the Code And Text Editor window.

2. Add the following *using* statements to the list at the top of the file:

```
using System.Security;
using System.Security.Permissions;
using System.Security.Principal;
```

3. Locate the *ListProducts* method in the *ProductsServiceImpl* class. Add the following attribute (shown in bold) to this method:

```
[PrincipalPermission(SecurityAction.Demand, Role="WarehouseStaff")]
public List<string> ListProducts()
{
    ...
}
```

The *PrincipalPermission* attribute specifies the authorization requirements of the method. In this case, the *SecurityAction.Demand* parameter indicates that the method requires that the user meet the criteria specified by the following parameters. The *Role* parameter indicates that the user must be a member of the *WarehouseStaff* role.

You can identify specific users by using the optional *Name* parameter. However, if you specify *Name* and *Role*, the user must match both criteria to be granted access (if the user is not a member of the specified role, they will not be allowed to invoke the operation). If you require users to be granted access to the method if they have a specific name *or* are a member of a specific group, you can use the *PrincipalPermission* attribute twice, like this:

```
[PrincipalPermission(SecurityAction.Demand, Role="WarehouseStaff")]
// LON-DEV-01\John is not a member of the WarehouseStaff group
[PrincipalPermission(SecurityAction.Demand, Name="LON-DEV-01\\John")]
public List<string> ListProducts()
{
    ...
}
```

You can also specify *SecurityAction.Deny* as the first parameter to the *PrincipalPermission* attribute. If you do this, the specified users and roles will be explicitly denied access to the method.

4. Apply the *PrincipalPermission* attribute with the *WarehouseStaff* group to the *GetProduct* and *CurrentStockLevel* methods, as shown in bold in the following:

```
[PrincipalPermission(SecurityAction.Demand, Role="WarehouseStaff")]
public Product GetProduct(string ProductNumber)
{
    ...
}
```

```
[PrincipalPermission(SecurityAction.Demand, Role="WarehouseStaff")]
public int CurrentStockLevel(string ProductNumber)
{
    ...
}
```

5. Locate the *ChangeStockLevel* method. Add the following code (shown in bold) to the start of this method:

```
public bool ChangeStockLevel(...)
{
    // Determine whether the user is a member of the StockControllers role
    WindowsPrincipal user = new WindowsPrincipal(
            (WindowsIdentity)Thread.CurrentPrincipal.Identity);
    if (!(user.IsInRole("StockControllers")))
    {
        // If the user is not in the StockControllers role,
        // throw a SecurityException
        throw new SecurityException("Access denied");
    }

    // Modify the stock level of the selected product.
    ...
}
```

The first statement retrieves the user identity information and uses it to create a *Windows Principal* object. Note that the identity returned by the current thread must be cast to a *WindowsIdentity* object. A *WindowsPrincipal* object is a representation of the user. It exposes the *IsInRole* method that this code uses to determine whether the user is a member of the *StockControllers* role. The *IsInRole* method returns *true* if the user is a member of the role or *false* if otherwise. If the user is not a member of the role, the code throws a *SecurityException* exception with the message "Access Denied."

 Warning It is tempting to provide more detail in the *SecurityException* exception. This practice is not recommended because it could provide an attacker with useful information that they might be able to use to try and infiltrate your system. Keep the exception message bland!

6. Edit the Program.cs file in the ProductsClient project. In the *Main* method, add the following exception handler (shown in bold) after the *FaultException* handler. This exception handler catches any exceptions that are not SOAP faults and displays them (this includes any possible *SecurityException* exceptions that might be thrown by the service):

```
static void Main(string[] args)
{
    ...
    catch (FaultException e)
```

```
    {
        Console.WriteLine("{0}: {1}", e.Code.Name, e.Reason);
    }
    catch (Exception e)
    {
        Console.WriteLine("General exception: {0}", e.Message);
    }
    ...
}
```

Test the Authorization for the WCF Service

1. Start the solution without debugging.

2. In the Products Service Host window, click Start. In the client console window, press Enter.

   Assuming that you are not currently logged in to Windows as Fred or Bert, the client application stops and reports the message "Access is denied" when attempting to invoke the *ListProducts* operation. This is because the authenticated Windows account for the client application must be a member of the *WarehouseStaff* role:

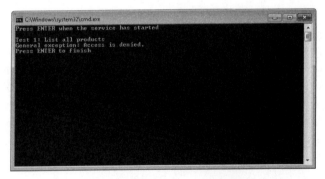

3. Press Enter to close the client console window, and then stop the service and close the Products Service Host window.

4. In Visual Studio, in the ProductsClient project, open the Program.cs file in the Code And Text Editor window.

5. In the *Main* method, add the following statements (shown in bold) immediately after the statement that creates the proxy object. Replace the value *"Domain"* specified in the *Domain* property with the name of your computer:

```
static void Main(string[] args)
{
    ...
    ProductsServiceClient proxy = new
        ProductsServiceClient("NetTcpBinding_IProductsService");
```

```
    proxy.ClientCredentials.Windows.ClientCredential.Domain = "Domain";
    proxy.ClientCredentials.Windows.ClientCredential.UserName = "Bert";
    proxy.ClientCredentials.Windows.ClientCredential.Password = "Pa$$w0rd";
    ...
}
```

These statements explicitly set the Windows credentials for the user to those of Bert. The WCF runtime on the client will send these credentials to the service rather than using those in the user's logon process.

6. Start the solution again, without debugging.

7. In the Products Service Host window, click Start. In the client console window, press Enter.

   This time, *Bert* is a member of the *WarehouseStaff* role and is granted access to the *ListProducts*, *GetProduct*, and *CurrentStockLevel* operations.

   When the *ListProducts* method runs, it displays the message box confirming that the identity of the authenticated user is Bert. Click OK to continue execution.

   The first three tests run successfully, but when the client application attempts to perform Test 4, which requires invoking the *ChangeStockLevel* operation, Bert has not been granted access to this method, and so the test fails with the "Access is denied" message:

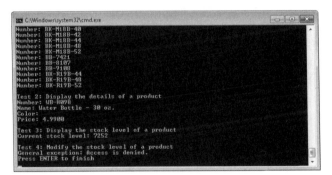

8. Press Enter to close the client console window, and then stop the service and close the Products Service Host window.

9. Return to the Program.cs file in the Code And Text Editor window.

10. In the *Main* method, change the Windows user name of the user to **Fred**, as follows:

```
static void Main(string[] args)
{
    ...
    proxy.ClientCredentials.Windows.ClientCredential.Domain = "Domain";
    proxy.ClientCredentials.Windows.ClientCredential.UserName = "Fred";
    proxy.ClientCredentials.Windows.ClientCredential.Password = "Pa$$w0rd";
    ...
}
```

11. Build and start the solution again without debugging.

12. In the Products Service Host window, click Start. In the client console window, press Enter.

    Fred is a member of the *WarehouseStaff* role and the *StockControllers* role, and so he is able to invoke all the operations in the *ProductsService* WCF service.

13. When the *ListProducts* method displays the message box with the name of the authenticated user, verify that the user name is *Fred*, and then click OK.

14. The client application performs all four tests successfully. Press Enter to close the client console window, and then stop the service and close the Products Service Host window.

Using Impersonation to Access Resources

Authenticating a user establishes the identity of the user to the WCF service, which can then perform authorization checks to verify that the user should be allowed to perform the requested operation. The method that implements the operation might require access to resources on the computer running the WCF service. By default, the service will attempt to gain access to these resources by using its own credentials. For example, when a method in the *ProductsService* WCF service connects to the *AdventureWorks* database, it does so as the account running the service. When using Windows authentication, it is possible to specify that the WCF service should access resources by using the authenticated identity of the user instead. So, if Fred has been granted access to the *AdventureWorks* database, the WCF service can connect to SQL Server as Fred and will have access to all the database resources to which Fred has been granted access. If the user connects as Bert, the WCF service might be able to use a different set of resources in the database, depending on Bert's access rights. The same principle applies to other resources, such as files, folders, and network shares. Using impersonation gives an administrator fine-grained control over the ability of a WCF service to read or write possibly sensitive information and can provide an additional degree of security—just because the user can connect to the WCF service, they might not be able to perform operations that retrieve or modify confidential data unless the administrator has explicitly granted the user access to this data.

You can enable impersonation for an operation by setting the *Impersonation* property of the *OperationBehavior* attribute, as shown in bold in the following:

```
[PrincipalPermission(SecurityAction.Demand, Role="WarehouseStaff")]
[OperationBehavior(Impersonation=ImpersonationOption.Required)]
public List<string> ListProducts
{
  ...
}
```

Specifying the value *ImpersonationOption.Required* enforces impersonation. The client application must also agree to this requirement and specify the level of impersonation that the WCF service application can use (you will see how to do this shortly). You can also specify either *ImpersonationOption.Allowed* or *ImpersonationOption.NotAllowed*. *ImpersonationOption. Allowed* (this is the default setting) enables the WCF service to impersonate the user if the client application permits, but executes as the identity running the service application if not; *ImpersonationOption.NotAllowed* disables impersonation.

WCF also provides an attribute of the *serviceAuthorization* service behavior element named *ImpersonateCallerForAllOperations*. If you set this element to *true*, the WCF runtime verifies that all operations in the service either support or require impersonation. It will also fail (and refuse to start the service) if any operations are marked as *ImpersonationOption.NotAllowed*. You can specify this attribute in the service configuration file, as shown in bold in the following:

```xml
<?xml version="1.0" encoding="utf-8" ?>
<configuration>
  ...
  <system.serviceModel>
    ...
    <behaviors>
      <serviceBehaviors>
        <behavior>
          <serviceAuthorization principalPermissionMode="UseWindowsGroups"
            impersonateCallerForAllOperations="true" />
        </behavior>
      </serviceBehaviors>
    </behaviors>
  </system.serviceModel>
</configuration>
```

You configure the client application to indicate the level of impersonation that the service can use by defining a behavior for the endpoint and specifying the *AllowedImpersonationLevel* property. The following fragments of a client configuration file highlight the pertinent elements:

```xml
<?xml version="1.0" encoding="utf-8" ?>
<configuration>
  <system.serviceModel>
    <behaviors>
      <endpointBehaviors>
        <behavior name="ImpersonationBehavior">
          <clientCredentials>
            <windows allowedImpersonationLevel="Impersonation" />
            ...
          </clientCredentials>
        </behavior>
      </endpointBehaviors>
    </behaviors>
    ...
```

```
   <client>
      ...
      <endpoint
        address="http://localhost:8010/ProductsService/ProductsService.svc"
        behaviorConfiguration="ImpersonationBehavior"
        binding="ws2007HttpBinding"
        contract="ProductsClient.ProductsService.IProductsService"
        name="WS2007HttpBinding_IProductsService" />
   </client>
  </system.serviceModel>
</configuration>
```

You can specify one of the following values for the *AllowedImpersonationLevel* property:

- *Impersonate*   The service can use the user's identity when accessing local resources on the computer hosting the service. However, the service cannot access resources on remote computers.

- *Delegation*   The service can use the user's identity when accessing local resources on the computer hosting the service and on remote computers. The service can pass the identity of the user on to remote services, which may authenticate the user and perform operations impersonating this user.

> **Warning** Use this setting with extreme caution. Essentially you are granting the service, and any other services that it might invoke (and any further services that they invoke, and so on) the ability to perform operations by using the identity and credentials of the user. This can open up a whole raft of security concerns.

- *Identify*   The service can use the user's credentials to authenticate the user and authorize access to operations but cannot impersonate the user.

- *Anonymous*   The service does not use the user's identity to authenticate the user but can use the user's credentials to perform access checks against resources accessed by the service. This setting is only valid for transport mechanisms such as named pipes that connect a client application to a service executing on the same computer. If the service is running on a remote computer, the setting is handled in the same way as the "Identify" option.

- *None*   The service does not attempt to impersonate the user.

Summary

In this chapter, you have seen how to use the features of three common WCF bindings to control the degree of protection afforded to a WCF service. You have seen how to configure encryption for messages flowing between a client application and a service, at the message level and at the transport level. You have learned how to specify the authentication mode for a binding and how to pass Windows credentials from a client application to a WCF service. You have also learned how to authorize access to operations for authenticated users and how to provide access to resources based on a user's authenticated identity by using impersonation.

You should now be aware that different bindings support different security configurations, and have default settings that are optimized for specific scenarios. For example, if you are deploying services that are accessible inside an organization you can use the *NetTcpBinding* or *NetNamedPipeBinding* bindings and implement transport-level security. However, if a service is intended to be accessible both inside an organization and externally, you may choose to provide a *NetTcpBinding* binding and a binding based on the HTTP protocol (either the *BasicHttpBinding* or *WS2007HttpBinding* binding), and implement either transport-level or message-level security, depending on the requirements of your service and the need to maintain compatibility with existing client applications and services. If you are building a WCF service that must be compatible with client applications and services that conform to the Basic Profile 1.1, you should use the *BasicHttpBinding* binding and configure it to use Basic authentication over transport-level security if authentication is required. If you need to build a service that conforms to the requirements of the WS-Security specification, you should use the *WS2007HttpBinding* binding and configure message-level security.

Chapter 5
Protecting a WCF Service over the Internet

After completing this chapter, you will be able to:

- Describe how to configure and use the ASP.NET Membership Provider and the ASP.NET Role Provider to store and query user identity and role information for a WCF service.

- Explain how to configure a WCF service to authenticate users by using certificates.

- Describe how to use certificates to authenticate a WCF service to a client application.

Managing client application and WCF service security inside an organization requires some thought, but WCF provides bindings and behaviors that you can use to simplify many of the tasks associated with protecting communications. Together with the authentication and authorization features included with the .NET Framework 4.0, you can help to ensure that clients and services transmit messages in a confidential manner and have a reasonable degree of confidence that only authorized users are submitting requests to services. However, bear in mind that an organization's internal network is a relatively benign environment because of its inherent privacy—hackers might be able to penetrate your network, but this is an exceptional circumstance rather than the norm. As long as your system and network administrators maintain the security of the organization's infrastructure, you can assume a certain degree of trust between client applications and services. Features such as message encryption, authentication, and authorization are important, but they can operate at the relatively unobtrusive level described in Chapter 4 "Protecting an Enterprise WCF Service."

When you start connecting client applications and services across a public network such as the Internet, you can no longer make any assumptions about the trustworthiness of client applications, services, or the communications passing between them. For example, how does a client application verify that the service to which it is sending messages is the real service and not some nefarious spoof that happens to have supplanted the real service? Or perhaps it is simply intercepting and logging messages before forwarding them on to the real service? Also, how does a service know that the user running the client application is who she says she is? How does a service distinguish genuine requests sent by an authenticated client application from those generated by some program written by an attacker? The attacker might probe the service by sending it messages and seeing whether the service responds with any error information that displays any potential security weaknesses.

The Internet is a potentially hostile environment, and you must treat all communications passing over it with the utmost suspicion. In this chapter, you will examine some techniques that you can use to help protect client applications, WCF services, and the information transmitted between them.

Authenticating Users and Services in an Internet Environment

Maintaining information about the users who can legitimately access a service and their credentials typically requires some form of database. In a Windows environment, Active Directory provides just such a database. A WCF service can use Windows Integrated Security to help authenticate users who are part of the same Windows domain as the service. When client applications connect to the service across the Internet, this approach is not always feasible; a client application will probably not be running using the same security domain as the service (it might not even be a Windows application). In this environment, you can use several alternative approaches for maintaining a list of authenticated users for a WCF service. For example, you can employ the ASP.NET Membership Provider (to store a list of users and their credentials in a SQL Server database) together with the ASP.NET Role Provider (to associate users with roles). Alternatively, you can use the Authorization Store Role Provider to record users and roles in XML files. In the exercises in this chapter, you will make use of the ASP.NET Membership Provider and ASP.NET Role Provider.

> **Important** Chapter 4 described how to use impersonation to allow a service to access resources. Impersonation requires that the service can identify the user as a Windows account in its local security domain, so it is not available when alternative authentication mechanisms such as the ASP. NET Membership Provider are used.

Authenticating and Authorizing Users by Using the ASP.NET Membership Provider and the ASP.NET Role Provider

To make a WCF service available across the Internet, you would typically host it by using Microsoft Internet Information Services (IIS) as described in Chapter 1, "Introducing Windows Communication Foundation." By hosting a WCF service in this way, you can use the ASP.NET Web Site Administration Tool to easily create a SQL Server database containing the security information for the service and, manage users and roles. You can then configure the WCF service to use the ASP.NET Membership Provider to authenticate users, and the ASP.NET Role Provider to retrieve role information for authorizing users. This is what you will do in the following set of exercises.

Additionally, it is good practice to use the Secure Sockets Layer (SSL) to protect communications when you build a service that is exposed to the Internet. Therefore, the first task is to configure IIS to support SSL by adding a certificate to identify the service and encrypt information passing to and from client applications. You can then bind this certificate to the Web site that hosts your WCF services.

Configure IIS Bindings to Support SSL

1. Open the Internet Information Services Manager console as an administrator, as follows:

    a. On the Windows Start menu, click Control Panel, click System And Security, and then click Administrative Tools. Right-click Internet Information Services (IIS) Manager, and then click Run As Administrator.

    b. Enter the administrator password if prompted.

2. In the Internet Information Services (IIS) Manager console window, in the Connections pane, click the node that corresponds to your computer.

3. In the middle pane, click the Features View tab.

4. In the Features View pane, in the IIS section, double-click Server Certificates.

    The Server Certificates pane appears, displaying possible certificates that you can use to configure IIS to use to implement SSL. It should display the HTTPS-Server certificate that you created in Chapter 4. For the purposes of this chapter, you will create another certificate; it is not considered good practice to use the same certificate for multiple Web sites.

5. In the Actions pane, click Create Self-Signed Certificate.

    The Create Self-Signed Certificate dialog box appears. This wizard creates a certificate in a manner similar to the *makecert* command that you used from the Visual Studio Command Line in Chapter 4. The same warnings and caveats apply; you should not use a self-signed certificate in a production environment. If you require a commercial-grade certificate, you should click the Create Certificate Request link in the Actions pane, create a certificate request that identifies your organization, and then send this request to a certificate provider, such as Active Directory Certificate Services or a trusted third-party organization to generate the certificate.

6. In the Create Self-Signed Certificate dialog box, in the Specify A Friendly Name For The Certificate box, type the name of your computer, and then click OK.

> **Note** It is important that you give the certificate a friendly name that is the same as your computer, otherwise you may run into some security errors later on when you attempt to access the Web site.

The certificate should be generated and added to the list in the Server Certificates pane, as shown in the following image (the name of your computer will probably be different from LON-DEV-01):

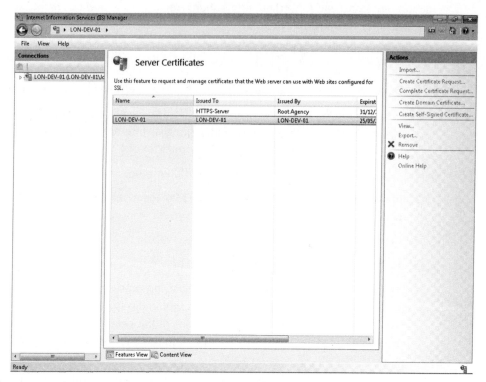

7. In the Connections pane, expand the node that corresponds to your computer, expand Sites, right-click Default Web Site, and then click Edit Bindings.

The Site Bindings dialog box appears, as shown in the following image, listing the protocols that IIS and WAS support for the Web site (your list may vary from that shown in the image):

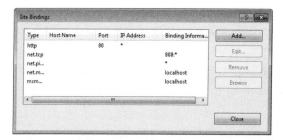

8. In the Site Bindings dialog box, if https is *not* configured, click Add; otherwise, select https, and then click Edit.

9. In the Add (or Edit) Site Binding dialog box, set Type to **https**, select the SSL certificate that is named after your computer, and then click OK.

10. In the Site Bindings dialog box, click Close.

11. Leave the Internet Information Services (IIS) Manager console open.

You can now add a Web application to the Web site that uses SSL to protect communications.

Create the InternetProductsService Web Application

1. Start Windows Explorer as an administrator and create the following folder:

   C:\inetpub\wwwroot\InternetProductsService

2. Return to the Internet Information Services (IIS) Manager console. In the Connections pane, right-click Default Web Site, and then click Add Application.

3. In the Add Application dialog box, specify the values shown in the following table, and then click OK.

Item	Value
Alias	InternetProductsService
Application Pool	ASP.NET v4.0
Physical Path	C:\inetpub\wwwroot\InternetProductsService

4. In the Connections pane, click the InternetProductsService application.

5. In the middle pane, click the Features View tab, and then double-click SSL Settings in the IIS section.

6. In the SSL Settings pane, check Require SSL, and then in the Actions pane, click Apply.

7. Leave the Internet Information Services (IIS) Manager console open.

You can now create the WCF service and host it by using this Web site.

Create an ASP.NET Web Site to Host the WCF Service

1. Start Visual Studio as an administrator.

2. Using Visual Studio, create a new Web site:

    ❏ Select New from the File menu, and then click Web Site.

3. In the New Web Site dialog box, click the WCF Service template. Set the Web location to **HTTP**, and type **https://*YourComputer*/InternetProductsService**, where *YourComputer* is the name of your computer, and then click OK.

> **Important** Make sure that you specify **https** as the scheme in this address.

4. In Solution Explorer, delete the Service.svc file and the Web.config file, and the IService.cs and Service.cs files in the App_Code folder.

> **Note** Although the Web site is configured to use SSL and support transport-level security, you can still perform message-level encryption as well if you need to provide end-to-end security rather than point-to-point. However, remember that encryption is a necessarily expensive operation. Encrypting at two levels will impact performance. Transport-level encryption tends to be much faster than message-level encryption. So, if performance is a limiting factor and you have to make a choice, go for transport-level security.

You will implement a version of the *ProductsService* WCF service in the IIS Web site. To save some time and avoid the need to retype the code, you will import the existing code for this service into your project.

Import the Code for the WCF Service into the IIS Web Site

1. In Solution Explorer, right-click the project, and then click Add Existing Item. Add the Web.config file located in the Microsoft Press\WCF Step By Step\Chapter 5 folder (located within your Documents folder) to the Web site.

    This configuration file contains the connection string for accessing the *AdventureWorks* database and the default configuration information generated for a WCF Service.

2. Right-click the App_Code folder, and then click Add Existing Item. In the Add Existing Item dialog box, move to the Microsoft Press\WCF Step By Step\Chapter 5 folder, select the ProductsService.cs file, and then click Add. Repeat this process for the IProductsService.cs file.

The ProductsService.cs file contains the code for the *ProductsService* service. This is almost the same code that you used in Chapter 4 (the statements that display the user identity in the *ListProducts* method have been removed because you should not attempt to display an interactive message box from a WCF service hosted by IIS).

3. Add a reference to the *ProductsEntityModel* assembly in the Microsoft Press\WCF Step By Step\Chapter 5 folder to the project.

4. Build the Web site, and then verify that everything compiles without errors.

Now that you have built the WCF service, you must configure it with an appropriate end-point and binding. For this service, you will use a *WS2007HttpBinding* binding that supports transport-level security for protecting messages, but with message-level credentials for authenticating and authorizing because this is the level at which the ASP.NET Role Provider operates. You will implement configuration-based activation for the service (as described in Chapter 1) so that you do not need to add a .svc file.

Configure the Activation and Binding for the WCF Service

1. Edit the Web.config file by using the Service Configuration Editor.

2. In the Configuration pane, expand the Advanced folder, expand the Hosting Environment folder, and then click the *serviceActivations* node.

3. In the Service Activations pane, click New.

4. In the Service Activation Editor dialog box, enter the values shown in the following table, and then click OK.

Item	Value
RelativeAddress	Service.svc
Service	Products.ProductsServiceImpl
Factory	*Leave blank*

5. In the Configuration pane, click the Services folder.

6. In the Services pane, click Create A New Service.

7. Proceed through the New Service Element Wizard; use the information in the following table to define the service. (When the warning messages concerning the service type and contract appear, click Yes to proceed.)

Page	Prompt	Value
What is the service type of your service?	Service type	Products.ProductsServiceImpl
What service contract are you using?	Contract	Products.IProductsService
What communications mode is your service using?		HTTP
What method of interoperability do you want to use?		Advanced Web Service interoperability (Simplex communication)
What is the address of your endpoint?	Address	https://*YourComputer*/InternetProductsService/Service.svc

8. In the Configuration pane, click the Bindings folder, and then click New Binding Configuration in the Bindings pane.

9. In the Create A New Binding dialog box, select **ws2007HttpBinding**, and then click OK.

10. In the right pane, in the *Name* property, type **ProductsServiceWS2007 HttpBindingConfig**.

11. Click the Security tab. Set the *Mode* property of the binding to **TransportWith MessageCredential**, set the *MessageClientCredentialType* property to **UserName**, and set the *TransportClientCredentialType* to **None**.

    The host Web site is configured to use the HTTPS protocol, so the WCF service must be configured to support transport-level security. The *TransportWithMessageCredential* mode uses HTTPS at the transport level to protect messages traversing the network and uses the server certificate to authenticate with the client. The user's credentials are authenticated by using message-level security. The credentials are passed as a *UserName* token (this is how the ASP.NET Role Provider presents them).

12. In the Configuration pane, expand the Endpoints folder under the *Products.Products ServiceImpl* node and click the *(Empty Name)* endpoint. In the Service Endpoint pane, set the *BindingConfiguration* property to **ProductsServiceWS2007HttpBindingConfig**.

13. In the Configuration pane, in the Advanced folder, expand the Service Behaviors folder, expand the *(Empty Name)* node, and then click the *serviceMetadata* element.

14. In the serviceMetadata pane, set the *HttpsGetEnabled* property to **True** and set the *HttpGetEnabled* property to **False**.

> **Note** If you are using the HTTPS protocol and you wish to enable the service to publish metadata, you must set the *HttpsGetEnabled* property of the *serviceMetadata* behavior to **True**. Additionally, you cannot set both the *HttpGetEnabled* and the *HttpsGetEnabled* properties to *True* at the same time (either the service is using HTTPS or it isn't).

15. Save the changes, and then exit the Service Configuration Editor.

16. In Visual Studio, open the Web.config file in the Code And Text Editor window.

17. In the *<serviceHostingEnvironment>* element, set the *multipleSiteBindingsEnabled* property to **false**, as shown in bold in the following.

```xml
<?xml version="1.0"?>
<configuration>
  ...
  <system.serviceModel>
  ...
    <serviceHostingEnvironment multipleSiteBindingsEnabled="false">
     <serviceActivations>
      <add relativeAddress="Service.svc" service="Products.ProductsServiceImpl" />
     </serviceActivations>
    </serviceHostingEnvironment>
  </system.serviceModel>
  ...
</configuration>
```

18. Save the Web.config file.

19. To quickly test that you have configured the service correctly, start Internet Explorer and go to the Web site *https://YourComputer/InternetProductsService/Service.svc* (where *YourComputer* is the name of your computer).

> **Note** If your computer is joined to a Windows domain, you may need to specify the fully qualified name of your computer in Internet Explorer. This has the form *YourComputer.YourDomain* and may include an extension such as ".net" or ".com". If you are not sure of the fully qualified name of your computer, consult the system administrator who manages your domain.

Internet Explorer opens the page *https://YourComputer/InternetProductsService/ProductsService.svc*, as shown in the following image:

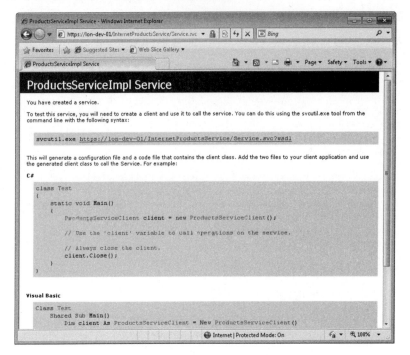

 Note If Windows 7 displays an error page with the message "There is a problem with this website's security certificate," this is because you might have mistyped the name of the computer when you created the certificate, or you have attempted to use *localhost* rather than the real name of your computer. If necessary, remove the certificate by using Internet Information Services (IIS) Manager, create a new one with the correct name, and bind the Default Web Site to this certificate as described earlier in this section.

   20. Close Internet Explorer.

Now that you have deployed, configured, and tested the WCF service by using IIS, you can use the ASP.NET Administration Tool to define the users and roles that will be permitted to access the service. To keep things simple, you will create roles (WarehouseStaff and StockControllers) and users (Fred and Bert) that mimic those you created by using Windows in Chapter 4.

Define Users and Roles for the WCF Service

   1. In Visual Studio, from the Website menu, choose ASP.NET Configuration.

   The ASP.NET Web Site Administration Tool starts. This is actually another Web application that runs by using the ASP.NET Development Server:

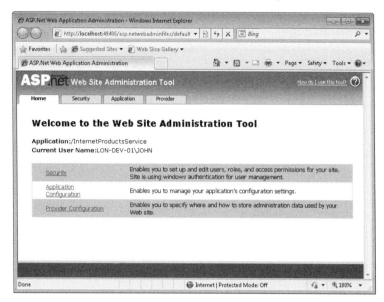

This tool provides pages with which you can add and manage users for your Web site, specify Web application settings that you want to be stored in the application configuration file (not WCF settings), and indicate how security information such as user names and passwords are stored. By default, the ASP.NET Web Site Administration Tool stores security information in a local SQL Server database called ASPNETDB.MDF that it creates in the App_Data folder of your Web site.

2. Click the Security tab.

   The Security page appears. You can use this page to manage users, specify the authentication mechanism that the Web site uses, define roles for users, and specify access rules for controlling access to the Web site.

   Note The first time you click the Security link there will be a delay before the page is displayed. This is because the tool creates the ASPNETDB.MDF database at this point.

3. In the Users section of the page, click the Select Authentication Type link.

   A new page appears asking how users will access your Web site. You have two options available:

   ❑ *From The Internet*   With this option, you can define users and roles in the SQL Server database. Users accessing your application must provide an identity that maps to a valid user.

Note The explanation given for the *From The Internet* option on the page assumes you are building an ASP.NET Web site rather than a WCF Web service, which is why it describes using forms-based authentication. A client application connecting to a WCF service can provide the user's credentials by populating the *ClientCredentials* property of the proxy object being used to send requests to the WCF service.

❑ *From A Local Network*   This option is selected by default. It configures the Web site to use Windows authentication; all users must be members of a Windows domain that your Web site can access.

4. Select the From The Internet option, and then click Done.

   You return to the Security page.

5. In the Users section, notice that the number of existing users that can access your Web site is currently zero. Click the Create User link.

   The Create User page appears.

6. In the Create User page, add a new user with the values shown in the following table (see also the image following the table):

Prompt	Response
User name	Bert
Password	Pa$$w0rd
Confirm password	Pa$$w0rd
E-mail	Bert@Adventure-Works.com
Security Question	What was the name of your first pet?
Security Answer	Tiddles

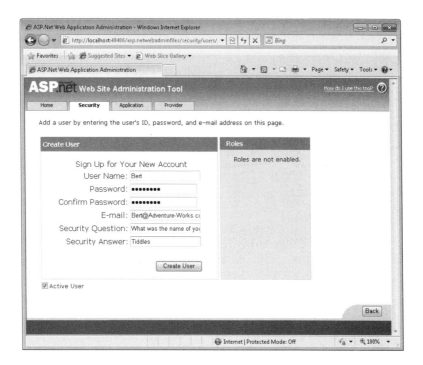

 Note You must supply values for all fields in this screen. The *E-mail*, *Security Question*, and *Security Answer* fields can be used by the ASP.NET *PasswordRecovery* control to recover or reset a user's password. Detailed discussion of the *PasswordRecovery* control is beyond the scope of this book.

7. Ensure that the Active User check box is selected, and then click Create User.

The message "Complete. Your account has been successfully created." appears in a new page.

8. Click Continue. The Create User page reappears, in which you can add more users. Add another user using the information shown in the following table:

Prompt	Response
User name	Fred
Password	Pa$$w0rd
Confirm password	Pa$$w0rd
E-mail	Fred@Adventure-Works.com
Security Question	What was the name of your first pet?
Security Answer	Rover

9. Again, ensure that the Active User check box is selected, and then click Create User.

10. Click Back to return to the Security page. Verify that the number of existing users is now set to *2*.

11. In the Roles section of the page, click the Enable Roles link.

12. When roles have been enabled, click the Create Or Manage roles link.

    The Create New Role page appears.

13. In the New Role Name text box, type **WarehouseStaff**, and then click Add Role.

    The new role appears on the page, together with links which you can use to add and remove users to or from this role.

14. Click the Manage link.

    Another page appears in which you can specify the users that are members of this role. You can search for users or list users whose names begin with a specific letter, and then add them to the role. Click the All link to display all users.

15. Select the User Is In Role check box for Bert and Fred, as shown in the following image:

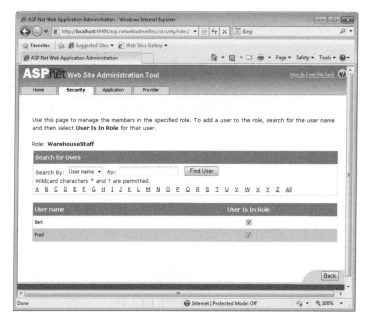

16. Wait for the page to be redisplayed, and then click Back.

> **Important** If you click Back before the page is redisplayed, the users might not be added to the roles correctly.

17. In the Create New Role page, in the New Role Name text box, type **StockControllers**, and then click Add Role.

18. Click the Manage link for the *StockControllers* role. Add Fred to the *StockControllers* role, wait for the page to be redisplayed, and then click Back.

19. Close the ASP.NET Web Site Administration Tool.

> **Note** The ASP.NET Web Site Administration Tool modifies the Web.config file of the WCF service; it adds *<roleManager>* and *<authentication>* elements to the *<system.Web>* section near the start of the file. When you return to Visual Studio, if you have the Web.config file open for editing in the Code And Text Editor window, you will be alerted that the file has been modified. In the message box, click Yes to reload the file; otherwise, you will lose the new settings.

The next step is to modify the behavior of the WCF service to perform authorization by using the users and roles defined in the SQL Server database created by the ASP.NET Role Provider and the Membership Provider, rather than by using Windows users and groups.

Configure the WCF service to use the ASP.NET Role Provider and the ASP.NET Membership Provider

1. In Visual Studio, edit the Web.config file by using the Service Configuration Editor.

2. In the Configuration pane, expand the Advanced folder, expand the Service Behaviors folder, and then click the *(Empty Name)* node.

3. In the Behavior pane, click Add.

4. In the Adding Behavior Element Extension Sections dialog box, click *serviceAuthorization*, and then click Add.

5. In the Configuration pane, click the *serviceAuthorization* node under the *(Empty Name)* node, under Service Behaviors. In the *serviceAuthorization* pane, set the *Principal PermissionMode* property to **UseAspNetRoles** and type **AspNetSqlRoleProvider** in the *RoleProviderName* property.

   The *RoleProviderName* property identifies a particular configuration for the identity role provider that will be used to map users to roles. The value *"AspNetSqlRoleProvider"* is actually defined in the Machine.config file and specifies the version of the ASP.NET Role Provider to use to authorize users, together with information, about how to connect to the database holding the user and role information.

4. In the Configuration pane, under Service Behaviors, right-click the *(Empty Name)* node again, and then click Add Service Behavior Element Extension. In the Adding Behavior Element Extension Sections dialog box, click *serviceCredentials*, and then click Add.

5. In the Configuration pane, click the *serviceCredentials* node. In the serviceCredentials pane, set the *UserNamePasswordValidationMode* property to **MembershipProvider** and type **AspNetSqlMembershipProvider** in the *MembershipProviderName* property.

   The membership provider is responsible for authenticating users based on their names and passwords stored in the SQL Server database. The value *"AspNetSqlMembership Provider"* is also defined in the Machine.config file.

> **Note** Try not to get too confused by the role provider and the membership provider. WCF uses the membership provider for authenticating users, and it uses the role provider for authorizing users' access to resources after they have been authenticated.

6. Save the configuration file, and then exit the Service Configuration Editor.

> **Important** Depending on how you have configured the application pool used by the Internet-ProductsService Web application in IIS, you may need to amend the identity used by the application pool. The default configuration of the ASP.NET v4.0 application pool will result in a failure when the WCF runtime attempts to access the SQL Server membership database (ASPNETDB.MDF in the App_Data folder of the Web application). Rather confusingly, the error is reported by the WCF runtime as "An unsecured or incorrectly secured fault was received from the other party," but if you examine the Windows Application Event Log you will find an exception with the message "Failed to generate a user instance of SQL Server due to a failure in retrieving the user's local application data path. Please make sure the user has a local profile on the computer." To circumvent this problem, you can run the ASP.NET v4.0 application pool with the NETWORK SERVICE identity, as follows:
>
> 1. In the Internet Information Services (IIS) Manager console, in the Connections pane, click Application Pools.
>
> 2. In the Application Pools pane, right-click the ASP.NET v4.0 application pool, and then click Advanced Settings.
>
> 3. In the Advanced Settings dialog box, in the Process Model section, click Identity, and then click the ellipsis button that appears on the right-hand side.
>
> 4. In the Application Pool Identity dialog box, click Built-In Account, select NetworkService from the drop-down list, and then click OK.
>
> 5. In the Advanced Settings dialog box, click OK.

You can now test the WCF service by using the client application developed in the previous chapters. First, you must make some changes so that the client application connects to the WCF service by using the correct binding and address.

Modify the WCF Client Application to Connect to the Updated WCF Service

1. In Visual Studio, add the ProductsClient project located in the Microsoft Press\WCF Step By Step\Chapter 5\ProductsClient folder (within your Documents folder) to the *Internet-ProductsService* solution.

2. Open the app.config file for the ProductsClient project by using the Service Configuration Editor.

3. In the Configuration pane, right-click the Bindings folder, and then click New Binding Configuration. In the Create A New Binding dialog box, click *ws2007HttpBinding*, and then click OK.

4. In the right pane, in the *Name* property, type **ProductsClientWS2007HttpBinding Config**.

5. Click the Security tab, set the *Mode* property to **TransportWithMessageCredential**, set the *MessageClientCredentialType* property to **UserName**, and set the *TransportClient CredentialType* property to **None**.

6. In the Configuration pane, in the Endpoints folder under the Client folder, click the *WS2007HttpBinding_IProductsService* endpoint.

7. In the Client Endpoint pane, change the *Address* property to **https://*YourComputer*/ InternetProductsService/Service.svc** and set the *BindingConfiguration* property to **ProductsClientWS2007HttpBindingConfig**.

8. Save the configuration file, and then exit the Service Configuration Editor.

9. In Solution Explorer, open the Program.cs file in the ProductsClient project. In the Code And Text Editor window, in the Main method, change the statement that calls the *PermissiveCertificatePolicy.Enact* method to refer to the certificate named after your computer (replace *LON-DEV-01* shown in the code sample with the name of your computer). Modify the statement that creates the proxy to refer to the *WS2007HttpBinding_ IProductsService* endpoint, as shown in bold in the following:

```
static void Main(string[] args)
{
    Console.WriteLine("Press ENTER when the service has started");
    Console.ReadLine();

    // Create a proxy object and connect to the service
    PermissiveCertificatePolicy.Enact("CN=LON-DEV-01");
    ProductsServiceClient proxy =
        new ProductsServiceClient("WS2007HttpBinding_IProductsService");

    ...
}
```

10. Remove the three statements that set the *Domain*, *UserName*, and *Password* properties of the *ClientCredentials.Windows.ClientCredential* property of the proxy object and replace them with the following statements:

```
proxy.ClientCredentials.UserName.UserName = "Bert";
proxy.ClientCredentials.UserName.Password = "Pa$$w0rd";
```

The client application uses message-level authentication to send the user's credentials to the WCF service. You specify the credentials to send by using the *ClientCredentials. UserName* property of the proxy object.

Important To reiterate the point made in Chapter 4, this code is for illustrative purposes in this exercise only. You should never hard-code user names and passwords directly into an application.

Test the WCF Service

1. In Solution Explorer, right-click the ProductsClient project, and then click Set As Startup Project.

2. Start the solution without debugging. When the client console window appears, press Enter to connect to the service.

The first three tests should run successfully, but the final test fails with the error shown in the following image:

```
C:\Windows\system32\cmd.exe
Number: BB-7421
Number: BB-8107
Number: BB-9108
Number: BK-R19B-44
Number: BK-R19B-48
Number: BK-R19B-52

Test 2: Display the details of a product
Number: WB-H098
Name: Water Bottle - 30 oz.
Color:
Price: 4.9900

Test 3: Display the stock level of a product
Current stock level: 8552

Test 4: Modify the stock level of a product
Receiver: The server was unable to process the request due to an internal error.
  For more information about the error, either turn on IncludeExceptionDetailInF
aults (either from ServiceBehaviorAttribute or from the <serviceDebug> configura
tion behavior) on the server in order to send the exception information back to
the client, or turn on tracing as per the Microsoft .NET Framework 3.0 SDK docum
entation and inspect the server trace logs.
Press ENTER to finish
```

The *PrincipalPermission* attributes implementing security demands for the first three methods automatically use the currently configured role provider. In Chapter 4, they used the Windows Token Role Provider and authorized users based on their Windows identity. In these exercises, they are using the ASP.NET Role Provider. The problem is that the method executed by Test 4 does not use the *PrincipalPermission* attribute—the authorization check is performed by using code. In particular, the following statement attempts to retrieve the identity of the user assuming it was a Windows principal, which it no longer is:

```
WindowsPrincipal user = new WindowsPrincipal(
    (WindowsIdentity)Thread.CurrentPrincipal.Identity);
```

3. Press Enter and return to Visual Studio.

4. Edit the ProductsService.cs file in the App_Code folder of the InternetProductsService Web site project. Locate the *ChangeStockLevel* method and modify the two lines of code that create the user variable; test this variable to determine whether the user is a member of the *StockControllers* role, as shown in bold in the following:

```
public bool ChangeStockLevel(string productNumber, short newStockLevel,
                             string shelf, int bin)
{
    // Determine whether the user is a member of the StockControllers role
    IIdentity user = ServiceSecurityContext.Current.PrimaryIdentity;
    if (!(System.Web.Security.Roles.IsUserInRole(user.Name, "StockControllers")))
    {
        ...
    }
    ...
}
```

The *ServiceSecurityContext* class contains information about the current security context for the WCF operation being performed. This security context information includes the identity if the user requesting the operation, which is available in the static *Current. PrimaryIdentity* property. You can use the name held in this identity object to determine whether the user is a member of a specific role by using the *IsInRole* method of the *System.Web.Security.Roles* class. The *Roles* class accesses the data in the currently configured role provider for the WCF service to perform its work.

5. Start the solution without debugging. Press Enter when the client application window appears. This time, Test 4 fails with the error "Access is denied." This is because Bert is not a member of the *StockControllers* role.

6. Press Enter again to close the application.

7. Edit the Program.cs file in the ProductsClient project. Change the user name sent to the WCF service through the proxy as follows:

```
proxy.ClientCredentials.UserName.UserName = "Fred";
```

8. Start the solution without debugging. Press Enter when the client application window appears. Fred is a member of both the *WarehouseStaff* and *StockControllers* roles, and all tests should run successfully.

9. Press Enter to close the application.

Authenticating and Authorizing Users by Using Certificates

Using a user name and password to identify a user provides a degree of security, but you are probably all too familiar with the shortcomings of many implementations that follow this approach. It is very easy to disclose a password (possibly unwittingly) to another user. Many people use passwords that are easy for them to remember, and typically passwords are often short, or easily guessed (how many times have you used "password," or "1234," or something equally insecure?). Even your mother's maiden name, suitably scrambled, is not that secure—this information is frequently available in the public domain, which is why it is nonsense for banks to use this as a piece of information to identify yourself whenever you need to contact them (I will get off my security hobbyhorse now).

Using a public key infrastructure (PKI) can help to overcome some of the shortcomings of passwords. PKI provides a mechanism both for encrypting messages and for authenticating them.

PKI is based on pairs of keys (a key is a long sequence of random numbers): a public key that you can use to encrypt messages, and a private key that you can use to decrypt them again. These keys should be unique. If you want to communicate with a third party, you can send them a copy of your public key. The third party can encrypt their messages using this key and transmit them to you. You can decrypt these messages using your private key. The theory is that only your private key can decrypt a message that was encrypted by your public key, so it does not matter if someone else intercepts the message because they will not be able to read it. In practice, it is possible to decrypt messages even if you don't have the private key, but it takes a lot of effort, and the longer the key, the more time and effort it takes—use keys with 128 bits or more.

Public and private keys can also work the other way around. If you encrypt a message with your private key, anyone with the public key can decrypt it. This does not sound too useful until you consider that this provides a convenient mechanism for verifying the source of a message. If a third party receives an encrypted message that purports to come from you but that it cannot decrypt by using the public key that you provided, then the chances are that this message was actually from someone else pretending to be you (only you can send messages that can be decrypted using your public key). The third party should probably discard the message in this case.

Where do you get keys? Well, you can request a pair of keys in a certificate from a certification authority, or CA. The CA will perform various checks to ensure that you are who you actually say you are, and if they are satisfied, they will issue you with a certificate containing a public key and a private key (you usually have to pay for this service). The certificate also contains other bits of identity information about you and about the CA itself.

When you wish to communicate with a third party, you can send them a message that includes a hash (a calculated summary, similar to a checksum but more complicated) of the message contents encrypted with your private key—this is referred to as your signature. You can arrange for a copy of your certificate, minus your private key, to be installed in the certificate store on the third-party computer as an out-of-band operation by the administrator at that end or attach a copy of your certificate, minus the private key, with the message when you send it. When the third party examines your certificate, it can verify that it was issued by a recognized and trusted CA, and that it has not been revoked before continuing (a certificate can be withdrawn if the service no longer wishes to trust the client, and the service can maintain a list of withdrawn certificates in its certificate revocation list).

If the third party does not recognize or trust the CA, they can simply reject the message. Assuming that the third party does trust the CA, it can use the public key from your certificate to decrypt the signature and verify the unencrypted hash against the message (the third party generates its own hash of the message contents using the same algorithm that you did and compares his hash to yours). If this is successful, the third party will then have a reasonable degree of assurance that the message was sent by you. It can also be very confident that the message has not been corrupted or otherwise tampered with as it passed across the network. The third party can use the identity information from your certificate to determine your level of authorization and process your request if you have the appropriate authority.

A service can also use a certificate to authenticate itself to a client application, reducing the likelihood of the client connecting to a spoof service.

> **Note** This discussion has been primarily concerned with signing messages for authentication purposes. You can use certificates to encrypt messages as well, but the process is slightly more complex. When a client application wants to send an encrypted and signed message to a service, it first signs the message by using its own private key and then encrypts the complete, signed message by using the service's public key. The service decrypts the signed message using its private key and then authenticates the message by using the client application's public key.
>
> If the service sends an encrypted and signed response back to the client, the process is reversed; the service signs the message with its private key and encrypts the message with the client application's public key. The client application decrypts the signed message with its private key and uses the service's public key to authenticate the message.
>
> You can see that communications that require the use of certificates include a complex protocol involving an initial exchange of certificates and keys. However, the additional security that certificates provide makes this overhead very worthwhile.

You should always obtain the certificates that you use to identify yourself and secure your communications from a reputable certification authority that is trusted by you and those parties with whom you wish to communicate. And you should never, ever disclose your own personal private key!

In the exercises in this section, you will see how you can use certificates to sign messages and authenticate users to a WCF service application.

Modify the WCF Service to Require Client Applications to Authenticate by Using Certificates

1. In Visual Studio, edit the Web.config file for the InternetProductsServive Web site project by using the Service Configuration Editor.

2. In the Configuration pane, expand the Bindings folder, and then click the *Products ServiceWS2007HttpBindingConfig* binding configuration.

3. In the right pane, click the Security tab. Change the *MessageClientCredentialType* property to **Certificate**.

   The WCF service now requires that client applications supply a certificate to authenticate users. The *NegotiateServiceCredential* property on this page specifies how the client application sends the certificate to the WCF service. If this property is set to *True* (the default value), the WCF service expects the client application to include the certificate with the messages that it sends (actually, a series of initial messages occur while the client and WCF service exchange certificates). If this property is set to *False*, the administrator for the WCF service must install the client certificate manually in the *Trusted People* certificate store of the computer running the service.

   Set this property to **False**, as you will manually install the client certificates in a later step.

4. In the Configuration pane, expand the Advanced folder, expand the Service Behaviors folder, expand the *(Empty Name)* node, expand the *serviceCredentials* node, and then click the *clientCertificate* node.

   The *CertificateValidationMode* property in the upper part of the *clientCertificate* pane is where you specify how the WCF service verifies the trustworthiness of client certificates. It can have the following values:

   - **ChainTrust** (the default)   The service will verify that the CA that issued the certificate is valid and can be trusted—the CA must either have a certificate that is stored in the Trusted Root Certification Authorities store on the service's computer, or have a certificate that was issued by another CA that is recorded in the Trusted Root Certification Authorities store, or have a certificate that was issued by a CA that has a certificate that was issued by another CA recorded in Trusted Root Certification Authorities store, and so on. The service will navigate its way up the chain of CA certificates until it either finds a trusted CA or reaches the end of the chain. If the service fails to establish that the chain ends in a trusted CA, the client certificate is not trusted, and it is rejected.

   - **PeerTrust**   The service searches the Trusted People store for the client certificate. If the service finds a matching certificate, the client is trusted. If not, the client request is rejected.

❏ **PeerOrChainTrust**   The service deems that the client certificate is valid if it is in the Trusted People store, or it can verify that the certificate was issued by a trusted CA by means of the ChainTrust mechanism described above.

❏ **Custom**   The service uses a class that implements your own custom certificate validation process. You specify the class that implements the custom validation by using the CustomeCertificateValidatorType property.

❏ **None**   The service does not attempt to verify the client certificate and just accepts it as valid.

By default, when validating certificates, the service will look in stores in the *LocalMachine* store location. This is useful if you are hosting the WCF service in IIS. If you are creating a self-hosted service that runs in the security context of a specific user account, you can configure the WCF service to look in the *CurrentUser* store location instead by changing the *TrustedStoreLocation* property.

The *RevocationMode* property specifies whether the service should also check to see whether the client certificate has been revoked (the client is no longer trusted). The service can query its online revocation list (*Online*), its cached revocation list (*Offline*), or not bother checking (*NoCheck*).

5. In the right pane, set the *CertificateValidationMode* property to **PeerTrust**.

> **Important**   In the following exercises, you will use test certificates generated by the *make-cert* utility to identify users. These certificates do not have a trusted CA. For the WCF service to be able to use these certificates, you must either disable validation checking (which is very dangerous and never recommended) or arrange for the certificates to be placed in the Trusted People store, which is what you have specified here.

6. Save the configuration file, and then close the Service Configuration Editor.

You can now configure the client application to send a certificate to the WCF service.

Modify the Client Application to Authenticate with the WCF Service by Using a Certificate

1. Edit the app.config file for the ProductsClient project by using the Service Configuration Editor.

2. In the Configuration pane, expand the Bindings folder, and then click the *ProductsClient WS2007HttpBindingConfig* binding configuration.

3. In the right pane, click the Security tab. Set the *MessageClientCredentialType* property to **Certificate**, and set the *NegotiateServiceCredential* property to **False**.

4. Save the configuration file, and then close the Service Configuration Editor.

The next step is to create certificates for the two test users, Bert and Fred, and then modify the client application to send a certificate that identifies the user to the WCF service.

Create Certificates to Identify the Test Users

1. Open a Visual Studio Command Prompt window as Administrator.

2. In the Visual Studio Command Prompt window, type the following command:

   ```
   makecert -sr CurrentUser -ss My -n CN=Bert -sky exchange
   ```

   This command creates a certificate with the subject "Bert" and places it in the Personal store of the currently logged on user.

3. In the Visual Studio Command Prompt window, type the following command:

   ```
   makecert -sr CurrentUser -ss My -n CN=Fred -sky exchange
   ```

   This command creates another certificate with the subject "Fred."

The certificates for Bert and Fred are in the Personal certificate store of the current user. The WCF service requires the administrator to install a copy of these certificates into the Trusted People store of the computer hosting the WCF service. In the next exercise, you will export a copy of the personal certificates to a pair of files, and then import the certificates to the Trusted People store for the local computer.

> **Note** The *certmgr* utility that you use in the following exercise provides options with which you can copy a certificate directly from one store to another in a single command. However, in the real world you would more likely export a certificate to a file, transport the file (in a secure manner) to the computer hosting the service, and then import the certificate into the certificate store. This is the approach used in the following exercise.

Export the Users' Certificates, and Import Them into the Server's Certificate Store

1. In the Visual Studio Command Prompt window, move to your Documents folder and type the following command:

   ```
   certmgr.exe -put -c -n Bert -r CurrentUser -s My bert.cer
   ```

   This command retrieves a copy of Bert's certificate from the Personal store (My) for the current user and creates a file called Bert.cer. This file contains a copy of the certificate including its public key, but *not* the private key.

> **Note** It is important that you include the ".exe" extension when you run the *certmgr* utility because there is also a Microsoft Management Console called certmgr, and this may run instead if you omit the extension (certmgr.msc is located in the \Windows\System32 folder). If the Certificates – Current User dialog box appears, you have started the certmgr console, not the *certmgr* utility.

2. Type the following command:

```
certmgr.exe -add bert.cer -c -r LocalMachine -s TrustedPeople
```

This command imports the certificate into the Trusted People store for the local computer.

3. Type the following commands to export Fred's certificate and import it into the Trusted People store on the local computer:

```
certmgr.exe -put -c -n Fred -r CurrentUser -s My fred.cer
certmgr.exe -add fred.cer -c -r LocalMachine -s TrustedPeople
```

4. Leave the Visual Studio Command Prompt window open.

> **Note** Using the commands shown in the previous exercise, you can automate the process of creating, exporting, and importing certificates by using scripts. However, the *certmgr* utility also provides a graphical user interface if you wish to manipulate certificates interactively. To display the user interface, simply run the *certmgr* utility without any parameters. The following image shows the user interface for the *certmgr* utility.

Update the Client Application to Send a Certificate to the WCF Service

1. In Visual Studio, open the Program.cs file in the ProductsClient project to display it in the Code And Text Editor window.

2. In the *Main* method of the *Program* class, replace the two statements that set the *User-Name* and *Password* properties of the *ClientCredentials.UserName* property of the proxy object with the following statement (shown in bold):

```
static void Main(string[] args)
{
    ...
    // Create a proxy object and connect to the service
    PermissiveCertificatePolicy.Enact("CN=LON-DEV-01");
    ProductsServiceClient proxy =
        new ProductsServiceClient("WS2007HttpBinding_IProductsService");

    proxy.ClientCredentials.ClientCertificate.SetCertificate(
        StoreLocation.CurrentUser, StoreName.My,
        X509FindType.FindBySubjectName, "Bert");
    ...
}
```

This statement retrieves Bert's certificate from the Personal store of the current user and adds it to the credentials sent to the WCF service.

3. Start the solution without debugging. In the client console window, press Enter.

The first test fails with the message "Access is denied." The WCF service has authenticated the client certificate (you would get a different exception if the authentication had failed—"An unsecured or incorrectly secured fault was received from the other party"), but the service is still attempting to authorize users based on the information stored in the SQL Server database used by the ASP.NET Role Provider.

4. Press Enter to close the client console window.

You need to modify the definitions of the users and roles in the SQL Server database to map user identities retrieved from user's certificates to roles. But first, you need to understand the identifiers that the WCF service uses when clients authenticate by using certificates.

Investigate the Identifiers of Users Authenticated by Using Certificates

1. Open the ProductsService.cs file in the App_Code folder in the InternetProductsService Web site project.

2. Comment out the *PrincipalPermission* attribute for the *ListProducts* method in the *ProductsServiceImpl* class. Add the following statements (shown in bold) to the start of the method:

```
//[PrincipalPermission(SecurityAction.Demand, Role="WarehouseStaff")]
public List<string> ListProducts()
{
  string userIdentifier = ServiceSecurityContext.Current.PrimaryIdentity.Name;
  List<string> tempList = new List<string>();
  tempList.Add(userIdentifier);
  return tempList;
  ...
}
```

The *Current.PrimaryIdentity.Name* property of the *ServiceSecurityContext* object contains the identifier of the currently authenticated user. This code returns a list of one string that contains the user's identifier.

> **Note** Using an existing operation in the WCF service in this way means that you don't need to regenerate the proxy for the client. Visual Studio will generate a warning, "Unreachable code detected," for the remaining code in the method. You can ignore this warning because you will remove the statements you have just added when you have finished with them.

3. Start the solution without debugging. In the client console window, press Enter. Test 1 now succeeds and displays the identity of the user, as shown in the following image:

```
C:\Windows\system32\cmd.exe
Press ENTER when the service has started

Test 1: List all products
Number: CN=Bert: DDFD773F76C8E6A6D76E20155140D9A8166BA8EF

Test 2: Display the details of a product
General exception: Access is denied.
Press ENTER to finish
```

The identifier for the authenticated user consists of two parts: the subject name, and the thumbprint of the certificate. The thumbprint uniquely identifies the certificate (multiple certificates can have the same subject name), so yours will probably be different from the one shown here. This is the information that you need to store in the SQL Server database, so make a note of the thumbprint.

4. Press Enter to close the client console window.

Update the User Information in the SQL Server Database

1. In Visual Studio, select the WCF service project in Solution Explorer. From the Website menu, select ASP.NET Configuration to run the ASP.NET Web Site Administration Tool.

2. In the ASP.NET Web Site Administration Tool, click the Security tab, and then click the Create User link.

3. On the Create User page, set the *User Name* field to the value displayed by the client application in the previous exercise. Include the subject name prefixed with "CN=Bert," followed by a semicolon, a space, and the thumbprint of the certificate you recorded in the previous exercise (be sure that there are no spaces in the thumbprint).

   Fill in the remaining fields with dummy values (the ASP.NET Web Site Administration Tool insists that you fill in all fields) and select the *WarehouseStaff* role. Click Create User when you have finished:

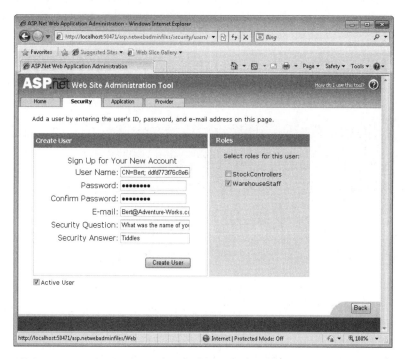

4. Click Continue, but leave the ASP.NET Web Site Administration Tool running (you will need it again shortly) and return to Visual Studio.

5. Run the solution again without debugging. In the client console window, press Enter.

   Test 1 still displays Bert's identifier, but Tests 2 and 3 now succeed. The user has been identified as a member of the *WarehouseStaff* role, although Test 4 still fails because Bert is not a member of the *StockControllers* role.

6. Press Enter to close the client console window.

7. Return to the Visual Studio Command Prompt window and start the *certmgr* utility without specifying any parameters:

```
certmgr.exe
```

The user interface for the *certmgr* utility starts and displays the Certificates dialog box.

8. In the Certificates dialog box, click the Personal tab, select the certificate for Fred, and then click View.

The certificate for Fred appears in the Certificate dialog box.

9. In the Certificate dialog box, click the Details tab, scroll down the list of fields, click the *Thumbprint* field, and make a note of the value.

10. Return to the ASP.NET Web Site Administration Tool. Add another user with the name "CN=Fred", followed by a semicolon, a space, and the thumbprint you noted in the previous step (remove the spaces from the thumbprint). Make this user a member of the *StockControllers* and *WarehouseStaff* roles.

11. When the user has been created, close the ASP.NET Web Site Administration Tool.

12. Return to the Certificate dialog box for the *certmgr* utility, and then click OK. Close the Certificates dialog box, but leave the Visual Studio Command Prompt window open.

13. In Visual Studio, return to the Program.cs file in the ProductsClient project.

14. In the *Main* method of the *Program* class, change the statement that sets the client credentials to use Fred's certificate, as shown in bold in the following:

```
static void Main(string[] args)
{
    ...
    proxy.ClientCredentials.ClientCertificate.SetCertificate(
        StoreLocation.CurrentUser, StoreName.My,
        X509FindType.FindBySubjectName, "Fred");
    ...
}
```

15. Open the ProductsService.cs file containing the code for the WCF service in the Code and Text Editor window.

16. Uncomment the *PrincipalPermission* attribute for the *ListProducts* method and remove the four lines of code you added earlier, returning the method to its original state:

```
[PrincipalPermission(SecurityAction.Demand, Role="WarehouseStaff")]
public List<string> ListProducts()
{
    // Create a list for holding product numbers
    List<string>  productsList = new List<string>():
    ...
}
```

17. Run the solution again without debugging. In the client console window, press Enter.

All four tests should execute successfully. Fred is a member of the *WarehouseStaff* and *StockControllers* roles.

18. Press Enter to close the client console window.

You have seen how to use certificates to authenticate users and how to authenticate users identified by certificates. Note that with IIS you can also map client certificates to Windows accounts if you prefer not to use the ASP.NET Role Provider. For more information, see the "Configure Client Certificate Mapping Authentication (IIS 7)" page, on the Microsoft Technet Web site at *http://technet.microsoft.com/en-us/library/cc732996(WS.10).aspx*.

There is one further feature worth mentioning at this point: the client application currently hard-codes the details and location of the user's certificate. This is almost as bad a practice as hard-coding user names and passwords. However, it is also a little unreasonable to expect users to know the details of their certificates, so prompting them for this information is not a feasible alternative. In addition, an administrator might not actually *want* the user to know too much about their certificates; this information could be dangerous in the hands of a naive user. An alternative approach is for an administrator to put the details of the certificate in the application configuration file for the client. You can define a client endpoint behavior that contains the client credentials and reference this behavior from the endpoint. The code below highlights the relevant fragments from a client application configuration file (you can, of course, create this behavior and attach it to the endpoint by using the Service Configuration Editor—endpoint behaviors are listed in the Advanced folder in the Configuration pane):

```xml
<?xml version="1.0" encoding="utf-8" ?>
<configuration>
  <system.serviceModel>
    <behaviors>
      <endpointBehaviors>
        <behavior name="ClientCertificateBehavior">
          <clientCredentials>
            <clientCertificate findValue="Fred" x509FindType="FindBySubjectName" />
          </clientCredentials>
        </behavior>
      </endpointBehaviors>
    </behaviors>
    <bindings>
      ...
      <ws2007HttpBinding>
        <binding name="ProductsClientWS2007HttpBindingConfig">
          <security mode="TransportWithMessageCredential">
            <transport clientCredentialType="None" />
            <message clientCredentialType="Certificate"
                     negotiateServiceCredential="false"/>
          </security>
        </binding>
```

```
        </ws2007HttpBinding>
      </bindings>
      <client>
        ...
        <endpoint address="https://lon-dev-01/InternetProductsService/Service.svc"
            behaviorConfiguration="ClientCertificateBehavior" binding="ws2007HttpBinding"
            bindingConfiguration="ProductsClientWS2007HttpBindingConfig"
            contract="ProductsClient.ProductsService.IProductsService"
            name="WS2007HttpBinding_IProductsService" />
      </client>
    </system.serviceModel>
</configuration>
```

Authenticating Service Messages by Using a Certificate

Using the HTTPS protocol with a service gives a client application a reasonable degree of confidence that communications with the service are secure. The service sends the client a certificate with a key that the client application uses for encrypting communications, and the client application verifies that the certificate sent by the service has originated from a trusted CA. However, HTTPS is primarily concerned with ensuring the confidentiality of communications. Authentication for the purpose of establishing an SSL session is not the same as performing message authentication, which can verify the identity of the message sender. The client application frequently assumes that it is sending messages in a secure manner to a specific, trusted service, but is this assumption always valid? The client might actually be securely exchanging messages with a totally different spoof service—it is not unknown for hackers to infiltrate DNS servers and arrange for messages addressed to one server to be rerouted elsewhere. To help alleviate concerns of this type, you can implement message-level security with mutual authentication in place of using transport-level security.

The protocol and mechanism used for authenticating a service to a client is very similar to that used by the service to authenticate a client. The service signs the messages it sends to the client application by using its private key. The client application uses a public key from a copy of the service's certificate held in its own certificate store to decode and verify the signature. If the decoding fails, the service's signature is not recognized (it is possibly a different service pretending to be the real service), and the client can reject the message from the service. All communications are also encrypted, as described when using message-level security in Chapter 4.

In the following exercises, you will create another ASP.NET Web site to host a copy of the WCF service that implements message-level security. You will then configure a certificate for the WCF service that the client application will use to authenticate the messages sent by the WCF service.

Create an ASP.NET Web Site to Host the WCF Service That Will Implement Message-Level Security

1. Return to the Internet Information Services (IIS) Manager console (if you have closed it, restart it again as an administrator).

2. In the Connections pane, expand the node that corresponds to your computer, and then click Application Pools.

3. In the Application Pools pane, right-click the ASP.NET v4.0 application pool, and then click Recycle.

    This step is necessary to close any resources (such as the ASPNETDB.MDF database) that the Web application has open.

4. Start Windows Explorer as an administrator and move to the C:\inetpub\wwwroot folder.

5. Create a copy of the InternetProductsService folder and rename it as **Mutual AuthenticationProductsService**.

6. Return to the Internet Information Services (IIS) Manager console. In the Connections pane, under the node that corresponds to your computer, expand Sites, right-click Default Web Site, and then click Add Application.

7. In the Add Application dialog box, specify the values shown in the following table, and then click OK.

Item	Value
Alias	MutualAuthenticationProductsService
Application Pool	ASP.NET v4.0
Physical Path	C:\inetpub\wwwroot\MutualAuthenticationProductsService

8. Close the Internet Information Services (IIS) Manager console.

Configure the WCF Service to Authenticate Itself to Client Applications by Using the Localhost Certificate

1. Return to the Visual Studio Command Prompt window and type the following command:

    ```
    makecert -sr LocalMachine -ss My -n CN=localhost -sky exchange
    ```

    This command creates a certificate with the subject "localhost" and places it in the Personal store of the local computer. The subject name for a service certificate should match the name of host computer in the URL that the client application uses to connect to the service (unlike the earlier exercises which used an SSL certificate with a name that had to match the real name of your computer, you can specify *localhost* this time).

If you are hosting a WCF service by using IIS, as you are in this exercise, you must grant the NETWORKSERVICE account read access to the certificate by using the procedure in the next step. If you are using a self-hosted service, the following step is not necessary, depending on the authority of the account you use to execute the self-hosted service.

2. Move to the Microsoft Press\WCF Step By Step\Chapter 5 folder and type the following command:

```
FindPrivateKey My LocalMachine -n CN=localhost -a
```

The *FindPrivateKey* utility displays information about the location of the private key file for a specified certificate. The source code for this utility is available as part of the Windows Communication Foundation Samples, which can be obtained from Microsoft. The output from this command is the name of a private key file associated with the local host certificate in the certificate store. It should look something like the following (the hexadecimal UUID identifying the certificate will be different on your computer):

```
C:\ProgramData\Microsoft\Crypto\RSA\MachineKeys\7b90a71bfc56f
2582e916a51aed6df9a_dc9d1a42-7732-4bec-8b74-a1df0d4465ef
```

This is the file that you need to grant read access on for the NETWORKSERVICE account.

> **More Info** For more information about the FindPrivateKey utility, see the "FindPrivateKey" page on the Microsoft Web site at *http://msdn.microsoft.com/en-us/library/aa717039.aspx*.

4. Type the following command on a single line (replacing the UUID of the certificate with your own value):

```
cacls "C:\ProgramData\Microsoft\Crypto\RSA\MachineKeys\7b90a71bfc56f
2582e916a51aed6df9a_dc9d1a42-7732-4bec-8b74-a1df0d4465ef"
/E /G NETWORKSERVICE:R
```

> **Note** This command assumes that you are running the ASP.NET v4.0 application pool with the NetworkService identity. If you are using a different identity for this application pool, replace NETWORKSERVICE in the previous command with the name of the identity that you are using.

5. Type the following command to stop and restart IIS:

```
iisreset
```

Leave the Visual Studio Command Prompt window open (you will need it later).

6. In Visual Studio, in the Solution Explorer, right-click the InternetProductsService solution, point to Add, and then click Existing Web Site.

7. In the Add Existing Web Site dialog box, ensure that Local IIS is selected, click the *Mutual AuthenticationProductsService* site, clear the Use Secure Sockets Layer check box, and then click Open.

8. Edit the Web.config file of the MutualAuthenticationProductsService Web site by using the Service Configuration Editor.

9. In Configuration pane, expand the Bindings folder, and then click the *ProductsService WS2007HttpBindingConfig* binding configuration.

10. In the right pane, click the Security tab. Set the *Mode* property to **Message**.

11. In the Configuration pane, expand the Advanced folder, expand the Service Behaviors folder, expand the *(Empty Name)* node, expand the *serviceCredentials* node, and then click the *serviceCertificate* node.

12. In the serviceCertificate pane, set the *FindValue* property to **localhost** and set the *X509FindType* property to **FindBySubjectName**. Verify that the *StoreLocation* property is set to *LocalMachine* and that the *StoreName* property is set to *My*.

13. In the Configuration pane, expand the Services folder, expand the *Products.Products ServiceImpl* service, expand the Endpoints folder, and then click the *(Empty Name)* endpoint.

14. In the Service Endpoint pane, change the *Address* of the service to **http://localhost/ MutualAuthenticationProductsService/Service.svc**

    Note that this address specifies the HTTP protocol and not HTTPS.

15. Save the configuration file, and then close the Service Configuration Editor.

You have now enabled the WCF service to authenticate itself to client applications by signing messages with the localhost certificate. In the real world, the administrator for the computer hosting the WCF service would export this certificate, and then distribute it to all computers running the client application. The next exercise simulates this process.

Export the WCF Service Certificate and Import It into the Client Certificate Store

1. Return to the Visual Studio Command Prompt window and type the following command:

```
certmgr.exe -put -c -n localhost -r LocalMachine -s My localhost.cer
```

This command retrieves a copy of the localhost certificate used by the WCF service to authenticate itself and creates a file called localhost.cer. Remember that this file contains a copy of the certificate including its public key but *not* the private key. The administrator can distribute this file to all client computers.

2. Type the following command:

```
certmgr.exe -add localhost.cer -c -r CurrentUser -s My
```

This command imports the certificate into the certificate store for the current user. This is typically what an administrator would do to make the certificate available to the client application.

Leave the Visual Studio Command Prompt window open.

You can now configure the client application to authenticate the WCF service by using the localhost certificate in the CurrentUser certificate store.

Configure the WCF Client Application to Authenticate the WCF Service

1. In Visual Studio, edit the app.config file of the ProductsClient project by using the Service Configuration Editor.

2. In the Configuration pane, in the Endpoints folder under the Client folder, click the *WS2007HttpBinding_IProductsService* node.

3. In the right pane, change the *Address* property to **http://localhost/Mutual AuthenticationProductsService/Service.svc**. This is the address of the WCF service. Notice that it uses the HTTP protocol, and not HTTPS, and the name of the server is now localhost.

4. In the Configuration pane, expand the Bindings folder, and then select the *ProductsClient WS2007HttpBindingConfig* binding configuration.

5. In the right pane, click the Security tab. Set the *Mode* property to **Message**.

6. In the Configuration pane, expand the Advanced folder, right-click the Endpoint Behaviors node, and then click New Endpoint Behavior Configuration.

7. In the right pane, type **AuthenticationBehavior** for the *Name* property, and then click Add.

8. In the Adding Behavior Element Extension Sections dialog box, select *clientCredentials*, and then click Add.

9. In the Configuration pane, expand the *clientCredentials* node, expand the *service Certificate* node, and then click the *defaultCertificate* node.

10. In the *defaultCertificate* pane, enter **localhost** for the *FindValue* property and set the *X509FindType* property to **FindBySubjectName**.

11. In the Configuration pane, click the *WS2007HttpBinding_IProductsService* endpoint in the Endpoints folder under the Client folder.

12. In the Client Endpoint pane, set the *BehaviorConfiguration* property to **AuthenticationBehavior**.

13. Save the configuration file, and then close the Service Configuration Editor.

14. Edit the Program.cs file for the ProductsClient application. In the *Main* method, comment out the code that overrides the validity check of the certificate exported by the HTTPS implementation of the WCF service (shown in bold)—this statement is not required by this version of the client:

```
static void Main(string[] args)
{
    ...
    // Create a proxy object and connect to the service
    // PermissiveCertificatePolicy.Enact("CN=LON-DEV-01");
    ...
}
```

The final step is to verify that the client application can connect to the WCF service and authenticate it successfully.

Verify that the Client Application Authenticates the WCF Service

1. Start the solution without debugging. In the client console window, press Enter.

   The client application should complete all four tests successfully.

> **Tip** If the client application fails with a message stating that the service could not be activated, check to make sure that you provided the correct endpoint address for the service in the configuration file and that you have granted read permission over the correct certificate file to the NETWORKSERVICE account.

2. Press Enter to close the client console window.

3. Return to the command prompt window and type the following command:

   ```
   certmgr.exe –del –c –n localhost –r LocalMachine –s My
   ```

   This command removes the *localhost* certificate from the *LocalMachine* certificate store.

4. Type the following command:

   ```
   makecert –sr LocalMachine –ss My –n CN=localhost –sky exchange
   ```

   This command creates another certificate with the same subject name as before. When you run the WCF service, it will find this certificate and present it to the client application.

5. Restart IIS by running the following command:

   ```
   iisreset
   ```

   When IIS has restarted, close the command prompt window.

6. Return to Visual Studio and start the solution without debugging. In the client console window, press Enter.

The client application should now fail with a *MessageSecurityException* "An unsecured or incorrectly secured fault was received from the other party...".

The private key in the *localhost* certificate used by the WCF service to sign messages has changed, so the client cannot use the public key in its copy of the *localhost* certificate to verify the signature of the messages sent by the WCF service. This situation is analogous to a rogue version of the WCF service being placed at the same address as the real service and highlights the benefits of authenticating a service in a client application.

 Important The only way the rogue service can imitate the real WCF service is if it has access to the same private key as the real WCF service. This shows once again the importance of keeping your private keys private.

7. Press Enter to close the client console window.

Identifying a Service

The example presented in the previous set of exercises is primarily intended to be used in configurations involving message-level security, and authentication occurs on a message-by-message basis. It requires a significant degree of cooperation between an administrator responsible for configuring a service who must be prepared to provide the details of the service's public key and the (possibly many) administrators responsible for managing the clients that connect to the service by configuring them to use this public key. This mechanism can be very secure, but the robust security comes at the cost of the additional processing required to sign and encrypt all communications. As an alternative, you can implement service authentication. This approach does not protect messages in quite the same way, but it does give you a degree of confidence that your client application is at least communicating with a *bona fide* service.

When you configure a client endpoint for connecting to a service, you can specify the expected identity of the service in the *<identity>* element. Depending on the security requirements of the service this identity can take the form of a certificate, the DNS name of the server hosting the service, an RSA key, a service principal name (SPN), or a user principal name specifying the account under which the service runs. The following example shows a client endpoint configuration with the expected identity of the service specified as an SPN.

```
<configuration>
  <system.serviceModel>
    ...
    <client>
      <endpoint address="http://lon-dev-01/ProductsServiceWithSpnIdentity/Service.svc"
                binding="ws2007HttpBinding" bindingConfiguration="..."
                contract="..." name="...">
        <identity>
          <servicePrincipalName value="host/LON-DEV-01" />
        </identity>
      </endpoint>
    </client>
  </system.serviceModel>
</configuration>
```

When the client application runs and connects to the service, the WCF runtime queries the identity of the service and verifies that it matches the identity specified in the client configuration; it does this before sending the first message from the client application. If the identities match, then the service is considered to be authenticated and the client application is allowed to send and receive messages. If the identities are different, then the service is treated as a spoof or fake service (possibly attempting a phishing attack), and communications from the client application will not proceed.

> **Note** The identity of a service can be defined as part of the service metadata. When you create a client proxy for a service by using the *svcutil* utility or the Add Service Reference Wizard, the client endpoint configuration generated automatically includes any identity information provided by the service.

Summary

In this chapter, you have seen how to authenticate and authorize users and services when they are running in different Windows domains across the Internet. You have learned how to configure the ASP.NET Membership Provider to authenticate users against credentials held in a SQL Server database, and the ASP.NET Role Provider to specify the roles that a user has for authorization purposes. You also should understand how client applications and services can use certificates to authenticate messages that they send to each other and explain how they can use public and private keys to help protect the privacy of communications in a potentially hostile network environment. Finally, you saw how you can provide the expected identity of a service as part of the endpoint configuration for a client application, and how the WCF runtime can use this information to determine whether a service is real or bogus.

Chapter 6
Maintaining Service Contracts and Data Contracts

After completing this chapter, you will be able to:

- Describe how to protect the individual operations in a service contract.

- Explain which changes to a service require that client applications to be updated.

- Implement different versions of a service contract in a service.

- Modify a data contract and explain which changes will break existing client applications.

- Describe how WCF can generate default values for missing items in a data contract.

In Chapter 1, "Introducing Windows Communication Foundation," you learned that one of the fundamental tenets of Service Oriented Architectures (SOA) is that services share schemas and contracts, not classes or types. When you define a service, you specify the operations that it supports by defining a service contract. The service contract describes each operation, together with its parameters, and any return types. A WCF service can publish its service contract definition, and a developer can use this information to build client applications that communicate with the service. A developer can generate a proxy class for the client application from the Web Services Description Language (WSDL) description of the service by using the Add Service Reference Wizard in Visual Studio or by using the *svcutil* utility from the command line, and then communicate with the service through this proxy.

The service contract is only one part of the story, however. The operations in a service contract can take parameters and return values. Client applications must provide data formatted in a manner that the service expects. Many of the primitive types in the .NET Framework have pre-defined formats, but more complex data types, such as classes, structures, and enumerations require the service to specify how client applications should package this information in messages that it sends to the service and the format for any information sent by the service back to client applications. You encapsulate this information in data contracts. Each complex data type used by a service should have a corresponding data contract. The service publishes this information together with the service contract, and the definitions of each complex type are included in the proxy code generated by the *svcutil* utility or the Add Service Reference Wizard in Visual Studio.

You should be able to see how service contracts and data contracts are fundamental parts of a service. If a client application does not understand the set of operations that a service exposes or the type of data used by these services, then it will have severe trouble communicating with the service.

Modifying a Service Contract

A service contract is an interface that the WCF tools and infrastructure can convert into a WSDL document, listing the operations for a service as a series of SOAP messages and message responses. You provide an implementation of these methods in a class in the service. When a WCF service starts, the WCF runtime creates a channel stack by using the bindings specified in the service configuration file and listens for client requests in the form of one of these messages. The WCF runtime then converts each SOAP message sent by a client application into a method call and invokes the corresponding method in an instance of the class implementing the service (you will learn how and when the WCF runtime actually creates this instance in Chapter 7, "Maintaining State and Sequencing Operations"). Any data returned by the method is converted back into a SOAP response message and is sent back through the channel stack for transmission to the client application.

You can draw two conclusions from the preceding discussion:

1. The service contract does not depend on the communication mechanism that the service uses to send and receive messages. The communications mechanism is governed by the channel stack constructed from the binding information specified in the service configuration file. You can change the network protocol or address of a service without modifying the code in the service or in any client applications that access the service (although client applications must use compatible endpoints in their configuration files). To a large extent, the security requirements of a service are also independent of the service contract, although there are exceptions, as you will see in the first part of this chapter.

2. Client applications wishing to communicate with the service must be able to construct the appropriate SOAP messages. These messages depend on the service contract; if the service contract changes, then the client must be provided with an up-to-date version; otherwise, it runs the risk of sending messages that the service does not understand or that are formatted incorrectly. Additionally, if the response messages returned by a service change, a client application might not be able to handle them correctly.

You will examine what these conclusions mean from a practical perspective in the exercises in this section.

Selectively Protecting Operations

The previous two chapters have shown how to protect the messages passing between client applications and services. However, the techniques shown have concentrated on using bindings and behaviors of a service to protect the service as a whole. By modifying the service contract, you can specify different security requirements for operations in the same service.

> **Note** Protecting a service by modifying binding and behavior information is an example of the fourth tenet of SOA—compatibility is based on policy. You can protect a service in a variety of ways without modifying the service contract, as long as the client applications and service follow compatible security policies. However, selectively protecting an operation *is* a change to the service contract because now the protection mechanism becomes tightly coupled to the operation, rather than being a policy attribute of the service. You will see the effects that this has on a client application in the next exercise.

Specify the Security Requirements for Operations in the WCF Service

1. Using Visual Studio, open the solution file ProductsService.sln located in the Microsoft Press\WCF Step By Step\Chapter 6\ProductsService folder, located within your Documents folder.

   This solution contains an amended copy of the ProductsClient, ProductsServiceLibrary, and ProductsServiceHost projects from Chapter 4, "Protecting an Enterprise WCF Service". In this version of the code, the service does not display a message box showing the identity of the user, and the service only exposes a single non-SSL endpoint using the *WS2007HttpBinding* binding. Note that the *WS2007HttpBinding* binding implements message-level security and authenticates users by using Windows tokens by default.

> **Important** The ProductsServiceHost application exposes the *ProductsService* service over an HTTP endpoint, listening on port 8010. You reserved this port in exercises in a previous chapter, but if you have since removed this reservation you must add it again. You can do this by opening a Visual Studio Command Prompt window as Administrator and typing the following command (replace *UserName* with your Windows user name):
>
> ```
> netsh http add urlacl url=http://+:8010/ user=UserName
> ```

2. Open the IProductsService.cs file for the ProductsServiceLibrary project in the Code And Text Editor window. Add the following *using* statement to the list at the top of the file:

   ```
   using System.Net.Security;
   ```

3. Locate the *IProductsService* interface that defines the service contract and amend the *OperationContract* attribute for the *ListProducts* and *GetProduct* methods, as shown in bold in the following:

```
[ServiceContract]
public interface IProductsService
{
    // Get the product number of every product
    [FaultContract(typeof(SystemFault))]
    [FaultContract(typeof(DatabaseFault))]
    [OperationContract(ProtectionLevel = ProtectionLevel.EncryptAndSign)]
    List<string> ListProducts();

    // Get the details of a single product
    [OperationContract(ProtectionLevel = ProtectionLevel.EncryptAndSign)]
    Product GetProduct(string productNumber);
    ...
}
```

The *ProtectionLevel* property of the *OperationContract* attribute specifies how messages invoking this operation—and output by this operation—are protected. In this case, *EncryptAndSign* specifies that calls to the *ListProducts* and *GetProduct* operations must be signed by the client and encrypted by using a key negotiated with the service. This requires that the security mode of the binding used by the client and service implements message-level authentication and that the client and service specify the same value for the *AlgorithmSuite* property (go back and look at Chapter 4 if you need to refresh your memory about these properties). In fact, this is the default protection level for operations when you configure message-level security by using the *WS2007HttpBinding* binding.

4. Modify the *OperationContract* attribute for the *CurrentStockLevel* and *ChangeStockLevel* methods, as shown in bold in the following:

```
[ServiceContract]
public interface IProductsService
{
    ...
    // Get the current stock level for a product
    [OperationContract(ProtectionLevel = ProtectionLevel.Sign)]
    int CurrentStockLevel(string productNumber);

    // Change the stock level for a product
    [OperationContract(ProtectionLevel = ProtectionLevel.Sign)]
    bool ChangeStockLevel(string productNumber, int newStockLevel,
                          string shelf, int bin);
}
```

The *Sign* protection level specifies that calls that client applications make to these operations must be signed but not encrypted. The protection level specified here overrides the message-level security configured for the binding.

You can also specify a value of *ProtectionLevel.None* if you don't want to sign or encrypt messages, although you should use this setting with caution as it has obvious security implications.

5. Edit the App.config file for the ProductsServiceHost project by using the Service Configuration Editor.

6. In the Configuration pane, click the Diagnostics folder. In the right pane, verify that the *MessageLogging* property is set to *On* (click Enable Message Logging if it is off).

    You configured message logging in Chapter 4, and you enabled tracing at the transport and message level.

7. In the right pane, click the MessageLog link. In the Listener Settings dialog box, change the path of the log file so that the trace output is sent to the ProductsService.svclog file in the Microsoft Press\WCF Step By Step\Chapter 6 folder, and then click OK.

8. In the Configuration pane, expand the Diagnostics folder, and then click Message Logging.

9. In the Message Logging pane, set *LogMessagesAtServiceLevel* to **False** and verify that *LogMessagesAtTransportLevel* is set to *True*.

    To minimize the logging overhead, you will trace messages only as they flow in and out of the transport level. At this level, you will be able to see the effects of the message-level security applied by the binding and the service contract—logging at the service (message) level will only show unencrypted messages as they are received and sent by the service.

10. Save the changes, and then exit the Service Configuration Editor.

> **Important** The *ProductsService* service requires that the user invoking the operations in the client application is a member of the *WarehouseStaff* and *StockControllers* security groups. The client application specifies the credentials for *Fred*, who should be a member of both of these groups. You created these groups and the user in the exercise "Create Groups for Warehouse Staff and Stock Controller Staff" on page 154 in Chapter 4. If these groups and user are missing from your computer, please go back and perform this exercise before continuing.

Test the Modified Service

1. Start the solution without debugging. In the Products Service Host window, click Start (if a Windows Security Alert message box appears, click Allow Access to enable the service to open the TCP port it uses for listening for client requests). In the client console window, press Enter.

Tests 1 and 2 complete successfully because the binding implements a policy of encryption and signing, and this automatically meets the requirements of the operation contract for the *ListProducts* and *GetProduct* operations. However, Test 3 raises the exception, "The primary signature must be encrypted," because the *CurrentStockLevel* operation specifies only signing in the operation contract, but the client binding is also encrypting information as well because the default mechanism is to encrypt and sign messages. The problem is that you have modified the service contract, but you have not updated the corresponding code in the client application; the proxy used by the client application is still expecting to send signed and encrypted messages to the service for Tests 3 and 4.

2. Press Enter to close the client console window. In the Products Service Host window, click Stop, and then close the window.

3. In Visual Studio, open the Products.cs file in the ProductsClient project.

    This file contains the code for the proxy that you generated by using the *svcutil* tool in Chapter 3, "Making Applications and Services Robust." Normally, when you make changes to a service contract you should regenerate the proxy again. However, in this example, where you have made a small change to the contract for a couple of operations, it is simpler and more informative for you to directly modify the code so that you can see the changes required in the proxy.

4. Scroll through the Products.cs file to locate the definition of the *IProductsService* interface (this should be somewhere around line 231).

    You should recognize the methods in this interface as they correspond very closely to the methods in the service contract. The return type of the *ListProducts* method is slightly different—it is an array of strings rather than a generic list (for reasons described in Chapter 1), and the *OperationContract* and *FaultContract* attributes for each operation include *Action* and *ReplyAction* properties; these items specify the types of the SOAP messages that the WCF runtime uses when communicating with the WCF service.

5. Modify the *ProtectionLevel* property of the *OperationContract* attribute for the *Current StockLevel* and *ChangeStockLevel* methods, as shown in bold in the following (do not modify the *Action* and *ReplyAction* properties):

```
[System.ServiceModel.OperationContractAttribute
    (ProtectionLevel=System.Net.Security.ProtectionLevel.Sign, Action= ...)]
int CurrentStockLevel(string productNumber);

[System.ServiceModel.OperationContractAttribute
    (ProtectionLevel = System.Net.Security.ProtectionLevel.Sign, Action = ...)]
bool ChangeStockLevel(string productNumber, int newStockLevel, string shelf, int bin);
```

6. Using Windows Explorer, delete the Products.svclog file in the Microsoft Press\WCF Step By Step\Chapter 6 folder.

7. In Visual Studio, start the solution without debugging. In the Products Service Host window, click Start. In the client console window, press Enter.

   All tests should now complete successfully.

8. Press Enter to close the client console window. In the Products Service Host form, click Stop, and then close the window.

9. Start the Service Trace Viewer (in the Microsoft Visual Studio 2010\Microsoft Windows SDK Tools program group).

10. In the Service Trace Viewer, open the Products.svclog file in the Microsoft Press\WCF Step By Step\Chapter 6 folder.

11. In the left pane, click the Message tab.

    You should see six messages concerned with negotiating the encryption keys used by the client and service; these messages have an *Action* in the *http://docs.oasis-open.org* namespace. Following these are ten messages corresponding to the messages received by the service and the responses sent back to the client application with an *Action* in the *http://tempuri.org* namespace. There are two further messages at the end, again with an *Action* in the *http://docs.oasis-open.org* namespace.

> **Tip** Expand the Action column in the left pane to see more of the name for each action.

12. Click the message with the *Action http://tempuri.org/IProductsService/ListProducts*. In the lower-right pane, click the Formatted tab and scroll to the bottom of the pane to display the Envelope Information section (if the Envelope Section is not visible, expand the Message Log area in this pane). In the *Parameters* box, note that the *Method* used to send the data is *e:EncryptedData* and that the parameter sent by the client application has been encrypted, as highlighted in the image that follows.

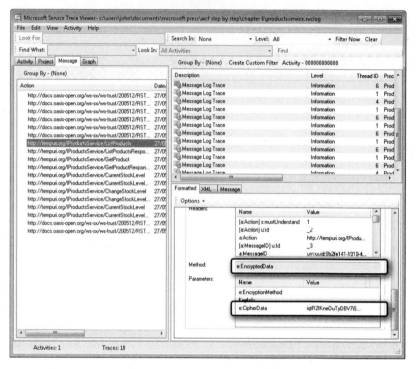

13. In the left pane, click the message with the *Action http://tempuri.org/IProductsService/ ListProductsResponse*. In the lower-right pane, verify that this response message is also encrypted. Follow the same procedure to examine the *http://tempuri.org/IProducts Service/GetProduct* and *http://tempuri.org/IProductsService/GetProductResponse* messages and verify that they are also encrypted.

14. In the left pane, click the *http://tempuri.org/IProductsService/ChangeStockLevel* message (this message occurs after the first *ChangeStockLevel* and *ChangeStockLevelResponse* messages in the log). In the lower-right pane, you should observe that the Method is *ChangeStockLevel* and that the parameters are not encrypted:

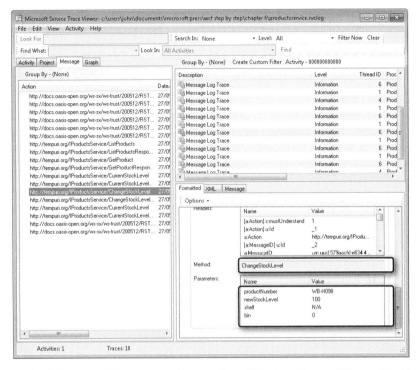

15. In the left pane, click the *http://tempuri.org/IProductsService/ChangeStockLevelResponse* message. This message should also be unencrypted. Examine the *http://tempuri.org/ IProductsService/CurrentStockLevel* and *http://tempuri.org/IProductsService/ CurrentStockLevelResponse* messages. These messages should be unencrypted, as well.

16. From the File menu, choose Close All to close the log file, but leave the Service Trace Viewer open.

Versioning a Service

Change happens. It is almost inevitable that a widely used service will evolve as circumstances and business processes change. In many cases, these changes will manifest themselves as modifications to the code that implements the operations in a service. However, it is also possible that the definitions of operations might need to change as well; you might need to add new operations, retire old or redundant operations, or change the parameters and return types of existing operations. Clearly, these modifications require updating the service contract. However, client applications depend on the service contract to specify the messages that the service receives and the responses it sends. If the service contract changes, what happens to clients that used the previous version of the contract? Will they still work or do you need to go and visit every client installation and update the code? Do you actually know where to locate every client? If client applications connect across the Internet, there could be a large number of them located anywhere in the world.

You can see that modifying a service is not a task that you should undertake lightly and, as far as possible, you should take steps to ensure that existing clients will continue to function without the need to be updated. To this end, it helps to understand what actually happens when you change a service or a service contract and the strategies that you can follow to minimize any detrimental impact of these changes. The following exercises illustrate some common scenarios.

Add a Method to the WCF Service and Amend the Business Logic of Operations

1. Using Visual Studio, open the ProductsService.cs file for the ProductsServiceLibrary project in the Code And Text Editor window.

2. Add the following method to the start of the *ProductsServiceImpl* class, above the *ListProducts* method:

```
public class ProductsServiceImpl : IProductsService
{
    public bool ProductExists(string productNumber, AdventureWorksEntities database)
    {
        // Check to see whether the specified product exists in the database
        int numProducts = (from p in database.Products
                            where string.Equals(p.ProductNumber, productNumber)
                            select p).Count();

        return numProducts > 0;
    }

    [PrincipalPermission(Security.Demand, Role="WarehouseStaff")]
    public List<string> ListProducts()
    {
        ...
    }
    ...
}
```

This method simply determines whether a product with the specified product number exists in the *AdventureWorks* database, returning *true* if it does and *false* if it does not.

3. Scroll down to the *GetProduct* method and add the *if* statement (shown in bold in the example that follows) around the code in the *using* block that retrieves the details of the specified product from the *AdventureWorks* database (don't forget to add the corresponding closing brace as well):

```
public Product GetProduct(string productNumber)
{
    ...
    try
    {
        // Connect to the AdventureWorks database by using the Entity Framework
        using (AdventureWorksEntities database = new AdventureWorksEntities())
        {
            // Check that the specified product exists
            if (ProductExists(productNumber, database))
            {
                // Find the first product that matches the specified product number
                Product matchingProduct = database.Products.First(...);

                productData = new ProductData()
                {
                    ...
                }
            }
        }
    }
    ...
}
```

4. Add the following *if* statement and closing brace (shown in bold) to the *CurrentStock-Level* method:

```
public int CurrentStockLevel(string productNumber)
{
    ...
    try
    {
        // Connect to the AdventureWorks database by using the Entity Framework
        using (AdventureWorksEntities database = new AdventureWorksEntities())
        {
            // Check that the specified product exists
            if (ProductExists(productNumber, database))
            {
                // Calculate the sum of all quantities for the specified product
                Product matchingProduct = database.Products.First(...);
                ...
            }
        }
    }
    ...
}
```

If the user provides a suspect product number, the method returns a stock level of *0*.

5. Add the *if/else* statement and closing brace (shown in bold) to the *ChangeStockLevel* method. Note that the *else* block wraps the existing code in the *using* block:

```
public bool ChangeStockLevel(string productNumber, int newStockLevel,
                             string shelf, int bin)
{
    ...
    try
    {
        // Connect to the AdventureWorks database by using the Entity Framework
        using (AdventureWorksEntities database = new AdventureWorksEntities())
        {
            // Check that the specified product exists
            if (!ProductExists(productNumber, database))
                return false;
            else
            {
                // Find the ProductID  for the specified product
                int productID = ...
                ...
                database.SaveChanges();
            }
        }
    }
    ...
}
```

If the product is not found the method returns *false* and does not update the database.

6. Start the solution without debugging. In the Products Service Host window, click Start. In the client console window, press Enter.

All tests should execute successfully.

7. Press Enter to close the client console window. In the Products Service Host window, click Stop, and then close the window.

8. In Visual Studio, edit the Program.cs file in the ProductsClient project. In the *Main* method, locate the block of code that invokes the *GetProduct* operation and displays the results. Change the parameter that the client sends to this operation to **AA-A999** and add code that checks whether the result returned by the *GetProduct* method is *null*. If the value returned is not *null*, then display the details, otherwise print the message "No such product", as shown in bold in the following code:

```
static void Main(string[] args)
{
    ...
    // Test the operations in the service

    try
    {
        ...
        Console.WriteLine("Test 2: Display the details of a product");
        ProductData product = proxy.GetProduct("AA-A999");
```

```csharp
        if (product != null)
        {
            Console.WriteLine("Number: {0}", product.ProductNumber);
            Console.WriteLine("Name: {0}", product.Name);
            Console.WriteLine("Color: {0}", product.Color);
            Console.WriteLine("Price: {0}", product.ListPrice);
            Console.WriteLine();
        }
        else
        {
            Console.WriteLine("No such product");
            Console.WriteLine();
        }

        // Query the stock level of this product
        ...
    }
    ...
}
```

9. Start the solution without debugging. In the Products Service Host window, click Start. In the client console window, press Enter.

Tests 1, 2, and 4 perform successfully, but the output from Test 2 displays the message "No such product"—there is no product in the *AdventureWorks* database with this number:

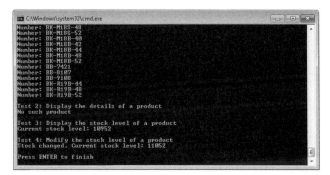

10. Press Enter to close the client console window. In the Products Service Host window, click Stop, and then close the window.

11. Edit the Program.cs file in the ProductsClient project, and change the line that calls the *GetProduct* method back to its original state (see the bold text):

```csharp
Product product = proxy.GetProduct("WB-H098");
```

Although the service has changed and a new public method has been added, the service contract has not been modified. Therefore, the *ProductExists* method is not accessible to client applications, which can continue to access the service exactly as before. This is an example of a nonbreaking change to a service.

Add a Parameter to an Existing Operation in the Service Contract

1. Open the IProductsService.cs file for the ProductsServiceLibrary project in the Code And Text Editor window.

2. Locate the definition of the *IProductsService* interface and add a parameter to the *ListProducts* method, as follows:

```
public interface IProductsService
{
    // Get the product number of every product
    [FaultContract(typeof(SystemFault))]
    [FaultContract(typeof(DatabaseFault))]
    [OperationContract(ProtectionLevel=ProtectionLevel.EncryptAndSign)]
    List<string> ListProducts(string match);
    ...
}
```

The AdventureWorks organization has dramatically increased the number of products that they manufacture. The original *ListProducts* method returns a list comprising thousands of rows. It has therefore been decided to modify this operation to give the user the option to constrain the list of products returned to just those for which the name matches a string value specified by the user.

3. Open the ProductsService.cs file in the Code And Text Editor window and locate the *ListProducts* method. Change the definition of this method and add the string parameter, shown in bold in the following code example:

```
[PrincipalPermission(SecurityAction.Demand, Role="WarehouseStaff")]
public List<string> ListProducts(string match)
{
    ...
}
```

4. Modify the code that retrieves the product numbers from the database and use a LINQ query to limit the products retrieved to those with a name that contains the string in the *match* parameter, as shown in bold in the following (you might also want to modify the comment in the code, which is now out of date):

```
[PrincipalPermission(SecurityAction.Demand, Role="WarehouseStaff")]
public List<string> ListProducts(string match)
{
    ...
    try
    {
        // Connect to the AdventureWorks database by using the Entity Framework
        using (AdventureWorksEntities database = new AdventureWorksEntities())
        {
            // Fetch the product number of every product in the database
```

```
        var products = from product in database.Products
                       where product.Name.Contains(match)
                       select product.ProductNumber;

        productsList = products.ToList();
    }
}
...
}
```

5. Start the solution without debugging. In the Products Service Host window, click Start in the client console window, and then press Enter.

   Test 1 fails to return any data:

The client application currently invokes the *ListProducts* operation without passing it a parameter. When the WCF runtime hosting the WCF service receives the message, it deserializes the message, finds that there is no data in the body of the message, and passes a null value as the parameter to the *ListProducts* method. The *ListProducts* method consequently returns an empty list (there are no matching products).

6. Press Enter to close the client console window. In the Products Service Host window, click Stop, and then close the window.

You may be surprised at the result of this exercise, but generally you will find that you can add parameters to an operation (and even remove parameters from an operation), and existing client applications will still be able to call them. If you add a parameter to an operation, and the client application fails to provide a value for this parameter, it will be assigned a default value that depends on its type; null for a reference type, 0 for a numeric or character type, and false for a Boolean type. Note that these default values (null, 0 or false) apply even if you attempt to make the parameter optional and assign it a different default value when you declare the method that implements the operation. For example, if you defined the *ListProducts* method as shown in the code fragment that follows, the default value specified for the *match* parameter ("W") will be ignored if the client application omits this parameter, and a null string will be used instead.

```
[PrincipalPermission(SecurityAction.Demand, Role="WarehouseStaff")]
public List<string> ListProducts(string match = "W")
{
    ...
}
```

If you change the type of a parameter, the formatter used by the WCF runtime to deserialize messages for the service will attempt to convert the data passed by the client application to the type required by the operation, if possible, but if no conversion is available, the formatter will throw an exception. However, adding, removing, or modifying parameters is not considered to be good practice, and you should treat the resulting behavior of an operation with extreme caution. For example, if you remove a parameter from the middle of a list of parameters for an operation, the data passed by the client application may be deserialized into the wrong parameters.

If you change the return type of an operation a similar set of rules apply. If the value returned by the operation cannot be converted to the type expected by the client application, an exception will occur in the formatter used by the client application to process response messages.

In general, you should avoid modifying types or numbers of parameters for an operation. Instead, if you need to modify a service contract for new client applications to use while maintaining compatibility with existing clients, you should actually define a new version of the service contract and leave the existing contract in place. You will see how to do this after the next exercise.

 Note If you want to call the updated version of the *ListProducts* operation from the client application, you should use the *svcutil* utility to generate a new version of the proxy class.

Add a New Operation to the WCF Service

1. Using Visual Studio, open the IProductsService.cs file for the ProductsService project in the Code And Text Editor window.

2. In the *IProductsService* interface, remove the *match* parameter from the *ListProducts* method and add another version of the *ListProducts* method, called *ListMatching Products* that includes this parameter to the interface, as follows:

```
[ServiceContract]
public interface IProductsService
{
    // Get the product number of every product
    [FaultContract(typeof(SystemFault))]
    [FaultContract(typeof(DatabaseFault))]
    [OperationContract(ProtectionLevel= ProtectionLevel.EncryptAndSign)]
    List<string> ListProducts();
```

```
// Get the product numbers of matching products
[FaultContract(typeof(SystemFault))]
[FaultContract(typeof(DatabaseFault))]
[OperationContract(ProtectionLevel =  ProtectionLevel.EncryptAndSign)]
List<string> ListMatchingProducts(string match);
    ...
}
```

> **Note** C# permits you to have multiple methods in an interface and a class that have the
> same name as long as their signatures differ. This is called "overloading." So, in theory, you
> could create two versions of the same method, both called *ListProducts*, one of which takes
> no parameters and the other which takes a single string parameter. However, the SOAP
> standard does not allow a service to expose multiple operations that share the same name
> in the same service, so this approach would fail.
>
> Apart from giving the operations different names in the C# interface, an alternative
> approach is to use the *Name* property of the *OperationContract* attribute in the service
> contract, like this:
>
> ```
> [OperationContract(Name="ListMatchingProducts", ...]
> List<string> ListProducts(string match);
> ```
>
> WCF uses this property to generate the names for the SOAP request and response mes-
> sages. If you don't provide a value for the *Name* property, WCF uses the name of the
> method instead. You should also notice that the name of an operation in a service contract
> impacts the SOAP request and response messages, and is therefore a breaking change
> to the service contract which will render existing client applications unable to invoke this
> operation; instead, they may trip the *UnknownMessageReceived* event of the service host,
> as described in Chapter 3.

 3. Open the ProductsService.cs file in the Code And Text Editor window. In the
 ProductsServiceImpl class, change the name of the *ListProducts* method to
 ListMatchingProducts:

```
public class ProductsServiceImpl : IProductsService
{
    ...
    [PrincipalPermission(SecurityAction.Demand, Role = "WarehouseStaff")]
    public List<string> ListMatchingProducts(string match)
    {
        ...
    }
    ...
}
```

 4. After the *ListMatchingProducts* method, add a new implementation of the original
 ListProducts method to the *ProductsServiceImpl* class, as shown in bold in the following:

```
public class ProductsServiceImpl : IProductsService
{
    ...
    [PrincipalPermission(SecurityAction.Demand, Role = "WarehouseStaff")]
```

```
public List<string> ListMatchingProducts(string match)
{
    ...
}

[PrincipalPermission(SecurityAction.Demand, Role = "WarehouseStaff")]
public List<string> ListProducts()
{
    return ListMatchingProducts("");
}
...
}
```

The *ListProducts* method uses the *ListMatchingProducts* method, passing in an empty string as the parameter. The LINQ query in the *ListMatchingProducts* method will therefore return all products; the criteria that the LINQ query generates will be *where product.Name.Contains("")*.

5. Start the solution without debugging. In the Products Service Host window, click Start. In the client console window, press Enter. All tests should succeed, and the call to the *ListProducts* operation should return a complete list of product numbers.

6. Press Enter to close the client console window. In the Products Service Host window, click Stop, and then close the window.

Adding a new operation to a service contract is a nonbreaking change. If you are building a new WCF client application, you can generate a proxy that includes the new operation by using the *svcutil* utility. Existing client applications using the old version of the proxy still continue to function, but they are not aware that the new operation exists.

There is still a potential issue, however. If you want new client applications to be able to call only the new operation (*ListMatchingProducts*) and not use the older operation (*ListProducts*), how can you hide this operation from them? The answer is to use multiple service contracts. Keep the existing service contract unchanged, and define a new service contract that includes the new version of the operation but not the old version. The code fragments that follow show the existing contract (*IProductsService*), and the new one (*IProductsServiceV2*). The code fragments also show the recommended mechanism for identifying and naming the different versions of a service contract by using the *Namespace* and *Name* properties of the *ServiceContract* attribute. By default, the service contract uses the namespace *"http://tempuri.org,"* and takes its name from the name of the interface (if you recall, when using the Service Trace Viewer to examine the messages sent to the *ProductsService*, you saw that they were all of the form *"http://tempuri.org/IProductsService/..."*). When defining a new version of a service contract, use the *Namespace* property to identify the version by including the date, but keep the *Name* property the same for each version. However, be warned that modifying the *Namespace* or *Name* properties of a service contract constitutes a breaking change because these items are used to help identify the SOAP messages sent between the client application and the service:

```
// Service contract describing the operations provided by the WCF service
[ServiceContract(Namespace="http://adventure-works.com/2010/02/28", Name="IProductsService")]
public interface IProductsService
{
    // Get the product number of every product
    [FaultContract(typeof(SystemFault))]
    [FaultContract(typeof(DatabaseFault))]
    [OperationContract(ProtectionLevel = ProtectionLevel.EncryptAndSign)]
    List<string> ListProducts();

    // Get the details of a single product
    ...
}

// Version 2 of the service contract
[ServiceContract(Namespace="http://adventure-works.com/2010/05/31", Name="IProductsService")]
public interface IProductsServiceV2
{
    // Get the product number of matching products
    [FaultContract(typeof(SystemFault))]
    [FaultContract(typeof(DatabaseFault))]
    [OperationContract(ProtectionLevel = ProtectionLevel.EncryptAndSign)]
    List<string> ListMatchingProducts(string match);

    // Get the details of a single product
    ...
}
```

The service implementation class, *ProductsServiceImpl*, should implement both of these interfaces. The code for the methods common to both interfaces (*GetProduct*, *CurrentStockLevel*, and *ChangeStockLevel*) needs to be provided only once in this class:

```
public class ProductsServiceImpl : IProductsService, IProductsServiceV2
{
    // Implement ListProducts, ListSelectedProducts,
    // GetProduct, CurrentStockLevel, and ChangeStockLevel
    ...
}
```

Finally, create a separate set of endpoints for the new version of the service contract (one for each binding). You can use the WCF Service Configuration Edito, or edit the service configuration file by hand, adding an endpoint with the contract attribute set to **Products.IProductsServiceV2**, as shown in the following:

```
<system.serviceModel>
    ...
    <services>
        <service behaviorConfiguration="..." name="Products.ProductsServiceImpl">
            <endpoint ... contract="Products.IProductsServiceV2" />
        </service>
    </services>
</system.serviceModel>
```

Making Breaking and Nonbreaking Changes to a Service Contract

Strictly speaking, you should consider a service contract to be immutable; any changes that
you make to the contract are likely to affect client applications, which might no longer be able
to communicate with the service correctly. In practice, you have seen that you can make some
changes to a service contract without breaking the terms of this contract, as far as a WCF
client application is concerned. Table 6-1 summarizes some common changes that developers
frequently make to service contracts and the effects that these changes can have on existing
client applications.

TABLE 6-1 Service Contract Changes

Change	Effect
Adding a new operation	This is a nonbreaking change. Existing client applications are unaffected, but the new operation is not visible to WCF client applications connecting to the service by using a proxy generated from the WSDL description of the original service contract. Existing client applications that dynamically query services and construct messages can use the new operation. For more details, see Chapter 11, "Programmatically Controlling the Configuration and Communications."
Removing an operation	This is a breaking change. Existing client applications that invoke the operation will no longer function correctly, although client applications that do not use the operation may remain unaffected.
Changing the name of an operation	This is a breaking change. Existing client applications that invoke the operation will no longer work, although client applications that do not use the operation may remain unaffected.
	Note that the name of an operation defaults to the name of the method in the service contract. You can change the name of a method but retain the original name of the operation by using the *Name* property in the *OperationContract* attribute of the method, as follows:
	`[OperationContract (Name="ListProducts")]` `List<string>ListAllProducts();`
	This is good practice because it removes any dependency between the service contract and the name of the physical method that implements the operation.

Change	Effect
Changing the protection level of an operation	This is a breaking change. Existing client applications will not be able to invoke the operation.
Adding a parameter to an operation	This is a nonbreaking change. Existing client applications will be able to invoke the operation, but the formatter used by the WCF runtime will initialize missing parameter values to default values, depending on their type.
Reordering parameters in an operation	This is a breaking change. The results are not easily predictable (some existing client applications might continue to work).
Removing a parameter from an operation	This may be a nonbreaking change as long as the parameter is removed from the end of the parameter list, in which case any data passed by the client application for this parameter will be ignored. If a parameter is removed from the start or middle of a parameter list, then this is a breaking change for the same reasons as reordering parameters is a breaking change.
Changing the types of parameters or the return type of an operation	This may be breaking change if the formatter used by the WCF runtime cannot convert data from the original types to the new types. Existing client applications might continue to function, but there is a significant risk that data in SOAP messages will be lost or misinterpreted. This includes applying or removing the *ref* and *out* modifiers to parameters, even if the underlying type does not change. For more information, see the section "Modifying a Data Contract" on page 224.
Adding a FaultContract to an operation	This is a breaking change. Existing client applications can be sent fault messages that they will not be able to interpret correctly.
Removing a FaultContract from an operation	This is a nonbreaking change. Existing client applications will continue to function correctly, although any handlers for trapping the faults specified by this fault contract will be rendered obsolete.
Changing the *Name* or *Namespace* property of the *ServiceContract* attribute for a service contract	This is a breaking change. Existing client applications that use the previous name or namespace will no longer be able to send messages to the service.

If you make a breaking change to a service contract, you must update the client applications that use the service. If client applications use WCF proxies, you will need to regenerate these proxies. However, the recommended approach for modifying a service contract is to create a new version and to leave the existing version intact, as described in the previous section. This removes the requirement for you to update existing client applications, although they will not be able to use any new features of the service.

Modifying a Data Contract

The methods in a service contract can take parameters and return values. The data for these parameters and return values is included in the SOAP messages that pass between the client application and service. SOAP messages encode data values as tagged XML text. The WCF runtime uses the built-in XML serialization features of the .NET Framework to serialize and deserialize primitive .NET Framework data types, such as integers, real numbers, or even strings. For more complex structured types, the service must specify the exact format for the serialized representation; there could be several ways to depict the same structured data as XML. You define structured types by using data contracts. The WCF runtime can then use a data contract serializer (an instance of the *DataContractSerializer* class) to serialize and deserialize these types.

Using a data contract, you can specify exactly how the service expects the data to be formatted as XML. The data contract is used by a data contract serializer in WCF client applications to describe how to serialize the data for parameters into XML. It is also used by a data contract serializer in the service to deserialize the XML back into data values that it can process. Values returned by a service are similarly serialized as XML and transmitted back to the client application that deserializes them.

Data Contract and Data Member Attributes

In Chapter 1, you saw how to define a simple data contract representing product data that the service returns to client applications. To remind you, this is what the data contract looks like:

```
// Data contract describing the details of a product passed to client applications
    [DataContract]
public class ProductData
{
    [DataMember]
    public string Name;

    [DataMember]
    public string ProductNumber;

    [DataMember]
    public string Color;

    [DataMember]
    public decimal ListPrice;
}
```

Tagging a class with the *DataContract* attribute marks it as serializable by using the data contract serializer. The data contract serializer will serialize and deserialize each member of the class marked with the *DataMember* attribute. In the example shown in the following code, the members of the class are .NET Framework primitive types, and the serializer uses its own built-in rules to convert these types into a form that can be included in an XML message, like this:

```
<GetProductResponse xmlns="http://adventure-works.com/2010/02/28">
  <GetProductResult xmlns:d4p1="http://schemas.datacontract.org/2004/07/Products"
  xmlns:i="http://www.w3.org/2001/XMLSchema-instance">
    <d4p1:Color i:nil="true"></d4p1:Color>
    <d4p1:ListPrice>4.9900</d4p1:ListPrice>
    <d4p1:Name>Water Bottle - 30 oz.</d4p1:Name>
    <d4p1:ProductNumber>WB-H098</d4p1:ProductNumber>
  </GetProductResult>
</GetProductResponse>
```

If any of the members of a data contract are themselves structured types, they should also be marked with the *DataContract* attribute. The data contract serializer can then recursively apply its own serialization and deserialization process to these members.

The *DataContract* and *DataMember* attributes have optional properties that you can use to tailor the way in which the data contract serializer performs its work. You will investigate some of these properties in the exercises in this section.

Change the Order of Members in the *ProductData* Data Contract

1. Using Visual Studio, open the solution file, ProductsService.sln, located in the Microsoft Press\WCF Step By Step\Chapter 6\ProductsServiceWithVersionedServiceContract folder.

    This solution contains the implementation of the *ProductsService* service that provides two versions of the service contract, as described in the previous section of this chapter. The client application still uses version 1 of the service contract.

2. Open the IProductsService.cs file in the ProductsServiceLibrary project and locate the *ProductData* class. Note that the order of the members of this class is *Name*, *Product-Number*, *Color*, and *ListPrice*.

3. Edit the App.config file for the ProductsServiceHost project by using the Service Configuration Editor.

4. In the Configuration pane, click the Diagnostics folder. In the right pane click the MessageLog link. In the Listener Settings dialog box, change the path of the log file so that the trace output is sent to the ProductsService.svclog file in the Microsoft Press\ WCF Step By Step\Chapter 6 folder, and then click OK.

 Note The WCF service configuration file for this version of the solution enables tracing at the service level rather than the transport level. All messages are traced in their unencrypted format to make it easier for you to examine their contents.

5. Save the changes, and then exit the Service Configuration Editor.

6. Using Windows Explorer, delete the Products.svclog file in the Microsoft Press\WCF Step By Step\Chapter 6 folder.

7. In Visual Studio, start the solution without debugging. In the Products Service Host window, click Start. In the client console window, press Enter.

   All tests should run successfully.

8. Press Enter to close the client console window. In the Products Service Host window, click Stop, and then close the window.

9. Return to the Service Trace Viewer and open the Products.svclog file in the Microsoft Press\WCF Step By Step\Chapter 6 folder.

10. In the left pane, click the Message tab. Click the fourth message in the *http://adventure-works.com/2010/02/28* namespace. This is the *GetProductResponse* message sent by the service to the client when replying to a *GetProduct* message.

11. In the lower-right pane, click the Message tab. Examine the body of the SOAP message; note that the order of the fields in this message is *Color*, *ListPrice*, *Name*, and *ProductNumber*.

    This sequence is different from the order of the members in the *Product* class. This is because the data contract serializer serializes the members of a data contract in alphabetic order.

12. Close the Products.svclog trace file, but leave the Service Trace Viewer open.

13. Return to Visual Studio and edit the IProductsService.cs file in the ProductsService Library project. Amend the *DataMember* attributes of each member, as shown in bold in the following:

```
[DataContract]
public class Product
{
    [DataMember(Order=0)]
    public string Name;

    [DataMember(Order=1)]
    public string ProductNumber;

    [DataMember(Order=2)]
    public string Color;

    [DataMember(Order=3)]
    public decimal ListPrice;
}
```

Rather than let the names of members imply an order, it is recommended that you use the *Order* property of the *DataMember* attribute to explicitly specify the sequence of the members. The data contract serializer will serialize members of the *Product* class in the sequence defined by the *Order* property, starting with the member with the lowest *Order* value. If two members have the same *Order* value, then they will be serialized in alphabetic order.

14. Using Windows Explorer, delete the Products.svclog file in the Microsoft Press\WCF Step By Step\Chapter 6 folder.

15. In Visual Studio, start the solution without debugging. In the Products Service Host window, click Start. In the client console window, press Enter.

All tests appear to run successfully. However, if you examine the output from Test 2 displaying the details of a product more closely, you should see that the *Price* is *0* rather than $4.99. Changing the order of members in a data contract is a breaking change, and the formatter used by the client application has not deserialized the data correctly (you will fix the client application later).

> **Note** The *Color* is also missing for the same reason, but this is less obvious because product WB-H098 has a null value in the database for the color. However, if the color value in the database was not null, it would be missing from the data displayed by the client application.

16. Press Enter to close the client console window. In the Products Service Host window, click Stop, and then close the window.

17. Return to the Service Trace Viewer and open the Products.svclog file in the Microsoft Press\WCF Step By Step\Chapter 6 folder.

18. In the left pane, click the Message tab. Click the fourth message in the *http://adventure-works.com/2010/02/28* namespace. In the lower-right pane, click the Message tab. Note that the order of the fields in this message is now *Name*, *ProductNumber*, *Color*, and *ListPrice*. This sequence now matches the order of the members in the *Product* class. You can see that the service is emitting the data in the products contract in the correct sequence even though the client application is not handling this data correctly when it receives it.

19. Close the Products.svclog trace file, but leave the Service Trace Viewer open.

You need to regenerate the proxy for the client application to make things work properly. Before doing that though, it is worth looking at how changing the names of data members also affects a data contract.

In a manner similar to the service contract, the data contract serializer uses the name of each data member to form the name of each serialized field. Consequently, changing the name of a data member is also a breaking change that requires updating client applications. Like the operations in a service contract, you can provide a logical name for data members that the data contract serializer will use in place of the physical name of the data members; the

DataMember attribute provides the *Name* property for this purpose. You can use this feature to rename the physical members of a data contract while keeping the logical names the same, as shown in bold in the following:

```
[DataContract]
public class Product
{
    [DataMember(Order=0)]
    public string Name;   // Serializer uses physical name of member

    [DataMember(Order=1, Name="ProductNumber")]
    public string Number; // Field renamed. Serializer uses Name property
    ...
}
```

The *DataContract* attribute provides a *Namespace* property. By default, WCF uses the namespace "*http://schemas.datacontract.org/2004/07*" with the .NET Framework namespace containing the data contract appended to the end. In the *ProductsService* service, the *ProductData* data contract is a member of the *Products* .NET Framework namespace, so messages are serialized with the namespace "*http://schemas.datacontract.org/2004/07/Products*." You can override this behavior by specifying a value for the *Namespace* property of the *DataContract* attribute. This is good practice; you can include date information in the namespace to help identify a specific version of the data contract. If you update the data contract, then modify the namespace to include the date of the update.

Change the Namespace of the *ProductData* Data Contract

1. In Visual Studio, edit the IProductsService.cs file in the ProductsServiceLibrary project.

2. Modify the *DataContract* attribute for the *ProductData* class, as shown in bold in the following:

```
[DataContract(Namespace="http://adventure-works.com/datacontract/2010/06/01/Products")]
public class ProductData
{
    ...
}
```

(For the purposes of this exercise, assume that the current date is 1 June, 2010.)

3. Using Windows Explorer, delete the Products.svclog file in the Microsoft Press\WCF Step By Step\Chapter 6 folder.

4. In Visual Studio, start the solution without debugging. In the Products Service Host window, click Start. In the client console window, press Enter.

   All tests should run, but this time Test 2 is also missing the product number and name (previously, only the price and color were omitted). Changing the namespace for a data contract is another example of a breaking change.

5. Press Enter to close the client console window. In the Products Service Host window, click Stop, and then close the window.

6. Return to the Service Trace Viewer and open the Products.svclog file in the Microsoft Press\WCF Step By Step\Chapter 6 folder.

7. In the left pane, click the Message tab. Click the fourth message in the *http://adventure-works.com/2010/02/28* namespace. In the lower-right pane, click the Message tab. Verify that the namespace for the fields in the message body is the new namespace; the *<GetProductResult>* element creates an alias for the namespace called *"d4p1,"* and the fields in the message are prefixed with this alias.

8. Close the Products.svclog trace file, but leave the Service Trace Viewer open.

You can see that the *ProductsService* service is formatting messages as expected, although the client application is not currently processing them correctly. The next step is to regenerate the proxy for the client application. You will also take the opportunity to switch the client application to use the *IProductsServiceV2* interface.

Regenerate the Proxy Class and Update the WCF Client Application

1. Open a Visual Studio Command Prompt window and move to the folder \Microsoft Press\WCF Step By Step\Chapter 6\ProductsServiceWithVersionedServiceContract\ProductsServiceLibrary\bin\Debug folder.

2. Run the following command to generate the schema files and WSDL description file for the *ProductsService* service:

```
svcutil ProductsServiceLibrary.dll
```

This command generates the following files:

- ❑ adventure-works.com.2010.02.28.wsdl
- ❑ adventure-works.com.2010.05.31.wsdl
- ❑ adventure-works.com.2010.02.28.xsd
- ❑ adventure-works.com.2010.05.31.xsd
- ❑ schemas.microsoft.com.2003.10.Serialization.xsd
- ❑ schemas.microsoft.com.2003.10.Serialization.Arrays.xsd
- ❑ Products.xsd
- ❑ adventure-works.com.datacontract.2010.06.01.Products.xsd

Notice that as the service now contains two service contracts, this command generates two WSDL description files with their corresponding schemas.

3. Type the following command on a single line to generate the proxy class from the WSDL description file for the version 2 interface (2010.05.31) and the schema files. The /out parameter specifies the name of the .cs file generated for the proxy class.

```
svcutil /namespace:*,ProductsClient.ProductsService
    adventure-works.com.2010.05.31.wsdl *.xsd /out:ProductsV2.cs
```

> **Note** If you need to generate a proxy for the version 1 interface (2010.02.28), then simply specify the appropriate WSDL file.

4. Leave the Visual Studio Command Prompt window open and return to Visual Studio.

5. In the ProductsClient project, delete the Products.cs file.

6. Add the file, ProductsV2.cs, located in the Microsoft Press\WCF Step By Step\Chapter 6\ ProductsServiceWithVersionedServiceContract\ProductsServiceLibrary\bin\Debug folder to the ProductsClient project.

7. Open the ProductsV2.cs file in the Code And Text Editor and locate the *IProducts Service* interface. Notice that the *Action* and *ReplyAction* message in the *Operation Contract* definitions for each method now specify messages the *http://adventure-works. com/2010/05/31/IProductsService* namespace.

8. The client application currently invokes the *ListProducts* operation. This operation is not available in version 2 of the *ProductsService* service. Open the Program.cs file in the *ProductsClient* project in the Code And Text Editor window. In the *Main* method, change the code that performs Test 1 to call the *ListMatchingProducts* method, passing in a product name that matches all bicycle frames, as shown in bold in the following:

```
static void Main(string[] args)
{
    ...
    // Test the operations in the service

    try
    {
        // Obtain a list of all bicycle frames
        Console.WriteLine("Test 1: List all bicycle frames");
        string[] productNumbers = proxy.ListMatchingProducts("Frame");
        foreach (string productNumber in productNumbers)
        {
            Console.WriteLine("Number: {0}", productNumber);
        }
        Console.WriteLine();
        ...
    }
    ...
}
```

9. Start the solution without debugging. In the Products Service Host window, click Start. In the client console window, press Enter.

   All tests should run successfully. Test 1 should display fewer items than before (the product numbers should all begin with the text "FR" to indicate that they are bicycle frames), and Test 2 should now display valid data for product WB-H098 (a 30 oz. water bottle of unspecified color that costs $4.99).

10. Press Enter to close the client console window. In the Products Service Host form, click Stop, and then close the window.

You can now see that you should carefully assess the impact of updating a data contract; doing so can cause client applications to malfunction in ways that are not always obvious. The nature of SOAP serialization means that reorganized or misplaced fields end up being assigned default values, which are very easy to miss.

You can also add new members to a data contract. Under some circumstances, you can perform this task without breaking existing client applications. You should notice that adding a member to a data contract changes the schema exported by WCF. Client applications use this schema to determine the format of the data they send and receive in SOAP messages. Many client applications that use SOAP (including those built by using WCF and ASP.NET Web services) will happily ignore additional fields in SOAP messages. However, a small number of client applications created by using other technologies can enable strict schema validation. If you have to support these types of client applications, you cannot add new fields to a data contract without updating those client applications, as well. In these cases, you should adopt a data contract versioning strategy similar to that shown for versioning service contracts. For more information, see the topic, Best Practices: Data Contract Versioning in the documentation provided with Visual Studio (also available on the Microsoft Web site at *http://msdn.microsoft.com/en-us/library/ms733832.aspx*).

In the following exercises you will examine the effects of adding a new field to a data contract in a WCF service, and see how a WCF client application handles this unexpected data.

Add a New Field to the *ProductData* Data Contract

1. Using Visual Studio, edit the IProductsService.cs file in the ProductsServiceLibrary project.

2. Add the following member (shown in bold) to the end of the *ProductData* class:

```
public class ProductData
{
    ...
    [DataMember(Order=0)]
    public decimal StandardCost;
}
```

The *StandardCost* in the *Product* table in the *AdventureWorks* database records the cost of the product to the AdventureWorks organization. The difference between the value in the *ListPrice* column and *StandardCost* is the profit that AdventureWorks makes whenever it sells an item. Adding this member with the *Order* property set to *0* causes it to be serialized as the second member of the data contract. The *Name* member, which also has the *Order* property set to *0*, will be output first, as it comes alphabetically before *StandardCost*.

Note As mentioned earlier, I would not normally recommend that you rely on alphabetical order to determine the sequence of members in a data contract, but in this case there is a reason for this approach; you will quickly be able to see what happens in a client application when an unexpected data member appears in the middle of a data contract.

3. In the ProductsService.cs file, find the *GetProduct* method in the *ProductsServiceImpl* class. In this method, update the statement that retrieves product information from the database and populates the *productData* object returned by this method, as shown in bold in the following:

```
public ProductData GetProduct(string productNumber)
{
    ...
    try
    {
        // Connect to the AdventureWorks database by using the Entity Framework
        using (AdventureWorksEntities database = new AdventureWorksEntities())
        {
            // Check that the specified product exists
            if (ProductExists(productNumber, database))
            {
                ...
                productData = new ProductData()
                {
                    Name = matchingProduct.Name,
                    ProductNumber = matchingProduct.ProductNumber,
                    Color = matchingProduct.Color,
                    ListPrice = matchingProduct.ListPrice,
                    StandardCost = matchingProduct.StandardCost
                };
            }
        }
    }
    ...
}
```

4. Using Windows Explorer, delete the Products.svclog file in the Microsoft Press\WCF Step By Step\Chapter 6 folder.

5. In Visual Studio, start the solution without debugging. In the Products Service Host window, click Start. In the client console window, press Enter.

All tests should run successfully, including Test 2, which completely ignores the new member of the data contract. Adding a new member in the middle of a data contract does not appear to affect the client application at all.

6. Press Enter to close the client console window. In the Products Service Host form, click Stop, and then close the window.

7. Return to the Service Trace Viewer and open the Products.svclog file in the Microsoft Press\WCF Step By Step\Chapter 6 folder.

8. In the left pane, click the Message tab. Click the fourth message in the *http://adventure-works.com/2010/05/31* namespace. Remember that this is the *GetProductResponse* message sent by the service to the client when replying to a *GetProduct* message.

9. In the lower-right pane, click the Message tab. Scroll this pane to display the body of the SOAP message. Notice that the *StandardCost* field appears between the *Name* and *ProductNumber* fields.

   The data contract serializer serializes every member of the data contract. The WCF client application is not expecting the *StandardCost* field, and as it does not perform strict schema validation, the client application simply ignores this extra field.

10. Close the Products.svclog trace file, and then close the Service Trace Viewer.

11. Regenerate the proxy class for the client application:

    a. Return to the Visual Studio Command Prompt window in the Microsoft Press\WCF Step By Step\Chapter 6\ProductsServiceV2\ProductsService\bin folder. Run the command:

    ```
    svcutil ProductsServiceLibrary.dll
    ```

    b. Run the command:

    ```
    svcutil /namespace:*,ProductsClient.ProductsService
        adventure-works.com.2010.05.31.wsdl *.xsd /out:ProductsV2.cs
    ```

12. Return to Visual Studio. In the ProductsClient project, delete the ProductsV2.cs file and replace it with the new file located in the Microsoft Press\WCF Step By Step\Chapter 6\ProductsServiceWithVersionedServiceContract\ProductsServiceLibrary\bin\Debug folder.

13. Edit the Program.cs file in the ProductsClient project. In the *Main* method, add a statement (shown in bold in the following code) after the code that performs Test 2 to display the standard cost:

```
static void Main(string[] args)
{
    ...
    try
    {
        ...
        Console.WriteLine("Test 2: Display the details of a product");
```

```
        ProductData product = proxy.GetProduct("WB-H098");
        if (product != null)
        {
            Console.WriteLine("Number: {0}", product.ProductNumber);
            Console.WriteLine("Name: {0}", product.Name);
            Console.WriteLine("Color: {0}", product.Color);
            Console.WriteLine("Price: {0}", product.ListPrice);
            Console.WriteLine("Standard Cost: {0}", product.StandardCost);
            Console.WriteLine();
        }
        ...
    }
    ...
}
```

14. Start the solution without debugging. In the Products Service Host window, click Start. In the client console window, press Enter.

    All tests should run successfully, and Test 2 should now include the standard cost ($1.8663).

15. Press Enter to close the client console window. In the Products Service Host window, click Stop, and then close the window.

While it is acceptable for a client application to discard a field sent by the service, this scenario can cause complications if the client application is later expected to send data to the service that includes this missing field. You will examine this scenario in the next exercise.

Add Another Operation to the WCF Service for Investigating Data Contract Serialization

1. In Visual Studio, edit the IProductsService.cs file in the ProductsServiceLibrary project.

2. Add the following operation (shown in bold) to the *IProductServiceV2* service contract:

```
public interface IProductServiceV2
{
    ...
    // Update the details of the specified product in the database
    [OperationContract]
    void UpdateProductDetails(ProductData product);
}
```

A client application can use this operation to modify the details of a product in the database.

3. Add the implementation of the *UpdateProductDetails* method to the end of the *Products ServiceImpl* class in the ProductsService.cs file, as shown in the following:

```
public class ProductsServiceImpl : ...
{
    ...
```

```
public void UpdateProductDetails(ProductData product)
{
    MessageBox.Show("Updating: " + product.Name, "UpdateProductDetails",
                MessageBoxButton.OK, MessageBoxImage.Information);
    try
    {
        // Connect to the AdventureWorks database by using the Entity Framework
        using (AdventureWorksEntities database = new AdventureWorksEntities())
        {
            if (!ProductExists(product.ProductNumber, database))
                return;
            else
            {
                // Find the product, using the ProductNumber as the key
                Product productToUpdate =
                    (from p in database.Products
                     where
                     String.Compare(p.ProductNumber, product.ProductNumber) == 0
                     select p).First();

                // Update the product
                productToUpdate.Name = product.Name;
                productToUpdate.ListPrice = product.ListPrice;
                productToUpdate.StandardCost = product.StandardCost;
                productToUpdate.Color = product.Color;

                // Save the change back to the database
                database.SaveChanges();
            }
        }
    }
    catch(Exception e)
    {
        MessageBox.Show("Error updating product: " + e.Message,
                    "UpdateProductDetails",
                        MessageBoxButton.OK, MessageBoxImage.Error);
    }
}
```

 Note   The code for this method is available in the UpdateProductDetails.txt file, which is in the Microsoft Press\WCF Step By Step\Chapter 6 folder.

This method displays the product number and name sent by the client application and then updates the corresponding product in the database. Note that for reasons described in previous chapters it is not normal, and certainly not good practice—to display messages in a WCF service; these statements are for instructional purposes for this exercise only—so that you can verify that the client application successfully invokes the *UpdateProductDetails* operation.

4. Build the solution.

5. Regenerate the proxy class for the client application:

    a. In the Visual Studio Command Prompt window, run the following command:

```
svcutil ProductsServiceLibrary.dll
```

    b. Run the following command to rebuild the proxy class:

```
svcutil /namespace:*,ProductsClient.ProductsService
       adventure-works.com.2010.05.31.wsdl *.xsd /out:ProductsV2.cs
```

6. Return to Visual Studio. In the ProductsClient project, delete the ProductsV2.cs file and replace it with the new file located in the Microsoft Press\WCF Step By Step\Chapter 6\ProductsServiceV2\ProductsService\bin folder.

7. Edit the Program.cs file in the ProductsClient project. In the *Main* method, add the following statements that test the new operation to the *try* block:

```
static void Main(string[] args)
{
    ...
    try
    {
        ...
        // Modify the details of this product
        Console.WriteLine("Test 5: Modify the details of a product");
        product.ProductNumber = "WB-H098";
        product.Name = "Water Bottle - 1 liter";
        proxy.UpdateProductDetails(product);
        Console.WriteLine("Request sent");
        Console.WriteLine();

        // Disconnect from the service
        proxy.Close();
    }
    ...
}
```

8. Start the solution without debugging. In the Products Service Host window, click Start. In the client console window, press Enter.

When Test 5 runs, a message box appears displaying the product number and the new product name.

Click OK to close the message box.

9. Press Enter to close the client console window. In the Products Service Host window, click Stop, and then close the window.

The client application successfully sends a *Product* object to the WCF service using the definition from the data contract. But what happens if the client application uses a version of the data contract that is missing a field?

Add Another Field to the *ProductData* Data Contract and Examine the Default Value

1. In Visual Studio, edit the IProductsService.cs file in the ProductsServiceLibrary project.

2. Add the following member (shown in bold) to the end of the *ProductData* data contract:

```
public class ProductData
{
    ...
    [DataMember(Order = 4)]
    public bool FinishedGoodsFlag;
}
```

The *FinishedGoodsFlag* in the *Product* table in the *AdventureWorks* database indicates whether the product is a complete item (such as a water bottle) or a component used to construct other parts (such as a chaining nut).

3. In the *UpdateProductDetails* method in the *ProductsServiceImpl* class in the Products Service.cs file, modify the statement that displays the product details to include the *FinishedGoodsFlag* member:

```
public class ProductsServiceImpl : ...
{
    ...
    public void UpdateProductDetails(ProductData product)
    {
        MessageBox.Show("Updating: " + product.Name + "\nFinished Goods Flag: " +
                product.FinishedGoodsFlag, "UpdateProductDetails",
                MessageBoxButton.OK, MessageBoxImage.Information);
        try
        {
            ...
        }
        ...
    }
}
```

4. Start the solution without debugging. In the Products Service Host window, click Start. In the client console window, press Enter.

   When Test 5 runs, the message box displays the value *False* for the *FinishedGoodsFlag*. The client application is still using the old version of the Product data contract and did not populate this field—this is the default value for a Boolean field in a SOAP message.

   Click OK to close the message box.

5. Press Enter to close the client console window. In the Products Service Host window, click Stop, and then close the window.

As when changing the order of data members, you should be very mindful of existing client applications when adding a new member to a data contract. If the client application does not populate every field in a serialized object, WCF will use default values—*False* for Booleans, *0* for numerics, and *null* for objects. If these default values are unacceptable, you can customize the serialization and deserialization process by implementing serialization callback methods in the WCF service.

> **More Info** The details of customizing the serialization process are beyond the scope of this book, but for more information, examine the topic Version Tolerant Serialization in the documentation supplied with Visual Studio (also available on the Microsoft Web site at *http://msdn.microsoft.com/en-us/library/ms229752.aspx*).

Data Contract Compatibility

If you need to version a data contract, you should do so in a manner that maintains compatibility with existing client applications. The *DataMember* attribute provides two properties that can assist you:

- *IsRequired*   If you set this property to true, then the SOAP message that the service receives must include a value in this data member. By default, the value of this property is *false*, and the WCF runtime will generate default values for any missing fields.

- *EmitDefaultValue*   If you set this property to *true*, the WCF runtime on the client will generate a default value for a data member if it is not included in the SOAP message sent by the client application. This property is *true* by default.

If you need to maintain strict conformance to a data contract in future versions of the service, you should set the *IsRequired* property of each data member in the data contract to **true** and set the *EmitDefaultValue* property to **false** when building the first version of a service. You should *never* make a data member mandatory (*IsRequired* set to *true*) in a new version of a data contract if it was previously optional (*IsRequired* set to *false*). This helps to maintain backward compatibility with older clients.

There is one further question that you should consider: it is possible for a client application to request data conforming to a data contract from a service, modify that data, and then submit it back to the service in a manner similar to calling the *GetProduct* method followed by the *UpdateProductDetails* method in the *ProductsService* example? If a client application uses the old version of a data contract that is missing one or more members, such as the *FinishedGoodsFlag*, what happens to this information when the client sends the data back to the service? The WCF runtime implements a technique called *round-tripping* to ensure that data does not become lost. You will examine how this feature works in the next exercise.

Examine How the WCF Runtime Performs Round-Tripping

1. In Visual Studio, edit the ProductsService.cs file in the ProductsServiceLibrary project.

2. In the *GetProduct* method in the *ProductsServiceImpl* class, add the following statement (shown in bold) to the end of the block of code that populates the *ProductData* object returned by the method:

```
public ProductData GetProduct(string productNumber)
{
    ...
    try
    {
        // Connect to the AdventureWorks database by using the Entity Framework
        using (AdventureWorksEntities database = new AdventureWorksEntities())
        {
            // Check that the specified product exists
            if (ProductExists(productNumber, database))
            {
                ...
                productData = new ProductData()
                {
                    Name = matchingProduct.Name,
                    ProductNumber = matchingProduct.ProductNumber,
                    Color = matchingProduct.Color,
                    ListPrice = matchingProduct.ListPrice,
                    StandardCost = matchingProduct.StandardCost,
                    FinishedGoodsFlag = true
                };
            }
        }
    }
    ...
}
```

This code sets the *FinishedGoodsFlag* to *true*. Remember that the default value for Booleans is *false*.

3. Start the solution without debugging. In the Products Service Host window, click Start. In the client console window, press Enter.

When Test 5 runs, the message box displays the value *True* for the *FinishedGoodsFlag* field. This is the value originally provided by the service; it has been sent through the client application and back to the service. Although the client application does not know anything about this field, it has managed to preserve its value.

Click OK to close the message box.

4. Press Enter to close the client console window. In the Products Service Host window, click Stop, and then close the window.

The WCF runtime implements round-tripping by using the *IExtensibleDataObject* interface. If you examine the code in the ProductsV2.cs file, you will see that the client proxy version of the *ProductData* class implements this interface. This interface defines a single property called *ExtensionData*, of type *ExtensionDataObject*. The *ExtensionData* property generated for the client proxy simply reads and writes data to a private field of type *ExtensionObjectData*, as follows:

```
public partial class ProductData : object,
    System.Runtime.Serialization.IExtensibleDataObject
{
    private System.Runtime.Serialization.ExtensionDataObject
        extensionDataField;
    ...

    public System.Runtime.Serialization.ExtensionDataObject ExtensionData
    {
        get
        {
            return this.extensionDataField;
        }
        set
        {
            this.extensionDataField = value;
        }
    }
    ...
}
```

The *extensionDataField* field acts as a "bucket" for all undefined data items received by the client; rather than discarding them, the proxy automatically stores them in this field. When the client proxy transmits the *ProductData* object back to the service, it includes the data in this field. If you need to disable this feature (for example, if you want to ensure strict schema compliance in client applications), you can set the *IgnoreExtensionDataObject* property of the data contract serializer in the endpoint behavior to *true* for the endpoint that the client is using. You can perform this task by defining an endpoint behavior in the client application configuration file, such as this:

```
<?xml version="1.0" encoding="utf-8" ?>
<configuration>
  <system.serviceModel>
    <behaviors>
      <endpointBehaviors>
        <behavior name="IgnoreExtensionDataBehavior">
          <dataContractSerializer ignoreExtensionDataObject="true"/>
        </behavior>
      </endpointBehaviors>
    </behaviors>
```

```
    <client>
      <endpoint address="http://localhost:8010/ProductsService/Service.svc"
          binding="ws2007HttpBinding" bindingConfiguration=""
          contract="ProductsClient.ProductsService.IProductsService"
          name="WS2007HttpBinding_IProductsService"
          behaviorConfiguration="IgnoreExtensionDataBehavior"/>
    </client>
  </system.serviceModel>
</configuration>
```

You can also disable extension data objects on the server-side by setting the *IgnoreExtension DataObject* property of the data contract serializer for a single service endpoint or for all server endpoints by adding a service behavior.

Data Contract Serialization and Security

A data contract provides a potential entry point for a malicious user to hack into your system. You must design your data contracts to be resistant to misuse such as this.

A common example is a *Denial of Service* attack. In this type of attack, a user invokes methods in your service by sending them vast quantities of data. Your service then spends much of its time simply trying to receive and read this data, and performance suffering accordingly. To avoid this type of attack, don't define data contracts that involve large, nested data structures, arrays, or collections of indeterminate length. If you must define data contracts that allow a user to send an array, collection, or nested data, then limit the size of the data that they can send by using the *readerQuota* properties of the service bindings, as shown in bold in the following:

```
<system.serviceModel>
    <bindings>
        <netTcpBinding>
            <binding name="ProductsServiceTcpBindingConfig">
                <readerQuotas maxDepth="2" maxStringContentLength="1024"
                              maxArrayLength="1024" />
                ...
            </binding>
        </netTcpBinding>
    </bindings>
    <services>
        <service ...>
            <endpoint binding="netTcpBinding"
            bindingConfiguration="ProductsServiceTcpBindingConfig" .../>
            ...
        </service>
    </services>
</system.serviceModel>
```

The *readerQuotas* properties include:

- *MaxArrayLength*   This is the maximum length of any array (in bytes) that the user can send to the service.

- *MaxDepth*   If a data structure contains nested data structures, this value specifies the maximum level of nesting allowed.

- *MaxStringContentLength*   This is the maximum length of any string (in characters) that the user can send to the service.

If a client application attempts to send a message that exceeds these parameters, WCF will abort the request. You will learn more about *readerQuota* properties in Chapter 13, "Implementing a WCF Service for Good Performance."

Summary

In this chapter, you have learned how WCF uses service and data contracts to define the operations that a service exposes to client applications and the information that client applications can send to, or receive from, these operations. You have seen why it is important to design service and data contracts carefully, and how to create new versions of service and data contracts while maintaining compatibility with existing client applications.

Chapter 7
Maintaining State and Sequencing Operations

After completing this chapter, you will be able to:

- Describe how WCF creates an instance of a service.

- Explain the different options available for creating service instances.

- Manage state information in a WCF service in a scalable manner.

- Fine tune the way in which the WCF runtime manages service instances.

- Describe how to control the life cycle of a service instance.

- Describe how to create durable services that can persist their state to a database.

In all the exercises that you have performed so far, the client application has invoked a series of operations in a WCF service. The order of these operations has been immaterial, so calling one operation before another has had no impact on the functionality of either; the operations are totally independent. In the real world, a Web service might require that operations be invoked in a particular sequence. For example, if you are implementing shopping cart functionality in a service, it does not make sense to allow a client application to perform a check-out operation to pay for goods before actually putting anything into the shopping cart.

The issue of sequencing operations should naturally lead you to consider the need to maintain state information between operations. Taking the shopping cart example, where should you store the data that describes the items in the shopping cart? You have at least two options:

- Maintain the shopping cart in the client application. With this method, you pass the information that describes the shopping cart contents as a parameter to each server-based operation and return the updated shopping cart contents from the operation back to the client. This is a variation of the solution implemented by traditional Web applications (including ASP.NET Web applications) that used cookies stored on the user's computer to store information. It relieved the Web application of the burden of maintaining state information between client calls, but there was nothing to stop the client application directly modifying the data in the cookie or even inadvertently corrupting it in some manner. Additionally, cookies can be a security risk, and as a result, many Web browsers implement features that let users disable them. This makes it difficult to store state information on the user's computer. In a Web service environment (as opposed to a Web application and browser combination), a client application can maintain state information using its own code rather than relying on cookies. However, this strategy ties the client application to the Web service and can result in a very tight coupling between the two, with all the inherent fragility and maintenance problems that this can cause.

- Maintain the shopping cart contents in the service. The first time the user running the client application attempts to add something to the shopping cart, the service creates a data structure to represent the items being added. As the user adds further items to the shopping cart, they are stored in this data structure. When the user wants to pay for the items in the shopping cart, the service can calculate the total, perform an exchange with the user through the client application to establish the payment method, and then arrange for dispatch of the items. In a WCF environment, all interactions between the client application and the service are performed by invoking well-defined operations, specified by using a service contract. Additionally, the client application does not need to know how the service actually implements the shopping cart.

The second approach sounds like the more promising of the two, but there are several issues that you must address when building a Web service to handle this scenario. In this chapter, you will investigate some of these issues and see how you can resolve them.

Managing State in a WCF Service

It makes sense to look at how to manage and maintain state in a WCF service first and then return to the issue of sequencing operations later.

The exercises that you performed in previous chapters involved stateless operations. All the information required to perform an operation in the *ProductsService* service was passed in as a series of parameters by the client application. When the operation completes, the service "forgets" that the client ever invoked it. In the shopping cart scenario, the situation is different. You must maintain the shopping cart between operations. In the exercises in this section, you will learn that this approach, although apparently simple, requires a little thought and careful design to work reliably in a scalable manner.

Create the *ShoppingCartService* Service

1. Using Visual Studio, create a new project by using the WCF Service Library template in the WCF folder (within the Visual C# folder), in the Installed Templates pane. Specify the following properties for the solution:

Property	Value
Name	ShoppingCartService
Location	Microsoft Press\WCF Step By Step\Chapter 7
Solution name	ShoppingCart

2. In Solution Explorer, rename the IService1.cs file to **IShoppingCartService.cs** and allow Visual Studio to rename all references to *IService1* to *IShoppingCartService* when prompted.

3. Change the name of the Service1.cs file to **ShoppingCartServce.cs**. Again, allow Visual Studio to rename all references to *Service1* to *ShoppingCartService*.

4. Add a reference to the *ProductsEntityModel* assembly, which is located in the Microsoft Press\WCF Step By Step\Chapter 7 folder (within your Documents folder). Remember that this assembly contains a copy of the entity model for the *Product* and *Product-Inventory* tables in the *AdventureWorks* database.

5. Add a reference to the *System.Data.Entity* assembly. This assembly is required by the *ProductsEntityModel* assembly.

6. Open the IShoppingCartService.cs file in the Code And Text Editor window. Delete all the comments and code except the *using* statements at the top of the file and the *ShoppingCartService* namespace.

7. Add the following class (shown in bold) to the *ShoppingCartService* namespace:

```
namespace ShoppingCartService
{
    // Shopping cart item
    class ShoppingCartItem
    {
        public string ProductNumber { get; set; }
        public string ProductName { get; set; }
        public decimal Cost { get; set; }
        public int Volume { get; set; }
    }
}
```

This class defines the items that can be stored in the shopping cart, which will contain a list of these items. Notice that this is not a data contract; this type is for internal use by the service. If a client application queries the contents of the shopping cart, the service will send it a simplified representation as a string. This way, there should be no dependencies between the structure of the shopping cart and the client applications that manipulate instances of it.

8. Add the following service contract to the *ShoppingCartService* namespace, after the *ShoppingCartItem* class:

```
namespace ShoppingCartService
{
    ...

    [ServiceContract(Namespace = "http://adventure-works.com/2010/06/04",
                    Name = "ShoppingCartService")]
    public interface IShoppingCartService
    {
        [OperationContract(Name="AddItemToCart")]
        bool AddItemToCart(string productNumber);
```

```
        [OperationContract(Name = "RemoveItemFromCart")]
        bool RemoveItemFromCart(string productNumber);

        [OperationContract(Name = "GetShoppingCart")]
        string GetShoppingCart();

        [OperationContract(Name = "Checkout")]
        bool Checkout();
    }
}
```

The client application will invoke the *AddItemToCart* and *RemoveItemFromCart* operations to manipulate the shopping cart. The *AdventureWorks* database identifies items by their product number. To add more than one instance of an item, you must invoke the *AddItemToCart* operation for each instance. These operations will return *true* if they are successful or *false* if otherwise.

The *GetShoppingCart* operation returns a string representation of the shopping cart contents that the client application can display.

The client application will call the *Checkout* operation if the user wants to purchase the goods in the shopping cart. Again, this operation will return *true* if it is successful or *false* if it is not.

> **Note** For the purposes of this example, assume that the user has an account with Adventure Works, and so the *Checkout* operation simply arranges dispatch of the goods to the customer's address. The customer will be billed separately.

9. Open the ShoppingCartService.cs file in the Code And Text Editor window. As you did with the IShoppingCartService.cs file, delete all the comments and code except the *using* statements at the start of the file and the *ShoppingCartService* namespace. Add the following *using* statement to the list at the top of the file:

```
using ProductsEntityModel;
```

10. Add the following class to the *ShoppingCartService* namespace in the ShoppingCart Service.cs file:

```
namespace ShoppingCartService
{
    public class ShoppingCartServiceImpl : IShoppingCartService
    {
    }
}
```

This class will implement the operations for the *IShoppingCartService* interface.

11. Add the following private *shoppingCart* field to the *ShoppingCartServiceImpl* class:

```
public class ShoppingCartServiceImpl : IShoppingCartService
{
    private List<ShoppingCartItem> shoppingCart =
        new List<ShoppingCartItem>();
}
```

This variable will hold the user's shopping cart, which comprises a list of *Shopping CartItem* objects. This list represents state information that the service must maintain between calls made by a client application.

12. Add the following private *find* method (shown in bold) to the *ShoppingCartServiceImpl* class:

```
public class ShoppingCartServiceImpl : IShoppingCartService
{
    ...
    // Examine the shopping cart to determine whether an item with a
    // specified product number has already been added.
    // If so, return a reference to the item, otherwise return null
    private ShoppingCartItem find(List<ShoppingCartItem> shoppingCart,
                            string productNumber)
    {
        foreach (ShoppingCartItem item in shoppingCart)
        {
            if (string.Compare(item.ProductNumber, productNumber) == 0)
            {
                return item;
            }
        }

        return null;
    }
}
```

The *AddItemToCart* and *RemoveItemFromCart* operations will make use of this utility method.

> **Note** The code for this method is available in the file Find.txt, which is located in the Chapter 7 folder.

13. Implement the *AddToCart* method in the *ShoppingCartServiceImpl* class, as shown in bold in the following:

```
public class ShoppingCartServiceImpl : IShoppingCartService
{
    ...
    public bool AddItemToCart(string productNumber)
```

```
        {
            // Note: For clarity, this method performs very limited
            // security checking and exception handling
            try
            {
                // Check to see whether the user has already added this
                // product to the shopping cart
                ShoppingCartItem item = find(shoppingCart, productNumber);

                // If so, then simply increment the volume
                if (item != null)
                {
                    item.Volume++;
                    return true;
                }

                // Otherwise, retrieve the details of the product from the database
                else
                {
                    // Connect to the AdventureWorks database
                    // by using the Entity Framework
                    using (AdventureWorksEntities database = new AdventureWorksEntities())
                    {
                        // Retrieve the details of the selected product
                        Product product = (from p in database.Products
                                          where string.Compare(p.ProductNumber,
                                              productNumber) == 0
                                          select p).First();

                        // Create and populate a new shopping cart item
                        ShoppingCartItem newItem = new ShoppingCartItem
                        {
                            ProductNumber = product.ProductNumber,
                            ProductName = product.Name,
                            Cost = product.ListPrice,
                            Volume = 1
                        };

                        // Add the new item to the shopping cart
                        shoppingCart.Add(newItem);

                        // Indicate success
                        return true;
                    }
                }
            }
            catch
            {
                // If an error occurs, finish and indicate failure
                return false;
            }
        }
    }
```

Note The code for this method is available in the file AddItemToCart.txt, which is located in the Chapter 7 folder.

Important For clarity, this method does not perform any security checking, and exception handling is minimal. In a production application, you should address these aspects robustly, as described in the preceding chapters. Additionally, for simplicity, this method assumes that there is always sufficient stock of the select item available. You will add further checking to this method in Chapter 9, "Supporting Transactions."

14. Add the following *RemoveItemFromCart* method (shown in bold) to the *Shopping CartServiceImpl* class:

```
public class ShoppingCartServiceImpl : IShoppingCartService
{
    ...
    public bool RemoveItemFromCart(string productNumber)
    {
        // Determine whether the specified product has an
        // item in the shopping cart
        ShoppingCartItem item = find(shoppingCart, productNumber);

        // If so, then decrement the volume
        if (item != null)
        {
            item.Volume--;

            // If the volume is zero, remove the item from the shopping cart
            if (item.Volume == 0)
            {
                shoppingCart.Remove(item);
            }

            // Indicate success
            return true;
        }

        // No such item in the shopping cart
        return false;
    }
}
```

Note The code for this method is available in the file RemoveItemFromCart.txt, which is located in the Chapter 7 folder.

15. Implement the *GetShoppingCart* method in the *ShoppingCartServiceImpl* class, as follows:

```
public class ShoppingCartServiceImpl : IShoppingCartService
{
    ...
    public string GetShoppingCart()
    {
        // Create a string holding a formatted representation
        // of the shopping cart
        string formattedContent = String.Empty;
        decimal totalCost = 0;

        foreach (ShoppingCartItem item in shoppingCart)
        {
            string itemString = String.Format(
                "Number: [0]\tName: {1}\tCost: {2:C}\tVolume: {3}",
                item.ProductNumber, item.ProductName, item.Cost,
                item.Volume);
            totalCost += (item.Cost * item.Volume);
            formattedContent += itemString + "\n";
        }

        string totalCostString = String.Format("\nTotalCost: {0:C}", totalCost);
        formattedContent += totalCostString;
        return formattedContent;
    }
}
```

 Note The code for this method is available in the file GetShoppingCart.txt, which is located in the Chapter 7 folder.

This method generates a string describing the contents of the shopping cart. The string contains a line for each item, with the total cost of the items in the shopping cart at the end.

16. Add the *Checkout* method to the *ShoppingCartServiceImpl* class, as shown in bold in the following:

```
public class ShoppingCartServiceImpl : IShoppingCartService
{
    ...
    public bool Checkout()
    {
        // Not currently implemented - just return true
        return true;
    }
}
```

This method is simply a placeholder. In a production system, this method would perform tasks such as arranging the dispatch of items, billing the user, and updating the database to reflect the changes in stock volume, according to the user's order.

17. Build the solution.

You now need to build a host application for this service. You will use a simple console application for this purpose.

Create a Host Application for the *ShoppingCartService* Service

1. Add a new project to the *ShoppingCartService* solution. Specify the following properties for the project:

Property	Value
Template	Console Application, in the Windows folder, within the Visual C# folder, in the Installed Templates pane
Name	ShoppingCartHost
Location	Microsoft Press\WCF Step By Step\Chapter 7\ShoppingCart

2. Add a reference to the ShoppingCartService project for the ShoppingCartHost project. Also add references to the *System.ServiceModel* and *System.Data.Entity* assemblies.

3. Add the App.config file located in the Microsoft Press\WCF Step By Step\Chapter 7 folder to the ShoppingCartHost project.

   This configuration file currently contains only the definition of the connection string that the service uses for connecting to the *AdventureWorks* database.

> **Tip** On the Project menu, click Add Existing Item to add a file to a project. You will also need to select All Files (*.*) from the drop-down in the Add Existing Item dialog box to display the App.config file.

4. Edit the App.config file for the ShoppingCartHost project by using the Service Configuration Editor. In the Services pane, click Create A New Service. Proceed through the New Service Element Wizard, using the information in the following table to define the service.

Page	Prompt	Value
What is the service type of your service?	Service type	ShoppingCartService.ShoppingCartServiceImpl
What service contract are you using?	Contract	ShoppingCartService.IShoppingCartService
What communications mode is your service using?		HTTP
What method of interoperability do you want to use?		Advanced Web Service interoperability (Simplex communication)
What is the address of your endpoint?	Address	http://localhost:9000 /ShoppingCartService/ShoppingCartService.svc

The wizard adds the service to the configuration file and creates an endpoint definition for the service.

5. Save the configuration file, and then exit the Service Configuration Editor.

6. Open the App.config file for the ShoppingCartHost project in the Code And Text Editor window. The *<system.serviceModel>* section should look like this:

```
<system.serviceModel>
  <services>
    <service name="ShoppingCartService.ShoppingCartServiceImpl">
      <endpoint
        address= "http://localhost:9000/ShoppingCartService/ShoppingCartService.svc"
        binding="ws2007HttpBinding" bindingConfiguration=""
        contract="ShoppingCartService.IShoppingCartService" />
    </service>
  </services>
</system.serviceModel>
```

7. Open the Program.cs file for the ShoppingCartHost project in the Code And Text Editor window. Add the following *using* statement to the list at the top of the file:

```
using System.ServiceModel;
```

8. Add the following statements (shown in bold) to the *Main* method in the *Program* class:

```
class Program
{
    static void Main(string[] args)
    {
        ServiceHost host = new ServiceHost(
            typeof(ShoppingCartService.ShoppingCartServiceImpl));
        host.Open();
        Console.WriteLine("Service running");
        Console.WriteLine("Press ENTER to stop the service");
        Console.ReadLine();
        host.Close();
    }
}
```

This code creates a new instance of the *ShoppingCartService* service, listening on the HTTP endpoint you specified in the configuration file.

The next task is to build a client application to test the *ShoppingCartService* service. You will create another Console Application to do this.

Create a Client Application to Test the *ShoppingCartService* Service

1. Add another new project to the ShoppingCartService solution. Specify the following properties for the project:

Property	Value
Template	Console Application, in the Windows folder, within the Visual C# folder, in the Installed Templates pane
Name	ShoppingCartClient
Location	Microsoft Press\WCF Step By Step\Chapter 7\ShoppingCart

2. In the ShoppingCartClient project, add a reference to the *System.Service Model* assembly.

3. Generate a proxy class for the client application by using the following procedure:

   a. Open a *Visual Studio Command Prompt* window and move to the ShoppingCart\ ShoppingCartService\bin\Debug folder in the Microsoft Press\WCF Step By Step\ Chapter 7 folder.

   b. In the Visual Studio Command Prompt window, run the command:

   ```
   svcutil ShoppingCartService.dll
   ```

   c. Run the command:

   ```
   svcutil /namespace:*,ShoppingCartClient.ShoppingCartService
       adventure-works.com.2010.06.04.wsdl *.xsd /out:ShoppingCartServiceProxy.cs
   ```

4. Close the Visual Studio Command Prompt window and return to Visual Studio. Add the ShoppingCartServiceProxy.cs file in the ShoppingCart\ShoppingCartService\bin\Debug folder to the ShoppingCartClient project.

5. Add a new application configuration file to the ShoppingCartClient project. Name this file **App.config**.

Tip To add a new file to a project, select Project | Add New Item.

6. Edit the App.config file in the ShoppingCartClient project by using the Service Configuration Editor. In the Configuration pane, click the Client folder. In the Client pane, click Create A New Client. Use the New Client Element Wizard to add a new client endpoint to the configuration file by using the information in the following table:

Page	Prompt	Value
What method do you want to use to create the client?	From service config	Microsoft Press\WCF Step By Step\Chapter 7\ShoppingCart\ShoppingCartHost\App.config
Which service endpoint do you want to connect to?	Service endpoint	ShoppingCartService.ShoppingCartServiceImpl- http://localhost:9000/ShoppingCartService/ShoppingCartService.svc- ws2007HttpBinding- ShoppingCartService.IShoppingCartService **Note**: This is the default endpoint.
What name do you want to use for the client configuration?		WS2007HttpBinding_IShoppingCartService

The wizard adds the client definition to the configuration file and creates an endpoint called *WS2007HttpBinding_IShoppingCartService* that the client application can use to connect to the ShoppingCartService service. However, the name of the type implementing the contract in the client proxy has a different name from that used by the service, so you must change the value added to the client configuration file.

7. In the Configuration pane, in the Endpoints folder under the Client folder, click the *WS2007HttpBinding_IShoppingCartService* endpoint. In the Client Endpoint pane, set the *Contract* property to **ShoppingCartClient.ShoppingCartService.ShoppingCartService** (the type is *ShoppingCartService* in the *ShoppingCartClient.ShoppingCartService* namespace in the client proxy).

8. Save the configuration file and exit the Service Configuration Editor. Allow Visual Studio to reload the modified App.config file, if prompted.

9. Open the App.config file for the ShoppingCartClient application in the Code And Text Editor window. It should appear as follows:

```
<?xml version="1.0" encoding="utf-8" ?>
<configuration>
  <system.serviceModel>
    <client>
      <endpoint address="http://localhost:9000/ShoppingCartService/
          ShoppingCartService.svc"
          binding="ws2007HttpBinding" bindingConfiguration=""
          contract="ShoppingCartClient.ShoppingCartService.ShoppingCartService"
```

```
            name="WS2007HttpBinding_IShoppingCartService" kind=""
            endpointConfiguration="">
            <identity>
              <certificateReference storeName="My" storeLocation="LocalMachine"
                x509FindType="FindSubjectDistinguishedName" />
            </identity>
          </endpoint>
        </client>
      </system.serviceModel>
    </configuration>
```

Remove the *<identity>* element and its child *<certificateReference>* element from the configuration file. This version of the service does not use certificates.

10. In Visual Studio, open the Program.cs file for the ShoppingCartClient project in the Code And Text Editor window. Add the following *using* statements to the list at the top of the file.

```
using System.ServiceModel;
using ShoppingCartClient.ShoppingCartService;
```

11. Add the following statements (shown in bold) to the *Main* method of the *Program* class:

```
static void Main(string[] args)
{
    Console.WriteLine("Press ENTER when the service has started");
    Console.ReadLine();
    try
    {
        // Connect to the ShoppingCartService service
        ShoppingCartServiceClient proxy =
            new ShoppingCartServiceClient("WS2007HttpBinding_IShoppingCartService");

        // Add two water bottles to the shopping cart
        proxy.AddItemToCart("WB-H098");
        proxy.AddItemToCart("WB-H098");

        // Add a mountain seat assembly to the shopping cart
        proxy.AddItemToCart("SA-M198");

        // Query the shopping cart and display the result
        string cartContents = proxy.GetShoppingCart();
        Console.WriteLine(cartContents);

        // Disconnect from the ShoppingCartService service
        proxy.Close();
    }
    catch (Exception e)
    {
        Console.WriteLine("Exception: {0}", e.Message);
    }
    Console.WriteLine("Press ENTER to finish");
    Console.ReadLine();
}
```

Note Complete code for the *Main* method is available in the file Main.txt, which is located in the Chapter 7 folder.

The code in the *try* block creates a proxy object for communicating with the service. The application then adds three items to the shopping cart—two water bottles and a mountain seat assembly—before querying the current contents of the shopping cart and displaying the result.

12. Open a Visual Studio Command Prompt window as an administrator and enter the following command to return port 9000 for your service (replace *UserName* with your Windows user name):

```
netsh http add urlacl url=http://+:9000/ user=UserName
```

13. Close the Visual Studio Command Prompt window and return to Visual Studio. In Solution Explorer set the ShoppingCartClient and ShoppingCartHost projects as the startup projects for the solution.

> **Tip** To set multiple projects as startup projects, right-click the *ShoppingCartService* solution and then click Set StartUp Projects. In the right pane of the Solution 'ShoppingCartService' Property Pages dialog box, select Multiple Startup Projects, set the *Action* property for the ShoppingCartClient and ShoppingCartHost projects to **Start** and then click OK.

14. Start the solution without debugging. In the client console window displaying the message "Press ENTER when the service has started," press Enter.

 Note If a Windows Security Alert message box appears, click Unblock to allow the service to use HTTP port 9000.

The client application adds the three items to the shopping cart and displays the result, as shown in the following image (your currency symbol might be different if you are not in the United Kingdom):

15. Press Enter to close the client application console window. In the host application con-
    sole window, press Enter to stop the service.

You can see that the *ShoppingCartService* service has maintained information about the
shopping cart for the client application between calls, so this technique for maintaining state
information in the service appears to work well. But, this is one of those situations that should
leave you feeling a little bit suspicious—everything appears to be just a bit too easy.

Service Instance Context Modes

If you think for a minute about what is going on, the service creates an instance of the
shopping cart when an instance of the service is itself created by the host; the *shoppingCart*
variable is a private instance variable in the *ShoppingCartServiceImpl* class. What happens
if two clients attempt to use the service simultaneously? The answer is that each client gets
their own instance of the service, with its own instance of the *shoppingCart* variable. This is
an important point. By default, the first time each client invokes an operation in a service, the
host creates a new instance of the service just for that client. How long does the instance last?

You can see from the shopping cart example that the instance hangs around between operation calls; otherwise, it would not be able to maintain its state in an instance variable. The
service instance is only destroyed after the client has closed the connection to the host (in
true .NET Framework fashion, you do not know exactly how long the instance will hang around
after the client application closes the connection because it depends on when the .NET
Framework garbage collector decides it is time to reclaim memory). Now think what happens if
you have 10 concurrent clients—you get 10 instances of the service. What if you have 10,000
concurrent clients? You get 10,000 instances of the service. If the client is an interactive application that runs for an indeterminate period while the user browses the product catalog and
decides which items to buy, you had better be running the host application on a machine
with plenty of memory!

An instance of a WCF service that is created to handle requests from a specific client application and maintain state information between requests from that client application is called a
Session. To be explicit, when a client application uses a proxy object to connect to a service,
the WCF runtime for the service host creates a session to hold an instance of the service and
any state data required by that instance. The session is terminated when the client application
closes the proxy object.

Note If you are using the TCP, or named pipe transport, you can restrict the maximum number of
concurrent sessions for a service by setting the *MaxConnections* property of the binding configuration. For these transports, the default limit is 10 connections. If you are using IIS to host a WCF
service using the HTTP or HTTPS transports, you can configure IIS to limit the number of concurrent
connections it should allow—the details of how to do this are beyond the scope of this book.

You can control the relationship between client applications and instances of a service by using the *InstanceContextMode* property of the *ServiceBehavior* attribute of the service. You specify this attribute when defining the class that implements the service contract, as follows:

```
[ServiceBehavior(InstanceContextMode = InstanceContextMode.PerSession)]
public class ShoppingCartService : IShoppingCartService
{
    ...
}
```

The *InstanceContextMode* property can take one of the following three values: *InstanceMode. PerSession*, *InstanceMode.PerCall*, and *InstanceMode.Single*. The following sections describe these instance context modes.

The *PerSession* Instance Context Mode

The *PerSession* instance context mode specifies that the service instance is created when a client application first invokes an operation, and the instance remains active, responding to client requests, until the client application closes the connection. Each time a client application creates a new session, it gets a new instance of the service. Two sessions cannot share a service instance when using this instance context mode, even if both sessions are created by the same instance of the client application.

It is possible for a client application to create multiple threads and then attempt to invoke operations in the same session simultaneously. By default, a service is single-threaded and will not process more than one request at a time. If a new request arrives while the service is still processing an earlier request, the WCF runtime causes the new request to wait for the earlier one to complete. The new request could possibly time-out while it is waiting to be handled. You can modify this behavior; The *ServiceBehavior* attribute has another property called *ConcurrencyMode*, you can set that property to specify how to process concurrent requests in the same session, as shown in the following:

```
[ServiceBehavior(..., ConcurrencyMode = ConcurrencyMode.Single)]
public class ShoppingCartService : IShoppingCartService
{
    ...
}
```

The default value for this property is *ConcurrencyMode.Single*, which causes the service to behave as just described. You can also set this property to *ConcurrencyMode.Multiple*, in which case the service instance is multithreaded and can accept simultaneous requests. However, setting the *Concurrency* property to *ConcurrencyMode.Multiple* does not make any guarantees about synchronization. You must take responsibility for ensuring that the code you write in the service is thread-safe.

There is a third mode called *ConcurrencyMode.Reentrant*. In this mode, the service instance is single-threaded, but it allows the code in your service to call out to other services and applications, which can then subsequently call back into your service. However, this mode makes no guarantees about the state of data in your instance of the service. It is the responsibility of your code to ensure that the state of service instance remains consistent and that the service doesn't accidentally deadlock itself.

The *PerCall* Instance Context Mode

The *InstanceContextMode.PerCall* instance context mode creates a new instance of the service every time the client application invokes an operation. The instance is destroyed when the operation completes. The advantage of this instance context mode is that it releases resources in the host between operations, greatly improving scalability. If you consider the situation with 10,000 concurrent users and the *PerSession* instance context mode, the main issue is that the host must hold 10,000 instances of the service, even if 9,999 of them are not currently performing any operations (perhaps because the users have gone to lunch without closing their copy of the client application and terminating their sessions). If you use the *PerCall* instance context mode instead, then the host will only need to hold an instance for the one active user.

The disadvantage of using this instance context mode is that maintaining state between operations is more challenging. You cannot retain information in instance variables in the service, so you must save any required state information in persistent storage such as a disk file or database. It also complicates the design of operations because a client application must identify itself so that the service can retrieve the appropriate state from storage (you will investigate a couple of ways of achieving this later in this chapter; a more comprehensive approach is described in Chapter 8, "Implementing Services by Using Workflows").

You can see that the lifetime of a service instance depends on how long it takes the service to perform the requested operation, so keep your operations concise. You should be very careful if an operation creates additional threads; the service instance will live on until all of these threads complete, even if the main thread has long-since returned any results to the client application. This can seriously affect scalability. You should also avoid registering callbacks in a service. Registering a callback does not block service completion, and the object calling back might find that the service instance has been reclaimed and recycled. The .NET Framework Common Language Runtime (CLR) traps this eventuality so it is not a security risk, but it is inconvenient to the object calling back as it will receive an exception.

The Single Instance Context Mode

The *InstanceContextMode.Single* instance context mode creates a new instance of the service the first time a client application invokes an operation and then uses this same instance to handle all subsequent requests from this client and *every other client that connects to the same service*. The instance is destroyed only when the host application shuts the service down. The main advantage of this instance context mode, apart from the reduced resource requirements, is that all users can easily share data. Arguably, this is also the principal disadvantage of this instance context mode.

The *InstanceContextMode.Single* instance context mode minimizes the resources used by the service at the cost of expecting the same instance to handle every single request. If you have 10,000 concurrent users, that could be a lot of requests. Also, if the service is single-threaded (the *ConcurrencyMode* property of the *ServiceBehavior* attribute is set to *ConcurrencyMode. Single*), then you should expect many timeouts unless operations complete very quickly. Consequently, you should set the concurrency mode to **ConcurrencyMode.Multiple** and implement synchronization to ensure that all operations are thread-safe.

> **More Info** Detailed discussion of synchronization techniques in the .NET Framework is beyond the scope of this book, but for more information, see the topic "Synchronizing Data For Multi-threading" in the documentation provided with Visual Studio (also available on the Microsoft Web site at *http://msdn.microsoft.com/en-us/library/z8chs7ft.aspx*).

In the next exercise, you will examine the effects of using the *PerCall* and *Single* instance context modes.

Investigate the *InstanceContextMode* Property of the *ServiceBehavior*

1. In Visual Studio, edit the ShoppingCartService.cs file in the ShoppingCartService project.

2. Add the *ServiceBehavior* attribute to the *ShoppingCartServiceImpl* class. Set the *Instance ContextMode* property to **InstanceContextMode.PerCall**, as shown in bold in the following:

   ```
   [ServiceBehavior(InstanceContextMode = InstanceContextMode.PerCall)]
   public class ShoppingCartService : IShoppingCartService
   {
       ...
   }
   ```

3. Start the solution without debugging. In the *ShoppingCartClient* console window that is displaying the message "Press ENTER when the service has started," press Enter.

   The client application adds the three items to the shopping cart as before, but the result displayed after retrieving the shopping cart from the service shows no items and a total cost of zero.

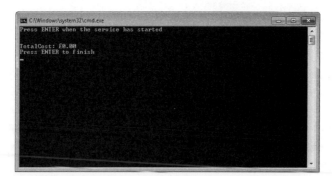

Every time the client application calls the service, it creates a new instance of the service. The shopping cart is destroyed each time an operation completes, so the string returned by the *GetShoppingCart* operation is a representation of an empty shopping cart.

4. Press Enter to close the client application console window. In the host application console window, press Enter to stop the service.

5. In Visual Studio, change the *InstanceContextMode* property of the *ServiceBehavior* attribute of the ShoppingCartService to **InstanceContextMode.Single**, as follows:

```
[ServiceBehavior(InstanceContextMode = InstanceContextMode.Single)]
public class ShoppingCartService : IShoppingCartService
{
    ...
}
```

6. Start the solution again, without debugging. In the *ShoppingCartClient* console window press Enter.

This time, the client application displays the shopping cart containing two water bottles and a mountain seat assembly. All appears to be well at first glance.

7. Press Enter to close the client application console window, but leave the service host application running.

8. In Solution Explorer, right-click the ShoppingCartClient project, point to Debug, and then click Start New Instance.

This action runs the client application again without restarting the service host application.

9. In the *ShoppingCartClient* console window, press Enter.

The shopping cart displayed by the client application now contains four water bottles and two mountain seat assemblies:

The second run of the client application used the same instance of the service as the first run, and the items were added to the same instance of the shopping cart.

10. Press Enter to close the client application console window. In the host application console window, press Enter to stop the service.

Tip The *PerSession* instance context mode is the default when you use an endpoint with a configuration that requires sessions. This is actually most of the time, unless you disable security (absolutely not recommended) or use the *BasicHttpBinding* binding, which does not support sessions when the service host defaults to using the *PerCall* instance context mode. This can be quite confusing, so it is better to always explicitly state the instance context mode your service requires by using the *ServiceBehavior* attribute.

Maintaining State with the PerCall Instance Context Mode

The exercises so far in this chapter have highlighted what happens when you change the instance context mode for a service. In the *ShoppingCartService* service, which instance context mode should you use? In a real-world environment, using a proper client application rather than the test code you have been working with, the user could spend a significant amount of time browsing for items of interest before adding them to their shopping cart. In this case, it makes sense to use the *PerCall* instance context mode. But you must provide a mechanism to store and recreate the shopping cart each time the client application invokes an operation. There are several ways you can achieve this, including generating an identifier for the shopping cart when the service first creates it, returning this identifier to the client application, and forcing the client to pass this identifier in to all subsequent operations as a parameter. This technique, and its variations, are frequently used, but suffer from many of the same security drawbacks as cookies, as far as the service is concerned; it is possible for a client application to forge a shopping cart identifier and hijack another user's shopping cart.

An alternative strategy is to employ the user's own identity as a key for saving and retrieving state information. In a secure environment, this information is transmitted as part of the request anyway, and so it is transparent to client applications—for example, the *ws2007Http Binding* binding uses Windows Integrated Security and transmits the user's credentials to the WCF service by default. You will make use of this information in the following exercise.

 Note The same mechanism works even if you are using a non-Windows specific mechanism to identify users, such as certificates. Thus, it is a valuable technique in an Internet security environment. The important thing is that you have a unique identifier for the user—it does not have to be a Windows user name.

Maintain State in the *ShoppingCartService* Service

1. In Visual Studio, open the IShoppingCartService.cs file for the ShoppingCartService project in the Code And Text Editor window.

2. Add the following *using* statement to the list at the top of the file:

```
using System.Xml.Serialization;
```

You will use classes in these namespaces to serialize the user's shopping cart and save it in a text file.

3. Modify the definition of the *ShoppingCartItem* class; mark it with the *Serializable* attribute and change its visibility to public, as shown in bold in the following:

```
[Serializable]
public class ShoppingCartItem
{
    ...
}
```

You can only serialize publicly accessible classes by using the XML serializer.

4. Open the ShoppingCartService.cs file in the Code And Text Editor window. Add the following *using* statements to the list at the top of the file:

```
using System.Xml.Serialization;
using System.IO;
```

5. Add the private *saveShoppingCart* method (shown in bold in the following code) to the *ShoppingCartServiceImpl* class:

```
public class ShoppingCartServiceImpl : IShoppingCartService
{
    ...
    // Save the shopping cart for the current user to a local XML
    // file named after the user
    private void saveShoppingCart()
    {
        string userName = ServiceSecurityContext.Current.PrimaryIdentity.Name;
        foreach (char badChar in Path.GetInvalidFileNameChars())
        {
            userName = userName.Replace(badChar, '!');
        }

        string fileName = userName + ".xml";
        TextWriter writer = new StreamWriter(fileName);
        XmlSerializer ser = new XmlSerializer(typeof(List<ShoppingCartItem>));
        ser.Serialize(writer, shoppingCart);
        writer.Close();
    }
    ...
}
```

Note The code for this method is available in the file SaveShoppingCart.txt, which is located in the Chapter 7 folder.

This private utility method retrieves the name of the user running the client application and creates a file name based on this user name, with the ".xml" file extension. The user name could include a domain name with a separating "\" character. This character is not allowed in file names, so the code replaces any "\" characters—and any other characters in the user name that are not allowed in filenames—with a "!" character.

Note If you are using certificates rather than Window's user names to identify users in an Internet environment, the file names will still be legal, although they will look a little strange because user identities in this scheme have the form "CN=*user*; FA097524718BDz8765D6E4AA7654891245BCAD85."

The method then uses an *XmlSerializer* object to serialize the user's shopping cart to this file before closing the file and finishing.

Note For clarity, this method does not perform any exception checking. In a production environment, you should be prepared to be more robust.

6. Add the following private *restoreShoppingCart* method (shown in bold) to the *ShoppingCartServiceImpl* class:

```
public class ShoppingCartServiceImpl : IShoppingCartService
{
    ...
    // Restore the shopping cart for the current user from the local XML
    // file named after the user
    private void restoreShoppingCart()
    {
        string userName = ServiceSecurityContext.Current.PrimaryIdentity.Name;
        foreach (char badChar in Path.GetInvalidFileNameChars())
        {
            userName = userName.Replace(badChar, '!');
        }

        string fileName = userName + ".xml";
        if (File.Exists(fileName))
        {
            TextReader reader = new StreamReader(fileName);
            XmlSerializer ser = new XmlSerializer(typeof(List<ShoppingCartItem>));
            shoppingCart = (List<ShoppingCartItem>)ser.Deserialize(reader);
            reader.Close();
        }
    }
    ...
}
```

> **Note** The code for this method is available in the file RestoreShoppingCart.txt, which is
> located in the Chapter 7 folder.

This method uses the user name to generate a file name using the same strategy as the *saveShoppingCart* method. If the file exists, this method opens the file and deserializes its contents into the *shoppingCart* variable before closing it. If there is no such file, the *shoppingCart* variable is left at its initial value of *null*.

> **Note** In a production environment, you should verify that the file contains a valid rep-
> resentation of a shopping cart before attempting to cast its contents and assign it to the
> shoppingCart variable.

7. In the *AddItemToCart* method, call the *restoreShoppingCart* method before examining the shopping cart, as follows in bold:

```
public bool AddItemToCart(string productNumber)
{
    // Note: For clarity, this method performs very limited security
    // checking and exception handling
    try
    {
        // Check to see whether the user has already added this
        // product to the shopping cart
        restoreShoppingCart();
        ShoppingCartItem item = find(shoppingCart, productNumber);
        ...
    }
    ...
}
```

8. In the block of code that increments the volume field of an item, following the *if* statement, call the *saveShoppingCart* method to preserve its contents before returning:

```
public bool AddItemToCart(string productNumber)
{
    // Note: For clarity, this method performs very limited security
    // checking and exception handling
    try
    {
        ...
        if (item != null)
        {
            item.Volume++;
            saveShoppingCart();
            return true;
        }
        ...
    }
    ...
}
```

9. In the block of code that adds a new item to the shopping cart, call the *saveShopping Cart* method before returning, as shown in bold in the following:

```
public bool AddItemToCart(string productNumber)
{
    // Note: For clarity, this method performs very limited security
    // checking and exception handling
    try
    {
        ...
        else
        {
            ...
            using (AdventureWorksEntities database = new AdventureWorksEntities())
            {
                ...
                // Add the new item to the shopping cart
                shoppingCart.Add(newItem);
                saveShoppingCart();

                // Indicate success
                return true;
            }
        }
    }
    ...
}
```

There is no need to save the shopping cart whenever the method fails (returns *false*).

10. In the *RemoveItemFromCart* method, call the *restoreShoppingCart* method before examining the shopping cart, as follows:

```
public bool RemoveItemFromCart(string productNumber)
{
    // Determine whether the specified product has an
    // item in the shopping cart
    restoreShoppingCart();
    ShoppingCartItem item = find(shoppingCart, productNumber);
    ...
}
```

11. Add the following code (shown in bold) to save the shopping cart after successfully removing the specified item and before returning *true*:

```
public bool RemoveItemFromCart(string productNumber)
{
    ...
    // Indicate success
    saveShoppingCart();
    return true;
}
```

12. In the *GetShoppingCart* method, call the *restoreShoppingCart* method before iterating through the contents of the shopping cart, as shown in bold in the following:

```
public string GetShoppingCart()
{
    ...
    restoreShoppingCart();
    foreach (ShoppingCartItem item in shoppingCart)
    {
        ...
    }
}
```

13. Change the *InstanceContextMode* property of the *ServiceBehavior* attribute of the *ShoppingCartServiceImpl* class back to **InstanceContextMode.PerCall**:

```
[ServiceBehavior(InstanceContextMode = InstanceContextMode.PerCall)]
public class ShoppingCartServiceImpl : IShoppingCartService
{
    ...
}
```

Remember that this instance context mode releases the service instance at the end of each operation and destroys any state information held in the memory of the service instance. Hopefully, the state of the user's shopping cart should be persisted to disk. You will test that this is the case in the next exercise.

Test the State Management Capabilities of the *ShoppingCartService* Service

1. Start the solution without debugging. In the *ShoppingCartClient* console window, press Enter.

The client application adds three items to the shopping cart and then displays the contents. The service saves the data in the user's shopping cart to a file between operations.

2. Press Enter to close the client application console window. In the host application console window, press Enter to stop the service.

3. Start the solution again. In the *ShoppingCartClient* console window, press Enter. This time, the client displays a shopping cart containing four water bottles and two mountain seat assemblies. Because the state information is stored in an external file, it persists across service shutdown and restart.

> **Note** As an additional exercise, you could add some code to the *Checkout* method to delete the shopping cart file for the user after they have paid for their goods.

4. Press Enter to close the client application console window. In the host application console window, press Enter to stop the service.

5. Using Windows Explorer, move to the Chapter 7\ShoppingCart\ShoppingCartHost \bin\Debug folder. You should see an XML file in this folder called *YourDomain!Your Name*.xml, where *YourDomain* is either the name of your computer or the name of the domain of which you are a member, and *YourName* is your Windows user name.

6. Open this file by using Notepad. It should look like this:

```xml
<?xml version="1.0" encoding="utf-8"?>
<ArrayOfShoppingCartItem xmlns:xsi="http://www.w3.org/2001/XMLSchema-
instance" xmlns:xsd="http://www.w3.org/2001/XMLSchema">
  <ShoppingCartItem>
    <ProductNumber>WB-H098</ProductNumber>
    <ProductName>Water Bottle - 30 oz.</ProductName>
    <Cost>4.9900</Cost>
    <Volume>4</Volume>
  </ShoppingCartItem>
  <ShoppingCartItem>
    <ProductNumber>SA-M198</ProductNumber>
    <ProductName>LL Mountain Seat Assembly</ProductName>
    <Cost>133.3400</Cost>
    <Volume>2</Volume>
  </ShoppingCartItem>
</ArrayOfShoppingCartItem>
```

This is the data from your shopping cart. Remember that the *saveShoppingCart* method writes the data by using an *XmlSerializer* object to save it as an XML document.

7. Close Notepad and return to Visual Studio. Edit the Program.cs file in the Shopping CartClient project by adding the following statements (shown in bold) to the *Main* method (replace *Domain* with the name of your domain or computer):

```csharp
static void Main(string[] args)
{
    ...
    try
    {
        // Connect to the ShoppingCartService service
        ShoppingCartServiceClient proxy =
            new ShoppingCartServiceClient("WS2007HttpBinding_ShoppingCartService");

        // Provide credentials to identify the user
        proxy.ClientCredentials.Windows.ClientCredential.Domain = "Domain";
        proxy.ClientCredentials.Windows.ClientCredential.UserName = "Fred";
        proxy.ClientCredentials.Windows.ClientCredential.Password = "Pa$$w0rd";

        // Add two water bottles to the shopping cart
        proxy.AddItemToCart("WB-H098");
        ...
    }
    ...
}
```

> **Note** You created the user Fred in the exercise, "Create Groups for Warehouse Staff and Stock Controller Staff," on page 154 in Chapter 4, "Protecting an Enterprise WCF Service."

8. Start the solution without debugging. In the client application console window, press Enter. The client application displays a shopping cart containing only three items—this is Fred's shopping cart and not the one created earlier.

9. Press Enter to close the client application console window. In the host application console window, press Enter to stop the service.

10. In Windows Explorer, you should see another XML file in the Chapter 7\Shopping CartService\ShoppingCartHost\bin\Debug folder, called *YourDomain*!Fred.xml.

This solution implements a balance between resource use and responsiveness. Although a new service instance must be created for every operation, and it takes time to restore and save session state, you do not need to retain a service instance in memory for every active client application, so the solution should scale effectively as more and more users access your service.

There are three other points worth making about the sample code in this exercise:

1. The *restoreShoppingCart* and *saveShoppingCart* methods are not currently thread-safe. This might not seem important as the *ShoppingCartService* service uses the *PerCall* instance context mode and the single-threaded concurrency mode. However, if the same user (such as Fred) runs two concurrent instances of the client application, it will establish two concurrent instances of the service, which will both attempt to read and write the same file. The file access semantics of the .NET Framework class library prevents the two service instances from physically writing to the same file at the same time, but both service instances can still interfere with each other. Specifically, the *save ShoppingCart* method simply overwrites the XML file, so one instance of the service can obliterate any data saved by the other instance. In a production environment, you should take steps to prevent this situation from occurring, such as using some sort of locking scheme or maybe using a database rather than a set of XML files.

2. The *saveShoppingCart* method creates human-readable XML files. In a production environment, you should arrange for these files to be stored in a secure location other than the folder where the service executables reside. For reasons of privacy, you don't want other users to be able to access these files or modify them.

3. The solution relies on users being authenticated and having unique identifiers; they cannot be anonymous. Without authentication and identification, there is no primary identity for each user and the *ShoppingCartService* service will not be able to generate unique names for files holding the state for each user's session.

You will revisit these issues later in this chapter and see how you can resolve them in a scalable manner by using a durable service and defining durable operations. Before that, however, it is worth looking at some other features of services and how you can control the sequence of operations that a client application performs. This too can have a bearing on the way in which you maintain state information.

Selectively Controlling Service Instance Deactivation

The service instance context mode determines the lifetime of service instances. This property is global across the service; you set it once for the service class, and the WCF runtime handles client application requests and directs them to an appropriate instance of the service (possibly creating a new instance of the service), irrespective of the operations that the client application actually invokes.

With the WCF runtime, you can selectively control when a service instance is deactivated, based on the operations being called. You can tag each method that implements an operation in a service with the *OperationBehavior* attribute. This attribute has a property called *ReleaseInstanceMode* that you can use to modify the behavior of the service instance context mode. You use the *OperationBehavior* attribute like this:

```
[OperationBehavior(ReleaseInstanceMode = ReleaseInstanceMode.AfterCall)]
public bool Checkout()
{
    ...
}
```

The *ReleaseInstanceMode* property can take one of these values:

- *ReleaseInstanceMode.AfterCall*   When the operation completes, the WCF runtime will release the service instance for recycling. If the client invokes another operation, the WCF runtime will create a new service instance to handle the request.

- *ReleaseInstanceMode.BeforeCall*   If a service instance exists for the client application, the WCF runtime will release it for recycling and create a new one for handling the client application request.

- *ReleaseInstanceMode.BeforeAndAfterCall*   This is a combination of the previous two values; the WCF runtime creates a new service instance for handling the operation and releases the service instance for recycling when the operation completes.

- *ReleaseInstanceMode.None*   This is the default value. The service instance is managed according to the service instance context mode.

You should be aware that you can only use the *ReleaseInstanceMode* property to reduce the lifetime of a service instance, and you should understand the interplay between the *Instance ContextMode* property of the *ServiceBehavior* attribute and the *ReleaseInstanceMode* property of any *OperationBehavior* attributes adorning methods in the service class. For example, if you specify an *InstanceContextMode* value of *InstanceContextMode.PerCall* and a *ReleaseInstance Mode* value of *ReleaseInstanceMode.BeforeCall* for an operation, the WCF runtime will still release the service instance when the operation completes. The semantics of *InstanceContext Mode.PerCall* cause the service to be released at the end of an operation, and the *Release InstanceMode* property cannot force the WCF runtime to let the service instance live on. On the other hand, if you specify an *InstanceContextMode* value of *InstanceContextMode.Single* and a *ReleaseInstanceMode* value of *ReleaseInstanceMode.AfterCall* for an operation, the WCF runtime will release the service instance at the end of the operation, destroying any shared resources in the process (there are some threading issues that you should also consider as part of your design if the service is multi-threaded, in this case).

The *ReleaseInstanceMode* property of the *OperationBehavior* attribute is most commonly used in conjunction with the *PerSession* instance context mode. If you need to create a service that uses *PerSession* instancing, you should carefully assess whether you actually need to hold a service instance for the entire duration of a session. For example, if you know that a client always invokes a particular operation or one of a set of operations at the end of a logical piece of work, you can consider setting the *ReleaseInstanceMode* property for the operation to *ReleaseInstanceMode.AfterCall*.

An alternative technique is to make use of some operation properties that you can use to control the sequence of operations in a session, which you will look at next.

Sequencing Operations in a WCF Service

When using the *PerSession* instance context mode, it is often useful to be able to control the order in which a client application invokes operations in a WCF service. Revisiting the *Shopping CartService* service, suppose that you decide to use the *PerSession* instance context mode rather than *PerCall*. In this scenario, it might not make sense to allow the client application to remove an item from the shopping cart, query the contents of the shopping cart, or per-form a checkout operation if the user has not actually added any items to the shopping cart. Equally, it would be questionable practice to allow the user to add an item to the shopping cart after the user has already checked out and paid for the items in the cart. There is actu-ally a sequence to the operations in the *ShoppingCartService* service, and the service should enforce this sequence:

1. Add an item to the shopping cart.

2. Add another item, remove an item, or query the contents of the shopping cart.

3. Check out and empty the shopping cart.

When you define an operation in a service contract, the *OperationContract* attribute provides two Boolean properties that you can use to control the order of operations and the consequent lifetime of the service instance:

- *IsInitiating*   If you set this property to *true*, a client operation can invoke this operation to initiate a new session and create a new service instance. If a session already exists, this property has no further effect. By default, this property is set to *true*. If you set this property to *false*, then a client application cannot invoke this operation until another operation has initiated the session and created a service instance. At least one operation in a service contract must have this property set to *true*.

- *IsTerminating*   If you set this property to *true*, the WCF runtime will terminate the session and release the service instance when the operation completes. The client application must create a new connection to the service before invoking another operation, which must have the *IsInitiating* property set to *true*. The default value for this property is *false*. If no operations in a service contract specify a value of *true* for this property, the session remains active until the client application closes the connection to the service.

> **Note** These properties are specific to WCF and do not conform to any current WS-* standards. Using them can impact the interoperability of your service with client applications created by using other technologies.

The WCF runtime checks the values of these properties for consistency at runtime in conjunction with another property for the service contract called *SessionMode*. The *SessionMode* property of the service contract specifies whether the service implements sessions. It can have one of the following values:

- *SessionMode.Required*   The service will create a session to handle client requests if a session does not already exist for this client; otherwise, it will use the existing session for the client. The binding used by the service must support sessions. For example, the *ws2007HttpBinding* binding supports sessions, but the *basicHttpBinding* binding does not.

- *SessionMode.Allowed*   The service will create or use a session if the service binding supports them; otherwise, the service will not implement sessions.

- *SessionMode.NotAllowed*   The service will not use sessions, even if the service binding supports them.

If you specify a value of *false* for the *IsInitiating* property of any operation, then you must set the *SessionMode* property of the service contract to *SessionMode.Required*. If you do not, the WCF runtime will throw an exception. Similarly, you can only set the *IsTerminating* property to *true* if the *SessionMode* property of the service is set to *SessionMode.Required*.

> **More Info**   You will learn more about the *SessionMode* property of a service contract and reliable sessions in Chapter 10, "Implementing Reliable Sessions."

In the next set of exercises, you will see how to apply the *IsInitiating* and *IsTerminating* properties of the *OperationBehavior* attribute.

Control the Sequence of Operations in the *ShoppingCartService* Service

1. In Visual Studio, open the IShoppingCartService.cs file for the ShoppingCartService project in the Code And Text Editor window.

2. Add the *SessionMode* property to the *ServiceContract* attribute for the *IShopping CartService* interface, as shown in bold in the following:

```
[ServiceContract(SessionMode = SessionMode.Required,
                 Namespace = "http://adventure-works.com/2007/03/01",
                 Name = "ShoppingCartService")]
public interface IShoppingCartService
{
    ...
}
```

Remember that this setting enforces the requirement for the service to create a session to handle requests from client applications. The service currently implements the *PerCall* instance context mode, and you will change this setting shortly.

3. Modify the operations in the *IShoppingCartService* interface by specifying which operations initiate a session and which operations cause a session to terminate, as follows:

```
public interface IShoppingCartService
{
    [OperationContract(Name="AddItemToCart", IsInitiating = true)]
    bool AddItemToCart(string productNumber);

    [OperationContract(Name = "RemoveItemFromCart", IsInitiating = false)]
    bool RemoveItemFromCart(string productNumber);

    [OperationContract(Name = "GetShoppingCart", IsInitiating = false)]
    string GetShoppingCart();

    [OperationContract(Name = "Checkout", IsInitiating = false, IsTerminating = true)]
    bool Checkout();
}
```

4. Open the ShoppingCartService.cs file for the ShoppingCartService project in the Code And Text Editor window. Change the *InstanceContextMode* property of the service to create a new instance of the service for each session, as shown in bold in the following:

```
[ServiceBehavior(InstanceContextMode = InstanceContextMode.PerSession)]
public class ShoppingCartServiceImpl : IShoppingCartService
{
    ...
}
```

5. In the *AddItemToCart* method, comment out the single statement that calls the *restore ShoppingCart* method and the two statements that call the *saveShoppingCart* method.

   The service is using the *PerSession* instance context mode. Therefore, the session will maintain its own copy of the user's shopping cart in memory, which renders these method calls unnecessary.

6. In the *RemoveItemFromCart* method, comment out the statement that calls the *restore ShoppingCart* method and the statement that calls the *saveShoppingCart* method.

7. In the *GetShoppingCart* method, comment out the statement that calls the *restore ShoppingCart* method.

You can test the effects of these changes by modifying the client application.

Test the Operation Sequencing in the *ShoppingCartService* Service

1. Open the ShoppingCartServiceProxy.cs file for the ShoppingCartClient project. This is the proxy class that you generated earlier. You have modified the service contract, so you must update this class to reflect these changes. You can use the *svcutil* utility to generate a new version of the proxy, but the changes are quite small so it is easier to add them by hand, as follows:

   a. Modify the *ServiceContract* attribute for the *ShoppingCartService* interface and specify the *SessionMode* property:

   ```
   [System.ServiceModel.ServiceContractAttribute(
       SessionMode=System.ServiceModel.SessionMode.Required, Namespace="...", ...)]
   public interface ShoppingCartService
   {
       ...
   }
   ```

   b. Add the *IsInitiating* property to the *OperationContract* attribute of the *AddItem ToCart*, *RemoveItemFromCart*, and *GetShoppingCart* methods:

```
[System.ServiceModel.OperationContractAttribute(IsInitiating = true,
    Action="...", ...)]
bool AddItemToCart(string productNumber);

[System.ServiceModel.OperationContractAttribute(IsInitiating = false,
    Action="...", ...)]
bool RemoveItemFromCart(string productNumber);

[System.ServiceModel.OperationContractAttribute(IsInitiating = false,
    Action="...", ...)]
string GetShoppingCart();
```

   c. Add the *IsInitiating* property and the *IsTerminating* property to the *Operation Contract* attribute of the Checkout method:

```
[System.ServiceModel.OperationContractAttribute(
    IsInitiating = false, IsTerminating = true, Action="...", ...)]
bool Checkout();
```

2. Edit the Program.cs file in the ShoppingCartClient project. Add the following statements (shown in bold) between the code that displays the shopping cart and the statement that closes the proxy:

```
static void Main(string[] args)
{
    ...
    try
    {
        ...
        // Query the shopping cart and display the result
        string cartContents = proxy.GetShoppingCart();
        Console.WriteLine(cartContents);

        // Buy the goods in the shopping cart
        proxy.Checkout();
        Console.WriteLine("Goods purchased");

        // Go on another shopping expedition and buy more goods
        // Add a road seat assembly to the shopping cart
        proxy.AddItemToCart("SA-R127");

        // Add a touring seat assembly to the shopping cart
        proxy.AddItemToCart("SA-T872");

        // Remove the road seat assembly
        proxy.RemoveItemFromCart("SA-R127");

        // Display the shopping basket
        cartContents = proxy.GetShoppingCart();
        Console.WriteLine(cartContents);
```

```
            // Buy these goods as well
            proxy.Checkout();
            Console.WriteLine("Goods purchased");

            // Disconnect from the ShoppingCartService service
            proxy.Close();
        }
        ...
}
```

The first statement that invokes the *Checkout* operation terminates the session and destroys the shopping cart. The statements that follow create and use a new session, with its own shopping cart.

3. Start the solution without debugging. In the *ShoppingCartClient* console window, press Enter.

   The client application adds the three items to the shopping cart and outputs the contents. It then displays an error:

This demonstrates that the first call to the *Checkout* operation successfully terminated the session. However, the service has closed the connection that the client application was using when the session finished. Therefore, the client application must open a new connection and create a new session before it can communicate with the service again.

4. Press Enter to close the client application console window. In the host application console window, press Enter to stop the service.

5. The simplest way to create a new connection is to rebuild the proxy. However, you must ensure that you provide the user's credentials again because these will be lost when the new instance of the proxy is created.

   In Visual Studio, add the following statements after the code that performs the first *Checkout* operation in the *Main* method:

```
static void Main(string[] args)
{
    ...
    try
```

```
    {
        ...
        // Buy the goods in the shopping cart
        proxy.Checkout();
        Console.WriteLine("Goods purchased");

        // Go on another shopping expedition and buy more goods
        proxy = new ShoppingCartServiceClient(
            "WS2007HttpBinding_IShoppingCartService");

        // Provide credentials to identify the user
        proxy.ClientCredentials.Windows.ClientCredential.Domain = "Domain";
        proxy.ClientCredentials.Windows.ClientCredential.UserName = "Fred";
        proxy.ClientCredentials.Windows.ClientCredential.Password = "Pa$$w0rd";

        // Add a road seat assembly to the shopping cart
        proxy.AddItemToCart("SA-R127");
        ...
    }
    ...
}
```

6. Start the solution again. In the *ShoppingCartClient* console window, press Enter.

   This time, the client application creates a second session after terminating the first.
   The second session has its own shopping cart:

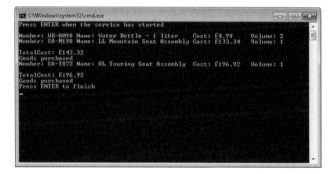

7. Press Enter to close the client application console window. In the host application console window, press Enter to stop the service.

As an additional exercise, you can test the effects of invoking the *RemoveItemFromCart*,
GetShoppingCart, or *Checkout* operations without calling *AddItemToCart* first. These operations do not create a new session, and the client application should fail, with the exception
shown in Figure 7-1.

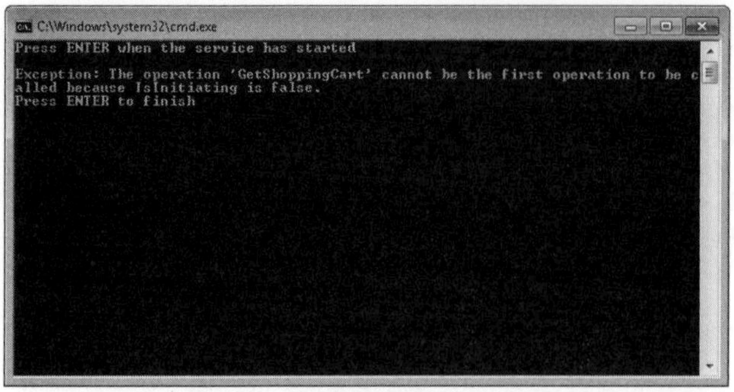

FIGURE 7-1 Invoking operations in the wrong sequence.

Bindings and Sessions

You should be aware that sessions require support from the underlying protocol used to connect to a WCF service. Not all protocols provide this level of support, and consequently not all of the standard bindings available with WCF enable sessions. If you attempt to configure a service to implement sessions by using a binding that does not support sessions, the service will fail to start. The following table lists the standard WCF bindings and indicates whether each binding supports sessions.

Binding	Supports Sessions?
BasicHttpBinding	No
BasicHttpContextBinding	No
WSHttpBinding	Yes
WSHttpContextBinding	Yes
WS2007HttpBinding	Yes
WSDualHttpBinding	Yes
WebHttpBinding	No
WSFederationHttpBinding	Yes
WS2007FederationHttpBinding	Yes
NetTcpBinding	Yes
NetTcpContextBinding	Yes
NetPeerTcpBinding	No
NetNamedPipeBinding	No
NetMsmqBinding	No
MsmqIntegrationBinding	No

Maintaining State by Using a Durable Service

In the earlier section, "Maintaining State with the *PerCall* Instance Context Mode," on page 262, you saw how to maintain state in a session-less service by providing your own code to serialize and deserialize state information. You were also made aware of some of the complications that you need to address if you wish to follow this approach in a professional application. These are non-trivial issues. Fortunately, WCF provides the notion of durable services and durable operations that can help you.

A durable service is a WCF service that uses sessions to maintain state information. However, you can suspend or even halt a session, releasing the resources associated with the service instance while preserving the state of the session. Later, you can start a new service instance, resume a session, and reload the state for that session into the service instance. Durable services are ideal for long-running sessions, during which a client application may be inactive for a period of time; the session and resources associated with an inactive client can be swapped out and reloaded when the client becomes active again. The workflow model for building scalable WCF services relies heavily on durable services (as you will see in Chapter 8), as does Windows Server AppFabric, if you are hosting WCF services in an enterprise environment. However, you can also use durable services outside of these scenarios. You will investigate how in the set of exercises to follow.

You indicate that a service is durable by tagging it with the *DurableService* attribute. A durable service requires a data store to persist the state of its sessions. WCF and Workflow Foundation provide the SQL Persistence Provider for storing session state in a SQL Server database. You can also build your own custom persistence provider if you wish to use some other mechanism. You configure a durable service to reference a persistence provider and provide the details for connecting to the persistence store used by that provider.

When a service instance is started and a new session is created, the WCF runtime generates a unique instance ID for that session. This instance ID is passed in the header of SOAP messages that flow between the client application and the service, and the WCF runtime uses this instance ID to correlate the client requests with the corresponding service instance. When the client closes the connection to the service, the WCF runtime saves the state of the session, including the instance ID, to the persistence store. Later on, if the client application resumes, it can populate the header of the request messages that it sends to the WCF service host with the instance ID of the earlier session. The WCF runtime for the service can create a new session, look up the session state from the persistence store, and use this information to populate the session. To the client application, this new session appears to be exactly the same as the old one.

As well as marking a service as durable, you also need to specify which operations can cause the service to save and resume session state. You do this with the *DurableOperation* attribute. This attribute provides similar functionality to the *IsInitiating* and *IsTerminating* properties of the *OperationBehavior* attribute; you can set a property named *CanCreateInstance* to *true* to specify that the WCF runtime can create a new instance of a durable service when the operation is invoked. You can also set this property to *false* to indicate that the operation can only run by using an existing instance. Additionally, you can set the *CompletesInstance* property to *true* to indicate that the operation finishes the session, and any saved state held in the persistence store should be removed when the operation completes.

In the following exercises, you will modify the *ShoppingCartService* to be a durable service, and examine how to interact with this service from a simple graphical client application.

Examine the ShoppingCartGUIClient Application

1. In Visual Studio, open the ShoppingCart solution located in the DurableShoppingCart folder in the Microsoft Press\WCF Step By Step\Chapter 7 folder.

   This solution contains a version of the *ShoppingCartService* but with the *Operation Behavior* attributes removed. The service implements the *PerSession* instance context mode. The ShoppingCartGUIClient project is a WPF application that invokes the operations in the *ShoppingCartService* service and displays the results in a GUI.

2. In the ShoppingCartGUIClient project, open the MainWindow.xaml file in the Design View window.

   When the user runs the application, she can enter a product number and then click *Add Item* to add the specified item to the shopping cart. The contents of the shopping cart are displayed in the text area below the buttons. The user can remove an item from the shopping cart by clicking the *Remove Item* button, and the contents of the shopping cart will be redisplayed. The user can click the *Checkout* button to invoke the *Checkout* operation, which also clears the shopping cart.

3. Start the solution without debugging. In the Shopping Cart GUI Client window, enter **WB-H098** in the Product Number text box, and then click Add Item. After a short delay, the contents of the shopping cart will appear, displaying a water bottle, as shown in the following image:

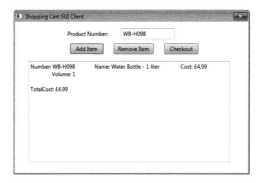

4. Click Add Item again and verify that the volume and total cost are updated.

5. In the Product Number text box, type **SA-M198**, and then click Add Item one more time. A mountain seat assembly should be added and appear in the shopping cart displayed in the window.

6. Click Remove Item. The mountain seat assembly should be removed from the shopping cart.

7. Click Checkout. The shopping cart should be emptied.

8. Close the Shopping Cart GUI Client window. In the service host application console window, press Enter to stop the service.

 9 In Solution Explorer, expand the *MainWindow.xaml* node in the ShoppingCartGUI Client project, and then open the MainWindow.xaml.cs file in the Code And Text Editor window.

This file contains the code behind the user interface. The highlights are reproduced in the following code example:

```
public partial class MainWindow : Window
{
    private ShoppingCartServiceClient proxy = null;
    ...
    private void Window_Loaded(object sender, RoutedEventArgs e)
    {
        // Connect to the ShoppingCartService service
        proxy = new ShoppingCartServiceClient(
            "WS2007HttpBinding_IShoppingCartService");
    }

    private void Window_Unloaded(object sender, RoutedEventArgs e)
    {
        // Disconnect from the service
        proxy.Close();
    }

    // Add the item specified in the productNumber Text Box to the shopping cart
    private void addItem_Click(object sender, RoutedEventArgs e)
    {
        try
        {
            // Add the item to the shoppping cart
            proxy.AddItemToCart(productNumber.Text);

            // Display the shopping cart
            string cartContents = proxy.GetShoppingCart();
            shoppingCartContents.Text = cartContents;
        }
```

```
                catch (Exception ex)
                {
                    MessageBox.Show(ex.Message, "Error adding item to cart",
                        MessageBoxButton.OK, MessageBoxImage.Error);
                }
            }

            // Remove the item specified in the productNumber Text Box from the shopping cart
            private void removeItem_Click(object sender, RoutedEventArgs e)
            {
                try
                {
                    // Remove the item from the shoppping cart
                    proxy.RemoveItemFromCart(productNumber.Text);

                    // Display the shopping cart
                    string cartContents = proxy.GetShoppingCart();
                    shoppingCartContents.Text = cartContents;
                }
                catch (Exception ex)
                {
                    MessageBox.Show(ex.Message, "Error removing item from cart",
                        MessageBoxButton.OK, MessageBoxImage.Error);
                }
            }

            // Checkout
            private void checkout_Click(object sender, RoutedEventArgs e)
            {
                try
                {
                    proxy.Checkout();

                    // Clear the shopping cart displayed in the window
                    shoppingCartContents.Clear();
                }
                catch (Exception ex)
                {
                    MessageBox.Show(ex.Message, "Error checking out",
                        MessageBoxButton.OK, MessageBoxImage.Error);
                }
            }
        }
```

The connection to the service is held in the *proxy* variable. The connection is established when the window appears, and it is terminated when the window disappears.

The *addItem_Click* method runs when the user clicks Add Item. This method invokes the *AddItemToCart* operation, passing the product number specified in the *productNumber* text box as the parameter. The method then calls *GetShoppingCart* to retrieve the contents of the shopping cart from the service, which it then displays in the *shoppingCart Contents* text area in the window.

The logic behind the *removeItem_Click* method is similar. This method runs when the user clicks Remove Item, and it calls the *RemoveItemFromCart* operation followed by *GetShoppingCart* to retrieve the updated shopping cart information.

The *checkout_Click* method runs when the user clicks Checkout. This method calls the *Checkout* operation and then clears the shopping cart displayed in the window.

This client application is straightforward, but it exhibits some very poor practice that does not lend itself to building a professional, scalable system. The problem is that the connection to the service is established and the session initiated when the user starts the application and opens the window, and this connection and session remain in memory in the service host until the user closes the window and stops the application. If the user *forgets* to close the client application before she goes off on holiday for two weeks, the resources associated with the session will remain in memory for this time. Additionally, if the service host is shut down during this period, the session state information (the shopping cart) will be lost.

Reconfiguring *ShoppingCartService* as a durable service and making some adjustments to the code in the client application can rectify these problems. You will start by creating the persistence store for the durable service.

Create the Persistence Store for the SQL Persistence Provider

1. In Visual Studio, select View | Server Explorer.

2. In Server Explorer, right-click Data Connections, and then click Create New SQL Server Database. In the Create New SQL Server Database dialog box, set the Server Name to **.\SQLExpress**, click Use Windows Authentication, enter **WCFPersistence** in the New Database Name text box, and then click OK.

3. From the File menu, click Open, and then click File. In the Open File dialog box move to the folder C:\Windows\Microsoft.NET\Framework\v4.0.30319\SQL\en, select the SqlPersistenceProviderSchema.sql file, and then click Open.

This SQL script creates the *InstanceData* table in the persistence database. The SQL Persistence Provider uses this table to store session information.

> **Note** The name of the folder (v4.0.30319) may change as newer versions of the .NET Framework are released.

4. From the Data menu, click Transact-SQL Editor, click Connection, and then click Connect. In the Connect to Database Engine dialog box, in the Server Name text box, enter **.\SQLExpress**. Ensure that Authentication is set to *Windows Authentication*, and then click Connect.

5. In the Visual Studio toolbar, in the Database drop-down, click **WCFPersistence**.

> **Important** This step is important; otherwise, the script will be run in the SQL Server *master* database.

6. From the Data menu, click Transact-SQL Editor, and then click Execute SQL. Verify that the SQL script runs and displays the message "Command(s) completed successfully."

7. Follow the process described in steps 3 through 6 to open and run the SqlPersistence ProviderLogic.sql script located in the C:\Windows\Microsoft.NET\Framework\ v4.0.30319\SQL\en folder.

   This script creates the stored procedures required by the SQL Persistence Provider to insert, update, and delete information about sessions in the *InstanceData* table. These operations are performed in a thread-safe manner by using logic that locks the session data while it is being manipulated.

You can now modify the service and configure it as a durable service that uses this persistence store.

Reconfigure the *ShoppingCartService* Service as a Durable Service

1. In Solution Explorer, click the ShoppingCartService project. From the Project menu, select *ShoppingCartService* Properties.

2. In the ShoppingCartService Properties window, click the Application tab. In the Target Framework drop-down, click **.NET Framework 4**. In the Target Framework Change message box, click Yes to allow Visual Studio to change the target framework.

   The project was originally built by using the more lightweight version of the .NET Framework provided by the Client Profile. However, the persistence functionality of durable services requires assemblies that are only available with the full-blown version of the .NET Framework.

3. Add a reference to the *System.WorkflowServices* assembly to the ShoppingCartService project.

   This assembly contains the implementation of the *DurableService* and *DurableOperation* attributes.

4. Open the IShoppingCartService.cs file for the ShoppingCartService project in the Code And Text Editor window. Examine the *ShoppingCartItem* class.

   Remember that this class holds the session data for each service instance. You marked this class as serializable earlier so you could save instances of this class as XML data. The SQL Persistence Provider also requires that this—and any other data stored as part of the session state—is serializable, so leave the *Serializable* attribute in place.

5. Open the ShoppingCartService.cs file for the ShoppingCartService project in the Code And Text Editor window. Add the following *using* statement to the list at the top of the file:

   ```
   using System.ServiceModel.Description;
   ```

   The *DurableService* and *DurableOperation* attributes implemented by the *System.Work flowServices* assembly are defined in this namespace.

6. Verify that the *InstanceContextMode* property of the *ServiceBehavior* attribute for the *ShoppingCartServceImpl* class is set to *InstanceContextMode.PerSession*.

   All durable services must implement sessions.

7. Add the *Serializable* and *DurableService* attributes (shown in bold in the following) to the *ShoppingCartServiceImpl* class.

   ```
   [ServiceBehavior(InstanceContextMode=InstanceContextMode.PerSession)]
   [Serializable]
   [DurableService]
   public class ShoppingCartServiceImpl : IShoppingCartService
   {
       ...
   }
   ```

   The SQL Persistence Provider requires that all durable services are also serializable so that their state can be saved to the persistence database.

8. Locate the *AddItemToCart* method in the *ShoppingCartServiceImpl* class. Tag this method as a durable operation and set the *CanCreateInstance* property to **true**, as shown in the following.

   ```
   [DurableOperation(CanCreateInstance = true)]
   public bool AddItemToCart(string productNumber)
   {
       ...
   }
   ```

Following the same logic described in the section "Sequencing Operations in a WCF Service" on page 271, a client application can use this operation to start a new session if one has not already been created.

9. Mark the *RemoveItemFromCart* method as a durable operation, but set the *CanCreate Instance* property to **false**. Do the same for the *GetShoppingCart* method.

```
[DurableOperation(CanCreateInstance = false)]
public bool RemoveItemFromCart(string productNumber)
{
    . . .
}
. . .
[DurableOperation(CanCreateInstance = false)]
public string GetShoppingCartCart()
{
    . . .
}
```

Neither of these methods can be invoked unless a session already exists.

10. Tag the *Checkout* operation with the *DurableOperation* attribute. Set the *CanCreate Instance* property to **false** and set the *CompletesInstance* property to **true**.

```
[DurableOperation(CanCreateInstance = false, CompletesInstance = true)]
public bool Checkout()
{
    . . .
}
```

This operation finishes a session and removes the state from the persistence store when it completes.

11. In Solution Explorer, click the ShoppingCartHost project. From the Project menu, select ShoppingCartHost Properties. In the ShoppingCartHost Properties window, click the Application tab. In the Target Framework drop-down, click **.NET Framework 4**. In the Target Framework Change message box, click Yes to allow Visual Studio to change the target framework.

The ShoppingCartHost project references the ShoppingCartService project and must run by using the same version of the .NET Framework.

12. Open the App.config file for the ShoppingCartHost project in the Code And Text Editor window. Add the following connection string (shown in bold) to the *connectionStrings* section.

```
<?xml version="1.0"?>
<configuration>
  <connectionStrings>
    <add name="AdventureWorksEntities" connectionString="..."/>
```

```
  <add name="DurableServiceConnectionString" connectionString=
"Data Source=.\SQLExpress;Initial Catalog=WCFPersistence;IntegratedSecurity=True"/>
  </connectionStrings>
  ...
</configuration>
```

This connection string contains the information that the SQL Persistence Provider requires for connecting to the SQL Server database that you created in the previous exercise. You will reference this connection by its name, *DurableServiceConnectionString*, in the WCF configuration for the service host.

13. Save the App.config file, and then edit it again using the Service Configuration Editor.

14. In the Configuration pane, expand the Advanced folder, and then click Service Behaviors. In the Service Behaviors pane, click New Service Behavior Configuration.

15. In the Behavior: NewBehavior() pane, in the Name field, enter **DurableServiceBehavior**. In the lower pane, click Add.

16. In the Adding Behavior Element Extension Sections dialog box, click persistenceProvider, and then click Add.

17. In the Configuration pane, under the DurableServiceBehavior node, click the *persistence Provider* node.

18. In the PersistenceProvider pane, in the Type field, enter **System.ServiceModel. Persistence.SqlPersistenceProviderFactory**.

19. In the Configuration pane, expand the *persistenceProvider* node, and then click persistence ProvideArguments.

20. In the PersistenceProviderArguments pane, click New.

21. In the Persistence Provider Arguments Editor dialog box, in the Name field, enter **connectionStringName**. In the Value field enter **DurableServiceConnectionString**, and then click OK.

These parameters specify that the WCF runtime should use the *SqlPersistenceProvider Factory* class to create a *SqlPersistenceProvider* object for persisting session data. This object will use the information specified by the *connectionStringName* parameter to connect to the SQL Server database.

> **Note** The *SqlPersistenceProviderFactory* class is implemented in the *System.WorkflowServices* assembly.

22. In the Configuration pane, under the Services folder, click the *ShoppingCartService. ShoppingCartServiceImpl* service. In the Service:ShoppingCartService.ShoppingCart ServiceImpl pane, set the *BehaviorConfiguration* property to **DurableServiceBehavior**.

23. In the Configuration pane, expand the *ShoppingCartService.ShoppingCartServiceImpl* service, expand the Endpoints folder, and then click the *(Empty Name)* endpoint.

24. In the Service Endpoint pane, change the *Binding* property to **wsHttpContextBinding**.

As mentioned earlier, the instance ID generated by the durable service is passed in the header of the SOAP messages that are exchanged by the client application and the service. The protocol used by the service must populate and examine this information automatically; the *wsHttpContextBinding* binding provides this functionality.

Note Remember from Chapter 2, "Hosting a WCF Service," that WCF provides three built-in bindings that can pass context information; *wsHttpContextBinding*, *basicHttpContext Binding*, and *netTcpContextBinding*. As described here, the *wsHttpContextBinding* binding passes information in the SOAP header of messages, as does the *netTcpContextBinding* binding. The *basicHttpContextBinding* binding uses cookies.

25. Save the configuration file, and then exit the Service Configuration Editor.

Note If you examine the app.config file by using the Code And Text Editor window, you may receive a warning that the *connectionStringName* attribute is not allowed in the *persistenceProvider* element. You can ignore this warning.

The next step is to modify the client application. You must configure it to use the same binding as the service (*wsHttpContextBinding*), and you will also update it to take better advantage of the durable service. Specifically, you will modify the code behind the *MainWindow* window to open and close connections to the service as they are required rather than creating a connection when the application starts and holding this connection open until the application finishes.

Update the ShoppingCartGUIClient Application

1. Open the app.config file for the ShoppingCartGUIClient project in the Code And Text Editor window. Modify the client endpoint to use the *wsHttpContextBinding* binding, and change the name of the endpoint to **WSHttpContextBinding_IShoppingCart Service**, for consistency, as shown in bold in the following:

```
<?xml version="1.0" encoding="utf-8" ?>
<configuration>
  <system.serviceModel>
    <client>
      <endpoint address="http://localhost:9000/ShoppingCartService/ShoppingCart
          Service.svc"
          binding="wsHttpContextBinding" bindingConfiguration=""
          contract="ShoppingCartClient.ShoppingCartService.ShoppingCartService"
```

```
      name="WSHttpContextBinding_IShoppingCartService" kind=""
         endpointConfiguration="">
      </endpoint>
    </client>
  </system.serviceModel>
</configuration>
```

2. Open the MainWindow.xaml.cs file in the Code And Text Editor window. Comment out the code in the *Window_Loaded* and *Window_Unloaded* methods.

3. Add the following *using* statements to the list at the top of the file:

```
using System.ServiceModel;
using System.ServiceModel.Channels;
```

4. In the *MainWIndow* class, add the private *context* variable (shown in bold in the following) after the definition of the *proxy* variable:

```
public partial class MainWindow : Window
{
    private ShoppingCartServiceClient proxy = null;
    private IDictionary<string, string> context = null;
    ...
}
```

You will use the *context* variable to capture the context generated by the service when it creates the session on the initial call to the *AddItemToCart* operation. The context is a dictionary of key/value pairs and will include the instance ID (with the key *"instanceId"*) that the WCF runtime creates and uses to identify the session and correlate with the client application. You will pass this context in the SOAP header of subsequent calls to operations.

5. Modify the code in the *try* block of the *addItem_Click* method, as shown in bold in the following:

```
// Add the item specified in the productNumber Text Box to the shopping cart
private void addItem_Click(object sender, RoutedEventArgs e)
{
    try
    {
        // Create the proxy and connect to the service
        using (proxy = new ShoppingCartServiceClient(
            "WSHttpContextBinding_IShoppingCartService"))
        {
            // If the context is not null, then the client application
            // has already created the durable session.
            // Set the context in the IContextManager object for
            // the proxy so that this context is passed in the SOAP
            // header of the AddItemToCart and
            // GetShoppingCart requests.
            IContextManager contextManager =
                proxy.InnerChannel.GetProperty<IContextManager>();
            if (context != null)
```

```
        {
            contextManager.SetContext(context);
        }

        // Add the item to the shoppping cart
        proxy.AddItemToCart(productNumber.Text);

        // If the context is null, then this was the first call
        // made to the session.
        // Capture the context and save it so it can be
        // passed to subsequent requests
        if (context == null)
        {
            context = contextManager.GetContext();
            MessageBox.Show(context["instanceId"], "New context created",
                        MessageBoxButton.OK, MessageBoxImage.Information);
        }

        // Display the shopping cart
        string cartContents = proxy.GetShoppingCart();
        shoppingCartContents.Text = cartContents;
    }
}
catch (Exception e)
{
    ...
}
}
```

The main items to notice in this code are:

❏ The method now creates the proxy object which it uses to communicate with the service. The method also destroys the proxy object when it has finished with it; this action closes the communications channel with the service and releases the in-memory resources associated with the session. At this point the WCF runtime for the service persists the session state to the persistence store.

❏ The name of the endpoint used to create the proxy is *WSHttpContextBinding_IShoppingCartService*; this is the name that you specified in the application configuration file.

❏ The method creates an *IContextManager* object which provides access to the context information held in the SOAP header of messages sent and received by using the proxy. Notice that you obtain a reference to this object by using the *GetProperty* method of the *InnerChannel* property of the proxy. The *InnerChannel* property gives you direct access to the communications channel used by the proxy.

❏ The method examines the *context* variable, and if this variable is not *null*, then the user must have clicked the Add Item button previously to initiate the session and create the shopping cart. In this case, before calling *AddItemToCart* again, the code invokes the *SetContext* method of the *IContextManager* object with the previously saved context information. The *IContextManager* object will pass this information in the SOAP header as part of the subsequent *AddItemToCart* and *GetShoppingCart* request messages, and the WCF runtime for the service will use this information to resurrect the session state associated with this context.

❑ The code that retrieves the context from the SOAP header of the response received from the service after calling the *AddItemToCart* operation and saves it if the *context* variable is *null*. In this case, this is the first time that the user has clicked the *Add Item* button, so the WCF runtime has created an entirely new session. The context is passed back to the client application in the SOAP header of the response message, and the client application can access it through the *GetContext* method of the *IContextManager* object. For your information, the code also displays the instance ID found in the context. You will see that the instance ID is simply a GUID that the SQL Persistence Provider uses as the key for storing and retrieving information in the persistence database.

6. Make the changes highlighted in bold in the code that follows to the *removeItem_Click* method. Remember that this method calls the *RemoveItemFromCart* operation which cannot be used to initiate a session. The logic in this method therefore assumes that the session has already been created, and so it simply populates the *IContextManager* object with the previously saved context information. This context is transmitted to the service in the SOAP header as part of the *RemoveItemFromCart* and *GetShoppingCart* request messages.

```
// Remove the item specified in the productNumber Text Box from the shopping cart
private void removeItem_Click(object sender, RoutedEventArgs e)
{
    try
    {
        // Create the proxy and connect to the service
        using (proxy =
            new ShoppingCartServiceClient("WSHttpContextBinding_IShoppingCartService"))
        {
            // Set the context in the IContextManager object for the proxy so
            // that this context s passed in the SOAP header of the
            // RemoveItemFromCart and GetShoppingCart requests.
            IContextManager contextManager =
                proxy.InnerChannel.GetProperty<IContextManager>();
            contextManager.SetContext(context);

            // Remove the item from the shoppping cart
            proxy.RemoveItemFromCart(productNumber.Text);

            // Display the shopping cart
            string cartContents = proxy.GetShoppingCart();
            shoppingCartContents.Text = cartContents;
        }
    }
    catch (Exception e)
    {
        ...
    }
}
```

7. Update the *checkout_Click* method, as shown in bold in the code that follows. The logic is similar to that in the *removeItem_Click* method. The principal difference is that the method sets the *context* variable to *null* as it finishes. This is because the *Checkout* operation terminates the session, so the context is no longer valid; a subsequent call to the *AddItemToCart* method must create a new session with a new context.

```
// Checkout
private void checkout_Click(object sender, RoutedEventArgs e)
{
    try
    {
        // Create the proxy and connect to the service
        using (proxy = new ShoppingCartServiceClient(
            "WSHttpContextBinding_IShoppingCartService"))
        {
            // Set the context in the IContextManager object for the proxy
            // so that this context is passed in the SOAP header of the
            // Checkout request.
            IContextManager contextManager =
                proxy.InnerChannel.GetProperty<IContextManager>();
            contextManager.SetContext(context);
            proxy.Checkout();

            // Clear the shopping cart displayed in the window
            shoppingCartContents.Clear();

            // Clear the context - the session has completed
            context = null;
        }
    }
    catch (Exception e)
    {
        ...
    }
}
```

Test the Durable Service

1. Start the solution without debugging. In the Shopping Cart GUI Client window, enter **WB-H098** in the Product Number text box, and then click Add Item.

   A message box similar to that shown in the following image should appear, displaying the instance ID of the session that has been created by the durable service (the GUID for your session will be different from that shown in the image):

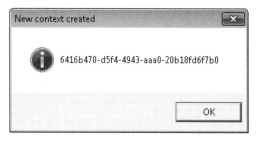

2. Click OK and verify that a water bottle has been added to the shopping cart.

3. Leave the Shopping Cart GUI Client window and the service host console application window running and return to Visual Studio.

4. In the Server Explorer pane, expand the Data Connections folder, expand the *Your Computer\sqlexpress.WCFPersistence.dbo* connection (where *YourComputer* is the name of your computer), expand Tables, right-click the *InstanceData* table, and then click Show Table Data.

    The SQL Persistence Provider stores session information in this table. You should see a single row in this table, and the value in the *id* column should be the same as the instance ID displayed previously by the message box in the client application. The session data is held in a binary format in the *instance* column.

5. Return to the Shopping Cart GUI Client window. Enter **SA-M198** in the Product Number text box, and then click Add Item.

    This time, no message box appears because the *addItem_Click* ascertains that the *context* variable has a value, so a session must have already been created. The context is passed to the *ShoppingCartService* service. The WCF runtime for the service creates a new service instance, extracts the instance ID from the context, retrieves the session data for this instance ID from the *InstanceData* table in the *WCFPersistence* database, and uses this data to populate the service instance. The mountain seat assembly is added to the shopping cart in this service instance. When the *addItem_Click* method finishes, the WCF runtime for the service saves the session data back to the *InstanceData* table before destroying the service instance.

6. Leave the Shopping Cart GUI Client window running, but close the service host console application window. In Solution Explorer, right-click the ShoppingCartHost project, point to Debug, and then click Start New Instance.

    This step simulates a user leaving the client application running while the service host is shut down and restarted.

7. Return to the Shopping Cart GUI Client window. Enter **PU-M044** in the Product Number text box, and then click Add Item.

A mountain bike pump is added to the shopping cart. Notice that the WCF runtime has successfully restored the existing contents of the shopping cart, despite the fact that the service host has been shut down and restarted in the period since the previous request.

8. Click Checkout.

   This operation completes the session, and the shopping cart is emptied.

9. Leave the Shopping Cart GUI Client window and the service host console application window running and return to Visual Studio displaying the data from the *InstanceData* table. In the Visual Studio toolbar, click the Execute SQL button (it has an image of a red exclamation mark). The table should now be empty.

   When the *Checkout* operation completed, the session was terminated, and the session information saved in the persistence store was removed.

> **Note** If you now click the Add Item button in the Shopping Cart GUI Client window, the client application will initiate a new session with its own unique session ID and shopping cart.

10. Close the Shopping Cart GUI Client window and the service host console application window.

Summary

In this chapter, you have seen the different options that the WCF runtime provides for creating an instance of a service. A service instance can exist for the duration of a single operation or for the entire session, until the client application closes the connection. In many cases, a service instance is private to a client, but WCF also supports singleton service instances that can be shared by multiple instances of a client. You have also seen how you can selectively control which operations create a new session and which operations close a session. Finally, you saw how you can create a durable service with which you can maintain session state without requiring that the corresponding service instance is active. Durable services are ideal for building systems that involve potentially long-running sessions that need to be able to survive service shutdown and restart.

Chapter 8
Implementing Services by Using Workflows

After completing this chapter, you will be able to:

- Describe how to build WCF–services-based Windows Workflow Foundation (WF) workflows.

- Build client applications that can consume WCF services based on WF workflows.

- Explain how to use the WF messaging activities to implement common messaging patterns.

- Manage state and correlate messages in a WCF service built by using WF.

- Configure the WF host environment to support long-running, durable services.

One of the principal reasons that organizations use WCF is to build service-oriented wrappers around existing components and applications so that they can be reused in an easily adaptable manner. This strategy gives organizations the flexibility to more easily respond to rapidly changing business requirements and create or adapt systems quickly that can meet those requirements.

The business processes followed by most organizations comprise a distinct series of steps that must be performed in a specific order. Some of these steps may involve invoking an operation in a service. This implies that there may be a requirement to ensure that the operations in a WCF service should be invoked in a sequence that matches the steps in the underlying business process. You have seen that you can tag methods in a service to specify which operations can initiate or terminate a session, but other than that, a service has little control over the sequence in which a client application invokes its operations. That makes it difficult to enforce an ordering and could possibly lead to bugs that are difficult to spot (and rectify). Defining a service by using a WF workflow can help to address this issue and enforce an ordering between operations.

Another potential issue is that of who should actually define and implement the logic for a business process. A business analyst might be best positioned to understand the processes that an organization follows. However, you could not necessarily expect a business analyst to be well versed in WCF or to understand how to implement the operations for a WCF service; this is clearly a task for a developer. On the other hand, a developer might be highly skilled in building reusable components and services but may not have a full understanding of the business processes that use them. WF can help to address this problem as well. A business analyst can work with a developer using WF to define a graphical model of the various business processes required, and a developer can implement the code required to perform the various tasks described by the model.

Yet another consideration (as discussed in Chapter 7, "Maintaining State and Sequencing Operations") is that of scalability. WF provides an ideal framework for implementing long-running business processes as workflows. WCF services that you build by using WF workflows can easily take advantage of the persistence functionality described in Chapter 7 for maintaining durable state information, swapping sessions out of memory as they become inactive, and reloading them when they are reactivated. Additionally, you can use Window Server AppFabric to host and manage WCF services based on WF workflows in an enterprise environment.

In this chapter, you will see how to build WCF services based on business processes modeled by using WF workflows, and how you can construct client applications that interact with these services.

> **Note** The documentation provided with Visual Studio refers to WCF services built by using WF workflows simply as "Workflow services". To save space and avoid unnecessary repetition, I will use the same terminology throughout this chapter.

Building a Simple Workflow Service and Client Application

A good place to start is to use WF to build a simple service that exposes a single stateless operation. You can then see how you can invoke this operation from a client application.

Implementing a Workflow Service

In the first set of exercises in this chapter, you will revisit the *ProductsService* service that a client application can use to obtain information about products sold by AdventureWorks. You will implement the *GetProduct* operation, which takes a product number and returns the details of that product, as part of a WF service.

> **Note** The exercises in this chapter assume that you are familiar with building workflows by using Windows Workflow Foundation and Visual Studio 2010.

Create the *ProductsWorkflowService* Service

1. Using Visual Studio, create a new WCF Workflow Service Application project:

   a. In the New Project dialog box, navigate to the Visual C# | WCF folder in the Installed Templates pane.

   b. Choose the WCF Workflow Service Application template.

c. Specify the following properties for the solution:

Property	Value
Name	ProductsWorkflowService
Location	Microsoft Press\WCF Step By Step\Chapter 8 (within your Documents folder)
Solution name	ProductsWorkflow

Visual Studio generates a new workflow service called Service1.xamlx in the Products WorkflowService project (all workflow services have the .xamlx file extension). The following image shows this service:

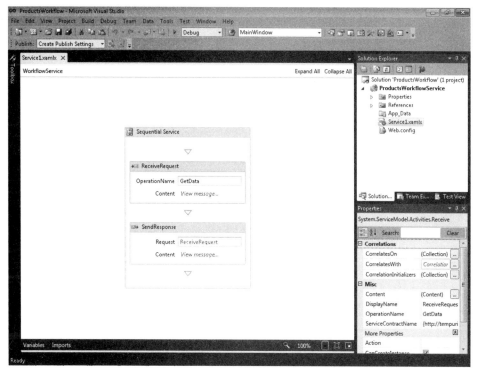

This is a simple sequential service consisting of a *WorkflowService* activity that contains a series of steps defined in a Sequence activity. The *ReceiveRequest* activity waits for an incoming request message from a client application specifying an operation called *GetData*. The *SendResponse* activity sends a response message back to the client application. Currently there is no additional processing performed by this operation; you are expected to add the necessary logic between the *ReceiveRequest* and *SendResponse* activities.

The *ReceiveRequest* and *SendResponse* activities define the service interface. You will see in the following steps how you can change the name of the operation and the service contract that is generated if you do not want to use the default values.

2. In Solution Explorer, rename the Service1.xamlx file to **ProductsService.xamlx**.

3. In the Design View window that is displaying the workflow, click the background, outside the bounds of the Sequential Service activity. In the Properties window, set the *ConfigurationName* and *Name* properties to **ProductsService**.

   The *ConfigurationName* property of a workflow service specifies the name of the service in the Web.config file for configuring this service. The *Name* property is the name of the service that appears in the WSDL description of the metadata for the service.

4. Click the *ReceiveRequest* activity in the Design View window. In the *OperationName* box, type **GetProduct**. This is the name of the operation that will be generated in the service contract.

5. In the Properties window, change the *ServiceContractName* property to **{http://adventure-works.com/}IProductsService**.

   The curly bracket characters shown above act as delimiters for the namespace generated for the service.

6. Ensure that the *ReceiveRequest* activity is still selected, and then click the Variables tab in the lower-left corner of the Design View window. Change the name of the *data* variable to **localProductNumber** and change the type of the variable to **String**. The *GetProduct* operation will expect a message that contains a product number provided by the client application; it will respond with another message that contains the details of this product. You will use this variable to hold the product number retrieved from the request message sent by the client application.

   Be careful not to modify or delete the *handle* variable. The workflow uses this variable to correlate the *SendResponse* activity with the *ReceiveRequest* activity; message correlation will be described in more detail later in this chapter.

   When you are done, click the Variables tab again to hide the variable definitions.

> **Note** Renaming the *data* variable causes several validation errors to appear in the workflow (they are displayed as exclamation marks in red circles). This is because the *Receive Request* and *SendResponse* activities still reference the original *data* variable. You will modify the *ReceiveRequest* activity in the next step, and update the *SendResponse* activity later in the exercise to reference the correct variables and fix the validation errors.

7. In the *ReceiveRequest* activity, in the *Content* property, click View Message.

The Content Definition dialog box appears. You use this dialog box to specify the data passed to the operation. You can specify this information either as a message object or a list of parameters. A message object is a type that implements the *IMessage* interface. You will learn more about *Message* objects and the *IMessage* interface in Chapter 11, "Programmatically Controlling the Configuration and Communications."

8. In the Content Definition dialog box, select the Parameters option, and then click Add New Parameter. Use the information in the following table to specify the details of the parameter, and then click OK:

Property	Value
Name	ProductNumber
Type	String
Assign To	localProductNumber

The SOAP message for this operation should contain the data specified by any parameters that you define here (the client application must populate the message with this data). The Assign To field in the parameter definition causes the workflow runtime to retrieve the parameter into the specified variable so that you can access it in other activities in the workflow.

> **Note** If you are unfamiliar with Windows Workflow Foundation, you may be surprised to see that the value in the Assign To field is designated as a Visual Basic expression, despite the fact that you are using Visual C#. This is not an error. When you design a workflow and have to specify an expression as part of the definition of an activity, you always use Visual Basic syntax. However, when you are writing the code to support activities and workflows, you use the language that you specified when you created the project (Visual C# in this case).

9. In the Design View window, click the *ReceiveRequest* activity. In the Properties window, verify that the *CanCreateInstance* check box is selected (select it if it is not currently checked).

This property specifies that a client application can invoke this operation to create a new instance of the service and start a new session. At least one operation in a service must enable this property; otherwise, the client application has no way of initiating a service instance.

You have now defined the request message for the *GetProduct* operation. If you recall from the earlier chapters, the purpose of this operation is to retrieve the details of the product from the *AdventureWorks* database, create a *ProductData* object and populate it with this information, and then return the *ProductData* object back to the client. To refresh your memory, the code that follows shows how you implemented this operation in Chapter 6, "Maintaining Service Contracts and Data Contracts."

```csharp
public class ProductsServiceImpl : IProductsService
{
    public bool ProductExists(string productNumber, AdventureWorksEntities database)
    {
        // Check to see whether the specified product exists in the database
        int numProducts = (from p in database.Products
                           where string.Equals(p.ProductNumber, productNumber)
                           select p).Count();

        return numProducts > 0;
    }
    ...
    public ProductData GetProduct(string productNumber)
    {
        // Create a reference to a ProductData object
        // This object will be instantiated if a matching product is found
        ProductData productData = null;

        try
        {
            // Connect to the AdventureWorks database by using the Entity Framework
            using (AdventureWorksEntities database = new AdventureWorksEntities())
            {
                // Check that the specified product exists
                if (ProductExists(productNumber, database))
                {
                    // Find the first product that matches the specified product number
                    Product matchingProduct = database.Products.First(
                        p => String.Compare(p.ProductNumber, productNumber) == 0);

                    productData = new ProductData()
                    {
                        Name = matchingProduct.Name,
                        ProductNumber = matchingProduct.ProductNumber,
                        Color = matchingProduct.Color,
                        ListPrice = matchingProduct.ListPrice
                    };
                }
            }
        }
        catch
        {
            // Ignore exceptions in this implementation
        }

        // Return the product
        return productData;
    }
}
```

It is possible to implement the basic logic of this operation by using the standard workflow activities provided with Visual Studio. However, none of the activities provided as standard with WF help you interact with a database. Consequently, in the next exercise you will create some custom code activities for querying the *AdventureWorks* database, and then you will incorporate these activities into the workflow that defines the *GetProduct* operation.

The code activities that you will implement are:

- *ProductExists*   This activity will test whether a product with a specified product number exists in the *AdventureWorks* database, and then return a Boolean value. You will connect to the database by using the Entity Framework and the same *ProductsEntityModel* assembly that you have employed in earlier chapters. You will pass the *AdventureWorks Entities* object that connects to the database, and the product number, as input arguments to the activity.

- *FindProduct*   This activity will retrieve the details of a specified product from the *AdventureWorks* database and populate a *ProductData* object. As before, for input arguments to the activity, you will pass the *AdventureWorksEntities* object that connects to the database along with the product number, and the activity will return the populated *ProductData* object.

Create the *ProductData* type, and Implement the *ProductExists* and *FindProduct* Activities

1. In Visual Studio, add a new item to the ProductsWorkflowService project using the information in the following table:

Property	Value
Template	Code Activity (in the Workflow templates list in the Add New Item dialog box)
Name	ProductsService.Activities.cs

> **Hint** It is common practice to implement activities for a workflow in a file that follows this naming convention.

2. Add a reference to the *ProductsEntityModel* assembly located in the Microsoft Press\ WCF Step By Step\Chapter 8 folder. Remember that this assembly contains a copy of the entity model for the *Product* and *ProductInventory* tables in the *AdventureWorks* database.

3. Add references to the *System.Data.Entity* assembly and the *System.Runtime.Serialization* assembly.

4. In the Code And Text Editor window displaying the ProductsService.Activities.cs file, add the following *using* statements to the list at the top of the file:

```
using System.Runtime.Serialization;
using System.ServiceModel;
using ProductsEntityModel;
```

5. In the *ProductsWorkflowService* namespace, before the *ProductsService* class, add the *ProductData* class shown in the code that follows. This is the same class that you used in the earlier chapters. Notice that the *ProductData* class is defined as a data contract so that it can be easily serialized by the WCF runtime.

```
// Data contract describing the details of a product passed to client applications
[DataContract]
public class ProductData
{
    [DataMember]
    public string Name;

    [DataMember]
    public string ProductNumber;

    [DataMember]
    public string Color;

    [DataMember]
    public decimal ListPrice;
}
```

 Note The code for this class is available in the ProductData.txt file, which is located in the Microsoft Press\WCF Step By Step\Chapter 8 folder.

6. In the Code And Text Editor window, change the name of the *ProductsService* class to **ProductExists**, as shown in bold in the following:

```
public sealed class ProductExists : CodeActivity
{
    ...
}
```

All code activities inherit from the *CodeActivity* class. The *CodeActivity* class provides a method called *Execute* that runs when the code activity is invoked from a workflow. You override this method with the code that you wish to perform when the activity runs.

7. In the *ProductExists* class, replace the *Text* property above the *Execute* method with the following pair of properties.

```
public sealed class ProductExists : CodeActivity
{
    public InArgument<AdventureWorksEntities> Database { get; set; }
    public InArgument<string> ProductNumber { get; set; }
```

```
    // If your activity returns a value, derive from CodeActivity<TResult>
    // and return the value from the Execute method.
    protected override void Execute(CodeActivityContext context)
    {
        ...
    }
}
```

You pass information into an activity from a workflow by defining one or more input arguments. An input argument is a property based on the *InArgument* generic type. You can also define output arguments by using the *OutArgument* generic type, but in this exercise, you will return a value from the activity directly rather than by passing an output argument.

8. When you return a value from the *Execute* method of an activity, you must specify the return type in the activity definition.

Modify the definition of the *ProductExists* class so that it inherits from the *CodeActivity<Boolean>* generic class. Change the *Execute* method so it returns a Boolean value, as shown in bold in the example that follows.

```
public sealed class ProductExists : CodeActivity<Boolean>
{
    ...
    // If your activity returns a value, derive from CodeActivity<TResult>
    // and return the value from the Execute method.
    protected override bool Execute(CodeActivityContext context)
    {
        ...
    }
}
```

9. Remove the existing comment and line of code in the *Execute* method, and replace it with the code shown in bold in the following:

```
protected override bool Execute(CodeActivityContext context)
{
    // Retrieve the product number and database reference from the input arguments
    string productNumber = ProductNumber.Get(context);
    AdventureWorksEntities database = Database.Get(context);

    // Check to see whether the specified product exists in the database
    int numProducts = (from p in database.Products
                       where string.Equals(p.ProductNumber, productNumber)
                       select p).Count();

    return numProducts > 0;
}
```

This code is very similar to the code for the *ProductExists* method shown earlier. The principal difference is that it retrieves the values for the *productNumber* and *database* variables from the input arguments rather than from input parameters. At runtime, the workflow host packages up the input arguments specified by the workflow into a

CodeActivityContext object and passes it to the *Execute* method. You retrieve the value of an input argument by using the *Get* method and specifying this *CodeActivityContext* object.

> **Note** The code for this method is available in the ProductExists.txt file, which is located in the Microsoft Press\WCF Step By Step\Chapter 8 folder.

10. In the *ProductsWorkflowService* namespace, after the *ProductExists* class, add the *Find Product* class shown in the following code example:

```
public sealed class FindProduct : CodeActivity<ProductData>
{
    public InArgument<AdventureWorksEntities> Database { get; set; }
    public InArgument<string> ProductNumber { get; set; }

    protected override ProductData Execute(CodeActivityContext context)
    {
        // Retrieve the product number and database reference from the input arguments
        string productNumber = ProductNumber.Get(context);
        AdventureWorksEntities database = Database.Get(context);

        // Find the first product that matches the specified product number
        Product matchingProduct = database.Products.First(
            p => String.Compare(p.ProductNumber, productNumber) == 0);

        ProductData productData = new ProductData()
        {
            Name = matchingProduct.Name,
            ProductNumber = matchingProduct.ProductNumber,
            Color = matchingProduct.Color,
            ListPrice = matchingProduct.ListPrice
        };

        return productData;
    }
}
```

This class is another code activity. It retrieves the details of a product and returns a *ProductData* object. Notice that, like the *ProductExists* code activity, you specify the database to which you want to connect as well as the product number as input arguments. The *Execute* method returns a *ProductData* object, so the class inherits from the *CodeActivity<ProductData>* type.

> **Note** The code for this class is available in the FindProduct.txt file, which is located in the Microsoft Press\WCF Step By Step\Chapter 8 folder.

11. Build the solution.

You will receive the following error message: "Compiler error(s) encountered processing expression data.ToString(). ToString is not a member of 'Data'". This is caused by the validation errors in the *SendResponse* activity in the workflow which you have not yet fixed. You can ignore this error for the time being. If you have any other error messages, you will need to correct them before moving on to the next stage.

You can now return to the workflow that defines the *GetProduct* operation and implement the business logic. Assuming that your code compiled successfully (apart from the one error just described), you will find that the ToolBox for the Design View window contains the *FindProduct* and *ProductExists* activities.

Implement the Logic for the *GetProduct* Operation

1. Return to the *ProductsService.xamlx* service in the Design View window. In the Toolbox, verify that the *FindProduct* and *ProductExists* activities have been added:

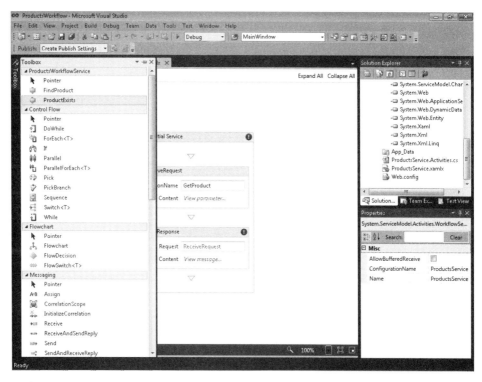

2. In the Design View window, click the *Sequential Service* activity to hide the Toolbox, and then click the Variables tab in the lower-left corner of the Design View window. Add the variables specified in the following table to the workflow. Notice that the values in the Default column use Visual Basic notation.

Name	Variable type	Scope	Default
database	ProductsEntityModel. AdventureWorksEntities	Sequential Service	New AdventureWorksEntities()
productData	ProductsWorkflowService. ProductData	Sequential Service	Nothing
exists	Boolean	Sequential Service	False

To specify the type for the *database* variable, in the Variable type drop-down list, click Browse For Types. In the Browse And Select A .Net Type dialog box, under *<Referenced assemblies>*, expand *ProductsEntityModel [1.0.0.0]*, expand *ProductsEntityModel*, click *AdventureWorksEntities*, and then click OK.

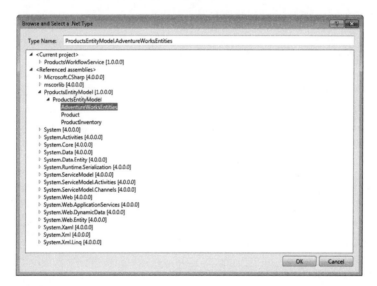

To specify the type for the *productData* variable, in the Browse And Select A .Net Type dialog box, expand *<Current Project>*, expand *ProductsWorkflowService [1.0.0.0]*, expand *ProductsWorkflowService*, click *ProductData*, and then click OK.

3. In the Toolbox, drag the *ProductExists* activity into the *Sequential Service* activity, between the *ReceiveRequest* and *SendResponse* activities. Your workflow should now look like the image that follows.

4. In the Properties window, set the *Database* property of the *ProductExists* activity to
    database, the *ProductNumber* property of the *ProductExists* activity to **localProduct
    Number**, and the *Result* property to **exists**.

    The *Database* and *ProductNumber* properties are the input arguments that you defined
    for the *ProductExists* code activity. The *localProductNumber* variable contains the product
    number from the message sent to the *ReceiveRequest* activity, and the *database* vari-
    able contains a new instance of the *AdventureWorksEntities* type for connecting to the
    AdventureWorks database. The *Result* property is the value returned by the *Execute*
    method, and this step assigns this value to the *exists* variable.

> **Note** The *ProductExists* and *FindProduct* activities only provide the default mechanism
> for binding input parameters and results to workflow variables. You can also implement an
> Activity Designer for each activity with which you can specify the input values in a more
> user-friendly manner in the Design View window, in the same way as the *ReceiveRequest* and
> the *SendResponse* activities. However, this technique is beyond the scope of this book.

5. In the Toolbox, expand the Control Flow section, drag the *If* activity into the *Sequential
    Service* activity, between the *ProductExists* and *SendResponse* activities. In the Condition
    box, type **exists**.

6. In the Toolbox, drag the *FindProduct* activity into the *Then* box of the *If* activity. The
    workflow should now appear as shown in the image that follows.

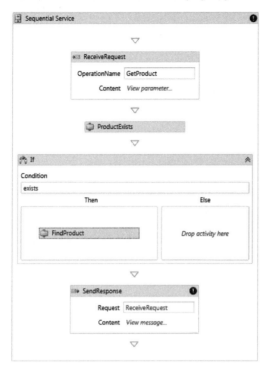

7. In the Properties window, set the *Database* property of the *FindProduct* activity to **database**, the *ProductNumber* property of the *FindProduct* activity to **localProduct Number**, and the *Result* property to **productData**.

   The *FindProduct* activity is invoked only when the *exists* variable is *true*. The *Database* and *ProductNumber* properties are the input arguments that you defined for the *Find Product* activity. The *Result* property is the *ProductData* object containing the details of the product retrieved from the *AdventureWorks* database.

   If the *exists* variable is *false*, then the value in the *productData* variable will remain set to *Nothing* (a null value in C# terminology).

8. In the Design View window, click the *SendResponse* activity, and then click View Message in the Content box. In the Content Definition dialog box, select the Parameters option, and then click Add New Parameter. Use the values in the following table to define the parameter. You can click Browse For Types to specify the type for this parameter. Click OK when you have finished.

Property	Value
Name	Product
Type	ProductsWorkflowService.ProductData
Value	productData

These settings specify the message that the *SendResponse* activity sends back to the client. In this case, the message contains the details of the product retrieved by calling the *FindProduct* activity.

You have now completed the workflow that defines the *GetProduct* operation. You can add further operations to the service if you require additional functionality, but you need to remember that this is a workflow; that carries some implications about when and how a client application can invoke these operations (this will be discussed in more detail later in this chapter).

As it currently stands, the ProductsWorkflowService project contains a WCF service that you can deploy and access from a client application in much the same way as any other WCF service. If you examine the Web.config file, you will see that it contains the basic, minimal configuration information required, so you can retrieve the metadata for the service and build a client application:

```
<?xml version="1.0" encoding="utf-8" ?>
<configuration>
  <system.web>
    <compilation debug="true" targetFramework="4.0" />
  </system.web>
  <system.serviceModel>
    <behaviors>
      <serviceBehaviors>
        <behavior>
          <!-- To avoid disclosing metadata information, set the value below
to false and remove the metadata endpoint above before deployment -->
          <serviceMetadata httpGetEnabled="true"/>
          <!-- To receive exception details in faults for debugging purposes,
set the value below to true.  Set to false before deployment to avoid disclosing
exception information -->
          <serviceDebug includeExceptionDetailInFaults="false"/>
        </behavior>
      </serviceBehaviors>
    </behaviors>
    <serviceHostingEnvironment multipleSiteBindingsEnabled="true" />
  </system.serviceModel>
  <system.webServer>
    <modules runAllManagedModulesForAllRequests="true"/>
  </system.webServer>
</configuration>
```

You can modify the configuration and define service endpoints if you wish to use non-default bindings.

The next step is to test that the service works and that the *GetProduct* operation returns the correct information. The simplest way to do this is to use the default WCF Test Client Application that was described in Chapter 2, "Hosting a WCF Service."

Test the *ProductsWorkflowService* Service

1. Open the Web.config file for the ProductsWorkflowService project in the Code And Text Editor window. Add the following connection string to the *<configuration>* section of the file.

```
<?xml version="1.0" encoding="utf-8" ?>
<configuration>
  <connectionStrings>
    <add name="AdventureWorksEntities"
connectionString="metadata=res://*/ProductsModel.csdl|res://*/ProductsModel.
ssdl|res://*/ProductsModel.msl;provider=System.Data.SqlClient;provider connection
string=&quot;DataSource=.\SQLExpress;Initial Catalog=AdventureWorks;Integrated
Security=True;MultipleActiveResultSets=True&quot;"
providerName="System.Data.EntityClient" />
  </connectionStrings>
  ...
</configuration>
```

This connection string is used by the *ProductsEntityModel* assembly to connect to the *AdventureWorks* database.

> **Note** Make sure that you enter the *<add name ... />* element on a single line without any breaks. A copy of this connection string is available in the ConnectionString.txt file, which is located in the Microsoft Press\WCF Step By Step\Chapter 8 folder.

2. Save the Web.config file, and then return to the *ProductsService.xamlx* workflow in the Design View window.

3. On the Debug menu, click Start Debugging.

The ASP.NET Development Server starts and acts as the host for your service. The WCF Test Client application also starts and connects to your service. The WCF Test Client application queries the metadata for your service and displays the operations that your service provides in the left pane, as shown in the following image:

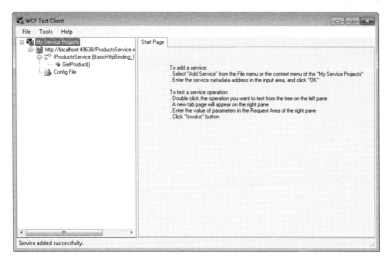

 Note If Internet Explorer starts instead of the WCF Test Client application, make sure that the *ProductsService.xamlx* workflow is displayed in the Design View window, and then start debugging again.

4. In the WCF Test Client application, in the left pane, double-click *GetProduct()*.

5. In the GetProduct pane, in the Request area at the top, type **WB-H098** into the Value field, and then click Invoke. If a Security Warning message box appears, click OK—you are only sending test messages to a local service running on your computer, so security is not an issue.

6. Verify that the service sends a response that contains the details of product *WB-H098* (a water bottle with a list price of 4.9900):

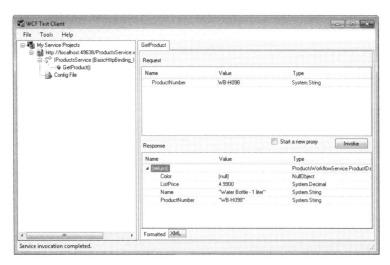

7. Click the XML tab at the bottom of the right pane.

The pane displays the XML content of the request and response messages. You can see how the *ProductData* object has been serialized as part of the response.

8. Close the WCF Test Client window.

Debugging a Workflow Service

You can debug and step through the activities in a workflow in a manner similar to stepping through C# code. If you right-click an activity in the Design View window and point to the Breakpoint command, you can set a breakpoint on that activity. When you start the service in debug mode, you can step through the workflow one activity at a time, displaying the values of the workflow variables at each step, as shown in Figure 8-1.

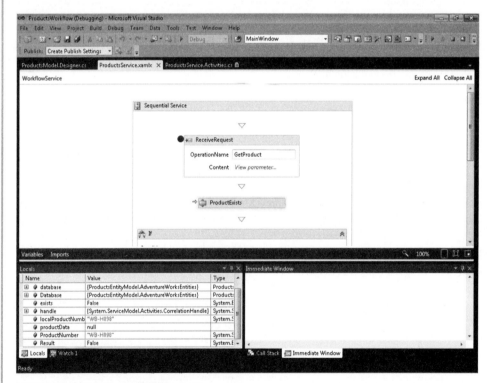

FIGURE 8-1 Debugging a workflow service.

And of course, if you have defined any code activities, you can set breakpoints in the code for these activities in the usual manner.

Implementing a Client Application for a Workflow Service

A client application does not need to understand how a service has been implemented or even be aware of the technology used to create and host it. The important thing is that the developer building the client application has access to the service metadata and knows which protocol to use to connect to the service. Consequently, you can implement a client application that consumes a workflow service in exactly the same way as you create a client application for any other type of WCF service.

However, you can also build a client application by using a workflow. Because it's instructive to see this approach, this is what you will do in the next exercise.

Create the Workflow Client Application

1. In Visual Studio, add a new project to the ProductsWorkflow solution. Use the Workflow Console Application template in the Workflow folder under the Visual C# folder in the Installed Templates pane. Specify the following properties for the project:

Property	Value
Name	ProductsWorkflowClient
Location	Microsoft Press\WCF Step By Step\Chapter 8\ProductsWorkflow within your Documents folder

2. In Solution Explorer, rename the Workflow1.xml file to **ClientWorkflow.xaml**.

3. Open the ClientWorkflow.xaml file in the Design View window.

    This workflow is currently empty. You will add activities to the workflow to connect to the *ProductsWorkflowService* and invoke the *GetProduct* operation shortly.

4. In the Properties window, change the workflow's *Name* property to **ProductsWorkflowClient.ClientWorkflow**.

5. Open the Program.cs file in the Code And Text Editor window. In the *Main* method, modify the statement that starts the default *Workflow1* workflow so it starts the *ClientWorkflow* workflow instead, as shown in bold in the following:

    ```
    static void Main(string[] args)
    {
        WorkflowInvoker.Invoke(new ClientWorkflow());
    }
    ```

    The static *Invoke* method of the *WorkflowInvoker* class loads and runs the specified workflow.

6. Add a service reference for the *ProductsWorkflowService* service to the ProductsWork flowClient project as follows:

    a. Right-click the ProductsWorkflowClient project, and then click Add Service Reference.

    b. In the Add Service Reference dialog box, click Discover. Verify that the *ProductsService.xamlx* service appears in the Services list.

    c. In the Namespace box, type **ProductsWorkflowService**; and then click OK.

    d. If the Microsoft Visual Studio message box appears stating that the operation has completed successfully, click OK.

    e. Rebuild the project.

7. Return to the *ClientWorkflow* workflow in the Design View window and display the Toolbox.

Notice that a new section appears at the top of the Toolbox, called *ProductsWork flowClient.ProductsWorkflowService.Activities*. This section contains a code activity called *GetProduct*.

When you add a service reference to a workflow application, the Add Service Reference Wizard generates a code activity for each operation exposed by the service. You can use these code activities to invoke the service operations. Each activity acts as a proxy, connecting to the service, sending a request message, and waiting for the response.

8. In the Toolbox, expand the Control Flow section, drag the *Sequence* activity onto the empty *ClientWorkflow* workflow in the Design View window.

9. Drag the *GetProduct* activity in the Toolbox onto the *Sequence* activity in the Design View window.

10. In the Properties window, change the *DisplayName* property of the *GetProduct* activity to **Get Water Bottle**.

11. Examine the other properties for this activity.

The *EndpointConfiguration* property specifies the name of the client endpoint in the app.config file that the workflow will use to connect to the service. The app.config file was generated by the Add Service Reference Wizard, and you can edit it if you need to reconfigure the bindings used by the client application if the service application changes or relocates to a different address (you will do this later, when you deploy the service to a different host environment).

The *ProductNumber* property corresponds to the parameter expected by the Receive Request activity for the *GetProduct* operation in the service. You should populate this property with the number that identifies a product before calling the operation. The details of the product found by the service and transmitted in the parameter specified by the *SendResponse* activity are returned in the *Product* property.

12. In the Design View window, click the *Get Water Bottle* activity. Using the Variables tab, add the following variable to the workflow:

Name	Variable type	Scope	Default
productReturned	ProductsWorkflowClient.ProductsWorkflowService. ProductData	Sequence	Nothing

> **Hint** To set the variable type, click Browse For Types in the drop-down list. In the Browse And Select a .NET Type dialog box, expand *<Current project>*, expand *ProductsWorkflow Client [1.0.0.0]*, expand *ProductsClientWorkflow.ProductsWorkflowService*, click *ProductData*, and then click OK.

13. Click the *Get Water Bottle* activity in the Design View window. In the Properties window for the Get Water Bottle activity, in the *ProductNumber* property, type **"WB-H098"** (including the quotes). In the *Product* property, type **productReturned**.

When the workflow performs the *Get Water Bottle* activity, it will call the *GetProduct* operation in the service and pass it the string *WB-H098*. The data returned by the operation will be stored in the *productReturned* variable.

14. In the Toolbox, expand the Primitives section. Drag the *WriteLine* activity into the *Sequence* activity below the Get Water Bottle activity. In the Text box for the *WriteLine* activity, type **productReturned.Name**, as shown in the following image:

This activity displays the name of the product retrieved by the *GetProduct* operation in a console window.

15. Add another *GetProduct* activity to the workflow, below the *WriteLine* activity. Set the properties for this activity as follows:

Property	Value
DisplayName	Get Mountain Seat Assembly
EndpointConfiguration	BasicHttpBinding_IProductsService *(this is the default value)*
Product	productReturned
ProductNumber	"SA-M198" *(include the quotes)*

16. In the Design View window, copy the *WriteLine* activity and paste the copy underneath the *Get Mountain Seat Assembly* activity.

Hint To copy an activity in the Design View window, right-click the activity, and then select Copy.

The complete workflow should look like this:

17. Build the solution.

Test the Workflow Client Application

1. In Solution Explorer, right-click the ProductsWorkflow solution, and then click Properties.

2. In the Solution 'ProductsWorkflow' Property Pages window, in the left pane, click Startup Project under Common Properties. In the right pane, click Multiple Startup Projects, and then set the *Action* property for the ProductsWorkflowClient and ProductsWorkflowService projects to **Start**. Click OK when you are done.

3. Start the solution without debugging.

   The ASP.NET Development Server starts and hosts the *ProductsWorkflowService* service. The client application also runs and displays the full names of products WB-H098 and SA-M198 in the console window:

> **Note** If Internet Explorer also starts and displays a list of files for the *ProductsWorkflow Service* service, close it.

4. Press Enter to close the client console window and return to Visual Studio.

Handling Faults in a Workflow Service

You saw in Chapter 3, "Making Applications and Services Robust," that catching exceptions in a service and reporting them back to a client application are an important part of building a resilient system. To recap, the basic steps are:

1. Define the structure of strongly-typed faults as classes tagged with the *DataContract* attribute.

2. In the logic for each service operation, catch any exceptions that might occur.

3. In the exception handlers, determine the cause of the exception, construct an instance of the appropriate fault class, and populate it with the relevant information.

4. Throw a strongly-typed *FaultException<>* exception that wraps the fault object.

You can apply the same logic to a workflow service; the way in which you can catch exceptions in a workflow service and report them as strongly-typed faults to a client application is very similar to the technique used when you construct a service by using procedural code. The issue with workflow services is how do you actually send the *FaultException<>* exception back to a client application?

In a procedural service implemented by using C#, you tagged operations with the *Fault Contract* attribute to specify the faults that they could generate. In the body of the method that defined an operation, you simply threw a *FaultException<>* exception, and the WCF runtime did the rest for you; it constructed a fault message with the data specified in the *FaultException<>* exception and transmitted this message back to the client as the response. When you build a workflow service, the operations are derived from the properties specified for the *Receive* activities in your service. You can specify items such as the operation name, the service contract name, and the shape of the request messages that the operation expects, but you cannot apply the *FaultContract* attribute. Consequently, to throw a *FaultException<>* exception from an operation in a workflow service, you need to perform some tasks explicitly, as part of the workflow. Specifically, you must add additional *SendReply* activities at the appropriate points in your workflow and configure them to send the different types of *Fault Exception<>* exception that can occur.

In the following set of exercises, you will reimplement the *SystemFault* and *DatabaseFault* classes from Chapter 3 in the *ProductsWorkflowService* service. You will modify the *GetProduct* operation to catch any exceptions. If the cause of the exception is a database problem, the operation will throw a *DatabaseFault*; otherwise, it will throw a *SystemFault*.

Add Fault-Handling to the *ProductsWorkflowService* Service

1. In the ProductsWorkflowService project, open the ProductsService.Activities.cs file in the Code And Text Editor window.

2. Add the following classes (shown in bold) to the *ProductsWorkflowService* namespace, above the existing classes in this namespace. These new classes define types that you will use for passing the details of faults from the service back to a client:

```
namespace ProductsWorkflowService
{
    // Classes for passing fault information back to client applications
    [DataContract]
    public class SystemFault
```

```
{
    [DataMember]
    public string SystemOperation { get; set; }

    [DataMember]
    public string SystemReason { get; set; }

    [DataMember]
    public string SystemMessage { get; set; }
}

[DataContract]
public class DatabaseFault
{
    [DataMember]
    public string DbOperation { get; set; }

    [DataMember]
    public string DbReason { get; set; }

    [DataMember]
    public string DbMessage { get; set; }
}

// Data contract describing the details of a product passed to client applications
[DataContract]
public class ProductData
{
    ...
}

    ...
}
```

3. Rebuild the project.

   This step is important; otherwise, these new types will not be available when you edit the workflow in the following steps.

4. Open the *ProductsService.xamlx* file in the Design View window. In the Toolbox, expand the Error Handling section and drag a *TryCatch* activity into the *Sequential Service* activity, between the *ReceiveRequest* activity and the *ProductExists* activity.

5. In the Toolbox, drag a *Sequence* activity from the Control Flow section into the Try box of the *TryCatch* activity in the Design View window.

6. In the Design View window, drag the *ProductExists*, *If*, and *SendResponse* activities and their contents into the *Sequence* activity located in the Try box of the *TryCatch* activity, as shown in the image that follows.

7. In the Catches section of the *TryCatch* activity, click Add New Catch. In the Exception drop-down list that appears, click System.Exception, and then press Enter. The Catches section expands and displays an area in which you can add activities to handle the exception.

8. Add an *If* activity from the Control Flow section of the Toolbox to the Exception handler in the Catches section of the *TryCatch* activity. In the Condition box, type **TypeOf exception.InnerException Is System.Data.SqlClient.SqlException**.

   This expression examines the type of the *InnerException* property of the exception to determine whether it is a *SqlException*.

9. Click the Variables tab and use the information in the following table to add a variable to the workflow:

Name	Variable type	Scope	Default
dbf	ProductsWorkflowService.DatabaseFault	TryCatch	Nothing

> **Hint** To set the variable type, click Browse For Types in the drop-down list. In the Browse And Select A .Net Type dialog box, expand *<Current project>*, expand *ProductsWorkflow Service [1.0.0.0]*, expand *ProductsWorkflowService*, click *DatabaseFault*, and then click OK.

10. Add a *Sequence* activity to the *Then* section of the *If* activity in the Exception handler.

11. Add an *Assign* activity from the Primitives section of the Toolbox to the new *Sequence* activity.

    In the To box of the *Assign* activity, type **dbf**. In the Properties window, click the ellipsis (...) button adjacent to the *Value* property.

    In the Expression Editor dialog box that appears, type the following expression, and then click OK:

    ```
    New DatabaseFault() With {
        .DbOperation = "Connect to database",
        .DbReason = "Exception accessing database",
        .DbMessage = exception.InnerException.Message
    }
    ```

    This expression is Visual Basic code that creates a new *DatabaseFault* object and populates it with the details of the exception that caused the fault. You will send this object back in a *FaultException<>* message to the client application.

    You send a response message by using a *SendReply* activity. You won't find this activity in the Toolbox. Instead, Visual Studio can generate a preconfigured *SendReply* activity for you directly from a *Receive* activity.

12. In the Design View window, locate the *ReceiveRequest* activity near the start of the workflow. Right-click this activity, and then click Create SendReply.

    The designer adds a *SendReply* activity called *SendReplyToReceiveRequest* to the workflow directly beneath the *ReceiveRequest* activity. Drag the *SendReplyToReceiveRequest* activity down to the *Sequence* activity in the *If* activity for the Exception handler, after the *Assign* activity.

    In the Properties window, change the *DisplayName* property of this activity to **Send DatabaseFault**.

13. In the *Send DatabaseFault* activity, click Define in the Content box. The Content Definition dialog box appears. Select the Parameters option, and then add the parameter specified in the following table to the message. Click OK when you are done.

Name	Type	Value
databaseFaultException	System.ServiceModel.Fault Exception<ProductsWorkflow Service.DatabaseFault>	New FaultException(Of DatabaseFault)(dbf)

Hint To specify the type for this parameter, in the Type drop-down list, click Browse For Types. In the Browse And Select A .Net Type dialog box, expand *<Referenced assemblies>*, expand *System.ServiceModel [4.0.0.0]*, expand *System.ServiceModel*, and then click *FaultException<TDetail>*. At the top of the dialog box, in the System.ServiceModel.Fault Exception drop-down list, click Browse For Types again. In the Browse And Select A .Net Type dialog box, expand *<Current Project>*, expand *ProductsWorkflowService [1.0.0.0]*, expand *ProductsWorkflowService*, click *DatabaseFault,* and then click OK. Click OK again to return to the Content Definition dialog box.

14. Using the Variables tab, add another variable to the workflow using the following:

Name	Variable type	Scope	Default
sf	ProductsWorkflow.SystemFault	TryCatch	Nothing

 Hint The *SystemFault* type is in the *<Current project>* | *ProductsWorkflowService [1.0.0.0]* | *ProductsWorkflowService* folder, in the Browse And Select a .Net Type dialog box.

15. Add a *Sequence* activity to the Else section of the *If* activity in the Exception handler, and then add an *Assign* activity to this *Sequence* activity.

In the To box of the *Assign* activity, type **sf** and enter the following code for the expression assigned to *sf*.

```
New SystemFault() With {
    .SystemOperation = "GetProduct",
    .SystemReason = "Exception finding product details",
    .SystemMessage = exception.Message
}
```

This expression creates a new *SystemFault* object and populates it with the details of the exception that caused the fault. This will be a non-database exception.

16. In the Design View window, find the *ReceiveRequest* activity near the start of the workflow, right-click this activity, and then click Create SendReply again.

Drag the *SendReplyToReceiveRequest* activity down to the *Sequence* activity in the Else part of the *If* activity for the Exception handler, after the *Assign* activity.

In the Properties window, change the *DisplayName* property of this activity to **Send SystemFault**.

17. In the *Send SystemFault* activity, click Define in the Content box. In the Content Definition dialog box, select the Parameters option, and then add the parameters in the following table to the message. Click OK when you are done.

Name	Type	Value
systemFaultException	System.ServiceModel.FaultException< ProductsWorkflowService.SystemFault>	New FaultException(Of SystemFault)(sf)

18. Rebuild the ProductsWorkflowService project.

You can quickly verify whether the service has been implemented correctly by examining the metadata. To do this, right-click the ProductsService.xamlx file in ProductsWorkflowService project in Solution Explorer, and then click View In Browser. Internet Explorer will appear displaying the *ProductsService* Service page. In this page, click the *http://localhost:99999/ ProductsService.xamlx?wsdl* link (replace 99999 with the port number displayed for your service). If you examine the WSDL description of the service, you should see that the *GetProduct* operation can generate *DatabaseFaultFault* and *SystemFaultFault* messages, as highlighted in bold in the following:

```
<?xml version="1.0" encoding="utf-8"?>
...
    <wsdl:binding name="BasicHttpBinding_IProductsService" type="i0:IProductsService">
      <soap:binding transport="http://schemas.xmlsoap.org/soap/http"/>
      <wsdl:operation name="GetProduct">
         <soap:operation soapAction="http://adventure-works.com/IProductsService/
GetProduct" style="document"/>
         <wsdl:input>
             <soap:body use="literal"/>
         </wsdl:input>
         <wsdl:output>
             <soap:body use="literal"/>
         </wsdl:output>
         <wsdl:fault name="DatabaseFaultFault">
         <soap:fault name="DatabaseFaultFault" use="literal"/>
         </wsdl:fault>
         <wsdl:fault name="SystemFaultFault">
             <soap:fault name="SystemFaultFault" use="literal"/>
         </wsdl:fault>
      </wsdl:operation>
    </wsdl:binding>
    <wsdl:service name="ProductsService">
       <wsdl:port name="BasicHttpBinding_IProductsService"
binding="tns:BasicHttpBinding_IProductsService">
          <soap:address location="http://localhost:99999/ProductsService.xamlx"/>
       </wsdl:port>
    </wsdl:service>
</wsdl:definitions>
```

You can test the fault handling capabilities of the service by adding a *TryCatch* activity to the client application that catches *FaultException<SystemFault>* and *FaultException<DatabaseFault>* exceptions. However, to save some repetition, and also to demonstrate that a workflow service works perfectly well with non-workflow client applications, you will test the service by using a stripped-down version of the procedural C# client application that you used in Chapter 3.

Test the Fault Handling in the *ProductsWorkflowService* Service

1. In Visual Studio, remove the ProductsWorkflowClient project from the ProductsWorkflowSolution.

2. Add the ProductsClient project to the solution. This project is located in the Microsoft Press\WCF Step By Step\Chapter 8\ProductsClient folder.

3. Open the Program.cs file for the ProductsClient project in the Code And Text Editor window.

   You can see that the application creates a proxy object to connect to the service and calls the *GetProduct* operation. The exception handlers trap and handle the various *FaultException* exceptions that can occur.

   Notice that there are some missing references highlighted by Visual Studio. This is because the project does not have a service reference yet. You will fix this now.

4. Right-click the Services References folder in Solution Explorer, and then click Add Service Reference. In the Add Service Reference dialog box, click Discover. In the Namespace box, type **ProductsService**, and then click OK.

5. Using the solution properties dialog box, configure the ProductsClient and Products WorkflowService projects as startup projects for the solution.

6. Start the solution without debugging. In the client console window, press Enter to connect to the service and verify that the details of the Water Bottle are displayed. Press Enter again to close the client console window.

> **Note** If an Internet Explorer window also appears displaying the files for the service, just close it.

7. In the ProductsWorkflowService project, open the Web.config file in the Code And Text Editor window. In the *<add>* element of the *<connectionStrings>* section, change the *Initial Catalog* part of the *connectionString* attribute to refer to the *Junk* database rather than *AdventureWorks*, as follows (do not change any other parts of the *connectionString* attribute):

```
<connectionStrings>
  <add ... connectionString="...;Initial Catalog=Junk;..." />
</connectionStrings>
```

8. Build and run the solution again. In the client console window, press Enter to connect to the service. This time, the service should return a *FaultException<DatabaseFault>* message stating that it cannot open the database "Junk" and that the attempt to log on to the database has failed, as shown in the following illustration:

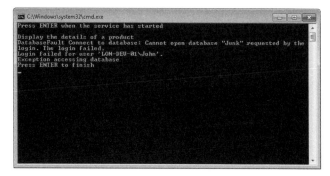

9. Close the client console window and return to Visual Studio.

10. In the ProductsWorkflowService project, edit the Web.config file, restore the *Initial Catalog* part of the *connectionString* attribute to refer to the *AdventureWorks* database as shown in the following code, and then save the Web.config file:

```
<connectionStrings>
  <add ... connectionString="...;Initial Catalog=AdventureWorks;..." />
</connectionStrings>
```

Hosting a Workflow Service

So far, you have used the ASP.NET Development Server to host the workflow service. However, as with regular WCF services, you can host a workflow service in other environments, such as IIS/WAS or a custom host application.

Hosting a Workflow Service in IIS

The technique for hosting a workflow service in IIS is very similar to hosting a regular WCF service, except that you can take advantage of the Build Deployment Package Wizard in Visual Studio if you prefer, rather than the Publish Web Site Wizard described in Chapter 1, "Introducing Windows Communication Foundation." You will use this wizard in the next exercise.

Deploy the *ProductsWorkflowService* Service to IIS

1. In Visual Studio, right-click the ProductsWorkflowService project in Solution Explorer, and then click Package/Publish Settings.

   The Properties page for the ProductsWorkflowService project appears and is opened at the Package/Publish Web tab.

2. In the Location Where The Package Will Be Created box, specify the file **ProductsWork flowService.zip** in the **Microsoft Press\WCF Step By Step\Chapter 8** folder.

> **Note** Visual Studio might change this path to ..\..\ProductsWorkflowService.zip. This is OK.

3. In the IIS Web Site/Application Name To Use On The Destination Server box, change the default value to **Default Web Site/ProductsWorkflowService**.

4. In Solution Explorer, right-click the ProductsWorkflowService project again, and then click Build Deployment Package. Wait until the message "Publish succeeded" appears in the Visual Studio status bar.

5. Using Windows Explorer, move to the Microsoft Press\WCF Step By Step\Chapter 8 folder and verify that the file ProductsWorkflowService.zip has been created.

   This file contains the deployment package for the service. You can copy this file to the server running IIS and then install this package on that server. In this exercise, you will use IIS running on the same computer, so there is no need to copy the file.

> **Note** The following steps assume that you have installed the Web Deployment Tool with Visual Studio 2010. This tool provides the Import Application Package Wizard in IIS. If you have not installed this utility, you can download it from the Web Deploy site at *http://www.iis.net/download/webdeploy*.
>
> If you are unable to install the Web Deployment Tool, you can still deploy the service to IIS. The Chapter 8 folder should contain some additional files generated at the same time as the ProductsWorkflowService.zip package: ProductsWorkflowService.deploy.cmd, Products WorkflowService.deploy-readme.txt, ProductsWorkflowService.SetParameters.xml, and ProductsWorkflowService.SourceManifest.xml. To deploy the service, open a command prompt as Administrator, move to the Microsoft Press\WCF Step By Step\Chapter 8 folder, and type the following command:
>
> ```
> ProductsWorkflowService.deploy.cmd /Y
> ```
>
> You can resume the exercise at step 13.

6. Start Internet Information Services Manager as an administrator.

7. In the Connections pane, expand the node that corresponds to your computer, expand Sites, and then click Default Web Site.

8. In the Actions pane, click Import Application. The Import Application Package Wizard starts.

9. On the Select The Package page of the wizard, click Browse, move to the Microsoft Press\WCF Step By Step\Chapter 8 folder, select the file ProductsWorkflowService.zip, and then click Open. On the Select The Package page, click Next.

10. On the Select The Contents Of The Package page, verify that the entire contents of the package is selected (all listed items have a check mark against them), and then click Next.

11. On the Enter The Application Package Information page, verify that the Application Path box specifies the name *ProductsWorkflowService*. You can also examine the connection string and verify that it references the *AdventureWorks* database (if the name of the database or server is different in your production environment, you can change it here). Click Next.

> **Important** Depending on how you have previously configured IIS, the Import Application Package dialog may appear with the message "The application you're installing requires a .NET 4.0 application pool. Do you want to change this application to run in the default .NET 4.0 application pool?" If this message box appears, click Yes.

12. Wait while the service is installed. In the Installation Progress And Summary page, verify that the summary indicates that the wizard added two directories and five files, and then click Finish.

13. In Internet Information Services Manager, expand the Default Web Site node in the Connections pane. You should see the *ProductsWorkflowService* application listed.

14. Click the ProductsWorkflowService application, and then click the Content View tab below the middle pane. You should see that the application contains the following items:

    ❑ A bin folder

    ❑ The ProductsService.xamlx file

    ❑ The Web.config file

    The bin folder should contain the binary executables for the service:

    ❑ ProductsEntityModel.dll

    ❑ ProductsWorkflowService.dll

    ❑ ProductsWorkflowService.pdb

15. In the Connections pane, right-click the ProductsWorkflowService application, point to Manage Application, and then click Advanced Settings. In the Advanced Settings dialog box, verify that the Application Pool property is set to *ASP.NET v4.0*, and then click OK.

16. In the Content View pane for the the ProductsWorkflowService application, right-click the ProductsService.xamlx file, and then click Browse. Internet Explorer should start and open the *ProductsService* Service page. Click the *http://localhost/ProductsWorkflow Service/ProductsService.xamlx?wsdl* link and verify that Internet Explorer successfully displays the metadata for your service.

17. Close Internet Explorer and return to Visual Studio.

You can test that the service is functioning correctly by reconfiguring the client application to connect to the service in IIS.

Test the *ProductsWorkflowService* Hosted by IIS

1. Return to Visual Studio and open the app.config file for the ProductsClient application in the Code And Text Editor window.

2. In the *<client>* section of the configuration file, change the endpoint address to match that of the *ProductsWorkflowService* hosted by IIS, as shown in bold in the following:

```xml
<?xml version="1.0" encoding="utf-8" ?>
<configuration>
    <system.serviceModel>
        ...
        <client>
          <endpoint address=
                "http://localhost/ProductsWorkflowService/ProductsService.xamlx"
                binding="basicHttpBinding"
                bindingConfiguration="BasicHttpBinding_IProductsService"
                contract="ProductsService.IProductsService"
                name="BasicHttpBinding_IProductsService" />
        </client>
    </system.serviceModel>
</configuration>
```

3. In Solution Explorer, right-click the ProductsClient project, click Set As StartUp Project, and then start the solution without debugging.

4. In the client application console window, press Enter to connect to the service. Verify that the client application successfully connects to the service, which returns the details for a water bottle.

5. Close the client console window and return to Visual Studio.

Hosting a Workflow Service in a Custom Application

Hosting a workflow service in a custom application is similar but not identical to hosting a non-workflow service. The primary difference is that the host application must provide run-time support for creating and managing workflows. Fortunately, the .NET Framework provides the *WorkflowServiceHost* class which includes this support. The *WorkflowServiceHost* class lives in the *System.ServiceModel.Activities* namespace, so to use it, you should add a reference to the *System.ServiceModel.Activities* assembly to your application.

Important Rather confusingly, there are actually two *WorkflowServiceHost* classes available; there is another one located in the *System.ServiceModel* namespace. The class in the *System. ServiceModel* namespace was built for the .NET Framework 3.0, which implemented a different model for workflows. If you are hosting workflow services built by using the .NET Framework 4.0 or later, always use the *WorkflowServiceHost* class in the *System.ServiceModel.Activities* namespace.

The *WorkflowServiceHost* class is analogous to the *ServiceHost* class that you should now be familiar with, and it provides a similar set of methods, properties, and events, with one or two additions that are specific to hosting workflow services. The most noticeable difference is that the *WorkflowServiceHost* class provides a constructor that can take an activity that defines the root of a workflow service (such as the *Sequence* activity encapsulating the workflow in the *ProductsWorkflowService* service) and starts the specified activity when a request is received by the host. Another useful constructor—and the one that you will use in the following exercise—takes a *WorkflowService* object. The *WorkflowService* class provides a wrapper around a workflow service that you can use to configure and modify the properties of the service.

Build a Custom Application for Hosting the *ProductsWorkflowService* Service

1. Add a new project to the ProductsWorkflow solution by using the Workflow Console Application template. Specify the following properties for the project:

Property	Value
Name	ProductsWorkflowHost
Location	Microsoft Press\WCF Step By Step\Chapter 8\ProductsWorkflow

2. Delete the file Workflow1.xaml from the ProductsWorkflowHost project.

3. Add a reference to the ProductsWorkflowService project.

4. Open the Program.cs file for the ProductsWorkflowHost project in the Code And Text Editor window. Add the following *using* statements to the list at the top of the file:

   ```
   using System.ServiceModel.Activities;
   using System.Xaml;
   ```

5. Delete the existing statement in the *Main* method that uses the *WorkflowInvoker* class to create and start a workflow. Replace this statement with the code shown in bold in the following:

   ```
   static void Main(string[] args)
   {
       WorkflowService service =
           XamlServices.Load(@"..\..\..\ProductsWorkflowService\ProductsService.xamlx")
           as WorkflowService;

       WorkflowServiceHost host = new WorkflowServiceHost(service);
       host.Open();
       Console.WriteLine("Service running. Press ENTER to stop");
       Console.ReadLine();
       host.Close();
   }
   ```

The first statement creates a *WorkflowService* object based on the ProductsService. xamlx file in the ProductsWorkflowService project. Remember that this file contains the description of the *ProductsWorkflowService* service. The static *Load* method of the *XamlServices* class can read any file that contains the description of a workflow and parse it into an object graph (you can actually read any XAML file by using this method, not just a workflow). The ProductsService.xamlx file contains a workflow service, so it is safe to cast the result into a *WorkflowService* object.

The next statement creates a *WorkflowServiceHost* object that hosts the workflow service. Like the *ServiceHost* class, the *WorkflowServiceHost* class lets you configure the service endpoint in code or by reading the configuration information specified in the App. config file. In this exercise, you will configure the service by using the App.config file.

The remainder of the code should be familiar to you. The *Open* method of the *WorkflowServiceHost* class starts the host listening for requests; the *Close* method stops the service.

6. Open the App.config file for the ProductsWorkflowHost project by using the Service Configuration Editor.

7. In the Configuration pane, click the *Services* node. In the Services pane, click Create A New Service to start the New Service Element Wizard and create a new service endpoint. Step through the wizard and enter the information shown in the following table:

Page	Prompt	Value
What is the service type of your service?	Service type:	ProductsService
What service contract are you using?	Contract:	IProductsService
What communication mode is your service using?		TCP
What is the address of your endpoint?	Address	net.tcp://localhost:8080/Products Service.xamlx

These setting configure the service to communicate with client applications by using a TCP connection (as a variation from HTTP). Remember that you named the service by setting the *Name* property of the *WorkflowService* activity in step 3 of the exercise "Create the *ProductsWorkflowService* Service," earlier in this chapter. You also defined the service contract, *IProductsService*, in step 5 of the same exercise.

8. Save the configuration file and exit the Service Configuration Editor.

9. Open the App.config file in the Code And Text Editor window and add the connection string for connecting to the *AdventureWorks* database to the *<configuration>* section of the file, above the *<startup>* section, as shown in bold in the following.

```
<?xml version="1.0" encoding="utf-8" ?>
<configuration>
  <connectionStrings>
    <add name="AdventureWorksEntities"
  connectionString="metadata=res://*/ProductsModel.csdl|res://*/ProductsModel.
  ssdl|res://*/ProductsModel.msl;provider=System.Data.SqlClient;provider
  connection string=&quot;DataSource=.\SQLExpress;Initial Catalog=AdventureWorks;
  Integrated Security=True;MultipleActiveResultSets=True&quot;"
  providerName="System.Data.EntityClient" />
  </connectionStrings>
  <startup>
    ...
  </startup>
  ...
</configuration>
```

 Note A copy of this connection string is available in the ConnectionString.txt file, which is located in the Microsoft Press\WCF Step By Step\Chapter 8 folder.

10. Save the App.config file.

Test the Hosted Service

1. Open the app.config file for the ProductsClient application in the Code And Text Editor window. Add the following *<endpoint>* definition (shown in bold) to the *<client>* section of the file, after the existing *<endpoint>* that connects to the version of the *ProductsWorkflowService* service hosted by IIS:

```
<?xml version="1.0" encoding="utf-8" ?>
<configuration>
  <system.serviceModel>
    ...
    <client>
      <endpoint address=
              "http://localhost/ProductsWorkflowService/ProductsService.xamlx"
              binding="basicHttpBinding"
              bindingConfiguration="BasicHttpBinding_IProductsService"
              contract="ProductsService.IProductsService"
              name="BasicHttpBinding_IProductsService" />
      <endpoint address="net.tcp://localhost:8080/ProductsService.xamlx"
              binding="netTcpBinding" contract="ProductsService.IProductsService"
              name="NetTcpBinding_IProductsService" />
    </client>
  </system.serviceModel>
</configuration>
```

2. Open the Program.cs file for the ProductsClient project in the Code And Text Editor window. Modify the statement that creates the proxy to connect to the service by using the *NetTcpBinding_IProductsService* endpoint, as shown in bold in the following:

```
static void Main(string[] args)
{
    Console.WriteLine("Press ENTER when the service has started");
    Console.ReadLine();

    // Create a proxy object and connect to the service
    ProductsServiceClient proxy = new ProductsServiceClient(
        "NetTcpBinding_IProductsService");

    // Test the operations in the service
    ...
}
```

3. Using the Properties dialog box for the ProductsWorkflow solution, set the Products Client and ProductsWorkflowHost as startup products. Verify that the startup action for the ProductsWorkflowService project is set to *None*.

4. Start the solution without debugging. If a Windows Security Alert appears, click Allow Access to enable the ProductsServiceHost application to open TCP port 8080.

5. In the client application console window, press Enter to connect to the service. Verify that the client application functions as before and successfully connects to the service to retrieve the details for a water bottle.

6. Close the client console window, close the service host console window, and return to Visual Studio.

Implementing Common Messaging Patterns in a Workflow Service

You have seen that you can build workflow services that behave in the classic "Wait for request, Send Response" cycle of message processing. However, this is just one of the messaging patterns that client applications and services commonly implement. In this mode of operation, as far as a client application is concerned, there is essentially a single synchronous thread of control that passes from the client to the service and back again; when a client application sends a request to a service it acts as though it were invoking a local method call and does not resume processing until the service sends a response. You will see in Chapter 12, "Invoking One-Way and Asynchronous Operations," that you can build WCF client applications and services that act in other ways and implement other messaging patterns. For example, not all request messages necessarily expect a response, so a client application can send a one-way message to a service and then carry on processing immediately.

The asynchronous messaging pattern enables a client application to send a request and then carry on running while the service processes the request. If the service needs to send a reply, it can do so, but the client application needs to be configured to listen for a response on a separate thread and be prepared to handle it.

Another common messaging pattern concerns callbacks. In this pattern, a service can call in to a client application and possibly alert it about some change in state in the service. In this pattern, a single request message from a client application can open a channel to the service that the service uses to send any number of informational messages back to the client, or even send request messages that expect a response from the client (effectively, turning the client into a service and vice versa for the purposes of that message exchange). You will learn more about callbacks in Chapter 16, "Using a Callback Contract to Publish and Subscribe to Events."

WCF provides attributes and properties that you can use to configure service contracts, operation contracts, services, and client applications when you are implementing them by using procedural code. If you are using workflows to implement services and client applications, you can implement these and many other messaging patterns by using the messaging activities.

Messaging Activities

You may have noticed that the Workflow Toolbox has a section named *Messaging*. The activities in this section are designed for use by workflow services for sending, receiving, and correlating messages. The following table summarizes the purpose of some of these activities. If you need more information, consult the documentation provided with Visual Studio.

Activity	Description
Receive	This activity encapsulates the functionality for listening to an endpoint and waiting for an incoming message. You can set properties that specify the expected *shape* of the information of the incoming message by using the *Content* property and assign this information to variables in the workflow (you did this earlier). You can also specify the *OperationName* and *ServiceContractName* properties, which the Workflow runtime uses to derive the service contract.
	Another important property is *CanCreateInstance*. If this property is *true*, an incoming message of the type specified by this activity can start a new service instance and establish a new session for the client if one is not already running. If the *CanCreateInstance* property is *false*, then a session must already exist for the client before the service will accept and process this message.
	If you wish to implement message-level security, you can use the *Protection Level* property to sign and encrypt messages.

Activity	Description
SendReply	As mentioned earlier, this activity does not actually appear in the Toolbox, although you will use it very frequently. The purpose of this activity is to send a response message back to a client. Every *SendReply* activity in a workflow should have a corresponding *Receive* activity, and you can generate a correctly configured *SendReply* activity by right-clicking the appropriate *Receive* activity and selecting Create *SendReply*.
ReceiveAndSendReply	This is a composite activity that consists of a *Sequence* activity containing a *Receive* activity and its corresponding *SendReply* activity. The WCF Workflow Service Application template in Visual Studio generates a workflow that contains a single *ReceiveAndSendReply* activity that you can use as the starting point for defining an operation.
Send	A client application can use the *Send* activity to send a request message to a service. As with the *Receive* activity, the *Content* property specifies the type of the message to send. You are expected to provide the details of the endpoint to send the message to as well as the endpoint configuration to use by using a combination of the *Endpoint*, *EndpointAddress*, and *EndpointConfiguration* properties. You must also specify the *OperationName* and *ServiceContractName* properties to identify the operation to invoke in the service.
	If the service implements message-level security, you should set the *ProtectionLevel* property of the *Send* activity to match that of the corresponding *Receive* activity in the service.
ReceiveReply	Like the *SendReply* activity, you will not find this activity in the Toolbox. When a client application sends a request message by using a *Send* activity, it should provide a corresponding *ReceiveReply* activity for obtaining the response message from the service. You can generate a configured *ReceiveReply* activity for a *Send* activity by right-clicking the *Send* activity and selecting Create ReceiveReply.
SendAndReceiveReply	Like *ReceiveAndSendReply*, this activity is a composite that comprises a *Sequence* activity containing a *Send* activity and its corresponding *ReceiveReply* activity.

Notice that when you created the workflow client application earlier in this chapter, you did not explicitly use the *Send* or *SendAndReceiveReply* activities. Instead, you used the custom *GetProduct* activity generated by the Add Service Reference Wizard. In fact, the *GetProduct* activity is simply a composite activity containing a *Sequence* activity with nested *Send*, *Receive Reply*, and *Assign* activities, as shown in the Figure 8-2. The *Send* activity sends the *GetProduct* message to the service and waits for the response message. The value passed back by the service to the response message is assigned to a temporary variable, which is passed back as the value returned by the custom *GetProduct* activity.

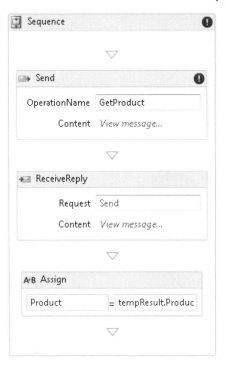

FIGURE 8-2 The *GetProduct* custom activity generated by the Add Service Reference Wizard.

Correlating Request and Reply Messages in a Workflow Service Instance

Previous chapters have shown you that a single service host can support multiple instances of a service. When a client application connects to a service instance, it creates a channel that it uses to send request messages to the instance, and the WCF runtime ensures that the responses are sent back down the appropriate channel to the correct client application. When you send a message to a workflow service, the *Receive* activity creates an identifier for the request and ensures that the corresponding reply is sent down the correct channel to the client application by associating the *SendReply* activity with the same identifier. This identifier is called a *correlation handle*. You can see this correlation handle in the *Correlation Initializers* property of a *Receive* activity. When you create a *SendReply* activity for a *Receive* activity, the WF Designer creates a *CorrelationHandle* variable for you automatically and populates the *Correlation Initializers* property of the *Receive* activity with this variable—these variables are typically called *_handle1*, *_handle2*, and so on. You do not need to understand the internal details of how correlation handles work or the data that they contain (much of the mechanism is hidden from you anyway), just accept that they uniquely identify a request and ensure that the reply is routed correctly.

The same logic applies when you add a *Send* activity to a workflow and then create a *Receive Reply* activity. The *Correlation Initializers* property of the *Send* activity is populated with a correlation handle, and the *ReceiveReply* activity is associated with this same correlation handle.

> **Important** Do not confuse request/reply correlation in a single workflow service instance with context-based correlation used to identify an instance of a long-running durable service. Request/reply correlation is implemented internally inside a service instance, and a client application has no knowledge of how the various *Receive* and *SendReply* activities are correlated. Context-based correlation, on the other hand, is used explicitly by a client application to ensure that it sends messages to a specific service instance; we will revisit context-based correlation toward the end of this chapter.

Using Messaging Activities to Implement Messaging Patterns

The most common messaging pattern for a service is the receive request/send reply message cycle, which you can implement as shown earlier by using the *ReceiveAndSendReply* composite activity. To recap, you simply configure the *Receive* activity with the name of the operation, the service contract, and the message type. When a workflow reaches a *Receive* activity, it blocks until a matching message is received. You can provide the necessary logic to handle the message and construct a response, which you send back to the client by using the *Send Reply* activity. Remember that the *SendReply* activity uses the same communications channel that was used to receive the message. If the service detects an exception, you can configure additional *SendReply* activities to send *FaultException* messages back to the client.

In this pattern, the client application uses a *SendAndReceiveReply* composite activity, usually in the preconfigured form of a proxy activity generated by the Add Service Reference Wizard. The *SendAndReceiveReply* activity mirrors the actions of the service; the *Send* activity sends the message to the service and then performs the *ReceiveReply* activity, which blocks until a response has been received on the channel used to send the message. Like the *Receive AndSendReply* activity utilized by the service, the *Send* and *ReceiveReply* activities are held as part of a *Sequence* activity, so you can insert additional logic after sending the request but before receiving the response. However, you should endeavor to keep any processing short, because if the client is not performing the *ReceiveReply* when the service sends the response, the service will be blocked.

You can implement a simple form of one-way messaging by using the *Send* activity in a client application, and not waiting for a response. The service should use a *Receive* activity to accept the message but must not attempt to send a response; otherwise, it will be blocked, possibly indefinitely—this includes sending any fault messages.

The basic asynchronous messaging pattern requires a little more configuration. A client application can use a *Send* activity to submit a request to a service and then carry on performing whatever processing it requires. However, the client must be prepared to receive a response from the service and not block the service unduly. A good way to achieve this is to employ the *Parallel* activity in the client; one sequence in this activity can wait for the response from the service while another performs the client processing.

In the asynchronous model, the service listens for the request by waiting on a *Receive* activity and then generates a response message. However, there is nothing to stop the service from generating more than one reply. Consider the scenario in which a client application sends a message to a brokerage service asking for the price of a product. The service might send requests to many other services operated by suppliers who are requesting price information. When the service receives a response from each supplier, it can send a corresponding reply back to the client. If more than one supplier responds, the service might send multiple replies to the client. In this pattern, the client must therefore be prepared to receive multiple responses. You can achieve this by using a *While* activity in the part of the client workflow that listens for response messages, receiving and processing each response message in turn.

Managing Sessions and Maintaining State in a Workflow Service

The example workflow service that you have investigated so far in this chapter is a very simple creature, exposing a single, stateless operation to client applications. In the real world, workflow services are more complex; they frequently need to maintain session state and typically provide more than one operation. When you implement a WCF service by using procedural code, you can specify the session mode of the service and implement each operation as a method. The WCF runtime manages the service instances, and the operations can be implemented in any sequence because the order of methods in a C# class has no significance.

However, the same is not true for workflow services. The whole point of a workflow is to define an order for the various tasks that it performs. You implement a workflow service by using *Receive* and *SendReply* activities for each operation, but in which order do you place these activities if you need to implement more than one operation and listen for different request messages? Additionally, how do you keep a service instance alive and maintain session state information? For example, consider the shopping cart service that you implemented in Chapter 7. This service exposed four operations; *AddItemToCart*, *RemoveItem FromCart*, *GetShoppingCart*, and *Checkout*. The business rules of the service specified that a client application had to call *AddItemToCart* as the first request to initiate a session, create the service instance and initialize any session state, and that the *Checkout* operation terminated the session and discarded any state information. Other than that, a client could make calls to *AddItemToCart*, *RemoveItemFromCart*, and *GetShoppingCart* in any sequence. If you think about how the WCF runtime handles this situation, you can see that essentially, it simply performs some sort of loop, waiting for request messages and dispatching them to the appropriate method. To provide the same functionality in a workflow service, you can implement the same logic by using *While* and *Pick* activities, which is what you will do in the following exercises.

Create the *ShoppingCartService* Workflow Service

1. Using Visual Studio, create a new solution by using the WCF Workflow Service Application template. Specify the following properties for the solution:

Property	Value
Name	ShoppingCartService
Location	Microsoft Press\WCF Step By Step\Chapter 8
Solution name	ShoppingCart

2. In Solution Explorer, rename the Service1.xamlx file to **ShoppingCartService.xamlx**.

3. In the Design View window, click the background, outside the bounds of the *Sequential Service* activity. In the Properties window, set the *ConfigurationName* and *Name* properties to **ShoppingCartService**.

4. Add a reference to the *ProductsEntityModel* assembly located in the Microsoft Press\ WCF Step By Step\Chapter 8 folder. Also, add a reference to the *System.Data.Entity* assembly.

   The *ShoppingCartService* service will use these assemblies to access the *AdventureWorks* database.

5. Add the ShoppingCartService.Activitities.cs file to the ShoppingCartService project. This file is located in the Microsoft Press\WCF Step By Step\Chapter 8 folder.

   The ShoppingCartService.Activities.cs file contains three items:

   ❑ The *ShoppingCartItem* class.   This is the same class that you created in Chapter 7. It defines the structure of the shopping cart. Each session will create its own instance of this class, and it will hold the state of the shopping cart for the session between requests made by a client.

   ❑ The *FindItem* code activity.   This is an implementation of the *find* utility method that examines a shopping cart to determine whether it already contains an item with the specified product number. The shopping cart and product number are specified as input arguments to the activity. The activity returns a reference to the item if it is found in the shopping cart, or a null reference if it is not.

❑ The *GetItemFromDatabase* code activity.   This is another utility that retrieves the details for a specified product from the database by using the Entity Framework. The entity context for connecting to the database and the product number are provided as input arguments. The activity creates a Product object and returns it if a matching product is found in the database, or a null reference if not.

6. Build the solution.

7. Return to the Design View window that is displaying the ShoppingCartService.xamlx file and delete the *Sequential Service* activity and its contents. The workflow should now be empty.

8. From the Control Flow section in the Toolbox, add a *Sequence* activity to the workflow.

9. Add a *While* activity (in the Control Flow section of the Toolbox) to the *Sequence* activity.

10. Using the Variables tab, add a Boolean variable called *serviceRunning* to the workflow. Limit the scope to the *While* activity and set the default value to **True**.

11. In the *While* activity, set the Condition expression to **serviceRunning**.

   You will add activities to this *While* activity that listen for request messages. The *While* activity will halt and the service instance will shut down when the *serviceRunning* variable is set to *False*.

12. Click the Imports tab at the base of the Design View window. In the Enter Or Select Namespace box, type **ShoppingCartService**, and then press Enter.

   The *ShoppingCartItem* class and the *FindItem* and *GetItemFromDatabase* code activities are defined in this namespace in the ShoppingCartService.Activities.cs file. Using the Imports tab, you can bring a namespace into scope in the same way that a *using* statement does when you are writing C# code.

13. In the Variables tab, add another variable called *shoppingCart*. The type of this variable should be *System.Collections.Generic.List<ShoppingCartService.ShoppingCartItem>*. Set the scope of this variable to the *While* activity and specify the following default value:

```
New List(Of ShoppingCartItem)()
```

   This variable is the shopping cart that the various operations implemented by the *ShoppingCartService* service will manipulate.

Note The *System.Collections.Generic.List<T>* type is defined in the *mscorlib* assembly.

12. Add a *Pick* activity from the Control Flow section of the Toolbox to the *While* activity.

The *Pick* activity is extremely useful for building workflows that need to respond to events that can occur in any order. It contains one or more *PickBranch* activities, and a *PickBranch* has two elements: a trigger and an action. In the Trigger section, you specify an activity that waits for an event, such as an incoming message, and in the Action section you specify the workflow that runs when this event occurs. When a workflow reaches a *Pick* activity, it halts until one of the specified events occurs, and then it performs the corresponding actions.

13. Click the *Branch1 PickBranch* activity, and in the Properties window change the *Display Name* property to **Add Item To Cart**.

14. In the Variables tab, add a string variable called *productNumber* with a default value of *Nothing*. Set the scope of this variable to the *Add Item To Cart* activity.

15. From the Messaging section of the Toolbox, add a *Receive* activity to the *Trigger* section of the *Add Item To Cart* activity. Set the properties of this *Receive* activity to the values shown in the following table:

Property	Value
DisplayName	Receive AddItemToCart Request
CanCreateInstance	*Checked*
OperationName	AddItemToCart
ServiceContractName	{http://adventure-works.com/}IShoppingCartService

Remember that the *CanCreateInstance* property specifies whether this message can be used to create a new instance of the service and start a new session.

16. In the Properties window for the *Receive* activity, click the ellipsis (...) button adjacent to the *Content* property. In the Content Definition dialog box, select the Parameters option, add the following parameter to the incoming message, and then click OK:

Property	Value
Name	ProductNumber
Type	String
Assign To	productNumber

The message received by the *AddItemToCart* operation contains the product number of the product to add to the shopping cart.

17. Add the AddItemToCart.xaml file to the ShoppingCartService project. This file is located in the Microsoft Press\WCF Step By Step\Chapter 8 folder.

The AddtemToCart.xaml file contains a custom activity (I created it by using the Activity template). If you examine this activity, you will see that it contains the workflow equivalent of the logic for the *AddItemToCart* operation that you implemented in Chapter 7. The product number for the product to add to the cart and the shopping cart itself are defined as input arguments (click the Arguments tab to see them). The activity performs the following tasks:

   ❑ It calls the *FindItem* code activity, passing the product number and shopping cart as input arguments. The *FindItem* code activity determines whether the specified product has already been added to the shopping cart. The value returned by the *FindItem* activity is stored in a variable called *item*, of type *ShoppingCartItem*.

   ❑ If the value of *item* is not *Nothing*, then the product has already been added to the shopping cart, so the *Volume* property of the item in the cart is simply incremented.

   ❑ If the value of *item* is *Nothing*, then the product has not previously been added to the shopping cart. The *Else* branch of the *If* activity calls invokes the *GetItemFrom Database* activity to obtain the details of the product and creates a new Shopping CartItem product with this information, which it assigns to the *item* variable. The object referenced by the item variable is added to the shopping cart by using an *AddToCollection* activity.

   ❑ If either branch of the *If* activity is successful, the value *True* is assigned to the *Result* argument. The *Result* argument is an output argument that is used to pass an indication back to the caller of whether the activity was successful or not.

   ❑ If an exception occurs, the *Catches* section of the *TryCatch* activity that encloses the entire activity sets the value of the *Result* argument to *False* to indicate that the activity was unsuccessful.

18. Rebuild the solution.

19. Return to the ShoppingCartService.xamlx file in the Design View window. In the Action section of the *Add Item To Cart* activity, add a *Sequence* activity and define the following variable for this sequence:

Property	Value
Name	result
Type	Boolean
Scope	Sequence
Default	False

20. From the *ShoppingCartService* section of the Toolbox, add an *AddItemToCart* activity to the *Sequence* activity in the *Action* section of the *Add Item To Cart* activity. In the Properties window, set the following properties for this activity (these properties are the input and output arguments for the activity):

Property	Value
ProductNumber	productNumber
Result	Result
ShoppingCart	shoppingCart

21. In the *Trigger* section of the *Add Item To Cart* activity, right-click the *Receive AddItem ToCart Request* activity, and then click Create SendReply.

    Visual Studio displays a message box stating that the activity has been created and copied to the clipboard. Click OK to close this message box.

22. Right-click the Sequence activity in the *Action* section of the *Add Item To Cart* activity, and then click Paste. If necessary, drag the *SendReplyToReceive AddItemToCart* activity below the *AddItemToCart* activity. In the Properties window, change the *DisplayName* property to *Send AddItemToCart Response*.

23. In the *Send AddItemToCart Response* activity, click Define, which is adjacent to the *Content* property. In the Content Definition dialog box, select the Parameters option, add the following parameter to the incoming message, and then click OK:

Property	Value
Name	Result
Type	Boolean
Value	result

The activity sends back a Boolean value in the response message indicating whether the product was successfully added to the shopping cart or not.

You have now implemented the *AddItemToCart* operation for the *ShoppingCartService* service. You can implement the *RemoveItemFromCart*, *GetShoppingCart*, and *Checkout* operations in a similar manner, by defining the logic for these operations in custom activities and adding *PickBranch* activities for each possible request message. To save you some time and avoid unnecessary repetition, you can find a copy of the completed *ShoppingCartService* service in the ShoppingCart folder within the Chapter 8\Completed folder. You will use this project in the remaining exercises in this chapter.

Host the *ShoppingCartService* Workflow Service

1. Using Visual Studio, open the ShoppingCart solution in the Microsoft Press\WCF Step By Step\Chapter 8\Completed\ShoppingCart folder.

2. Open the ShoppingCartService.xamlx file in the Design View window.

3. In the *Trigger* section of the *Remove Item From Cart* activity, click the *Receive Remove ItemFromCart Request* activity. In the Properties window, notice that the *CanCreate Instance* property is not selected. The same applies to the *Receive GetShoppingCart Request* and *Receive Checkout Request activities*. Only the *AddItemToCart* operation can create a new session.

4. Examine the *Action* section of the *Checkout* activity. After the response message has been sent, an Assignment activity sets the *serviceRunning* variable to *False*. This action causes the *While* activity encompassing the *Pick* activity to finish, terminating the workflow and stopping the service instance.

5. Add a new Workflow Console Application project to the ShoppingCart solution. Name the project ShoppingCartHost.

6. In Solution Explorer, delete the Workflow1.xamlx file.

7. Add a reference to the ShoppingCartService project to the ShoppingCartHost project.

8. Open the Program.cs file in the Code And Text Editor window. Add the following *using* statements to the list at the top of the file:

```
using System.ServiceModel.Activities;
using System.Xaml;
```

9. In the *Main* method, replace the statement that uses the *WorkflowInvoker* class to start and run the *Workflow1* workflow with the code shown in bold in the following:

```
static void Main(string[] args)
{
    WorkflowService service =
        XamlServices.Load(@"..\..\..\ShoppingCartService\ShoppingCartService.xamlx")
        as WorkflowService;

    WorkflowServiceHost host = new WorkflowServiceHost(service);
    host.Open();
    Console.WriteLine("Service running. Press ENTER to stop");
    Console.ReadLine();
    host.Close();
}
```

This code is very similar to that which you saw previously, except that it starts the *ShoppingCartService.xamlx* service.

10. Open the App.config file in the Code And Text Editor window. Add the following connection string (shown in bold) to the *<configuration>* section of the file.

```xml
<?xml version="1.0" encoding="utf-8" ?>
<configuration>
  <connectionStrings>
    <add name="AdventureWorksEntities"
connectionString="metadata=res://*/ProductsModel.csdl|res://*/ProductsModel.
ssdl|res://*/ProductsModel.msl;provider=System.Data.SqlClient;provider
connection string=&quot;DataSource=.\SQLExpress;Initial Catalog=AdventureWorks;
Integrated Security=True;MultipleActiveResultSets=True&quot;"
providerName="System.Data.EntityClient" />
  </connectionStrings>
  ...
</configuration>
```

> **Note** As before, you can use the copy of this connection string that is available in the ConnectionString.txt file, which is located in the Microsoft Press\WCF Step By Step\ Chapter 8 folder.

11. Add a *<system.serviceModel>* section to the file, and then add the following service endpoint.

```xml
<?xml version="1.0"?>
<configuration>
  ...
  <system.serviceModel>
    <services>
      <service name="ShoppingCartService">
        <endpoint address="net.tcp://localhost:8080/ShoppingCartService.xamlx"
                  binding="netTcpContextBinding" contract="IShoppingCartService" />
      </service>
    </services>
  </system.serviceModel>
</configuration>
```

The service host listens for requests by using the TCP protocol. Note that the host uses the *NetTcpContextBinding* binding. This is necessary because, by default, when a workflow service receives a request message, it attempts to create a new service instance if the incoming request does not contain any context information that identifies an existing service instance.

12. Rebuild the solution.

To test the *ShoppingCartService*, you will use the version of the ShoppingCartGUIClient application from Chapter 7 that communicates with the non-durable version of the *Shopping CartService* service. (A copy of this application is provided in the Chapter 8 folder.) In the next exercise, you will add the ShoppingCartGUIClient application to the solution, configure it to connect to the ShoppingCartHost by using the TCP protocol, and then test the Shopping CartService service.

Test the *ShoppingCartService* Workflow Service

1. Add the ShoppingCartGUIClient project to the ShoppingCart solution. This project is located in the Microsoft Press\WCF Step By Step\Chapter 8\ShoppingCartGUIClient folder.

2. In Solution Explorer, right-click the Service References folder in the ShoppingCartGUI Client project, and then click Add Service Reference. In the Add Service Reference dialog box, click Discover. In the Namespace box, type **ShoppingCartService**, and then click OK.

   This action generates the proxy that the client application can use to connect to the service and configures the client. However, the Add Service Reference Wizard generates client endpoint information based on the HTTP protocol, whereas the ShoppingCart Host application exposes the service by using the TCP protocol. Therefore, you need to amend the client configuration.

3. Open the app.config file for the ShoppingCartGUIClient project in the Code And Text Editor window. Delete the contents of the *<system.serviceModel>* section and replace it with the client endpoint configuration, shown in bold in the following:

```xml
<?xml version="1.0" encoding="utf-8" ?>
<configuration>
  <system.serviceModel>
    <client>
      <endpoint address="net.tcp://localhost:8080/ShoppingCartService.xamlx"
                binding="netTcpContextBinding"
                contract="ShoppingCartService.IShoppingCartService"
                name="NetTcpContextBinding_IShoppingCartService" />
    </client>
  </system.serviceModel>
</configuration>
```

4. Open the MainWindow.xaml.cs file for the ShoppingCartGUIClient project in the Code And Text Editor window. In the *MainWindow* class, locate the *clientEndpointName* variable. The various methods in the client application use this variable to specify the name of the client endpoint through which to connect. Verify that it is set to *NetTcpContext Binding_IShoppingCartService*, as shown in bold in the following:

```csharp
public partial class MainWindow : Window
{
    private ShoppingCartServiceClient proxy = null;
    private IDictionary<string, string> context = null;
    private string clientEndpointName = "NetTcpContextBinding_IShoppingCartService";
    ...
}
```

5. Set the ShoppingCartGUIClient and ShoppingCartHost projects as the startup projects for the ShoppingCart solution.

6. Build and run the solution without debugging. In the Shopping Cart GUI Client window, in the Product Number box, type **WB-H098**, and then click Add Item. Verify that a water bottle is added to the shopping cart and appears in the client window.

7. Type **SA-M198**, and then click Add Item again. A Mountain Seat Assembly should be added to the shopping cart.

8. Click Remove Item, and verify that the Mountain Seat Assembly disappears from the shopping cart.

9. Click Checkout. The shopping cart should be emptied.

10. Close the Shopping Cart GUI Client window. Stop the service, and then return to Visual Studio.

Correlating Clients and Service Instances

Chapter 7 described how client applications and services can use the *WSHttpContext Binding* binding to pass context information in the SOAP header of request and response messages to identify to which service instance a client application should connect. The discussion in Chapter 7 focused on durable services, but the same principles apply to workflow services. When an operation is marked as *CanCreateInstance*, the workflow service host can create a new service instance and generates an instance ID (a unique identifier) which it passes back to the client as part of the response message. The client can provide this same instance ID in the header of subsequent requests, and the workflow service host will direct these requests to the correct service instance. The *NetTcpContextBinding* binding provides the same facility. However, you can also correlate client applications and service instances by using other bindings that don't support this form of automatic correlation. To do this, you must configure the *Receive* activities for the service and specify the data it should use to correlate request messages with service instances.

The *Receive* activity provides the *CorrelatesOn* property. You can use this property to specify that one or more message parameters should be used to identify the service instance rather than an instance ID generated by the workflow runtime. When the service host receives a request message, the workflow runtime examines the values of these parameters and uses them to direct the request to the appropriate service instance, or create a new service instance as necessary (assuming that the *CanCreateInstance* property of the corresponding *Receive* activity is set to *True*). You should be careful to ensure that the corresponding fields are populated as part of any requests sent by client applications; otherwise, correlation will not occur as expected. Additionally, if two or more clients provide the same information as message parameters, the workflow service runtime will assume that they are the same client and will direct them both to the same workflow service instance; this may be useful if you need to share session data between clients, but it may also pose a security risk if this sharing is unintentional.

For more information about configuring this form of correlation, look up Content Based Correlation in the documentation provided with Visual Studio (also available on the Microsoft Web site at *http://msdn.microsoft.com/en-us/library/ee358755.aspx*).

Building Durable Workflow Services

A key aspect of workflow services is their support for scalability. Like the procedural services described in Chapter 7, workflow services can be durable, enabling service instances to survive the service host shutting down and restarting. Additionally, you can configure a workflow service to temporarily suspend a service instance if it becomes idle for a period of time, save its state to the persistence store, and remove it from memory. If a request is received for this instance subsequently, the workflow host can load the instance state from the persistence store and resume the service instance.

> **Note** Windows Server AppFabric provides extensions to Internet Information Services Manager with which you can configure persistence for workflow services hosted by using IIS. An administrator can examine the state of services, forcibly terminate service instances, and even restart failed service instances. The details of Windows Server AppFabric are outside the scope of this book, but by employing the techniques presented in this section, you can build workflow services that can take full advantage of the AppFabric environment.

In the final set of exercises in this chapter, you will configure the *ShoppingCartService* as a durable workflow service.

Configure the *ShoppingCartService* Workflow Service as a Durable Service

1. Open the ShoppingCartService.xamlx file for the ShoppingCartService project in the Design View window.

2. In the *Action* section of the *Add Item To Cart* activity, click the *Send AddItemToCart Response* activity. In the Properties window, select the *PersistBeforeSend* property check box.

   When the service instance sends the response message, the state of the service instance will be automatically saved to the persistence store.

3. Check the *PersistBeforeSend* property of the *Send RemoveItemFromCart Response* and *Send GetShoppingCart Response* activities. The state of the service instance will also be saved whenever either of these messages is sent by the service.

4. Leave the check box for the *PersistBeforeSend* property of the *Send Checkout Response* activity cleared.

   The *Checkout* operation is the final action that a client performs, and the session should terminate when this operation completes. By not selecting the *PersistBeforeSend* property, the state is removed from the persistence store when the operation completes.

   The persistence store for workflow services employs a different database schema from that of durable procedural services described in Chapter 7. Scripts for creating the schema and stored procedures needed by durable workflow services are available in the C:\Windows\Microsoft.NET\Framework\v4.0.30319\SQL\en folder, in the SqlWorkflow InstanceStoreSchema.sql and SqlWorkflowInstanceStoreLogic.sql files.

> **Note** The following steps assume that you have created the *WCFPersistence* SQL Server database, as described in Chapter 7. If you have not already created this database, perform the following steps:
>
> 1. In Server Explorer, right-click Data Connections, and then click Create New SQL Server Database.
>
> 2. In the Create New SQL Server Database dialog box, set the Server Name to **.\SQLExpress**, click Use Windows Authentication, enter **WCFPersistence** in the New Database Name text box, and then click OK.

5. On the File menu, point to Open, and then click File. In the Open File dialog box move to the C:\Windows\Microsoft.NET\Framework\v4.0.30319\SQL\en folder, select the SqlWorkflowInstanceStoreSchema.sql file, and then click Open.

6. On the Data menu, point to Transact-SQL Editor, point to Connection, and then click Connect. In the Connect to Database Engine dialog box, in the Server Name text box enter **.\SQLExpress**, ensure that Authentication is set to Windows Authentication, and then click Connect.

7. In the Visual Studio toolbar, in the Database drop-down, click WCFPersistence.

8. On the Data menu, point to Transact-SQL Editor, and then click Execute SQL. Verify that the SQL script runs and displays the message "Command(s) completed successfully".

9. Follow the process described in steps 5 through 8 to open and run the SqlWorkflow InstanceStoreLogic.sql script, which is located in the C:\Windows\Microsoft.NET\ Framework\v4.0.30319\SQL\en folder.

10. Add references to the *System.Activities.DurableInstancing* and *System.Runtime.Durable Instancing* assemblies to the ShoppingCartHost project.

11. Open the Program.cs file for the ShoppingCartHost project in the Code And Text Editor window, and add the following *using* statement to the file:

```
using System.Activities.DurableInstancing;
```

12. Add the following statements (shown in bold) to the *Main* method.

```
static void Main(string[] args)
{
    WorkflowService service =
        XamlServices.Load(@"..\..\..\ShoppingCartService\ShoppingCartService.xamlx")
        as WorkflowService;

    WorkflowServiceHost host = new WorkflowServiceHost(service);

    string persistenceStoreConnectionString =
        @"Data Source=.\SQLExpress;Initial Catalog=WCFPersistence;
         Integrated Security=True";
    SqlWorkflowInstanceStore instanceStore =
        new SqlWorkflowInstanceStore(persistenceStoreConnectionString);
    host.DurableInstancingOptions.InstanceStore = instanceStore;

    host.Open();
    Console.WriteLine("Service running. Press ENTER to stop");
    Console.ReadLine();
    host.Close();
}
```

This code specifies that the *WorkflowServiceHost* object should support persistence and specifies the connection string for the persistence database. You can also provide this information in the application configuration file by defining a service behavior and adding the *workflowRuntime* element. For more information, consult the documentation provided with Visual Studio.

Test the Durable Service

1. Start the solution without debugging. In the Shopping Cart GUI Client window, enter **WB-H098** in the Product Number text box, and then click Add Item. Verify that a water bottle has been added to the shopping cart.

2. Leave the Shopping Cart GUI Client window and the service host console application window running. Return to Visual Studio.

3. In the Server Explorer pane, expand the Data Connections folder, expand the *Your Computer\sqlexpress.WCFPersistence.dbo* connection (where *YourComputer* is the name of your computer), expand Tables, right-click the *InstancesTable* table, and then click Show Table Data.

The workflow host stores session information in this table. You should see a single row in this table. The session data is held in a binary format in the PrimitiveDataProperties, ComplexDataProperties, WriteOnlyPrimitiveDataProperties, and WriteOnlyPrimitive-DataProperties columns (some of these columns may be empty). Other properties in this table provide information about the state of the service instance.

4. Leave the Shopping Cart GUI Client window running, but press Enter in the service host console application window to stop the service.

 Important Do not simply close the service host console window; wait for the service host to finish first. Otherwise, the session information for the client application may not be persisted fully.

5. In Solution Explorer, right-click the ShoppingCartHost project, point to Debug, and then click Start New Instance.

6. Return to the Shopping Cart GUI Client window. Enter **PU-M044** in the Product Number text box, and then click Add Item.

   A mountain bike pump is added to the shopping cart. Notice that the workflow runtime has successfully restored the existing contents of the shopping cart from the state information in the persistence store.

7. Click Checkout.

   This operation completes the session, and the shopping cart is emptied.

8. Leave the Shopping Cart GUI Client application and the service host console application running, and return to Visual Studio. Click the InstancesTable tab, and in the Visual Studio toolbar, click the Execute SQL button (the button with the red exclamation mark). The table should now be empty.

   When the Checkout operation completed, the session was terminated, and the session information saved in the persistence store was removed.

8. Close the Shopping Cart GUI Client window and the service host console application window.

Summary

In this chapter, you have seen how to use the Workflow Foundation to build robust workflow services. WF provides a small but complete set of messaging activities. You can use these activities to build services that implement almost any messaging pattern.

You learned how to listen for requests by using a *Receive* activity and how to send a response by using a *SendReply* activity. You also saw how to deploy a workflow service and include activities that can detect and handle faults. You learned how to build workflow client applications and how the Add Service Reference Wizard can create custom activities that encapsulate sending a request message and waiting for the response.

Finally, you learned how workflow services correlate client applications with service instances and how to configure a workflow service as a durable service.

Chapter 9
Supporting Transactions

After completing this chapter, you will be able to:

- Describe the transaction management protocols available with WCF.

- Use transactions with WCF services and operations.

- Describe the impact that using transactions can have on the design of a WCF service.

- Explain how to implement secure, distributed transactions by using the WS-AtomicTransaction protocol.

- Describe how to implement transactions in a workflow service.

Most applications commonly need to ensure the internal consistency of the data that they manipulate. You can use transactions to help achieve this consistency. A transaction is an atomic unit of work or a series of operations that should either *all* be performed successfully, or, if something unexpected happens, none should be performed. The classic example of a transaction is transferring funds between two bank accounts, deducting an amount of money from one account and adding an equivalent amount to the other account. If the addition operation fails, then the deduction operation must be undone, otherwise the money is lost (and the bank risks losing its trading license!). Similarly, if the deduction operation fails, the addition operation must not occur, either. Traditionally, transactions were associated with database systems, but the semantics of transactions can be applied to any series of operations that involve making changes to data.

In a Service-Oriented Application (SOA) environment, a transaction can span several services, possibly running on different computers within different organizations—this is called a *distributed transaction*. In this environment, the underlying infrastructure must be able to guarantee consistency across a network and between potentially heterogeneous data stores. Making such a guarantee is a complex task because of the number of possible failure points in a network. This problem has been the subject of much research. The commonly accepted standard mechanism for handling distributed transactions is the two-phase commit protocol. The OASIS organization has proposed the *Web Services Atomic Transaction* (WS-AtomicTransaction) specification, which describes a standard mechanism for handling transactions in a Web services infrastructure. The WS-AtomicTransaction specification defines the semantics of the two-phase commit protocol between Web services. Web services running on an infrastructure that conforms to the WS-AtomicTransaction specification should be interoperable with each other from a transactional perspective.

> **More Info** There are two versions of the WS-AtomicTransaction specification in use: the 2004 version, and the more recent version 1.1. Prior to the .NET Framework 4.0, WCF implemented only the 2004 version, but WCF 4.0 now supports both. For detailed information about the WS-Atomic Transaction specification, see the "Transaction Specification Index Page" page on the Microsoft Web site at *http://msdn.microsoft.com/en-us/library/ms951262.aspx*

The WS-AtomicTransaction specification is primarily useful when building Web services. However, WCF is not just concerned with Web services; you can use WCF to build applications based on many other technologies, such as COM, MSMQ, and .NET Framework Remoting. Microsoft has provided its own transaction management features, which are built in to the current family of Microsoft Windows operating systems under the name Distributed Transaction Coordinator, or DTC. DTC uses its own optimized transaction protocol. Transactions based on the DTC transaction protocol are referred to as OLE transactions (OLE was the name of a technology that was the forerunner of COM). OLE transactions are ideal if you are building solutions based on Microsoft technologies.

The .NET Framework 4.0 provides a number of classes, structures, interfaces, delegates, and enumerations in the *System.Transactions* namespace. These types provide an interface to the transaction management features of WCF, letting you develop code that is independent of the technology used to control the transactions that your code performs. In this chapter, you will see how to create a WCF service that supports transactions and how to build client applications that can initiate and control those transactions.

Using Transactions in a WCF Service

The *ShoppingCartService* service that you implemented in previous chapters currently lets users add items to their shopping cart, but it does not perform many of the consistency checks that a production application should include. For example, the service always assumes that goods are in stock when a user adds them the shopping cart. Similarly, the service currently makes no attempt to update stock levels. You will rectify these shortcomings in the exercises in this section. You will make the service transactional to ensure that any changes made to the data result in a consistent state.

Implementing OLE Transactions

You will start by examining how to configure a WCF service to use transactions with a TCP endpoint. Endpoints established by using the TCP transport can incorporate OLE transactions.

Enable Transactions in the *ShoppingCartService* Service

1. Using Visual Studio, open the ShoppingCart solution located in the Microsoft Press\WCF Step By Step\Chapter 9\ShoppingCartService folder, located within your Documents folder.

   This solution contains a modified copy of the non-durable *ShoppingCartService*, as well as the ShoppingCartServiceHost and ShoppingCartClient projects from Chapter 7, "Maintaining State and Sequencing Operations." The ShoppingCartHost project exposes a TCP endpoint rather than the HTTP endpoint that you configured in Chapter 7, and the ShoppingCartClient application has been simplified and modified to communicate with the service by using that TCP endpoint.

2. Add a reference to the *System.Transactions* assembly to the ShoppingCartService project. This assembly contains some of the classes and attributes required to manage transactions. You'll also use other types and attributes from the *System.ServiceModel* assembly, which the ShoppingCartService project already references.

3. Open the ShoppingCartService.cs file for the ShoppingCartService project in the Code And Text Editor window.

4. Add the following *using* statement to the list at the top of the file:

   ```
   using System.Transactions;
   ```

5. Locate the *ServiceBehavior* attribute that precedes the *ShoppingCartServiceImpl* class. Add the following *TransactionIsolationLevel* property (shown in bold) to this attribute:

   ```
   [ServiceBehavior(InstanceContextMode = InstanceContextMode.PerSession,
       TransactionIsolationLevel=IsolationLevel.RepeatableRead)]
   public class ShoppingCartServiceImpl : IShoppingCartService
   {
       ...
   }
   ```

   The *TransactionIsolationLevel* property determines how the database management system (SQL Server in the exercises in this book) lets concurrent transactions overlap. In a typical system, multiple concurrent users access the database at the same time. However, this can lead to problems when two users try to modify the same data at the same time, or when one user tries to query data that another user is modifying. You must ensure that concurrent users cannot interfere adversely with each other—they must be isolated. Typically, whenever a user modifies, inserts, or deletes data during a transaction, the database management system locks the affected data until the transaction completes. If the transaction commits, the database management system makes the changes permanent. If an error occurs and the transaction rolls back, the database management system cancels the changes. The *TransactionIsolationLevel* property specifies how the locks applied during a data-modification transaction affect other transactions attempting to access the same data. The *TransactionIsolationLevel* property can take one of several values. The most common isolation levels are:

❑ *IsolationLevel.ReadUncommitted*   This isolation level enables the transaction to read data that another transaction has modified and locked, but not yet committed. This isolation level provides the most concurrency; however, there is the risk of the user being presented with "dirty" data that might change unexpectedly if the modifying transaction rolls back the changes rather than committing them.

❑ *IsolationLevel.ReadCommitted*   This isolation level prevents the transaction from reading data that another transaction has modified, but not yet committed. The reading transaction will be forced to wait until the modified data is unlocked. Although this isolation level prevents read access to dirty data, it does not guarantee consistency; if the transaction reads the same data twice, there is the possibility that another transaction might have modified the data in between reads, thus the reading transaction would be presented with two different versions of the data.

❑ *IsolationLevel.RepeatableRead*   This isolation level is similar to the *ReadCommitted* isolation level, but it causes the transaction reading the data to lock this data until the reading transaction finishes (the *ReadCommitted* isolation level does not cause a transaction to lock data that it reads). The transaction can then safely read the same data as many times as it wants without the data being changed by another transaction until this transaction has completed. This isolation level therefore provides more consistency, at the cost of reduced concurrency.

❑ *IsolationLevel.Serializable*   This isolation level takes the *RepeatableRead* isolation level one stage further. When using the *RepeatableRead* isolation level, data read by a transaction cannot change. However, it is possible for a transaction to execute the same query twice and obtain different results if another transaction inserts data that matches the query criteria: new rows suddenly appear. The *Serializable* isolation level prevents this inconsistency from occurring by restricting the rows that other concurrent transactions can add to the database. This isolation level provides the greatest level of consistency, but the degree of concurrency can be significantly reduced.

Unless you have a good reason to choose otherwise, use the *IsolationLevel.Repeatable Read* isolation level.

6. In the *ShoppingCartServiceImpl* class, add the following *OperationBehavior* attribute to the *AddItemToCart* method:

```
[OperationBehavior(TransactionScopeRequired=true, TransactionAutoComplete=false)]
public bool AddItemToCart(string productNumber)
{
    ...
}
```

You are going to modify the *AddItemToCart* method to check the level of stock for the selected product and modify the stock level if the product is available. This work will be transactional, and the client application should invoke this operation only in the context of a transaction, which ensures that the changes can be undone if some sort of failure occurs. Setting the *TransactionScopeRequired* property of the *OperationBehavior* attribute to *true* forces the operation to execute as part of a transaction; either the client application must initiate the transaction (you will see how to do this shortly) or the WCF runtime will automatically create a new transaction when this operation runs.

The *TransactionAutoComplete* property specifies what happens to the transaction when the operation finishes. If you set this property to *true*, the transaction automatically commits and makes all its changes permanent. Setting this property to *false* keeps the transaction active; the changes are not committed yet. The default value for this property is *true*. In the case of the *AddItemToCart* method, you don't want to commit changes and finish the transaction until the user has checked out and paid for the goods, so the code sets this property to *false*.

7. Open the IShoppingCartService.cs file in the Code And Text Editor window. Add the *TransactionFlow* attributes (shown in bold in the following code) to all the method definitions in the *IShoppingCartService interface*, just after the *OperationContract* attribute:

```
public interface IShoppingCartInterface
{
    [OperationContract(Name = "AddItemToCart", IsInitiating = true)]
    [TransactionFlow(TransactionFlowOption.Mandatory)]
    public bool AddItemToCart(string productNumber)

    [OperationContract(Name = "RemoveItemFromCart", IsInitiating = false)]
    [TransactionFlow(TransactionFlowOption.Mandatory)]
    bool RemoveItemFromCart(string productNumber);

    [OperationContract(Name = "GetShoppingCart", IsInitiating = false)]
    [TransactionFlow(TransactionFlowOption.Mandatory)]
    string GetShoppingCart();

    [OperationContract(Name = "Checkout", IsInitiating = false, IsTerminating = true)]
    [TransactionFlow(TransactionFlowOption.Mandatory)]
    bool Checkout();
}
```

The description of the *TransactionScopeRequired* property in the previous step mentioned that the WCF runtime automatically creates a new transaction when invoking an operation, if necessary. In the shopping cart scenario, you want the client application to be responsible for creating its own transactions and invoking the operations in the *ShoppingCartService* service in the context of these transactions. You can enforce this rule by applying the *TransactionFlow* attribute to the operation contract. Specifying a parameter of *TransactionFlowOption.Mandatory* indicates that the client application *must* create a transaction before calling this operation and must send the details of this transaction as part of the SOAP message header when invoking the operation. The other values you can specify are *TransactionFlowOption.Allowed*, which will use a transaction created by the client if one exists (the WCF runtime will create a new transaction if not), and *TransactionFlowOption.NotAllowed*, which causes the WCF runtime to disregard any client transaction and always create a new one.

The default value is *TransactionFlowOption.NotAllowed*.

8. You can now amend the code in the *ShoppingCartServiceImpl* class to check stock levels and update them in the database, safe in the knowledge that this functionality is protected by transactions—if anything should go wrong, the changes will be rolled back automatically.

In the ShoppingCartService.cs file, add the *decrementStockLevel* method shown below to the *ShoppingCartServiceImpl* class:

```
private bool decrementStockLevel(string productNumber)
{
    // Decrement the current stock level of the selected product
    // in the ProductInventory table.
    // If the update is successful then return true, otherwise return false.

    // The Product and ProductInventory tables are joined over the
    // ProductID column.

    try
    {
        // Connect to the AdventureWorks database by using the Entity Framework
        using (AdventureWorksEntities database = new AdventureWorksEntities())
        {
            // Find the ProductID for the specified product
            int productID =
                (from p in database.Products
                 where String.Compare(p.ProductNumber, productNumber) == 0
                 select p.ProductID).First();

            // Update the first row for this product in the ProductInventory table
            // that has a quantity value greater than zero.
            ProductInventory productInventory = database.ProductInventories.First(
                pi => pi.ProductID == productID && pi.Quantity > 0);

            // Update the stock level for the ProductInventory object
            productInventory.Quantity --;

            // Save the change back to the database
            database.SaveChanges();
        }
    }
    catch
    {
        // If an exception occurs, return false to indicate failure
        return false;
    }

    // Return true to indicate success
    return true;
}
```

> **Note** The code for this method is available in the file DecrementStockLevel.txt, which is located in the Chapter 9 folder.

This method verifies that the specified product is available, and then updates the stock level for that product, decrementing the *Quantity* by one. You may recall from Chapter 1, "Introducing Windows Communication Foundation," that a product can be stored in more than one location; thus it may exist in more than one row in the *ProductInventory* table. This method simply updates the first matching product row in the *ProductInventory* table that has a quantity greater than zero. If the update fails to modify a row, this method returns *false* to indicate either insufficient stock (all rows have a zero for the quantity) or that no such product exists (there are no rows). If the update changes exactly one row, then this method returns *true* to indicate success.

> **Note** Strictly speaking, the service should record and save the value in the rowguid column of the row it updates in the *ProductInventory* table, so that the corresponding row can be incremented again if the user decides to remove the item from the shopping cart later. However, this functionality is left as an exercise for readers to perform.
>
> It is also possible for this method to cause a database deadlock if multiple service instances execute it simultaneously. In this situation, SQL Server picks one of the transactions (referred to rather prosaically as the "victim" by SQL Server) and aborts it, releasing any locks held, and possibly letting other concurrent transactions complete. Aborting the transaction will cause the *SaveChanges* method of the Entity Framework to fail and throw an exception. When that happens, the method returns *false*. The important point to learn from this is that using transactions ensures that the database will remain consistent, even in the face of unforeseen eventualities.

9. In the *AddItemToCart* method, change the code that increments the volume of an item in the shopping cart so that it calls the *decrementStockLevel* method you just created, as shown in bold in the following:

```
public bool AddItemToCart(string productNumber)
{
    // Note: For clarity, this method performs very limited
    // security checking and exception handling
    try
    {
        // Check to see whether the user has already added this
        // product to the shopping cart
        ShoppingCartItem item = find(shoppingCart, productNumber);

        // If so, then simply increment the volume
        if (item != null)
        {
            if (decrementStockLevel(productNumber))
```

```
            {
                item.Volume++;
                return true;
            }
            else
            {
                return false;
            }
        }

        // Otherwise, retrieve the details of the product from the database
        else
        {
            ...
        }
    }
    ...
}
```

10. Modify the *else* block in the *AddItemToCart* method so that it checks whether sufficient stock is available in the database before retrieving the details of the product from the database, as shown in bold in the following:

```
public bool AddItemToCart(string productNumber)
{
    // Note: For clarity, this method performs very limited
    // security checking and exception handling
    try
    {
        // Check to see whether the user has already added this
        // product to the shopping cart
        ShoppingCartItem item = find(shoppingCart, productNumber);

        // If so, then simply increment the volume
        if (item != null)
        {
            ...
        }

        // Otherwise, retrieve the details of the product from the database
        else if (decrementStockLevel(productNumber))
        {
            ...
        }
        else
        {
            return false;
        }
    }
    catch
    {
        ...
    }
}
```

Leave the block of code that connects to the database and retrieves the product details untouched. Also, be sure to add the additional *else* statement to the end of the block, immediately before the *catch* block, as shown in the previous example.

11. Add an *OperationBehavior* attribute to the *RemoveItemFromCart* method, setting the *TransactionScopeRequired* property to **true** and the *TransactionAutoComplete* property to **false**. The method should look like this:

```
[OperationBehavior(TransactionScopeRequired=true, TransactionAutoComplete=false)]
public bool RemoveItemFromCart(string productNumber)
{
    ...
}
```

> **Note** If you have the time, you might want to add the appropriate code to this method to increment the stock level in the database after removing the item from the shopping cart.

12. Add another *OperationBehavior* attribute to the *GetShoppingCart* method, setting the *TransactionScopeRequired* property to **true** and the *TransactionAutoComplete* property to **false**:

```
[OperationBehavior(TransactionScopeRequired=true, TransactionAutoComplete=false)]
public bool GetShoppingCart()
{
    ...
}
```

The *GetShoppingCart* method does not actually query or modify the database, but it could be (and probably would be) called by the client application during a transaction. It is important that this method does not commit the transaction; hence, the need to set the *TransactionAutoComplete* property to *false*. You cannot set the *TransactionAuto Complete* property to *false* without setting the *TransactionScopeRequired* property to *true*.

13. Add a final *OperationBehavior* attribute to the *Checkout* method, setting the *Transaction-ScopeRequired* property to **true** and the *TransactionAutoComplete* property to **false**:

```
[OperationBehavior(TransactionScopeRequired=true, TransactionAutoComplete=false)]
public bool Checkout()
{
    ...
}
```

Having modified the code in the service, you must also change the configuration of the service endpoint to enable the WCF runtime to "flow" transactions from the client application into the service. Information about transactions is included in the headers of the SOAP messages sent by client applications invoking the operations.

Note Not all bindings allow you to flow transactions from client applications into a service. The bindings that do not support transactions include *BasicHttpBinding, NetMsmqBinding, NetPeer TcpBinding,* and *WebHttpBinding.*

Configure the *ShoppingCartService* Service to Flow Transactions from Client Applications

1. Edit the App.config file for the ShoppingCartHost project by using the Service Configuration Editor.

2. In the Service Configuration Editor, in the Configuration pane, click the Bindings folder. In the right pane, click New Binding Configuration.

3. In the Create A New Binding dialog box, select the **netTcpBinding** binding type, and then click OK.

4. In the right pane, change the *Name* property of the binding to **ShoppingCartService NetTcpBindingConfig**. In the General section of the pane, set the *TransactionFlow* property to **True**. Verify that the *TransactionProtocol* property is set to *OleTransactions*.

   The *TransactionFlow* property indicates that the service should expect to receive information about transactions in the SOAP messages it receives.

   The *TransactionProtocol* property specifies the transaction protocol the service should use. By default, endpoints based on the TCP transport use the internal DTC protocol when performing distributed transactions. However, you can configure them to use transactions that follow the WS-AtomicTransaction protocol by changing this property to **WSAtomicTransactionOctober2004** (for services that need to conform to the 2004 version of the specification), or **WSAtomicTransaction11** (for services that need to conform to the more recent version 1.1 of the specification).

5. In the Configuration pane, in the Services folder, expand the *ShoppingCartService. ShoppingCartServiceImpl* node, expand the Endpoints folder, and then click the (*Empty Name*) node. In the Service Endpoint pane, set the *BindingConfguration* property of the endpoint to **ShoppingCartServiceNetTcpBindingConfig**.

6. Save the configuration file then close the Service Configuration Editor.

You have configured the *ShoppingCartService* service to expect the client application to invoke operations within the scope of a transaction. You now need to modify the client application to actually create this transaction.

Create a Transaction in the Client Application

1. In Visual Studio, add a reference to the *System.Transactions* assembly to the Shopping CartClient project.

2. Open the Program.cs file for the ShoppingCartClient project in the Code And Text Editor window and add the following *using* statement to the list at the top of the file:

```
using System.Transactions;
```

3. In the *Main* method, add the code shown below in bold, and surround the statements that invoke the operations in the *ShoppingCartService* service with a *using* block:

```
static void Main(string[] args)
{
    ...
    try
    {
        // Connect to the ShoppingCartService service
        ShoppingCartServiceClient proxy =
            new ShoppingCartServiceClient("NetTcpBinding_IShoppingCartService");

        TransactionOptions tOpts = new TransactionOptions();
        tOpts.IsolationLevel = IsolationLevel.RepeatableRead;
        tOpts.Timeout = new TimeSpan(0, 1, 0);
        using (TransactionScope tx =
            new TransactionScope(TransactionScopeOption.RequiresNew, tOpts))
        {
            // Add two water bottles to the shopping cart
            proxy.AddItemToCart("WB-H098");
            proxy.AddItemToCart("WB-H098");

            // Add a mountain seat assembly to the shopping cart
            proxy.AddItemToCart("SA-M198");

            // Query the shopping cart and display the result
            string cartContents = proxy.GetShoppingCart();
            Console.WriteLine(cartContents);

            // Buy the goods in the shopping cart
            proxy.Checkout();
            Console.WriteLine("Goods purchased");
        }

        // Disconnect from the ShoppingCartService service
        proxy.Close();
    }
    catch (Exception e)
    {
        ...
    }
    ...
}
```

You can create a new transaction in several ways: a service can initiate a new transaction automatically by setting the *TransactionScopeRequired* attribute of the *OperationBehavior* property to *true* as described earlier; an operation can explicitly start a new transaction by creating a *CommittableTransaction* object; or the client application can implicitly create a new transaction. In a WCF client application, the recommended approach is to use a *TransactionScope* object.

When you create a new *TransactionScope* object, any transactional operations that follow are automatically enlisted into a transaction. If the WCF runtime detects that there is no active transaction when you create a new *TransactionScope* object, it can initiate a new transaction and performs the operations in the context of this transaction. In this case, the transaction remains active until the *TransactionScope* object is destroyed. For this reason, it is common practice to employ a *using* block to explicitly delimit the scope of a transaction.

The *TransactionScopeOption* parameter of the *TransactionScope* constructor determines how the WCF runtime utilizes an existing transaction. If this parameter is set to *Transaction ScopeOption.RequiresNew*, the WCF runtime will always create a new transaction. The other values you can specify are *TransactionScopeOption.Required*, which will create a new transaction only if no other transaction is currently in scope (referred to as the "ambient transaction"), and *TransactionScopeOption.Suppress*, which causes all operations in the context of the *TransactionScope* object to be performed without using a transaction (operations will not participate in the ambient transaction, if there is one).

> **Note** The *TransactionScopeOption.Suppress* option is useful for situations in which you need to include non-transactional code within transactional code; the operations in the non-transactional code can fail without causing the enclosing transaction to abort, and vice versa. Scenarios include performing logging or audit operations; you want the log or audit data to be saved, regardless of whether the enclosing transaction commits or aborts.

The transaction isolation level of any new transactions should match the requirements of the service. You can specify the isolation level by creating a *TransactionOptions* object and referencing it in the *TransactionScope* constructor, as shown in the previous example. You can also specify a timeout value for transactions. This can improve the responsiveness of an application because transactions will not wait an indeterminate period for resources locked by other transactions to become available; instead, the WCF runtime throws an exception that the client application should be prepared to handle when a timeout occurs. In this example, the timeout period is set to one minute.

4. Add an *if* block and the statement shown in the following around the code that invokes the *Checkout* operation:

```
// Buy the goods in the shopping cart
if (proxy.Checkout())
{
    tx.Complete();
    Console.WriteLine("Goods purchased");
}
```

By default, when the flow of control leaves the *using* block (either by the natural flow of the code or because of an exception), unless you specify otherwise, the transaction will be aborted and the work it performed undone. This is probably not what you want. Calling the *Complete* method of the *TransactionScope* object before destroying it indicates that work has been completed successfully and that the transaction should be committed. In the *ShoppingCartService* service; the *Checkout* method returns *true* if the checkout operation is successful and *false* if otherwise. If the *Checkout* method fails and returns *false*, the *Complete* method will not be called and any changes made to the database by the transaction will be rolled back.

> **Note** Calling the *Complete* method does not actually guarantee that your work *will* be committed. It indicates only that the work performed inside the transaction scope was successful and *can* be committed in the absence of any other problems. You can nest transaction scopes; you can create a new *TransactionScope* object inside the *using* state-ment of another *TransactionScope* object. If the nested *TransactionScope* object creates a new transaction (called a nested transaction), calling the *Complete* method on the nested *TransactionScope* object commits the nested transaction *with respect to* the transaction (called the parent transaction) used by the outer *TransactionScope* object. If the parent transaction aborts, then the nested transaction will also be aborted.

5. In an earlier exercise, you modified the contract for the *ShoppingCartService* by adding the *TransactionFlow* attribute to each operation. You must therefore update the proxy that the client application uses to ensure that the proxy sends the details of transactions to the service. You can perform this task either by regenerating the code for the proxy class using the *svcutil* utility (Chapter 7 contains the steps for doing this), or you can modify the code manually. For this exercise, perform this task manually by editing the code as follows:

    a. Open the ShoppingCartServiceProxy.cs file for the ShoppingCartClient project in the Code And Text Editor window.

    b. Add the following *using* statement at the start of the file:

    ```
    using System.ServiceModel;
    ```

    c. Locate the *ShoppingCartService* interface. This is the first interface in the *Shopping CartClient.ShoppingCartService* namespace.

d. Add the *TransactionFlow* attribute to each method in this interface, as shown in bold in the code that follows. Do not change any other code or attributes in this interface (the properties of the *OperationContractAttribute* for each method have been omitted, for clarity—leave those intact in your code):

```
public interface ShoppingCartService
{
    [System.ServiceModel.OperationContractAttribute(...)]
    [TransactionFlow(TransactionFlowOption.Mandatory)]
    bool AddItemToCart(string product
            Number);

    [System.ServiceModel.OperationContractAttribute(...)]
    [TransactionFlow(TransactionFlowOption.Mandatory)]
    bool RemoveItemFromCart(string productNumber);

    [System.ServiceModel.OperationContractAttribute(...)]
    [TransactionFlow(TransactionFlowOption.Mandatory)]
    string GetShoppingCart();

    [System.ServiceModel.OperationContractAttribute(...)]
    [TransactionFlow(TransactionFlowOption.Mandatory)]
    bool Checkout();
}
```

The final step is to configure the endpoint for the client application to send information about its transactions across the network to the service.

Configure the Client Application to Flow Transactions to the *ShoppingCartService* Service

1. Edit the App.config file for the ShoppingCartClient project using the Service Configuration Editor.

2. In the Service Configuration Editor, in the Configuration pane, click the Bindings folder. In the right pane, click New Binding Configuration.

3. In the Create A New Binding dialog box, select the **netTcpBinding** binding type, and then click OK.

4. In the right pane, change the *Name* property of the binding to **ShoppingCartClient NetTcpBindingConfig**. In the General section of the pane, set the *TransactionFlow* property to **True** and verify that the *TransactionProtocol* property is set to *OleTransactions*.

5. In the Configuration pane, select the *NetTcpBinding_IShoppingCartService* node in the Endpoints folder within the Client folder. In the Client Endpoint pane, set the Binding Configuration property of the endpoint to **ShoppingCartClientNetTcpBindingConfig**.

6. Save the configuration file then close the Service Configuration Editor.

You can now test the transactional version of the *ShoppingCartService* service and the client application.

Test the Transactional Implementation of the *ShoppingCartService* Service

1. On the Windows Start menu, open the Control Panel, click System And Security, click Administrative Tools, right-click Component Services, and then click Run As Administrator. Provide the administrator password if you are prompted.

   The Component Services console appears. You can use this console to monitor the transactions being processed by DTC.

2. In the left pane of the Component Services console, click Services. In the right pane, click the Distributed Transaction Coordinator service, and then click Restart The Service.

   Stopping and restarting DTC clears its statistics so you can more easily monitor the progress of your transactions.

3. In the left pane, expand the Component Services node, expand the Computers folder, expand My Computer, expand the Distributed Transaction Coordinator folder, expand Local DTC, and then click Transaction Statistics.

   The right pane displays the statistics summarizing the activity since the DTC service was last started. Currently all values should be set to zero.

4. Return to Visual Studio and start the solution without debugging.

> **Note** If a Windows Security Alert appears, click Allow Access to enable the service to open TCP port 8080.

In the ShoppingCartClient console window that is displaying the message "Press ENTER when the service has started," press Enter.

The client application displays the shopping cart containing two water bottles and a mountain seat assembly, followed by the "Goods purchased" message. However, there also appears to be a problem because the application throws an exception reporting, "The transaction has aborted."

```
C:\Windows\system32\cmd.exe
Press ENTER when the service has started

Number: WB-H098 Name: Water Bottle - 1 liter    Cost: £4.99      Volume: 2
Number: SA-M198 Name: LL Mountain Seat Assembly Cost: £133.34   Volume: 1

TotalCost: £143.32
Goods purchased
Exception: The transaction has aborted.
Press ENTER to finish
```

Press Enter to close the client application console window. In the host application console window, press Enter to stop the service.

5. Switch to the Component Services console. It should confirm that the one transaction you have performed since you restarted DTC has aborted:

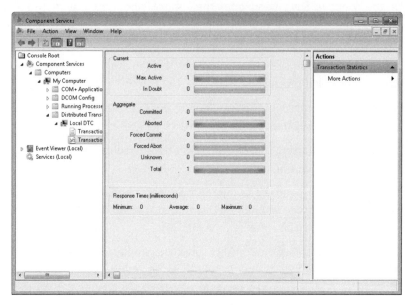

The problem is actually quite subtle. Remember that the *Complete* method of a *TransactionScope* object indicates only that the transaction can be committed. However, before committing a transaction, the transaction must have actually done some work and completed this work successfully. Although the *AddItemToCart* operation invoked in the *ShoppingCartService* service clearly updates the database, it never actually indicates that the work was successfully completed. The same is true of the other operations. Consequently, when the runtime examines the state of the transaction created for the *TransactionScope* object, in the absence of any information indicating success, it decides to abort the transaction and rollback the changes.

You need to make some modifications to the *ShoppingCartService* service to indicate when a transaction has completed successfully. Bear in mind that you can complete a transaction only once, so in the shopping cart scenario, the best place to do this is in the *Checkout* method.

6. In Visual Studio, open the ShoppingCartService.cs file for the ShoppingCartService project in the Code And Text Editor window and find the *Checkout* method, toward the end of the file. The *OperationBehavior* attribute for this method currently sets the *TransactionAutoComplete* property to *false*. You could set this property to *true*, and this would cause the transaction to complete successfully at the end of the method, as long as it did not throw an unhandled exception (if the method throws an exception that you handle in the same method, the transaction will not abort). But in the real world,

you would probably want to be a bit more selective than this; for example, the transaction should only commit if this method ascertains that the user has a valid account with AdventureWorks, for billing purposes. However, for this exercise you will simply add a statement that indicates that the transaction can be committed.

Modify the code in the *Checkout* method, as shown in bold in the following:

```
[OperationBehavior(TransactionScopeRequired = true,
                   TransactionAutoComplete = false)]
public bool Checkout()
{
    // Not currently implemented
    // - just indicate that the transaction completed successfully
    // and return true
    OperationContext.Current.SetTransactionComplete();
    return true;
}
```

The static *Current* property of the *OperationContext* class provides access to the execution context of the operation. The *SetTransactionComplete* method indicates that the current transaction has completed successfully and can be committed when the client application calls the *Complete* method of the *TransactionScope* object containing this transaction. If you need to abort the transaction, just exit the method without calling the *SetTransactionComplete* method, as you did before.

> **Note** Calling the *SetTransactionComplete* method indicates that you have finished all the transactional work. If a transaction spans multiple operations, you cannot invoke any further operations that have the *TransactionScopeRequired* property of the *OperationBehavior* attribute set to *true* and that execute in the same transaction scope. Additionally, you can call the *SetTransactionComplete* method only once in a transaction. A subsequent call to this method inside the scope of the same transaction will raise an exception. Finally, if you call the *SetTransactionComplete* method, but later fail to call the *Complete* method of the *TransactionScope* object, the transaction will be rolled back silently.

7. Start the solution without debugging. In the ShoppingCartClient console window, press Enter.

   This time, the client application executes without reporting that the transaction aborted.

8. Press Enter to close the client application console window. In the host application console window, press Enter to stop the service.

9. Return to the Component Services console. This time, as shown in the image that follows, you can see that the transaction committed.

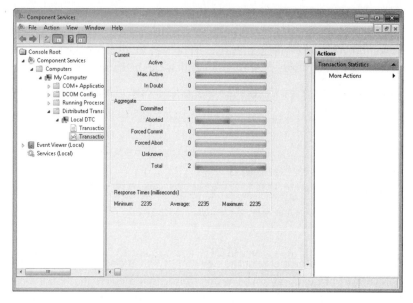

10. To verify that the database is being updated, open a Visual Studio command prompt window and move to the Microsoft Press\WCF Step By Step\Chapter 9 folder. Type the following command:

   StockLevels

   This command executes a script that queries the *AdventureWorks* database, displaying the current stock level of water bottles and mountain seat assemblies:

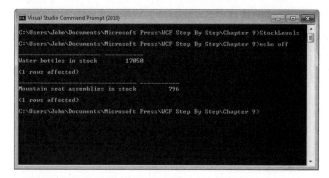

   Make a note of these stock levels.

Note Your stock levels might be different from those shown in the previous image.

11. Leave the command prompt window open and return to Visual Studio. Start the solution again without debugging. In the ShoppingCartClient console window, press Enter. When the client application has finished, press Enter to close the client application console window. In the host application console window, press Enter to stop the service.

12. Return to the command prompt window and execute the *StockLevels* command again. Verify that the stock level for water bottles has decreased by two and the stock level for mountain seat assemblies has decreased by one.

13. Examine the transaction statistics in the Component Services console. You should see that the number of committed transactions is now two.

14. Close the Component Services console.

Implementing the WS-AtomicTransaction Protocol

The *NetTcpBinding* binding uses OLE transactions and Microsoft's own protocol for communicating through DTC to other Microsoft-specific services such as SQL Server. In a heterogeneous environment involving services based on non-Microsoft technologies, you may not be able to employ OLE transactions. Instead, you should apply a more standardized mechanism, such as the WS-AtomicTransaction protocol. When using the *NetTcpContextBinding*, *NetTcp Binding*, or *NetNamedPipeBinding* bindings, you can explicitly specify which transaction protocol to use by setting the *TransactionProtocol* property that these bindings provide. With the HTTP family of bindings, the WCF runtime itself selects the transaction protocol based on the Windows configuration, the transport you are using, and the format of the SOAP header used to flow the transaction from the client application to the service.

For example, a WCF client application connecting to a WCF service through an endpoint based on the "http" scheme will use OLE transactions. If the computers hosting the WCF client application and WCF service are configured to support the WS-AtomicTransaction protocol over a specific port, and the client application connects to the service through an endpoint based on the "https" scheme that uses this port, then transactions will follow the WS-Atomic Transaction protocol (either the October 2004 specification, or version 1.1 as appropriate).

The choice of transaction protocol should be transparent to your services and client applications. The code that you write to initiate, control, and support transactions based on the WS-AtomicTransaction protocol is the same as that for manipulating OLE transactions, so the same service can execute using OLE transactions or WS-AtomicTransaction transactions, depending on how you configure the service.

 Important The *BasicHttpBinding* binding does not support transactions (OLE or WS-Atomic Transaction).

If you wish to exploit the implementation of the WS-AtomicTransaction protocol provided by the .NET Framework 4.0 with the HTTP bindings, you must configure support for the WS-AtomicTransaction protocol in DTC.

The .NET Framework 4.0 includes the wsatConfig.exe utility in the C:\Windows\Microsoft.NET\ Framework\v4.0.30319 folder. This is a command line tool that you can use to configure WS-AtomicTransaction protocol support. The Microsoft Windows SDK provides a graphical user interface component that performs many of the same tasks and that plugs into the Component Services console, as shown in Figure 9-1. You can access this interface by opening the Properties dialog box for Local DTC in the Distributed Transaction Coordinator folder under My Computer, and then clicking the WS-AT tab.

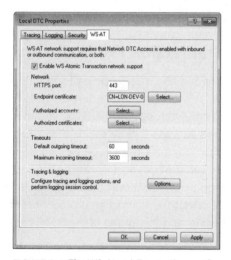

FIGURE 9-1 The WS-AtomicTransaction configuration tab in the Component Services console.

> **Note** You must register the assembly that implements the user interface before you can use it in the Component Services console. Open a Visual Studio command prompt as administrator, move to the C:\Windows\Microsoft.NET\Framework\v4.0.30319 folder (or the C:\Windows\Microsoft. NET\Framework64\v4.0.30319 folder if you are running a 64-bit implementation of Windows 7) and type the following command:
>
> ```
> regasm /codebase wsatui.dll
> ```

To enable WS-AtomicTransaction support, you must first enable network DTC access and permit inbound and outbound communications to and from DTC. You can perform these tasks by using the Security tab in the Local DTC Properties dialog box.

The implementation of the WS-AtomicTransaction protocol over HTTP requires mutual authentication, integrity, and confidentiality for all messages. This means that you must configure the HTTPS transport. If the WCF service listens on a port other than 443 (the default

HTTPS port), you should specify the port in the WS-AT tab. You must also provide a certificate that the service can use to encrypt messages. Additionally, the WS-AT tab lets you specify which users are authorized to access your service, identifying these accounts by their Windows credentials or certificates.

> **More Info** If you require more information about configuring the WS-AtomicTransaction support with DTC, visit the "Configuring WS-Atomic Transaction" support page on the Microsoft Web site at *http://msdn.microsoft.com/en-us/library/ms733943.aspx*.

Designing a WCF Service to Support Transactions

The previous sections have shown you how to implement transactions in a WCF service, but there are a number of issues you should be aware of when designing a WCF service that requires transactions.

Transactions, Sessions, and Service Instance Context Modes

If you set the *TransactionAutoComplete* property of the *OperationBehavior* attribute of one or more operations in a WCF service to *false*, you must use the *PerSession* service instance context mode. This is because the WCF runtime needs to maintain transactional state between calls to operations. If you set the *TransactionAutoComplete* property to *true* for every operation, the WCF runtime does not need to maintain transactional state because it completes the current transaction at the end of each operation, and you can use the *PerCall* or *Single* service instance context modes.

When you use the *PerSession* instance context mode, WCF provides two additional properties you can specify as part of the *ServiceBehavior* attribute:

- *ReleaseServiceInstanceOnTransactionComplete*   If you set this property to *true*, the WCF runtime will automatically end the session and recycle the service instance at the end of each transaction. If a client application invokes another operation, it must create and connect to a new instance of the service, as described in Chapter 7. Setting this property to *false* allows a session to handle multiple transactions. The default value of this property is *true*.

- *TransactionAutoCompleteOnSessionClose*   If you set this property to *true*, the WCF runtime will automatically complete the current transaction when the client application closes the session. The default value for this property is *false*, which causes the transaction to be aborted and any transactional work to be undone.

An important point to bear in mind from the points just raised is that transactions cannot span multiple sessions. What this means in practical terms is that if a client application initiates a transaction, performs some work by sending requests to a service, and then closes the connection, the transaction will be terminated. The outcome of the transaction depends on whether the most recent operation completed the transaction successfully or not, either by calling *SetTransactionComplete* or by virtue of the *TransactionAutoComplete* attribute of the operation being set to *true*. If neither of these cases apply, then the transaction will be aborted and all transactional work done will be rolled back.

It may sound like this is a shortcoming, but in fact it makes sense. If transactions could outlive sessions, then there would be no guarantee that a transaction would ever terminate, and any resources locked by a transaction might have those locks retained indefinitely.

Transactions and Messaging

A transactional operation sends information back to the client application about the state of the transaction. All the operations you have defined so far have followed the request/response model; the client application sends a request and waits for a response from the service. You will see in Chapter 12, "Implementing One-Way and Asynchronous Operations," that you can define one-way operations that do not send a response back to the client application. One-way operations cannot be transactional.

Transactions and Multi-Threading

You saw in Chapter 7 that a WCF service can enable multiple concurrent calls to operations if you set the *ConcurrencyMode* property of the *ServiceBehavior* attribute to *ConcurrencyMode.Multiple*. You should note the following points when attempting to use this mode:

- The *TransactionAutoComplete* property of the *OperationBehavior* attribute must be set to *true* for every operation in the service. Transactions cannot span multiple operations.

- The *ReleaseServiceInstanceOnTransactionComplete* property of the *ServiceBehavior* attribute for the service must be set to *false*. You must explicitly release the service instance by closing the connection from the client.

- The *TransactionAutoCompleteOnSessionClose* property of the *ServiceBehavior* property for the service must be set to *true*. All transactions on all threads must be terminated when the session closes.

Implementing Transactions in a Workflow Service

Windows Workflow Foundation provides the *TransactedReceiveScope* activity in the Messaging section of the Toolbox for implementing transactional operations in a workflow service. This activity exposes two properties:

- *Request*   This must be a *Receive* activity that defines a message received by the service, effectively marking the start of an operation.

- *Body*   This contains an activity that defines the logic of the operation. Typically you will implement this as a *Sequence* activity that processes the data sent by the client. This element should also include a *SendReply* activity that sends a response message back to the client.

Figure 9-2 shows an example of the *TransactedReceiveScope* activity implementing the *Change StockLevel* operation in the products service. This operation updates the stock level of a product in the *AdventureWorks* database. The code for this service is available in *ProductsWorkflow* Service project in the ProductsWorkflow solution, in the Chapter 9 folder. Notice that the *Request* property contains a *Receive* activity that listens for *ChangeStockLevel* messages. The *Body* property comprises a *Sequence* activity that invokes the *ChangeStockLevel* custom activity (this activity actually does the work of modifying the stock level), and a *SendReply* activity that sends the result of the update (*true* if the modification is successful, *false* if otherwise).

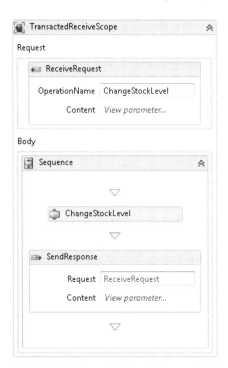

FIGURE 9-2 A *TransactedReceiveScope* activity implementing the *ChangeStockLevel* operation.

Compared to the way you define and control transactions in a procedural WCF service, a transactional activity in a workflow service has some fundamental differences:

- You cannot explicitly specify how the workflow runtime completes the transaction (there is no notion of the *TransactionAutoComplete* attribute as there is for a procedural operation). In a workflow service, the *TransactedReceiveScope* activity decides the outcome of the operation; if the *Sequence* activity defining the body of the *TransactedReceiveScope* activity finishes without throwing an exception, then the operation is deemed to have completed successfully and will be subject to commit processing when the transaction finishes. If the body throws an exception, then the transaction will be aborted.

- The transactional work does not finish with the *SendReply* activity. The *Sequence* activity defining the body of the *TransactedReceiveScope* activity can contain additional logic after you send a reply. Any work implemented by this logic is performed within the scope of the transaction. Only when the *Sequence* activity finishes is the outcome of the transactional work known. Note that this means that a workflow service may send a response message to a client and then carry on with some additional processing that may fail and abort the transaction; but in this situation the client application may not be immediately aware of the failure, so use this feature with care.

- Implementing an operation with a *TransactedReceiveScope* activity implies *Transaction FlowOption.Allowed* semantics. You cannot specify that an operation *must* be performed in the context of an existing transaction (*TransactionFlowOption.Mandatory*); if a client application does not flow a transaction into the operation, the workflow runtime will create a transaction automatically. Additionally, the default isolation level of the transaction is *Serializable*, although this will be overridden if the client application creates a transaction scope with a different isolation level.

You can initiate a transaction in a workflow client application by using the *TransactionScope* activity in the Transaction section of the Toolbox. This activity provides properties with which you can specify the isolation level and timeout of the transaction (you set these same properties in the procedural client application, shown earlier in the constructor of the *Transaction Scope* object). Figure 9.3 shows the workflow for a simple client application that invokes the *ChangeStockLevel* operation (this code is also available as part of the ProductsWorkflow solution, in the ProductsWorkflowClient project).

FIGURE 9-3 A workflow client using a *TransactionScope* activity to initiate a transaction.

The workflow creates a *TransactionScope* activity encompassing a sequence that makes two calls to the *ChangeStockLevel* operation. These two calls are made as part of the same transaction. You can verify this by viewing the Transaction Statistics in the Component Services console as the application runs. As an additional check, the code in the *ChangeStockLevel* custom activity prints the details of the transaction that has been created in the service host console window, as shown in Figure 9-4. Notice that the transaction identifier is the same for both invocations of the operation.

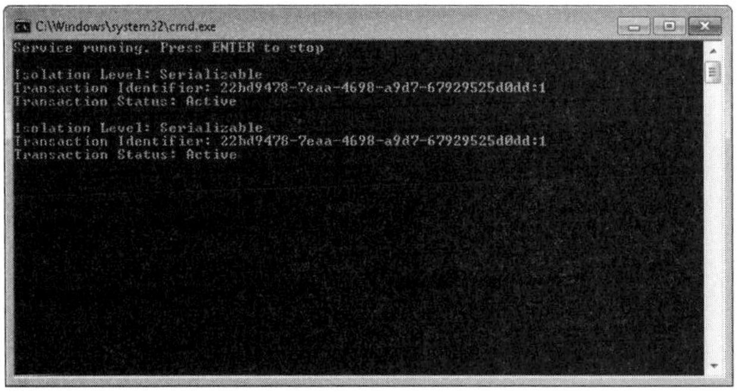

FIGURE 9-4 The output of the workflow service showing the transaction details.

Long-Running Transactions

Transactions lock resources. To minimize the impact on other users and to maintain through-put and concurrency, you should design transactions to be as short-lived as possible. Avoid performing tasks such as waiting for user input while executing a transaction. For example, although this chapter used the shopping cart service to illustrate transactions, the implementation shown is not necessarily good practice; if a user ran the GUI client application from the previous chapters to access the service, the transaction could last for a considerable time (you have no control over when the user invokes the *Checkout* operation), keeping resources locked for this duration.

Another common scenario concerns business-to-business solutions. It is common for inter-business transactions to take a significant period of time (possibly days). Such long-running transactions require you to adopt an alternative strategy to the techniques shown in this chapter. The most common solution is for a service to perform any updates and release any locks on resources immediately, effectively treating each modification as a singleton trans-action in its own right. The service should maintain a list of changes it has made. At some later point, if the service needs to rollback these changes, it can consult this list and perform updates that reverse their effect. This undo operation is sometimes referred to as a "compen-sating transaction." Windows Workflow Foundation provides the *CompensableActivity* activity in the Transaction section of the Toolbox for just this purpose.

The *CompensableActivity* activity provides a *Body* property with which you can define the workflow for a long-running task, such as waiting for input from a client application or a mes-sage from another service. If some sort of failure occurs, you can define compensation logic in the *CancellationHandler* property to undo any changes made so far by the *Body* workflow. If the logic in the *Body* workflow has completed, you can still undo the work performed by defining the appropriate logic in the *CompensationHandler* property. Only when the work performed by a *CompensableActivity* activity has been confirmed are the changes considered permanent. To confirm the work performed by a *CompensableActivity*, you use a *Confirm* activity.

Building compensating transactions raises a number of issues. For example, it might not be possible to undo an operation if another user has made further changes to the same data in the interim. Additionally, other users can see the changes that have been made, so if you undo these changes, other users' transactions might result in some inconsistencies.

A detailed discussion of creating and rolling back long-running transactions by using the *CompensableActivity* activity is outside the scope of this book, but for more information see the "Compensation" page on the Microsoft Web site at *http://msdn.microsoft.com/en-us/ library/dd489432.aspx*.

Summary

In this chapter, you have seen how to define and control transactions in a WCF client application and service. An application can enlist in an existing transaction, or create a new transaction by instantiating a *TransactionScope* object with the appropriate parameters. Transactions can flow from a client application, across the network, and to the service. You can specify the transactional requirements of a WCF service by using the *ServiceBehavior* and *Operation Behavior* attributes. The operations in a WCF service can indicate that the transaction can be committed by executing the *OperationContext.Current.SetTransactionComplete* method. An application can then finish a transaction by calling the *Complete* method of the *Transaction Scope* object.

You learned how to configure a WCF service and client application to include information about the transactions they are performing in the SOAP messages that they send and receive. You have also learned how using transactions can affect the design of a WCF service.

Finally, you have seen how to implement transactions in a workflow service by using the *TransactedReceiveScope* activity. The *TransactedReceiveScope* activity is intended for implementing short-lived transactions. If your service needs to support long-running operations, then it may be more appropriate to define compensating logic by using the *Compensable Activity* activity and avoid locking resources for an extended period of time.

Chapter 10
Implementing Reliable Sessions

After completing this chapter, you will be able to:

- Explain how to implement reliable sessions in a WCF service and client application.
- Describe how the WS-ReliableMessaging protocol works with the WCF runtime.
- Create a custom binding that implements replay detection.

Most of the time when building WCF client applications and services (apart from when you are performing the exercises in this book), you will expect them to be deployed to different computers and communicate with each other across a connecting network—after all, that's the principal reason for using WCF. Aside from the concerns surrounding security issues, the other main problem with networks is that they can be unreliable. It is very easy for a cable or wireless connection to be interrupted and for messages to be intercepted, interfered with, or just lost. This is clearly unacceptable.

Additionally, if a WCF service is running using the *PerSession* service instance mode, a conversation between a client application and the WCF service can comprise several messages. In a wide area network such as the Internet, different messages can take different routes when traveling to their destination, and so it is possible for messages to arrive in a sequence different from that in which they were sent. It could be important for a service to process messages in the same order that the client sent them rather than the order that they were received, so the client application and service may need to implement a protocol that indicates the sequence of messages.

Messages traveling across an open network are vulnerable. They can be intercepted, corrupted, diverted, or have a variety of other nasty things happen to them. Several of the Web service (WS-*) specifications are intended to help protect messages, and you have seen how WCF implements some of these specifications in earlier chapters. Another common security issue is the "replay attack," in which a third party intercepts messages and repeatedly forwards them on to the intended destination. A relevant specification when you need to send messages reliably and mitigate replay attacks is WS-ReliableMessaging.

Strictly speaking, reliable messaging and reliable sessions are different but related concepts. Reliable messaging is concerned with ensuring that messages are delivered exactly once, and a reliable session provides a context for sending and receiving a series of reliable messages. However, in WCF, reliable sessions have a dependency on reliable messaging; you use reliable messaging to provide an end-to-end reliable session between a client application and a service. This chapter examines both aspects together; you will look at the ways in which you can use WCF to provide reliable sessions and messaging, and configure replay detection.

Using Reliable Messaging

To handle the problems of lost messages, or messages arriving in the wrong order, the OASIS organization has proposed the *WS-ReliableMessaging* specification. This specification defines an interoperable protocol for transmitting messages in a reliable manner between a single source and a single destination. Messages can pass through any number of intermediary sites en route to the destination. WCF provides an implementation of this protocol that attempts to ensure that all messages sent from the source will arrive at the destination without duplication (in other words, they will arrive exactly once). The protocol implemented by the WCF runtime also attempts to detect missing messages and resend them if possible. At worst, the WCF runtime will throw an exception if a message disappears irrevocably. This means that if a message is lost, either the client application or the service, or both, will be made aware of the problem and can take corrective action.

WCF optionally supports sequencing, ensuring that messages are processed by the destination in the order in which they were sent. Using this protocol, messages might arrive in a different order, but the WCF infrastructure can buffer them to present them to a service in the correct sequence.

> **More Info** For detailed information about the WS-ReliableMessaging specification, see the "WS-ReliableMessaging Specification Index Page" page on the Microsoft Web site at *http://msdn.microsoft.com/en-us/library/ms951271.aspx.*

It is important to understand that reliable messaging as specified by the WS-ReliableMessaging specification does not imply any form of message persistence or message queuing. The protocol requires that both the source application sending the message and the destination application receiving the message are running at the same time. If it is not possible to receive messages, either because the destination application is not running or because of a network failure, the source application will receive an error. In other words, when using reliable messaging, the WCF runtime will guarantee to deliver a message if it can, or it will alert the sender if it cannot—WCF will not silently lose messages.

> **More Info** Message queuing implements its own form of reliable messaging through the use of transactions and message durability rather than the WS-ReliableMessaging protocol. You will learn about using message queues as a transport mechanism for WCF messages in Chapter 12, "Implementing One-Way and Asynchronous Operations."

Implementing Reliable Sessions with WCF

Configuring reliable messaging with a WCF service is straightforward. The WS-ReliableMessaging protocol generates a number of additional messages used by the WCF runtime on the client and service to coordinate their activities. It is instructive to enable tracing, because that can help you understand how it all works.

Enable Reliable Sessions in the *ShoppingCartService* Service and Client Application

1. Using Visual Studio, open the solution file ShoppingCart.sln located in the Microsoft Press\WCF Step By Step\Chapter 10\ShoppingCartService folder (within your Documents folder).

   This solution contains a copy of the completed *ShoppingCartService*, and Shopping CartHost and ShoppingCartClient projects from Chapter 9, "Supporting Transactions." Remember that the *ShoppingCartService* service exposes a TCP endpoint and requires the client application to create a transaction to maintain the integrity of the database.

> **Note** This set of exercises uses the *NetTcpBinding* binding and transport-level security. As such, you can easily examine the messages and headers generated by the reliable messaging protocol. Reliable messaging works with the *WSHttpBinding* over an HTTP endpoint with message-level security in exactly the same way. However, in this configuration the messages are intermingled with other messages negotiating the various security tokens, and the messages also contain encrypted data and additional headers making it more difficult to pick out the elements associated with reliable messaging.

2. In Solution Explorer, edit the App.config file for the ShoppingCartHost project by using the Service Configuration Editor.

3. In the Configuration pane, expand the Bindings folder, and then select the *Shopping CartServiceNetTcpBindingConfig* binding configuration. In the right pane, scroll down to display the *ReliableSession* Properties section, and then set the *Enabled* property to **True**. Verify that the *Ordered* property is also set to *True*, and note that the *Inactivity Timeout* property is set to *10* minutes (00:10:00) by default.

   The WCF runtime uses the *Ordered* property to determine whether to pass messages to the service in the same order that the client sent them; this is an optional but useful feature of reliable messaging. The WCF runtime will wait for the time period specified by the *InactivityTimeout* property between messages before deciding that something has gone wrong and messages have gone missing. If this timeout expires, the WCF runtime sends a "sequence terminated" SOAP fault message to the client application (which it might not receive if the client application is no longer running or communications have failed) and then terminates the session, rolling back any changes that have occurred if the service uses transactions.

> **Note** If you are using the *NetTcpBinding* or *NetNamedPipeBinding* bindings you must also verify that the *TransferMode* property in the *General* section of the binding configuration page is set to *Buffered*.
>
> Setting the *TransferMode* property to *Buffered* specifies that the WCF runtime buffers complete messages in memory before passing them to the service or sending out responses. The TCP and named pipe transports also support streaming, so you can send large messages as a series of small chunks. In streaming mode, the receiver does not have to wait for the sender to finish transmitting the message before it can start processing it. Using streaming removes the need for holding large messages in memory and can improve scalability. However, the implementation of reliable sessions in WCF requires that an entire message has been received before it can be processed, so buffering is mandatory.
>
> If you are using the *WSHttpBinding* binding, messages are automatically buffered (the HTTP protocol does not support streaming).
>
> Incidentally, transactions and message-level security also require WCF to buffer messages before transmitting them.

You will examine the messages generated by the WS-ReliableMessaging protocol, so the next step is to configure tracing.

4. In the Configuration pane, click the Diagnostics folder. In the Diagnostics pane, click EnableMessageLogging.

5. In the Configuration pane, expand the Diagnostics folder, and then click the Message Logging node. In the Message Logging pane, set the *LogEntireMessage* property to **True** and set the *LogMalformedMessages* property to **False**.

6. In the Configuration pane, expand the Listeners folder, and then click the ServiceModel MessageLoggingListener node. In the right pane, change the path in the *InitData* property to refer to the file app_messages.svclog in the Microsoft Press\WCF Step By Step\ Chapter 10 folder.

7. Save the configuration file, and then exit the Service Configuration Editor.

8. The binding configuration for the client endpoint must match the properties used by the service endpoint.

Edit the App.config file for the ShoppingCartClient project by using the Service Configuration Editor. Display the properties for the *ShoppingCartClientNetTcpBindingConfig* binding configuration in the Bindings folder, and set the *Enabled* property in the *Reliable Session* Properties section to **True**. Verify that the *Ordered* property is set to *True*, and the *InactivityTimeout* property is set to *10* minutes (00:10:00).

Reliable messaging in the client application can cause a timeout and throw an exception if it doesn't receive any messages within the period specified by the *InactivityTimeout* property. However, a client application normally only receives messages in response to a request (in Chapter 16, "Using a Callback Contract to Publish and Subscribe to Events," you will see that it is also possible for a client application to receive messages at other times). It is possible for a client application to become quiescent on the network but remain active even if it is not sending messages to a service (it might be busy displaying data, or gathering user input, for example).

Similarly, as mentioned earlier, a WCF service can timeout if it doesn't receive any messages within the period specified by its own *InactivityTimeout* property. To prevent this from happening unnecessarily, the WCF runtime on the client computer periodically sends a "keep alive" message to the service if the client application has not sent any messages recently. The point at which this happens is approximately half the value of the *InactivityTimeout* period specified in the client application configuration file. This "keep alive" message actually serves a dual purpose: it lets the service know the client application is still running, and it probes to make sure that the service is still accessible. The WCF runtime on the client computer expects the WCF runtime on the server computer to reply with an acknowledgment message; if it doesn't receive that acknowledgment within the period specified by the *InactivityTimeout* property, the WCF runtime on the client application assumes that the service has died and generates a "sequence terminated" SOAP fault message that the client application should handle.

9. Save the configuration file, and then exit the Service Configuration Editor.

Examine the Trace Messages Generated by the Client Application

1. Start the solution without debugging. In the ShoppingCartClient console window that is displaying the message "Press ENTER when the service has started," press Enter.

The client application executes as before, displaying the shopping cart containing two water bottles and a mountain seat assembly, followed by the "Goods purchased" message. Press Enter to close the client application console window. In the host application console window, press Enter to stop the service and close the application.

2. Start the Service Trace Viewer (in the Windows Start menu, click All Programs, click Microsoft Visual Studio 2010, click Microsoft Windows SDK Tools, and then click Service Trace Viewer).

3. In the Service Trace Viewer, open the app_messages.svclog file in the Microsoft Press \WCF Step By Step\Chapter 10 folder.

4. In the left pane, click the Message tab, and then click the first message. In the lower-right pane, click the Message tab. Examine the contents of this message; it should look like the following text (although your *MessageID* and *Identifier* properties will be different from those shown here):

```
<s:Envelope ...>
  <s:Header>
    <a:Action s:mustUnderstand="1">
        http://schemas.xmlsoap.org/ws/2005/02/rm/CreateSequence</a:Action>
```

```
    <a:MessageID>urn:uuid:fe0e4bbe-4eeb-4e85-85f0-46a133195754</a:MessageID>
    <a:To s:mustUnderstand="1">net.tcp://localhost:8080/ShoppingCartService</a:To>
  </s:Header>
  <s:Body>
    <CreateSequence xmlns="http://schemas.xmlsoap.org/ws/2005/02/rm">
      <AcksTo>
        <a:Address>http://www.w3.org/2005/08/addressing/anonymous</a:Address>
      </AcksTo>
      <Offer>
        <Identifier>urn:uuid:e170f8ff-4715-4ace-bc81-76a2a6e63245</Identifier>
      </Offer>
    </CreateSequence>
  </s:Body>
</s:Envelope>
```

The WS-ReliableMessaging protocol organizes messages in a conversation between a client application and a service by associating them with a unique identifier known as a sequence number. The first message in the protocol is this *CreateSequence* message, sent by the WCF runtime on the client computer. This message initiates the reliable session. All messages in the same reliable session must share the same set of identifiers. The body of this message contains a unique identifier generated by the WCF runtime (highlighted in bold in the previous example) that the service should use when responding to the client application.

5. In the left pane, click the second message, and then examine the contents of this message in the lower-right pane. It should look like this:

```
<s:Envelope ...>
  <s:Header>
    <a:Action s:mustUnderstand="1">
      http://schemas.xmlsoap.org/ws/2005/02/rm/CreateSequenceResponse</a:Action>
    <a:RelatesTo>urn:uuid:fe0e4bbe-4eeb-4e85-85f0-46a133195754</a:RelatesTo>
    <a:To s:mustUnderstand="1">http://www.w3.org/2005/08/addressing/anonymous</a:To>
  </s:Header>
  <s:Body>
    <CreateSequenceResponse xmlns="http://schemas.xmlsoap.org/ws/2005/02/rm">
      <Identifier>urn:uuid:efae0f85-cd33-438e-a8f1-bc6e0818de1e</Identifier>
      <Accept>
        <AcksTo>
          <a:Address>net.tcp://localhost:8080/ShoppingCartService</a:Address>
        </AcksTo>
      </Accept>
    </CreateSequenceResponse>
  </s:Body>
</s:Envelope>
```

This is the *CreateSequenceResponse* message, sent back to the client by the WCF runtime on the service computer. The *RelatesTo* header specifies the same message ID generated by the WCF runtime on the client computer for the *CreateSequence* message (so the WCF runtime for the client application knows to associate this response message with the original *CreateSequence* message; it is possible for a client application to start multiple reliable sessions simultaneously). Note that the body of this message contains a new identifier (shown in bold in the previous example). The WCF runtime on the client must provide this identifier when sending further messages to the service.

6. Examine the contents of the third message. It should look like this (some elements have been removed for clarity):

```
<s:Envelope ...>
  <s:Header>
    <r:AckRequested>
      <r:Identifier>urn:uuid:efae0f85-cd33-438e-a8f1-bc6e0818de1e</r:Identifier>
    </r:AckRequested>
    <r:Sequence s:mustUnderstand="1">
      <r:Identifier>urn:uuid:efae0f85-cd33-438e-a8f1-bc6e0818de1e</r:Identifier>
      <r:MessageNumber>1</r:MessageNumber>
    </r:Sequence>
    ...
  </s:Header>
  <s:Body>
    <AddItemToCart xmlns="http://adventure-works.com/2010/06/04">
      <productNumber>WB-H098</productNumber>
    </AddItemToCart>
  </s:Body>
</s:Envelope>
```

This is the first *AddItemToCart* message sent by the client application. The key thing to notice in this message is the *<Sequence>* block, shown in bold. The identifier in this block is the same as the identifier returned in the *CreateSequenceResponse* message by the service. All messages transmitted from the client application to the service participating in the reliable session must include this information in the SOAP header. They should also include a message sequence number—in this case message "1"—which enables the WCF runtime on the server computer to ensure that messages are passed to the service in the correct order. You should also notice that the SOAP header includes an *<AckRequested>* block. When the WCF runtime on the server computer receives this message, it must send an acknowledgment message back to the client computer so that the client knows it has been received.

7. Examine the contents of the fourth message. It should look like this:

```
<s:Envelope ...>
  <s:Header>
    <r:SequenceAcknowledgement>
      <r:Identifier>urn:uuid:efae0f85-cd33-438e-a8f1-bc6e0818de1e</r:Identifier>
      <r:AcknowledgementRange Lower="1" Upper="1"></r:AcknowledgementRange>
      <netrm:BufferRemaining xmlns:netrm=
        "http://schemas.microsoft.com/ws/2006/05/rm">8</netrm:BufferRemaining>
    </r:SequenceAcknowledgement>
    <a:Action s:mustUnderstand="1">http://schemas.xmlsoap.org/ws/2005/02/rm/
      SequenceAcknowledgement</a:Action>
    <a:To s:mustUnderstand="1">http://www.w3.org/2005/08/addressing/anonymous</a:To>
  </s:Header>
  <s:Body></s:Body>
</s:Envelope>
```

This is the acknowledgment message sent from the WCF runtime on the server computer back to the WCF runtime on the client computer. The data in the *<Sequence Acknowledgement>* block indicates that the service has verified that it has received the *AddItemToCartMessage*; it has acknowledged receipt of a message with the same identifier and sequence number included in the *AddItemToCart* message. Note that the *AcknowledgementRange* element indicates the sequence numbers of the messages that the service has successfully received to date. Some of these messages might have already been acknowledged, but the service includes them as a failsafe in case the previous acknowledgment messages were not received by the client (the protocol does not go as far as sending an acknowledgment in response to acknowledgment messages). The client can discard acknowledgments for messages that have already been acknowledged.

8. Look at the fifth message:

```
<s:Envelope ...>
  <s:Header>
    <r:AckRequested>
      <r:Identifier>urn:uuid:e170f8ff-4715-4ace-bc81-76a2a6e63245</r:Identifier>
    </r:AckRequested>
    <r:Sequence s:mustUnderstand="1">
      <r:Identifier>urn:uuid:e170f8ff-4715-4ace-bc81-76a2a6e63245</r:Identifier>
      <r:MessageNumber>1</r:MessageNumber>
    </r:Sequence>
    <a:Action s:mustUnderstand="1">
       http://adventure-works.com/2010/06/04/ShoppingCartService/AddItemToCartResponse
    </a:Action>
    ...
  </s:Header>
  <s:Body>
    <AddItemToCartResponse xmlns="http://adventure-works.com/2010/06/04">
      <AddItemToCartResult>true</AddItemToCartResult>
    </AddItemToCartResponse>
  </s:Body>
</s:Envelope>
```

This is the *AddItemToCartResponse* message, indicating that the service successfully added the specified item to the shopping cart. Notice that this message requires the client to acknowledge its receipt; that the identifier used in the *<Sequence>* block is the identifier specified by the client at the start of the session; and that this is also message "1" (in the opposite direction from the client message). If you examine the sixth message, you will see that it is the acknowledgment for this *AddItemToCartResponse* message from the client, sent back to the service.

9. Examine messages 7 through 14. You can see that things settle down at this point, and the conversation consists of request messages sent by the client application and the response messages sent back from the service. These messages all contain a *<Sequence>* block with the appropriate identifier. Each message also has a message number, which is incremented for each new message in each direction (the next message in the sequence sent from the client application to the service is message "2," and the response message sent by the service back to the client is also message "2").

> **Note** If it helps, think of the request/response messages as a series of two synchronized one-way conversations. Each message traveling in one direction forms part of a sequence, and the messages in this sequence are numbered starting at 1. The messages traveling in the opposite direction form part of a different sequence and are also numbered starting at 1. The message numbers do not tie messages together; response message 1 might or might not be the response for request message 1.

As a further optimization mechanism, after the initial request/response messages, the message acknowledgments are incorporated into the next request or response messages sent by the client application or service—in other words, the header in a message being sent contains the acknowledgment for the previous message received.

> **Note** The *<SequenceAcknowledgement>* block in message four and messages eight through fourteen also includes a *BufferRemaining* element. As already mentioned, to handle messages arriving out of order, the WCF runtime buffers them before handing them off to the application. If a message with a high message number is received when the runtime was expecting a lower message number, the higher-numbered message will be held in a buffer until the lower-numbered message has been received and passed to the application.
>
> The WCF runtime provides a finite number of buffers for a session. If a client application sends a large volume of messages to a service and many arrive out of order, the WCF runtime on the server computer may run out of buffers and start to drop messages (they are resent when more space is available). Therefore, when acknowledging a message, the WCF runtime also provides the number of free buffers it currently has in the *Buffer Remaining* element. The WCF runtime on the client computer can examine this value and suspend sending messages if this number (minus the number of messages the client has sent but have not yet been acknowledged—these are still in transit) drops below a certain threshold (currently 2 by default).
>
> As the WCF runtime on the server receives the missing messages it can pass them to the service and hopefully free up some of the buffers. Subsequent acknowledgment messages from the service should indicate that more buffer space is available, and the WCF runtime on the client computer can resume sending messages. This is a WCF-specific feature—if an application built using another technology does not understand this element, it will be ignored.

10. Examine message 15. It should look like this:

```
<s:Envelope ...>
  <s:Header>
    <r:SequenceAcknowledgement>
      <r:Identifier>urn:uuid:e170f8ff-4715-4ace-bc81-76a2a6e63245</r:Identifier>
      <r:AcknowledgementRange Lower="1" Upper="5"></r:AcknowledgementRange>
      <netrm:BufferRemaining xmlns:netrm=
          "http://schemas.microsoft.com/ws/2006/05/rm">8</netrm:BufferRemaining>
    </r:SequenceAcknowledgement>
    <r:Sequence s:mustUnderstand="1">
      <r:Identifier>urn:uuid:efae0f85-cd33-438e-a8f1-bc6e0818de1e</r:Identifier>
      <r:MessageNumber>6</r:MessageNumber>
      <r:LastMessage></r:LastMessage>
    </r:Sequence>
    <a:Action s:mustUnderstand="1">
      http://schemas.xmlsoap.org/ws/2005/02/rm/LastMessage
    </a:Action>
    <a:To s:mustUnderstand="1">net.tcp://localhost:8080/ShoppingCartService</a:To>
  </s:Header>
  <s:Body></s:Body>
</s:Envelope>
```

This is a *LastMessage* message. It is sent by the WCF runtime on the client computer to indicate that this is the final message in the sequence. This message is sent when the client application starts to close the session. The WCF runtime on the server computer acknowledges this message (see message 16) and then sends its own *LastMessage* message to indicate that it has also finished (message 17). The WCF runtime on the client computer sends an acknowledgment (message 19).

11. Examine message 18:

```
<s:Envelope ...>
  <s:Header>
    <a:Action s:mustUnderstand="1">http://schemas.xmlsoap.org/ws/2005/02/rm/
        TerminateSequence</a:Action>
    ...
  </s:Header>
  <s:Body>
    <TerminateSequence xmlns="http://schemas.xmlsoap.org/ws/2005/02/rm">
      <Identifier>urn:uuid:e170f8ff-4715-4ace-bc81-76a2a6e63245</Identifier>
    </TerminateSequence>
  </s:Body>
</s:Envelope>
```

This is a *TerminateSequence* message. The WCF runtime on the server computer sends this message to indicate that it is not going to send any more messages using the sequence specified by the identifier and that the WCF runtime on the client computer can release any resources associated with this session. Notice that the server sends this message without necessarily waiting for the acknowledgment of the *LastMessage* message from the client (which, ironically, is why the messages appear to be out of order).

The WCF runtime on the client computer also sends a *TerminateSequence* message to the server (message 20), identifying the sequence used by the client to send messages to the server. At the end of this exchange, the session terminates.

12. Close the Microsoft Service Trace Viewer and delete the trace file.

These exercises should make two things apparent to you:

- It is easy to implement reliable messaging with WCF. You need only set a few binding configuration properties. You don't need to write any additional code; it is all transparent to your client applications and services.

- Reliable sessions can generate a significant amount of additional network traffic, both in terms of the extra protocol messages and the increased size of each message. The more messages a client application sends in a session, the smaller this overhead becomes, proportionally. However, if you use short sessions (for example, comprising a single request and response), each request sent by a client application establishes a new reliable session that is thrown away after a response has been received. This is expensive, so in this situation you should consider very carefully whether you really need reliable messaging or whether you should rework the client application to make more efficient use of reliable sessions.

It was mentioned at the start of this chapter that reliable sessions have a dependency on reliable messaging. However, the converse is not true, and you can employ reliable messaging without implementing sessions. What this means is that although reliable messaging works best with the *PerSession* instance context mode, it also functions with the *PerCall* service instance context mode. In the *PerCall* instance context mode, even though the WCF runtime creates a new service instance for each request, it actually creates the sequence for the reliable messaging conversation when the client application makes the first call to the service and only terminates the sequence when the client closes the connection and the conversation ends.

You should also be aware that not all binding configurations support the WS-ReliableMessaging protocol. The ones that do are *netTcpBinding*, *wsDualHttpBinding* (this binding always uses reliable messaging; you cannot disable it), *wsFederationHttpBinding*, and *wsHttpBinding*. The MSMQ bindings (*msmqIntegrationBinding* and *netMsmqBinding*) implement their own version of reliable messaging that is based on message persistence and queuing technologies rather than WS-ReliableMessaging. The common bindings that do not support reliable messaging include *basicHttpBinding*, *netNamedPipeBinding*, and *netPeerTcpBinding*.

Note You can also create custom bindings that support reliable sessions. You will see how to define a custom binding later in this chapter, and explore that further in Chapter 11, "Programmatically Controlling the Configuration and Communications."

The *DeliveryRequirements* Attribute

When you enabled reliable messaging for the *ShoppingCartService* service, you saw that the ReliableSession Properties section in the Service Configuration Editor included a property named *Ordered*, which was set to *true*. This property guaranteed that messages will be processed by the service in the order in which they were sent by the client, and the service host will buffer them if necessary if it receives any messages out of order. If you set the *Ordered* property to *false*, the service will still implement reliable messaging, but will no longer make the guarantee of ordered delivery (this is useful if the service is very busy, but only has a finite amount of memory available for buffering messages).

If you absolutely insist that the service provides ordered delivery, you can apply the *DeliveryRequirements* attribute either to the class that implements the service or to the service contract, and set the *RequireOrderedDelivery* property to **true**, as shown in the following code example:

```
[DeliveryRequirements(RequireOrderedDelivery=true)]
public class ShoppingCartServiceImpl : IShoppingCartService
{
    ...
}
```

When you specify this attribute, the service must be deployed with a binding configuration that implements ordered delivery; otherwise, it will fail to start and the service host will throw an *InvalidOperationException* exception.

Detecting and Handling Replay Attacks

In Chapter 4, "Protecting an Enterprise WCF Service," you learned a little about replay attacks. In a replay attack, a hacker intercepts and stores messages flowing over the network and then sends them at some time in the future. At best, this can become a nuisance if, for example, a hacker repeatedly replays the same intercepted purchase order sent by a genuine customer to an online bookstore; the bookstore may receive hundreds of orders and send the books to the customer who has not ordered them. At worst, it can lead to large-scale fraud; consider an attacker intercepting a request to credit his bank account and then repeatedly replaying that message to the bank's servers.

Using reliable sessions can help to mitigate simple replay attacks, because each message must provide a valid sequence identifier and a unique message number. When the session has completed, the sequence identifier becomes invalid, so any subsequent attempt to replay the message should be rejected by the receiver. However, consider the following hypothetical scenario: if a session is long-running, it might be possible for an attacker to edit the *<Sequence>* block in an intercepted message, modify the message number, set it to some value higher than the message that was received, and then forward this message to the service if the session is still active. When the application hosting the service receives this message, if no message with this number has yet been received, the host will buffer it and then pass it to the service when all the intermediate messages have been received. When a genuine message from the client with that message number is subsequently received, the genuine message will be rejected. How can you handle this situation?

You can configure transport-level security to encrypt messages as they traverse the network from machine to machine. Additionally, many implementations of transport-level security include automatic replay detection of packets at the transport layer. But remember that transport-level security operates on a point-to-point basis, and when a service receives the message, it has unrestricted access to its contents. If the service is expected to forward the request on to a service running elsewhere, it can modify the message before it does so. The usual way to protect data, if you cannot trust any intermediate services, is to implement message-level security. However, message-level security is predominantly concerned with protecting the body of a message rather than the data in message headers, which is where the sequence identifiers and message numbers are held.

> **More Info** Review Chapter 4, "Protecting an Enterprise WCF Service," and Chapter 5, "Protecting a WCF Service over the Internet," for more information about implementing message-level security with WCF.

So, to prevent a reply attack, the receiver requires a more secure mechanism than simple sequence identifiers and message numbers that uniquely identify messages. Fortunately, WCF provides just such a mechanism in the replay detection protocol.

Configuring Replay Detection with WCF

When you enable replay detection, the WCF runtime generates a random, unique, signed, time-stamped identifier for each message. These identifiers are referred to as *nonces*. Upon receiving a message, a service can use the signature to verify that the nonce has not been corrupted and extract and examine the timestamp to ascertain that the message was sent *reasonably* recently (the service can allow for a certain amount of clock-skew between computers and should also recognize that it takes some time for data to physically traverse the network from the client application). The service can then save the nonce in a cache. When another message is received, the service can retrieve the nonce from the message header. If it finds a matching nonce in its cache then the new message is a copy of an earlier message and should be discarded. If it is not, the service can process the message and add the new nonce to the cache.

The WCF security channel implements replay detection by default, although the relevant properties for configuring it are not immediately visible when using the standard WCF bindings. However, it is quite simple to create a custom binding that makes them available. You will adopt this approach in the following exercises.

Create a Custom Binding for the *ShoppingCartService* Service

1. In Visual Studio, edit the App.config file for the ShoppingCartHost project by using the Service Configuration Editor.

2. In the Configuration pane, click the Bindings folder. In the right pane, click New Binding Configuration. In the Create A New Binding dialog box, select **customBinding**, and then click OK.

3. In the right pane, change the *Name* property of the binding configuration to **ShoppingCartServiceCustomBindingConfig**.

   If you recall from Chapter 2, "Hosting a WCF Service," the WCF runtime creates a channel stack for sending and receiving messages. Incoming messages arrive at a particular address (such as a port or a URL) using an appropriate transport (such as TCP or HTTP). When you host a service, the WCF runtime "listens" for incoming request messages sent by client applications to the specified address by using a transport channel. Incoming messages pass through the transport channel to an encoding channel, which parses the message. The WCF runtime can then invoke the relevant operation in the service using the information in this parsed data. Outgoing response messages are encoded by the encoding channel (a message can be encoded as text, or as binary data) before being passed to the transport channel for transmission back to the client application.

   A channel stack must always have at least these two channels: a transport channel and an encoding channel. When you create a new custom binding, the Service Configuration Editor automatically adds elements for using the HTTP transport and text encoding. You have been using the TCP transport in previous exercises in this chapter, so you will change the transport channel accordingly.

4. In the lower-right pane, select the *httpTransport* stack element, click Remove, and then click the Add button. In the Adding Binding Element Extension Sections dialog box, select *tcpTransport* then click Add.

   A point worth emphasizing from Chapter 2 is that the order of the channels in the channel stack is important. The transport channel must always be the final item, and conventionally, the encoding channel resides immediately above the transport channel. Verify that the *tcpTransport* element is in position 2 in the list and that the *textMessageEncoding* element is in position 1. If the positions differ, use the Up and Down buttons to swap them.

5. Click the Add button in the lower-right pane again. In the Adding Binding Element Extension Sections dialog box, select the *security* binding extension element, and then click Add. Use the Up and Down buttons to place the *security* element in position 1 at the top of the stack, above the *textMessageEncoding* element.

6. In the Configuration pane, click the security node underneath the *ShoppingCartService CustomBindingConfig* node. In the right pane, set the *AuthenticationMode* property to **SecureConversation**. This mode implements the protocol defined by the WS-Secure Conversation specification to establish a secure session between the service and client applications (see the sidebar that follows this exercise for details).

7. In the right pane, click the Service tab. Verify that the *DetectReplays* property is set to *True*.

8. Examine the *ReplayCacheSize* property.

   When implementing replay detection, the WCF runtime on the server computer will cache nonces in memory. The value of this property determines the maximum amount of memory it will use, specified as a number of cached nonces. When this limit is reached, the oldest nonce is removed from the cache before a new one is added. The default value (900000) should be sufficient for most cases, but you might want to consider reducing it if memory is at a premium. However, don't make it so small that nonces are discarded too quickly; doing so can render the service vulnerable to replay attacks again.

9. Examine the *ReplayWindow* and *MaxClockSkew* properties.

   The *ReplayWindow* property specifies the duration for which nonces are considered valid (five minutes by default). If the timestamp in a received nonce is outside the time window specified here, it is discarded as being too old. However, WCF recognizes that the system clock on different computers might not be completely synchronized. To compensate, you can use the *MaxClockSkew* property to specify the maximum clock difference to allow (again, five minutes by default). It is also possible that the timestamp for a nonce could appear to be a short time in the future if the clock on the server com-puter is slower, so the *MaxClockSkew* property allows the service to accept nonces with a future timestamp—provided they are within the specified range.

 Note You can use the *security custom binding* element to configure replay detection for client applications as well, by using the properties in the Client tab.

10. In the Configuration pane, click the *ShoppingCartServiceCustomBindingConfig* node.

The *ShoppingCartService* service uses transactions and reliable sessions, so you must add channels that implement these features, as follows:

❑ In the lower-right pane, click Add. In the Adding Binding Element Extension Sections dialog box, select the *reliableSession* binding extension element, and then click Add.

❑ Repeat this process and add the *transactionFlow* binding extension element to the binding.

❑ Rearrange the channel stack so that the *transactionFlow* element is in position 1, the *reliableSession* element is in position 2, the *security* element is in position 3, the *textMessageEncoding* element is in position 4, and the *tcpTransport* element is in position 5, as shown in the following image (this is the recommended order for these channels):

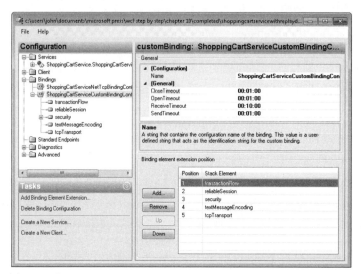

11. In the Configuration pane, expand the *ShoppingCartService.ShoppingCartServiceImpl* service in the Services folder, right-click the Endpoints folder, and then click New Service Endpoint. In the right pane, set the properties of this endpoint using the values in this table:

Property	Value
Name	ShoppingCartServiceCustomEndpoint
Address	net.tcp://localhost:8090/ShoppingCartService (**Note**: This address specifies port 8090, to avoid clashing with the service listening on port 8080)
Binding	customBinding
BindingConfiguration	ShoppingCartServiceCustomBindingConfig
Contract	ShoppingCartService.IShoppingCartService

12. Save the file, and then exit the Service Configuration Editor.

The WS-SecureConversation Specification

The WS-SecureConversation specification is yet another specification developed by members of OASIS. It allows two participants (a service and a client application) to establish and share a security context for exchanging multiple messages (a conversation) in a secure and optimal manner without the need to include comprehensive security credential information in every message. Participants exchange and validate credentials at the start of the session, and then negotiate security tokens derived from the authorized credentials. Subsequent messages in the conversation contain these derived tokens rather than a complete set of credentials as a means for the recipient to authenticate the source. The process of validating these derived tokens is faster than fully authenticating each message from the original set of credentials.

The WS-SecureConversation specification builds on other WS-* specifications, such as WS-Security, so you can create a security context based on a variety of authentication and encryption mechanisms, as described in Chapter 4.

For detailed information about the WS-SecureConversation specification, see the "Web Services Security Specifications Index Page" page on the Microsoft Web site at *http://msdn.microsoft.com/en-us/library/ms951273.aspx.*

You can now add a corresponding binding to the client application and then configure the client to use this binding.

Create a Custom Binding for the ShoppingCartClient Application

1. In Visual Studio, edit the App.config file for the ShoppingCartClient project by using the Service Configuration Editor.

2. In the Configuration pane, add a new *customBinding* binding configuration to the Bindings folder and set the *Name* property to **ShoppingCartClientCustomBindingConfig**.

3. Remove the *httpTransport* element and replace it with a *tcpTransport* element.

4. Add a *security* element and set the *AuthenticationMode* property of this *security* element to *SecureConversation*.

5. Add a *reliableSession* element and a *transactionFlow* element to the custom binding.

6. Rearrange the channel stack so that the *transactionFlow* element is in position 1, the *reliableSession* element is in position 2, the *security* element is in position 3, the *text MessageEncoding* element is in position 4, and the *tcpTransport* element is in position 5.

7. In the Configuration pane, add a new endpoint to the Endpoints folder under the Client folder. Set the properties for this endpoint using the following values:

Property	Value
Name	CustomBinding_IShoppingCartService
Address	net.tcp://localhost:8090/ShoppingCartService
Binding	customBinding
BindingConfiguration	ShoppingCartClientCustomBindingConfig
Contract	ShoppingCartClient.ShoppingCartService.ShoppingCartService

8. Save the file, and then exit the Service Configuration Editor.

9. In Visual Studio, open the Program.cs file for the ShoppingCartClient project in the Code And Text Editor window. In the *Main* method, change the statement that creates the *proxy* object to reference the *CustomBinding_IShoppingCartService* endpoint, as shown in bold in the following:

```
static void Main(string[] args)
{
    ...
    try
    {
        // Connect to the ShoppingCartService service
        ShoppingCartServiceClient proxy = new
            ShoppingCartServiceClient("CustomBinding_IShoppingCartService");
        ...
    }
    ...
}
```

10. Start the solution without debugging. In the ShoppingCartClient console window that's displaying the message "Press ENTER when the service has started," press Enter.

   The client application executes exactly as before, except that this time it is using the custom binding, with replay detection enabled, to communicate with the *Shopping CartService* service.

11. Press Enter to close the client application console window. In the host application console window, press Enter to stop the service.

When you run the client application, you may observe that there is a small but noticeable delay before it displays the results of the first response message received from the service. If you examine the trace file for the service by using the Service Trace Viewer, you can see why this is the case. The secure conversation protocol generates a significant number of messages to establish the security context. In addition, the body of each request message sent by the client application, and the corresponding response messages (the messages in the adventure-works.com namespace) are signed, encrypted, and include nonce information. So, although the secure conversation protocol provides a good degree of protection, it comes at a price. If you are building client applications and services that communicate directly with each other, point-to-point, then you may find that implementing transport-level security provides a more efficient solution.

Summary

In this chapter, you configured a WCF service and client application to communicate by using a reliable session. You have seen how WCF implements the protocol defined by the WS-ReliableMessaging specification and how it uses sequences, message numbers, and acknowledgment messages to verify that messages have been received and assembled in the correct order. You have also seen how to create a custom binding that you can use to configure replay detection.

Chapter 11
Programmatically Controlling the Configuration and Communications

After completing this chapter, you will be able to:

- Describe the main elements of the WCF Service Model.

- Create bindings by using code.

- Implement a custom service behavior and add it to a service.

- Connect to a service from a client application by using the service contract.

- Send messages directly to a service without using a proxy object.

By now, you should have a good understanding of how to create WCF client applications and services and how to configure them so that they can communicate with each other. A compelling feature of WCF is the ability to perform many of these tasks by using configuration files. Behind the scenes, the WCF runtime takes this configuration information and uses it to build an infrastructure that can send and receive messages using specified protocols, encoding them in the appropriate manner and directing them to the appropriate methods implementing the operations in a service.

There will inevitably be occasions when you need to perform configuration tasks programmatically, possibly because an application or service needs to adapt itself dynamically according to its environment without intervention from an administrator. Alternatively, for security reasons you may not want anyone to be able to modify the configuration for an application. For example, you might not want an administrator to be able to enable or disable metadata publishing for a service. Beyond that, it's instructive to see the sorts of things the WCF runtime does when it executes your client applications and services. So, in this chapter you will look at how to create and use bindings in code and how to send and receive messages programmatically.

The WCF Service Model

WCF provides a comprehensive infrastructure for sending and receiving messages by creating a number of objects that manage and control the communications. This infrastructure is extensible, and you can augment it with your own functionality if you need to customize the way it works. For example, in Chapter 10, "Implementing Reliable Sessions," you saw how to compose the channels provided with WCF into a custom binding. If you have a very specific requirement, or need to transmit messages using a protocol that has no corresponding channel in the .NET Framework class library, you can develop your own channel (or buy one from a third party) and then easily integrate it into your configuration without needing to modify the code for a service or client application. You can also customize other parts of the WCF infrastructure, such as the way that WCF maps incoming messages to operations. You will see some examples of this in Chapter 14, "Discovering Services and Routing Messages."

> **More Info**   A detailed discussion about creating a custom channel is beyond the scope of this book. For information about creating custom channels, see the "Developing Channels" page on the Microsoft Web site at *http://msdn.microsoft.com/en-us/library/ms788753.aspx*.
>
> For more information about how to add your own functionality to the WCF infrastructure, consult the topics in the "Extending WCF" section in the documentation provided with Visual Studio (also available on the Microsoft Web site at *http://msdn.microsoft.com/en-us/library/ms733848.aspx*).

This section introduces you to some of the main components in the WCF infrastructure, sometimes referred to as the *WCF Service Model*.

Services and Channels

You can think of a binding as a description of the channels in a channel stack. When a host application starts a service running, the WCF runtime uses the bindings defined for each endpoint to instantiate a *ChannelListener* object and a channel stack. A *ChannelListener* object connects an endpoint to the transport channel for the channel stack. The WCF runtime creates a *ChannelListener* object for each URI on which the service can accept messages. When a request message arrives at a URI, the corresponding *ChannelListener* object receives the message and passes it to the transport channel at the bottom of the corresponding channel stack. To the transport channel, a message is nothing more than a stream of bytes; it makes no attempt to understand the contents of the message. The transport channel passes the message to the next channel in the stack, which by convention is an encoding channel.

The purpose of an encoding channel is to parse the incoming request message and convert it into a format that the channels above it in the channel stack can understand—usually SOAP. When sending an outgoing response message, the encoding channel converts a SOAP message passed in from the channels above it in the stack into a specified format for transmission by the transport channel. The .NET Framework 4.0 class library provides encoding channels for converting between SOAP messages and plain text, binary data, and an optimized format called the Message Transmission Optimization Mechanism, or MTOM. You will learn more about MTOM in Chapter 13, "Implementing a WCF Service for Good Performance." The transport and encoding channels are mandatory parts of a binding. Above the encoding channel, you can add channels handling reliability, security, transactions, and other non-functional aspects of SOAP messaging.

> **Note** The binary encoding channel implements a WCF-specific encoding. You cannot use it to communicate with non-WCF client applications and services, so you should only use it in situations where interoperability is not an issue. If you need to transmit data in a binary format in an interoperable manner, you should use MTOM, which is an OASIS-approved specification.
>
> Additionally, each transport channel will load a default encoding channel unless you specify one in the channel stack. The HTTP and HTTPS transport channels load the text encoding channel, but the TCP channel defaults to using the binary encoding channel.

When an incoming request message reaches the top of the channel stack, a *Channel Dispatcher* object takes the message, examines it, and passes it to an *EndpointDispatcher* object that invokes the appropriate method in the service, passing the data items in the message as parameters to the method. WCF creates *ChannelDispatcher* and *EndpointDispatcher* objects automatically when you use a *ServiceHost* object to run a service.

> **Note** It is possible to associate multiple endpoints with the same URI. When a WCF service receives a message, the *ChannelDispatcher* object queries the *EndpointDispatcher* object for each endpoint in turn to establish which one, if any, can process the message. You will learn more about this process in Chapter 14.

When a method implementing an operation in a service completes, the data it returns passes back through the channel stack to the transport channel where it is transmitted back to the client application. The WCF runtime on the client builds a structure similar to that used by the service, but somewhat simpler, because the client does not have to listen for requests or manage multiple instances of the application the way a service does. The WCF client runtime creates a *ChannelFactory* object and uses this object to construct a channel from the binding definition. The proxy object in the client application is responsible for converting method calls into outgoing request messages and passing them to the channel for transmission. Incoming response messages received on the transport channel work their way back up through the channel stack where the proxy object converts them into the format expected by the client code and returns them as the results of the original method call.

Behaviors

You can customize the way that components in the WCF infrastructure operate by applying behaviors. In a configuration file, a behavior contains one or more behavior elements. For example, the .NET Framework 4.0 provides a number of built-in endpoint behavior elements that you can use to modify the way that an endpoint serializes data, how it batches operations together in a transaction, the specific credentials it uses when sending messages or receiving messages, and so on.

Behaviors have scope; you can apply them to an entire service, a specific operation, a contract, or an endpoint. An example of a behavior element that applies to an entire service is *serviceDebug*. In a configuration file, you can define a service behavior and add the *service Debug* behavior element to specify that the service should transmit complete error information to the client application when an exception occurs.

Bear in mind that in a configuration file, behaviors can be named or anonymous. Anonymous behaviors are applied automatically to a service or endpoint, whereas named behaviors are applied only if they are referenced explicitly by a service or endpoint configuration.

You can also define your own custom behaviors and enable an administrator to reference them from a configuration file by defining a corresponding behavior element extension class. You will see an example of a custom service behavior and service behavior element extension class later in this chapter.

> **Note** The terminology used by the WCF documentation and the distinction between a behavior and a behavior element can be a little confusing. In the .NET Framework, a behavior is a class that implements one of the behavior interfaces (*IServiceBehavior*, *IOperationBehavior*, *IContract Behavior*, or *IEndpointBehavior*; these interfaces are described later in this chapter). To enable an administrator to reference these behavior classes from a configuration file, you can create custom behavior element extension classes.
>
> In a configuration file, the term "behavior" means a collection of references to one or more behavior classes, configured by using behavior element extension classes. For example, *service Debug* is just a friendly name for the *ServiceDebugElement* behavior element extension class, which configures the *ServiceDebugBehavior* behavior class. You will see later in this chapter how you can create a behavior element extension class and provide a friendly name for it in a configuration file.

You can also specify behaviors for services, endpoints, operations, and contracts declaratively by using attributes, or imperatively by adding code that instantiates these items and sets their properties.

Not all behaviors are configurable through all mechanisms. In particular, the configuration file for a WCF service does not provide a simple means for an administrator to specify contract and operation behaviors. Behaviors are typically the concern of the developers building a service rather than an administrator configuring it, and the general rule is that you should only be able to change behaviors that are critical to the way in which a service functions (such as operation and contract behaviors) by applying an attribute or writing code. On the other hand, service and endpoint behaviors are commonly a matter of administrative policy rather than implementation strategy, so WCF provides a means for you to apply and configure these behaviors through the configuration file.

Composing Channels into Bindings

The channels in a channel stack implement the various protocols and specifications required by the service. The binding used by a client application should correspond to the binding implemented by the service with which the client application communicates. If a channel is omitted, substituted for a different channel, or placed in a different position in the channel stack, it's possible that either the client application or the service will not be able to interpret messages correctly, and communications will fail.

In Chapter 2, "Hosting a WCF Service," you were first introduced to the predefined bindings in the .NET Framework 4.0, such as *basicHttpBinding*, *ws2007HttpBinding*, and *netTcpBinding*. These predefined bindings combine channels in configurations that meet the requirements of many common scenarios. The .NET Framework 4.0 contains classes that correspond to these bindings in the *System.ServiceModel* namespace. These classes expose properties with which you can configure the channels used by these bindings. You can also create your own custom bindings by combining binding elements and setting the properties of each of these binding elements to determine exactly which channels the WCF runtime uses.

You build a custom binding by adding binding elements to a *CustomBinding* object. The predefined bindings restrict the channels in a binding to various meaningful combinations. However, when you create a custom binding, you must ensure that you combine binding elements in a sensible manner. To some extent, the WCF runtime protects you and will throw an exception if, for example, you try to add two encoding binding elements to a binding. However, the WCF runtime is not able to perform complete sanity checking of your custom bindings. If you get it wrong, the client application and service might not understand each other's messages, which will consequently cause faults, timeouts, and exceptions.

The order of the binding elements in a custom binding is important. It has been mentioned before that the transport channel must be at the bottom of the stack, followed by the encoding channel. Microsoft recommends that you layer channels according to the function they perform. Table 11-1 lists the layers and the channels appropriate to each layer. The class names for the binding element classes associated with the corresponding channels provided by the .NET Framework 4.0 in each layer are shown in italics.

TABLE 11-1 **Recommended Channel Organization**

Layer	Function	Channel Binding Element Class
1 (*top*)	Transaction Flow	*TransactionFlowBindingElement*
2	Reliable Sessions	*ReliableSessionBindingElement*
3	Security	*AsymmetricSecurityBindingElement, SymmetricSecurityBinding Element,* or *TransportSecurityBindingElement*, and others created by factory methods in the *SecurityBindingElement* class.
4	Stream Upgrades	*SslStreamSecurityBindingElement* or *WindowsStreamSecurityBindingElement*
5	Encoding	*BinaryMessageEncodingBindingElement, MtomMessageEncoding BindingElement, TextMessageEncodingBindingElement,* or *WebMessageEncodingBindingElement*
6 (*bottom*)	Transport	*HttpTransportBindingElement, HttpsTransportBindingElement, PeerTransportBindingElement, TcpTransportBindingElement, NamedPipeTransportBindingElement, MsmqTransportBinding Element,* or *MsmqIntegrationBindingElement*

This table lists the most commonly-used binding elements. There are others, and you will see some of them later. Most of these binding elements are self-explanatory, but some warrant a little more explanation.

■ The *SecurityBindingElement* class acts as a factory for security binding elements and exposes methods that you can use to create channels that implement them. You will see an example of this in the exercise that follows this section.

■ The *AsymmetricSecurityBindingElement* and *SymmetricSecurityBindingElement* classes represent channels that implement message-level security. The *TransportSecurityBindingElement* class represents a channel that implements transport-level security. (For more information about message-level and transport level-security, refer back to Chapter 4.) However, you are more likely to use channels for specific scenarios, such as *CreateAnonymousForCertificate-BindingElement,* which creates a symmetric binding element that supports anonymous client authentication and certificate-based server authentication. You can create these channels by using the factory methods of the *SecurityBindingElement* class.

■ Stream upgrades such as the *SslStreamSecurityBindingElement* and *WindowsStream SecurityBindingElement* classes do not actually represent channels but rather objects that can modify the way in which data is transmitted over the network. You can use them in conjunction with a transport that supports a stream-oriented protocol, such as TCP and named pipes. A stream upgrade operates on a stream of data rather than individual WCF messages. For example, with the *WindowsStreamSecurityBindingElement* class, you can specify that data should be encrypted and/or signed before being transmitted. Another example (not currently implemented by the .NET Framework 4.0) would be to use a streaming upgrade channel that compresses the data using a specified algorithm before transmission.

When you define a binding in a configuration file, you are not necessarily aware of which binding elements you are using. For example, when you specify a *<security>* element, the "mode" attribute determines whether the WCF runtime uses a message-level security binding element or a transport-level element. Setting other attributes in the *<security>* element enables the WCF runtime to determine exactly which of the many possible security binding elements it should employ when constructing the channel. When you create a binding programmatically, you need to be explicit.

That's the theory. The exercises that follow show how to put some of what you have just read into action. You will start by implementing a custom binding in code in the *ShoppingCart Service* service.

Programmatically Create and Use a Custom Binding in the *ShoppingCartService* Service

1. Using Visual Studio, open the solution file ShoppingCart.sln located in the Microsoft Press\WCF Step By Step\Chapter 11\ShoppingCartService folder (within your Documents folder).

   This solution contains a slightly modified copy of the *ShoppingCartService*, and Shopping CartClient projects from Chapter 10. The ShoppingCartHost project is significantly different though. The binding and service endpoint information in the configuration file for the *ShoppingCartService* service has been removed, leaving only the connection string for the *AdventureWorks* database. Additionally, the *Main* method in the Program.cs file in the ShoppingCartHost project is currently empty.

2. In Solution Explorer, open the Program.cs file for the ShoppingCartHost project in the Code And Text Editor window. Add the following *using* statement to the list at the top of the file:

   ```
   using System.ServiceModel.Channels;
   ```

   The *System.ServiceModel.Channels* namespace contains the classes defining the various channels and bindings provided by the WCF.

3. In the *Main* method of the *Program* class, add the following statement shown in bold:

   ```
   static void Main(string[] args)
   {
       CustomBinding customBinding = new CustomBinding();
   }
   ```

   This statement creates a new, empty custom binding object. You will add binding elements to the custom binding object in the next step.

> **Note** If you want to use one of the standard bindings, you can create them in much the same way. For example, to create a standard HTTP binding object for the *ws2007Http Binding* binding configuration, you could use:
>
> ```
> WS2007HttpBinding httpBinding = new WS2007HttpBinding();
> ```

4. The *ShoppingCartService* service implements transactions and requires reliable sessions. Instantiate the binding elements that correspond to the channels that implement the transaction and reliable messaging protocols, set their properties, and then add them to the custom binding, as shown in bold in the following:

```
static void Main(string[] args)
{
    CustomBinding customBinding = new CustomBinding();

    TransactionFlowBindingElement txFlowBindElement =
        new TransactionFlowBindingElement();
    txFlowBindElement.TransactionProtocol = TransactionProtocol.OleTransactions;
    customBinding.Elements.Add(txFlowBindElement);

    ReliableSessionBindingElement rsBindElement = new ReliableSessionBindingElement();
    rsBindElement.FlowControlEnabled = true;
    rsBindElement.Ordered = true;
    customBinding.Elements.Add(rsBindElement);
}
```

The transaction flow binding element is configured to implement OLE transactions; the alternative is to specify *WSAtomicTransactionOctober2004* which implements the WS-AtomicTransactions specification from October 2004, or *WSAtomicTransaction11* which implements the more recent version of the specification. Refer back to Chapter 9, "Supporting Transactions," for further details.

The reliable sessions binding element enables flow control and ensures that the order of messages is preserved, as described in Chapter 10, "Implementing Reliable Sessions".

It is worth emphasizing again that the order in which you add the elements to the custom binding is important. Binding elements higher up the channel stack must be added to the custom binding *before* those that should reside lower down in the stack.

5. The *ShoppingCartService* service also needs to implement secure conversations and replay detection. Use the *SecurityBindingElement* class to create a *SecureConversation- BindingElement,* as follows:

```
static void Main(string[] args)
{
    ...
```

```
SecurityBindingElement secBindElement =
    SecurityBindingElement.CreateSecureConversationBindingElement(
        SecurityBindingElement.CreateSspiNegotiationBindingElement());
secBindElement.LocalServiceSettings.DetectReplays = true;
customBinding.Elements.Add(secBindElement);
}
```

The secure conversation protocol uses a handshaking mechanism between the client application and the service to establish a security context token that both parties can use to authenticate the messages that pass between them. This handshake also needs to be protected, and the security binding element passed as a parameter to the *Create SecureConversationBindingElement* method specifies how to guard the handshake messages that flow while negotiating the security context. The code in this exercise uses SOAP SSPI negotiation to authenticate messages while performing handshaking (this is the default mechanism).

After creating the security binding element, the code enables server-side replay detection before adding it to the custom binding.

6. Add binding elements that implement a text encoding channel and a TCP transport channel, as shown in the following:

```
static void Main(string[] args)
{
    ...
    customBinding.Elements.Add(new TextMessageEncodingBindingElement());
    TcpTransportBindingElement tcpBindElement = new TcpTransportBindingElement();
    tcpBindElement.TransferMode = TransferMode.Buffered;
    customBinding.Elements.Add(tcpBindElement);
}
```

The reliable sessions channel requires the transport to buffer messages. The transport channel must be the last item in the custom binding.

7. After the statements that create and configure the custom binding, add the following statement to instantiate a *ServiceHost* object:

```
static void Main(string[] args)
{
    ...
    ServiceHost host = new ServiceHost(
        typeof(ShoppingCartService.ShoppingCartServiceImpl));
}
```

This should be a familiar statement to you, but you now appreciate what a *ServiceHost* object does: it constructs a channel stack, it manages the lifetimes of various instances of the service defined by the specified type, and it ensures that client requests are dispatched to the correct service instance. It performs these tasks in conjunction with *ChannelListener*, *ChannelDispatcher*, and *EndpointDispatcher* objects that it creates by using the code you will add in the following steps.

8. Previously, you specified the endpoint definition for the *ShoppingCartService* in the application configuration file, and the *ServiceHost* constructor used this information to construct an endpoint and a *ChannelListener*. You no longer have this information in the application configuration file, so add the endpoint by using code, as shown below:

```
static void Main(string[] args)
{
    ...
    host.AddServiceEndpoint(typeof(ShoppingCartService.IShoppingCartService),
        customBinding, "net.tcp://localhost:8090/ShoppingCartService");
}
```

The parameters to the *AddServiceEndpoint* method are the service contract that the service implements, the binding, and the URI for the listener.

9. You can now start the service running. Add the following statements to the *Main* method:

```
static void Main(string[] args)
{
    ...
    host.Open();
    Console.WriteLine("Service running");
    Console.WriteLine("Press ENTER to stop the service");
    Console.ReadLine();
}
```

You have seen this code before, but now you should understand that the *Open* method starts a *ChannelListener* object listening for client requests. When a request arrives, the *ChannelListener* passes it to the channel. The *ChannelDispatcher* object retrieves the message from the top of the channel and passes it through the *EndpointDispatcher* object to an instance of the *ShoppingCartService* service.

10. Start the solution without debugging. In the ShoppingCartClient console window that's displaying the message "Press ENTER when the service has started," press Enter.

The client application runs exactly as before; it creates a shopping cart, adds two water bottles and a mountain seat assembly, and then purchases the goods.

11. Press Enter to close the client application console window. In the host application console window, press Enter to stop the service.

Inspecting Messages

An interesting feature of the WCF service model is the ability to intercept messages as they are dispatched to a service method, and again as they leave the service method prior to traversing the channel stack and being transmitted back to the client application. Using message interception, you can examine messages as they are sent and received. You can also modify an incoming message prior to it being processed by a service or before an outgoing message is transmitted to a client. Message interception is therefore a very powerful technique, although you must manage it carefully to avoid introducing security flaws and other loopholes into your system.

You can intercept messages by creating a message inspector; you create a class that implements the *IDispatchMessageInspector* interface and insert it into the WCF infrastructure by defining a behavior. The behavior that you create determines the scope of the message interception. If you specify message interception as a service behavior, all messages sent to the service will be intercepted. You can also apply message interception by using operation, endpoint, or contract behaviors; in which case, interception applies only to the specified operation, endpoint, or contract.

You can implement message inspection in a client application or a service. In the exercise that follows, you will see how to create and integrate a message inspector into the dispatch mechanism of the WCF runtime for the service. This message inspector will displays messages as they are received by a service. To continue in the spirit of this chapter, you will perform these tasks programmatically.

Create a Message Inspector for the *ShoppingCartService* Service

1. In Visual Studio, select the ShoppingCartService project in Solution Explorer. From the Project menu, select Add Class and add a new class file called ShoppingCartInspector.cs to the project.

2. In the ShoppingCartInspector.cs file, add the following *using* statements to the list at the top:

   ```
   using System.ServiceModel.Dispatcher;
   using System.ServiceModel.Description;
   ```

3. Modify the definition of the *ShoppingCartInspector* class to make it public and implement the *IDispatchMessageInspector* interface, as follows:

   ```
   public class ShoppingCartInspector : IDispatchMessageInspector
   {
   }
   ```

   The *IDispatchMessageInspector* interface defines two methods (described in the next step) with which you can view and modify messages flowing into and out of the service.

4. In the code view window, right-click *IDispatchMessageInspector*, point to Implement Interface, and then click Implement Interface.

   Visual Studio generates stubs for the two methods in the *IDispatchMessageInspector* interface. These methods are called *AfterReceiveRequest*, which is invoked immediately before the service method is called, and *BeforeSendReply*, which runs when the service method has completed. Notice that the first parameter to both methods is a reference to a *Message* object. This is the message that has just been received or is about to be sent. The important point to realize is that you can modify the contents of this message, and any changes you make will be passed to the service method or returned to the client application, depending on whether this is an inbound message (*AfterReceive Request*) or an outbound message (*BeforeSendReply*). For this reason, you should be especially careful that you don't implement any code that inadvertently changes the contents of messages.

5. Remove the *throw* statement in the *AfterReceiveRequest* method and replace it with the code shown in bold in the following:

```
public object AfterReceiveRequest(ref System.ServiceModel.Channels.Message request,
    System.ServiceModel.IClientChannel channel,
    System.ServiceModel.InstanceContext instanceContext)
{
    Console.WriteLine("Message received: {0}\n{1}\n\n",
        request.Headers.Action, request.ToString());
    return null;
}
```

The first statement displays the action that identifies the message (this is the fully quali-fied name of the message, including the namespace to which it belongs), followed by the message itself.

It is sometimes useful to be able to correlate messages in the *AfterReceiveRequest* method with the corresponding response sent by the *BeforeSendReply* method. If you examine the *BeforeSendReply* method, you will see that it has a second parameter called *correlation State*. If you need to correlate request and reply messages, you can create a unique identifier in the *AfterReceiveRequest* method and return it. The WCF runtime will pass this same identifier in as the *correlationState* parameter to the *BeforeSendReplyMethod*. In this example, you are not correlating request and reply messages, so the *AfterReceive Request* method simply returns *null*.

Caution The *Message* object contains a SOAP message that comprises XML text. If you are familiar with the types in the *System.Xml* namespace in the .NET Framework, you may be tempted to use the generic *GetBody<>* method to parse the contents of the message and retrieve the data in the *<Body>* element, such as in the following:

```
System.Xml.XmlElement data = request.GetBody<System.Xml.XmlElement>();
```

However, the *GetBody<>* method is destructive. You can use it only once on a message, so doing this destroys the message, and the service method receives incorrect data. To examine a message safely, use the *CreateBufferedCopy* method of the request message to create a *System.ServiceModel.Channels.MessageBuffer* object containing a copy of the message. You can then extract the copy of the message from this *MessageBuffer* object into a *System. ServiceModel.Channels.Message* object by using the *CreateMessage* method, like this:

```
MessageBuffer requestBuffer = request.CreateBufferedCopy(10000);
Message requestCopy = requestBuffer.CreateMessage();
```

6. Replace the *throw* statement in the *BeforeSendReply* method by using the code shown in bold in the following:

```
public void BeforeSendReply(ref System.ServiceModel.Channels.Message reply,
    object correlationState)
{
    Console.WriteLine("Reply sent: {0}\n{1}\n\n",
        reply.Headers.Action, reply.ToString());
}
```

This statement displays the action and the reply message on the console.

7. Rebuild the solution.

Creating a Custom Behavior

You will integrate the behavior implemented by the *ShoppingCartInspector* class into the WCF runtime by using a service behavior. Sadly, there is no built-in "IntegrateShopping CartInspector" service behavior in WCF. Fortunately, it is not difficult to write one yourself by creating a class that implements the *IServiceBehavior* interface.

The *IServiceBehavior* interface defines three methods that a class must implement to be able to act as a service behavior in the WCF infrastructure. These methods are:

- *AddBindingParameters*   Some behaviors can take additional data items as parameters to the binding elements, and an administrator or developer can supply this information in *the BindingParameterCollection* passed to this method. The WCF runtime invokes the *AddBindingParameters* method once for each URI to which the service is listening.

- *ApplyDispatcherBehavior*   With this method, you can modify the behavior of *Service Host* object hosting the service. The *ServiceHost* object is passed in as the second parameter to this method. Use this method to perform tasks such as adding custom error handlers or message inspector objects into the runtime.

- *Validate*   The WCF runtime invokes this method to verify that the service meets your own custom requirements. For example, you can examine the service description passed in as the first parameter, and if the contract for the service does not conform to expectations (it doesn't specify how to handle faults, for example), you can reject it and throw an exception.

If you are implementing an operation behavior, an endpoint behavior, or a contract behavior, you can implement the *IOperationBehavior*, *IEndpointBehavior*, or *IContractBehavior* interfaces instead of *IServiceBehavior*. The principles behind these interfaces are very similar to the *IServiceBehavior*; they expose the *AddBindingParameters*, *ApplyDispatcherBehavior*, and *Validate* methods whose purpose is as described previously, although their parameters are different because their scope is limited to an operation, endpoint, or contract rather than an entire service. Additionally, these three interfaces provide a method called *ApplyClientBehavior*. This method takes a reference to the WCF client runtime in the form of a *ClientRuntime* object. You can modify the properties of this object to configure the way in which the client runtime operates, and you can insert a message inspector into the client runtime if you need to monitor and manage the messages that a client sends and receives.

In the following exercise, you will implement the *IServiceBehavior* interface and create a service behavior that you can use to add the message inspector to the *ShoppingCartService* service.

Create a Service Behavior for the *ShoppingCartService* Service

1. Add the following public class to the ShoppingCartInspector.cs file, just below the *ShoppingCartInspector* class:

   ```
   public class ShoppingCartBehavior: IServiceBehavior
   {
   }
   ```

2. In the code view window, right-click *IServiceBehavior*, point to Implement Interface, and then click Implement Interface.

   Visual Studio adds the following three methods (described earlier) to the *Shopping CartBehavior* class:

   ❏ *AddBindingParameters* The *ShoppingCartBehavior* service behavior does not require this facility, so simply remove the *throw* statement and leave the method blank. Note that even if you do not require this method you must still implement it (it is part of the *IServiceBehavior* interface), and the WCF runtime will call it when it starts the service host running, so if you leave the *throw* statement in place the service host will stop with a *NotImplementedException* exception.

   ❏ *ApplyDispatcherBehavior* The *ShoppingCartBehavior* service behavior will use this method to insert the message inspector into the processing path for each *Endpoint Dispatcher* object used by the service.

   ❏ *Validate* The *ShoppingCartBehavior* service behavior does not use this feature either, so remove the *throw* statement and leave the method empty.

3. Comment out the *throw* statements in the *AddBindingParameters* and *Validate* methods.

4. Replace the *throw* statement in the *ApplyDispatchBehavior* method with the code shown in bold in the following:

   ```
   public void ApplyDispatchBehavior(ServiceDescription serviceDescription,
       System.ServiceModel.ServiceHostBase serviceHostBase)
   {
       foreach (ChannelDispatcher chanDispatcher in serviceHostBase.ChannelDispatchers)
       {
           foreach (EndpointDispatcher epDispatcher in chanDispatcher.Endpoints)
   ```

```
        {
            epDispatcher.DispatchRuntime.MessageInspectors.Add
                (new ShoppingCartInspector());
        }
    }
}
```

This block of code iterates through each *EndpointDispatcher* object for each *Channel Dispatcher* object created by the *ServiceHost* object and adds a *ShoppingCartInspector* object into the *MessageInspectors* collection of each endpoint. Subsequently, whenever an *EndpointDispatcher* object dispatches a service method or whenever a service method returns to the *EndpointDispatcher* object, the message will pass through the *ShoppingCartInspector* object.

The final step is to apply the *ShoppingCartBehavior* to the *ShoppingCartService* when it runs.

5. Open the Program.cs file for the ShoppingCartHost project in the Code And Text Editor. In the *Main* method insert the code (shown in bold in the following) between the statement that adds the service endpoint to the service and the statement that opens the service:

```
static void Main(string[] args)
{
    ...
    host.AddServiceEndpoint(typeof(ShoppingCartService.IShoppingCartService),
        customBinding, "net.tcp://localhost:8090/ShoppingCartService");
    host.Description.Behaviors.Add(new ShoppingCartService.ShoppingCartBehavior());
    host.Open();
    ...
}
```

> **Note** The *Description* property of a *ServiceHost* object provides programmatic access to some of the metadata of the hosted service. The *Behaviors* collection is the set of service behaviors applied to the service. You can add or remove behaviors in code but only before you call the *Open* method of the *ServiceHost* object. Once the service has started, you cannot change its behaviors without first stopping it and then restarting it.
>
> You can query and modify the endpoint behaviors of a service by using the *Endpoints* collection of the *Description* property. You have seen that a service can expose more than one endpoint, and you can apply different behaviors to each endpoint. The code fragment below configures the behavior for the first endpoint for a service and applies the *MyEndpoint Behavior* behavior:
>
> ```
> host.Description.Endpoints[0].Behaviors.Add(new MyEndpointBehavior());
> ```

6. Start the solution without debugging. In the ShoppingCartClient console window, press Enter.

The client application runs as before (albeit a little more slowly). However, the console window running the service host now displays the SOAP messages being sent and received, as shown in the image below (this is the same data that you can capture when you configure message logging for a service):

7. Press Enter to close the client application console window. In the host application console window, press Enter to stop the service.

Defining a Behavior Extension Element

In the previous exercise, you hard-coded the *ShoppingCartBehavior* behavior into the service host application by explicitly adding it to the *Behaviors* collection in the *Description* property of the *ServiceHost* object. However, this behavior is an example of non-critical functionality that would be best left to an administrator to selectively enable or disable by using a configuration file.

To support configuring a behavior in a configuration file, you must provide a behavior extension element. A behavior extension element is a class that the WCF runtime uses to configure a behavior when it starts a service running and reads the configuration file. The behavior extension element enables the WCF runtime to locate the type that implements the behavior, instantiate it, and set its properties (if it has any).

The simplest way to implement a behavior extension element is to extend the *Behavior ExtensionElement* class located in the *System.ServiceModel.Configuration* namespace. This is an abstract class that provides most of the functionality required, although you can override it if necessary. The only elements that you must provide are a read-only property called *Behavior Type* that returns the type of the behavior, and a protected method called *CreateBehavior* that instantiates the behavior.

In the following exercises, you will create a behavior extension element called *ShoppingCart BehaviorExtensionElement*, and then update the configuration file for the *ShoppingCartService* service to reference this behavior extension element.

Create a Behavior Extension Element for the *ShoppingCartBehavior* Behavior

1. In Visual Studio, add a reference to the *System.Configuration* assembly to the Shopping CartService project.

2. Return to the ShoppingCartInspector.cs file in the Code And Text Editor window and add the following *using* statement to the list at the top of the file:

```
using System.ServiceModel.Configuration;
```

3. At the end of the file, after the *ShoppingCartBehavior* class, add another public class called *ShoppingCartBehaviorExtensionElement* that inherits from the *BehaviorExtension Element* class.

```
public class ShoppingCartBehaviorExtensionElement: BehaviorExtensionElement
{
}
```

4. In the *ShoppingCartBehaviorExtensionElement* class, override the public *BehaviorType* property and add a *get* accessor that returns the type of the *ShoppingCartBehavior* class, as shown in bold in the following:

```
public class ShoppingCartBehaviorExtensionElement: BehaviorExtensionElement
{
    public override Type BehaviorType
    {
        get
        {
            return typeof(ShoppingCartBehavior);
        }
    }
}
```

5. In the *ShoppingCartBehaviorExtensionElement* class, after the *BehaviorType* property, override the protected *CreateBehavior* method. This method creates an instance of the behavior and returns it as an object:

```
public class ShoppingCartBehaviorExtensionElement: BehaviorExtensionElement
{
    ...
    protected override object CreateBehavior()
    {
        return new ShoppingCartBehavior();
    }
}
```

6. Rebuild the solution.

The next step is to remove the statement from the *ShoppingCartHost* application that hard-codes the reference to the *ShoppingCartBehavior* behavior and add this behavior to the configuration file instead. You will create an anonymous service behavior in the configuration file so that it will be automatically picked up and referenced by the service host.

1. Open the Program.cs file for the ShoppingCartHost project in the Code And Text Editor
   window.

2. In the *Main* method, locate the statement that adds the *ShoppingCartBehavior* behavior
   to the list of behaviors for the service host and comment this statement out, as shown in
   bold in the following:

```
static void Main(string[] args)
{
    ...
    host.AddServiceEndpoint(typeof(ShoppingCartService.IShoppingCartService),
        customBinding, "net.tcp://localhost:8090/ShoppingCartService");
    // host.Description.Behaviors.Add(new ShoppingCartService.ShoppingCartBehavior());
    host.Open();
    ...
}
```

3. Open the App.config file for the ShoppingCartHost project by using the Service
   Configuration Editor.

4. In the Configuration pane, expand the Advanced folder, expand the Extensions folder,
   and then click Behavior Element Extensions.

   The list of extension binding elements provided with WCF appears in the Behavior
   Element Extensions pane. This list displays the friendly name of each extension, and
   the type that implements each behavior extension element. Some of these items, such
   as *serviceDebug*, should be familiar to you, others less so. The important point to realize is that all the behaviors provided with WCF are simply examples of *Behavior* classes
   that you can replace with your own types, or augment if you wish to implement a new
   behavior.

5. Click the New button at the bottom of the Behavior Element Extensions pane. In the
   Extension Configuration Element Editor dialog box, type **messageInspector** for the *Name*
   property.

   Click the *Type* property, and then click the ellipsis (...) button that appears. In the Behavior
   Extension Type Browser dialog box, browse to the ShoppingCartService\ShoppingCart
   Service\bin\Debug folder (within the Chapter 11 folder), click ShoppingCartService.dll,
   and then click Open. The *ShoppingCartService.ShoppingCartBehaviorExtensionElement*
   type that you created in the previous exercise should be listed:

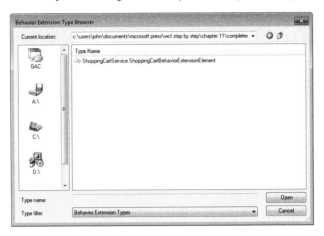

 Hint If the *ShoppingCartService.ShoppingCartBehaviorExtensionElement* does not appear, make sure that you successfully built the solution at the end of the previous exercise.

6. Click the *ShoppingCartService.ShoppingCartBehaviorExtensionElement* type, and then click Open again. The full name of the type should appear in the Extension Configuration Element Editor dialog box.

7. In the Extension Configuration Element Editor dialog box, click OK. The *messageInspector* behavior extension element should be listed in the Behavior Element Extensions pane:

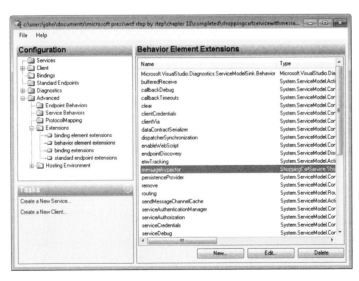

8. In the Service Configuration Editor, in the Configuration pane, click the Service Behaviors folder within the Advanced folder. In the Service Behaviors pane, click New Service Behavior Configuration.

9. In the right pane, clear the *Name* property of the behavior (it must be anonymous to be used automatically by the service host). In the lower part of the pane, click the Add button. In the Adding Behavior Element Extension Sections dialog box, click the *message Inspector* element, and then click Add.

10. Save the configuration file, and then close the Service Configuration Editor.

11. In Visual Studio, open the App.config file for the ShoppingCartHost project in the Code And Text Editor window. The file should now look like this:

```xml
<?xml version="1.0"?>
<configuration>
  <connectionStrings>
    <add name="AdventureWorksEntities" ... />
  </connectionStrings>
  <system.serviceModel>
    <behaviors>
      <serviceBehaviors>
        <behavior name="">
          <messageInspector />
        </behavior>
      </serviceBehaviors>
    </behaviors>
    <extensions>
      <behaviorExtensions>
        <add name="messageInspector"
type="ShoppingCartService.ShoppingCartBehaviorExtensionElement, ShoppingCartService,
Version=1.0.0.0, Culture=neutral, PublicKeyToken=null" />
      </behaviorExtensions>
    </extensions>
  </system.serviceModel>
</configuration>
```

The *<extensions>* element specifies the details of the behavior element extension and gives this extension the name *messageInspector*. The *<serviceBehaviors>* section defines an anonymous behavior that references the *messageInspector* behavior element extension to apply the *ShoppingCartBehavior* behavior class to the service.

> **Note** The *messageInspector* element in the *<serviceBehaviors>* section might be displayed with a warning stating that this element is invalid. You can ignore this warning.

12. Start the solution without debugging. In the ShoppingCartClient console window, press Enter.

    The client application and service run as before, and the ShoppingCartHost console window displays the messages output by the *ShoppingCartInspector* object.

13. Press Enter to close the client application console window. In the host application console window, press Enter to stop the service.

You can easily verify that the behavior has been picked up from the configuration file and not as the result of code in the host application by setting the *Name* property of the service behavior to a value other than the empty string. A named behavior will only be used if it is explicitly referenced from a service definition. There are no service definitions in the App.config file because the service is configured by using code in the ShoppingCartHost project; consequently, the behavior will not be applied and the messages from the *ShoppingCartInspector* object will not appear in the ShoppingCartHost console window.

Controlling Client Communications

You have now seen how to configure the channel stack for a service and how to create a behavior that can modify the way in which the WCF runtime processes messages. In this section, you will examine how to programmatically connect a client application to a service, send messages, and process responses.

Connecting to a Service Programmatically

When a client application runs and connects to a service, the WCF runtime creates an infrastructure that is a simplified mirror of that created for the service. When you use a proxy object to connect to a service, behind the scenes the WCF runtime creates a binding object using the binding elements specified in the configuration file and an endpoint based on the selected endpoint definition. It then uses these items to construct a *ChannelFactory* object. The WCF runtime uses the *ChannelFactory* object to instantiate the channel stack and connect it to the URI specified by the endpoint. When the client application invokes operations through the proxy object, the WCF runtime routes these requests through the channel stack and transmits them to the service. When a response message arrives from the service, it passes back up through the channel stack to the WCF runtime, and the proxy object then passes it back to the client application code.

You can create a client proxy class for a service by using the *svcutil* utility or Add Service Reference Wizard to query the metadata for the service and generate an assembly that you can add to the client project (you have performed this task at regular intervals during the exercises in this book). For security reasons, the administrator managing the host computer running a WCF service can elect to disable service metadata publishing. However, the WCF service developer can distribute an assembly containing the service contract, and you can use this to create the channel stack dynamically. This approach can also have some performance benefits. For instance, you might find that the proxy types generated by using the *svcutil* utility and Add Service Reference Wizard are not necessarily optimal; they are robust because they cannot make any assumptions about the technology used to implement the service, but this robustness adds bulk which can impact performance. If you know that the service was generated using WCF, you can construct a *ChannelFactory* object for the client directly from an assembly containing the service contract and eliminate the need to create a proxy. This is the approach that you will follow in the next set of exercises.

Connect to the *ProductsService* Service by Using a *ChannelFactory* Object

1. In Visual Studio, close the ShoppingCartService solution and then open the Products Service solution in the Microsoft Press\WCF Step By Step\Chapter 11\ProductsService folder.

   This solution contains a copy of the *ProductsService* service and ProductsServiceHost application from Chapter 6, "Maintaining Service Contracts and Data Contracts," and a version of the ProductsClient application from which most of the code in the Program.cs file has been removed. The application configuration file and the file containing the proxy class definition have also been removed from the client application.

   The ProductsServiceHost application exposes the *ProductsService* service over the HTTP protocol, at the address *http://localhost:8010/ProductsService/Service.svc*. The host is configured to implement message-level security to encrypt and sign messages by using basic 128-bit encryption.

   > **Note** If you have not already done so in Chapter 4, open a Visual Studio Command Prompt window as administrator and type the following command to add an HTTP reservation for port 8010 (replace *UserName* with the name of your Windows account).
   >
   > ```
   > netsh http add urlacl url=http://+:8010/ user=UserName
   > ```

2. In Solution Explorer, add a link to the IProductService.cs file in the ProductsServiceLibray project to the ProductsClient project as follows:

   a. Right-click the ProductsClient project, point to Add, and then click Existing Item.

   b. In the Add Existing Item – ProductsClient dialog box, browse to the Products Service\ProductsServiceLibrary folder and select the IProductsService.cs file.

   c. Click the drop-down arrow on the Add button, and then click Add As Link.

   This technique enables you to reference the same source file from more than one project rather than creating a copy and ending up with possible versioning issues. You can edit the source file in any of the projects that reference the file.

   The IProductsService.cs file contains the definition of the service contract for the *Products Service* service. If you don't wish to share the source code for a service contract, you can compile it into a separate assembly and distribute this assembly to developers building client applications.

3. In Solution Explorer, open the Program.cs file in the ProductsClient project. This file contains the basic framework for the client application in the *Main* method, but the code that connects to the service and invokes operations is currently missing.

Add the following *using* statement to the list at the top of the file:

```
using System.ServiceModel.Security;
```

4. In the *Main* method, in the *try* block, add the following statements, as shown in bold:

```
static void Main(string[] args)
{
    ...
    try
    {
        WS2007HttpBinding httpBinding = new WS2007HttpBinding(SecurityMode.Message);
        WSHttpSecurity httpSec = httpBinding.Security;
        httpSec.Message.AlgorithmSuite = SecurityAlgorithmSuite.Basic128;
        httpSec.Message.ClientCredentialType = MessageCredentialType.Windows;
    }
    ...
}
```

The *WS2007HttpBinding* class implements the standard *WS2007HttpBinding* binding. The ProductsServiceHost exposes an HTTP endpoint with the URI, *http://localhost:8010/ ProductsService/Service.svc*. As mentioned earlier, if you examine the application configuration file for the ProductsServiceHost project, you will see that the binding configuration for the service endpoint uses message-level security, with 128-bit encryption of messages and Windows authentication. The code you have just added sets the corresponding security properties for the *WS2007HttpBinding* object in the client application.

5. Add the following statement (shown in bold) to the *try* block in the *Main* method:

```
static void Main(string[] args)
{
    ...
    try
    {
        ...
        EndpointAddress address = new EndpointAddress(
            "http://localhost:8010/ProductsService/Service.svc");
    }
    ...
}
```

The *EndpointAddress* object encapsulates the address that the client application uses to communicate with the service.

6. Add the following code (shown in bold) to the *try* block:

```
static void Main(string[] args)
{
    ...
    try
    {
        ...
        Products.IProductsServiceV2 channel =
            ChannelFactory<Products.IProductsServiceV2>.CreateChannel(
                httpBinding, address);
    }
    ...
}
```

The generic *ChannelFactory* class creates a channel by calling the static *CreateChannel* method. The new channel uses the binding specified in the first parameter and connects to the address provided in the second parameter. The value returned is a reference to the channel just created. A channel has a type based on the service contract, and this type determines the methods exposed by the channel to the client application. In this case, the channel is assigned to a variable of type *Products.IProductsServiceV2*. Remember that *IProductsServiceV2* is the interface implemented by the service contract in the ProductsServiceContract.cs file. You can create channels based on any interface that is annotated with the *ServiceContract* attribute.

7. You can now invoke methods through the *channel* variable. In the *try* block, add the following statements that call the *ListMatchingProducts* operation to retrieve a list of bicycle frames and display the results:

```
static void Main(string[] args)
{
    ...
    try
    {
        ...
        Console.WriteLine("Test 1: List all bicycle frames");
        List<string> productNumbers = channel.ListMatchingProducts("Frame");
        foreach (string productNumber in productNumbers)
        {
            Console.WriteLine("Number: {0}", productNumber);
        }
        Console.WriteLine();
    }
    ...
}
```

There is one very subtle difference between this code and the corresponding code you used in Chapter 6: the value returned by the *ListMatchingProducts* method is now passed back as a *List<string>* object rather than the array of strings returned when using the generated proxy (remember that the Add Service Reference Wizard enables you to specify how collections should be handled and converted by the proxy when they are returned to the client application).

8. Close the connection to the service and set the *channel* variable to *null* to release any associated resources at the end of the *try* block, as follows:

```
static void Main(string[] args)
{
    ...
    try
    {
        ...
        channel = null;
    }
    ...
}
```

The completed *Main* method should look like this (comments have been added to help clarify the code):

```
static void Main(string[] args)
{
    Console.WriteLine("Press ENTER when the service has started");
    Console.ReadLine();

    try
    {
        // Create the HTTP binding and configure security
        WS2007HttpBinding httpBinding = new WS2007HttpBinding(SecurityMode.Message);
        WSHttpSecurity httpSec = httpBinding.Security;
        httpSec.Message.AlgorithmSuite = SecurityAlgorithmSuite.Basic128;
        httpSec.Message.ClientCredentialType = MessageCredentialType.Windows;

        // Create an endpoint to connect to the service
        EndpointAddress address = new EndpointAddress(
            "http://localhost:8010/ProductsService/Service.svc");

        // Build the channel stack for communicating with the service
        Products.IProductsServiceV2 channel =
            ChannelFactory<Products.IProductsServiceV2>.CreateChannel(
                httpBinding, address);

        // Obtain a list of bicycle frames
        Console.WriteLine("Test 1: List all bicycle frames");
        List<string> productNumbers = channel.ListMatchingProducts("Frame");
        foreach (string productNumber in productNumbers)
        {
            Console.WriteLine("Number: {0}", productNumber);
        }
        Console.WriteLine();

        // Close the connection to the service
        channel = null;
    }
```

```
        catch (Exception e)
        {
            Console.WriteLine("Exception: {0}", e.Message);
        }

        Console.WriteLine("Press ENTER to finish");
        Console.ReadLine();
    }
```

10. Build the solution and then exit Visual Studio.

Before you run the client application, you must make one configuration change to the security of your computer: you need to add your user account to the *WarehouseStaff* group. This is because the *ProductsService* service expects the user requesting the *ListMatchingProducts* operation to be a member of this group.

Configure Security and Test the Client Application

1. Open the Windows Start menu, right-click Computer, and then select Manage. Enter the administrator password if you are prompted.

2. In the Computer Management console, under the System Tools node, expand the Local Users And Groups node, and then click the Users folder.

3. In the right pane, right-click the user name for your account, and then click Properties.

4. In the Properties dialog box, click the Member Of tab, and then click Add.

5. In the Select Groups dialog box, type **WarehouseStaff** in the text box, and then click OK.

6. In the Properties dialog box, click OK.

7. Close the Computer Management console.

8. Log off Windows and then log back on again.

This step is necessary for Windows to recognize your new membership of the *WarehouseStaff* group.

9. Start Visual Studio then open the ProductsService solution again.

10. Start the solution without debugging. In the Products Service Host window, click Start. In the client console window, press Enter.

The client application connects to the service, requests a list of bicycle frames, and displays the results, as shown in the following image:

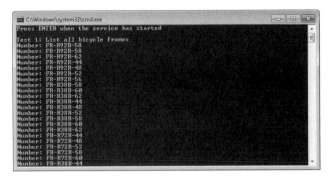

11. Press Enter in the client console window to close the client application. In the Products Service Host window, click Stop, and then close the form. Note that the Products Service Host window takes a little while to respond to the Stop button. This is because it must wait to ensure that the client application has disconnected before closing the connection and tidying up the various network resources. The client application only disconnects when the .NET Framework garbage collector frees the resources associated with the *channel* variable in the client application sometime after it has been set to *null*.

Using the *ClientBase Abstract* Class

In earlier chapters, you used the *ClientCredentials* property of the proxy object to specify the credentials to send to the service. The *Products.IProductsServiceV2* interface does not include this functionality. If you need to provide credentials other than your current Windows identity, you must define a class that extends the *System.ServiceModel.ClientBase* generic abstract class and use this class to connect to the service. The *ClientBase* class incorporates the client-side *ChannelFactory* infrastructure through a series of constructors. You can expose whichever of the base class constructors are appropriate for your situation. The class should also provide an implementation of the interface that defines service contract. You use the *Channel* property of the base class to route method calls through the channel to the service in each method implementing the service interface. The code below shows an example, creating a *ClientBase* class based on the *Products.IProductsServiceV2* service contract and implementing the methods of the *Products.IProductsServiceV2* interface. This example also implements one of the 12 available *Client Base* constructors.

> **Note** You can find copy of this code in the ProductsService solution in the ProductsService WithManualProxy folder, which is located within the Chapter 11 folder.

```
class ProductsServiceProxy : ClientBase<Products.IProductsServiceV2>,
                Products.IProductsServiceV2
{
    public ProductsServiceProxy(Binding binding, EndpointAddress address) :
        base(binding, address)
    {
    }

    public List<string> ListMatchingProducts(string match)
    {
        return base.Channel.ListMatchingProducts(match);
    }

    public Products.ProductData GetProduct(string productNumber)
    {
        return base.Channel.GetProduct(productNumber);
    }

    public int CurrentStockLevel(string productNumber)
    {
        return base.Channel.CurrentStockLevel(productNumber);
    }

    public bool ChangeStockLevel(string productNumber, short newStockLevel,
                                 string shelf, int bin)
    {
        return base.Channel.ChangeStockLevel(productNumber, newStockLevel, shelf,
            bin);
    }
}
```

You can instantiate this class and call its methods as your proxy object. The *ClientBase* class provides the *ClientCredentials* property that you can populate to specify the credentials to transmit to the service by using the following familiar code:

```
ProductsServiceProxy channel = new ProductsServiceProxy(httpBinding, address);
channel .ClientCredentials.Windows.ClientCredential.UserName = "Fred";
channel .ClientCredentials.Windows.ClientCredential.Password = "Pa$$wOrd";
channel .ClientCredentials.Windows.ClientCredential.Domain = "LON-DEV-01";
```

If you examine the code for any client proxy class generated by using the *svcutil* utility, you will see that it follows this approach.

The *ClientBase* class has one further advantage; it provides a *Close* method that explicitly terminates the communication channel and frees any associated resources in the client application immediately rather than waiting for the .NET Framework garbage collector to perform these tasks.

Sending Messages Programmatically

A major objective of WCF is to provide a platform for interoperability. You can build WCF client applications that communicate with services created by using other, non-WCF technologies, such as Java. In this situation, if the administrator of the computer hosting the service disables service metadata publishing, the service developer is unlikely to be able to provide you with C# code or a .NET Framework assembly containing the service contract. However, if you have documentation describing the SOAP messages that the service can accept and the responses the service emits, you can still access the service from a WCF client application; you can send messages directly through the channel. This is a very low-level, but extremely flexible approach that also gives a valuable insight into how the WCF runtime on the client converts method calls for a channel into SOAP messages. This is the subject of the final exercise in this chapter.

Send a Message and Process the Response in the Client Application

1. In Visual Studio, close the ProductsService solution. Open the SimpleProducts Service solution in the Microsoft Press\WCF Step By Step\Chapter 11\Simple ProductsService folder within your Documents folder.

   This solution contains a simplified version of the *ProductsService* service called *Simple ProductsService*. The settings in the App.config file cause the host application, Products ServiceHost, to publish the service with an HTTP endpoint using the *BasicHttpBinding* binding at the URI *http://localhost:8010/SimpleProductsService/Service.svc*.

2. Open the ISimpleProductsService.cs file in the ProductsServiceLibrary project. Locate the *ISimpleProductsService* interface defining the service contract. It looks like this:

   ```
   [ServiceContract(Namespace="http://adventure-works.com/2010/06/29",
                   Name="SimpleProductsService")]
   public interface ISimpleProductsService
   {
       [OperationContract(Name = "ListProducts")]
       List<string> ListProducts();
   }
   ```

   The service contract defines a single operation: *ListProducts* (this is the same as the corresponding operation in the original *ProductsService* service). Note the namespace and name of the service contract. WCF uses the service contract namespace and name in conjunction with the name of the operations to define the SOAP messages, or actions, that the service publishes. In this case, the service will accept and process SOAP messages using the action *http://adventure-works.com/2010/06/29/SimpleProductsService/ ListProducts*. Also, notice that the return type is *List<string>*, so the service will return a SOAP message containing a serialized list of strings.

> **Note** If you don't want to base the name of an action on the name and namespace properties of the service contract, you can provide your own name by specifying the *Action* and *ReplyAction* properties for the *OperationContract* attribute. You will learn more about the *Action* and *ReplyAction* properties in Chapter 14.

3. Open the Program.cs file for the ProductsClient project in the Code And Text Editor window. The *Main* method in this project currently creates a default *BasicHttpBinding* object and an *EndpointAddress* object. The URI in this endpoint is *http://localhost:8010/ SimpleProductsService/Service.svc*; this is the address that the *SimpleProductsService* is configured to listen on.

   Add the following *using* statement to the list at the top of the file:

   ```
   using System.ServiceModel.Channels;
   ```

4. In the *try* block in the *Main* method, add the following statements (shown in bold) immediately after the code that creates the *EndpointAddress* object:

   ```
   static void Main(string[] args)
   {
       ...
       try
       {
           ...
           EndpointAddress address = new EndpointAddress(
               "http://localhost:8010/SimpleProductsService/Service.svc");

           IChannelFactory<IRequestChannel> factory =
               httpBinding.BuildChannelFactory<IRequestChannel>();
           factory.Open();
       }
       ...
   }
   ```

   The first statement creates a client-side *ChannelFactory* object that the client application can use for building a channel that can send and receive messages by using the specified binding. The *Open* method instantiates the channel factory ready for constructing the channel stack.

   A channel implements interfaces that specify the messaging pattern that it supports. A channel can be an input channel; an output channel; an input and output channel (a duplex channel); a special form of output channel known as a *request channel*; or an equivalent input channel known as a *reply channel*. These interfaces are collectively referred to as channel shapes. The shapes available to a transport channel depend on several factors, including the type of the transport channel and the current value of its properties. For example, a TCP transport channel cannot act as a reply channel if it uses the buffered transfer mode; it can only operate as a bi-directional duplex channel in this case. However, the HTTP protocol operates using a send/receive pattern, and by default, the HTTP transport channel conforms to the request channel shape in a client application and the reply channel shape in a service.

The next step is to create the client-side channel stack by using the channel factory and connect to the service listening at the address specified earlier.

5. Add the following statements to the *try* block to perform this task:

```
static void Main(string[] args)
{
    ...
    try
    {
        ...
        IRequestChannel channel = factory.CreateChannel(address);
        channel.Open();
    }
    ...
}
```

6. You can now send messages and receive replies through the channel stack. You create a message by using the static *CreateMessage* method of the *Message* class. When creating a message, you must specify the message version and a string specifying the requested action.

Add the following statement to the *try* block:

```
static void Main(string[] args)
{
    ...
    try
    {
        ...
        Message request = Message.CreateMessage(MessageVersion.Soap11,
            "http://adventure-works.com/2010/06/29/SimpleProductsService/ListProducts");
    }
    ...
}
```

The SOAP messaging specification has undergone several changes since it was first released, and the various bindings in WCF support different versions of the specification. The *BasicHttpBinding* binding is intended to be compatible with SOAP 1.1 messaging. The constant *MessageVersion.Soap11* specified as the first parameter to *CreateMessage* indicates that the message should be formatted according to this specification. If you are using the *WS2007HttpBinding* binding, you can send messages by using the SOAP 1.2 format.

As discussed earlier, the action string combines the namespace and name of the service with the name of the operation. This is the value passed as the second parameter to *CreateMessage*.

The *CreateMessage* method is overloaded. Other overloads enable you to specify the data for the message body if the operation expects parameters and to generate SOAP fault messages (useful if you are creating a service using this low-level mechanism).

To actually send a message by using the request/response pattern, you use the *Request* method of the channel.

7. Add the following statements to the *try* block:

```
static void Main(string[] args)
{
    ...
    try
    {
        ...
        Message reply = channel.Request(request);
        Console.WriteLine(reply);
    }
    ...
}
```

The *Request* method blocks until a response is received from the service. The incoming response message is passed back as the return value from the *Request* method. After the application has received the response, the client simply displays it to the console and does not make any attempt to parse the contents.

> **Note** You can use the generic *GetBody< >* method of the reply message to parse a SOAP message, as described earlier in this chapter.

At this point, you can send further requests to the service, but this simple client application will simply disconnect and finish.

8. Add these statements at the end of the *try* block.

```
static void Main(string[] args)
{
    ...
    try
    {
        ...
        request.Close();
        reply.Close();
        channel.Close();
        factory.Close();
    }
    ...
}
```

Messages, channels, and channel factories all consume resources, so you should close them when you have finished using them.

9. Build and start the solution without debugging. In the Products Service Host window, click Start. In the client application console window, press Enter.

   The client application sends the *ListMatchingProducts* request to the service, which responds with a message containing a list of products. The client application displays the SOAP message containing this list, which has the following format:

```
<s:Envelope xmlns:s="http://schemas.xmlsoap.org/soap/envelope/">
  <s:Header />
  <s:Body>
    <ListProductsResponse xmlns="http://adventure-works.com/2010/06/29">
      <ListProductsResult
xmlns:a="http://schemas.microsoft.com/2003/10/Serialization/Arrays"
xmlns:i="http://www.w3.org/2001/XMLSchema-instance">
        <a:string>AR-5381</a:string>
        <a:string>BA-8327</a:string>
        ...
        <a:string>VE-C304-S</a:string>
        <a:string>WB-H098</a:string>
      </ListProductsResult>
    </ListProductsResponse>
  </s:Body>
</s:Envelope>
```

10. Press Enter to close the client application console window. In the Products Service Host window, click Stop, and then close the window.

Summary

In this chapter, you have examined some of the internal mechanisms that the WCF runtime uses to send and receive messages. You have seen how to create bindings in code and how to use a *ServiceHost* object to create a channel for listening for requests. You have explored how you can employ a message inspector to examine the messages flowing from the channel stack into a service and how to create a service behavior for modifying the way in which the WCF runtime manages a service. You have also examined ways of sending messages from a client to a service when you don't have access to a proxy class generated by using the *svcutil* utility, or when you wish to avoid the overhead sometimes associated with the proxy—by creating your own "lean and mean" channel stack using the *ChannelFactory* class or taking advantage of the low-level messaging interface.

Chapter 12
Implementing One-Way and Asynchronous Operations

After completing this chapter, you will be able to:

- Explain the behavior of one-way operations, and how service behavior and binding properties impact such operations.

- Implement one-way operations in a WCF service and invoke them from a WCF client application.

- Implement asynchronous operations in a WCF service and invoke operations asynchronously in a WCF client application.

- Explain the difference between invoking an operation asynchronously and implementing an operation that supports asynchronous execution.

- Use a message queue to send requests to a service asynchronously.

WCF client applications and services frequently follow the request/response messaging pattern for performing operations; the client application issues a request and then waits patiently while the message crosses the network, the service receives and processes the message, the service generates a reply, and the reply wends its way back across the network to the client application. If the client application does not require the service to send a response, then waiting for one is a waste of time and can impact the responsiveness of the client application. In this situation, you might find that a one-way operation can improve performance of the client application.

If the client application does require a response but can safely perform other tasks while waiting for this response, then you should implement asynchronous method invocation. Using this technique, the client application can send a request and then continue execution. When a reply message arrives from the service, a separate thread in the client application handles the response.

One-way operations and asynchronous operations both require the client application and the service to be running at the same time. If this is not the case, then you should consider using message queues as the transport medium between the client application and the service. A message queue can provide durable storage for messages. However, you must design client applications and services carefully if you are planning on using message queues because the request/response messaging pattern is not appropriate in this case.

Chapter 8, "Implementing Services by Using Workflows," provided a brief discussion on implementing common messaging patterns—including one-way and asynchronous operations—by using workflows. In this chapter, you will look in detail at options for implementing these styles of operations in a procedural service and how you can maximize the scope for parallelism in your applications.

> **Note** It is also possible for a client to provide a callback method for a service. The service can send a message that invokes this method. WCF client applications and services can use this mechanism to implement events, enabling the service to notify a client application of some significant occurrence. You will examine this feature in more detail in Chapter 16, "Using a Callback Contract to Publish and Subscribe to Events."

Implementing One-Way Operations

When a client application invokes a one-way operation, it can continue running without waiting for the service to complete the operation. You indicate that an operation is one way by specifying that behavior in the operation contract. The simplest way to achieve this is to set the *IsOneWay* property to **true** in the *OperationContract* attribute when defining the operation. You will see an example of this in the exercises in this section.

The Effects of a One-Way Operation

Defining an operation as one way has several implications, the most important of which is that such an operation cannot pass any data back to the client application; it must return a *void* and cannot have parameters marked as *out* or *ref*. When a one-way operation starts running in the service, the client application has no further contact with it and will not even be aware of whether the operation was successful or not. If the operation raises an exception that would normally generate a SOAP fault message, this SOAP fault message is simply discarded and never sent to the client.

> **Note** If you invoke a one-way operation by using the *Request* method of an *IRequestChannel* object as described in Chapter 11, "Programmatically Controlling the Configuration and Communications," the value of the response message returned will be *null*.

Invoking a one-way operation is not simply a matter of generating a message and throwing it at an endpoint where, hopefully, the service is listening. Although a client application does not know when a one-way operation has completed (successfully or not), it is still important for the client application to know that the service has received the message. If the service is not listening on the specified endpoint, the client will be alerted with an exception. Additionally, if the service is very busy, it might not be able to accept the message immediately.

Some transports implement a buffering mechanism for requests and will not accept further messages if there are too many outstanding requests. For example, the *TcpTransport* channel has a configurable property called *ListenBacklog* that specifies the maximum number of connection requests that can be pending. When pending requests reach this number, subsequent requests will be blocked until the number of pending requests drops; in this situation, the client application will wait until the request is accepted. If you want to be absolutely certain that the service has received the message and that the transport has not just buffered it, you can invoke the one-way operation in a reliable session. The service will send back an acknowledgment to the client when it starts processing the message, as described in Chapter 10, "Implementing Reliable Sessions." Reliable messaging has some other beneficial side effects on one-way operations, as you will see in the exercises in this chapter.

One-Way Operations and Transactions

You may recall from Chapter 9, "Supporting Transactions," that a client application can initiate a transaction and flow it into operations performed by a service. The transaction protocol enables a service to indicate that an operation has failed, causing the transaction to abort. This requires that the service is able to transmit information about the outcome of the operation back to the client. However, when you implement a one-way operation, there is no channel available for a service to send this data back. You should bear this in mind when you design a service and mark all one-way operations in a service contract with the *Transaction Flow(TransactionFlowOption.NotAllowed)* attribute—refer back to Chapter 9 for more details. When you start a service, the WCF runtime performs a sanity check and throws an *Invalid OperationException* exception if any one-way operations in the service mandate or allow transactions.

One-Way Operations and Timeouts

There are several possible failure points when sending messages over a network. If a client application does not receive a response to a request within a specified period of time, the WCF runtime on the client computer assumes that something has gone wrong and throws a *System.TimeoutException* to the client application. The duration of this timeout period is configurable as the *SendTimeout* property of the client binding and has a default value of one minute. If a client application invokes a one-way operation, the service needs only to accept the message within this timeout period; it does not need to complete message processing within the timeout duration.

In WCF, many bindings implement a buffering model for requests. If you recall from Chapter 7, "Maintaining State and Sequencing Operations," services that implement sessions are single threaded by default. When a client application sends a request to a service that implements sessions, the request is directed to a session that is specific to the client connection. If the application sends a second request over the same connection, it will be sent to the same session. If the instance running this session is still busy processing the first request, the second request will be buffered pending receipt. Bindings have a *ReceiveTimeout* property, which is used by the WCF runtime managing the service to manage and control buffered requests. If a service instance takes longer than the amount of time specified by the *ReceiveTimeout* value to actually receive a request because it is busy handling an earlier one, the WCF runtime aborts the request and throws a *Timeout* exception back to the client. The default value for the *ReceiveTimeout* property is 10 minutes. This is a long time for a client application to wait for a request to be rejected, and you should consider reducing this value unless you genuinely have operations that could run for this duration.

Implementing a One-Way Operation

In the following exercises, you will implement a one-way operation and investigate what happens when you invoke it from a client application. The Web service that you will create will provide administrative functions for the AdventureWorks organization.

The first operation you will implement provides an administrator with a mechanism to request a report for the current day's sales. This report could take several minutes to run, so you don't want to hold up the administrator while this is happening. Therefore, you will implement this feature as a one-way operation.

Create the AdventureWorks Administrative Operations Service

1. Start Visual Studio and create a new Web site by using the WCF Service template. In the New Web Site dialog box, specify the following properties for the project to create and host the Web site by using the ASP.NET Development Web Server:

Property	Value
Web location	File System
Folder	Microsoft Press\WCF Step By Step\Chapter 12\AdventureWorksAdmin within your Documents folder (create the folder, if prompted by Visual Studio)

2. In Solution Explorer, select the C:\...\AdventureWorksAdmin\ project. In the Properties window, set the *Use Dynamic Ports* property to **False** and set the *Port Number* to **9090** (you may need to wait for a few seconds before you can change the port number).

   By default, the ASP.NET Development Web Server picks an unused port when it starts running; however, for this exercise, it is useful to know in advance exactly which port the service will use. Disabling the *Dynamic Ports* property lets you specify a fixed port.

3. In Solution Explorer, expand the App_Code folder and open the IService.cs file in the Code And Text Editor window.

4. In the IService.cs file, remove everything below the *using* statements (leave the *using* statements intact).

5. Add a new service interface called *IAdventureWorksAdmin* to the file and mark it as a service contract. In the *ServiceContract* attribute, set the *Namespace* property to **http://adventure-works.com/2010/06/30** (assume that it is June 30, 2010 and that you use the recommended approach of incorporating the creation date into namespaces), and set the *Name* property to **AdministrativeService**, as shown here:

```
[ServiceContract(Namespace="http://adventure-works.com/2010/06/30",
                 Name="AdministrativeService")]
public interface IAdventureWorksAdmin
{
}
```

6. Add an operation called *GenerateDailySalesReport* (shown in bold in the following code), to the service contract. Mark it as a one-way operation by setting the *IsOneWay* property of the *OperationContract* attribute to **true**:

```
[ServiceContract(Namespace="http://adventure-works.com/2010/06/30",
                 Name="AdministrativeService")]
public interface IAdventureWorksAdmin
{
    [OperationContract(IsOneWay = true)]
    void GenerateDailySalesReport(string id);
}
```

Notice that this method returns a *void*. All one-way methods must be *void* methods. One-way methods can take parameters, as long as they are not marked with *ref* or *out* modifiers. You'll use the string parameter passed to the *GenerateDailySalesReport* method to identify an invocation of the operation.

7. In Solution Explorer, right-click the C:\...\AdventureWorksAdmin\ project, and then click Add Reference. In the Add Reference dialog box, add a reference to the *Presentation Framework* assembly, and then click OK.

You will display a message box in the service, and the *MessageBox* class is defined in this assembly.

8. Open the Service.cs file in the App_Code folder, remove everything underneath the *using* statements, and add a public class called *AdventureWorksAdmin* to the file. This class should implement the *IAdventureWorksAdmin* interface and provide the *Generate DailySalesReport* method, as follows:

```
public class AdventureWorksAdmin : IAdventureWorksAdmin
{
    public void GenerateDailySalesReport(string id)
    {
        // Simulate generating the report
        // by sleeping for 1 minute and 10 seconds
        System.Threading.Thread.Sleep(70000);
```

```
        string msg = String.Format("Report {0} generated", id);
        System.Windows.MessageBox.Show(msg);
    }
}
```

This version of the WCF service simulates the process of generating the report by sleep-ing for 70 seconds (you will understand why the duration is just over 1 minute in the next exercise). After the report has been generated, the method displays a message box.

> **Important** The message box displayed by this method is solely for example purposes—it allows you to observe when the method completes. You should never incorporate interac-tive message boxes like this into a production service. If you need to output messages for testing or debugging purposes, you should generally use the *System.Diagnostics.Debug. WriteLine* method and send messages to a trace listener.

9. Open the Service.svc file in the Code And Text Editor window. Modify this file to refer to the *AdventureWorksAdmin* class, as shown in bold in the following:

```
<%@ServiceHost Language=C# Debug="true" Service="AdventureWorksAdmin"
    CodeBehind="~/App_Code/Service.cs" %>
```

10. In Solution Explorer, edit the Web.config file by using the Service Configuration Editor.

11. In the Configuration pane, click the Services folder. In the Services pane, click Create A New Service.

12. Proceed through the New Service Element Wizard, using the information in the follow-ing table to define the service. (When the warning messages concerning the service type and contract appear, click Yes to proceed.)

Page	Prompt	Value
What is the service type for your service?	Service type	AdventureWorksAdmin
What service contract are you using?	Contract	IAdventureWorksAdmin
What communications mode is your service using?		HTTP
What method of interoperability do you want to use?		Advanced Web Service interoperability (Simplex communication)
What is the address of your endpoint?	Address	http://localhost:9090/AdventureWorks Admin/Service.svc

13. In the Configuration pane, click the Bindings folder. In the Bindings pane, click New Binding Configuration.

14. In the Create A New Binding dialog box, select **ws2007HttpBinding**, and then click OK.

15. In the right pane, in the *Name* property, type **AdventureWorksAdminWS2007 HttpBindingConfig**.

16. It should never take more than five minutes to generate the daily report, so in the General section displaying the properties of the new binding, set the *ReceiveTimeout* property to **00:05:00**.

17. In the Configuration pane, expand the Endpoints folder under the *AdventureWorks Admin* service, and then click the *(Empty Name)* endpoint.

18. In the Service Endpoint pane, set the *BindingConfiguration* property to **Adventure WorksAdminWS2007HttpBindingConfig**.

19. In the Configuration pane, expand the Advanced folder, expand the ServiceBehaviors folder, expand the *(Empty Name)* behavior, and then click the *serviceDebug* behavior element. In the ServiceDebug pane, set the *IncludeExceptionDetailInFaults* property to **True**.

20. In the Configuration pane, click the *serviceMetadata* behavior element under the *(Empty Name)* behavior. In the ServiceMetadata pane, verify that the *HttpGetEnabled* property is set to *True* (set it to **True** if it is currently *False*).

21. Save the configuration file, and then exit the Service Configuration Editor.

22. Open the Web.config file in the Code And Text Editor window.

23. In the *<serviceHostingEnvironment>* element, set the *multipleSiteBindingsEnabled* property to **false**, as shown in bold in the following.

```xml
<?xml version="1.0"?>
<configuration>
  ...
  <system.serviceModel>
    ...
    <serviceHostingEnvironment multipleSiteBindingsEnabled="false">
  </system.serviceModel>
  ...
</configuration>
```

24. Save the Web.config file.

25. In Solution Explorer, right-click Service.svc, and then click View In Browser.

The ASP.NET Development Server will start (if it is not already running) and display an icon in the lower-right corner of the Windows taskbar. Internet Explorer will run, navigate to the site **http://localhost:9090/AdventureWorksAdmin/Service.svc**, and display the page that describes how to generate the WSDL description for the service and how to use the service in a client application, as shown in the image that follows.

 Tip If Internet Explorer displays a blank page, manually enter the address **http://localhost:9090/AdventureWorksAdmin/Service.svc** in the address bar, and then press Enter to display the page for the service.

26. Close Internet Explorer then return to Visual Studio.

27. In Solution Explorer, right-click the C:\...\AdventureWorksAdmin\ project, and then click Start Options. From the Start Options page, select the option "Don't Open A Page. Wait For A Request From An External Application," and then click OK.

    When you start this project in subsequent exercises, you need the service to start running, but you don't want Internet Explorer to open.

Create a WCF Client Application to Test the AdventureWorks Administrative Operations Service

1. In Visual Studio, add a new project to the AdventureWorksAdmin solution by using the Console Application template (use the Console Application template, and not the Workflow Console Application template). Specify the following properties for the project:

Property	Value
Name	AdventureWorksAdminTestClient
Location	Microsoft Press\WCF Step By Step\Chapter 12 (within your Documents folder)

2. In Solution Explorer, right-click the AdventureWorksAdminTestClient project, and then click Add Service Reference. In the Add Service Reference dialog box click Discover, type **AdventureWorksAdmin** in the Namespace text box, and then click OK.

   This action creates a proxy that the client application can use to connect to the *AdventureWorksAdmin* service.

3. Open the app.config file in the Code And Text Editor and examine its contents. Note that Visual Studio has added and configured a client endpoint for communicating with the *AdventureWorksAdmin* service called *WS2007HttpBinding_AdministrativeService*, after the value of the *Name* attribute in the service contract when you created the service.

4. In Solution Explorer, in the AdventureWorksAdminTestClient project, open the file Program.cs in the Code And Text Editor window. Add the following *using* statement to the list at the start of the file:

   ```
   using AdventureWorksAdminTestClient.AdventureWorksAdmin;
   ```

   The proxy class generated in the earlier step is in this namespace.

5. Add the following code (shown in bold) to the *Main* method:

   ```
   static void Main(string[] args)
   {
       try
       {
           AdministrativeServiceClient proxy = new AdministrativeServiceClient(
               "WS2007HttpBinding_AdministrativeService");

           Console.WriteLine("Requesting first report at {0}", DateTime.Now);
           proxy.GenerateDailySalesReport("First Report");
           Console.WriteLine("First report request completed at {0}", DateTime.Now);
           Console.WriteLine("Requesting second report at {0}", DateTime.Now);
           proxy.GenerateDailySalesReport("Second Report");
           Console.WriteLine("Second report request completed at {0}", DateTime.Now);

           proxy.Close();
       }
       catch (Exception e)
       {
           Console.WriteLine("Exception: {0}", e.Message);
       }
       Console.WriteLine("Press ENTER to finish");
       Console.ReadLine();
   }
   ```

This code creates a proxy object and then invokes the *GenerateDailySalesReport* operation twice in quick succession, displaying the date and time before and after each request is sent.

6. In Solution Explorer, right-click the AdventureWorksAdmin solution, and then click Set Startup Projects. In the Property Pages dialog box, select the **Multiple Startup Projects** option. Set the action for both projects to Start, and then click OK.

7. Start the solution without debugging.

The request for the first report completes quickly (it might take a few seconds, depending on whether the WCF service is still running or Visual Studio needs to start it, but it will require less time than the 70 seconds that the operation runs for). However, the second request causes the client application to stop. If you wait for one minute, the client application eventually times out with an error (the default value of the *SendTimeout* property of the binding is 1 minute):

You should also notice that the *AdventureWorksAdmin* service eventually (after 70 seconds) completes the first request successfully and displays a message box:

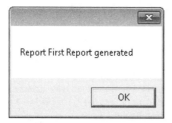

Click OK to close the message box. If you wait for a couple more seconds, the message box for the second request appears as well. This shows that the request was actually received successfully by the *AdventureWorksAdmin* service, although something appears to have gone awry with the client application.

Click OK to close the second message box and then press Enter to close the client application console window.

So, what went wrong? The problem lies partly in the fact that the service uses sessions and partly in the concurrency mode of the service. Remember from the earlier discussion in the section, "One-Way Operations and Timeouts" on page 435, that sessions are single threaded by default, and a service instance will not accept a new request if it is still processing an earlier one. If you disable sessions (by using a binding that does not support them or by setting the *SessionMode* property of the *ServiceContract* attribute of the *IAdventureWorksAdmin* interface to *SessionMode.NotAllowed*), then the concurrent calls to the service are not blocked; instead, each call is sent to a different instance of the service.

> **Note** The blocking problem is exacerbated because the *AdventureWorksAdmin* service uses the HTTP transport, which does not support request queuing like the TCP transport does. If you had used a TCP endpoint instead, the client would be able to continue as soon as the second request was queued by the transport channel rather than waiting for the request to be accepted by the service; however, the second request would still not be processed until the first had completed.

In the next exercise you will see how to address this situation.

Resolve the Blocking Problem with the One-Way Request

1. In Solution Explorer, edit the Service.cs file in the App_Code folder in the C:\...\Adventure WorksAdmin\ project. Add the *ServiceBehavior* attribute to the *AdventureWorksAdmin* class, as shown in bold on the following:

```
[ServiceBehavior(ConcurrencyMode=ConcurrencyMode.Multiple)]
public class AdventureWorksAdmin : IAdventureWorksAdmin
{
    ...
}
```

As described in Chapter 7, you can use the *ConcurrencyMode* property of the *Service Behavior* attribute to change the threading model used by the session. Selecting the value *ConcurrencyMode.Multiple* allows the service to process multiple concurrent requests in the same session, although you must ensure that the code you write in each method is thread-safe (as it is in this example).

2. Start the solution without debugging.

   This time, both requests are submitted successfully (the client application displays the message "Second Report Request Completed At …"), but the client application now stops and times out at the end of the *Main* method (see the image that follows).

Press Enter to close the client console window, and then press OK when the two message boxes displayed by the service appear.

This time, the blockage is caused by a combination of the security implemented by the service and the call to the *Close* method of the proxy. Remember that the *ws2007Http Binding* binding uses sessions and message-level security by default. When terminating a session, the client application and service exchange messages to ensure that the session terminates in a secure and controlled manner. The client application will not finish until this message exchange completes, and the service does not send its final message until all operations have completed—consequently, a timeout occurs.

Two of the possible solutions are to disable security (absolutely not recommended) or to switch to transport-level security (which requires installing a certificate and configuring HTTPS). However, there is a third option available if you want to employ message-level security: you can configure reliable sessions.

3. In the C:\...\AdventureWorksAdmin\ project, edit the Web.config file by using the Service Configuration Editor.

In the Configuration pane, expand the Bindings folder and select the *AdventureWorks AdminWS2007HttpBindingConfig* binding configuration. In the right pane, set the *Enabled* property in the *ReliableSession Properties* section to **True**.

Save the file, and then close the Service Configuration Editor.

5. Follow the same procedure to edit the app.config file of the client application and enable reliable sessions in the *WS2007HttpBinding_AdministrativeService* binding configuration.

6. Start the solution without debugging.

The client should successfully send both requests and quickly close the session without timing out. After 70 seconds, the first message box should appear from the service; the second will be displayed shortly after.

In Chapter 10, you investigated the acknowledgment messages sent by the reliable sessions protocol implemented by WCF. The purpose of this protocol is to assure both parties (the client and the service) that the messages they have sent have been received. When the client application closes its session, it does not need to wait for the service to actually complete its processing as long as the service has acknowledged all messages sent by the client application; the *Close* method can complete before the service actually terminates the session.

> **Tip** If you need to implement one-way operations but cannot guarantee the thread-safe status of the corresponding methods, you *should not* set the *ConcurrencyMode* attribute of the service to *ConcurrencyMode.Multiple*. Just enable reliable sessions.
>
> When you enable reliable sessions, the client will not wait for a single-threaded service to accept each message before continuing; instead, the client will be able to carry on as soon as the service has acknowledged the message. Message acknowledgments are generated by the WCF runtime hosting the service before the message is dispatched to the service instance; they are not blocked by a single-threaded service instance.
>
> If you are curious, try disabling multiple-threading for the *AdventureWorksAdmin* service, but keep reliable sessions enabled and then run the solution. The client application will run without blocking. However, you should observe the difference in the behavior of the service. Previously, both calls to the *GenerateDailySalesReport* method executed concurrently, and the second message box appeared a couple of seconds after the first. If you use reliable messaging rather than multiple threads, the method calls run sequentially, and the second message box will appear at least 70 seconds after the first.

Recommendations for Using One-Way Operations

You have seen that one-way operations are a very useful mechanism for improving the responsiveness of a client application by allowing it to continue executing without waiting for the service to complete processing operation requests. However, to maximize the concurrency between a client application and a service, you should bear in mind the following points, summarizing what you have seen in the exercises:

- Services that don't use sessions provide the greatest degree of parallelism by default. If a service requires or allows sessions, then depending on how the transport used by the binding buffers messages, the service can block one-way requests if it is already busy processing a message in the same session. This is true even if the service uses the *PerCall* service instance context mode; it is the fact that the service uses sessions that causes the service to block requests.

- Services that use sessions can set the concurrency mode to enable multi-threading, but you must ensure that the operations in the service are thread-safe. Enabling multi-threading allows the service to execute requests in the same session simultaneously.

- Using reliable sessions enables a client application to close a connection to a service before the service has completed processing of all outstanding requests.

As a word of caution, malicious users have been known to exploit one-way operations to perform *Denial of Service* attacks; they bombard a service with a large number of requests, hop-
ing to cause it to grind to a halt as it attempts to process all the messages. If you implement a
multi-threaded service that supports asynchronous operations, you must take steps to ensure
that an attacker cannot send an inordinate number of requests in a short period of time and
cause your system to collapse under the strain.

Invoking and Implementing Operations Asynchronously

A one-way operation is useful for "fire and forget" scenarios, in which the client application
does not expect the service to pass back any information. However, many operations do not
fit into this scheme—they do return data to the client application. To cater to these situations,
WCF supports asynchronous operations and the *IAsyncResult* design pattern. You can implement the *IAsyncResult* design pattern in two ways using WCF: in the client application invoking the operation, and in the WCF service implementing the operation.

> **More Info** The *IAsyncResult* design pattern is commonly used throughout the .NET Framework
> and is not specific to WCF. For details, see the topic, "Asynchronous Programming Design Patterns,"
> available in the documentation provided with Visual Studio (also available on the Microsoft Web
> site at *http://msdn.microsoft.com/en-us/library/ms228969.aspx*).

Invoking an Operation Asynchronously in a Client Application

Using WCF, you can generate a version of the proxy class that a client application can use to
invoke operations asynchronously by using the */async* flag with the *svcutil* utility when you
create the proxy class. You can also generate an asynchronous proxy by using the Add Service
Reference Wizard in Visual Studio. To do that, click the Advanced button and then select the
Generate Asynchronous Operations check box in the Service Reference Settings dialog box.

An asynchronous proxy provides *begin* and *end* pairs of methods for each operation. The
client application can invoke the *begin* method to initiate the operation. The *begin* method
returns after sending the request, but a new thread created by the .NET Framework runtime
in the client waits for the response. When you invoke the *begin* method, you also provide the
name of a callback method. When the service finishes the operation and returns the results
to the client proxy, the callback method executes on this new thread. You use the callback
method to retrieve the results from the service. You should also call the *end* method for the
operation to indicate that you have processed the response.

It is important to understand that you do not need to modify the service in any way to support this form of asynchronous programming. Indeed, the service itself does not necessarily
need to be a WCF service; it could be a service implemented by using other technologies. The

code that makes the operation appear asynchronous to the client application is encapsulated inside the proxy generated on the client side and the .NET Framework runtime. All the threading issues are handled by code running in the WCF runtime on the client. As far as the service is concerned, the operation is being invoked in the exact same, synchronous manner that you have seen in all the preceding chapters in this book.

Implementing an Operation Asynchronously in a WCF Service

As mentioned earlier, with WCF, you can also implement an operation that can execute asynchronously. In this case, the service provides its own pair of *begin* and *end* methods that constitute the operation. The code in the client application invokes the operation through the proxy object using the ordinary operation name (not the *begin* method). The WCF runtime transparently routes the operation to the *begin* method, so the client application is not necessarily aware that the service implements the operation as an asynchronous method.

As a variation, the developer of the service can add logic to the *begin* method to choose whether the operation should run synchronously or asynchronously. For example, if the current workload of the service is light, it might make sense to perform the operation synchronously to allow it to complete as soon as possible. As the workload increases, the service might choose to implement the operation asynchronously. Implementing operations in this manner in a service can improve the scalability and responsiveness of a service without the need to modify client applications. You should use this implementation for any operation that returns data to a client application after performing a lengthy piece of processing.

> **Important** You should understand the important distinction between asynchronous operation invocation in the client application and asynchronous operation implementation in the service. Asynchronous invocation in the client application enables the client to initiate the operation and then continue its own processing while waiting for a response. Asynchronous implementation in the service enables the service to offload the processing to another thread or sleep while waiting for some background process to complete. A client application invoking an operation implemented asynchronously by the service still waits for the operation to complete before continuing.

You can specify that an operation supports asynchronous processing by setting the *Async Pattern* property to **true** in the *OperationContract* attribute when defining the operation, and providing a pair of methods that follow a prescribed naming convention and signature and that implement the *IAsyncResult* design pattern.

In the next set of exercises, you will add another operation called *CalculateTotalValueOfStock* to the *AdventureWorksAdmin* service. The purpose of this operation is to determine the total value of every item currently held in the AdventureWorks warehouse. This operation could take a significant time to run, so you will implement it as an asynchronous method.

Add an Asynchronous Operation to the AdventureWorks Administrative Service

1. In Visual Studio, open the IService.cs file in the App_Code folder for the C:\...\Adventure-
WorksAdmin\ project in the Code And Text Editor window. Add the following operation
(shown in bold) to the *IAdventureWorksAdmin* service contract:

```
[ServiceContract(Namespace="http://adventure-works.com/2010/06/30",
                 Name="AdministrativeService")]
public interface IAdventureWorksAdmin
{
    [OperationContract(IsOneWay = true)]
    void GenerateDailySalesReport(string id);

    [OperationContract(AsyncPattern = true)]
    IAsyncResult BeginCalculateTotalValueOfStock(string id, AsyncCallback cb,
        object s);
    int EndCalculateTotalValueOfStock(IAsyncResult r);
}
```

This operation consists of two methods: *BeginCalculateTotalValueOfStock* and *End
CalculateTotalValueOfStock*. Together, they constitute a single asynchronous operation
called *CalculateTotalValueOfStock*. It is important that you name both methods in the
operation following this convention in order for them to be recognized correctly when
you build the client proxy. You can specify whatever parameters the operation requires
in the *begin* method (in this case, the client application will pass in a string parameter
to identify each invocation of the operation), but the final two parameters must be an
AsyncCallback object that will reference a callback method in the client application and
an *object* holding state information provided by the client application. The return type
must be *IAsyncResult*. The *end* method must take a single parameter of type *IAsync
Result*, but the return type should be the type appropriate for the operation. In this case,
the *CalculateTotalValueOfStock* operation returns an *int* containing the calculated value.

The other key part of this operation is the *AsyncPattern* property of the *Operation
Contract* attribute. You apply the *OperationContract* attribute only to the *begin* method.
When you generate the metadata for this service (when building the client proxy, for
example), this property causes the *begin* and *end* methods to be recognized as the
implementation of a single asynchronous operation.

2. In Solution Explorer, right-click the App_Code folder in the C:\...\AdventureWorksAdmin\
project, and then click Add Existing Item. Add the file AsyncResult.cs, located in the
Microsoft Press\WCF Step By Step\Chapter 12 folder.

3. Open the AsyncResult.cs file and examine its contents. It contains a single generic class
called *AsyncResult* that implements the *IAsyncResult* interface. Detailed discussion of this
class and the *IAsyncResult* interface is beyond the scope of this book, but the purpose
of the *AsyncResult* class is to provide synchronization methods and state information
required by other classes that implement asynchronous methods. For this exercise, the
important members of the *AsyncResult* class are:

❏   *Data*   This property provides access to the data returned by the asynchronous operation. In this example, the *CalculateTotalValueOfStock* operation will populate this property and return the *AsyncResult* object to the client application when it executes the *end* method.

❏   *AsyncResult*   This is the constructor. It takes two parameters which it stores in private fields. The service will use the *synchronous* parameter to indicate whether it really is invoking the operation synchronously, and the *stateData* parameter will be a reference to the object passed in as the final parameter to the *begin* method (it is important to save this object because it must be returned to the client application to enable it to complete processing).

4. Open the Service.cs file in the App_Code folder the for the C:\...\AdventureWorksAdmin\ project in the Code And Text Editor window. Add the following delegate to the start of the *AdventureWorksAdmin* class:

```
public class AdventureWorksAdmin : IAdventureWorksAdmin
{
    private delegate void AsyncSleepCaller(int millisecondsTimeout);
    ...
}
```

You will use this delegate in the methods that you will add in the next steps.

5. Add the following method to the *AdventureWorksAdmin* class:

```
public class AdventureWorksAdmin : IAdventureWorksAdmin
{
    ...
    // CalculateTotalValueOfStock operation
    // Service can elect to perform the operation
    // synchronously or asynchronously
    public IAsyncResult BeginCalculateTotalValueOfStock(string id,
        AsyncCallback callback, object state)
    {
        AsyncResult<int> calcTotalValueResult;

        // Generate a random number.
        // The value generated determines the "complexity" of the operation
        Random generator = new Random();

        // If the random number is even, then the operation is simple
        // so perform it synchronously
        if ((generator.Next() % 2) == 0)
        {
            calcTotalValueResult = new AsyncResult<int>(true, state);
            System.Threading.Thread.Sleep(20000);
            System.Windows.MessageBox.Show("Synchronous sleep completed");
            calcTotalValueResult.Data = 5555555;
            calcTotalValueResult.Complete();
        }
        // Otherwise, the operation is complex so perform it asynchronously
        else
```

```
        {
            // Perform the operation asynchronously
            calcTotalValueResult = new AsyncResult<int>(false, state);
            AsyncSleepCaller asyncSleep = new AsyncSleepCaller(
                System.Threading.Thread.Sleep);
            IAsyncResult result = asyncSleep.BeginInvoke(30000,
                new AsyncCallback(EndAsyncSleep), calcTotalValueResult);
        }

        callback(calcTotalValueResult);
        System.Windows.MessageBox.Show(
            "BeginCalculateTotalValueOfStock completed for " + id);
        return calcTotalValueResult;
    }
    ...
}
```

 Note You can find this code in the file BeginCalculateTotalValueOfStock.txt, which is located in the Chapter 12 folder.

Again, the exact details of how this method works are beyond the scope of this book (strictly speaking, it has nothing to do with WCF). But to summarize, the method generates a random number, and if this number is even, it performs the operation synchronously (simulating a lightly-loaded server in the scenario outlined earlier), otherwise it performs it asynchronously (simulating a busier server). In the synchronous case, the code creates a new *AsyncResult* object, sleeps for 20 seconds to simulate the time taken to perform the calculation, and then populates the *AsyncResult* object with the result—5555555. In the asynchronous case, the code also creates an *AsyncResult* object, but spawns a thread that sleeps for 30 seconds in the background. It does not populate the *AsyncResult* object because this happens in the background when the sleeping thread wakes up later. In both cases, the code invokes the callback method in the client application, passing the *AsyncResult* object as its parameter. The client application will retrieve the results of the calculation from this object. The same *AsyncResult* object is also returned as the result of this method (this is a requirement of the *IAsyncResult* design pattern).

The method also displays message boxes that help you to trace the execution of the method and establish whether the operation is running synchronously or asynchronously.

6. Add the *end* method shown below to the *AdventureWorksAdmin* class:

```
public class AdventureWorksAdmin : IAdventureWorksAdmin
{
    ...
    public int EndCalculateTotalValueOfStock(IAsyncResult r)
```

```
    {
        // Wait until the AsyncResult object indicates the
        // operation is complete
        AsyncResult<int> result = r as AsyncResult<int>;
        if (!result.CompletedSynchronously)
        {
            System.Threading.WaitHandle waitHandle = result.AsyncWaitHandle;
            waitHandle.WaitOne();
        }

        // Return the calculated value in the Data field
        return result.Data;
    }
    ...
}
```

> **Note** You can find this code in the file EndCalculateTotalValueOfStock.txt, which is located in the Chapter 12 folder.

This method is invoked when the *begin* method completes. The purpose of this method is to retrieve the result of the calculation from the *Data* property in the *AsyncResult* object passed in as the parameter. If the operation is being performed asynchronously, it might not have completed yet. (Applications invoking the *begin* method for an asynchronous operation can call the *end* method at any time after the *begin* finishes, so the *end* method should ensure that the operation has completed before returning.) In this case, the method waits until the *AsyncResult* object indicates that the operation has finished before extracting the data and returning.

7. Add the following private method to the *AdventureWorksAdmin* class:

```
public class AdventureWorksAdmin : IAdventureWorksAdmin
{
    ...
    private void EndAsyncSleep(IAsyncResult ar)
    {
        // This delegate indicates that the "complex" calculation
        // has finished
        AsyncResult<int> calcTotalValueResult = (AsyncResult<int>)ar.AsyncState;
        calcTotalValueResult.Data = 9999999;
        calcTotalValueResult.Complete();

        System.Windows.MessageBox.Show("Asynchronous sleep completed");
    }
    ...
}
```

> **Note** You can find this code in the file EndAsyncSleep.txt, which is located in the Chapter 12 folder.

If the *begin* method decides to perform its task asynchronously, it simulates performing the calculation by creating a new thread and sleeping for 30 seconds. The *EndAsyncSleep* method is registered as a callback when the background sleep starts. When the 30 seconds have expired, the operating system reawakens the thread and invokes this method. This method populates the *Data* field of the *AsyncResult* object, and then indicates that the operation is now complete. This releases the main thread in the service, which was waiting in the *end* method and allows it to return the data to the client application.

Notice that the values returned are different depending on whether the service performs the operation synchronously (*5555555*) or asynchronously (*9999999*).

8. Rebuild the solution.

Invoke the *CalculateTotalValueOfStock* Operation in the WCF Client Application

1. In the AdventureWorksAdminTestClient project, expand the Service References folder, right-click the *AdventureWorksAdmin* service reference, and then click Update Service Reference.

This action generates a new version of the client proxy, including the *CalculateTotal ValueOfStock* operation.

2. In the Solution Explorer, ensure that the Show All Files check box is selected.

3. Expand the *AdventureWorksAdmin* service reference, expand the Reference.svcmap folder, and open the Reference.cs file in the Code And Text Editor window. Examine the definition of the service contract in the *AdministrativeService* interface. Notice that the new operation is called *CalculateTotalValueOfStock* and that there is no sign of the *begin* and *end* methods that implement this operation; the fact that the operation is implemented asynchronously is totally transparent to the client application.

4. Edit the Program.cs file. Remove the statements in the *try* block that invoke the *Generate DailySalesReport* operation and the *Console.WriteLine* statements. Replace them with the following code shown in bold:

```
static void Main(string[] args)
{
    try
    {
        AdministrativeServiceClient proxy = new AdministrativeServiceClient(
            "WS2007HttpBinding_AdministrativeService");

        int totalValue = proxy.CalculateTotalValueOfStock("First Calculation");
        Console.WriteLine("Total value of stock is {0}", totalValue);

        totalValue = proxy.CalculateTotalValueOfStock("Second Calculation");
        Console.WriteLine("Total value of stock is {0}", totalValue);

        totalValue = proxy.CalculateTotalValueOfStock("Third Calculation");
```

```
Console.WriteLine("Total value of stock is {0}", totalValue);

        proxy.Close();
    }
    ...
}
```

These statements simply invoke the *CalculateTotalValueOfStock* method three times and display the results. Hopefully, the service will execute at least one of these calls in a different manner from the other two (either synchronously or asynchronously).

5. Start the solution without debugging.

   What happens next depends on the value of the random number generated by the service to determine whether it should perform the operation synchronously or asynchronously. If you are unlucky, you must wait for 20 seconds before you see the first message box appear.

   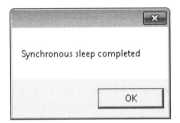

   This is because the random number generator in the *BeginCalculateTotalValueOfStock* method produced an even number and is executing the method synchronously. This should be followed by the following message box:

   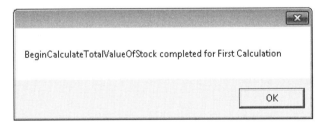

   You will see the result (*5555555*) displayed in the client application console window as soon as you click OK in the message box.

   If you only see the second message box, the *BeginCalculateTotalValueOfStock* has decided to execute the method asynchronously. You will then need to wait for up to 30 seconds after closing the message box, until you see the following one appear.

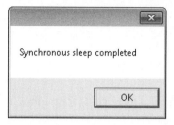

The value *9999999* should also appear in the client application console window. This process will be repeated for each of the three calls that the client application makes to the *CalculateTotalValueOfStock* operation.

6. Press Enter to close the client application console window.

This is all very well, but so far, you have gone to a lot of trouble to allow the service to determine the best strategy for running a potentially lengthy or expensive operation. Worse, as far as the client application is concerned, everything is still synchronous; each call to the *CalculateTotalValueOfStock* operation was blocked until it completed. Fortunately, you can also enable asynchronous operations on the client by regenerating the proxy with the */async* flag, as mentioned earlier. That is what you will do in the next exercise.

Invoke the *CalculateTotalValueOfStock* Operation Asynchronously

1. In the AdventureWorksAdminTestClient project, expand the Service References folder, right-click the *AdventureWorksAdmin* service reference, and then click Configure Service Reference. In the Service Reference Settings dialog box, select the Generate Asynchronous Operations check box, and then click OK.

This action generates another version of the proxy that enables the client application to invoke operations in the services asynchronously.

2. Examine the Reference.cs file under the Reference.svcmap folder in the *AdventureWorks Admin* service reference folder.

> **Tip** If you still have this file open in the Code And Text Editor window from earlier exercises, close the file and reopen it to refresh the display.

You should see that the client proxy now contains *begin* and *end* methods for both of the operations in the service contract, so you can call them asynchronously (the synchronous versions of each method are still present). These changes are implemented only in the client proxy; the service is not actually aware of them.

3. Edit the Program.cs file in the AdventureWorksAdminTestClient project. Remove the
statements that invoke the *CalculateTotalValueOfStock* operation, the *Console.WriteLine*
statements, and the statement that closes the proxy. Replace them with the following
code shown in bold:

```
static void Main(string[] args)
{
    try
    {
        AdministrativeServiceClient proxy = new AdministrativeServiceClient(
            "WS2007HttpBinding_AdministrativeService");

        proxy.BeginCalculateTotalValueOfStock("First Calculation",
            CalculateTotalValueCallback, proxy);
        proxy.BeginCalculateTotalValueOfStock("Second Calculation",
            CalculateTotalValueCallback, proxy);
        proxy.BeginCalculateTotalValueOfStock("Third Calculation",
            CalculateTotalValueCallback, proxy);

    }
    ...
}
```

This code invokes the client-side asynchronous version of the *CalculateTotalValueOf
Stock* method three times. The results will be handled by a method called *Calculate
TotalValueCallback*, which you will add next. A reference to the proxy is passed in as the
state parameter.

It is important that you remove the *proxy.Close* statement. If you close the proxy at this
point, the WCF runtime will destroy the channel stack on the client side before the asynchronous calls have completed, and the client application will be unable to obtain the
responses from the service.

4. Add the following method immediately after the end of the *Main* method in the
Program class:

```
static void CalculateTotalValueCallback(IAsyncResult asyncResult)
{
    int total = ((AdministrativeServiceClient)asyncResult.AsyncState).
        EndCalculateTotalValueOfStock(asyncResult);
    Console.WriteLine("Total value of stock is {0}", total);
}
```

This is the callback method. When the *CalculateTotalValueOfStock* operation completes,
the proxy will run this method. It retrieves the object passed back from the service (this
is the state object, which is a reference to the proxy passed in by the client application
as the third parameter in the *BeginCalculateTotalValueOfStock* method) and uses this
object to invoke the *EndCalculateTotalValueOfStock* method. The value returned by the
end method is the calculated total value of the stock from the service.

5. Start the solution without debugging.

The client application starts and immediately displays the message "Press ENTER to finish." This is because the calls to the *BeginCalculateTotalValueOfStock* method are no longer blocking the client application.

Do not press Enter just yet; allow the application to continue running. After 20 or 30 seconds, you should see the message boxes that appeared in the previous exercise, indicating whether the service is executing each request synchronously or asynchronously. The results of the calculations should appear in the client console window as the operations complete.

6. After all three results have been displayed, press Enter to close the client application console window.

From these exercises, you should now understand the difference between invoking an operation asynchronously in a client application and implementing an operation that supports asynchronous processing in the service. A developer can decide whether to implement an operation as a pair of methods implementing the *IAsyncResult* design pattern independently from any client applications. These methods appear as a single operation to the client application, and the implementation is totally transparent.

Similarly, when creating a WCF client application, developers wishing to invoke operations asynchronously need only generate an asynchronous proxy (either by using the Add Service Reference Wizard, or by specifying the */async* flag with the *svcutil* utility). Whether the client application invokes an operation synchronously is transparent to the service.

Finally, you should also realize that although a client application can invoke an operation asynchronously, the service may choose to implement the operation synchronously, and vice versa. The result is complete flexibility on the part of both client applications and services.

There is one further point worth making. You can define both synchronous and asynchronous versions of the same operation in a service contract, as shown in the following:

```
[ServiceContract(...)]
public interface IAdventureWorksAdmin
{
    ...
    // Synchronous operation
    [OperationContract]
    int CalculateTotalValueOfStock(string id);

    // Asynchronous version
    [OperationContract(AsyncPattern = true)]
    IAsyncResult BeginCalculateTotalValueOfStock(string id, AsyncCallback cb, object s);
    int EndCalculateTotalValueOfStock(IAsyncResult r);
}
```

However, if you do this, both operations appear in the WSDL description of the service as the same action (*CalculateTotalValueOfStock*). In this case, WCF will not throw an exception but will always use the synchronous version of the operation in preference to the asynchronous version (WCF assumes that the synchronous version achieves faster throughput). So, don't define synchronous and asynchronous versions of the same operation in the same service contract.

Using Message Queues

Message queues are the ultimate in asynchronous technology. Message queues can provide a durable, reliable, transacted transport for messages. Furthermore, a client application sending messages and a service receiving them do not need to be running at the same time. You pay a price for this flexibility though: message queues are inherently a one-way transport, so implementing applications and services that send requests and expect to receive responses requires much careful design. Message queues are also slower than other transports, primarily because of their support for reliability and durability; the Windows operating system stores messages in files on disk. While this means that messages held in a message queue can survive machine shutdown and power failure, that robustness comes at the cost of the additional I/O involved in creating and transmitting the messages.

 Note You can specify that messages are not durable if performance is more important than reliability. So-called *volatile* messages are cached in memory rather than disk and consequently do not survive machine restarts or crashes.

If you have already built message queuing applications using Microsoft Message Queue Server (MSMQ), you will appreciate that although the programming model is straightforward, it is fundamentally different than the programming practices you adopt when building a more traditional client/server application. However, one of the goals of WCF is to provide a consistent model for sending and receiving, irrespective of the underlying transport, so using message queues with WCF is very similar to using most other transports. However, it is somewhat different from the message queuing techniques you might have used in the past.

In the final set of exercises in this chapter, you will see just how easy it is to use message queues as a transport for asynchronous one-way operations.

Implement a WCF Service that Uses Message Queuing

1. Using Visual Studio, open the solution file AdventureWorksAdmin.sln located in the Microsoft Press\WCF Step By Step\Chapter 12\MSMQ folder within your Documents folder.

   This solution contains two projects: AdventureWorksAdminHost, which is a self-hosted version of the *AdventureWorksAdmin* WCF service, and AdventureWorksAdminTest Client, which is a client application for testing the service.

    Note Don't try to build this solution yet; it is not complete.

2. In Solution Explorer, open the IService.cs file for the AdventureWorksAdminHost project in the Code And Text Editor window.

   This is the code that defines the service contract in the *IAdventureWorksAdmin* interface. It should look familiar because it is very similar to the service you created in the first set of exercises in this chapter. The service contains a single operation: *GenerateDailySales Report*. Notice that the operation contract still specifies that this is a one-way operation. This is important because all operations in a service accessed through a message queue must be one-way operations.

3. Open the Service.cs file in the Code And Text Editor window.

   This file contains the *AdventureWorksAdmin* class that implements the *IAdventureWorks Admin* interface. Notice that the *GenerateDailySalesReport* method now only waits for 10 seconds (assume that you are running on a faster machine than before, so the processing takes less time).

4. Open the HostController.xaml file in the Design View window. This is a version of the window that you previously used to host the *ProductsService* service.

5. Examine the code behind this window in the HostController.xaml.cs file. The logic in this form is the same as before. The only difference is that this form now hosts the *Adventure WorksAdmin* service.

6. Edit the app.config file for the AdventureWorksAdminHost project by using the Service Configuration Editor. The application configuration file does not currently contain any information about the service.

7. In the Configuration pane, right-click Services, and then click New Service.

   A new, empty service definition is added to the configuration file that you can configure manually. This approach is an alternative to using the Create A New Service Wizard.

8. In the right pane, in the *Name* property, type **AdventureWorksAdmin** (this is the name of the class implementing the service).

9. In the Configuration pane, right-click the Endpoints folder under the *AdventureWorks-Admin* service, and then click New Service Endpoint.

10. In the right pane, set the properties of the endpoint by using the values in the following table. Leave any other properties at their default values.

Property	Value
Name	AdventureWorksAdminMsmqBinding
Address	net.msmq://localhost/private/AdventureWorksAdmin
Binding	netMsmqBinding
Contract	IAdventureWorksAdmin

The format for a message queuing URI consists of the scheme "net.msmq" followed by the name of the queue. MSMQ identifies queues using a syntax very similar to HTTP URLs, although the semantics are somewhat different. The "private" part of the URI indicates that this is a private message queue, meaning that it can be accessed only from applications running on the local computer. If you are using a computer that is a member of a Windows domain, you can also create public message queues that can be accessed by code running on other computers. The actual name of the message queue is "AdventureWorksAdmin."

> **More Info** For a detailed description of message queues, see the topic "Using Messaging Components" in the documentation provided with Visual Studio (also available on the Microsoft Web site at *http://msdn.microsoft.com/en-us/library/fzc40kc8.aspx*).

11. In the Configuration pane, right-click the Bindings folder, and then click New Binding Configuration. In the Create A New Binding dialog box, click the *netMsmqBinding* binding type, and then click OK.

12. In the right pane, set the *Name* property of this binding configuration to **AdventureWorksAdminMsmqBindingConfig**.

You can set binding properties that control many aspects of the way the message queue works. For example, the *Durable* property determines whether messages should be capable of surviving process failure or machine shutdown and restart; setting this property to *False* makes messages volatile. The *ExactlyOnce* property is the MSMQ analog of reliable messaging; setting this property to *True* guarantees that messages will be received once and once only, and messages will not be lost or inadvertently retrieved more than once by concurrent instances of the service from the message queue. Setting this property to *True* requires the message queue to be transactional (you can specify whether a queue is transactional when you create it, by using the Computer Management Console).

13. Click the Security tab. Modify the security settings of the binding configuration, and set the *Mode* property to **None**.

    Message queues support message-level security and transport-level security, although the implementation of transport-level security is peculiar to MSMQ and does not require you to configure SSL. If you implement message-level security, you can specify the client credential type. You should note that the authentication mechanism implemented by MSMQ message-level security requires that the message queue server must be configured to provide a certificate for the message queue used by the binding.

> **Important** For simplicity, this example uses a local, unprotected private message queue that is accessible only on the host computer. In a production environment, you will most likely use public queues, which should be protected by using transport-level or message-level security.

14. In the Configuration pane, click the *AdventureWorksAdminMsmqEndpoint* endpoint definition in the Endpoints folder under the *AdventureWorksAdmin* service. In the right pane, set the *BindingConfiguration* property to *AdventureWorksAdminMsmqBinding Config*.

15. Save the configuration file then exit the Service Configuration Editor.

16. In Visual Studio, build the AdventureWorksAdminHost project. Do not try to build the entire solution, because the client application is not yet complete; that is your next task.

Send Messages to a Message Queue from a WCF Client Application

1. Open a Visual Studio Command Prompt window and move to the Microsoft Press\WCF Step By Step\Chapter 12\MSMQ\AdventureWorksAdminHost\bin\Debug folder. Type the following commands to generate the client proxy from the service contract compiled into the *AdventureWorksAdminHost.exe* assembly:

```
svcutil AdventureWorksAdminHost.exe

svcutil /namespace:*,AdventureWorksAdminTestClient.AdventureWorksAdmin
    adventure-works.com.2010.07.01.wsdl *.xsd /out:AdventureWorksAdminProxy.cs
```

   The code for the proxy is generated in the AdventureWorksAdminProxy.cs file. Note that you cannot easily use the Add Service Reference Wizard in Visual Studio to add a reference to a WCF service that uses the MSMQ transport.

2. Return to Visual Studio and add the AdventureWorksAdminProxy.cs file that you just created to the AdventureWorksAdminTestClient project.

3. Open the Program.cs file for the AdventureWorksAdminTestClient project in the Code And Text Editor window. Again, this code should look very familiar because it is almost identical to the client application you developed in the first set of exercises in this chapter for testing one-way operations. There is an additional prompt—"Press ENTER to send messages"—in the *try* block, and you must specify a binding to use when instantiating the proxy. Before you do this, you must define the binding you are going to use and add it to the application configuration file.

4. Edit the app.config file for the AdventureWorksAdminTestClient project by using the Service Configuration Editor.

5. In the Configuration pane, expand the Client folder, right-click the Endpoints folder, and then click New Client Endpoint. As before, you will enter the details of the client endpoint manually rather than by using the New Client Element Wizard.

6. In the Client Endpoint pane, set the properties of the endpoint using the values shown in the following table. Leave any other properties with their default values.

Property	Value
Name	MsmqBinding_AdventureWorksAdmin
Address	net.msmq://localhost/private/AdventureWorksAdmin
Binding	netMsmqBinding
Contract	AdventureWorksAdminTestClient.AdventureWorksAdmin.AdministrativeService

7. Add a binding configuration based on the *netMsmqBinding* type. Set the *Name* property of this binding configuration to **AdventureWorksAdminMsmqBindingConfig**. Change the security settings of the binding configuration and set the *Mode* property to **None**.

8. Return to the *MsmqBinding_AdventureWorksAdmin* endpoint definition and set the *BindingConfiguration* property to **AdventureWorksAdminMsmqBindingConfig**.

9. Save the configuration file and exit the Service Configuration Editor.

10. In the Program.cs file for the AdventureWorksAdminTestClient project, modify the statement that creates the proxy object and replace the text "INSERT ENDPOINT HERE" with the name of the MSMQ endpoint, as shown in bold in the following:

```
AdministrativeServiceClient proxy =
    new AdministrativeServiceClient("MsmqBinding_AdventureWorksAdmin");
```

This completes the code for the service and the client application. You can now create the message queue and then test the service.

Create the *AdventureWorksAdmin* Queue and Test the Service

1. On the Windows Start menu, right-click Computer, and then click Manage to open the Computer Management console.

2. In the Computer Management console, expand the Services And Applications node in the left pane, expand the Message Queuing node, right-click the Private Queues folder, point to New, and then click Private Queue.

3. In the New Private Queue dialog box, type **AdventureWorksAdmin** in the Queue name text box, select the Transactional option, and then click OK.

> **Note** If you don't want the overhead of transactional message queues, you must set the *ExactlyOnce* property of the binding configuration for the *netMsmqBinding* binding to **False**.

4. Leave the Computer Management console open and return to Visual Studio.

5. Start the solution without debugging.

   In the client console window, press Enter to send the two *GenerateDailySalesReport* messages—but don't start the service running yet. Notice that the client successfully sends the messages, even though the service is not running. Press Enter to close the client console window.

6. Return to the Computer Management console. Expand the *AdventureWorksAdmin* queue in the Private Queues folder under Message Queuing, and then click the Queue Messages folder. Two messages should be displayed in the right pane:

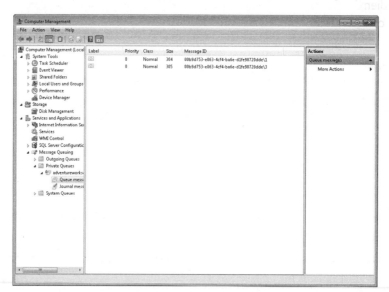

Tip If no messages appear, click Refresh on the Action menu to update the display.

If you double-click a message, you can display its properties, including the text in the body of the message.

7. In the AdventureWorks Admin Host window, click Start.

The service starts, retrieves each message from the queue in turn, and processes them (remember that each message takes at least 10 seconds to process, and the host application will be unresponsive while the messages are being processed because it is not multi-threaded, for simplicity). The operation displays a message box after processing each message.

Stop the service and close the AdventureWorks Admin Host window after the second message box has displayed.

8. Return to the Computer Management console that's displaying the messages in the message queue. From the Action menu, select Refresh to update the display. Both messages should disappear because they have now been removed from the message queue by the WCF service.

9. Close the Computer Management console.

MSMQ provides an easy-to-use mechanism for implementing asynchronous operations. However, the *netMsmqBinding* binding restricts you to implementing one-way operations. If a service needs to send a response, it can do so asynchronously by sending a message to a queue to which the client application can connect. This involves implementing a different message for each client (for privacy) and correlating messages so the client application knows which response corresponds to which request.

 More Info For more information and an example of using message queues to implement asynchronous request/response messaging, see the topic "Two-Way Communication" in the documentation provided with Visual Studio (also available on the Microsoft Web site at *http://msdn.microsoft.com/en-us/library/ms752264.aspx*).

Summary

In this chapter, you have seen three ways to send and process messages to improve the responsiveness of WCF client applications and services and exploit multiple threads in a service to improve throughput. You should use one-way messaging for long-running operations that do not return any data. For operations that do pass information back to the client application, you can generate an asynchronous client proxy and invoke these operations asynchronously. A service can also choose to implement a long-running operation asynchronously—independent from the way in which the client application actually invokes the operation—by setting the *AsyncPattern* property of the operation contract to *true*, and then implementing the IAsync Result design pattern. If client applications and services execute at different times, you can implement message queuing and the MSMQ transport.

Chapter 13
Implementing a WCF Service for Good Performance

After completing this chapter, you will be able to:

- Manage service scalability by using throttling to control use of resources.

- Use the Message Transmission Optimization Mechanism to transmit messages containing binary data in a standardized, efficient manner.

- Explain how to enable streaming for a binding and design operations that support streaming.

Good performance is a key factor in most applications and services. You can help to ensure that a WCF service maintains throughput, remains responsive, and is scalable by thoughtful design and by selecting the appropriate features that meet this design. The examples that you have seen so far include careful use of transactions, session state, reliable messaging, and asynchronous operations.

There are other aspects that can impact performance, such as security. As discussed in earlier chapters, implementing message-level security and secure conversations results in a complex exchange of messages to negotiate the protocol to use and the exchange of identity information. Messages themselves are also bigger because of the additional security information included in the message headers—they take longer to traverse the network and require more memory to process. Encryption and decryption are also very resource-intensive tasks. However, all these are necessary parts of a secure system, so most people are willing to trade some performance for assurance that their data and identity information remain private. (If decryption were quick and easy to perform it would also be fairly useless; the more resources it takes to decrypt a message, the better protected the message is.)

An important aspect of maintaining performance is ensuring that a service does not exhaust the resources available on the host computer, causing the system to slow down and possibly stop altogether. WCF provides *service throttling* to help control resource utilization. Using this feature can greatly aid the scalability of your service. Load-balancing is another technique that you can employ to distribute requests across multiple servers and maintain even throughput; Chapter 14, "Discovering Services and Routing Messages," describes a simple implementation of load balancing by building a specialized WCF service. You can also build a load-balancing infrastructure based on Microsoft Windows Network Load Balancing and Windows Server AppFabric, although the details of this technology are beyond the scope of this book.

Using the appropriate encoding mechanism when transmitting data can also have a signifi-cant effect on performance. As you have seen, WCF supports both text and binary encoding of messages. Binary encoding is often more compact and incurs less network overhead, but the format is proprietary and cannot easily be used with applications and services running on non-Microsoft platforms. However, WCF also supports Message Transmission Optimization Mechanism (MTOM), which provides a standardized, interoperable, and efficient format for transmitting large blocks of binary data.

MTOM is useful if you know how much data the service is going to transmit. Some services emit long data blocks of indeterminate size. This type of data is best transmitted as a stream, and WCF also provides support for outputting streams from a service.

In this chapter, you will examine how to use service throttling to assist in maintaining scalabil-ity, how to encode data by using MTOM to reduce the overhead of transmitting large binary data objects, and how to enable streaming to make best use of network bandwidth.

Using Service Throttling to Control Resource Use

You can use service throttling to prevent over-consumption of resources in a WCF service. You might recall from Chapter 11, "Programmatically Controlling the Configuration and Communications," that when a message received by a service host reaches the top of the channel stack, it passes to a *ChannelDispatcher* object, which in turn passes it to the appro-priate *EndpointDispatcher* object, which invokes the corresponding method in the appro-priate service instance. However, before forwarding the request to the *EndpointDispatcher* object, the *ChannelDispatcher* object can examine the current load on the service and elect to delay the request if it would cause the service to exceed the permissible load. In that case, the request is blocked and held in an internal queue until the load on the service eases. The *ChannelDispatcher* object has a property called *ServiceThrottle* that you can use to help con-trol how the *ChannelDispatcher* decides whether to block and queue requests or let them execute. The *ServiceThrottle* property is an instance of the *ServiceThrottle* class, which itself exposes three more integer properties:

- *MaxConcurrentInstances*   This property specifies the maximum number of concurrent service instances that the service host will permit.

- *MaxConcurrentCalls*   This property specifies the maximum number of concurrent mes-sages that the service host will process. If a client application makes a large number of concurrent calls, either as the result of invoking one-way operations or by using client-side multi-threading, it can quickly monopolize a service. In this scenario, you might want to limit each client to a single thread in the service by setting the *ConcurrencyMode* property of the service to *ConcurrencyMode.Single*. The client application can continue running asynchronously and should remain responsive to the user, but requests submit-ted by the client application will be processed in a serial manner by the service.

■ *MaxConcurrentSessions*   This property specifies the maximum number of concurrent sessions that the service host will permit. Client applications are responsible for establishing and terminating sessions and can make several calls to the service during a session. Clients that create long-running sessions can cause other clients to be blocked, so keep sessions as brief as possible and avoid performing tasks such as waiting for user input.

Configuring Service Throttling

By default, the *ServiceThrottle* property of the *ChannelDispatcher* object is set to *null* and the WCF runtime uses its own default values for the maximum number of concurrent instances, calls, and sessions (these default values are described later). To control scalability, you should arrange for the WCF runtime to create a *ServiceThrottle* object and explicitly set these properties to values suitable for your environment, taking into account the expected number of concurrent client applications and the work that they are likely to perform. You can perform this task in code by creating a *ServiceThrottlingBehavior* object, setting its properties (the *Service ThrottlingBehavior* class provides the same properties as the *ServiceThrottle* class), and adding it to the collection of behaviors attached to the *ServiceHost* object, as described in Chapter 11. You must do this before opening the *ServiceHost* object. The following code shows an example:

```
// Required for the ServiceThrottlingBehavior class
using System.ServiceModel.Description;
...
ServiceHost host = new ServiceHost(...);
ServiceThrottlingBehavior throttleBehavior = new ServiceThrottlingBehavior();
throttleBehavior.MaxConcurrentCalls = 40;
throttleBehavior.MaxConcurrentInstances = 20;
throttleBehavior.MaxConcurrentSessions = 20;
host.Description.Behaviors.Add(throttleBehavior);
host.Open();
...
```

However, be warned that the values of the properties in a *ServiceThrottle* object can have a drastic effect on the response time and throughput of a WCF service. You should actively monitor the performance of the WCF service and be prepared to change those settings if the computer hosting the service is struggling. Additionally, clients blocked by limits that are set too low can result in an excessive number of time-outs or other errors that will occur in the client application or the channel stack, so be prepared to catch and handle them.

Because you might need to change the *ServiceThrottle* property values, a more flexible way to create a *ServiceThrottle* object and set its properties is to add a service behavior that contains the *<serviceThrottling>* element to the service configuration file. This is the approach that you will adopt in the following exercise. You will also modify the service host to display the current throttle settings.

Apply Throttling to the *ShoppingCartService* Service

1. Using Visual Studio, open the solution file ShoppingCart.sln located in the Microsoft Press\WCF Step By Step\Chapter 13\Throttling folder (within your Documents folder).

    This solution contains a simplified non-transactional version of the *ShoppingCartService* service that does not actually update the database. It also contains an extended version of the client application that opens multiple concurrent sessions to the service.

    > **Note** The rationale behind not updating the database or using transactions is to allow you to concentrate on the throttling semantics of a service and not worry about any potential locking and concurrency issues in the database. In the real world, you would have to take all these factors into account.

2. Open the IShoppingCartService.cs file for the ShoppingCartService project in the Code And Text Editor window. Notice that the service specifies that sessions are required in the *ServiceContract* attribute of the *IShoppingCartService* interface. Open the Shopping CartServics.cs file and observe that the *ServiceBehavior* attribute of the *ShoppingCart ServiceImpl* class specifies the *PerSession* instance context mode.

3. Examine the *AddItemToCart* method in this class. This method starts with a *WriteLine* statement that displays the method name. A corresponding *WriteLine* statement has been added at each point at which the method can terminate. You will use these statements to trace the progress of each instance of the service as it runs. Also notice that the method contains the statement *System.Threading.Thread.Sleep(10000)* immediately after the first *WriteLine* statement. Although this method still queries the database, it no longer performs updates for reasons described in the previous note. This statement slows the method down by waiting for 10 seconds, simulating the time taken to perform the database update (assume the database update operation is very time consuming). The purpose of all this is to make it a little easier to observe the effects of the service throttling parameters. The other public methods, *RemoveItemFromCart*, *GetShopping-Cart*, and *Checkout*, have been amended in the same way for this example.

4. Open the Program.cs file in the ShoppingCartClient project and locate the *doClientWork* method. This method contains code that creates a new instance of the proxy object and then invokes the various operations in the *ShoppingCartService* service, in much the same way as you have seen in earlier chapters. The method contains *WriteLine* statements that display its progress in the console window. The output includes a number that identifies the client (this number is passed in as the parameter to the *doClientWork* method). The client connects to the service using a standard TCP binding.

5. Examine the *Main* method. This method employs the *Parallel.For* construct to asynchronously call the *doClientWork* method 10 times, passing in a value that identifies each iteration as the client number parameter. Each call creates a new parallel task. This simulates 10 different but identifiable clients connecting to the service at the same time.

6. Open the Program.cs file in the ShoppingCartHost project. This is the application that hosts the service. Add the following *using* statement to the top of the file:

```
using System.ServiceModel.Dispatcher;
```

This namespace contains the *ServiceThrottle* and *ChannelDispatcher* classes.

7. Add the following code (shown in bold) to the *Main* method, immediately after the statement that opens the *ServiceHost* object:

```
static void Main(string[] args)
{
    ...
    host.Open();

    ChannelDispatcher dispatcher = (ChannelDispatcher)host.ChannelDispatchers[0];
    ServiceThrottle throttle = dispatcher.ServiceThrottle;
    if (throttle == null)
        Console.WriteLine("Service is using default throttling behavior");
    else
        Console.WriteLine("Instances: {0}\nCalls: {1}\nSessions: {2}",
            throttle.MaxConcurrentInstances, throttle.MaxConcurrentCalls,
            throttle.MaxConcurrentSessions);

    Console.WriteLine("Service running");
    ...
}
```

This code retrieves a reference to the *ChannelDispatcher* object used by the service (in this example, the service has only a single binding, so the WCF runtime creates only a single *ChannelDispatcher* when the host starts the service running). The code then examines the *ServiceThrottle* property of this *ChannelDispatcher* object. If it is *null*, then the administrator or developer has not specified any customized throttling settings, so the service uses the default values. If the *ServiceThrottle* property is not *null*, then the service is using a customized throttling behavior, and it displays the values provided by the administrator or developer.

8. Start the solution without debugging. In the service console window, notice that the service is using the default throttling behavior.

Press Enter in the client application console window that's displaying the message "Press ENTER when the service has started."

The client console window displays messages in the form "Client *n*: 1st AddItemToCart," where *n* is the number that identifies the client instance. Note that the *Parallel.For* construct does not guarantee the order in which the clients start, so do not be surprised if, for example, messages from Client 5 appear before those of Client 0 in the client application console window.

In the service host console window, you should see the message "AddItemToCart opera-tion started" appear as each client sends an *AddItemToCart* request, as shown in the fol-lowing image (the client application console window is the upper image, and the service host is the lower one):

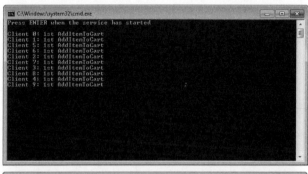

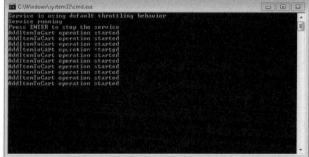

This indicates that the service is handling multiple clients simultaneously. As each method completes, the service displays "AddItemToCart operation completed" messages and the clients invoke further operations. At this point, the output might become a little more chaotic, but the important point is that in this "unthrottled" state, the service has not prevented any of the 10 clients from invoking operations at the same time (the default value for the maximum number of concurrent calls is greater than 10).

When the message "Tests complete: Press ENTER to finish" appears in the client appli-cation console window, press Enter. In the service host console window press Enter to terminate the service host.

The behavior you've just seen used the default settings. Next, you'll customize them.

9. In Visual Studio, edit the App.config file for the ShoppingCartHost project by using the Service Configuration Editor.

10. In the Configuration pane, expand the Advanced folder, and then click the Service Behaviors folder. In the right pane, click the New Service Behavior Configuration link.

    In the right pane, change the *Name* property of the new behavior to **ThrottleBehavior**.

12. In the lower part of the right pane, click Add then add a *serviceThrottling* element to the behavior.

13. In the Configuration pane, click the *serviceThrottling* behavior element under the *Throttle Behavior* behavior node.

The properties for this element appear: *MaxConcurrentCalls*, *MaxConcurrentInstances*, and *MaxConcurrentSessions*. Each property displays a default value:

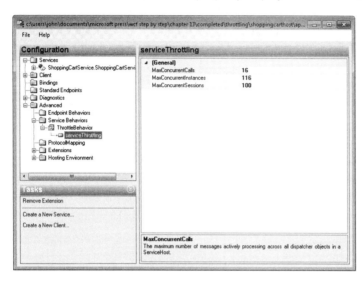

14. Change the value of the *MaxConcurrentCalls* property to **3**.

15. In the Configuration pane, click the *ShoppingCartService.ShoppingCartServiceImpl* service in the Services folder. In the right pane, set the *BehaviorConfiguration* property to **ThrottleBehavior**.

16. Save the configuration file but leave the Service Configuration Editor open.

17. In Visual Studio, start the solution without debugging. In the service host console window, you should see that the service is now using the throttling behavior you have just defined.

You may be a little surprised at the values shown in the service host console window (and the values that you see might be different from those shown, for reasons that I am about to describe). In the Service Configuration Editor, the values generated for the properties of the *serviceThrottling* element are not necessarily the actual values used by the service host unless you modify them. In WCF 4.0, the default values are determined based on the available resources of the host computer. For example on a machine with a single-core processor, the default value for the maximum number of concurrent instances is 116, the default value for the maximum number of concurrent calls is 16, and the default value for the maximum number of concurrent sessions is 100 (the values you saw displayed in the Service Configuration Editor).

On a dual-core machine, you will find that the defaults are doubled—even though the default values displayed for the *serviceThrottling* behavior element are still those shown in the image in step 13. Additionally, there is a relationship between the default values such that *MaxConcurrentInstances = MaxConcurrentCalls + MaxConcurrentSessions*. This means that if you change the *MaxConcurrentCalls* property but leave the others unchanged, the WCF runtime will generate values for them. I built and tested the service on a computer with a dual-core processor. This is why the maximum number of sessions displayed by the service host console window is 200 rather than 100, and the maximum number of instances is 203 (203 = 3 + 200).

Of course, if you specify your own values for *MaxConcurrentInstances* and *MaxConcurrent Sessions*, then WCF will use those rather than calculate them.

18. Press Enter in the client application console window.

In the client console window, all 10 clients output the message "Client *n*: 1st AddItemTo Cart," but the service host console shows something different than before; initially only three "AddItemToCart operation started" messages appear. This is because the service now supports only three concurrent operation calls. The *ChannelDispatcher* queues each subsequent request. As each call finishes, displaying the "AddItemToCart operation completed" message, the *ChannelDispatcher* releases the next request from its queue, and you see the message "AddItemToCart operation started" appear for the next client. Thereafter, each time an operation completes, the *ChannelDispatcher* releases the next request. You should see more or less (it probably won't be exact) alternating "completed" and "started" messages until all the clients have finished their work, because the time required by the service to process each request is at least 10 seconds, which is longer than the time each client takes to send the next request after the previous one completes.

Note The *ChannelDispatcher* releases requests from its queue on a first-come, first-served basis. Currently, WCF does not allow you to specify that the requests for one client should have a higher priority than another.

When the client application has finished, press Enter to close the client application console window, and then press Enter to close the service host console window.

19. Return to the Service Configuration Editor and click the *serviceThrottling* service behavior element in the Configuration pane. In the right pane, increase the *MaxConcurrentCalls* property to **16** (the default value) and set the *MaxConcurrentSessions* property to **3**. Save the configuration file then close the Service Configuration Editor.

20. In Visual Studio, start the solution without debugging. In the service host console window, you should see that the service is using the updated throttling behavior (*MaxConcurrentInstances* should now be calculated as 19 on a dual-core machine).

Press Enter in the client application console window.

Again, in the client console window, all 10 clients output the message "Client *n*: 1st AddItemToCart," and the service console window shows 3 calls to the *AddItemToCart* operation starting and completing. However, when these calls complete, if you observe the messages in the client console window, you will see that only the first clients invoke the *AddItemToCart* operation the second time; the other clients are held pending by the *ChannelDispatcher* because it has reached the maximum allowed number of concurrent sessions. The first 3 clients complete their cycle of work, calling *AddItemToCart* a third time, followed by the *GetShoppingCart* operation and the *Checkout* operation. Only when *Checkout* completes and a client closes its session before terminating is the next client allowed to continue. You should see messages occurring in batches of 3 in the client console window (3 "2nd AddItemToCart" messages, 3 "3rd AddItemToCart" messages, and so on), as each set of 3 sessions executes.

Some of the later sessions will report the exception "The operation did not complete within the allotted time-out of 00:01:00. ...." This occurs because the time between when they submitted their initial *AddItemToCart* request and when the service allowed that request to be handled exceeded the time-out limit specified for the client binding.

 Note Although the *ChannelDispatcher* queues the initial requests that create each session in the order in which they are received, once a session starts running, there is no guarantee that the session will be serviced before or after any other running session. For example, when sessions for clients 3, 4, and 5 are running, you might see messages indicating that operations for client 4 execute before those of client 3; this is due to the scheduling algorithm in the operating system which decides when to execute each thread in the client and in the service.

When the tests have completed, press Enter to close the client application console window, and then press Enter to close the service console window.

This exercise showed the effects of using service throttling to control the maximum number of concurrent calls and sessions that a service will permit. Unfortunately, this won't tell you the values you should use for your own services. You need to test your services against a realistic workload and observe whether client applications are blocked for extended periods. Remember that the purpose of service throttling is to prevent a service from being inundated with a flood of requests that it does not have the resources to cope with. You should set the service throttling properties to ensure that when a client request is accepted and execution actually starts, the computer hosting the service has sufficient resources available to be able to complete the operation before the client times out; otherwise, you would further hinder overall performance. Note that in a transactional environment, aborted client requests generate even more work for the service, because when a timeout occurs, it has to roll back all the transactional work it has already performed.

WCF and Service Instance Pooling

The WCF runtime creates service instances to handle client requests. If the service is using the *PerSession* instance context mode, the instance can last for several operations. If the service is using the *PerCall* instance context mode, each operation call results in a new service instance, which is discarded and destroyed when the operation ends. Creating and destroying instances are expensive, potentially time-consuming tasks. Service instance pooling would be very useful in this scenario.

When using instance pooling, the WCF runtime would create a pool of service instance objects when the service starts. When using the *PerCall* instance context mode, as client applications invoke operations, the WCF runtime would retrieve a pre-created service instance from the pool and then return it to the pool when the operation completes. When using the *PerSession* instance context mode, the same semantics apply, but the WCF runtime would obtain a service instance from the pool at the start of the session and return it at the end of the session. For security purposes, any data held by the service instance (fields in the class defining the service implementation) would be cleared as the instance was returned to the pool.

As you might have gathered from the tone of the previous paragraph, WCF does not provide service instance pooling directly, but it is possible to extend WCF by defining your own custom behavior that implements pooling. WCF supplies the *IInstanceProvider* interface in the *System.ServiceModel.Dispatcher* namespace that you can use to define your own service instance dispatch mechanism. This is a useful technique, but the details are beyond the scope of this book, (although Chapter 11 provides an example of how to implement a service behavior). For more information, see the topic "Pooling" in the Visual Studio documentation. This topic is also available on the Microsoft Web site at *http://msdn.microsoft.com/en-gb/library/ms751482.aspx*.

Specifying Memory Requirements

Applying a throttling behavior lets you limit the number of sessions and connections made to a service in an attempt to maintain throughput. However, services are simply applications that run on a computer, and if a service performs resource-intensive operations it may be better to ensure that sufficient resources are available before it starts running.

One common resource that frequently runs short is memory. For this reason, the WCF run-time enables you to specify the minimum amount of memory that should be available before activating a service. You can indicate this value as the *minFreeMemoryPercentageToActivate Service* attribute of the *<serviceHostingEnvironment>* element in the service configuration file. The default value is *5*, but the following example sets it to *10*.

```
<configuration>
  <system.ServiceModel>
    <serviceHostingEnvironment minFreeMemoryPercentageToActivateService="10" />
    ...
  </system.ServiceModel>
</configuration>
```

In this case, if less than 10% of total memory is available when the WCF runtime attempts to activate a service, it will fail with a *ServiceActivationException* exception.

You can also configure this parameter using the Service Configuration Editor. In the Configuration pane, expand the Advanced folder, and then click Hosting Environment. In the Hosting Environment pane, specify the minimum amount of memory required in the Memory Gates box, as shown in Figure 13-1.

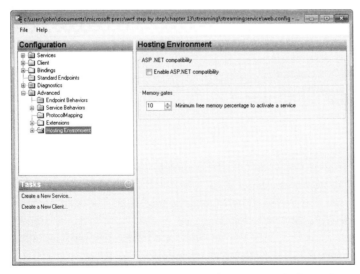

FIGURE 13-1 Setting the minimum amount of memory required to activate a service.

Transmitting Data by Using MTOM

MTOM is an optimization mechanism for sending and receiving SOAP messages that contain binary data. A SOAP message usually consists of a message header that provides addressing, routing, and security information, and a message body, which provides the data, or payload, of the message. The body is XML that contains the data for a request being transmitted to a service or the information being returned to a client application in response to a request. The actual structure of the information in the message body is specified by the WSDL description of the operation, which is in turn derived from the operation contract you specify in your services. For example, the *ProductsService* service that you created in Chapter 1, "Introducing Windows Communication Foundation," defined the *ChangeStockLevel* operation in the *IProducts Service* service contract as follows:

```
[ServiceContract]
public interface IProductsService
{
    ...
    [OperationContract]
    bool ChangeStockLevel(string productNumber, int newStockLevel,
                          string shelf, int bin);
}
```

When a client application invokes the *ChangeStockLevel* operation, the WCF runtime constructs a message that looks like this:

```
<s:Envelope xmlns:a="http://www.w3.org/2005/08/addressing"  xmlns:s="http://www.
w3.org/2003/05/soap-envelope">
    <s:Header>
        ...
    </s:Header>
    <s:Body>
        <ChangeStockLevel xmlns="http://tempuri.org/">
            <productNumber>WB-H098</productNumber>
            <newStockLevel>25000</newStockLevel>
            <shelf>N/A</shelf>
            <bin>40101</bin>
        </ChangeStockLevel>
    </s:Body>
</s:Envelope>
```

You can see that the message body contains the parameters for the operation, encoded as an XML infoset. This scheme works well for parameters that have easily definable representations. However, remember that the XML message is transmitted as a series of text characters when it traverses the network, and non-text data, such as the *<newStockLevel>* and the *<bin>* elements in the example above, must be converted to and from a text representation as the message is sent and received. This conversion incurs an overhead at two levels:

1. It takes time, memory, and computational power to convert from the binary representation of an integer (in the case of the *<newStockLevel>* and the *<bin>* elements) to text and back again.

2. The text representation of the data as it crosses the network might be less compact than the original binary representation; the bigger the value of the data, the more characters are required for the text representation.

In this example, this overhead is minimal. However, how would you handle lengthy binary data, such as an image? One possible solution is to convert the binary data into a text representation containing the corresponding series of "0" and "1" characters. But consider the overhead of this approach. Converting a megabyte of binary data into a string a million characters long requires a significant amount of memory and time. What actually happens in this case is that WCF converts the binary data to a Base64 encoded string rather than a string of "0" and "1" characters. The result is a more compact text representation of the data. However, on average, the Base64 encoding mechanism results in a string that is approximately 140% of the length of the original data. Additionally, this data must be converted back into its original binary format by the recipient of the data. Clearly, it makes sense to find an alternative representation when transmitting messages that include large amounts of binary data.

MTOM is a specification that provides just such an alternative representation. When you use MTOM to transmit a message that includes binary data, that data is not encoded as text, but is transmitted unchanged as an attachment to the message that follows the format of the well-known Multipurpose Internet Mail Extension (MIME) specification. Any text information in the original message is encoded as an XML infoset as before, but binary information is represented as a reference to the MIME attachment, as depicted in Figure 13-2.

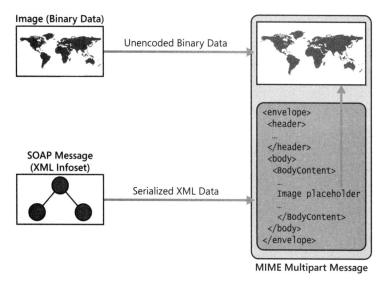

FIGURE 13-2 Encoding a message containing binary data.

> **Note** MTOM supercedes previously proposed standards that you might have heard of, such as the Direct Internet Message Encapsulation protocol (DIME) and the WS-Attachments specification. Don't confuse DIME with MIME.

As always, security is an important consideration. When signing MTOM messages, WCF computes a signature that includes the data in any MIME attachments. If any part of the message, including the MIME attachments, is changed between sending and receiving the message, the signature will be invalid. For more details about signing messages, refer back to Chapter 4, "Protecting an Enterprise WCF Service."

In WCF, MTOM is handled by a specific encoding channel. If you are using any of the standard HTTP bindings (*basicHttpBinding*, *wsDualHttpBinding*, *wsFederationHttpBinding*, or *ws2007HttpBinding*), you can change the *MessageEncoding* property of the binding configuration to **MTOM** to specify the MTOM encoding channel. Other transports, such as TCP, MSMQ, and Named Pipes, use their own proprietary binary encodings by default. The corresponding standard bindings do not have a *MessageEncoding* property, so if, for example, you want to transmit MTOM messages over TCP, you must create your own custom binding.

Sending Large Binary Data Objects to a Client Application

Consider this scenario: AdventureWorks wants to extend the functionality provided by the *ShoppingCartService* WCF service so that users can view photographs of the company's products. The database contains images of the products stored as binary data. The developers have built a prototype service called *ShoppingCartPhotoService* that provides an operation called *GetPhoto*, which retrieves the image data from the database and returns it to the client application. In the following exercises, you will examine this solution, and then see how to configure the service to take advantage of MTOM messaging.

Examine the *ShoppingCartPhotoService* Service

1. Using Visual Studio, open the solution file MTOMService.sln located in the Microsoft Press\WCF Step By Step\Chapter 13\MTOM folder.

    This solution contains a prototype WCF service called *ShoppingCartPhotoService* that implements the *GetPhoto* operation. The *ShoppingCartPhotoService* service is hosted by using the ASP.NET Development Web Server. The solution also contains a simple WPF client application that displays data in a WPF window.

2. Open the IShoppingCartPhotoService.cs file in the App_Code folder in the C:\...\ MTOMService\ project.

    Examine the *IShoppingCartPhotoService* interface defining the service contract. This interface contains the *GetPhoto* operation, which enables a client application to request a product photograph by passing the product number as a parameter. The service

retrieves the photograph and returns it to the client application in the *photo* parameter, which is marked as *out*. This parameter is of type *byte[]* because the photographic
images are held as raw binary data in the database. The return value is a Boolean that
indicates whether the operation was successful or not.

3. If you have time, look at the implementation of the *GetPhoto* method in the *Shopping
    CartPhotoServiceImpl* class in the ShoppingCartPhotoService.cs file. There is nothing
    WCF-specific about this method; all it does is to perform a LINQ query over the *Products
    PhotoModel* entity model (also defined in the App_Code folder) to retrieve the photo-
    graph for the specified product from the *ProductPhoto* table in the database. The data
    is returned from the query as a *ProductPhoto* object (this type was generated by the
    Entity Framework). Note that for clarity, this method does not perform any validation
    checking.

    The photograph is held in a *varbinary* column called *LargePhoto* in the database.
    The Entity Framework retrieves this *varbinary* data into a *byte* array (also called Large-
    Photo*) in the *ProductPhoto* object returned by the LINQ query. This value of this field
    is assigned to the *photo* output parameter. The method returns *true* if it successfully
    located and retrieved the photo, or *false* if an exception occurs.

4. Open the ClientWindow.xaml file in the ShoppingCartGUIClient application. This XAML
    file defines a WPF window containing an image control that occupies the main part of
    the form, together with a label, a text box, and a button. A user types a product number
    into the text box and clicks the Get Photo button.

5. Open the ClientWindow.xaml.cs code file behind this window (expand the Client
    Window.xaml node in Solution Explorer to display the file). The *getPhoto_Click* method
    in this file runs when the user clicks the Get Photo button.

    The code in this method creates an instance of the client proxy, reads the product number
    typed in by the user, creates a new *byte* array, and then invokes the *GetPhoto* opera-
    tion, passing in the *byte* array and the product number as parameters. If the operation
    returns *true*, the method uses the *byte* array containing the data for the photograph and
    uses it to populate a *BitmapImage* object, which it then displays in the image control on
    the WPF form.

6. Start the solution without debugging. The *ShoppingCartPhotoService* starts the ASP.NET
    Development Web Server and begins to listen on port 9080.

 Note If an Internet Explorer window appears displaying the files in the MTOMService
service, just close it and continue on.

When the Shopping Cart Client window appears, type **WB-H098** in the product number
text box, and then click Get Photo. An image showing a pair of water bottles appears in
the image control on the form, as shown in the image that follows.

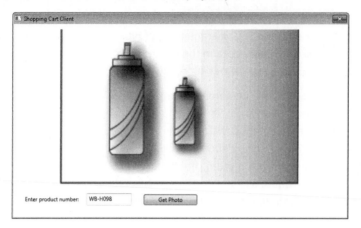

Type **PU-M044** in the product number text box, and then click Get Photo. This time the image displays a picture of a mountain bike pump.

7. Close the Shopping Cart Client window and return to Visual Studio.

8. In Solution Explorer, edit the web.config file for the C:\...\MTOMService\ project by using the Service Configuration Editor.

9. In the Configuration pane, click the Diagnostics folder. In the Diagnostics pane, click Enable Message Logging.

10. In the Configuration pane, expand the Diagnostics folder, and then click the Message Logging node. In the Message Logging pane, set the *LogEntireMessage* property to **True**.

11. In the Configuration pane, expand the Listeners folder, and then click the *ServiceModel MessageLoggingListener* node. In the right pane, set the *InitData* property to **web_ messages.svclog** in the Microsoft Press\WCF Step By Step\Chapter 13 folder within your Documents folder.

12. In the Configuration pane, expand the Sources folder under Diagnostics, and then click the *System.ServiceModelMessageLogging node*. In the right pane, set the *Trace Level* property to **Verbose**.

13. In the Configuration pane, click the Diagnostics node again. In the Diagnostics pane, click Enable Tracing. With this option, you can capture additional information about the activities in the WCF runtime that generate the messages being sent and received.

14. In the Configuration pane, click the *ServiceModelTraceListener* node in the Listeners folder. In the right pane, set the *InitData* property to **web_tracelog.svclog** in the Microsoft Press\WCF Step By Step\Chapter 13 folder within your Documents folder.

15. In the Configuration pane, click the *System.ServiceModel* node in the Sources folder. In the right pane, set the *Trace Level* property to **Verbose**.

16. Save the configuration file but leave the Service Configuration Editor open.

17. In Visual Studio, start the solution again without debugging.

Using the Shopping Cart Client window, retrieve and display the photographs for products **WB-H098** and **PU-M044**, and then close the Shopping Cart Client window. Stop the ASP.NET Web Development Server by right-clicking the ASP.NET Development Server icon in the Windows taskbar, and then clicking Stop.

18. Start the Service Trace Viewer (on the Windows Start menu, click All Programs, click Microsoft Visual Studio 2010, click Microsoft Windows SDK Tools, and then click Service Trace Viewer). In the Service Trace Viewer, open the file web_messages.svclog in the Microsoft Press\WCF Step By Step\Chapter 13 folder within your Documents folder.

19. In the left pane, click the Message tab. You should see four messages listed: one for each request and response (the *ShoppingCartPhotoService* service is configured to use the *BasicHttpBinding* binding, so there are no extraneous messages exchanging security credentials or establishing reliable messaging sessions, and so on).

20. Click the first message. In the lower-right pane, click the Message tab, and then scroll down to display the body of the message. You should see that this is the message requesting the photograph for product WB-H098.

21. In the left pane, click the second message. In the lower-right pane, examine the message body. This is the response containing the photographic data in the *<photo>* element. You can see that this data consists of a long string of characters containing the Base64 encoding of the binary data. Examine the remaining messages; the third message is the request for the photograph of product PU-M044, and the fourth is the response containing the Base64 encoded image data.

22. Open the web-tracelog.svclog file, and then click the Activity tab in the left pane. This file contains a log of the work performed by the WCF runtime, and the Activity pane displays a list of all the tasks the WCF runtime on the service performed.

23. Locate and click the first item named "Process action 'http://adventure-works.com/2010/07/01/ShoppingCartPhotoService/GetPhoto.'" The upper-right pane displays the tasks performed by this activity, including receiving the message over the channel, opening an instance of the service, executing the operation, creating a response message, sending the response message, and finally, closing the service instance.

24. In the upper-right pane, scroll down and click the task, "A Message Was Written." The lower-right pane displays information about the message. In the Message Properties And Headers section, note that the *Encoder* property is *text/xml; charset=utf-8*. This indicates that the message was encoded as text when it was transmitted, as shown in the image that follows.

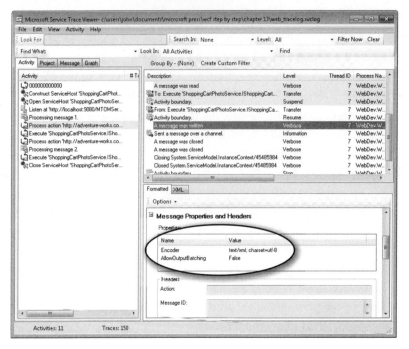

25. On the File menu, click Close All but leave the Service Trace Viewer running.

This exercise has shown you that, by default, the *ShoppingCartPhotoService* service sends all messages—including those containing potentially large amounts of binary data—by encoding them and transmitting them as text. For messages such as these binary images, it would be more efficient if the *ShoppingCartPhotoService* messages containing the photographic images were encoded using MTOM.

In the next exercise, you will see how to modify the binding configuration of the *Shopping CartPhotoService* service to encode binary data by using MTOM over HTTP when transmitting the photographic data from the service to the client application.

Configure the *ShoppingCartPhotoService* Service to Transmit MTOM-Encoded Messages

1. Return to the Service Configuration Editor that is currently displaying the contents of the web.config file for the *ShoppingCartPhotoService* service.

2. In the left pane, click the Bindings folder. In the Bindings pane, click New Binding Configuration. Add a new binding configuration for the *basicHttpBinding* binding. Name the binding **ShoppingCartPhotoServiceBasicHttpBindingConfig** and change the *MessageEncoding* property from *Text* to **Mtom**.

3. In the Configuration pane, expand the *ShoppingCartPhotoService.ShoppingCartPhoto Serviceimpl* node in the Services folder, expand the Endpoints folder, and then click the (*Empty Name*) endpoint. In the Service Endpoint pane, set the *BindingConfiguration* property of the endpoint to **ShoppingCartPhotoServiceBasicHttpBindingConfig**.

4. Save the configuration file, and then close the Service Configuration Editor.

5. In Visual Studio, open the app.config file for the ShoppingCartGUIClient project by using the Service Configuration Editor.

6. In the Configuration pane, expand the Bindings folder, and then click the *BasicHttp Binding_ShoppingCartPhotoService* binding configuration. This is the binding configuration referenced by the client endpoint; it was generated automatically by the Add Service Reference Wizard when the client application was being developed.

7. In the right pane, set the *MessageEncoding* property of the binding configuration to **Mtom**, to match that of the service.

8. Save the configuration file but leave the Service Configuration Editor open.

9. Using Windows Explorer, delete the files web_messages.svclog and web_tracelog.svc in the Microsoft Press\WCF Step By Step\Chapter 13\ folder.

10. In Visual Studio, start the solution without debugging. Fetch and display the photographs for products **WB-H098** and **PU-M044**. Close the Shopping Cart Client window, and then stop the ASP.NET Web Development Server.

11. In the Service Trace Viewer, open the web_tracelog.svclog file. In the Activity pane, locate and click the first item named "Process Action 'http://adventure-works.com/ 2010/07/01/ShoppingCartPhotoService/GetPhoto.'" In the upper-right pane, locate and click the task, "A Message Was Written." In the lower-right pane, examine the *Encoder* property in the Message Properties And Headers section. This time the *Encoder* property is set to *multipart/related; type='application/xop+xml.'* This indicates that the service transmitted the data as a MIME multipart message by using MTOM encoding as shown in the image that follows.

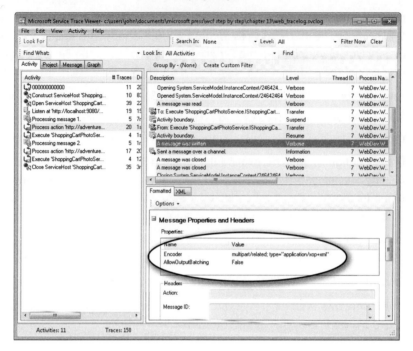

12. Close the Service Trace Viewer.

Note If you examine the SOAP messages in the web_messages.svclog file, you might be surprised—and possibly even a bit disappointed—to see that the *<photo>* parameter returned in the *GetPhotoResponse* message still appears to be encoded as a Base64 string embedded in the message. Do not be fooled. MTOM is actually transparent to WCF SOAP message logging in much the same way that it is transparent to your own applications, and so it is not aware that the *<photo>* parameter is being transmitted as an attachment. If you really want to see the SOAP message in its raw format with the attachment, you must use a network analyzer, such as Microsoft Network Monitor.

Controlling the Size of Messages

You have seen that configuring a binding to use the MTOM encoding is a straightforward task. Using MTOM does not affect the functionality of your applications, and you don't need to make any special coding changes to use it. However, you need to be aware that you have been using MTOM in an idealized environment. Services that can send and receive messages containing large amounts of binary data can be prone to *Denial of Service* attacks; if a service is configured to use MTOM, then an attacker might try to send some incredibly large messages to try to overwhelm the service. Similarly, a rogue service might reply to client requests with very large response messages in an attempt to disrupt a user's computer. Therefore, the WCF runtime enables you to place some limitations on the size of messages that client applications and services can receive.

In the following exercise you will examine what happens when you attempt to receive some data that is bigger than the WCF runtime allows, and how you can configure a binding to support larger messages, if necessary.

Attempt to Receive a Large Message in a WCF Application

1. In Visual Studio, start the solution without debugging. In the Shopping Cart Client application, specify the product number **BK-M38S-46** (this is a Mountain-400-W bicycle), and then click Get Photo.

   The Shopping Cart Client application displays a message box with the following exception:

   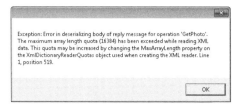

   The problem is that by default the WCF runtime places a limit of 16384 bytes (16 Kb) on the length of any arrays received as part of a message. In the *AdventureWorks* database, the photograph for the Mountain-400-W bicycle is larger than this. The WCF runtime happily lets the service send the data (there is no limit on the size of messages that a service can transmit), but it prevents the client application from receiving it.

2. In the message box, click OK, and then close the Shopping Cart Client window.

3. Return to the Service Configuration Editor editing the app.config file for the Shopping CartGUIClient project. In the Configuration pane, click the *BasicHttpBinding_Shopping CartPhotoService* binding in the Bindings folder.

4. In the right pane, scroll down to the *ReaderQuota Properties* section of the binding. Notice that the value of the *MaxArrayLength* property is set to *16384*. Change this value to **32768**. This setting enables the WCF runtime for the client application to receive a message containing an array of up to 32 Kb. Save the configuration file then close the Configuration File Editor.

5. Start the solution again without debugging. In the Shopping Cart Client application, fetch the photograph of product **BK-M38S-46**. This time the image should display successfully.

6. Close the Shopping Cart Client window.

Apart from the *MaxArrayLength* property, the *ReaderQuotas* element of all bindings provides several other properties: *MaxBytesPerRead*, *MaxDepth*, *MaxNameTableCharCount*, and *Max StringContentLength*. These properties determine the complexity of messages that the WCF runtime will process before throwing an exception. The data in the body of a message is an XML document; internally, the WCF runtime uses an *XmlDictionaryReader* object to parse the contents of message bodies and break them up into the appropriate parameters, returning values that a service or client application expects. The WCF runtime uses the reader quota properties to configure the *XmlDictionaryReader* object and to constrain the messages it processes to a manageable size and structure. The *MaxBytesPerRead* property specifies how many bytes the *XmlDictionaryReader* will read from the message at one time while processing it; the *MaxDepth* property specifies the maximum node depth of elements in the message; the *MaxNameTableCharCount* property limits the total number of characters in strings that are atomized in the *NameTable* for the *XmlDictionaryReader*; and the *MaxStringContentLength* determines the maximum length of string data that a message can contain. If you set any of these properties to zero, the *XmlDictionaryReader* will use its default settings.

> **More Info** A detailed discussion of the *XmlDictionaryReader* class is beyond the scope of this book, but if you want more information, consult the documentation provided with Visual Studio (also available online at *http://msdn.microsoft.com/en-us/library/system.xml.xmldictionaryreader. aspx*).

The reader quota properties you are most likely to amend are *MaxArrayLength* and *MaxString ContentLength*, because these relate directly to the size of the data in the messages that you send.

However, this is not the end of the story. A message may contain more than one array or string. The reader quota properties limit the size of individual elements but not the *number* of elements in a message, so it would still be possible to stage an effective *Denial of Service* attack. If you examine the General section for a binding configuration in the Service Configuration Editor, you will see that a binding also has a *MaxReceivedMessageSize* property. This property governs the maximum overall size of a message that can be received. Note that this property value includes any SOAP headers or other administrative information (if the binding does not use SOAP), not just the data.

The default value for this property is 65536 bytes (64 Kb), which should be adequate for most situations, but you can increase it if necessary. The maximum value you can specify is 2,147,483,647 (*Int32.MaxValue*), but you should never raise it anywhere near this level without having a very good reason to do so (see the discussion on streaming in the next section). However, you should always make sure that *MaxReceivedMessageSize* is at least as big as the greater of *MaxArrayLength* and *MaxStringContentLength*; if it is smaller, then this limitation will kick in before the reader quota restrictions are reached.

There is one other property that you should be aware of: *MaxBufferSize*. When a message is transmitted, it is sent as a stream of bytes over the network. When a message is received, this stream must be reconstituted back into a message. The WCF runtime uses an in-memory buffer to do this, and the maximum amount of memory it will allocate to this buffer is determined by the *MaxBufferSize* property. In most cases, the value of *Max BufferSize* must be the same as *MaxReceivedMessageSize* (the WCF runtime will throw an exception if they are different when it attempts to receive a message). However, there is one situation when *MaxBufferSize* should be significantly less—when you implement streaming.

> **Note** Unlike many other binding properties, the *MaxReceivedMessageSize* and *MaxBufferSize* properties are not considered to be service metadata. What this means is that if you use the *svcutil* utility or the Add Service Reference Wizard to generate a proxy for a service, the values for these properties are not propagated from the service to the client. It is an administrator's responsibility to ensure that these properties are configured appropriately in a client application.

Streaming Data from a WCF Service

MTOM is useful for encoding large binary data objects in messages, but if these objects become too large, they can consume significant amounts of memory in the computer hosting the WCF service and the client applications that receive them. Additionally, very large messages can take a long time to construct and transmit, and it is possible that the client application could time out while waiting for a response containing a large binary object.

In many cases, it does not make sense to even attempt to try to package up data into a single message. Consider a WCF service that provides an operation that emits audio or video data. In this scenario, it is far more efficient to send and receive the data as a stream than to try to transmit it as one big chunk. Streaming allows the client application to start receiving and processing bytes of data before the service has transmitted the end of the message, removing the need to create large buffers for holding an entire message in the service and the client application, and resolving the timeout issue.

Enabling Streaming in a WCF Service and Client Application

WCF provides streaming support for operations by providing you with a mechanism to modify the *TransferMode* property of binding configurations based on the *basicHttpBinding*, *netTcp Binding*, or *netNamedPipeBinding* bindings.

You can set the *TransferMode* property to one of the following values:

- *Buffered*   This is the default transfer mode. Messages are completely constructed in memory and transmitted only when they are complete.

- *StreamedRequest*   Request messages are streamed but response messages are buffered.

- *StreamedResponse*   Response messages are streamed but request messages are buffered.

- *Streamed*   Both request and response messages are streamed.

The maximum size of a streamed message that can be received is still determined by the *MaxReceivedMessageSize* property of the binding. However, when you enable streaming for a binding, only the message header needs to be buffered by the receiver, so you should reduce the value of the *MaxBufferSize* property.

Designing Operations to Support Streaming

There is more to streaming than just changing the *TransferMode* property of a binding—and not all operations are conducive to streaming. To support request streaming, an operation can take only a single input parameter, which must either be a stream object (a descendent of the *System.IO.Stream* class), a *Message* object (an instance of the *System.ServiceModel.Channel. Message* class or one of its descendants), or be serializable as XML. To support response streaming, an operation must either have a *non-void* return type or a single *out* parameter, and, like the input parameter, the type of this return type or parameter must either be a stream object or be serializable as XML. The reason for this restriction is that the input parameter (or output parameter or return type) must constitute the entire request or response message.

As an example, here is the service contract for a version of the *GetPhoto* operation from the *ShoppingCartPhotoService* service that supports streaming:

```
public interface IShoppingCartPhotoService
{
    [OperationContract(Name = "GetPhoto")]
    Stream GetPhoto(string productNumber);
}
```

The implementation of the *GetPhoto* method returns a *MemoryStream* object containing the data for the photograph, as shown in bold in the following code (remember that the *Large Photo* property of a *ProductPhoto* object is a byte array):

```
public Stream GetPhoto(string productNumber)
{
    try
    {
        // Connect to the AdventureWorks database by using the Entity Framework
        using (AdventureWorksEntities database = new AdventureWorksEntities())
        {
            // Retrieve the photograph of the selected product
            ProductPhoto photoData = (from p in database.Products
                                      where string.Compare(p.ProductNumber, productNumber)
                                          == 0
```

```
                          join ph in database.ProductProductPhotos
                          on p.ProductID equals ph.ProductID
                          join phd in database.ProductPhotos
                          on ph.ProductPhotoID equals phd.ProductPhotoID
                          select phd).First();

            // Return the photo as a stream
            MemoryStream data = new MemoryStream(photoData.LargePhoto);
            return data;
        }
    }
    catch (Exception e)
    {
        // If an exception occurs (possibly no such product) then return null
        return null;
    }
}
```

> **Note** A version of the *ShoppingCartPhotoService* and ShoppingCartGUIClient application that
> uses streaming is available in the Microsoft Press\WCF Step By Step\Chapter 13\Streaming folder.
> The purpose of this sample is simply to show how to define an operation that implements stream-
> ing. The client application still reads the streamed response in the foreground, and so it does not
> actually gain much advantage from streaming (the application still blocks until the message is
> fully transmitted and received). A real-world application should read the streamed response on
> a background thread by opening a *StreamReader* object over the *Stream* object returned by the
> *GetPhoto* operation and making the streamed data available for processing as it is read.

For reasons described in the next section, the service implements the *BasicHttpBinding*
binding with the *TransferMode* property set to *StreamedResponse* to enable streaming for
response messages only.

If you enable message logging, you will see that the body of the response message appears
like this:

```
<Addressing ...>
  ...
</Addressing>
<s:Envelope xmlns:s="http://www.w3.org/2003/05/soap-envelope">
  <s:Header>
    ...
  </s:Header>
  <s:Body>... stream ...</s:Body>
</s:Envelope>
```

The code in the client application reads the data returned by the *GetPhoto* operation as a
stream:

```
string prudctNumber = …;
Stream photo = proxy.GetPhoto(productNumber);
```

The *TransferMode* property of the *BasicHttpBinding* binding employed by the *ShoppingCart GUIClient* application is also set to *StreamedResponse*; otherwise, the WCF runtime will attempt to buffer response received from the *ShoppingCartService* service before passing it to the client application.

Security Implications of Streaming

Message-level security features such as signing and encryption that are commonly employed by the *ws2007HttpBinding* binding and its relatives require that the WCF runtime to have access to the entire message. When you enable streaming for a binding, this is no longer possible. For this reason, the *ws2007HttpBinding* and other related bindings do not support streaming. The solution is to implement transport-level security over the *basicHttpBinding* binding instead.

Additionally, you cannot exploit reliable messaging. This feature depends on buffering so that the protocol can acknowledge delivery of complete messages and optionally order them (if ordered delivery has been specified for the binding). Again, this is only really an issue for the *ws2007HttpBinding* family of bindings. This is because the TCP protocol and named pipes typically provide their own inherently reliable delivery mechanisms that are independent of the WCF implementation of the WS-ReliableMessaging protocol.

One final point concerning security: remember that, by default, bindings created by WCF allow a maximum received message size of 64 Kb. If a message being received exceeds this limit, the WCF runtime throws an exception and aborts the operation. As mentioned earlier, this limit is primarily intended to reduce the scope for *Denial of Service* attacks. This value is sufficient for most message-oriented operations but is too low for many streaming scenarios. In these cases, you will need to increase the value of the *MaxReceivedMessageSize* property of the binding. However, be aware that this is a global setting for the binding, and as such, it affects all operations exposed by the service through this binding. Consequently, if you implement streaming operations, it may be better to define them in a separate service contract from non-streaming operations.

> **More Info** For further details on implementing streaming in a WCF service, see the "Large Data and Streaming" page on the Microsoft Web site at *http://msdn.microsoft.com/en-us/library/ ms733742.aspx*.

Summary

In this chapter, you have seen how to use service throttling to control the requests submitted to a service and ensure that a service does not overcommit itself and attempt to handle too many concurrent operations. You have also seen how to use MTOM to optimize the way in which WCF encodes large binary objects for transmission. Finally, you have seen how to design operations and services that support streaming.

Chapter 14
Discovering Services and Routing Messages

After completing this chapter, you will be able to:

- Configure a WCF service to support discovery, and modify a client application to use discovery to locate services.

- Implement a discovery proxy.

- Describe how the WCF runtime for a service dispatches messages to operations.

- Build a WCF service that transparently routes client requests to other WCF services.

- Use the WCF *RoutingService* class to implement message routing.

When a client application sends a message to a WCF service, it sends the request through an endpoint. If you recall, an endpoint specifies three pieces of information: an address, a binding, and a contract. The address indicates where the message should go; the binding identifies the transport, format, and protocols to use to communicate with the service; and the contract determines the messages that the client can send and the responses it should expect to receive. It is possible for more than one service to implement the same contract, and it is also possible for a service to change its address. If a client application has the address of a specific service hard-coded into its configuration, then if that service moves, becomes temporarily unavailable, or is just too busy to handle requests, the client will not be able to communicate with it. WCF provides discovery and routing to address these issues.

In this chapter, you will see how to implement discovery in a WCF solution. You will also learn how you can configure a WCF service to route messages intelligently.

Implementing Discovery

WCF discovery is an implementation of the OASIS WS-Discovery specification. This feature enables a client application to locate a service dynamically, based on criteria such as the contract that the service implements. The location of the service can change, but as long as a service is discoverable, a client application can find it and connect to it.

In the simplest form of the WS-Discovery protocol, when a client application wishes to connect to a service, it broadcasts a *Probe* message containing information about the service with which it wishes to communicate. A service that supports discovery listens for *Probe* messages on an endpoint with a well-known address defined by the WS-Discovery specification. When the service receives a *Probe* request, it can examine its contents, and if the probe matches the contract implemented by the service, it can respond to the client with a *ProbeMatch* message. The *ProbeMatch* message contains the service addressing information that the client needs to connect to the service. This form of discovery is known as *ad hoc* mode.

With WCF, you can configure a service to support discovery simply by enabling the discovery behavior and adding a preconfigured discovery endpoint to the service. This endpoint is called *udpDiscoveryEndpoint* and is an example of one of several standard endpoints implemented by WCF. A standard endpoint implements a well-defined set of functionality and contains built-in configuration information; all you need to do is refer to it by name. The *udpDiscoveryEndpoint* endpoint has a fixed contract, a fixed HTTP binding, and a default address as specified in the WS-Discovery specification.

> **Note** The *udpDiscoveryEndpoint* standard endpoint is implemented by the *UdpDiscoveryEndpoint* class in the *System.ServiceModel.Discovery* namespace. If you want to create a discovery endpoint that listens on a non-default address or change other properties of the endpoint, you can create an instance of this class in your code, modify the values of its properties, and use that instead of the *udpDiscoveryService* standard endpoint. Alternatively, you can override the default settings for the standard endpoint by defining a standard endpoint configuration in the configuration file for a service (the following exercise takes this latter approach).

Configuring Ad Hoc Discovery

In the following exercises, you will configure the *ProductsService* service to support ad hoc discovery and add code to the client application that locates the *ProductsService* before establishing a connection.

Configure the *ProductsService* Service to Support Ad Hoc Discovery

1. Start Visual Studio as Administrator and open the solution file ProductsService.sln located in the Microsoft Press\WCF Step By Step\Chapter 14\ProductsService folder (within your Documents folder).

> **Note** It is important that you start Visual Studio as an administrator because you will be performing tasks that require administrative rights in a later exercise in this section.

This solution contains a copy of the *ProductsService* service that you have met at regular stages throughout the book. The service is hosted by using the ASP.NET Development Web Server, listening to port 8090. The solution also contains a version of the client application that connects directly to the *ProductsService* service by using a client endpoint called *WS2007HttpBinding_IProductsService* and invokes the various operations.

The app.config file in the client application specifies the address of the *ProductsService* service as part of the client endpoint definition, as shown in bold in the following:

```
<?xml version="1.0" encoding="utf-8" ?>
<configuration>
  <system.serviceModel>
    ...
    <client>
      <endpoint address="http://localhost:8090/ProductsService/ProductsService.svc"
                binding="ws2007HttpBinding" bindingConfiguration="..."
                contract="ProductsService.IProductsService"
                name="WS2007HttpBinding_IProductsService">
      </endpoint>
    </client>
  </system.serviceModel>
</configuration>
```

2. Start the solution without debugging.

> **Note** If Internet Explorer starts, just close it and continue on.

Notice that the ASP.NET Development Server starts and begins listening on port 8090. In the client application console window, verify that the address displayed is *http://localhost:8090/ProductsService/ProductsService.svc*, and then press Enter. The client application should perform its usual cycle of work; display the number of each product in the *AdventureWorks* database, display the details of product WB-H098 (a water bottle), display the current stock level of product WB-H098, and then increment it by 100.

Press Enter when the client application has finished then return to Visual Studio.

The client application does not currently use discovery to locate the *ProductsService* service—and the service itself does not support discovery. In the following steps, you will first configure discovery for the service, and then turn your attention to the client application.

3. Open the web.config file for the C:\...\ProductsService\ project using the Service Configuration Editor.

4. In the Configuration pane, expand the Advanced folder, expand the Service Behaviors folder, and then click the *(Empty Name)* behavior.

5. In the Behavior pane, click the Add button. In the Adding Behavior Element Extension Sections dialog box, select the *serviceDiscovery* behavior element, and then click Add.

The *serviceDiscovery* behavior element makes the endpoints that are exposed by the service discoverable. However, you also need to add a discovery endpoint that can listen for *Probe* requests from client applications. As mentioned earlier, you can achieve this by adding the *udpDiscoveryEndpoint* standard endpoint to the service.

6. In the Configuration pane, expand the Services folder, expand the *ProductsService. ProductsServiceImpl* service, right-click the Endpoints folder, and then click New Service Endpoint.

7. In the Service Endpoint pane, leave all the properties set to their default values except *Kind*; set this property to *udpDiscoveryEndpoint*.

   The *Kind* property specifies that this is a standard endpoint, and the value that you specify indicates the functionality exposed by this endpoint (the developers building WCF used the term "Kind" rather than "Type" to avoid causing confusion).

> **Note** The *udpDiscoveryEndpoint* standard endpoint is intended to be used by services that implement the ad hoc mode of discovery. In this mode, client applications send *Probe* requests to a well-known multicast address using the UDP protocol. You may have noticed that there is another standard endpoint, simply called *discoveryEndpoint*. This endpoint is intended for the *managed mode* of discovery, which implements unicast addressing. You will investigate managed mode discovery in a later exercise in this chapter.

As mentioned earlier, standard endpoints have a default configuration, but you can modify their properties by adding a standard endpoint configuration, which is what you will do for the *udpDiscoveryEndpoint* endpoint next.

8. In the Configuration pane, click the Standard Endpoints folder. In the Standard Endpoints pane, click New Standard Endpoint Configuration. In the Create A New Standard Endpoint dialog box, click the *udpDiscoveryEndpoint* endpoint type, and then click OK.

9. In the right pane, change the *Name* property of the endpoint to **AdHocDiscovery Endpoint**. In the General section, notice that the *DiscoveryMode* property is set to *Adhoc*, and the *DiscoveryVersion* property is set to *WSDiscovery11*.

   There are actually two commonly used versions of the WS-Discovery specification; an early version dating from April, 2005, and an updated version, 1.1. The *updDiscovery Endpoint* standard endpoint supports both but defaults to the more recent 1.1 version. If you wish to enable older client applications to discover your service, set the *Discovery Version* property to *WSDiscoveryApril2005*.

   The purpose of the *MaxResponseDelay* property is to prevent the service from causing a network storm by attempting to send a large number of *ProbeMatch* messages at the same time. If you specify a non-zero value, the service will wait for a random interval up to this period before sending each *ProbeMatch* response.

   Notice that you can change the multicast address on which the endpoint listens (the default value comes from the WS-Discovery specification); however, you should not modify it unless you also change client applications to send *Probe* requests to the same address.

10. In the Configuration pane, click the lower *(Empty Name)* endpoint in the Endpoints folder in the Services folder and return to the *udpDiscoveryEndpoint* endpoint. Set the *EndpointConfiguration* property to **AdHocDiscoveryEndpoint**.

Although you did not change any of the properties of the endpoint from their default values, this configuration lets you alter the values easily in the future if circumstances or discovery requirements change.

11. Save the configuration file then close the Service Configuration Editor.

In the next exercise, you will modify the client application to take advantage of discovery. The client application will create a *DiscoveryClient* object to broadcast a *Probe* message that specifies the contract implemented by *ProductsService* service. The *udpDiscoveryEndpoint* for the *ProductsService* service should receive this request, recognize that the service implements the requested contract, and respond with a *ProbeMatch* message containing the details of the service endpoint. The client application will retrieve the address of the service from the *Probe Match* message and use this to connect to the *ProductsService* service.

Modify the Client Application to Discover the *ProductsService* Service

1. In Solution Explorer, add a reference to the *System.ServiceModel.Discovery* assembly to the ProductsClient project. This assembly contains the types required by a client application to perform service discovery.

2. Open the Program.cs file for the ProductsClient project in the Code And Text Editor window. Add the following *using* statement to the list at the top of the file:

```
using System.ServiceModel.Discovery;
```

3. In the *Main* method, delete the first comment (it is not going to be true any longer) and the statement directly underneath that creates the *ProductsServiceClient* proxy object. Leave the two *Console.WriteLine* statements and the *Console.ReadLine* statement intact.

4. In the *Main* method, above the first *Console.WriteLine* statement, add the following code (shown in bold):

```
static void Main(string[] args)
{
    // Use Discovery to find the ProductsService service
    DiscoveryClient client = new DiscoveryClient(new UdpDiscoveryEndpoint());

    Console.WriteLine("Address of ProductsService is {0}", proxy.Endpoint.Address);
    Console.WriteLine("Press ENTER to continue");
    Console.ReadLine();
    ...
}
```

This code creates an instance of the *DiscoveryClient* class and opens a local instance of the *UdpDiscoveryEndpoint* endpoint for sending and receiving multicast discovery messages. The *DiscoveryClient* class is located in the *System.ServiceModel.Discovery* namespace. It provides the functionality required to issue *Probe* requests and wait for *ProbeMatch* responses.

> **Note** By default, the *UdpDiscoveryEndpoint* class builds an endpoint that supports ad hoc discovery over the address shown earlier conforming to the WS-Discovery version 1.1 protocol. You can modify the mode and address by providing parameters to the constructor of the *UdpDiscoveryEndpoint* class.

5. Add the following statement (shown in bold) to the *Main* method:

```
static void Main(string[] args)
{
    // Use Discovery to find the ProductsService service
    DiscoveryClient client = new DiscoveryClient(new UdpDiscoveryEndpoint());
    FindCriteria productsServiceFindCriteria =
        new FindCriteria(typeof(IProductsService));

    Console.WriteLine("Address of ProductsService is {0}", proxy.Endpoint.Address);
    ...
}
```

This statement creates a *System.ServiceModel.Discovery.FindCriteria* object. The information in this object will be transmitted as a *Probe* request in the next step. The constructor specifies the service contract to send in the *Probe* request.

6. Add the following statements (shown in bold) to the *Main* method:

```
static void Main(string[] args)
{
    // Use Discovery to find the ProductsService service
    DiscoveryClient client = new DiscoveryClient(new UdpDiscoveryEndpoint());
    FindCriteria productsServiceFindCriteria =
        new FindCriteria(typeof(IProductsService));
    FindResponse productsServices = client.Find(productsServiceFindCriteria);
    client.Close();

    Console.WriteLine("Address of ProductsService is {0}", proxy.Endpoint.Address);
    ...
}
```

The *Find* method of the *DiscoveryClient* class broadcasts a *Probe* message using the local *UdpDiscoveryEndpoint* endpoint. The parameter specifies the service to search for. The *Find* method returns a *FindResponse* object containing a collection of *EndpointAddress* objects that hold the address for each service that responded.

It is important to realize that the *Find* operation may take a significant time to run. In the WS-Discovery protocol, when a client sends a *Probe* message, zero or more services might respond. The client can elect to timeout if it receives no *ProbeMatch* messages within a given period. Equally important, any given service response might not be the most appropriate service for the client to use. Therefore, the client can continue waiting for a specified duration, and then examine all the *ProbeMatch* responses it has received to determine which service best meets its requirements (for example, the client might examine the URLs of each response and decide to connect to the service that is geographically closest to the client).

The *Find* method of the *DiscoveryClient* class hides much of this complexity from you. When you create a *FindCriteria* object, you can set its *Duration* and *MaxResults* properties. As their names imply, the *Duration* property specifies how long the *Find* method will wait for results (the default is 20 seconds), and *MaxResults* specifies the maximum number of expected results (the default is *Int32.MaxInt*). The *Find* method waits either until this period has expired or the maximum number of responses has been received. It then gathers all the data from the various *ProbeMatch* messages that have been sent and stores this information in the *Endpoints* collection in the *FindResponse* object that it passes back as the return value. If you do not wish to block the client application while discovery is occurring, you can invoke the *FindAsync* method, which returns immediately, but raises the *FindProgressChanged* event of the *DiscoveryClient* object each time the client receives a response. It also raises the *FindCompleted* event when the *Discovery Client* object determines that it has spent long enough waiting for results.

When the *DiscoveryClient* object has finished discovering services, the *Close* method closes the endpoint.

7. After the *Close* statement, add the following code (shown in bold) to the *Main* method:

```
static void Main(string[] args)
{
    // Use Discovery to find the ProductsService service
    DiscoveryClient client = new DiscoveryClient(new UdpDiscoveryEndpoint());
    FindCriteria productsServiceFindCriteria =
        new FindCriteria(typeof(IProductsService));
    FindResponse productsServices = client.Find(productsServiceFindCriteria);
    client.Close();

    EndpointAddress productsServiceAddress = productsServices.Endpoints[0].Address;
    ProductsServiceClient proxy = new ProductsServiceClient();
    proxy.Endpoint.Address = productsServiceAddress;

    Console.WriteLine("Address of ProductsService is {0}", proxy.Endpoint.Address);
    ...
}
```

This code retrieves the address for the first matching service from the *Endpoints* collection of the *FindResponse* object. It then creates a new instance of the *ProductsService Client* proxy and sets the address of this proxy to the just-retrieved address. The program then continues as before.

Note To keep the code simple, the client application assumes that at least one matching service is found; otherwise, it will throw an exception when it attempts to access the *Address* property of the object at element zero in the *Endpoints* collection of the *productsServices* variable. In a production application, you should ensure that at least one matching service was found before attempting to use the address (in other words, you should verify that *productsServices.Endpoints.Count* is greater than zero).

8. Rebuild the solution.

Before you can test the client application, you must deploy the service to a host environment that supports discovery. Sadly, discovery does not work with the ASP.NET Development Server, so you will publish the *ProductsService* service to IIS. This exercise will also give you a chance you prove to yourself that the client application can connect to the service even though the service has now moved and you have not specified the new address in the client configuration file.

Deploy the *ProductsService* Service to IIS and Test the Client Application

1. In Solution Explorer, right-click the C:\...\ProductsService\ project, and then click Publish Web Site.

2. In the Publish Web Site dialog box, in the Target Location box, type **http://localhost/ DiscoverableProductsService**, and then click OK. Wait for the message "Publish succeeded" to appear in the Visual Studio status bar.

Note If publication fails, ensure that you are running Visual Studio as Administrator.

3. Open Internet Information Services Manager as Administrator. In the Connections pane, expand the node that corresponds to your computer, expand Sites, expand Default Web Site, and then verify that the *DiscoverableProductsService* Web application appears (refresh the Connections pane if necessary).

4. Right-click the *DiscoverableProductsService* Web application, click Manage Application, and then click Advanced Settings. In the Advanced Settings dialog box, set the Application Pool property to **ASP.NET v4.0**, and then click OK.

This step is necessary because the Web service connects to the *AdventureWorks* database, and unlike the default application pool, the ASP.NET v4.0 application pool runs by using an identity that has been granted access to the database.

5. Click the Content View tab under the middle pane. If the *ProductsService* service has been deployed correctly, you should see the following files and folders in the *Discoverable ProductsService* Web application:

❑ The bin folder (holding the files App_Code.compiled, App_Code.dll, and Products EntityModel.dll)

❑ PrecompiledApp.config

❑ ProductsService.svc

❑ Web.config

6. Right-click ProductsService.svc, and then click Browse. Verify that Internet Explorer starts and displays the *ProductsServiceImpl* Service page. This action further verifies that your service has been deployed correctly.

Close Internet Explorer but leave Internet Information Services Manager running.

7. Return to Visual Studio and start the solution without debugging (you can ignore the version of the service running in the ASP.NET Development Web Server). After 20 seconds (the value of the *Duration* property of the *FindCriteria* object that was passed to the *Find* method), you should see the address of the *ProductsService* service that the client application has located, as shown in the following image (the name of your server will probably be different, but apart from that, the URL should be the same):

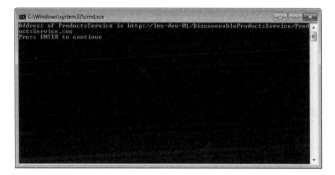

8. Press Enter. The client application should connect to this address and function exactly as before.

9. When the client application has finished, press Enter and return to Visual Studio.

Handling Service Announcements

Discovery is undoubtedly a very powerful technique, but ad hoc discovery can be a little time consuming and frustrating in a client application; basically, every time you want to connect to a service you must wait while its endpoint is discovered. You can tweak the *Duration* property of the *FindCriteria* object that you use to locate the service, but if you make this value too small, you run the risk of not finding the service if it does not respond in a timely manner to *Probe* requests. Ad hoc discovery can also be very network unfriendly, especially if you have a large number of clients in your organization; each time they connect to a service they will broadcast *Probe* requests across your network. One possible solution to these issues is to handle announcement messages.

A service that supports discovery "announces" its presence to the world when it starts up by broadcasting a multicast message over a well-known address. Client applications can listen for these multicast messages and capture the details of the service in a local collection acting as a cache (the address of the service and metadata describing the service is transmitted as part of the announcement). When a client wishes to send a message to a service, it can look up the address of the service in its local collection. The client can then connect to the service and invoke its operations, as before.

Similarly, when a service shuts down, it broadcasts a shutdown message. Client applications can capture these messages and use the information to remove the details of the service from their local caches.

In this case, the onus shifts from the discoverable service to the client applications. Clients no longer send *Probe* messages to the service, and consequently, the service does not need to implement a discovery endpoint. However, you need to modify the service to send announcement messages as it starts up and shuts down. WCF makes this easy; all you need to do is add a *udpAnnouncementEndpoint* standard endpoint to the *serviceDiscovery* behavior element. The WCF runtime does the rest.

A client application can listen for announcements by using the *AnnouncementService* class. This class resides in the *System.ServiceModel.Discovery* namespace. In a client application, you simply create an instance of this class, host it, and provide it with an endpoint to listen to. When a new service announces its arrival, the message triggers the *OnlineAnnouncement Received* event of the *AnnouncementService* object, and the details of the service are passed to this event. Similarly, when a service shuts down the *OfflineAnnouncementReceived* event occurs.

In the next batch of exercises, you will modify the *ProductsService* service to send announcement messages. You will then update the client application to capture these messages and store the details for a service as it comes on and off line.

Configure the *ProductsService* Service to Send Announcements

1. In Visual Studio, open the web.config file for the C:\...\ProductsService\ project by using the Service Configuration Editor.

2. In the Configuration pane, expand the *Products.ProductsServiceImpl* service in the Services folder, expand the Endpoints folder, and then click the second *(Empty Name)* endpoint. Verify that this is the *udpDiscoveryEndpoint* endpoint, right-click the endpoint, and then select Delete Endpoint to remove it. In the message box that's displaying the text, "This Item Will Be Deleted," click OK.

The service will now send announcements rather than responding to *Probe* messages, so this endpoint is no longer required. However, there is nothing to stop a service from implementing both mechanisms, in which case you could leave the discovery endpoint in place.

3. In the Configuration pane, expand the Advanced folder, expand the Service Behaviors folder, expand the *(Empty Name)* behavior, and then expand the *serviceDiscovery* behavior element.

   The *serviceDiscovery* behavior element contains a folder called Announcement Endpoints. You add endpoints to this folder that the service uses to send announcement messages.

4. Right-click the Announcement Endpoints folder, and then click New Client Endpoint. In the Client Endpoint pane, set the *Kind* property to **udpAnnouncementEndpoint**.

   The *udpAnnouncementEndpoint* endpoint is another standard endpoint preconfigured to send announcement messages by following the protocol defined by the WS-Discovery specification. If you need to change the address or the configuration of the announcement endpoint, you can create a standard endpoint configuration for the *udp AnnouncementEndpoint* type, as you did for the *udpDiscoveryEndpoint* type in the previous set of exercises.

5. Save the configuration file then close the Service Configuration Editor.

Modify the Client Application to Capture Announcement Messages

1. Open the Program.cs file for the ProductsClient project in the Code And Text Editor window.

2. In the *Program* class, add the following *using* statement to the list at the top of the file.

   ```
   using System.Collections.Concurrent;
   ```

3. In the *Program* class, add the following *ConcurrentDictionary* collection before the *Main* method.

   ```
   class Program
   {
       // Store data for announced services in a ConcurrentDictionary object

       private static ConcurrentDictionary<EndpointAddress,
           EndpointDiscoveryMetadata> services =
           new ConcurrentDictionary<EndpointAddress,EndpointDiscoveryMetadata>();

       static void Main(string[] args)
       {
           ...
       }
   }
   ```

The *ConcurrentDictionary* class is a thread-safe *Dictionary* collection, defined in the *System.Collections.Concurrent* namespace. When the client application receives service announcement messages, it will store the details of the services that are making the announcements in this collection.

4. In the *Main* method, remove all the comments and code up to the comment // *Test the operations in the service*. This code is no longer necessary (it sends the *Probe* request and waits for the *ProbeMatch* response) because you will be capturing announcement messages instead.

5. Add the following statements to the start of the *Main* method.

```
static void Main(string[] args)
{
    // Use Service Announcements events to track the location and status of services
    AnnouncementService announcementService = new AnnouncementService();
    ...
}
```

The preceding statement creates an *AnnouncementService* object that will listen for announcement messages.

6. Add the following code (shown in bold) to the *Main* method.

```
static void Main(string[] args)
{
    // Use Service Announcements events to track the location and status of services
    AnnouncementService announcementService = new AnnouncementService();

    announcementService.OnlineAnnouncementReceived += (sender, eventArgs) =>
    {
        Console.WriteLine("Online announcement received");
        try
        {
            services.TryAdd(eventArgs.EndpointDiscoveryMetadata.Address,
                eventArgs.EndpointDiscoveryMetadata);

            foreach (var contractName in
                eventArgs.EndpointDiscoveryMetadata.ContractTypeNames)
            {
                Console.WriteLine("Added service with contract {0} at address {1}",
                    contractName.ToString(),
                    eventArgs.EndpointDiscoveryMetadata.Address.ToString());
            }
        }
        catch (Exception e)
        {
            Console.WriteLine("Failed to add service at address {0}",
                data.Address.ToString());
            Console.WriteLine("Exception: {0}", e.Message);
        }
    };
    ...
}
```

This code subscribes to the *OnlineAnnouncementReceived* event that occurs when a new service starts up and sends announcement messages. The *eventArgs* parameter to the event is an instance of the *AnnouncementEventArgs* type. The principal property of interest in this type is *EndpointDiscoveryMetadata*, which among other details, contains the address and contracts implemented by the newly announced service. This event handler adds the service metadata to the *services* dictionary collection, specifying the *Address* as the key. (It also catches the exception that occurs if the event handler fails to add the service to the collection, possibly because another service already exists with the same address.) Finally, the event handler iterates through the list of contracts implemented by the service and displays them in the client console window, together with the address. This is purely so you can see when a service announcement occurs; you would not normally do this in a production client application.

7. Add the following code (shown in bold) to the *Main* method.

```
static void Main(string[] args)
{
    // Use Service Announcements events to track the location and status of services
    AnnouncementService announcementService = new AnnouncementService();

    announcementService.OnlineAnnouncementReceived += (sender, eventArgs) =>
    {
        ...
    };

    announcementService.OfflineAnnouncementReceived += (sender, eventArgs) =>
    {
        try
        {
            Console.WriteLine("Offline announcement received");
            EndpointDiscoveryMetadata data;
            services.TryRemove(eventArgs.EndpointDiscoveryMetadata.Address, out data);

            Console.WriteLine("Removed service at address {0}",
                data.Address.ToString());
        }
        catch (Exception e)
        {
            Console.WriteLine("Failed to remove service at address {0}",
                eventArgs.EndpointDiscoveryMetadata.Address.ToString());
            Console.WriteLine("Exception: {0}", e.Message);
        }
    };
    ...
}
```

This code subscribes to the *OfflineAnnouncementReceived* event that occurs when a service indicates that it is shutting down. The *AnnouncementEventArgs* parameter that's passed in contains the details of the service, as before. This event handler removes the service metadata from the *services* collection, catching and reporting any exceptions that occur.

8. Add the following statements (shown in bold) after the code that handles the events.

```
static void Main(string[] args)
{
    // Use Service Announcements events to track the location and status of services
    AnnouncementService announcementService = new AnnouncementService();

    announcementService.OnlineAnnouncementReceived += (sender, eventArgs) =>
    {
        ...
    };

    announcementService.OfflineAnnouncementReceived += (sender, eventArgs) =>
    {
        ...
    };

    ServiceHost announcementServiceHost = new ServiceHost(announcementService);
    announcementServiceHost.AddServiceEndpoint(new UdpAnnouncementEndpoint());
    announcementServiceHost.Open();

    Console.WriteLine("Client listening for announcements");
    Console.WriteLine("Press ENTER when the Products Service is available");
    Console.ReadLine();
    ...
}
```

This code creates a host for the *AnnouncementService* object and starts it listening for announcements on a *UdpAnnouncementEndpoint* standard endpoint object. The endpoint is configured by default to listen to the same broadcast address used by the *udpAnnouncementEndpoint* standard endpoint in the service. When the host has started, the program waits for the user to press Enter before continuing.

9. Add this code to the Main method, as shown in bold in the following:

```
static void Main(string[] args)
{
    ...
    Console.WriteLine("Client listening for announcements");
    Console.WriteLine("Press ENTER when the Products Service is available");
    Console.ReadLine();

    // Find the announced endpoint for the Products Service
    FindCriteria productsServiceCriteria = new FindCriteria(typeof(IProductsService));
    EndpointAddress productsServiceAddress =
        (from service in services
         where productsServiceCriteria.IsMatch(service.Value)
         select service.Key).First();
    ...
}
```

These statements are similar in principal to the original code that broadcast *Probe* messages, except that it retrieves the service details from the services collection rather than by following the WS Discovery protocol. The *IsMatch* method of the *FindCriteria* class compares the metadata of a service with that of a specified service contract and returns *true* if they match. In this case, the LINQ query searches the *services* collection for a service that implements the *IProductsService* contract and returns the address of the first matching service.

> **Note** If there are no matching services, the LINQ query will throw an exception. However, for clarity, this example assumes that a matching service exists and does not catch the exception.

10. Add the statements shown in bold in the following code to the *Main* method.

```
static void Main(string[] args)
{
    ...
    EndpointAddress productsServiceAddress =
        (from service in services
         where productsServiceCriteria.IsMatch(service.Value)
         select service.Key).First();

    // Connect to the Products Service
    ProductsServiceClient proxy = new ProductsServiceClient();
    proxy.Endpoint.Address = productsServiceAddress;
    ...
}
```

The preceding code creates an instance of the *ProductsServiceClient* proxy and attaches it to the address of the service retrieved from the *services* collection.

The remainder of the code in the client application that tests each of the operations in the service remains exactly the same as before.

11. Rebuild the solution.

The final step is to redeploy the updated service to IIS. After doing so, you can run the client application to verify that it receives service announcements correctly.

Test the *ProductsService* Service and Client Application

1. In Solution Explorer, right-click the C:\...\ProductsService\ project, and then click Publish Web Site. Publish the updated Web site to the location **http://localhost/Discoverable Service**, as before. In the message box that's displaying the text, "Existing Files In The Destination Location Will Be Deleted. Continue?", click Yes.

2. Start the solution without debugging. In the client console window, do not press Enter just yet because the *ProductsService* service has not sent any announcement messages, and the client application will therefore not be able to find it.

3. Return to Internet Information Services Manager. In the Connections pane, click the *DiscoverablePoductsService* Web application, and then click the Content View tab below the middle pane. Right-click ProductsService.svc, and then click Browse. This action starts the service, causing it to send announcement messages.

   Close Internet Explorer but leave Internet Information Services Manager running.

4. Return to the client console window. It should now be displaying a message indicating that it has received an announcement from a service that implements the *IProducts Service* interface and showing the address, like this:

6. In the client console window, press Enter. The application should run as before. When the application has finished, do not press Enter but leave the client console window open.

7. Return to Internet Information Services Manager. In the Connections pane, click Application Pools. In the middle pane, right-click the ASP.NET v4.0 application pool, and then click Recycle.

   Any active Web applications and services that run using the ASP.NET v4.0 application pool, including the *ProductsService*, will be shut down.

8. Return to the client console window. You should see a message triggered by the service sending an offline announcement, and the client application has removed the details of the service from the dictionary collection.

Press Enter to close the client console window and return to Visual Studio.

Using a Discovery Proxy

The use of service announcements can reduce the volume of network traffic associated with large numbers of *Probe* and *ProbeMatch* messages, but what happens if a client is not running when the service starts up? The answer is that it will miss the announcement messages and will not be aware of the service, so it will not be able to connect to it. The solution is to use a hybrid combination of discovery messages and announcements; build an intermediary service that lives at a well-known address that listens for announcement messages from other services and caches them. In your client applications, send *Probe* requests to this intermediary service. The intermediary service should accept these *Probe* requests, consult its cache of service addresses, and if it finds a match, it should return a *ProbeResponse* populated with the details of the matching service. Because the intermediary service lives at a fixed, well-known address, clients do not need to broadcast *Probe* messages to the world at large; instead, they can send them in a unicast manner directly to the intermediary service.

In WCF, the intermediary service is known as a *discovery proxy*. Furthermore, the *System.ServiceModel.Discovery* namespace contains an abstract class called *DiscoveryProxy* that you can use as the basis for building one these services.

To build a discovery proxy, you inherit from the *DiscoveryProxy* class and then override the abstract methods described in the following list. These methods implement the following set of asynchronous operations and they must be thread-safe:

- *OnBeginOnlineAnnouncement* and *OnEndOnlineAnnouncement*   The *DiscoveryProxy* effectively contains a built-in announcement service that listens for announcement messages. When you used the *AnnouncementService* class in the previous exercise, you added handlers for the *OnlineAnnouncementReceived* and *OfflineAnnouncementReceived* events. The *DiscoveryProxy* class does not expose these events in the same way, but expects you to provide the logic that these events invoke when they occur.

  The *OnBeginOnlineAnnouncement* method runs when a service indicates that it has just come online. The purpose of this method is to store the service metadata, in whatever way is appropriate to the discovery proxy (this data could be stored in memory, written to a file, or possibly held in a database). This may take some time, so this method implements the Asynchronous Programming design pattern. The parameters to this method include the metadata describing the service, passed in as an *EndpointDiscoveryMetadata* object, and an *AsyncCallback* object for calling back into the *DiscoveryProxy* object when the operation has completed. The method returns an *IAsyncResult* object. The *DiscoveryProxy* object calls the *OnEndOnlineAnnouncement* method to finish the operation, passing in the *IAsyncResult* object returned by the *OnBeginOnlineAnnouncement* method. This method blocks until the *IAsyncResult* object indicates that the service announcement has been processed and the details of the service have been stored.

■ *OnBeginOfflineAnnouncement* and *OnEndOfflineAnnouncement*   These methods provide the logic to handle an offline announcement message sent by a service when it shuts down. The purpose of these methods is to remove the details of the service from storage. These methods also follow the Asynchronous Programming design pattern.

■ *OnBeginFind* and *OnEndFind*   These methods run when a client application sends a *Probe* request. The details of the service to locate are passed in as a *FindRequestContext* object. The *OnBeginFind* method initiates a search for the service, and the *OnEndFind* method blocks until the search is complete.

■ *OnBeginResolve* and *OnEndResolve*   The WS-Discovery protocol also supports *Resolve* messages as the corollary of *Probe* messages; a *Probe* message specifies the contract to search for, and the resultant *ProbeMatch* contains the address of the service. A *Resolve* request specifies the address of a service, and the corresponding *ResolveMatch* message contains the metadata describing the service contract. The *OnBeginResolve* and *OnEnd Resolve* methods run when a client application sends a *Resolve* request. The *OnBegin Resolve* method should perform the search asynchronously, and the *OnEndResolve* method should block until the search has finished.

In the following set of exercises, you will implement a discovery proxy by extending the *DiscoveryProxy* class. You will then modify the client application to send *Probe* requests to the discovery proxy rather than catch service announcements.

Implement a Discovery Proxy

1. In Solution Explorer, add a new project to the ProductsService solution by using the Console Application template (in the Windows folder in the Installed Templates pane in the Add New Project dialog box). Name the project **ProductsServiceProxy** and save it in the **Microsoft Press\WCF Step By Step\Chapter 14\ProductsService** folder.

2. Add references to the *System.ServiceModel* and *System.ServiceModel.Discovery* assemblies to the ProductsServiceProxy project.

3. Add the existing AsyncResult.cs file located in the Chapter 14 folder to the *Products ServiceProxy* project. This file contains a copy of the generic *AsyncResult* class that implements the *IAsyncResult* interface (you employed this same class in Chapter 12, "Implementing One-Way and Asynchronous Operations").

4. Add a new class called *ProductsServiceProxy*, and save it in a file called **ProductsService Proxy.cs** to the *ProductsServiceProxy* project.

5. In the ProductsServiceProxy.cs file, add the following *using* statements to the list at the top of the file:

```
using System.ServiceModel;
using System.ServiceModel.Discovery;
using System.Threading.Tasks;
using System.Threading;
using System.Collections.Concurrent;
```

6. Tag the *ProductsServiceProxy* class with the following *ServiceBehavior* attribute, as shown in bold in the following:

```
[ServiceBehavior(InstanceContextMode = InstanceContextMode.Single,
                 ConcurrencyMode = ConcurrencyMode.Multiple)]
class ProductsServiceProxy
{
}
```

For simplicity, the *ProductsServiceProxy* is going to cache service information in a *ConcurrentDictionary* object in memory. Therefore, the *ProductsServiceProxy* service will be implemented as a reentrant (and thread-safe) single instance service.

7. Modify the *ProductsServiceProxy* class so that it inherits from the *DiscoveryProxy* class, as shown in bold in the following:

```
[ServiceBehavior(InstanceContextMode = InstanceContextMode.Single,
                 ConcurrencyMode = ConcurrencyMode.Multiple)]
class ProductsServiceProxy : DiscoveryProxy
{
}
```

8. In the *ProductsServiceProxy* class, add the *ConcurrentDictionary* collection, which will hold the following service information (shown in bold), and add a constructor that initializes this collection.

```
class ProductsServiceProxy : DiscoveryProxy
{
    // Store data for registered services in a ConcurrentDictionary object
    ConcurrentDictionary<EndpointAddress, EndpointDiscoveryMetadata> services;

    public ProductsServiceProxy()
    {
        this.services = new ConcurrentDictionary<EndpointAddress,
            EndpointDiscoveryMetadata>();
    }
}
```

9. Add the private *AddService* and *RemoveService* methods (shown in bold in the code that follows) to the *ProductsServiceProxy* class.

These methods add the metadata for a service to the services collection, remove the metadata from the collection, and output some diagnostic messages so that you can see what is going on. The code is similar to the client code that implemented announcement events in the previous set of exercises. You will call these methods when you implement the *OnBeginOnlineAnnouncement* and *OnEndOnlineAnnouncement* methods.

```
class ProductsServiceProxy : DiscoveryProxy
{
    ...
    // Add the specified service to the list of registered services
    private void AddService(EndpointDiscoveryMetadata metadata)
    {
        try
        {
            this.services.TryAdd(metadata.Address, metadata);

            foreach (var contractName in metadata.ContractTypeNames)
            {
                Console.WriteLine("Added service with contract {0} at address {1}",
                    contractName.ToString(), metadata.Address.ToString());
            }
        }
        catch (Exception e)
        {
            Console.WriteLine("Failed to add service at address {0}",
                data.Address.ToString());
            Console.WriteLine("Exception: {0}", e.Message);
        }
    }

    // Remove the specified service from the list of registered services
    private void RemoveService(EndpointDiscoveryMetadata metadata)
    {
        try
        {
            EndpointDiscoveryMetadata data;
            this.services.TryRemove(metadata.Address, out data);

            Console.WriteLine("Removed service at address {0}",
                data.Address.ToString());
        }
        catch (Exception e)
        {
            Console.WriteLine("Failed to remove service at address {0}",
                metadata.Address.ToString());
            Console.WriteLine("Exception: {0}", e.Message);
        }
    }
}
```

 Note The code for these methods is available in the AddServiceAndRemoveService.txt file, which is located in the Chapter 14 folder.

10. Add the following private method, called *FindService*, to the *ProductsServiceProxy* class.

```
class ProductsServiceProxy : DiscoveryProxy
{
    ...
    // Search through the list of registered services to find all matching services
```

```
private void FindService(FindRequestContext requestContext)
{
    try
    {
        // Find all services that match the criteria specified by the request
            context
        var matches = from service in this.services
                        where requestContext.Criteria.IsMatch(service.Value)
                        select service;

        // Iterate through the list of services and add them
        // to the list of services in the FindRequestContext parameter
        foreach (var data in matches)
        {
            Console.WriteLine("Found matching service endpoint at {0}",
                data.Value.Address);
            requestContext.AddMatchingEndpoint(data.Value);
        }
    }
    catch (Exception e)
    {
        Console.WriteLine("Failed to find service with criteria {0}",
            requestContext.Criteria.ToString());
        Console.WriteLine("Exception: {0}", e.Message);
    }
}
```

This method searches the services dictionary for a service that matches the data in the *FindRequestContext* parameter of the request. The *Criteria* property of this parameter holds the contract of the service to search for. The LINQ query searches the dictionary to find the relevant services, and the *foreach* loop adds the endpoint details to the *FindRequestContext* object passed in as the parameter.

> **Note** The code for this method is provided in the FindService.txt file, which is located in the Chapter 14 folder.

11. Add the private *ResolveService* method shown in bold in the following code to *Products ServiceProxy* class.

```
class ProductsServiceProxy : DiscoveryProxy
{
    ...
    // Search through the list of registered services to find a service
    // with and address that matches that in the specified ResolveCriteria
    private EndpointDiscoveryMetadata ResolveServiceRequest(ResolveCriteria criteria)
    {
        try
        {
            // Find the first service that matches the specified address
            var match = (from service in this.services
```

```
                    where service.Value.Address == criteria.Address
                    select service).First();

            Console.WriteLine("Resolved service endpoint at {0}",
                match.Value.Address);

            // Return the service
            return match.Value;
        }
        // If there is no matching service, the LINQ query throws an exception
        // In this case, return null
        catch (Exception e)
        {
            Console.WriteLine("Failed to resolve service with address {0}",
                criteria.Address);
            Console.WriteLine("Exception: {0}", e.Message);
            return null;
        }
    }
}
```

This method is similar in concept to the *FindService* method, but it searches for services
using the address specified in the *Address* property of the *ResolveCriteria* parameter. It
returns an *EndpointDiscoveryMetadata* object containing the service details.

> **Note** The code for this method is available in the ResolveService.txt file, which is located in
> the Chapter 14 folder.

12. Add the *WaitForAsyncResult* utility method shown in bold in the following code to the
ProductsServiceProxy class.

```
class ProductsServiceProxy : DiscoveryProxy
{
    ...
    private  void WaitForAsyncResult(IAsyncResult result)
    {
        // The IAsyncResult parameter should be an AsyncResult object
        // returned by the OnBegin method.
        // If it is some other type, then this method will return without waiting
        AsyncResult<object> r = result as AsyncResult<object>;

        // If the OnBeginOnlineAnnouncement did not complete synchronously
        // then wait until the AsyncWaitHandle property says that
        // the async operation is complete
        if ((r != null) && !r.CompletedSynchronously)
        {
            WaitHandle waitHandle = r.AsyncWaitHandle;
            waitHandle.WaitOne();
        }
    }
}
```

You will use this method when you implement the various *OnEnd* methods shortly. The purpose of this method is to block until the *IAsyncResult* object specified as the parameter indicates that the operation has completed (this operation could be an announcement request, a find request, or a resolve request).

> **Note** The code for this method is available in the WaitForAsyncResult.txt file, which is located in the Chapter 14 folder.

13. Override the *OnBeginOnlineAnnouncement* and *OnEndOnlineAnnouncement* methods of the *DiscoveryProxy* class, as follows:

```
class ProductsServiceProxy : DiscoveryProxy
{
    ...
    // Asynchronously add the specified service to the list
    // registered with this discovery proxy
    protected override IAsyncResult OnBeginOnlineAnnouncement(
        DiscoveryMessageSequence messageSequence,
        EndpointDiscoveryMetadata endpointDiscoveryMetadata,
        AsyncCallback callback, object state)
    {
        Console.WriteLine("Starting OnBeginOnlineAnnouncement");

        // Create an AsyncResult object to pass back for synchronization purposes
        AsyncResult<object> result = new AsyncResult<object>(false, state);
        // Use a Task to add the service in the background
        Task.Factory.StartNew(() =>
            {
                // Add the service to the collection of registered services
                this.AddService(endpointDiscoveryMetadata);

                // Indicate that the operation is complete
                result.Complete();

                // Invoke callback and pass the AsyncResult object as the parameter
                Console.WriteLine("Calling back after adding service");
                if (callback != null)
                    callback(result);
            });

        // Return the AsyncResult object
        Console.WriteLine("Returning after scheduling task to add service");
        return result;
    }

    protected override void OnEndOnlineAnnouncement(IAsyncResult result)
    {
        Console.WriteLine("Starting OnEndOnlineAnnouncement");
        WaitForAsyncResult(result);
        Console.WriteLine("Leaving OnEndOnlineAnnouncement");
    }
}
```

The *OnBeginOnlineAnnouncement* method creates a *Task* to asynchronously call the *AddService* method, which adds the service metadata specified in the parameter to the *services* dictionary. This method returns an *IAsyncResult* containing the state information needed to wait for the operation to complete.

The *OnEndOnlineAnnouncement* method takes this *IAsyncResult* object as a parameter and calls the *WaitForAsyncResult* method, which blocks until the *IAsyncResult* object indicates that the operation has completed.

 Note The code for this method is provided in the OnlineAnnouncement.txt file, which is located in the Chapter 14 folder.

14. Override the *OnBeginOfflineAnnouncement* and *OnEndOfflineAnnouncement* methods of the *DiscoveryProxy* class:

```
class ProductsServiceProxy : DiscoveryProxy
{
    ...
    // Asynchronously remove the specified service from the list
    // registered with this discovery proxy
    protected override IAsyncResult OnBeginOfflineAnnouncement(
        DiscoveryMessageSequence messageSequence,
        EndpointDiscoveryMetadata endpointDiscoveryMetadata,
        AsyncCallback callback, object state)
    {
        Console.WriteLine("Starting OnBeginOfflineAnnouncement");

        // The logic in this method is very similar
        // to that in OnBeginOnlineAnnouncement
        AsyncResult<object> result = new AsyncResult<object>(false, state);

        Task.Factory.StartNew(() =>
        {
            // Remove the service from the collection of registered servers
            this.RemoveService(endpointDiscoveryMetadata);
            result.Complete();

            Console.WriteLine("Calling back after removing service");
            if (callback != null)
                callback(result);
        });

        Console.WriteLine("Returning after scheduling task to remove service");
        return result;
    }

    protected override void OnEndOfflineAnnouncement(IAsyncResult result)
    {
        Console.WriteLine("Starting OnEndOfflineAnnouncement");
        WaitForAsyncResult(result);
        Console.WriteLine("Leaving OnEndOfflineAnnouncement");
    }
}
```

The logic behind these two methods is similar to that for the *OnBeginOnline Announcement* and *OnEndOnlineAnnouncement* methods, but the *OnBeginOffline Announcement* method calls *RemoveService* to delete the details of the service from the *services* dictionary.

> **Note** The code for this method is provided in the OfflineAnnouncement.txt file, which is located in the Chapter 14 folder.

15. Override the *OnBeginFind* and *OnEndFind* methods of the *DiscoveryProxy* class:

```
class ProductsServiceProxy : DiscoveryProxy
{
    ...
    protected override IAsyncResult OnBeginFind(
        FindRequestContext findRequestContext, AsyncCallback callback, object state)
    {
        Console.WriteLine("Starting OnBeginFind");
        AsyncResult<FindRequestContext> result =
            new AsyncResult<FindRequestContext>(false, state);

        Task.Factory.StartNew(() =>
        {
            this.FindService(findRequestContext);
            result.Complete();

            Console.WriteLine("Calling back after finding service");
            if (callback != null)
                callback(result);
        });

        Console.WriteLine("Returning after scheduling task to find service");
        return result;
    }

    protected override void OnEndFind(IAsyncResult result)
    {
        Console.WriteLine("Starting OnEndFind");
        WaitForAsyncResult(result);
        Console.WriteLine("Leaving OnEndFind");
    }
}
```

By now, the pattern should be familiar. The *OnBeginFind* method calls the *FindService* method to find services that match the criteria specified by the *FindRequestContext* object passed as a parameter. The caller expects the endpoint details of any matching services to be added to the *FindRequestContext* object passed in as the parameter.

> **Note** The code for this method is provided in the AsyncFind.txt file, which is located in the Chapter 14 folder.

16. Finally, override the *OnBeginResolve* and *OnEndResolve* methods of the *DiscoveryProy* class:

```
class ProductsServiceProxy : DiscoveryProxy
{
    ...
    protected override IAsyncResult OnBeginResolve(ResolveCriteria resolveCriteria,
        AsyncCallback callback, object state)
    {
        Console.WriteLine("Starting OnBeginResolve");
        AsyncResult<EndpointDiscoveryMetadata> result =
            new AsyncResult<EndpointDiscoveryMetadata>(false, state);
        result.Data = null;

        Task.Factory.StartNew(() =>
        {
            EndpointDiscoveryMetadata data = this.ResolveServiceRequest(resolve
                Criteria);
            result.Data = data;
            result.Complete();

            Console.WriteLine("Calling back after resolving service");
            if (callback != null)
                callback(result);
        });

        Console.WriteLine("Returning after scheduling task to resolve service");
        return result;
    }

    protected override EndpointDiscoveryMetadata OnEndResolve(IAsyncResult result)
    {
        Console.WriteLine("Starting OnEndResolve");
        WaitForAsyncResult(result);
        if (result is AsyncResult<EndpointDiscoveryMetadata>)
        {
            Console.WriteLine("Returning result from OnEndResolve");
                return ((AsyncResult<EndpointDiscoveryMetadata>)result).Data;
        }
        else
        {
            Console.WriteLine("Returning null from OnEndResolve");
            return null;
        }
    }
}
```

The *OnBeginResolve* invokes the *ResolveService* method to find the service metadata. There is a small difference in the pattern for the *OnEndResolve* method; it returns the service metadata directly rather than expecting the caller to retrieve it from the *Resolve Criteria* parameter.

Note The code for this method is provided in the AsyncResolve.txt file, which is located in the Chapter 14 folder.

17. Rebuild the solution.

You have now defined a *DiscoveryProxy* service that caches announcement requests in a dictionary collection, in memory. The next step is to provide a host for this service. To save you some time (and typing), and to provide a variation from using IIS, the code for a complete host is already provided, and you'll examine it in the next exercise. Additionally—again as a variation and to prove that discovery is not tied to the HTTP protocol—this host exposes the announcement and discovery endpoints using the TCP protocol.

Examine the Host for the *ProductsServiceProxy* Service

1. Delete the Program.cs file from the ProductsServiceProxy project and add the existing Host.cs file located in the Chapter 14 folder to the project in its place.

2. Open the Hosts.cs file in the Code And Text Editor window.

The *Program* class contains two string constants called *probeAddress* and *announcement Address*. These are both TCP addresses:

```
private const string probeAddress = "net.tcp://localhost:8001/Probe";
private const string announcementAddress = "net.tcp://localhost:8002/Announcement";
```

Client applications will send *Probe* messages to an endpoint that is listening to the *probe Address* address, and services will send announcement messages to an endpoint that is listening to the *announcementAddress* address.

The *Main* method creates a new *ServiceHost* object for hosting the *ProductsServiceProxy* service:

```
ServiceHost proxyService = new ServiceHost(new ProductsServiceProxy());
```

The *Main* method then creates a discovery endpoint by using the *DiscoveryEndpoint* and binds it to the address specified by the *probeAddress* constant.

Note The *DiscoveryEndpoint* class is the more generalized parent class of *UdpDiscovery Endpoint* that supports network protocols and addressing modes in addition to UDP multicasting. It is located in the *System.ServiceModel.Discovery* namespace:

```
// Create probe endpoint for discovery proxy
DiscoveryEndpoint discoveryEndpoint = new DiscoveryEndpoint();
discoveryEndpoint.Binding = new NetTcpBinding();
discoveryEndpoint.Address = new EndpointAddress(probeAddress);
discoveryEndpoint.IsSystemEndpoint = false;
```

> **Note** The *IsSystemEndpoint* property indicates whether the endpoint is a system-defined standard endpoint with a built-in configuration or an application-defined endpoint with application-defined settings. By default, a *DiscoveryEndpoint* endpoint is classified as a system endpoint, but in this case, you are modifying the configuration in your application (it is a TCP endpoint with an address specified by the application), so the *IsSystemEndpoint* property must be set to **false**. If you leave this property set to *true* (the default for the *DiscoveryEndpoint* class), then you will receive errors when you attempt to open the discovery proxy, indicating that you need to add a service discovery behavior to make the service discoverable.

The *Main* method creates an announcement endpoint in a similar way, by using the *AnnouncementEndpoint* class (also located in the *System.ServiceModel.Discovery* namespace).

```
// Create announcement endpoint for discovery proxy
AnnouncementEndpoint announcementEndpoint = new AnnouncementEndpoint();
announcementEndpoint.Binding = new NetTcpBinding();
announcementEndpoint.Address = new EndpointAddress(announcementAddress);
```

Next, the *Main* method adds these two endpoints to the *ServiceHost* object, and then starts the host running. At this point, the discovery proxy is available to receive announcement messages from services and to handle Probe and Resolve requests from client applications:

```
// Add endpoints to the service host
proxyService.AddServiceEndpoint(discoveryEndpoint);
proxyService.AddServiceEndpoint(announcementEndpoint);

// Start the service
proxyService.Open();
Console.WriteLine("Discovery Proxy Service running\n");
```

The service continues running until the user presses Enter, at which point the *Service-Host* object shuts down:

```
Console.WriteLine("Press ENTER to stop");
Console.ReadLine();

// Stop the service and finish
proxyService.Close();
```

   3. Rebuild the solution.

Before you start the *ProductsService* running, you must configure it to send announcement messages to the TCP endpoint created by the discovery proxy rather than broadcasting them to the world at large.

Configure the *ProductsService* Service to Send Announcement Messages to the Discovery Proxy

1. Open the web.config file for the C:\...\ProductsService\ project by using the Service Configuration Editor.

2. In the Configuration pane, expand the Advanced folder, expand the Service Behaviors folder, expand the *(Empty Name)* behavior, expand the *serviceDiscovery* behavior element, expand the Announcement Endpoint folder, and then click the *(Empty Name)* announcement endpoint.

    The service is currently configured to broadcast announcements over a UDP connection.

3. In the Client Endpoint pane, change the *Kind* property to **announcementEndpoint**.

    The *announcementEndpoint* endpoint is a standard endpoint for sending unicast announcement messages announcement messages. You can specify the address to send the messages to in the *Address* property.

4. In the *Address* property, enter **net.tcp://localhost:8002/Announcement**. As described earlier, this is the address that the discovery proxy listens to for announcement messages. Set the *Binding* property to **netTcpBinding**, because this is a TCP address.

5. Save the configuration file then close the Service Configuration Editor.

You also need to amend the client application. Previously, it included functionality that listened for announcement messages, but the discovery proxy is now performing this task. Therefore, you need to revert back to something approaching the version of the client application that you built in the first exercise and configure it to send *Probe* messages. However, as with the *ProductsService* service, the client should no longer broadcast these *Probe* requests; instead, it should direct them toward the discovery proxy.

Modify the Client Application to Send Probe Requests to the Discovery Proxy

1. Open the Program.cs file for the ProductsClient project in the Code And Text Editor window.

2. In the *Program* class, remove the definition of the *services ConcurrentDictionary* collection above the *Main* method and replace it with the following statement that specifies the address to which to send *Probe* messages:

```
class Program
{
    private const string probeAddress = "net.tcp://localhost:8001/Probe";

    static void Main(string[] args)
    {
        ...
    }
}
```

3. In the *Main* method, remove the *announcementService* variable and delete the code that implements the *OnlineAnnouncementReceived* and *OfflineAnnouncementReceived* events. Also remove the statements that create the *announcementHost ServiceHost* variable as well as those that connect this service to the UDP announcement endpoint and start it listening. The *Main* method should now start with the code that prompts the user to press Enter when the *ProductsService* service is running:

```
static void Main(string[] args)
{
    Console.WriteLine("Press ENTER when the Products Service is available");
    Console.ReadLine();
    ...
}
```

4. In the *Console.WriteLine* statement, change the message to **"Press ENTER when the Discovery Proxy has started"**.

```
static void Main(string[] args)
{
    Console.WriteLine("Press ENTER when the Discovery Proxy has started");
    Console.ReadLine();
    ...
}
```

5. After the *Console.ReadLine* statement, add the following code shown in bold:

```
static void Main(string[] args)
{
    Console.WriteLine("Press ENTER when the Discovery Proxy has started");
    Console.ReadLine();

    // Create a DiscoveryClient object that connects to the discovery proxy
    Uri discoveryProxyUri = new Uri(probeAddress);
    EndpointAddress discoveryProxyAddress = new EndpointAddress(discoveryProxyUri);
    DiscoveryEndpoint discoveryProxyEndpoint =
        new DiscoveryEndpoint(new NetTcpBinding(), discoveryProxyAddress);
    DiscoveryClient discoveryClient = new DiscoveryClient(discoveryProxyEndpoint);
    ...
}
```

These statements create a TCP endpoint for connecting to the discovery proxy and then instantiate a *DiscoveryClient* object that connects to this endpoint.

6. The next statement creates a *FindCriteria* object based on the type of the contract (*IProductsService*) implemented by the *ProductsService* service. Leave this statement intact, but remove the subsequent statement that attempts to locate the service in the services collection. Replace it with the following code (shown in bold) that submits a *Probe* request through the *DiscoveryClient* object to the discovery proxy and retrieves the address of the first endpoint returned by the *ProbeMatch* response:

```
static void Main(string[] args)
{
    ...
    DiscoveryClient discoveryClient = new DiscoveryClient(discoveryProxyEndpoint);

    // Find the announced endpoint for the Products Service
    FindCriteria productsServiceCriteria = new FindCriteria(typeof(IProductsService));
    FindResponse findResponse = discoveryClient.Find(productsServiceCriteria);
    EndpointAddress productsServiceAddress = findResponse.Endpoints[0].Address;

    // Connect to the Products Service
    ...
}
```

 Note As in the first set of exercises in this chapter, this code assumes that at least one matching service was found; otherwise, it will throw an exception when it attempts to access the *Address* property of the object at element zero in the *Endpoints* collection of the *find Response* variable.

7. The remainder of the code in the client application should stay unchanged. Rebuild the solution.

You can now test the discovery proxy, but first you need to deploy the updated version of the *ProductsService* service and configure the solution to start the discovery proxy, as well as the client application.

Test the Discovery Proxy

1. In Solution Explorer, right-click the C:\...\ProductsService\ project, and then click Publish Web Site. Publish the Web site to the location **http://localhost/DiscoverableService** and allow Visual Studio to overwrite the existing files deployed previously.

2. In the ProductsService solution, set the ProductsServiceProxy and ProductsClient projects as startup projects.

3. Start the solution without debugging but do not press Enter in the client console window just yet.

4. Return to Internet Information Services Manager and start the *DiscoverableProducts Service* Web application by browsing the ProductsService.svc file, as before. Close Internet Explorer but leave Internet Information Services Manager open.

5. Switch to the console window for the discovery proxy. You should see the trace messages output by the *OnBeginOnlineAnouncement* and *OnEndOnlineAnnouncement* methods that were triggered by the *ProductsService* service starting up, as shown in the image that follows.

6. Switch to the console window for the client application, and then press Enter. The client application should send a *Probe* message to the discovery proxy, which returns the address of the *ProductsService* service. The client application should then use this address to connect to the *ProductsService* service and use it to retrieve and update product information, as before.

7. Return to the console window for the discovery proxy. You should now see additional trace messages that were generated by the *OnBeginFind* and *OnEndFind* methods called when the client application submitted the *Probe* request:

8. Return to Internet Information Services Manager. In the Connections pane, click Application Pools. In the middle pane, right-click the ASP.NET v4.0 application pool, and then click Recycle. This action will shut down all Web applications services that use this application pool, including the *ProductsService* service.

9. Switch back to the console window for the discovery proxy. This window should now display further trace messages from the *OnBeginOfflineAnnouncement* and *OnEnd OfflineAnnouncement* methods; the *ProductsService* service announced that it was going offline as it shut down.

10. Press Enter to close the console windows for the discovery proxy and the client application, and then return to Visual Studio.

Implementing Routing

Routing is intended to handle a subtly different scenario from discovery.

Sometimes it is useful to be able to forward messages sent to a service to an entirely different service for handling. For example, suppose that client applications send requests to various WCF services hosted by an organization, but all these requests actually go through the same front-end service, which acts as a firewall to the real WCF services. The front-end service can run on a computer forming part of the organization's perimeter network, and the computers hosting the real WCF services can reside in a protected network inside the organization. The front-end service can implement a routing mechanism, forwarding requests on the real services by examining the action or address in each message. This technique is known as *address-based routing*. The front-end service can also filter messages, detecting rogue requests and blocking them, depending on the degree of intelligence you want to incorporate into the front-end service logic.

An alternative scheme is to route messages based on their contents rather than on the action being requested; this mechanism is known as *content-based routing*. For example, if you are hosting a commercial service, you might offer different levels of service to different users, depending on the fees that they pay you. A "premium" user (paying higher fees) could have requests forwarded to a high-performance server for a fast response, whereas a "standard" user (not paying as much) might have to make do with a lower level of performance. The client application run by both categories of user actually sends messages to the same front-end service, but the front-end service examines some aspect of the message, such as the identity of the user making the request, and then forwards the message to the appropriate destination.

A front-end service can also provide other features, such as load-balancing. Requests from client applications arrive at a single front-end server, which uses a load-balancing algorithm to distribute requests evenly across all servers running the WCF service.

WCF provides two primary mechanisms that you can employ to implement routing, depending upon the complexity of your requirements. The *RoutingService* class in the *System.Service Model.Routing* namespace enables you to provide configuration information to route messages to other services, based on criteria that examine the contents and addresses of these messages (address-based routing and content-based routing). Alternatively, if you need to implement a more dynamic or low-level approach such as that required by a load-balancing router, you can route messages manually, based on criteria such as the current workload of a service.

Before looking at how you can use the *RoutingService*, it is useful to explain a little more about what happens when a WCF service actually receives a request message from a client application and how you can use this information to implement your own custom routing service.

Routing Messages Manually

A service can expose multiple endpoints, each associated with the same or a different contract. When a WCF service receives a message, it must examine the message to determine which service endpoint should actually process it. You can customize the way in which WCF selects the endpoint to use, and this provides a mechanism for you to change the way in which WCF routes messages within a service.

ChannelDispatcher and *EndpointDispatcher* Objects Revisited

In Chapter 11, "Programmatically Controlling the Configuration and Communications," you saw that the WCF runtime for a service creates a channel stack for each distinct address and binding combination used to communicate with the service. Each channel stack has a *Channel Dispatcher* object and one or more *EndpointDispatcher* objects. The purpose of the *Channel Dispatcher* object is to determine which *EndpointDispatcher* object should handle the message. The role of the *EndpointDispatcher* object is to convert the message into a method call and invoke the appropriate method in the service.

> **Note** This is a very simplified view of the WCF Service Model. The *EndpointDispatcher* object does not directly invoke the method in the service itself; it uses a number of other helper objects instantiated by the WCF runtime. These objects have their own specific responsibilities for converting the message into a method call, selecting the appropriate service instance, handling the value returned by the method, and all the other low-level tasks associated with executing an operation. The WCF runtime is highly customizable, so you can replace many of the standard components provided by WCF that perform these tasks with your own implementations.

Each address and binding combination exposed by a service can be shared by multiple endpoints. For example, the configuration file for the ProductsServiceHost project in the ProductsServiceLibrary solution from Chapter 6, "Maintaining Service Contracts and Data Contracts," defined the following service and endpoints for the two versions of the service contract, *Products.IProductsService* and *Products.IProductsServiceV2*:

```
<services>
  <service name="Products.ProductsServiceImpl">
    <endpoint address="http://localhost:8010/ProductsService/Service.svc"
      binding="ws2007HttpBinding" bindingConfiguration=""
      name="WS2007HttpBinding_IProductsService"
      contract="Products.IProductsService" />
    <endpoint address="http://localhost:8010/ProductsService/Service.svc"
      binding="ws2007HttpBinding" bindingConfiguration=""
      name="WS2007HttpBinding_IProductsService"
      contract="Products.IProductsServiceV2" />
  </service>
</services>
```

Notice that this configuration defines two endpoints, but they share the same address/binding combination; the only difference is the contract associated with each endpoint. This configuration causes the WCF runtime to create a single channel stack with its own *ChannelDispatcher* object. However, the channel stack is associated with two possible endpoints; one for each of the contracts available. Consequently, the WCF runtime creates two *EndpointDispatcher* objects for the channel stack and adds them to the collection of *EndpointDispatcher* objects associated with the *ChannelDispatcher* object. If the ProductsServiceHost project additionally provided TCP endpoints for this service, as shown in the following configuration, then the WCF runtime would create two channel stacks (one for the HTTP endpoints, and another for the TCP endpoints), with their own *ChannelDispatcher* objects. The TCP endpoints would have their own *EndpointDispatcher* objects.

```
<service name="Products.ProductsServiceImpl">
  <endpoint address="http://localhost:8010/ProductsService/Service.svc"
    binding="ws2007HttpBinding" bindingConfiguration=""
    name="WS2007HttpBinding_IProductsService"
    contract="Products.IProductsService" />
  <endpoint address="http://localhost:8010/ProductsService/Service.svc"
    binding="ws2007HttpBinding" bindingConfiguration=""
    name="WS2007HttpBinding_IProductsService"
    contract="Products.IProductsServiceV2" />
  <endpoint address="net.tcp://localhost:8080/TcpProductsService"
    binding="netTcpBinding" bindingConfiguration=""
    name="NetTcpBinding_IProductsService"
    contract="Products.IProductsService" />
  <endpoint address="net.tcp://localhost:8080/TcpProductsService"
    binding="netTcpBinding" bindingConfiguration=""
    name="NetTcpBinding_IProductsService"
    contract="Products.IProductsServiceV2" />
</service>
```

Figure 14-1 shows the relationship between the endpoints, channel stack, and dispatcher object for this service configuration.

When the service receives a message on a channel, the *ChannelDispatcher* object at the top of the channel stack queries each of its associated *EndpointDispatcher* objects to determine which endpoint can process the message. If none of the *EndpointDispatcher* objects can accept the message, the WCF runtime raises the *UnknownMessageReceived* event on the *ServiceHost* object hosting the service. Chapter 3, "Making Applications and Services Robust," describes how to handle this event.

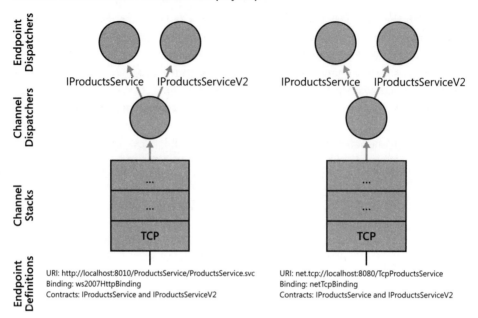

FIGURE 14-1 Channels and Dispatchers for the *ProductsServiceImpl* service.

EndpointDispatcher Objects and Filters

How does an *EndpointDispatcher* object indicate that it can process a message? An *Endpoint Dispatcher* object exposes two properties that the *ChannelDispatcher* can query: *AddressFilter* and *ContractFilter*.

The *AddressFilter* property is an instance of the *EndpointAddressMessageFilter* class. The *EndpointAddressMessageFilter* class provides a method called *Match* that takes a message as its input parameter and returns a Boolean value that indicates whether the *Endpoint Dispatcher* object recognizes the address contained in the header of this message.

The *ContractFilter* property is an instance of the *ActionMessageFilter* class. This class also provides a method called *Match* that takes a message as its input parameter, and it returns a Boolean value that indicates whether the *EndpointDispatcher* object can handle the action specified in the message header. Remember that the action identifies the method that the *EndpointDispatcher* will invoke in the service instance if it accepts the request. Internally, the *ActionMessageFilter* object contains a table of actions, held as strings, and all the *Match* method does is iterate through this table until it either finds a match or reaches the end of the table.

Note The *EndpointAddressMessageFilter* class and the *ActionMessageFilter* class are both descendents of the *MessageFilter* abstract class. They override the abstract *Match* method of the *MessageFilter* class with their own specialized implementations that match endpoints and contracts.

The *Match* method in *both* filters must return *true* for the *ChannelDispatcher* object to consider sending the message to the *EndpointDispatcher* object for processing. It is also possible for more than one *EndpointDispatcher* object to indicate that it can handle the message. In this case, the *EndpointDispatcher* class provides the *FilterPriority* property. This property returns an integer value. An *EndpointDispatcher* object can indicate its relative precedence compared to other *EndpointDispatcher* objects by returning a higher or lower number. If two matching endpoints have the same priority, the WCF runtime throws a *MultipleFilterMatches Exception* exception.

The WCF runtime creates the *EndpointAddressFilterMessage* and *ActionMessageFilter* objects for each *ChannelDispatcher* object, based on the endpoint definitions in the service configuration file (or in code, if you are creating endpoints dynamically by using the *AddService Endpoint* method of the *ServiceHost* object, as described in Chapter 11). You can override these filters by creating your own customized instances of these objects with your own address and table of actions and inserting these filters when the WCF runtime builds the service prior to opening it. One way to do this is to create a custom behavior, as you did when adding the message inspector in Chapter 11.

By default, the *EndpointDispatcher* invokes the method corresponding to the action in the service contract. However, you can modify the way in which the *EndpointDispatcher* processes an operation request by creating a class that implements the *IDispatchOperationSelector* interface and assigning it to the *OperationSelector* property of the *DispatchRuntime* object referenced by the *DispatchRuntime* property of the *EndpointDispatcher* object. This interface contains a single method called *SelectOperation*:

```
public string SelectOperation(ref Message message).
```

You can use this method to examine the message and return the name of a method that the *EndpointDispatcher* should invoke to handle it. This is useful if you want to manually control the way in which the dispatching mechanism works.

> **More Info** The Custom Demux sample included with the WCF samples that you can download from the Microsoft Web site (*http://www.microsoft.com/downloads/details.aspx?FamilyID=35ec8682-d5fd-4bc3-a51a-d8ad115a8792&displaylang=en*) provides more information on creating an endpoint behavior class that overrides the contract filter and operation selector for an endpoint dispatcher. This sample is based on the *MsmqIntegrationBinding* binding, but the general principles are the same for other bindings. You can find this sample online at *http://msdn.microsoft.com/en-us/library/ms752265.aspx*.

To summarize, the dispatching mechanism provides a highly customizable mechanism for determining which endpoint should process a message. You can make use of this knowledge to build services that can transparently route messages to other services.

Routing Messages to Other Services

The WCF runtime makes it a relatively simple matter to build a WCF service that accepts *specific messages* and sends them to another service for processing (I shall refer to this type of service as a *front-end service* from here on in this chapter). All you need to do is define a front-end service with a service contract that mirrors that of the target service. The methods defining the operations in the front-end service can perform any pre-processing required, such as examining the identity of the user making the request or the data being passed in as parameters and then forward the request on to the appropriate target service.

However, creating a generalized WCF service that can accept *any messages* and route them to another service running on a different computer requires a little more thought. There are at least three issues that you need to handle:

1. The service contract. A WCF service describes the operations that it can perform by defining a service contract. For a service to accept messages, those messages must be recognized by the *ContractFilter* of one or more *EndpointDispatcher* objects. At first glance, therefore, it would appear that any front-end service that accepts messages and forwards them on to another service must implement a service contract that is the same as that of the target service. While this is feasible when routing messages to a single service, if you are building a front-end service for many other services, this situation can quickly become unmanageable because the front-end service has to implement service contracts that match all these other services.

2. The contents of messages. In some ways this issue is related to the first problem. If a front-end service must implement the service contracts for a vast array of other services, it also must implement any data contracts that these other services use, describing how data structures are serialized into the bodies of the messages. Again, this can quickly become an unwieldy task.

3. The contents of message headers. Apart from the data in the body, a message also contains one or more message headers. These message headers contain information such as encryption tokens, transaction identifiers, and many other miscellaneous items used to control the flow of data and manage the integrity of messages. A front-end service must carefully manage this information in order to appear transparent to the client application sending requests and the services that receive and process those requests.

Fortunately, there are reasonably straightforward solutions to at least some of these problems, which you will investigate in the following set of exercises. In these exercises, you will see how to build a very simple load-balancing router for the *ShoppingCartService* service. You will run two instances of the *ShoppingCartService* service, and the load-balancing router will direct requests transparently from client applications to each service. The load-balancing routing will implement a very simple algorithm, sending alternate requests to each instance of the

ShoppingCartService service. Although all three services in this exercise will be running on the same computer, it would be very easy to arrange for them to execute on different machines, allowing you to spread the workload across different processors.

You will start by refamiliarizing yourself with the *ShoppingCartService* service and modifying it to execute in a more traditional Internet environment.

Revisit the Durable *ShoppingCartService* Service

1. Using Visual Studio, open the ShoppingCart.sln solution file in the Microsoft Press\WCF Step By Step\Chapter 14\LoadBalancingRouter folder.

    This solution contains an amended copy of the durable *ShoppingCartService*, *Shopping CartServiceHost*, and *ShoppingCartGUIClient* projects from Chapter 7, "Maintaining State and Sequencing Operations."

> **Note** This version of the *ShoppingCartService* service requires that you have created the *WCFPersistence* database as the persistence store and configured the SQL Server persistence provider, as described in Chapter 7. You must also have reserved port 9000. If you have removed this reservation since performing the exercises in Chapter 7, open a Visual Studio Command Prompt window as administrator, and enter the following command (replace *UserName* with your windows user name):
>
> ```
> netsh http add urlacl url=http://+:9000/ user=UserName
> ```

2. Open the IShoppingCartService.cs file for the ShoppingCartService project in the Code And Text Editor window and review the code in this file. Recall from Chapter 7 that the *ShoppingCartService* service implements the operations *AddItemToCart*, *RemoveItem FromCart*, *GetShoppingCart*, and *Checkout*.

3. Open the ShoppingCartService.cs file in the Code And Text Editor window and review the code in this file as well. Notice that the service employs the *PerSession* instance context mode and that it is tagged with the *DurableService* attribute. Session state is maintained between calls in the *WCFPersistence* SQL Server database.

4. Open the Program.cs file in the *ShoppingCartHost* project. This is the service host application. All it does is start the service running by using a *ServiceHost* object, and then it waits for the user to press Enter to close the host.

5. Open the App.config file for the ShoppingCartHost project in the Code And Text Editor window. Notice that the service host creates an HTTP endpoint with the URI *http:// localhost:9000/ShoppingCartService/ShoppingCartService.svc*. In this version of the application, the endpoint uses the *basicHttpContextBinding* binding without any additional settings beyond its default configuration. In an Internet environment, it is likely that you would implement transport-level security to protect messages travelling between a client application and a service. With WCF, you can configure transport-level security by

using the *basicHttpBinding* binding over HTTPS. The *basicHttpContextBinding* binding is simply an extended version of the *basicHttpBinding* binding that passes the instance ID of the session that the client application wishes to communicate with as a cookie in the Web request header.

Close the App.config file when you have finished.

> **Note** For simplicity, and to allow you to concentrate on the process of routing messages, in this exercise you will not actually configure the *ShoppingCartService* service to use HTTPS, but if you want to know how to do this, go back and read the "Protecting an HTTP Service at the Transport Level" section on page 135 in Chapter 4, "Protecting an Enterprise WCF Service."

6. Open the app.config file for the ShoppingCartGUIClient project in the Code And Text Editor window and verify that the client application uses an endpoint with the same URI and binding as the service (*http://localhost:9000/ShoppingCartService/ShoppingCart Service.svc*). Close the app.config file when you have finished.

7. Start the solution without debugging to refamiliarize yourself with the client application.

   In the Shopping Cart GUI Client window, enter **WB-H098** in the Product Number text box, and then click Add Item. After a short delay, a water bottle should be added to the shopping cart and displayed in the window.

   Enter **BK-M38S-46** in the Product Number text box, and then click Add Item again. This time, you should see a silver mountain bike added to the shopping cart.

   Click Checkout. The shopping cart should empty.

8. Close the Shopping Cart GUI Client window as well as the service host console application window.

At this point, you have a version of the *ShoppingCartService* service to which a client application can connect directly. The next step is to run multiple instances of this service and create another service that routes messages transparently from the client application to one of these instances, based on the load-balancing algorithm implemented by the routing service. In this example, you will simply send alternating requests to two instances of the *ShoppingCart Service* service.

Create the *ShoppingCartRouter* Service

1. Add a new project to the ShoppingCart solution by using the WCF Service Library template (in the WCF folder, located in the Installed Templates pane, in the Add New Project dialog box). Name the project **ShoppingCartServiceRouter** and save it in the **Microsoft Press\WCF Step By Step\Chapter 14\LoadBalancingRouter** folder within your Documents folder.

2. In the ShoppingCartServiceRouter project, rename the Service1.cs file to **Router.cs**, and rename the IService1.cs file to **IRouter.cs**. Allow Visual Studio to rename all *Service1* references to *Router* when prompted.

3. Open the IRouter.cs file in the Code And Text Editor window. Add the following *using* statement to the list at the top of the file:

```
using System.ServiceModel.Channels;
```

4. Remove the comment above the *ServiceContract* attribute for the *IRouter* interface, and then modify this attribute to set the *Namespace* and *Name* properties, as shown in bold in the following:

```
[ServiceContract(Namespace = "http://adventure-works.com/2010/15/07",
                 Name = "ShoppingCartServiceRouter")]
public interface IRouter
{
    ...
}
```

5. In the *IRouter* interface, remove the definitions of the *GetData* and *GetDataUsing DataContract* operations and the comment, and replace them with the *ProcessMessage* operation, as shown in bold in the following:

```
public interface IRouter
{
    [OperationContract(Action="*", ReplyAction="*")]
    Message ProcessMessage(Message message);
}
```

Understanding this rather simple-looking service contract is the key to appreciating how the router works.

In the earlier discussion, you saw that the problems that you have to overcome when designing a generalized front-end service that can forward any message on to another service concern the service contract and the contents of messages passing through the service. A service contract defines the operations that the service can process. Under normal circumstances, the WSDL description for an operation combines the *Namespace* and *Name* properties from the *ServiceContract* attribute with the name of the operation to generate an identifier, or action, defining the request message that a client application should send to invoke the operation as well as the reply action for the response message that the service will send back. For example, the *AddItemToCart* operation in the *ShoppingCartService* service is identified as follows:

```
http://adventure-works.com/2010/06/04/ShoppingCartService/AddItemToCart
```

When the WCF runtime constructs each *EndpointDispatcher* for a service, it adds the actions that the corresponding endpoint can accept to the table referenced by the *ContractFilter* property.

If you explicitly provide a value for the *Action* property of the *OperationContract* attribute when defining an operation, the WCF runtime uses your defined value instead of the operation name. If you specify a value of "*" for the *Action* property, the WCF runtime automatically routes all messages to this operation—regardless of the value of the action specified in the header of the message sent by the client application. Internally, the WCF runtime for the service replaces the *ActionMessageFilter* object referenced by the *ContractFilter* property of the *EndpointDispatcher* object with a *MatchAllMessageFilter* object. The *Match* method of this object returns *true* for all non-null messages passed to it, so the *EndpointDispatcher* will automatically indicate that it can accept all requests sent to it (the *AddressFilter* property is still queried by the *ChannelDispatcher*, however). In this exercise, when the *ShoppingCartClient* application sends *AddItemToCart*, *RemoveItemFromCart*, *GetShoppingCart*, and *Checkout* messages to the *ShoppingCartServiceRouter* service, it will accept them all and the *EndpointDispatcher* will invoke the *ProcessMessage* method.

You should also pay attention to the signature of the *ProcessMessage* method. The WCF runtime on the client packages the parameters passed into an operation as the body of a SOAP message. Under normal circumstances, the WCF runtime on the service converts the body of the SOAP message back into a set of parameters that are then passed into the method implementing the operation. If the method returns a value, the WCF runtime on the service packages it up into a message and transmits it back to the WCF runtime on the client, where it is converted back into the type expected by the client application.

The *ProcessMessage* method is a little different, because it takes a *Message* object as input. In Chapter 11, you saw that the *Message* class provides a means for transmitting and receiving raw SOAP messages. When the WCF runtime on the service receives a message from the client application, it does not unpack the parameters but instead passes the complete SOAP message to the *ProcessMessage* method. It is up to the *ProcessMessage* method to parse and interpret the contents of this *Message* object itself.

Similarly, the value returned by the *ProcessMessage* method is also a *Message* object. The *ProcessMessage* method must construct a complete SOAP message that contains the data in the format expected by the client application and return this object. This response message must also include a *ReplyAction* in the message header corresponding to the *ReplyAction* expected by the WCF runtime on the client. Usually, the WCF runtime on the service adds a *ReplyAction* based on the name of the service and the operation. For example, the message that the *ShoppingCartService* service sends back to a client application in response to an *AddItemToCart* message is identified like this:

```
http://adventure-works.com/2010/06/04/ShoppingCartService/AddItemToCartResponse
```

If you set the *ReplyAction* property of the *OperationContract* attribute to "*", the WCF runtime for the service expects you to provide the appropriate *ReplyAction* in code and add it to the message header when you create the response message. In this case, you will pass the *ReplyAction* returned from the *ShoppingCartService* back to the client application unchanged.

6. Remove the *CompositeType* class, including the *DataContract* attribute, from the IShoppingCartServce.cs file (it is not required by the *ShoppingCartServiceRouter* service).

7. Open the Router.cs file for the ShpppingCartServiceRouter project in the Code And Text Editor window.

8. Add the following *using* statement to the list at the top of the file:

```
using System.ServiceModel.Channels;
```

9. Remove the comment and the implementations of the *GetData* and *GetDataUsing DataContract* methods from the *Router* class.

10. Add the following *ServiceBehavior* attribute to the *Router* class:

```
[ServiceBehavior(InstanceContextMode = InstanceContextMode.Single,
                 ValidateMustUnderstand = false)]
public class Router : IRouter
{
}
```

The *Router* class will provide the implementation of the *ProcessMessage* method (you will add this method in a later step). If you are familiar with the SOAP protocol, you will be aware that you can include information in message headers that the receiving service must recognize and be able to process. In this example, the *ShoppingCartServiceRouter* service is not actually going to process the messages itself, it is simply going to forward them to an instance of the *ShoppingCartService* service. It therefore does not need to examine or understand the message headers, and should pass them on unchanged. Setting the *ValidateMustUnderstand* property of the *ServiceBehavior* attribute to *false* turns off any enforced recognition and validation of message headers by the service.

Additionally, the *ShoppingCartServiceRouter* service will be a singleton service, with a single instance accessed by all client applications.

11. Add the following private fields (shown in bold) to the *Router* class:

```
public class Router : IRouter
{
    private static IChannelFactory<IRequestChannel> factory = null;
    private EndpointAddress address1 = new EndpointAddress(
        "http://localhost:9010/ShoppingCartService/ShoppingCartService.svc");
    private EndpointAddress address2 = new EndpointAddress(
        "http://localhost:9020/ShoppingCartService/ShoppingCartService.svc");
    private static int routeBalancer = 1;
}
```

The *ShoppingCartServiceRouter* service will act as a client application to two instances of the *ShoppingCartService* service, sending each of them messages and waiting for responses. The generalized nature of the *ProcessMessage* method requires you to connect to the *ShoppingCartService* service using the low-level techniques described in Chapter 11 rather than by using a proxy object. You will use the *IChannelFactory* object to create a channel factory, based on the *IRequestChannel* shape for opening channels to each instance of the *ShoppingCartService* (refer back to Chapter 11 for a brief description of channel shapes).

The *EndpointAddress* objects specify the URI for each instance of the *ShoppingCart Service* service. You will configure the *ShoppingCartServiceHost* application to run two instances of the *ShoppingCartService* service at these addresses in a later step.

The *ProcessMessage* method will use the *routeBalancer* variable to determine to which instance of the *ShoppingCartService* service to send messages.

12. Add the following static constructor (shown in bold) to the *Router* class:

```
public class Router : IRouter
{
    ...
    static Router()
    {
        try
        {
            BasicHttpContextBinding service = new BasicHttpContextBinding();
            factory = service.BuildChannelFactory<IRequestChannel>();
            factory.Open();
        }
        catch (Exception e)
        {
            Console.WriteLine("Exception: {0}", e.Message);
        }
    }
}
```

The *ProcessMessage* method will use a *ChannelFactory* object to open a channel with the appropriate instance of the *ShoppingCartService* service. *ChannelFactory* objects are expensive to create and destroy, but as this is a singleton service all requests will reuse the same *ChannelFactory* object. Building this object in a static constructor ensures that it is created only once.

Also, notice that the *ChannelFactory* object is constructed by using a *BasicHttpContext Binding* object. This binding matches the addressing scheme (http) and requirements for the two instances of the *ShoppingCartService* service (they are durable services that pass context information in the SOAP headers of messages).

13. Add the *ProcessMessage* method to the *Router* class, as follows:

```
public class Router : IRouter
{
    ...
    public Message ProcessMessage(Message message)
    {
        IRequestChannel channel = null;

        Console.WriteLine("Action {0}", message.Headers.Action);
        try
        {
            if (routeBalancer % 2 == 0)
            {
                channel = factory.CreateChannel(address1);
                Console.WriteLine("Using {0}\n", address1.Uri);
            }
            else
            {
                channel = factory.CreateChannel(address2);
                Console.WriteLine("Using {0}\n", address2.Uri);
            }
            routeBalancer++;
            message.Properties.Remove("ContextMessageProperty");

            channel.Open();
            Message reply = channel.Request(message);
            channel.Close();
            return reply;
        }
        catch (Exception e)
        {
            Console.WriteLine(e.Message);
            return null;
        }
    }
}
```

This method contains several *Console.WriteLine* statements that let you follow the execution in the service console window when the service runs.

The *if* statement in the *try* block implements the load-balancing algorithm; if the value in the *routeBalancer* variable is even, the method creates a channel for forward requests to *address1* (*https://localhost:9010/ShoppingCartService/ShoppingCartService.svc*); otherwise, it creates a channel for *address2* (*https://localhost:9020/ShoppingCartService/ShoppingCartService.svc*). The method then increments the value in the *routeBalancer* variable. In this way, the *ProcessMessage* method sends all requests alternately to one instance or the other of the *ShoppingCartService* service.

There is one small complication to be aware of in this method, which is caused by the context protocol implemented by the binding. Remember that when you use one of the context bindings (*WSHttpContextBinding*, *BasicHttpContextBinding*, or *NetTcp ContextBinding*), the message can include context information that the durable service uses to correlate requests made by a client application and direct them to the appropriate session. By default, the channel that receives the message caches this context information internally and flows this same context on if it invokes other services. However, the message that has been received also contains the same context information, so the same context will be sent twice when the message is forwarded, causing errors in the service to which the router sends the message. The solution is to remove the context from the incoming message before forwarding it, which is what the *message.Properties. Remove("ContextMessageProperty")* statement does.

> **Note** You can examine the ambient information in the current operation, including any message properties that will be flowed on to other services, by querying the static *Operation Context.Current* property in the code for an operation.

The *Request* method of the *IRequestChannel* class sends the *Message* object through the channel to the destination service. The value returned is another *Message* object containing the response from the service. The *ProcessMessage* method passes this message unchanged to the client application.

> **Important** Note that the code explicitly closes the *IRequestChannel* object before the method finishes. This object is local to the *ProcessMessage* method, and so it is subject to garbage collection when the method finishes. If it were open at that time, it would be closed automatically. However, you can never be sure when the Common Language Runtime is going to perform its garbage collection, so leaving the *IRequestChannel* object open holds a connection to the service open for an indeterminate period, possibly resulting in the service refusing to accept further connections if you exceed the value of *MaxConcurrent Instances* for the *ShoppingCartService* service (Refer back to Chapter 13, "Implementing a WCF Service for Good Performance," for more details.)

Remember that the *Message* object sent by the client application can contain security and other header information. Other than the context data, the *ProcessMessage* method makes no attempt to examine or change this information, so the destination service is not even aware that the message has been passed through the *ShoppingCartService Router* service. Similarly, the *ProcessMessage* method does not modify the response in any way, and the router is transparent to the client application. However, there is nothing to stop you from adding code that changes the contents of a message or a response before forwarding it. This opens up some interesting security considerations, so you should ensure that you deploy the *ShoppingCartServiceRouter* service in a secure environment.

14. Rebuild the solution.

In a production environment, you would typically host the router using an environment such as IIS that is accessible to the outside world, but to keep things concise, in this example you will host the *ShoppingCartRouterService* service with the same application that hosts the *ShoppingCartService* service. You will also modify the host configuration and provide two endpoints for the *ShoppingCartService* service at the addresses expected by the *Shopping CartRouterService* service.

Configure the *ShoppingCartHost* Application to Host the *ShoppingCartRouterService* Service

1. Edit the app.config file for the ShoppingCartHost project by using the Service Configuration Editor.

2. In the Configuration pane, right-click the Services folder then click New Service. In the right pane, in the Name field, type **ShoppingCartServiceRouter.Router**.

3. In the Configuration pane, right-click the Endpoints folder under the new *Shopping-CartServiceRout.Router* service, and then click New Service Endpoint. In the Service Endpoint pane, specify the values shown in the following table (leave any unlisted properties set to their default values):

Property	Value
Address	http://localhost:9000/ShoppingCartService/ShoppingCartService.svc
Binding	basicHttpContextBinding
Contract	ShoppingCartServiceRouter.IRouter

Note that the address of the service is the same as that originally specified for the *ShoppingCartService* service. Existing client applications will now connect to the router without requiring reconfiguration.

4. In the Configuration pane, in the Services folder, expand the *ShoppingCartService. ShoppingCartServiceImpl* service, expand the Endpoints folder, and then click the *(Empty Name)* endpoint. In the Service Endpoint pane, set the name of this endpoint to **ShoppingCartServiceHttpEndpoint1** and change the address to **http:// localhost:9010/ShoppingCartService/ShoppingCartService.svc**.

5. In the Configuration pane, right-click the Endpoints folder under the *ShoppingCart Service.ShoppingCartServiceImpl* service, and then click New Service Endpoint to add a second endpoint to this service. Use the values in the following table to set the properties for this endpoint.

Property	Value
Name	ShoppingCartServiceHttpEndpoint2
Address	http://localhost:9020/ShoppingCartService/ShoppingCartService.svc
Binding	basicHttpContextBinding
Contract	ShoppingCartService.IShoppingCartService

6. Save the configuration file then exit the Service Configuration Editor.

7. In Solution Explorer, add a reference to the ShoppingCartServiceRouter project to the ShoppingCartHost project.

8. Open the Program.cs file for the ShoppingCartHost project in the Code And Text Editor window. In the *Main* method, add the following statements (shown in bold):

```
static void Main(string[] args)
{
    ServiceHost host = new ServiceHost(...)
    host.Open();
    ServiceHost routerHost = new ServiceHost(
        typeof(ShoppingCartServiceRouter.Router));
    routerHost.Open();
    Console.WriteLine("Service running");
    ...
}
```

These statements create and open a new *ServiceHost* object for the *ShoppingCart ServiceRouter* service.

9. The ShoppingCartHost application uses ports 9010 and 9020 as endpoints for the *ShoppingCartService* service. You must reserve these ports to enable the Shopping CartHost application to access them. Open a Visual Studio Command Prompt window as Administrator, and then enter the following commands (replace *UserName* with your Windows user name).

```
netsh http add urlacl url=http://+:9010/ user=UserName
netsh http add urlacl url=http://+:9020/ user=UserName
```

10. Close the Visual Studio Command Prompt window then return to Visual Studio.

Test the *ShoppingCartRouter* Service

1. Start the solution without debugging. In the Shopping Cart GUI Client window, enter **PU-M044** in the Product Number box, and then click Add Item. Add a water bottle to the shopping cart as well (item WB-H098), and then click Checkout.

The client application should function exactly as it did before. However, if you examine the service console window, you can see that the router has forwarded the messages to the two instances of the *ShoppingCartService* service in turn; the addresses alternate between port 9020 and port 9010:

2. Close the Shopping Cart GUI window, and then press Enter to close the service host console window.

Using the RoutingService Class

Implementing manual routing is undoubtedly a very powerful technique, but commonly all you want to do is to route a message to a service, based on some attribute of the request rather than by coding some dynamic algorithm. To handle these situations, WCF provides the *RoutingService* class, in the *System.ServiceModel.Routing* namespace.

The purpose of the *RoutingService* class is to implement request routing based on the contents of the messages that it receives. You can configure a *RoutingService* object to examine information in the headers of messages or even parse the contents in the body of messages and make a decision based on this data. You configure the *RoutingService* class by providing a filter table that contains one or more routing filters that specify criteria for matching messages and a destination to send the message when a match is successful. A routing filter is actually an instance of the *MessageFilter* class that you explored in the previous section.

You can construct *MessageFilter* objects dynamically and associate them with a *RoutingService* object, but the most common approach is to add the information for each routing filter statically to the configuration file for the application hosting the *RoutingService* object and let the WCF runtime create the necessary *MessageFilter* objects when the service starts up. This is the approach that you will take in the exercises in this section.

In the following exercises, you will change the routing strategy for the *ShoppingCartService* service. Instead of using a load-balancing mechanism that directs alternate requests to different instances of the *ShoppingCartService* listening at different endpoints, you will route messages based on the type of request, sending *AddItemToCart* and *RemoveItemFromCart* messages to one instance of the *ShoppingCartService* service, and *GetShoppingCart* and *Checkout* messages to another.

Host and Configure the *RoutingService* Service

1. Using Visual Studio, open the ShoppingCart.sln solution file in the Microsoft Press\WCF Step By Step\Chapter 14\ShoppingCartServiceWithRouter folder.

   This solution contains another copy of the durable *ShoppingCartService*, *ShoppingCart ServiceHost*, and *ShoppingCartGUIClient* projects from Chapter 7; it provides a starting point similar to that used in the previous set of exercises, except that this *ShoppingCart ServiceHost* application has already been configured with two HTTP endpoints that listen for *ShoppingCartService* service requests on ports 9010 and 9020. Both endpoints use the *BasicHttpContextBinding* binding.

2. Add a new project to the *ShoppingCart* solution by using the Console Application template (in the Windows folder, located in the Installed Templates pane, in the Add New Project dialog box). Name the project **StaticRouter** and save it in the **Microsoft Press\ WCF Step By Step\Chapter 14\ ShoppingCartServiceWithRouter** folder within your Documents folder.

3. Add references to the *System.ServiceModel* and *System.ServiceModel.Routing* assemblies and the ShoppingCartService project to the *StaticRouter* project.

4. Open the Program.cs file for the StaticRouter project in the Code And Text Editor window. Add the following *using* statements to the list at the top of the file:

```
using System.ServiceModel;
using System.ServiceModel.Routing;
```

5. Add the following statements (shown in bold) to the *Program* class:

```
static void Main(string[] args)
{
    try
    {
        ServiceHost routerHost = new ServiceHost(typeof(RoutingService));
        routerHost.Open();
        Console.WriteLine("Router running");
        Console.WriteLine("Press ENTER to stop the service");
        Console.ReadLine();
        routerHost.Close();
    }
    catch (Exception e)
    {
        Console.WriteLine(e.Message);
    }
}
```

   Most of this code should be familiar to you by now. All it does is create an instance of the *RoutingService* class and host it in an ordinary *ServiceHost* object. You will define the endpoint for the service in an application configuration file. You will also specify the addresses of the *ShoppingCartService* service to which to route requests as client endpoints in the configuration file.

6. Add a new application configuration file called App.config to the StaticRouter project. Edit the application configuration file by using the Service Configuration Editor.

7. In the Configuration pane, right-click the Services folder, and then click New Service. In the right pane, type **System.ServiceModel.Routing.RoutingService** in the Name field. This is the fully qualified name of the *RoutingService* class.

8. In the Configuration pane, right-click the Endpoints folder under the new service, and then click New Service Endpoint. In the Service Endpoint pane, specify the values shown in the following table (leave any unlisted properties set to their default values):

Property	Value
Address	http://localhost:9000/ShoppingCartService/ShoppingCartService.svc
Binding	basicHttpContextBinding
Contract	System.ServiceModel.Routing.IRequestReplyRouter

The contract determines the messaging pattern that the *RoutingService* object implements. The *IRequestReply* interface handles the basic two-way request/reply pattern over a channel, forwarding request messages from client applications and routing response messages back to the same client. Other contracts available are *IDuplexSessionRouter*, which enables the *RoutingService* object to route callback messages initiated by a service to a client; *ISimplexSessionRouter* for routing one-way messages to a service that implements sessions; and *ISimplexDatagramRouter*, which supports services that do not provide sessions.

 Note Chapter 16, "Using a Callback Contract to Publish and Subscribe to Events" describes how to create and use duplex channels in more detail.

The *IRequestReplyRouter* interface defined in the *System.ServiceModel.Routing* namespace looks like this:

```
[ServiceContract(Namespace="http://schemas.microsoft.com/netfx/2009/05/routing",
                 SessionMode = SessionMode.Allowed)]
public interface IRequestReplyRouter
{
    [OperationContract(AsyncPattern = true, IsOneWay= false, Action = "*",
        ReplyAction = "*")]
    [TransactionFlow(TransactionFlowOption.Allowed)]
    IAsyncResult BeginProcessRequest(Message message, AsyncCallback callback,
        object state);
    Message EndProcessRequest(IAsyncResult result);
}
```

The *IRequestReplyRouter* interface enables the *RoutingService* class to forward request and response messages asynchronously; it can also flow transactions. Note that the *Action* and *ReplyAction* properties of the *OperationContract* attribute specify the "*" value.

9. In the Configuration pane, expand the Advanced folder, and then click the Service Behaviors folder. In the Service Behaviors pane, click the New Service Behavior Configuration link.

10. In the right pane, clear the *Name* property of the behavior, and then click the Add button and add a *routing* behavior element. This element contains properties with which you can configure the behavior of the *RoutingService* service and specify the name of routing table (containing the routing rules for the service).

11. In the Configuration pane, expand the *(Empty Name)* behavior, and then click the *routing* element. In the right pane, enter **ShoppingCartServiceRoutingTable** in the *Filter TableName* field, verify that the *RouteOnHeadersOnly* property is set to *True* (this is the default value), and set the *SoapProcessingEnabled* property to **False**.

You will specify the message filters for the *ShoppingCartServiceRoutingTable* filter table later in this exercise. The *RouteOnHeadersOnly* property indicates whether the filters in this table can define rules that examine just the headers or include data from the body of messages routed through the *RoutingService* service. In this exercise, the messages will be routed based on the action specified in the request headers, so *RouteOnHeaders Only* is set to *true*.

When the *RoutingService* service receives a request, it can route this request to a target service over a different binding, one that possibly implements dissimilar messaging requirements. The *SoapProcessingEnabled* property of the routing behavior specifies whether the *RoutingService* service should convert the message between the formats required by the bindings. If this property is set to *false*, the message will be forwarded unchanged; otherwise, the *RoutingService* service will examine the message and change it to the format expected by the target service if necessary. In this exercise, the *Shopping CartService* service employs the *BasicHttpContextBinding* binding to transmit context information containing the service instance ID between the service and the client application. You need this information to pass verbatim through the *RoutingService* service without interference, so this property is set to **false**.

12. In the Configuration pane, expand the Client folder, right-click the Endpoints folder, and then click New Client Endpoint. In the Client Endpoint pane, specify the values shown in the following table (leave any unlisted properties set to their default values):

Property	Value
Name	ShoppingCartServiceHttpEndpoint1
Address	http://localhost:9010/ShoppingCartService/ShoppingCartService.svc
Binding	basicHttpBinding
Contract	*

The address matches that of the first endpoint for the *ShoppingCartService* service hosted by the *ShoppingCartHost* application. The "*" character in the contract field enables the service to accept any messages and not just those specified by a particular service contract.

Notice that the *Binding* property is set to *basicHttpBinding* and not *basicHttpContext Binding*. The client application connects to the *RoutingService* service by using the *Basic HttpContextBinding* binding, which enables it to include context information containing the service instance ID in the message header. If the *RoutingService* service connects to the *ShoppingCartService* service also by using a context binding, the *RoutingService* service will handle any context information it receives from the *ShoppingCartService* service itself, remove it from the message header, and not return it to the client application. Specifying *basicHttpBinding* prevents the *RoutingService* service from looking for this information and removing it as it flows back to the client. Additionally, as mentioned in the previous step, setting the *SoapProcessingEnabled* property of the behavior of the *RoutingService* service to *false* stops the *RoutingService* service from removing any context headers provided by the client, so they are passed on directly to the *Shopping CartService* service.

13. Add a second client endpoint with the following values.

Property	Value
Name	ShoppingCartServiceHttpEndpoint2
Address	http://localhost:9020/ShoppingCartService/ShoppingCartService.svc
Binding	basicHttpBinding
Contract	*

14. Save the configuration file, and then exit the Service Configuration Editor.

15. Open the App.config file for the StaticRouter project by using the Code And Text Editor window. Add the routing filter table and filters after the *<services>* section, as shown in bold in the following configuration:

```
<?xml version="1.0" encoding="utf-8" ?>
<configuration>
  <system.serviceModel>
    <services>
      ...
```

```
      </services>
      <routing>
        <filters>
          <filter name="ShoppingCart1" filterType="Action" filterData=
            "http://adventure-works.com/2010/06/04/ShoppingCartService/AddItemToCart"/>
          <filter name="ShoppingCart2" filterType="Action" filterData=
            "http://adventure-works.com/2010/06/04/ShoppingCartService/RemoveItemFromCart"/>
          <filter name="ShoppingCart3" filterType="Action" filterData=
            "http://adventure-works.com/2010/06/04/ShoppingCartService/GetShoppingCart"/>
          <filter name="ShoppingCart4" filterType="Action" filterData=
            "http://adventure-works.com/2010/06/04/ShoppingCartService/Checkout"/>
        </filters>
        <filterTables>
          <filterTable name="ShoppingCartServiceRoutingTable">
            <add filterName="ShoppingCart1" endpointName="ShoppingCartServiceHttp
                Endpoint1"/>
            <add filterName="ShoppingCart2" endpointName="ShoppingCartServiceHttp
                Endpoint1"/>
            <add filterName="ShoppingCart3" endpointName="ShoppingCartServiceHttp
                Endpoint2"/>
            <add filterName="ShoppingCart4" endpointName="ShoppingCartServiceHttp
                Endpoint2"/>
          </filterTable>
        </filterTables>
      </routing>
    </system.serviceModel>
</configuration>
```

The list of filters in the *<filters>* section defines the rules for routing messages. Each filter has a unique name and specifies a *filterType* that identifies a type of *Message Filter* object to create for filtering messages. The *Action* type causes the WCF runtime to create an *ActionMessageFilter* object that can filter requests based on the *Action* element in message headers. The *filterData* property indicates the data to match against. If a match is found, the WCF runtime looks up the entry in the *<filterTable>* section that matches the filter name and routes the message to the endpoint specified by the *endpointName* for this entry. For example, if a message is received with an action of *http:// adventure-works.com/2010/06/04/ShoppingCartService/AddItemToCart* in the header, the WCF runtime will route the message through the endpoint identified by the *Shopping Cart1* filter in the filter table. The *endpointName* property in this table refers to the name of the endpoint as defined in the *<client>* section of the configuration file.

With WCF, you can filter messages based on other criteria apart from the *Action* in the request header. For example, you can specify *EndpointAddress* to define an *Endpoint AddressMessageFilter* (the *filterData* property should identify the endpoint address to match). If you wish to perform filtering based on the data in message bodies, you specify *XPath* to create an *XPathMessageFilter* object. The *filterData* property defines the path to the data in the message and the value to match against as an *XPath* expression.

> **More Info** For further details about the different filter types that you can define, see the *FilterType Enumeration* topic in documentation provided with Visual Studio (also available on the Microsoft Web site at *http://msdn.microsoft.com/en-us/library/system.servicemodel. routing.configuration.filtertype.aspx*).

16. Rebuild the solution.

You can now test the *RoutingService* host application and configuration. However, to demonstrate that messages are being routed correctly to the two *ShoppingCartService* service endpoints, you will configure the *ShoppingCartHost* application and add a service behavior that displays the action and address of each message received and sent.

Test the *RoutingService* Service

1. In the *ShoppingCartHost* project, add a reference to the *MessageInspector* assembly, located in the Chapter 14 folder.

> **Note** The source code for the message inspector is available in the MessageInspector project, in the MessageInspector folder within the Chapter 14 folder. This type is very similar to the message inspector that you created in Chapter 11.

2. Open the App.config file for the ShoppingCartHost project in the Service Configuration Editor. In the Configuration pane, expand the Advanced folder, expand Extensions, and then click Behavior Element Extensions.

3. At the bottom of the right pane, click New. In the Extension Configuration Element Editor dialog box, in the Name property, type **messageInspector**.

Click the Type field, and then click the ellipsis (...) button that appears adjacent to this field. In the Behavior Extension Type Browser dialog box, move to the Chapter 14 folder, click the *MessageInspector* assembly, and then click Open. In the Behavior Extension Type Browser dialog box, click *MessageInspector.ShoppingCartBehaviorExtensionElement*, and then click Open.

In the Extension Configuration Element Editor dialog box, click OK.

4. In the Configuration pane, expand Service Behaviors in the Advanced folder, and then click the *DurableServiceBehavior* behavior. In the right pane, click Add, and then add the *messageInspector* behavior element to the *DurableServiceBehavior* behavior.

5. Save the configuration file and exit the Service Configuration Editor.

6. In Solution Explorer, right click the ShoppingCart solution, and then click Set StartUp Projects. Add the *StaticRouter* project to the list of startup projects for the solution then click OK.

When the solution runs, it should start the ShoppingCartGUIClient, StaticRouter, and ShoppingCartHost projects.

7. Start the solution without debugging. The Shopping Cart GUI Client window should appear, together with console windows for the ShoppingCartHost application and the StaticRouter application.

8. In the Shopping Cart GUI Client window, enter **SA-M198** in the Product Number box, and then click Add Item. Next, add a water bottle to the shopping cart (item **WB-H098**), and then click Checkout.

The client application should operate exactly as before.

9. Switch to the console window for the *ShoppingCartHost* project. You should see the messages displayed by the message inspector. Verify that all *AddItemToCart* requests are sent to the service listening on port 9010; *GetShoppingCart* and *Checkout* messages should be sent to the service listening on port 9020.

10. Close the Shopping Cart GUI window, and then press Enter to close the service host console window and the *StaticRouter* console window.

Summary

In this chapter, you have seen how you can decouple the location of a service from its implementation by configuring service discovery. You have seen the three common modes of discovery supported by WCF: *ad hoc*, *announced*, and *managed*.

You have also looked in detail at how you can implement routing for WCF services. You have seen how the WCF runtime for a service determines how to handle an incoming message. The *ChannelDispatcher* object receiving the message queries each of its *EndpointDispatcher* objects in turn. An *EndpointDispatcher* exposes the *AddressFilter* and *ContractFilter* properties that the *ChannelDispatcher* can use to ascertain whether the *EndpointDispatcher* can accept the message. The *EndpointDispatcher* selected to process the message invokes the appropriate method in the service. You can customize the way in which the *EndpointDispatcher* accepts and processes messages by providing your own *AddressFilter* and *ContractFilter* objects and implementing the *IDispatchOperationSelector* interface.

You have also seen how to define a generalized WCF service that can act as a router for other services, implementing a method that can accept almost any message and forward it for processing elsewhere.

Finally, you have seen how to use and configure the *RoutingService* class to implement routing, based on information defined in a configuration file.

Chapter 15
Building REST Services

After completing this chapter, you will be able to:

- Describe the REST model of Web services, and how it differs from the scheme implemented by SOAP Web services.

- Build and configure a REST Web service.

- Detect and handle error conditions in a REST Web service.

- Build a custom host application for a REST Web service.

- Implement a client proxy that enables an application to connect to a REST Web service.

- Use WCF Data Services to build a REST Web service based on an Entity Framework entity model.

There are two common architectures that organizations use for implementing Web services; services based on the Simple Object Access Protocol (SOAP), and services based on the Representational State Transfer (REST) model. Both architectures rely on the ubiquitous HTTP protocol and the addressing scheme implemented by the Internet, but they employ it in different ways. So far, the exercises in this book have concentrated on the SOAP model, but this style forces the designer to focus on the business processes implemented by the Web service and expose these processes as operations. In contrast, the REST model considers the data exposed by an organization and implements a scheme that enables client applications to access this data and manipulate it using their own business logic. The REST model is becoming increasingly common, and WCF provides attributes, methods, and types with which you can construct and access REST Web services quickly and easily. Additionally, the Entity Framework provides the WCF Data Services template, which you can use to expose the data and entities from an Entity Framework model to client applications as REST resources.

The purpose of this chapter is to provide an introduction to REST Web services and show you how to build and access them using WCF.

Understanding the REST Model

The REST model was first described in 2000 by Roy Fielding in his doctoral dissertation, "Architectural Styles and the Design of Network-based Software Architectures." As the name of the thesis implies, REST is an architectural style rather than a prescribed way of building Web services, and you can implement it by using any appropriate technology. The key point is that REST describes a stateless, hierarchical scheme for representing resources and business objects over a network, following a structure that is very similar to that implemented by the World

Wide Web (you could argue that the World Wide Web is simply a global example of the REST model). For example, AdventureWorks might provide access to customer and sales information in their database, exposing the details of each customer or order as a single resource. To retrieve a list of all customers from the AdventureWorks sales Web site, a Web application might access the following URL:

http://www.adventure-works.com/sales/customers

The data can be returned in a number of formats, but for portability the most common formats include XML (sometimes referred to as "Plain Old XML" or POX) and JavaScript Object Notation (or JSON). If AdventureWorks chooses to use POX, the result returned by querying the URL shown above might be something like this (some details have been omitted to keep the example concise):

```
<ArrayOfContact xmlns="...">
  <Contact z:Id="i1" xmlns:z="http://schemas.microsoft.com/2003/10/Serialization/">
    <ContactID>1</ContactID>
    <EmailAddress>gustavo0@adventure-works.com</EmailAddress>
    <EmailPromotion>2</EmailPromotion>
    <FirstName>Gustavo</FirstName>
    <LastName>Achong</LastName>
    <MiddleName i:nil="true" />
    <ModifiedDate>2005-05-16T16:33:33.06</ModifiedDate>
    ...
  </Contact>
  <Contact z:Id="i3" xmlns:z="http://schemas.microsoft.com/2003/10/Serialization/">
    <ContactID>2</ContactID>
    <EmailAddress>catherine0@adventure-works.com</EmailAddress>
    <EmailPromotion>1</EmailPromotion>
    <FirstName>Catherine</FirstName>
    <LastName>Abel</LastName>
    <MiddleName>R.</MiddleName>
    <ModifiedDate>2005-05-16T16:33:33.077</ModifiedDate>
    ...
  </Contact>
  <Contact z:Id="i5" xmlns:z="http://schemas.microsoft.com/2003/10/Serialization/">
    <ContactID>3</ContactID>
    <EmailAddress>kim2@adventure-works.com</EmailAddress>
    <EmailPromotion>0</EmailPromotion>
    <FirstName>Kim</FirstName>
    <LastName>Abercrombie</LastName>
    <MiddleName i:nil="true" />
    <ModifiedDate>2005-05-16T16:33:33.077</ModifiedDate>
    ...
  </Contact>
  ...
</ArrayOfContact>
```

Web services that follow the REST model typically enable a Web application to drill down into the data by specifying additional path elements. For example, to find the details of a single customer—customer 99 for example—the AdventureWorks Web site would enable a Web application to specify a URL such as this:

http://www.adventure-works.com/sales/customers/99

Additionally, it might be useful to enable a Web application to find all the orders placed by a given customer by querying a URL, such as the following:

http://www.adventure-works.com/sales/customers/99/orders

The key to designing a REST-based solution is to understand how to divide a business model into a set of resources and how to relate these resources together. In some cases, such as customers and orders, this might be straightforward, but in other situations this might be more of a challenge.

The REST model relies on the application that accesses the data sending the appropriate HTTP verb as part of the request used to access the data. For example, the requests shown previously should send an HTTP *GET* request to the Web service. HTTP supports other verbs as well, such as *POST*, *PUT*, and *DELETE*, which you can exploit in a REST service to create, modify, and remove resources, respectively. Using the REST model, you can exploit these verbs and build Web services that can insert, update, and delete data.

In contrast to SOAP, the messages sent and received by using the REST model tend to be much more compact. This is primarily because REST does not provide the same routing, policy, or security facilities described by the WS-* specifications, and you must rely on the underlying transport infrastructure implemented by the Web server to protect REST Web services. It is also important to bear in mind that a key aspect of the REST model is that it is stateless; there is no concept of sessions or transactions that can span interactions between a client application and a service (although there is nothing to stop a service implementing transactions internally to guarantee the integrity of individual insert, update, and delete operations). However, this minimalist approach means that a REST Web service is usually much more efficient than the equivalent SOAP Web service when transmitting and receiving messages.

Querying Data by Implementing a REST Web Service

Implementing a REST Web service by using WCF is a straightforward process, and WCF provides a number of types in the *System.ServiceModel.Web* assembly that can assist you. However, the most important part of the process is designing the scheme that you will use to provide access to the resources exposed by the service. In many cases, resources are naturally grouped into collections and have relationships with other resources and collections. The exercises in this section use the scheme described in the table that follows (which was introduced in the examples discussed earlier).

URI	Description
Customers	All customers in the AdventureWorks database.
Customers/{customerID}	A specific customer. For example, *Customers/99*.
Orders	All orders in the AdventureWorks database.
Orders/{orderID}	A specific order. For example, *Orders/43687*.
Orders/{orderID}/Customer	The customer that placed the specified order. For example, *Orders/43687/Customer* retrieves the customer that placed order *43687*.
Customers/{customerID}/Orders	The orders for a specific customer. For example, *Customers/99/Orders* retrieves the list of orders placed by customer 99.

Depending on the volume of data in the database, the *Customers* and *Orders* URIs might identify a large number of items. Therefore, it makes sense to provide additional query parameters that a user can specify to limit the number of items returned. In the following exercises, you will implement two optional query parameters called *skip* and *top*, which a user can specify as shown in the following examples:

```
Orders?top=10
Orders?skip=500
Orders?skip=9&top=20
```

The purpose of the *top* parameter is to retrieve only the first *n* items, where *n* is the value specified for this parameter. The first example shown above fetches only the first 10 orders. The *skip* parameter causes the query to omit the first *n* items and fetch data starting at item *n* + *1*. The second example omits the first 500 orders and fetches the data starting with order 501. You can combine the *skip* and *top* parameters. The third example retrieves 20 orders starting, at position 10 (it omits orders 1 through 9, and then fetches orders 10 through 29 inclusive). Combining the parameters in this way enables a client implementation to implement a paging mechanism that retrieves data in manageable block sizes.

As with a SOAP Web service, the first task in implementing a REST Web service is to define the service contract. This contract specifies the operations that the service exposes and associates these operations with the URIs that identify the various resources. Web client applications can then invoke these operations by querying these URIs.

Define the *ProductsSales* REST Web Service Contract

1. Using Visual Studio, create a new solution by using the information in the following table:

Item	Value
Template	Blank Solution (in the Other Project Types/Visual Studio Solutions folder in the Installed Templates pane)
Name	ProductsSales
Location	Microsoft Press\WCF Step By Step\Chapter 15 (within your Documents folder)

2. Add a new Class Library project to the ProductsSales solution (select the Class Library template in the Visual C# folder in the Installed Templates pane in the Add New Project dialog box). Name the project **ProductsSalesService** and save it in the **Microsoft Press\WCF Step By Step\Chapter 15\ProductsSales** folder.

3. In Solution Explorer, add the ProductsSalesModel.edmx file and the App.config file (both located in the Chapter 15 folder) to the ProductsSalesService project.

> **Hint** To display .edmx and .config files in the Add Existing Item dialog box, click All Files (*.*) in the drop-down list box adjacent to the File Name box.

The ProductsSalesModel.edmx file is an Entity Framework model that defines two entities called *Contact* and *SalesOrderHeader*. In the *AdventureWorks* database, the *Contacts* table contains the details of all contacts and customers, and the *SalesOrderHeader* table holds the information about the orders placed by customers. The App.config file contains the connection string that the entity model uses to connect to the *AdventureWorks* database.

4. Rebuild the solution. This action generates the code for *Contact* and *SalesOrderHeader* classes from the entity model.

5. Add references to the *System.ServiceModel* and *System.ServiceModel.Web* assemblies to the ProductsSalesService project.

6. In Solution Explorer, change the name of the Class1.cs file to **IProductsSales.cs**. Allow Visual Studio to change all references to the *Class1* class to *IProductsSales* when prompted.

7. Open the IProductsSales.cs file in the Code And Text Editor window. Add the following *using* statements to the list at the top of this file:

```
using System.ServiceModel;
using System.ServiceModel.Web;
using System.ComponentModel;
```

8. Change the *IProductsSales* class into a public interface and prefix it with the *Service Contract* attribute, as shown in bold in the following code example.

```
[ServiceContract(Namespace = "http://adventure-works.com/2010/07/28",
                 Name = "ProductsSales")]
public interface IProductsSales
{
}
```

9. In the *IProductsSales* interface, add the *GetAllOrders* method and annotate it with the attributes, as shown in bold in the following code example.

```
public interface IProductsSales
{
    [OperationContract]
    [WebGet(UriTemplate = "Orders?skip={skip}&top={top}")]
    [Description("Returns a list of all orders. By default, the list is limited to" +
                " the first 100 orders; specify the SKIP and TOP parameters to" +
                " implement paging.")]
    ICollection<SalesOrderHeader> GetAllOrders(int skip, int top);
}
```

This operation will return a collection of *SalesOrderHeader* objects, containing the data for each order. The *OperationContract* attribute marks this method as a Web service operation in exactly the same way that you have seen in previous chapters. The *Web-Get* attribute indicates that this is a REST operation that responds to HTTP *GET* requests and specifies the URI that Web client applications can use to invoke this operation in the *UriTemplate* property. This URI includes the optional *skip* and *top* query parameters. The items in the curly braces (*skip* and *top*) are placeholders that will be substituted with the values provided by the client application at runtime. The definition of the *GetAllOrders* method includes parameters with the same names; the WCF runtime will populate these parameters with the corresponding values passed in by the client application. Note that the order of these parameters is immaterial (a Web client application can specify the *top* and *skip* parameters in any order), but names of these parameters must match the names in the curly braces in the *UriTemplate* property of the *WebGet* attribute.

> **Note** You can also use the *WebGet* attribute to specify the format for request and response messages. By default, operations marked with *WebGet* send response messages formatted as XML data, and the WCF runtime serializes them as POX objects. However, you can send response messages in JSON format by specifying the *ResponseFormat* property of the *WebGet* attribute with the value **WebMessageFormat.Json**, as shown here:
>
> ```
> [WebGet(UriTemplate = "...", ResponseFormat = WebMessageFormat.Json)]
> ```

With the *Description* attribute (defined in the *System.ComponentModel* namespace), you can specify some simple documentation that can be displayed by the Help page for the service (you will learn more about this feature later in this section).

10. Add the *GetOrder* method shown below in bold to the *IProductsSales* interface:

```
public interface IProductsSales
{
    ...
    [OperationContract]
    [WebGet(UriTemplate = "Orders/{orderID}")]
    [Description("Returns the details of an order")]
    SalesOrderHeader GetOrder(string orderID);
}
```

This operation runs when a Web client application specifies a URI of the form Orders/ *orderID* and will retrieve the *SalesOrderHeader* object that corresponds to this order. As before, notice that the method takes a parameter that matches the placeholder specified in the URI. Another point worth noticing is that this parameter is passed as a string, although the equivalent column in the *SalesOrderHeader* table in the *AdventureWorks* database is an integer. The reason for this is that navigational elements in a URI must be strings. This restriction does not apply to query parameters (the *skip* and *top* parameters for the *GetAllOrders* method in the previous step are integers).

11. Add the *GetCustomerForOrder* method to the *IProductsSales* interface, as shown in bold below:

```
public interface IProductsSales
{
    ...
    [OperationContract]
    [WebGet(UriTemplate = "Orders/{orderID}/Customer")]
    [Description("Returns the details of the customer that placed the order")]
    Contact GetCustomerForOrder(string orderID);
}
```

This method runs when a Web client application specifies a URI that fetches the customer that placed the specified order.

12. Add the *GetAllCustomers*, *GetCustomer*, and *GetOrdersForCustomer* methods shown in bold in the following code example to the *IProductsSales* interface:

```
public interface IProductsSales
{
    ...
    [OperationContract]
    [WebGet(UriTemplate = "Customers?skip={skip}&top={top}")]
    [Description("Returns a list of all customers")]
    ICollection<Contact> GetAllCustomers(int skip, int top);
```

```
[OperationContract]
[WebGet(UriTemplate = "Customers/{customerID}")]
[Description("Returns the details of a customer")]
Contact GetCustomer(string customerID);

[OperationContract]
[WebGet(UriTemplate = "Customers/{customerID}/Orders")]
[Description("Returns the orders placed by a customer")]
ICollection<SalesOrderHeader> GetOrdersForCustomer(string customerID);
}
```

These methods define operations that enable a Web client application to retrieve all customers, the details of a specific customer, and the orders for a specific customer, respectively. They follow the same pattern as the operations defined in the preceding steps.

13. Rebuild the solution.

Implement the *ProductsSales* REST Web Service

1. Add a new class file to the ProductsSalesService project. Name the class file **Products Sales.cs**.

2. Open the ProductsSales.cs file in the Code And Text Editor window and add the following *using* statements to the list at the top of the file:

```
using System.ServiceModel;
using System.ServiceModel.Web;
using System.Net;
```

3. Modify the definition of the *ProductsSales* class so that it is public and implements the *IProductsSales* interface, as shown in bold in the following code example:

```
public class ProductsSales : IProductsSales
{
}
```

4. Add the following *GetAllOrders* method (shown in bold) to the *ProductsSales* class:

```
public class ProductsSales : IProductsSales
{
    // Return a list of orders
    public ICollection<SalesOrderHeader> GetAllOrders(int skip, int top)
    {
        List<SalesOrderHeader> salesOrders = null;

        if (top == 0)
        {
            top = 100;
        }
```

```
        try
        {
            using (AdventureWorksEntities database = new AdventureWorksEntities())
            {
                salesOrders = (from order in database.SalesOrderHeaders
                               orderby order.SalesOrderID
                               select order).Skip(skip).Take(top).ToList();
            }
        }
        catch
        {
            throw new WebFaultException(HttpStatusCode.BadRequest);
        }

        return salesOrders;
    }
}
```

> **Note** The code for this method is available in the file GetAllOrders.txt, which is located in
> the Microsoft Press\WCF Step By Step\Chapter 15 folder.

This method retrieves a list of orders from the *AdventureWorks* database and returns
it as a collection of *SalesOrderHeader* objects. Remember that a Web application can
invoke this operation by visiting the Orders URI exposed by the Web site hosting the
service. The Web application can optionally provide values for the *skip* and *top* arguments as query parameters. If the Web application does not specify values for these
parameters, they both default to zero. It is possible that the database may contain
hundreds, if not thousands, of orders. Therefore, the service will fetch only the first 100
orders unless the user explicitly constrains the number of orders requested. If an application actually requires every order in the database, it can fetch them in blocks by making repeated calls to the *GetAllOrders* operation and specifying appropriate values for
the *skip* and *top* parameters.

This method performs very limited parameter validation and error checking; for example, it does not verify that the values of the *skip* and *top* parameters are not negative. If
an exception occurs, the method throws a *WebFaultException* exception. This type is a
specialized version of the *FaultException* class that you encountered in Chapter 3, "Making
Applications and Services Robust," except that it generates an HTTP fault rather than a
SOAP fault. The parameter to the *WebFaultException* constructor specifies the HTTP status
code that the HTTP fault contains. The *HttpStatusCode* enumeration in the *System.Net*
namespace defines the list of codes that you can pass back to a Web application; the
value *HttpStatusCode.BadRequest* generates an HTTP 400 (Bad Request) error message,
which is a good catch-all if no other, more specific error applies. For security reasons, as
described in Chapter 3, you should avoid attempting to return too much information if
an error does occur (although it is commonly accepted practice to record the details of
errors locally on the server, often in the Application Event Log).

5. Add the *GetOrder* method shown in bold in the following code example to the *Products Sales* class:

```
public class ProductsSales : IProductsSales
{
    ...
    // Return the details of the specified order
    public SalesOrderHeader GetOrder(string orderID)
    {
        SalesOrderHeader header = null;

        try
        {
            int id = Convert.ToInt32(orderID);
            using (AdventureWorksEntities database = new AdventureWorksEntities())
            {
                header = (from order in database.SalesOrderHeaders
                            where order.SalesOrderID == id
                            select order).FirstOrDefault();
            }
        }
        catch
        {
            throw new WebFaultException(HttpStatusCode.BadRequest);
        }

        return header;
    }
}
```

 Note The code for this method is provided in the file GetOrder.txt, which is located in the Chapter 15 folder.

This method locates and returns the *SalesOrderHeader* object that matches the order ID passed in as the parameter. Note that the order ID is provided as a string, so it must be converted to an integer before being referenced by the LINQ query. The LINQ query itself generates a null reference which the service returns to the Web application if no matching order is found. As before, the method performs no error checking, but generates a Bad Request fault if an exception occurs.

6. Implement the *GetCustomerForOrder* method in the *ProductsSales* class, as shown below in bold:

```
public class ProductsSales : IProductsSales
{
    ...
    // Return the details of the customer for the specified order
    public Contact GetCustomerForOrder(string orderID)
    {
        Contact orderCustomer = null;
```

```
        try
        {
            int id = Convert.ToInt32(orderID);
            using (AdventureWorksEntities database = new AdventureWorksEntities())
            {
                orderCustomer = (from customer in database.Contacts
                                join order in database.SalesOrderHeaders
                                on customer.ContactID equals order.CustomerID
                                where order.SalesOrderID == id
                                select customer).FirstOrDefault();
            }
        }
        catch
        {
            throw new WebFaultException(HttpStatusCode.BadRequest);
        }

        return orderCustomer;
    }
}
```

> **Note**   The code for this method is provided in the file GetCustomerForOrder.txt, which is located in the Chapter 15 folder.

The preceding method retrieves the customer that placed the specified order. To do that, it joins the *Contact* and *SalesOrderHeader* tables in the *AdventureWorks* database on their ContactID and CustomerID columns, respectively. It returns the data as a *Contact* object.

7. Add the following *GetAllCustomers*, *GetCustomer*, and *GetOrdersForCustomer* methods (shown in bold) to the *ProductsSales* class:

```
public class ProductsSales : IProductsSales
{
    ...
    // Return a list of customers
    public ICollection<Contact> GetAllCustomers(int skip, int top)
    {
        List<Contact> orderCustomers = null;

        if (top == 0)
        {
            top = 100;
        }

        try
        {
            using (AdventureWorksEntities database = new AdventureWorksEntities())
```

```
        {
            orderCustomers = (from customer in database.Contacts
                              orderby customer.ContactID
                              select customer).Skip(skip).Take(top).ToList();
        }
    }
    catch
    {
        throw new WebFaultException(HttpStatusCode.BadRequest);
    }

    return orderCustomers;
}

// Return the details of the specified customer
public Contact GetCustomer(string customerID)
{
    Contact orderCustomer = null;

    try
    {
        int id = Convert.ToInt32(customerID);
        using (AdventureWorksEntities database = new AdventureWorksEntities())
        {
            orderCustomer = (from customer in database.Contacts
                             where customer.ContactID == id
                             select customer).FirstOrDefault();
        }
    }
    catch
    {
        throw new WebFaultException(HttpStatusCode.BadRequest);
    }

    return orderCustomer;
}

// Return the orders for the specified customer
public ICollection<SalesOrderHeader> GetOrdersForCustomer(string customerID)
{
    List<SalesOrderHeader> salesOrders = null;

    try
    {
        int id = Convert.ToInt32(customerID);
        using (AdventureWorksEntities database = new AdventureWorksEntities())
        {
            salesOrders = (from customer in database.Contacts
                           join order in database.SalesOrderHeaders
                           on customer.ContactID equals order.CustomerID
                           where customer.ContactID == id
                           select order).ToList();
        }
    }
    catch
```

```
    {
        throw new WebFaultException(HttpStatusCode.BadRequest);
    }

    return salesOrders;
    }
}
```

 Note The code for these methods are available in the GetAllCustomers.txt, GetCustomer.txt, and GetOrdersForCustomer.txt files, which are located in the Chapter 15 folder.

These methods follow a pattern similar to those you added in the previous steps, except that they focus on customers rather than orders.

8. Rebuild the solution.

As with a SOAP Web service, you can host a REST Web service by using IIS, or you can create a custom host application. WCF provides the *WebServiceHost* class in the *System.ServiceModel. Web* namespace, which is a specialized version of the *ServiceHost* class that provides the hosting environment for REST Web services. The *WebServiceHost* class adds an endpoint behavior called *WebHttpBehavior* to the services that it hosts. This behavior enables the service to receive and send messages as HTTP requests rather than SOAP requests. You will make use of this class in the next exercise.

Host the *ProductsSales* REST Web Service

1. Add a new Console Application project to the ProductsSales solution. Name the project **ProductsSalesHost** and save it in the **Microsoft Press\WCF Step By Step\Chapter 15\ProductsSales** folder.

2. Open the Properties page for the ProductsSalesHost project (right-click the Products SalesHost project in Solution Explorer then click Properties), and then click the Application tab. Set the Target Framework property to **.NET Framework 4** and allow Visual Studio to close and reopen the project.

   This application will use types from the *System.ServiceModel.Web* assembly. Note that this assembly is only available in the full version of the .NET Framework 4.0, not the .NET Framework 4.0 Client Profile.

3. Add a reference to the ProductsSalesService project. Also add references to the *System. ServiceModel* and *System.ServiceModel.Web* assemblies to the ProductsSalesHost project.

4. Open the Program.cs file in the Code And Text Editor window. Add the following *using* statement to the list at the top of the file.

```
using System.ServiceModel.Web;
```

5. In the *Program* class, add the following statements (shown in bold) to the *Main* method.

```
class Program
{
    static void Main(string[] args)
    {
        WebServiceHost host = new WebServiceHost(
            typeof(ProductsSalesService.ProductsSales));
        host.Open();
        Console.WriteLine("Service running");
        Console.WriteLine("Press ENTER to stop the service");
        Console.ReadLine();
        host.Close();
    }
}
```

This code creates a *WebServiceHost* object based on the *ProductsSalesService* class, and then starts it listening for requests. It is very similar to code shown in previous chapters for building a custom host.

6. Delete the app.config file from the ProductsSalesHost project and replace it with the App.config file, located in the Microsoft Press\WCF Step By Step\Chapter 15 folder.

Remember that this file contains the connection string for connecting to the *Adventure-Works* database.

7. Open the app.config file for the ProductsSalesHost project by using the Service Configuration Editor.

8. In the Configuration pane, right-click the Services folder, and then click New Service. In the right pane, in the Name property, type **ProductsSalesService.ProductsSales**.

9. In the Configuration pane, under the ProductsSalesService.ProductsSales service, right-click the Endpoints folder, and then click New Service Endpoint. In the Service Endpoint pane, enter the values shown in the following table:

Property	Value
Address	http://localhost:8000/Sales
Binding	webHttpBinding
Contract	ProductsSalesService.IProductsSales

The URIs specified by the *UriTemplate* property for the operations defined in the *WebGet* attribute applied to the *IProductsSales* service contract are applied relative to the address of the service. For example, the *GetCustomerForOrder* operation has the *UriTemplate* property set to *"Orders/{ordered}/Customer."* A Web client application can invoke this operation by visiting a URL such as *http://localhost:8000/Sales/Orders/54545/Customer*, where *54545* is the ID of an order.

The *webHttpBinding* binding configures endpoints for REST Web services exposed through HTTP requests instead of SOAP messages.

10. Save the configuration file and close the Service Configuration Editor.

11. Rebuild the solution.

The *ProductsSales* service responds to HTTP *GET* requests that you can submit from a Web application, but you can also use a Web browser such as Internet Explorer, which is what you will do in the following exercise. Note that the *WebServiceHost* class disables WSDL metadata publishing (WSDL applies only to SOAP Web services). However, you can still query a REST Web service to find out its capabilities if it is help-enabled. Therefore, in the following exercise, you will also configure the *ProductsSalesService* service to provide help information, listing the URLs that the service supports and the structure of the data returned when you query each URL.

> **Note** The ProductsSalesHost application assumes that you still have the reservation for port 8000 in place. If this is not the case, then open a Visual Studio Command Prompt window as Administrator and run the following command, replacing *UserName* with your Windows user name:
>
> ```
> netsh http add urlacl url=http://+:8000/ user=UserName
> ```

Test the *ProductsSales* REST Web Service by Using a Web Browser

1. In Solution Explorer, set the ProductsSalesHost project as the startup project for the solution, and then start the solution without debugging. Verify that the console window for the ProductsSalesHost application displays the message "Service Running."

2. Start Internet Explorer, type the URL **http://localhost:8000/Sales/Orders** into the address field, and then press Enter. Navigating to this URL invokes the *GetOrders* operation, which responds by returning a collection of *SalesOrderHeader* objects, serialized as XML. Internet Explorer displays this XML data, as shown in the image that follows.

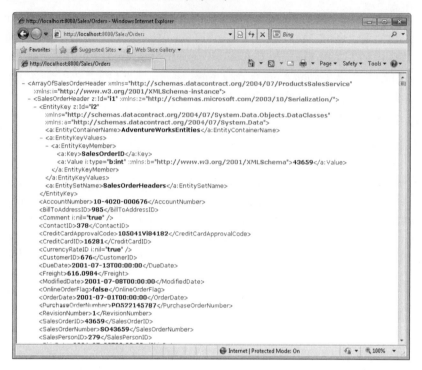

If you scroll through this list, you will see that the *ProductsSales* service has returned the first 100 orders. The ID of the first order is *43659*, and the ID of the final order is *43758*.

3. Specify a URL of **http://localhost:8000/Sales/Orders?skip=100&top=5**, and then examine the data returned by the ProductsSales service.

   This time the *ProductsSales* service retrieves five orders, starting with order ID *43759*.

4. Move to each of the URLs listed in the following table and verify that the results match those expected.

URL	Expected Result
http://localhost:8000/Sales/Orders?top=-10	An error page with the title "HTTP 400 Bad Request". The *GetOrders* operation attempts to retrieve –10 orders, so the *Take* method in the LINQ query throws an exception. The *GetOrders* method catches this exception and throws a *WebFaultException* exception with the value *HttpStatusCode.BadRequest*.
http://localhost:8000/Sales/Orders/43700	The details of the single order with ID 43700.
http://localhost:8000/Sales/Orders/30000	A blank page. There is no order with ID 30000 in the *AdventureWorks* database.

URL	Expected Result
http://localhost:8000/Sales/Orders/43700/Customer	The details for customer with ID 14501. This is the customer that placed order 43700.
http://localhost:8000/Sales/Customers	The details of the first 100 customers in the *AdventureWorks* database.
http://localhost:8000/Sales/Customers/100	The details of customer 100.
http://localhost:8000/Sales/Customers/100/Orders	The details of all orders placed by customer 100.

5. Return to the console application window for the *ProductsSales* service, press Enter to stop the service, and then close the console window but leave Internet Explorer running.

6. In Visual Studio, open the App.Config file for the ProductsSalesHost project by using the Service Configuration Editor.

7. In the Configuration pane, expand the Advanced folder, right-click the Endpoint Behaviors folder, and then click New Endpoint Behavior Configuration. In the right pane, clear the *Name* property. In the lower part of the right pane, click the Add button and add a *webHttp* behavior extension element to the endpoint behavior.

8. In the Configuration pane, click the *webHttp* node under the *(Empty Name)* endpoint behavior. In the WebHttp pane, set the *HelpEnabled* property to **True**. This property enables a REST Web service to publish a help page that describes the operations for the service, the XML schema of the response message, and an example JSON structure for the response message.

 Note The default value of the *HelpEnabled* property is *false*.

9. Save the configuration file, and then close the Service Configuration Editor.

10. In Visual Studio, start the solution without debugging.

11. Return to Internet Explorer and browse to the URL **http://localhost:8000/Sales/help**. The help page for the *ProductsSales* service appears (as shown in the following image), displaying the URI and description for each operation exposed by the service.

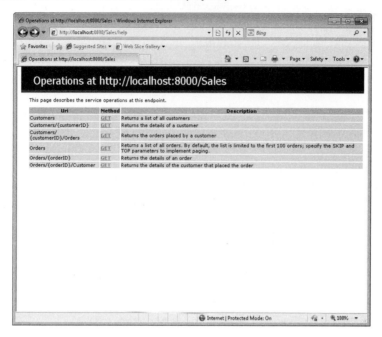

12. Click the *GET* link for the *Customers/{customerID}* URI. Another page appears that describes the format of the response message returned by the *GetCustomer* operation:

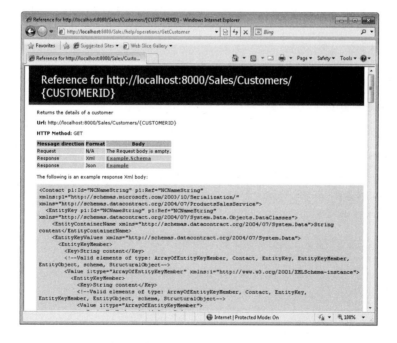

13. Examine the format of the response messages for the remaining operations, and then close Internet Explorer.

14. Return to the console application window for the *ProductsSalesService* service. Press Enter to stop the service, and then close the window.

As well as sending requests through URLs in a Web application or Web browser, you can also invoke the operations in a REST Web service from a procedural client application. The technique is very similar to building a client application for a SOAP Web service; you can create a proxy class and invoke the methods exposed by the service in the usual way. Unfortunately, Visual Studio does not currently provide the functionality to generate a proxy class for a REST Web service—but it is not difficult to implement a proxy class manually by extending the *System.ServiceModel.ClientBase* class (Chapter 11, "Programmatically Controlling the Configuration and Communications," introduced this class to you). This is the approach that you will take in the next exercise.

Build a Procedural Client Application for the *ProductsSales* REST Web Service

1. In Visual Studio, add a new Console Application project to the ProductsSales solution. Name the project **ProductsSalesClient**, and save it in the **Microsoft Press\WCF Step By Step\Chapter 15\ProductsSales** folder.

2. Open the Properties page for the ProductsSalesClient project and set the *Target Framework* property to **.NET Framework 4**. Allow Visual Studio to close and reopen the project.

   Like the ProducstSalesHost project, this application will use types from the *System. ServiceModel.Web* assembly, which is only available in the full version of the .NET Framework 4.0.

3. Add a reference to the ProductsSalesService project. In addition, add references to the *System.Data.Entity*, and *System.ServiceModel* assemblies to the ProductsSalesClient project.

   The client application needs access to the definition of the operations of the service contract exposed by the *ProductsSalesService* service in order to implement the proxy class.

4. Add a new class file to the ProductSalesClient project. Name the class file **Products-SalesProxy.cs**.

5. Open the *ProductsSalesProxy* class in the Code And Text Editor window. Add the following *using* statements to the list at the top of the file:

```
using System.ServiceModel;
using ProductsSalesService;
```

6. Modify the definition of the *ProductsSalesProxy* class so that it extends the *ClientBase<IProductsSales>* class and implements the *IProductsSales* interface, as shown in bold in the following code example:

```
class ProductsSalesProxy : ClientBase<IProductsSales>, IProductsSales
{
}
```

7. Implement the *GetAllOrders* method defined by the *IProductsSales* interface in the *ProductsSalesProxy* class as follows:

```
class ProductsSalesProxy : ClientBase<IProductsSales>, IProductsSales
{
    public ICollection<SalesOrderHeader> GetAllOrders(int skip = 0, int top = 0)
    {
        return this.Channel.GetAllOrders(skip, top);
    }
}
```

As described in Chapter 11, this method simply routes calls through the channel connected to the service and invokes the operation with the same name in the service (the *Channel* property is inherited from the *ClientBase* class). This implementation specifies the *skip* and *top* parameters as optional, with a default value of zero.

8. Add the *GetOrder*, *GetCustomerForOrder*, *GetAllCustomers*, *GetCustomer*, and *GetOrders ForCustomer* methods, shown in bold in the code example that follows, to the *Products-SalesProxy* class. These methods all follow the same pattern as the *GetAllOrders* method; they simply invoke the corresponding method in the service through the channel connected to the service.

```
class ProductsSalesProxy : ClientBase<IProductsSales>, IProductsSales
{
    ...
    public SalesOrderHeader GetOrder(string orderID)
    {
        return this.Channel.GetOrder(orderID);
    }

    public Contact GetCustomerForOrder(string orderID)
    {
        return this.Channel.GetCustomerForOrder(orderID);
    }

    public ICollection<Contact> GetAllCustomers(int skip = 0, int top = 0)
    {
        return this.Channel.GetAllCustomers(skip, top);
    }

    public Contact GetCustomer(string customerID)
    {
        return this.Channel.GetCustomer(customerID);
    }
```

```
    public ICollection<SalesOrderHeader> GetOrdersForCustomer(string customerID)
    {
        return this.Channel.GetOrdersForCustomer(customerID);
    }
}
```

9. Open the Program.cs file for the ProductsSalesClient project in the Code And Text Editor window. Add the following *using* statement to the list at the top of the file.

```
using ProductsSalesService;
```

10. Add the following statements (shown in bold) to the *Main* method.

```
static void Main(string[] args)
{
    Console.WriteLine("Press ENTER when the service has started");
    Console.ReadLine();

    // Create a proxy object and connect to the service
    ProductsSalesProxy proxy = new ProductsSalesProxy();

    // Test the operations in the service
    try
    {
        // Obtain a list of 30 orders, starting with the 11th
        Console.WriteLine("Test 1: List orders");
        ICollection<SalesOrderHeader> orders = proxy.GetAllOrders(10, 30);
        Console.WriteLine("Order\tDate Placed\tCustomer\tAmount Due");
        foreach (SalesOrderHeader order in orders)
        {
            Console.WriteLine("{0}\t{1:d}\t{2}\t\t{3:C}",
                order.SalesOrderID, order.OrderDate, order.CustomerID,
                order.TotalDue);
        }
        Console.WriteLine();

        // Find the details for order 43687
        Console.WriteLine("Test 2: Get details for order 43687");
        SalesOrderHeader salesOrder = proxy.GetOrder("43687");
        Console.WriteLine(
            "Order ID: {0}\nDate Placed {1}\nCustomer ID: {2}\nAmount Due: {3:C}\n\n",
            salesOrder.SalesOrderID, salesOrder.OrderDate, salesOrder.CustomerID,
            salesOrder.TotalDue);

        // Find the customer that placed order 43687
        Console.WriteLine("Test 3: Find the customer for order 43687");
        Contact salesCustomer = proxy.GetCustomerForOrder("43687");
        Console.WriteLine("Customer: {0} {1}\nEmail: {2}\nPhone: {3}\n\n",
            salesCustomer.FirstName, salesCustomer.LastName,
            salesCustomer.EmailAddress, salesCustomer.Phone);

        // Find all customers with an ID in the range 75 to 90
        Console.WriteLine("Test 4: List customers");
        ICollection<Contact> customers = proxy.GetAllCustomers(74, 15);
        Console.WriteLine("Name\t\tEmail\t\t\tPhone");
```

```
            foreach (Contact customer in customers)
            {
                Console.WriteLine("{0} {1}\t{2}\t{3}",
                    customer.FirstName, customer.LastName,
                    customer.EmailAddress, customer.Phone);
            }
            Console.WriteLine();

            // Find the details of customer 99
            Console.WriteLine("Test 5: Find the details for customer 99");
            salesCustomer = proxy.GetCustomer("99");
            Console.WriteLine("Customer: {0} {1}\nEmail: {2}\nPhone: {3}\n\n",
                salesCustomer.FirstName, salesCustomer.LastName,
                salesCustomer.EmailAddress, salesCustomer.Phone);

            // Find all orders placed by customer 99
            Console.WriteLine("Test 6: Find all orders for customer 99");
            orders = proxy.GetOrdersForCustomer("99");
            Console.WriteLine("Order\tDate Placed\tCustomer\tAmount Due");
            foreach (SalesOrderHeader order in orders)
            {
                Console.WriteLine("{0}\t{1:d}\t{2}\t\t{3:C}",
                    order.SalesOrderID, order.OrderDate,
                    order.CustomerID, order.TotalDue);
            }
            Console.WriteLine();

            // Disconnect from the service
            proxy.Close();
        }

        catch (Exception e)
        {
            if (e.InnerException != null)
            {
                Console.WriteLine("{0}", e.InnerException.Message);
            }
            else
            {
                Console.WriteLine("General exception: {0}", e.Message);
            }
        }

        Console.WriteLine("Press ENTER to finish");
        Console.ReadLine();
    }
```

 Note This code is available in the Main.txt file, which is located in the Chapter 15 folder.

This code creates an instance of the *ProductsSalesProxy* class and then exercises each of the methods available through the proxy with the following series of tests:

- ❏ Retrieve orders by using the *GetAllOrders* method, specifying values for the *skip* and *top* parameters to limit the number of orders returned.

- ❏ Retrieve the details of order *43687* by calling the *GetOrder* method.

- ❏ Find the customer that placed order *43687* by calling the *GetCustomerForOrder* method.

- ❏ Find the details of customers with IDs between 75 and 90 by calling the *GetAll Customers* method with values for the *skip* and *top* parameters.

- ❏ Retrieve the details of customer *99* by calling the *GetCustomer* method.

- ❏ Find all orders for customer *99* by calling the *GetOrdersForCustomer* method.

11. Open the app.config file for the ProductsSalesClient project by using the Service Configuration Editor.

12. In the Configuration pane, expand the Client folder, right-click the Endpoints folder, and then click New Client Endpoint.

13. In the Client Endpoint pane, specify the following values for the new endpoint:

Property	Value
Address	http://localhost:8000/Sales
Binding	webHttpBinding
Contract	ProductsSalesService.IProductsSales

14. In the Configuration pane, expand the Advanced folder, right-click the Endpoint Behaviors folder, and then click New Endpoint Behavior Configuration. In the right pane, clear the *Name* property. In the lower part of the right pane, click the Add button and add a *webHttp* behavior extension element to the endpoint behavior.

> **Note** Unlike a service hosted by using the *WebServiceHost* class, the endpoint for a client application for a REST service is not automatically configured to send HTTP requests, so you must always add the *WebHttpBehavior* behavior to the client endpoint.

15. Save the configuration file then close the Service Configuration Editor.

16. In Visual Studio, set the ProductsSalesClient and ProductsSalesHost projects as the startup projects for the solution, and then start the solution without debugging.

17. In the ProductsSalesClient console window, press Enter. The various tests should all perform successfully and produce output similar to that shown in the image that follows.

18. Press Enter to close the ProductsSalesClient console window, and then close the ProductsSalesHost console window.

Updating Data Through a REST Web Service

A REST Web service provides operations that can query data by responding to HTTP *GET* requests. However, the HTTP protocol supports other forms of requests, and you can exploit these message types to provide operations that can modify data in a REST Web service. The common convention is that you use HTTP *POST* requests to specify operations that can create new items, HTTP *PUT* requests for operations that update existing data, and HTTP *DELETE* requests to define operations that can remove items.

> **Note** This convention is not enforced, and you could use HTTP *POST* requests to update and delete data, but this is not considered to be good practice. The rationale behind the convention is that in the HTTP protocol, *POST* requests are non-idempotent, whereas *PUT* and *DELETE* requests are idempotent. What this means is that *PUT* and *DELETE* requests can be used for operations that may be repeated any number of times, and they have an effect that is the same as if they had been executed only once, whereas the same is not true of *POST* requests. So, if you implement an update operation by using a *PUT* request, you can repeatedly perform this update operation over the same data and the result should always be the same. This logic also applies to removing data by using *DELETE* requests; if you delete an item that has already been deleted, it is still deleted. However, repeatedly adding the same information by using *POST* requests may result in duplicate data.

In a WCF REST Web service, you mark operations that respond to HTTP *GET* requests with the *WebGet* attribute. You also provide a template that specifies the URI that Web clients can visit to invoke the operation. To support HTTP *POST*, *PUT*, and *DELETE* requests, WCF supplies the *WebInvoke* attribute. Again, you use this attribute to identify a URI, but you can also indicate the type of the request message to which to respond. When the REST Web service receives a message of the defined type directed at the specified URI, it will invoke the corresponding operation. This scheme makes it possible for multiple operations to respond to the same URI, as long as they expect different types of HTTP messages. This is extremely useful and prevents you from having to think up multiple URI schemes to support different operations over the same logical data. For example, the *GetCustomer* operation in the *IProductsSales* service contract looks like this:

```
[OperationContract]
[WebGet(UriTemplate = "Customers/{customerID}")]
[Description("Returns the details of a customer")]
Contact GetCustomer(string customerID);
```

You can define the *DeleteCustomer* operation that deletes a customer by reusing the same URI (which makes sense because you are referring to the same data), but by specifying that the operation responds to HTTP *DELETE* messages, as shown in the following:

```
[OperationContract]
[WebInvoke(Method = "DELETE", UriTemplate = "Customers/{customerID}")]
[Description("Deletes a customer")]
void DeleteCustomer(string customerID);
```

In the following set of exercises, you will extend the *ProductsSales* REST Web service to enable insert, update, and delete operations for Customer data.

Extend the *ProductsSales* REST Web Service to Support Data Updates

1. In Visual Studio, open the IProductsSales.cs file for the ProductsSalesService project by using the Code And Text Editor window.

2. Add the following operation to the *IProductsSales* interface:

```
public interface IProductsSales
{
    ...
    [OperationContract]
    [WebInvoke(Method = "POST", UriTemplate =
        "Customer?FirstName={firstName}&LastName={lastName}&EmailAddress={email}" +
        "&Phone={phone}")]
    [Description("Adds a new customer")]
    int CreateCustomer(string firstName, string lastName, string email, string phone);
}
```

You will implement the *CreateCustomer* method to add a new customer to the *Adventure Works* database. The operation is tagged with the *WebInvoke* attribute, and the *Method* property is set to *POST* because this is an insert operation. The *UriTemplate* property specifies arguments that provide the details for the customer (the *Customer* table in the *AdventureWorks* database contains more columns than the list of parameters, but you will generate default values for these columns). As with the *skip* and *top* arguments in the *GetAllOrders* and *GetAllCustomers* operations in the previous set of exercises, the order of these arguments is immaterial, as long as you define parameters with the same names in the *CreateCustomer* method.

A Web application can submit *POST* requests with a URI with the form indicated by the *UriTemplate* property to create new customers. For example, to add a record for John Sharp, an application could specify the following URI (note that the URI should be a single line):

```
Customers?FirstName=John&LastName=Sharp&
    EmailAddress=john@adventure-works.com&Phone=(123)456789
```

3. Add the following *UpdateCustomer* operation (shown in bold) to the *IProductsSales* interface.

```
public interface IProductsSales
{
    ...
    [OperationContract]
    [WebInvoke(Method = "PUT", UriTemplate =
      "Customers/{customerID}?EmailAddress={email}&Phone={phone}")]
    [Description("Updates the email address and/or telephone number for a customer")]
    void UpdateCustomer(string customerID, string email, string phone);
}
```

The *UpdateCustomer* method will modify the customer with the specified customer ID and change the email address and telephone number by using the values provided as arguments. It will respond to HTTP *PUT* requests.

4. Add the *DeleteCustomer* operation to the *IProductsSales* interface, as shown in the following code example:

```
public interface IProductsSales
{
    ...
    [OperationContract]
    [WebInvoke(Method = "DELETE", UriTemplate = "Customers/{customerID}")]
    [Description("Deletes a customer")]
    void DeleteCustomer(string customerID);
}
```

This method will respond to HTTP *DELETE* requests, removing the specified customer from the *AdventureWorks* database.

5. Open the ProductsSales.cs file for the ProductsSalesService project in the Code And Text Editor window and implement the *CreateCustomer* method in the *ProductsSales* class, as shown in bold below.

```
public class ProductsSales : IProductsSales
{
    ...
    // Create a new customer, and return the customer ID
    public int CreateCustomer(string firstName, string lastName,
                        string email, string phone)
    {
        try
```

```
        {
            using (AdventureWorksEntities database = new AdventureWorksEntities())
            {
                // Create and populate a new Contact object
                Contact newCustomer = new Contact()
                {
                    FirstName = firstName,
                    LastName = lastName,
                    EmailAddress = email,
                    Phone = phone,
                    PasswordHash = "",
                    PasswordSalt = "",
                    rowguid = Guid.NewGuid(),
                    ModifiedDate = DateTime.Now
                };

                // Add the new customer to the database and save the changes
                database.AddToContacts(newCustomer);
                database.SaveChanges();
                return newCustomer.ContactID;
            }
        }
        catch
        {
            throw new WebFaultException(HttpStatusCode.BadRequest);
        }
    }
}
```

> **Note** The code for this method is available in the file CreateCustomer.txt, which is located in the Chapter 15 folder.

This method uses the parameters passed in to create a new *Contact* object (remember that customers are stored in the Contact table in the *AdventureWorks* database) and then uses the Entity Framework to save this new object to the database. Notice that default values are generated for some of the columns. The *AdventureWorks* database automatically generates an ID for the new customer when the record is saved, and the *CreateCustomer* method returns that ID value. If an error occurs, the method throws a *WebFaultException* exception with an HTTP status code of 400 (Bad Request).

6. Add the following *UpdateCustomer* method (shown in bold) to the *ProductsSales* class:

```
public class ProductsSales : IProductsSales
{
    ...
    // Update the email address and/or telephone number
    // for the specified customer
    public void UpdateCustomer(string customerID, string email, string phone)
    {
        try
```

```
        {
            int id = Convert.ToInt32(customerID);
            using (AdventureWorksEntities database = new AdventureWorksEntities())
            {
                // Find the customer in the database
                var findCustomer = from customer in database.Contacts
                                   where customer.ContactID == id
                                   select customer;

                if (findCustomer.Count() > 0)
                {
                    // Update the details for the customer and save the changes
                    Contact customer = findCustomer.First();

                    if (email != null)
                        customer.EmailAddress = email;
                    if (phone != null)
                        customer.Phone = phone;

                    customer.ModifiedDate = DateTime.Now;
                    database.SaveChanges();
                }
                else
                {
                    throw new WebFaultException(HttpStatusCode.NotFound);
                }
            }
        }
        catch (Exception e)
        {
            if (e is WebFaultException)
            {
                throw;
            }
            else
            {
                throw new WebFaultException(HttpStatusCode.BadRequest);
            }
        }
    }
}
```

 Note The code for this method is available in the file UpdateCustomer.txt, which is located in the Chapter 15 folder.

The *UpdateCustomer* method first tries to locate the customer to be updated. When it finds a match, it sets the email address and telephone number to the values specified by the *email* and *phone* parameters. Note that if either of these parameters is *null* then the method ignores them; this enables a Web client application to omit either of these parameters if the corresponding columns in the database do not need to be modified. If there is no matching customer in the *AdventureWorks* database, the method throws a

WebFaultException exception with the HTTP status 404 (Not Found). If an error occurs, the method throws a *WebFaultException* exception with the HTTP status 400 (Bad Request).

7. Add the *DeleteCustomer* method to the *ProductsSales* class, as shown in bold in the following code example:

```
public class ProductsSales : IProductsSales
{
    ...
    // Delete the specified customer
    public void DeleteCustomer(string customerID)
    {
        try
        {
            int id = Convert.ToInt32(customerID);
            using (AdventureWorksEntities database = new AdventureWorksEntities())
            {
                // Find the customer in the database
                var findCustomer = from customer in database.Contacts
                                   where customer.ContactID == id
                                   select customer;

                if (findCustomer.Count() > 0)
                {
                    // Remove the customer and save the changes
                    Contact customer = findCustomer.First();
                    database.DeleteObject(customer);
                    database.SaveChanges();
                }
                else
                {
                    throw new WebFaultException(HttpStatusCode.NotFound);
                }
            }
        }
        catch (Exception e)
        {
            if (e is WebFaultException)
            {
                throw;
            }
            else
            {
                throw new WebFaultException(HttpStatusCode.BadRequest);
            }
        }
    }
}
```

Note The code for this method is available in the DeleteCustomer.txt file, which is located in the Chapter 15 folder.

This method is similar to *UpdateCustomer*, in so much as it locates the customer to be removed. When a match is found it deletes the corresponding record from the *Adventure Works* database. If there is no matching customer in the *AdventureWorks* database, the method throws a *WebFaultException* exception with the HTTP status 404 (Not Found). If an error occurs, the method throws a *WebFaultException* exception with the HTTP status 400 (Bad Request).

8. Rebuild the ProductsSalesService project.

Make sure that you only rebuild the ProductsSalesService project and not the entire solution; at this point, the ProductsSales client project will fail to build because the *CreateCustomer*, *UpdateCustomer*, and *DeleteCustomer* methods are missing from the client proxy. You will add these methods in the next exercise.

You can invoke the *CreateCustomer*, *UpdateCustomer*, and *DeleteCustomer* operations from a Web application that submits the appropriate *POST*, *PUT*, and *DELETE* requests. The following code fragment is taken from an ASP.NET Web application and shows how to submit an HTTP *DELETE* request that attempts to delete customer 101 from the *AdventureWorks* database:

```
System.Net.WebRequest request =
    System.Net.HttpWebRequest.Create("http://localhost:8000/Sales/Customers/101");
request.Method = "DELETE";
System.Net.HttpWebResponse response = request.GetResponse() as System.Net.HttpWebResponse;
if (response != null && response.StatusCode == System.Net.HttpStatusCode.OK)
{
    ... // Customer 101 was successfully deleted
}
else
{
    ... // Customer 101 was not deleted
}
```

You cannot easily invoke these operations directly by specifying a URI in the address bar of a Web browser such as Internet Explorer. This is because most Web browsers work by sending HTTP *GET* requests; by their nature they are intended to query data rather than modify it. To test these new operations, you can either create an ASP.NET Web application or you can invoke the operations by name from a procedural client application, as you did in the previous set of exercises; this is the approach that you will employ in the next exercise.

To call the new operations from the client application, you must first update the *Products SalesProxy* class.

Update the Procedural Client Application and Test the *ProductsSales* REST Web Service

1. Open the ProductsSalesProxy.cs file for the ProductsSalesClient project in the Code And Text Editor window. Add the *CreateCustomer, UpdateCustomer,* and *DeleteCustomer* methods shown in the following code in bold to the *ProductsSalesProxy* class.

```
class ProductsSalesProxy : ClientBase<IProductsSales>, IProductsSales
{
    ...
    public int CreateCustomer(string firstName, string lastName,
                              string email, string phone)
    {
        return this.Channel.CreateCustomer(firstName, lastName, email, phone);
    }

    public void UpdateCustomer(string customerID, string email=null,
                               string phone=null)
    {
        this.Channel.UpdateCustomer(customerID, email, phone);
    }

    public void DeleteCustomer(string customerID)
    {
        this.Channel.DeleteCustomer(customerID);
    }
}
```

These methods follow the same pattern as the methods you defined in the previous set of exercises; they simply route the requests to the service using the *Channel* property of the *ClientBase<IProductsSales>* class. Notice that the *UpdateCustomer* method provides default values for the *email* and *phone* parameters so that the client application can omit either of them if necessary.

2. Open the Program.cs file for the ProductsSales project in the Code And Text Editor window. In the *Main* method of the *Program* class, add the following statements (shown in bold) after Test 6, but before the statement that closes the *proxy* object.

```
static void Main(string[] args)
{
    ...
    // Test the operations in the service
    try
    {
        ...
        // Find all orders placed by customer 99
        Console.WriteLine("Test 6: Find all orders for customer 99");
        orders = proxy.GetOrdersForCustomer("99");
        Console.WriteLine("Order\tDate Placed\tCustomer\tAmount Due");
        foreach (SalesOrderHeader order in orders)
```

```
        {
            Console.WriteLine("{0}\t{1:d}\t{2}\t\t{3:C}",
                order.SalesOrderID, order.OrderDate,
                order.CustomerID, order.TotalDue);
        }
        Console.WriteLine();

        // Create a new customer
        Console.WriteLine("Test 7: Create a new customer");
        int customerID = proxy.CreateCustomer("John", "Sharp",
            "john@adventure-works.com", "(123)456789");
        salesCustomer = proxy.GetCustomer(customerID.ToString());
        Console.WriteLine("Customer ID: {0}\nName: {1} {2}\nEmail: {3}"+
            "\nPhone: {4}\n\n", salesCustomer.ContactID,
            salesCustomer.FirstName, salesCustomer.LastName,
            salesCustomer.EmailAddress, salesCustomer.Phone);

        // Change the email address for the new customer
        Console.WriteLine("Test 8: Change the email address for the new customer");
        proxy.UpdateCustomer(customerID.ToString(),
            email: "newaddress@adventure-works.com");
        salesCustomer = proxy.GetCustomer(customerID.ToString());
        Console.WriteLine("Customer ID: {0}\nName: {1} {2}\nEmail: {3}"+
            "\nPhone: {4}\n\n", salesCustomer.ContactID,
            salesCustomer.FirstName, salesCustomer.LastName,
            salesCustomer.EmailAddress, salesCustomer.Phone);

        // Delete the new customer
        Console.WriteLine("Test 9: Delete a customer");
        proxy.DeleteCustomer(customerID.ToString());
        salesCustomer = proxy.GetCustomer(customerID.ToString());
        if (salesCustomer == null)
            Console.WriteLine("Customer deleted");
        else
            Console.WriteLine("Customer not deleted");

        // Disconnect from the service
        proxy.Close();
    }
    ...
}
```

This code implements tests that invoke each of the new operations in turn. The first test creates a new customer, and then calls *GetCustomer* with the ID of the newly created customer to verify that the operation was successful. The second test changes the email address for this customer, and again calls *GetCustomer* to retrieve the updated details. The final test deletes the new customer. After the call to *DeleteCustomer*, the *Get Customer* method should return a null object if the delete operation was successful.

3. Rebuild the solution.

4. Start the solution without debugging. In the ProductsSalesClient console window, press Enter. The new tests should all perform successfully and add a new customer record (your customer ID might vary from that shown) before updating the email address and then deleting the customer.

5. Press Enter to close the ProductsSalesClient console window and then close the ProductsSalesHost console window.

Using WCF Data Services

The examples shown so far in this chapter have been very generalized. They illustrate how to utilize WCF to build a REST Web service that exposes data by using a scheme that you define manually through the *WebGet* and *WebInvoke* attributes. If you are constructing REST Web services that provide access to data through an ADO.NET Entity Framework entity model, you can employ WCF Data Services to automate many of these tasks. WCF Data Services provides an additional layer of abstraction for constructing REST Web Services through the WCF Data Service template and assemblies provided with Visual Studio 2010.

You can add a WCF Data Service to a Web application. You define the entity model describing the data that you want to publish and then add the WCF Data Service to the project. The WCF Data Service template generates a very basic data service class based on the generic *System. Data.Services.DataService* type, as shown in the following code fragment:

```
using System;
using System.Data.Services;
using System.Data.Services.Common;
using System.Collections.Generic;
using System.Linq;
using System.ServiceModel.Web;
```

```
public class WcfDataService : DataService< /* TODO: put your data source class name here */ >
{
    // This method is called only once to initialize service-wide policies.
    public static void InitializeService(DataServiceConfiguration config)
    {
        // TODO: set rules to indicate which entity sets and service operations are visible,
        // updatable, etc.
        // Examples:
        // config.SetEntitySetAccessRule("MyEntityset", EntitySetRights.AllRead);
        // config.SetServiceOperationAccessRule("MyServiceOperation",
        // ServiceOperationRights.All);
        config.DataServiceBehavior.MaxProtocolVersion = DataServiceProtocolVersion.V2;
    }
}
```

The type parameter for this class is the *ObjectContext* class generated for the entity model (in the previous examples, the *ObjectContext* class is the *AdventureWorksEntities* type), and you should replace the comment with this type. The *InitializeService* method executes automatically when the service starts running. You add statements to this method that identify the entities in the entity model that the service publishes and that specify the permissions client applications have over this data. For example, you can indicate that the data in one set of entities is read-only, while the data in another entity set allows write access.

The following exercises provide a basic introduction to building and consuming a REST Web service by using the WCF Data Services template.

Build a WCF Data Service to Expose Sales Information

1. Using Visual Studio, create a new Web site by using the ASP.NET Empty Web Site template. Set the Web Location to **File System** and save the project in the **Microsoft Press\ WCF Step By Step\Chapter 15\SalesData** folder within your Documents folder. Allow Visual Studio to create this folder when prompted.

2. In Solution Explorer, click the C:\...\SalesData project. In the Properties window, set the *Use Dynamic Ports* property for this project to **False**, and then set the *Port Number* property to **48000** (it is easier to reference the service from a client application if the port number is fixed).

3. In Solution Explorer, right-click the C:\...SalesData\ project, and then click Add New Item. In the Add New Item dialog box, select the *ADO.NET Entity Data Model* template. In the Name text box type **SalesDataModel.edmx**, and then click Add. Allow Visual Studio to add the data model to the App_Code folder in your project when prompted.

4. In the Entity Data Model Wizard, on the Choose Model Contents page, click Generate From Database, and then click Next.

5. On the Choose Your Data Connection page, click New Connection. In the Connection Properties dialog box, in the Server Name field, type **.\SQLExpress**. In the Select Or Enter A Database Name field, type **AdventureWorks**, and then click OK.

6. On the Choose Your Data Connection page, verify that the Save Entity Connection Settings In Web.Config As: check box is selected, change the name to **AdventureWorks Entities** if necessary, and then click Next.

7. On the Choose Your Database Objects page, expand Tables, and select the **Contact (Person)**, **SalesOrderDetail (Sales)**, and **SalesOrderHeader (Sales)** tables. Verify or specify the following values for the other items on this page, and then click Finish.

Item	Value
Pluralize or singularize generated object names	*Checked*
Include foreign key columns in the model	*Checked*
Model Namespace	AdventureWorksModel

The resulting entity model should look like this.

When a customer places an order, the order may contain multiple items. The *SalesOrder Header* table contains the information about the order (such as the date the order was placed, the customer that placed the order, and so on), and the *SalesOrderDetail* table contains a row for each item in the order (such as the product and quantity required).

8. Build the solution.

9. In Solution Explorer, add another new item to the C:\...SalesData\ project. In the Add New Item dialog box, select the **WCF Data Service** template. In the Name text box, type **SalesDataService.svc**, and then click Add.

The Visual Studio template generates a new file called SalesDataService.cs that contains a class called *SalesDataService*, which inherits from the *DataService* class, as described earlier.

10. In the SalesDataService.cs file, in the Code And Text Editor window, add the following *using* statement to the list at the top of the file:

```
using AdventureWorksModel;
```

11. In the definition of the *SalesDataService* class, delete the comment, */* TODO: put your data source class here */* between the opening and closing angle brackets and replace it with the *AdventureWorksEntities* type, as shown in below in bold:

```
public class SalesDataService : DataService<AdventureWorksEntities>
{
    ...
}
```

The *AdventureWorksEntities* class is the *ObjectContext* type generated by the ADO.NET Entity Model Wizard for accessing the data presented by the entity model.

For security reasons, the WCF Data Services template does not automatically expose any resources, such as entity collections that the entity model implements. You must specify a policy that enables or disables access to resources in the *InitializeService* method of your data service. This method takes a *DataServiceConfiguration* object, which you can use to define the access policy.

12. In the *InitializeService* method, remove the comments at the start of the method and add the following statements shown in bold.

```
public class SalesDataService : DataService<AdventureWorksEntities>
{
    // This method is called only once to initialize service-wide policies.
    public static void InitializeService(DataServiceConfiguration config)
    {
        config.DataServiceBehavior.MaxProtocolVersion = DataServiceProtocolVersion.V2;
        config.SetEntitySetAccessRule("Contacts", EntitySetRights.AllRead);
        config.SetEntitySetAccessRule("SalesOrderHeaders", EntitySetRights.AllRead);
        config.SetEntitySetAccessRule("SalesOrderDetails", EntitySetRights.AllRead);
    }
}
```

The *SetEntitySetAccessRule* method of the *DataServiceConfiguration* class specifies the level of access that client applications have to each of the entities defined in the underlying entity model. In this case, the WCF Data Service provides read-only access to the data.

The *SetEntitySetAccessRule* method takes two parameters:

❑ The name of the entity set. In the entity model, this is the same as the name of an entity but specified as a plural. This string can also contain the "*" wildcard character to indicate all entity sets, although this is not considered to be good practice.

> **Note** You can specify either the name of an entity or the string "*"; you cannot combine "*" with other characters to form entity set name patterns. If you need to provide access to multiple entity sets, you must call the *SetEntitySetAccessRule* method for each entity set.

❑ The access rights you want to grant to this entity set. This is a value from the *System.Data.Services.EntitySetRights* enumeration. This enumeration defines various read and write access rights. You can combine entity set rights by using the bitwise *OR* operator. The following table summarizes the values in the *EntitySet Rights* enumeration.

Value	Description
None	Denies all rights to access data. This is the default setting for all entities.
ReadSingle	Authorization to read single items in an entity set.
ReadMultiple	Authorization to read sets of data.
WriteAppend	Authorization to create new data items in datasets.
WriteReplace	Authorization to replace data.
WriteDelete	Authorization to delete data items from datasets.
WriteMerge	Authorization to merge data.
AllRead	Shorthand for *ReadSingle	ReadMultiple*.
AllWrite	Shorthand for *WriteAppend	WriteReplace	WriteDelete	WriteMerge*.
All	Shorthand for all read and write operations.

13. Add the following statement (shown in bold) to the end of the *InitializeService* method:

```
public static void InitializeService(DataServiceConfiguration config)
{
    ...
    config.SetEntitySetPageSize("*", 25);
}
```

Each entity set (*Contacts*, *SalesOrderHeaders*, *SalesOrderDetails*) could contain many thousands of rows, and a client application could potentially issue a query that fetches all this data. To prevent unconstrained queries that might tie up the network bandwidth, the *SetEntitySetPageSize* method limits the number of items returned by a query, in this case to *25*. The first parameter specifies the name of the entity set to constrain, and—like the *SetEntitySetAccessRule* method—you can provide the wildcard name "*" to apply the restriction to all entity sets. However, unlike the *SetEntitySetAccessRule* method, providing "*" as the first parameter is considered acceptable practice with the *SetEntitySet PageSize* method.

14. Build the solution.

That is all you need to do to build a simple REST Web service using the WCF Data Services template. At runtime, the *DataServices* class automatically exposes the data by using a scheme based on the names of the entities and their relationships in the entity model. You specify URIs that match the structure of the entity model. WCF Data Services also provides a number of operators that you can use to selectively retrieve data from individual columns, sort data, and perform aggregate calculations over data. You will investigate some of these operators in the next exercise.

Test the *SalesData* WCF Data Service

1. In Solution Explorer, open the SalesDataService.svc file in the Code And Text Editor window. This file contains the following code:

```
<%@ ServiceHost Language="C#" Factory="System.Data.Services.DataServiceHostFactory"
Service="SalesDataService" %>
```

The WCF runtime uses the information in this file to determine how to start the *Sales DataService* service. The *Factory* attribute specifies the *DataServiceHostFactory* type located in the *System.Data.Services* namespace. This type is provided with WCF Data Services, and its purpose is to create an instance of a WCF Data Service by using the type indicated by the *Service* attribute, call the *InitializeService* method of this type to set the security policy, and then start it running.

2. Right-click the SalesDataService.svc file, and then click View In Browser.

The service starts running and Internet Explorer opens, displaying the following data:

WCF Data Services utilize the Atom Publishing Protocol (AtomPub) to publish data. This page lists the names of each entity set as an Atom title.

> **Note** The AtomPub protocol is a simple HTTP-based protocol for creating and updating Web resources. This protocol was proposed as a standard by the Internet Engineering Task Force (IETF) and published as RFC 5023. For more information, visit the IETF Web site at *http://www.rfc-editor.org/rfc/rfc5023.txt.*

3. In the address bar of Internet Explorer, enter the URL **http://localhost:48000/ SalesData/SalesDataService.svc/Contacts**.

Internet Explorer displays the data for the first 25 contacts in the *AdventureWorks* database. The data is displayed as an Atom feed, again following the AtomPub protocol.

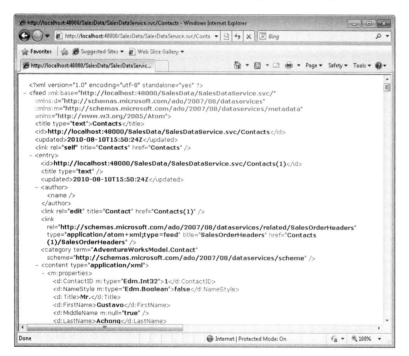

> **Note** Depending on how Internet Explorer is configured, you may need to turn off the feed-reading view to display the data in this format. To do this, on the Tools menu, click Internet Options. In the Internet Options dialog box, click the Content tab. In the Feeds And Web Slices section near the bottom of the dialog box, click Settings. In the Feed And Web Slice Settings dialog box, clear the Turn On Feed Reading View check box, and then click OK. Click OK again and then close Internet Explorer. Finally, open the SalesDataService.svc file by using Internet Explorer as described in step 2 of this exercise, and then browse to the URL **http://localhost:48000/SalesData/SalesDataService.svc/Contacts**.

4. Enter the URL **http://localhost:48000/SalesData/SalesDataService.svc/SalesOrder Details**. The data from the first 25 rows from the *SalesOrderDetails* table in the *Adventure Works* database should appear.

    If you need to access items beyond the first 25 rows, WCF Data Services allows you to fetch data in chunks by using query options it defines, called *$top* and *$skip*. These query options function in a manner similar to the *top* and *skip* query parameters that you implemented in the *ProductsSales* REST Web service earlier in this chapter.

5. Enter the URL **http://localhost:48000/SalesData/SalesDataService.svc/SalesOrder Details?$skip=50**.

    This time, Internet Explorer displays 25 *SalesOrderDetails* records, starting with the 51st item found in the *AdventureWorks* database. Notice that the data is displayed in ascending order of the SalesOrderID column; this is the primary key of the table in the database.

6. Change the URL to **http://localhost:48000/SalesData/SalesDataService.svc/Sales OrderDetails?$orderby=UnitPrice**.

    This time, the data is displayed in ascending order of the *UnitPrice* field. You can switch to descending order by specifying *desc*, like this:

    http://localhost:48000/SalesData/SalesDataService.svc/SalesOrderDetails?$order by=UnitPrice desc

7. WCF Data Services provides operators with which you can drill into the data for an entity. Enter the following URL in the address bar of Internet Explorer:

    http://localhost:48000/SalesData/SalesDataService.svc/SalesOrderHeaders?$ select=SalesOrderID,OrderDate,CustomerID,TotalDue

    This URL forms a projection that limits the data returned to the items in the *SalesOrderID*, *OrderDate*, *CustomerID*, and *TotalDue* columns. You can also specify predicates that limit the items returned according to criteria that you specify by using the *$filter* option. The following example displays the *SalesOrderID* and *TotalDue* for all *SalesOrderHeader* records for customer 99.

    http://localhost:48000/SalesData/SalesDataService.svc/SalesOrderHeaders?$ select=SalesOrderID,TotalDue&$filter=CustomerID eq 99

    Notice that you can use the standard "&" character in a query string in a URL to separate the different options.

8. WCF Data Services also makes it easy to traverse the relationships between entities and fetch related data. Enter the following URL:

    http://localhost:48000/SalesData/SalesDataService.svc/SalesOrderHeaders(43682)

This URL retrieves the data for a single *SalesOrderDetail* item, with the specified value for the primary key column (the SalesOrderID) in the *AdventureWorks* database. If you want to find the details of the contact that placed this order, you can append the text "**/Contact**" to the URL, as follows (Note that you specify the entity name as a singular noun rather than the plural that is used to identify an entity set. This is because the underlying entity model implements this relationship as a many-to-one relationship between the *SalesOderDetail* and *Contact* entities, and the name of the navigation property that connects these two entities in the entity model is called *Contact*):

http://localhost:48000/SalesData/SalesDataService.svc/SalesOrderHeaders (43682)/Contact

To find the *SalesOrderDetails* rows for this order, enter the following URL (note that *SalesOrderDetails* is plural because this is a one-to-many relationship between the *SalesOrderHeader* and *SalesOrderDetail* entities, and the name of the navigation property generated by the entity model is *SalesOrderDetails*):

http://localhost:48000/SalesData/SalesDataService.svc/SalesOrderHeaders (43682)/SalesOrderDetails

 9. Enter the following URL:

http://localhost:48000/SalesData/SalesDataService.svc/SalesOrderHeaders?$ expand=Contact

This query fetches the first 25 *SalesOrderHeader* rows, but the *$expand* option causes WCF Data Services to also fetch the related *Contact* information for each row.

 10. Close Internet Explorer and return to Visual Studio.

You have now built a WCF Data Service and seen how to access it from a Web browser. The service itself was hosted by using the ASP.NET Development Web server, but you can easily deploy this service to IIS. You can also build a custom host application by using the *Web ServiceHost* class, as you did in the exercises in the first part of this chapter.

Consuming a WCF Data Service in a Client Application

The *SalesData* service is very simple, and with it, a user can perform a variety of very complex queries. However, although the AtomPub protocol is widely accepted, the format of the data returned by this protocol is not always easy to understand or parse; you certainly should not expect end users to make sense of this data. Fortunately, you can build client applications that consume the data from a WCF Data Service and present it in a more understandable format. To do this, you must generate a WCF Data Services client library. This client library acts as a proxy for the service, providing access to the data published by the service.

You can generate a client library in two ways; you can use the *DataSvcUtil* utility from the command line, or you can use the Add Service Reference Wizard in Visual Studio. To use the *DataSvcUtil* utility, open a Visual Studio command prompt and type the following command while the WCF Data Service is running:

```
DataSvcUtl /out:SalesClient.cs /uri:http://localhost:48000/SalesData/SalesDataService.svc
```

This command creates a source file called SalesClient.cs that contains the methods that a client application can use to send requests to the WCF Data Service. The client library exposes the data through a series of collections and properties that closely resemble the underlying entity model in the WCF Data Service. The difference is that when a client application attempts to retrieve data from one of these collections, the client library formulates the corresponding HTTP request and sends it to the service. When the data is returned by the service, the client library converts the data from AtomPub format into .NET Framework collections and types that the client application can more easily consume.

In the following exercise you will build a test client application that connects to the *SalesData* service and performs queries similar to those that you ran by using Internet Explorer in the previous section.

Build a Test Client Application for the *SalesData* Service

1. In Visual Studio, add a new Console Application project to the SalesData solution. Name the project **SalesDataClient** and save it in the **Microsoft Press\WCF Step By Step\ Chapter 15** folder.

2. In Solution Explorer, right-click the new SalesDataClient project, and then click Add Service Reference. In the Add Service Reference dialog box, click Discover. In the Namespace box, type **SalesDataService**, and then click OK.

   At first glance, the Add Service Reference dialog box operates in exactly the same way as adding a reference to a SOAP Web service. However, the Visual Studio detects that the service is a WCF Data Service, and so generates a client library that matches the data exposed by the service rather than a series of methods that correspond to SOAP Web service operations.

   The client library for a WCF Data Service consists of a class that is derived from the *DataServiceContext* type. This class exposes one or more *DataServiceQuery* objects as properties. The name of this class is usually the same as the name of the *ObjectContext* object that is used by the entity model on which the WCF Data Service is based. For example, the *SalesDataService* service uses an *ObjectContext* object called *Adventure WorksEntities* to connect to the underlying entity model, so the name of the *DataService Context* type generated for the client library is also *AdventureWorksEntities*.

The *DataServiceContext* class performs a role similar to the *ObjectContext* class in the Entity Framework. A client application connects to the data source (in this case, a WCF Data Service) through a *DataServiceContext* object and fetches the data for the entities that the data service exposes by using the *DataServiceQuery* properties. Each *Data ServiceQuery* property is a generic collection object that presents data from one of the underlying entities that provides the data for the WCF Data Service. In the *SalesData* service, the entity model provides access to the *Contact, SalesOrderHeader,* and *Sales OrderDetail* tables in the *AdventureWorks* database. The *AdventureWorksEntities* class in the client library has *DataServiceQuery* properties called *Contacts, SalesOrderHeaders,* and *SalesOrderDetails.*

The client library also provides definitions of the types that each *DataServiceQuery* collection contains (*Contact, SalesOrderHeader,* and *SalesOrderDetail*). A client application can perform LINQ queries against the *DataServiceQuery* collection properties, and the client library constructs the appropriate HTTP request to fetch the corresponding data. The WCF Data Service fetches the matching data and populates the *DataServiceQuery* collection. The client application can then iterate through this collection and retrieve the data for each item.

3. Open the Program.cs file for the SalesDataClient project in the Code And Text Editor window. Add the following using statement to the list at the top of the file:

```
using SalesDataClient.SalesDataService;
```

This namespace contains the types in the client library that are generated by the Add Service Reference Wizard.

4. In the *Main* method in the *Program* class, add the following code shown in bold:

```
static void Main(string[] args)
{
    AdventureWorksEntities service = new AdventureWorksEntities(
        new Uri("http://localhost:48000/SalesData/SalesDataService.svc"));
}
```

This statement connects to the *SalesData* service. As described earlier, the *Adventure WorksEntities* type is a *DataServiceContext* object that acts like a proxy for sending requests to the *SalesData* service. The URI that you specify in the constructor is the address of the service.

5. Add the following code (shown in bold) to the *Main* method.

```
static void Main(string[] args)
{
    AdventureWorksEntities service = new AdventureWorksEntities(
        new Uri("http://localhost:48000/SalesData/SalesDataService.svc"));

    Console.WriteLine("Test 1: List details of contacts");
    foreach (Contact contact in service.Contacts)
```

```
    {
        Console.WriteLine("ID: {0}\nFirst Name: {1}\nLast Name: {2}\n",
            contact.ContactID, contact.FirstName, contact.LastName);
    }
    Console.WriteLine("Press ENTER to continue");
    Console.ReadLine();
}
```

These statements retrieve the details of contacts from the *SalesData* service and display the first name and last name of each contact. Note that when you reference the *Contacts* collection in the *AdventureWorksEntities* object, the client library sends the corresponding HTTP *GET* request (*http://localhost:48000/SalesData/SalesDataService.svc/Contacts*) to the *SalesData* service to populate this collection. This request is subject to the same constraints as any queries that you perform by using Internet Explorer; it will return only the first 25 contacts.

6. Add the following code to the *Main* method:

```
static void Main(string[] args)
{
    ...
    Console.WriteLine("Test 2: List sales order details");
    foreach (SalesOrderDetail detail in service.SalesOrderDetails)
    {
        Console.WriteLine("Order ID: {0}\nProduct: {1}\nQuantity: {2}\n"+
            "Unit Price: {3:C}\n", detail.SalesOrderID,
            detail.ProductID, detail.OrderQty, detail.UnitPrice);
    }
    Console.WriteLine("Press ENTER to continue");
    Console.ReadLine();
}
```

This code is similar to that in the previous step except that it queries the *SalesOrder Details* collection. As before, this action causes the *AdventureWorksEntities* object to send an HTTP *GET* request (*http://localhost:48000/SalesData/SalesDataService.svc/ SalesOrderDetails*) to the *SalesData* service, and also as before, the request returns only the first 25 rows.

7. Add the statements shown below in bold to the *Main* method:

```
static void Main(string[] args)
{
    ...
    Console.WriteLine("Test 3: Skip the first 50 order details records");
    foreach (SalesOrderDetail detail in service.SalesOrderDetails.Skip(50))
    {
        Console.WriteLine("Order ID: {0}\nProduct: {1}\nQuantity: {2}\n"+
            "Unit Price: {3:C}\n", detail.SalesOrderID,
            detail.ProductID, detail.OrderQty, detail.UnitPrice);
    }
    Console.WriteLine("Press ENTER to continue");
    Console.ReadLine();
}
```

This code retrieves 25 *SalesOrderDetails* records, starting with the 51st item in the *AdventureWorks* database. The *Skip* method, which normally causes a LINQ query to simply omit the specified number of items, in this case is overridden by code in the client library and the *System.Data.Services.Client* assembly, and causes the *Adventure WorksEntities* object to generate a URL with the query string *$skip=50*.

> **Note** The Add Service Reference Wizard added a reference to the *System.Data.Services. Client* assembly when you generated the client library for the *SalesData* service.

8. Add the code shown in the following example to the *Main* method:

```
static void Main(string[] args)
{
    ...
    Console.WriteLine("Test 4: Sort data by unit price");
    foreach (SalesOrderDetail detail in service.SalesOrderDetails.OrderBy((d) =>
        d.UnitPrice))
    {
        Console.WriteLine("Order ID: {0}\nProduct: {1}\nQuantity: {2}\n"+
            "Unit Price: {3:C}\n", detail.SalesOrderID,
            detail.ProductID, detail.OrderQty, detail.UnitPrice);
    }
    Console.WriteLine("Press ENTER to continue");
    Console.ReadLine();

    Console.WriteLine("Test 5: Sort data by unit price (most expensive first)");
    foreach (SalesOrderDetail detail in
        service.SalesOrderDetails.OrderByDescending((d) => d.UnitPrice))
    {
        Console.WriteLine("Order ID: {0}\nProduct: {1}\nQuantity: {2}\n"+
            "Unit Price: {3:C}\n", detail.SalesOrderID,
            detail.ProductID, detail.OrderQty, detail.UnitPrice);
    }
    Console.WriteLine("Press ENTER to continue");
    Console.ReadLine();
}
```

This block of code retrieves *SalesOrderDetails* records, but it sequences them according to the value of the *UnitPrice* field, in ascending and descending order. Again, the *OrderBy* method is overridden and generates a query string containing the text, *$orderby= UnitPrice*. Similarly, the *OrderByDescending* method generates the query string, *$orderby=UnitPrice desc*.

9. Add the following block of code to the *Main* method:

```
static void Main(string[] args)
{
    ...
    Console.WriteLine(
        "Test 6: Display the SalesOrderID and TotalDue "+
        "for all orders for customer 99");
```

```
foreach (var orderData in
        from o in service.SalesOrderHeaders
        where o.CustomerID == 99
        select new {o.SalesOrderID, o.TotalDue})
{
    Console.WriteLine("Order ID: {0}\nTotal Due: {1:C}\n",
        orderData.SalesOrderID, orderData.TotalDue);
}
Console.WriteLine("Press ENTER to continue");
Console.ReadLine();
}
```

This code uses LINQ syntax to filter and project data, listing the *SalesOrderID* and *Total Due* fields for all orders placed by customer 99. The client library generates a *$filter* query expression for the *where* clause in the LINQ query, and a *$select* query expression for the *select* clause. The result looks similar to this:

```
$filter=CustomerID eq 99 &$select=SalesOrderID,TotalDue
```

10. Add the code shown in bold to the *Main* method:

```
static void Main(string[] args)
{
    ...
    Console.WriteLine("Test 7: fetch the contact details for all orders");
    foreach (var orderData in
            from o in service.SalesOrderHeaders.Expand("Contact")
            select o)
    {
        Console.WriteLine("Order ID: {0}\nCustomer: {1} {2}\n",
            orderData.SalesOrderID, orderData.Contact.FirstName,
            orderData.Contact.LastName);
    }
    Console.WriteLine("Press ENTER to finish");
    Console.ReadLine();
}
```

This block of code retrieves orders and the corresponding contacts for each order. If an entity has related data in other entities, you can fetch the data from those entities by using the *Expand* method. This method causes the query to include the *$expand* option to automatically fetch the related data from these entities. If you omit the *Expand* method, then no related data will be fetched.

11. Rebuild the solution.

You can now test the client application. However, before doing that, it is useful to configure tracing for the *SalesData* service so that you can see the queries that the client application actually sends to the service.

Configure Tracing and Test the *SalesData* Service

1. In the C:\...\SalesData\ project, open the Web.config file by using the Service Configuration Editor.

2. In the Configuration pane, click the Diagnostics node. In the Diagnostics pane, click the Enable Tracing link.

3. Click the link adjacent to the Trace Level label. In the Tracing Settings dialog box, set the Trace Level property to **Information**, and then click OK.

4. Click the ServiceModelTraceListener link. In the Listener Settings dialog box, set the Log File property to **web_tracelog.svclog** under the **Microsoft Press\WCF Step By Step\ Chapter 15** folder within your Documents folder, and then click OK.

5. Save the configuration file then close the Service Configuration Editor.

6. In Solution Explorer, open the SalesData solution properties window, set the C:\...\Sales Data\ and SalesDataClient projects as startup projects for the SalesData solution, and then click OK.

7. Start the solution without debugging. Minimize Internet Explorer when it appears. In the client application console window, verify that the names of the first 25 customers appear:

8. Press Enter and then verify that the first 25 *SalesOrderDetails* records appear. These items have an order ID in the range *43659* to *43661* (there are multiple *SalesOrder Details* records for each order).

9. Press Enter again and verify that a different set of *SalesOrderDetails* records are displayed. This batch should be for orders in the range *43662* to *43666*.

10. Press Enter again. The *SalesOrderDetails* records should be sorted in ascending order of the *UnitPrice* field (the cheapest product costs $1.33).

11. Press Enter again. This time the *SalesOrderDetails* records should be displayed in descending order of the value in the *UnitPrice* field (the most expensive product costs $3578.27).

12. Press Enter again. You should see the *SalesOrderID* and *TotalDue* fields from the *Sales OrderHeader* table in the *AdventureWorks* database for orders placed by customer 99, starting with order ID *43682*, and finishing with order ID *69485*.

13. Press Enter again. This time you should see a list of order IDs and customer names for each order.

14. Press Enter to finish the application and close the client console window.

15. In the Windows task bar, right-click the ASP.NET Development Server icon, and then click Stop.

16. Start the Service Trace Viewer utility in the Microsoft Visual Studio 2010 | Microsoft Windows SDK Tools group on the Windows Start menu, and then open the web_tracelog. svclog file located in the Microsoft Press\WCF Step By Step\Chapter 15 folder.

17. In the Service Trace Viewer, click the Activity tab, and then click the first activity named "Process action". In the right pane, click the item named "Received a message over a channel". In the lower pane on the right side, scroll down to the Message Properties And Headers section to display the "To" address. The URI in this address should be *http:// localhost:48000/SalesData/SalesDataService.svc/Contacts*. This is the URI generated by the first test in the client application:

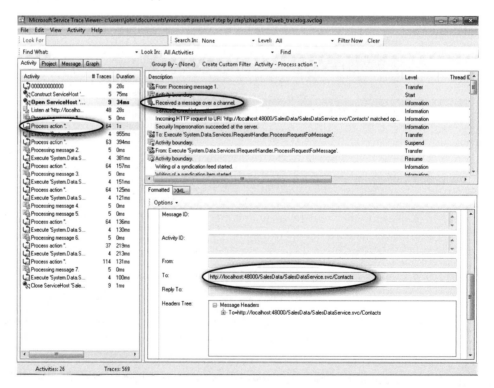

18. In the Activity pane, click the second "Process action" activity. In the right pane, click the "Received a request over a channel" item, and in the lower pane, verify that the To address is *http://localhost:48000/SalesData/SalesDataService.svc/SalesOrderDetails*. This is the URL generated by the second test in the client application.

19. Repeat this process for the remaining "Process action" activities. The following table lists the expected To addresses for each of the remaining tests (note that space characters are replaced with the sequence "%20" in URLs):

Test	To Address
3	http://localhost:48000/SalesData/SalesDataService.svc/SalesOrderDetails()?$skip=50
4	http://localhost:48000/SalesData/SalesDataService.svc/SalesOrderDetails()?$orderby= UnitPrice
5	http://localhost:48000/SalesData/SalesDataService.svc/SalesOrderDetails()?$orderby= UnitPrice%20desc
6	http://localhost:48000/SalesData/SalesDataService.svc/SalesOrderHeaders()?$filter= CustomerID%20eq%2099&$select=SalesOrderID,TotalDue
7	http://localhost:48000/SalesData/SalesDataService.svc/SalesOrderHeaders()?$expand= Contact

20. Close the Service Trace Viewer and return to Visual Studio.

Modifying Data by Using a WCF Data Service

As you might expect, with WCF Data Services, you can also build client applications that can modify data as well as query it. The client library implements a model with which you to make changes locally to the collections that correspond to the entity sets exposed by the service, and then send these changes to the service as a batch by using the *SaveChanges* method of the *DataServiceContext* object that you used to connect to the service. You should note, however, that the WCF Data Service must explicitly enable you to make changes to entities by specifying the appropriate access rights in the *InitializeService* method. The following code shows how to enable updates for the *Contacts* entity set in the SalesData service by specifying the *EntitySetRights.AllWrite* privilege:

```
public static void InitializeService(DataServiceConfiguration config)
{
    ...
    config.SetEntitySetAccessRule("Contacts",
        EntitySetRights.AllRead | EntitySetRights.AllWrite);
    ...
}
```

The code example that follows shows you how to create a new *Contact* entity object. When you create the client library for a WCF Data Service, the Add Service Reference Wizard generates a static *Create* method for each entity type, with a parameter for every non-nullable entity property. It also generates an *AddTo* method for every entity type; you call this method to add the new object to the appropriate collection in the *DataServiceContext* object before invoking *SaveChanges*.

```
AdventureWorksEntities service = new AdventureWorksEntities(
    new Uri("http://localhost:48000/SalesData/SalesDataService.svc"));
...
// Create a new Contact object
// The parameters to CreateContact are values for each field in the Contact type
Contact newContact = Contact.CreateContact(0, true, "John", Sharp", ...);

// Add the Contact object to the DataServiceContext object
service.AddToContacts(newContact);

// Send the new contact to the WCF Data service
service.SaveChanges();
```

The *SaveChanges* method generates an HTTP *POST* request, passing the data for the new contact as the body of the message.

To modify an object, you simply retrieve it by sending a query to the WCF Data Service, change the values required, and then call the *UpdateObject* method of the *DataServiceContext* object to notify it of the changes. When you call *SaveChanges* to send the updates back to the service, the *DataServiceContext* object generates either an HTTP *PUT* or an HTTP MERGE message for each object that has changed, and passes the data for the object in the body of the message. The following code shows how to modify the email address for contact *99*.

```
AdventureWorksEntities service = new AdventureWorksEntities(
    new Uri("http://localhost:48000/SalesData/SalesDataService.svc"));
...
// Fetch the details for contact 99
Contact contact = (from c in service.Contacts
                   where c.ContactID == 99
                   select c).First();

// Update the email address
contact.EmailAddress = "NewEmailAddress@Adventure-Works.com";

// Inform the DataServiceContext object of the change
service.UpdateObject(contact);

// Save the change to the WCF Data Service
service.SaveChanges();
```

Note By default, the *DataServiceContext* object will send a MERGE message if possible, but you can override this decision and explicitly request that it sends a *PUT* message by specifying the *SaveChangesOptions.ReplaceOnUpdate* flag as a parameter to the *SaveChanges* method.

To delete an object, the process is similar; you fetch the object to be deleted and then call *DeleteObject* on the *DataServiceContext* object followed by *SaveChanges*. The *SaveChanges* method generates an HTTP *DELETE* message which it sends to the WCF Data Service. The following code shows an example that attempts to delete contact *101*.

```
AdventureWorksEntities service = new AdventureWorksEntities(
    new Uri("http://localhost:48000/SalesData/SalesDataService.svc"));
...
// Fetch the details for contact 101
Contact contact = (from c in service.Contacts
                   where c.ContactID == 101
                   select c).First();

// Inform the DataServiceContext object that you want to delete this contact
service.DeleteObject(contact);

// Delete the object in the WCF Data Service
service.SaveChanges();
```

Note that these examples have shown the *SaveChanges* method being called after each operation. If you are making several changes (inserts, updates, deletes, or combinations of these operations) you only need to call *SaveChanges* once after you have made the final change. The *DataServiceContext* object tracks the state of all the objects in its various collections and generates the appropriate HTTP *POST*, *PUT*, MERGE, and *DELETE* messages for each modification, sending each of them to the WCF Data Service. As a further optimization, you can specify the *SaveChangesOptions.ReplaceOnUpdate.Batch* flag as a parameter to the *SaveChanges* method. This flag causes the *DataServiceContext* object to send all changes as a single message. This approach can reduce the number of round trips and improve the performance of the client application. Batches also behave like transactions, so either all of the operations in the batch succeed or they all fail. This can help with the design of data-integrity rules in the application. Each batch request results in a single HTTP response that contains the response results for all of the operations in the batch. If any individual operation fails, the batch response will contain just one response result for that failed operation.

As with any multiuser data application, concurrency exceptions may be raised and you need to handle them appropriately in the client application. You also need to ensure that you maintain data integrity when modifying relational data.

Handling Exceptions in a Client Application

When a client application sends a request to a WCF Data Service, that request may fail for many reasons. For example, the client application may have attempted to access data to which it does not have rights, or it tried to perform a query that requires functionality that the service has restricted.

If the failure is due to the way in which the client application interacts with the service (as opposed to a failure caused by some other problem, such as a network failure when attempting to connect to the service), the service responds by throwing a *DataServiceException* exception. The *DataServiceException* type is a serializable exception that is specifically designed to communicate the causes of a failure in a WCF Data Service. When the client library receives a *DataServiceException* exception, it actually deserializes it as a *DataServiceClientException* object, which it passes to your application.

If your application was performing a query when the exception occurred, the *DataService ClientException* exception is wrapped in a *DataServiceQueryException* object, with the message "An error occurred while processing the request." You can access the *DataService ClientException* exception that contains the reason for the exception by examining the *Inner Exception* property of the *DataServiceQueryException* object.

If a client application sends a request other than a query, the WCF Data Service can respond with a *DataServiceRequestException* exception.

A client application should be prepared to catch the *DataServiceQueryException* type when it performs query operations, and the *DataServiceRequestException* exception when it performs other types of operations, such as modifying data. A client application should also be prepared to catch the *DataServiceClientException* type to handle any other exceptions that the WCF Data Service throws when it performs other types of operations.

Summary

In this chapter, you have seen how to build WCF services that follow the REST model. You can use REST Web services to define a URL scheme that client applications can use to query and update data in a logical manner. When you build a REST Web service from scratch, you have full control over these URLs through the *WebGet* and *WebInvoke* attributes. You have also seen how to retrieve data by using a Web browser as well as how to construct a proxy class that a client application can use to connect to a REST Web service.

The second half of this chapter introduced WCF Data Services. This is a highly flexible framework with which you can build REST Web services based directly on an ADO.NET Entity Framework entity model. Visual Studio provides tools that can generate a client library that applications can use to connect to the service and query and modify the data. The client library hides all the complexity associated with building, sending, and receiving the appropriate HTTP messages, so developers can concentrate on the application's business logic. WCF Data Services is a very large topic in its own right, and this chapter has only just scratched the surface. For example, you can define custom business operations, and you can expose data that is not defined in an entity model. For more information, visit the WCF Data Services page on the Microsoft Web site at *http://msdn.microsoft.com/en-us/data/odata.aspx*.

Chapter 16

Using a Callback Contract to Publish and Subscribe to Events

After completing this chapter, you will be able to:

- Define a callback contract that enables a WCF service to call back in to a client application.

- Create a client application that implements a callback contract.

- Use a callback contract to build a simple mechanism for alerting client applications about significant events.

The examples and exercises that you have seen so far in this book have concentrated on the client/server model of processing. In this model, a server provides a service that waits passively for a request from a client application, handles that request, and then optionally sends a response back to the client application. The client application is the active participant, making requests and effectively determining when the service should perform its work. While this is the most common model, WCF supports other processing schemes, such as peer-to-peer networking and client callbacks.

In the peer-to-peer scenario, there are no passive services. All applications are autonomous clients that can communicate with each other as equals (or peers). There is no client/server relationship, so applications should be prepared to handle messages sent to them at any time.

 More Info Peer-to-peer technologies have been an integral part of the Windows operating system since Windows Vista. The .NET Framework includes a number of types in the *System.Net.Peer ToPeer* namespace that you can use to implement peer network functionality. Additionally, WCF provides the Peer Channel for communicating between peers and the *NetPeerTcpBinding* binding for configuring communication parameters and specifying security settings.

A detailed discussion of using WCF to build peer-to-peer applications is beyond the scope of this book, but the Visual Studio documentation provides information and examples in the Peer-to-Peer Networking section, under WCF Feature Details. This content is also available on the Microsoft Web site at *http://msdn.microsoft.com/en-us/library/ms733761.aspx*.

Using client callbacks, a service can invoke a method in a client application, in essence inverting the client/server relationship between the client application and the service. In this chapter, you will look at how to define a client callback and how to use it to implement a simple eventing mechanism for alerting interested client applications about a change of state in the service.

Implementing and Invoking a Client Callback

In the traditional client/server arrangement, a service listens for messages on one or more endpoints by using the WCF service infrastructure established when the host application opens a *ServiceHost* object, but a client application only expects to receive messages in response to explicit requests that it sends. However, once a client has opened a channel to a service, WCF also enables the service to send additional messages to the client, as long as the client application has a means to receive them. WCF provides two features that you can use to implement this functionality: callback contracts and duplex channels.

There is one key aspect that is important to understand; callbacks can only be sent as part of the processing for a request sent by a client, and the callback is invoked by using the communications channel that the client initiated to send this request.

Defining a Callback Contract

A callback contract defines operations that a service can invoke in a client application. A callback contract is very similar to a service contract in the respect that it is an interface or class that contains operations marked with the *OperationContract* attribute. The main syntactic difference is that you do not decorate it with the *ServiceContract* attribute. Here is an example defining a method that a service can call to alert a client application that the price of a product has been changed:

```
public interface IProductsServiceV3Callback
{
    // Inform the client application that the price of the specified
    // product has changed
    [OperationContract]
    void OnPriceChanged(ProductData product);
}
```

A client application listening for callbacks provides an implementation of each method in the callback contract. A service can discover the callbacks supported by a client by referencing the callback contract from the service contract that defines the operations implemented by the service. You achieve this by using the *CallbackContract* property of the *ServiceContract* attribute, as shown in the code example that follows. The intention in this example is that the client application calls the *ChangePrice* operation to update the price of a specified product. The service invokes the *OnPriceChanged* operation in the client when the price has been successfully modified and passes back a copy of the modified product. As an aside, you should note that any other operations in the *IProductsServiceV3* service contract shown in the example can also call the *OnPriceChanged* operation because the callback contract is tied to the service contract and not to a specific operation in the service contract:

```
[ServiceContract(..., CallbackContract=typeof(IProductsServiceV3Callback))]
public interface IProductsServiceV3
{
    // Any method in this contract can invoke the OnPriceChanged method
    // in the client application
    [OperationContract]
    List<string> ListProducts();
    ...
    [OperationContract]
    bool ChangePrice(string productNumber, decimal price);
    ...
}
```

> **Important** You can associate only a single callback contract with a service contract.

Implementing an Operation in a Callback Contract

When you create a client proxy class intended to access a service implementing a contract that has an associated callback contract, the proxy class generated is based on the generic *System.ServiceModel.DuplexClientBase* class (an ordinary client proxy extends the *ClientBase* generic class, as described in Chapter 11, "Programmatically Controlling the Configuration and Communications"). An abbreviated and edited version of the proxy code for the *Products Service* service looks like this:

> **Note** The names of the interfaces in the proxy in the following code sample have been changed for clarity. The *svcutil* utility actually generates different names for these items, depending on the *Name* attribute specified for the service contract when it is defined.

```
...
[System.ServiceModel.ServiceContractAttribute(...,
        CallbackContract=typeof(IProductsServiceV3Callback))]
public interface ProductsServiceV3
{
    [System.ServiceModel.OperationContractAttribute(Action=..., ReplyAction=...)]
    string[] ListProducts();
    ...
    [System.ServiceModel.OperationContractAttribute(Action=..., ReplyAction=...)]
    bool ChangePrice(string productNumber, decimal price);
    ...
}
...
public interface IProductsServiceV3Callback
```

```
{
    [OperationContractAttribute(Action=...)]
    void OnPriceChanged(ProductData product);
}
...
public partial class ProductsServiceV3Client :
  System.ServiceModel.DuplexClientBase<IProductsServiceV3>, IProductsServiceV3
{
    ProductsServiceV3Client(System.ServiceModel.InstanceContext callbackInstance) :
            base(callbackInstance)
    {
    }

    public ProductsServiceClient(System.ServiceModel.InstanceContext callbackInstance,
                                 string endpointConfigurationName) :
            base(callbackInstance, endpointConfigurationName)
    {
    }
    // Other constructors not shown
    ...
    public string[] ListProducts()
    {
        return base.Channel.ListProducts();
    }
    ...
    bool ChangePrice(string productNumber, decimal price);
    {
        return base.Channel.ChangePrice(productNumber,price);
    }
    ...
}
```

The bold statements in the preceding example highlight the important differences between
this code and the code for an ordinary proxy that does *not* define a callback contract. It is the
responsibility of the developer building the client application to provide a class that implements the *IProductsServiceV3Callback* interface, including the *OnPriceChanged* method.

The *ProductsServiceV3Client* proxy class extends the *DuplexClientBase<IProductsServiceV3>*
class and defines a number of constructors that the client application can use to instantiate
a proxy object. The preceding code fragment shows only two of these constructors, but the
main feature of all the constructors is that they expect you to provide an *InstanceContext*
object as the first parameter. This is the key property that enables the service to invoke the
operation in the client application.

You should already be familiar with the concept of "instance context" for a service as dictated
by the *InstanceContextMode* specified for the service, but to recap, each instance of a service
runs in its own context and holds state information (instance variables and pieces of system
information) for that instance. Each instance of a service has its own context. The WCF runtime creates and initializes this context automatically when it instantiates the service instance.
This can occur when:

- A client application starts a new session (if the services specifies the *PerSession* instance context mode)

- The client invokes an operation in the service (if the service specifies the *PerCall* instance context mode)

- The service host starts the service (if the service specifies the *Single* instance context mode)

When a client connects to a service instance, the communications channel used to transmit messages between the client and the service holds information about the specific service instance being used, so the WCF runtime can direct messages to the correct instance.

When you implement a client callback, you must provide the same facility so that the WCF runtime can route messages back to the appropriate client. To do this, you create an *Instance-Context* object that refers to a specific instance of the client application and pass that *Instance Context* to the service when you connect to it through the proxy. When the client application sends a request message through the proxy to the service, the WCF runtime automatically includes the client context with the request. If the service needs to invoke an operation in the callback contract, it uses the context object to direct the call to the appropriate instance of the client application (you will see how to do this shortly).

As an example, here is the code for part of a client application that implements the *IProducts ServiceV3Callback* interface defined in the client proxy:

```
class Client : IProductsServiceV3Callback, IDisposable
{
    private ProductsServiceV3Client proxy = null;

    public void DoWork()
    {
        // Create a proxy object and connect to the service
        InstanceContext context = new InstanceContext(this);
        proxy = new ProductsServiceV3Client(context, ...);
        ...

        // Invoke operations
        bool result = proxy.ChangePrice(...);
        ...
    }

    public void Dispose()
    {
        // Disconnect from the service
        if (proxy != null && proxy.State == CommunicationState.Opened)
        {
            proxy.Close();
        }
    }
}
```

```
// Method specified in the ProductsServiceCallback interface
public void OnPriceChanged(ProductData product)
{
    Console.WriteLine("Price of {0} changed to {1}",
        product.Name, product.ListPrice);
}
}
```

The parameter specified for the *InstanceContext* constructor (*this*) is a reference to the object implementing the *IProductsServiceV3Callback* contract. The statement that creates the proxy object in the *DoWork* method references this *InstanceContext* object. If the service invokes the *OnPriceChanged* operation through this context object, the WCF runtime will call the method on this instance of the client application.

Notice that the *client* class also implements the *IDisposable* interface; the *Dispose* method closes the proxy. A service could potentially call back into the client application at any time after the *Client* object has connected to the service and sent an initial message. If the client application closes the proxy immediately after sending requests to the service in the *DoWork* method, the service will fail if it attempts to call back into the *Client* object, because the client *InstanceContext* object would no longer be valid. In the code shown above, if a *Client* object continues to exist after the *DoWork* method finishes, closing the proxy in the *Dispose* method enables a service to invoke operations in the *Client* object at any time until the client application terminates or it explicitly disposes the *Client* object.

Invoking an Operation in a Callback Contract

To invoke an operation in a callback contract, a service must obtain a reference to the instance of the client application that sent the request. As you've just seen, the WCF runtime for the service makes this information available through the operation context for the service. You can access the operation context through the static *OperationContext.Current* property, which returns an *OperationContext* object. The *OperationContext* class provides the generic *GetCallbackChannel* method, which in turn returns a reference to a channel that the service can use to communicate with the instance of the client application that invoked the service. The value returned by the *GetCallbackChannel* method is a typed reference to the callback contract; you can invoke operations through this reference, as shown in the following:

```
// WCF service class that implements the service contract
public class ProductsServiceImpl : IProductsServiceV3
{
    ...
    public bool ChangePrice(string productNumber, decimal price)
    {
        // Update the price of the product in the database
        ...
```

```
    // Invoke the callback operation in the client application
    IProductsServiceV3Callback callback =
        OperationContext.Current.GetCallbackChannel<
        IProductsServiceV3Callback>();
    callback.OnPriceChanged(GetProduct(productNumber));
    ...
    }
}
```

It is possible that the client application could terminate or close the communication channel
in the period between invoking the operation in the service and the service calling back into
the service, especially if the operation in the service is a one-way operation. You should therefore check to ensure that the callback channel has not been closed before invoking a callback
operation:

```
IProductsServiceV3Callback callback =
    OperationContext.Current.GetCallbackChannel<
    IProductsServiceV3Callback>();

if (((ICommunicationObject)callback).State
    == CommunicationState.Opened)
{
    callback.OnPriceChanged(GetProduct(productNumber));
}
```

All WCF channels implement the *ICommunicationObject* interface. This interface provides the
State property, which you can use to determine whether the channel is still open. If the value
of the *State* property is anything other than *CommunicationState.Opened,* the service should
not attempt to use the callback.

> **Note** Channels exhibit the same set of states and state transitions that a *ServiceHost* object does
> (the *ServiceHost* class indirectly implements the *ICommunicationObject* interface). Refer to Chapter 3,
> "Making Applications and Services Robust," for a description of these states.

Reentrancy and Threading in a Callback Operation

If a service invokes an operation in a callback contract, it is possible for the client code implementing that contract to make another operation call back into the service. By default, the
WCF runtime in the service handling the callback executes by using a single thread, so calling
back into the service could possibly result in the service blocking the thread processing the
initial request. In this case, the WCF runtime detects the situation and throws an *InvalidOperation
Exception* exception, with the message "This operation would deadlock because the reply cannot be received until the current Message completes processing." To prevent this situation
from arising, you can set the concurrency mode of the class implementing the callback

contract in the client application either to enable multiple threading (if the client application code is thread-safe) or enable reentrancy (if the client application code is not thread-safe but the data it uses remains consistent across calls). You achieve this by applying the *Callback Behavior* attribute to the class in the client application implementing the callback contract and setting the *ConcurrencyMode* property to *ConcurrencyMode.Multiple* or *Concurrency-Mode.Reentrant*:

```
[CallbackBehavior(ConcurrencyMode = ConcurrencyMode.Reentrant)]
class Client : ProductsServiceCallback, IDisposable
{
    ...
}
```

Bindings and Duplex Channels

Not all bindings support client callbacks. Specifically, you must use a binding that supports bidirectional communications; either end of the connection must be able to initiate communications, and the other end must be able to accept them. Transports such as TCP and named pipes are inherently bidirectional, so you can use the *NetTcpBinding* and *NetNamedPipeBinding* bindings with a client callback. However, the model implemented by the HTTP protocol does not support bidirectional operations, so you cannot use the *BasicHttpBinding*, *WSHttpBinding*, or *WS2007HttpBinding* bindings. This sounds like a major shortcoming if you want to build an Intranet system based on the HTTP transport. However, WCF provides the *WSDualHttp Binding* binding for this purpose. This binding establishes two HTTP channels (one for sending requests from the client application to the service, and the other for the service to send requests to the client application) but hides much of the complexity from you, so you can treat it as a single bidirectional channel.

There are some important differences between the *WSDualHttpBinding* binding and the *WSHttpBinding* or *WS2007HttpBinding* bindings. Specifically, the *WSDualHttpBinding* binding does not support transport-level security, but it always implements reliable sessions (you cannot disable them).

Using a Callback Contract to Notify a Client of the Outcome of a One-Way Operation

The principal use of a callback contract is to provide a service with a means to inform a client application of the result of a one-way operation—which by definition does not return any information. The example in these exercises is based on an extended version of the price change scenario described earlier. When a client application invokes the *ChangePrice* operation in the *ProductsService* service, the service will call back to the client to notify it when the database has been updated.

Add a Callback Contract to the *ProductsService* Service and Invoke a Callback Operation

1. Using Visual Studio, open the solution file ProductsServiceV3.sln, located in the Microsoft Press\WCF Step By Step\Chapter 16\ProductsServiceV3 folder.

   This solution contains version 3 of the *ProductsService* service (versions 1 and 2 have been removed from the *ProductsService* service, to keep the project concise and focused). This service implements the operations you've already seen such as *ListProducts*, *Get Product*, *CurrentStockLevel*, and *ChangeStockLevel*. It also includes a new operation called *ChangePrice*, which a client application can invoke to change the price of a product. In addition, the solution contains a WPF application for hosting the service, and a client application that you will use to test the *ProductsService* service.

2. Build and run the solution. In the Products Service Host window, click Start. In the client console window, press Enter when the service has started.

   > **Note** The ProductsServiceHost application assumes that you still have the reservation for port 8010 in place. If this is not the case, open a Visual Studio Command Prompt window as Administrator and run the following command, replacing *UserName* with your Windows user name:
   >
   > ```
   > netsh http add urlacl url=http://+:8010/ user=UserName
   > ```

   The client application connects to the service, lists the product number of every product, displays the details for product FR-M21S-40 (a bicycle frame), changes the price of this product, and then displays the new price.

   When the client application has finished, close the client console window, click Stop in the Products Service Host window, close the Products Service Host window, and then return to Visual Studio.

3. In Solution Explorer, open the Program.cs file for the ProductsClient project in the Code And Text Editor window.

   Examine the code in the *Main* method. This method creates an instance of a class called *Client*, and then runs the *TestProductsService* method in this instance. The *Client* class is implemented in the same file. The *TestProductsService* method contains the now-familiar code that creates a proxy object to connect to *ProductsService* service (the endpoint is named *WS2007HttpBinding_IProductsServiceV3* in the application configuration file), and then exercises the *ListProducts* and *GetProduct* operations. The *TestProductsService* method also calls the *PriceChange* method to update the price of the specified product.

The *ChangePrice* operation currently blocks client applications that call it until the price has been changed, and then returns a Boolean value to the caller indicating whether the change was successful. As this operation may take some time to update the database, you will modify it to become a one-way operation and provide a callback contract that the *ProductsService* service can use to notify the client of the operation's outcome. This strategy lets the client application continue running while the change is made.

4. In Solution Explorer, open the IProductsService.cs file for the ProductsService project in the Code And Text Editor window. Add the following callback contract to the file, immediately before the *IProductsServiceV3* interface defining the service contract:

```
// Callback interface for notifying the client that the price has changed
public interface IProductsServiceV3Callback
{
    [OperationContract(IsOneWay = true)]
    void OnPriceChanged(ProductData product);
}
```

This callback contract contains a single operation called *OnPriceChanged*. You will modify the *ChangePrice* operation in the *ProductsService* service to invoke this operation in a later step. The purpose of this operation is to inform the client of a change in the price of the product passed in as the parameter. Notice that this operation is defined as a one-way operation; it simply alerts the client application and does not return any sort of response.

5. Modify the *ServiceContract* attribute for the *IProductsServiceV3* interface to reference this callback contract, as shown in bold in the following code example:

```
// Version 3 of the service contract
[ServiceContract(Namespace = "http://adventure-works.com/2010/07/22",
                 Name = "ProductsService",
                 CallbackContract = typeof(IProductsServiceV3Callback))]
public interface IProductsServiceV3
{
    ...
}
```

The value to the *CallbackContract* property must be a type, so this code uses the *typeof* operator to return the type of the *IProductsServiceV3Callback* interface.

6. In the *IProductsServiceV3* interface, modify the definition of the *ChangePrice* operation and mark it as a one-way operation. One-way methods cannot return a value, so change the return type to *void*, as shown in bold below:

```
public interface IProductsServiceV3
{
    ...
    [OperationContract(IsOneWay = true)]
    void ChangePrice(string productNumber, decimal price);
}
```

7. Open the ProductsService.cs file in the Code And Text Editor window. Locate the *ChangePrice* method at the end of the *ProductsServiceImpl* class (the *ProductsService Impl* class implements the *IProductsServiceV3* service contract). This method updates the *AdventureWorks* database with the new product price, returning *true* if the update was successful or *false* if otherwise (the method performs very limited error checking).

Change the return type of the method to *void*. Modify the two return statements that return *false* (to indicate failure) in the *if* statement and the *catch* block to simply finish without returning a value. Remove the final *return* statement that returns *true* and replace it with code that creates a *ProductData* object for the updated product and invokes the *OnPriceChanged* operation in the callback contract, as shown in bold in the following code (the comments in the method have also been updated to reflect the way in which the method now works):

```
public void ChangePrice(string productNumber, decimal price)
{
    // Modify the price of the selected product
    Product product = null;

    try
    {
        // Connect to the AdventureWorks database by using the Entity Framework
        using (AdventureWorksEntities database = new AdventureWorksEntities())
        {
            if (!ProductExists(productNumber, database))
                return;
            else
            {
                // Find the specified product
                product = (from p in database.Products
                        where String.Compare(p.ProductNumber, productNumber) == 0
                        select p).First();

                // Change the price for the product
                product.ListPrice = price;

                // Save the change back to the database
                database.SaveChanges();
            }
        }
    }
    catch
    {
        // If an exception occurs, just return
        return;
    }

    // Notify the client that the price has been changed successfully
    IProductsServiceV3Callback callback =
        OperationContext.Current.GetCallbackChannel<IProductsServiceV3Callback>();
```

```
        if (((ICommunicationObject)callback).State == CommunicationState.Opened)
        {
            ProductData productData = new ProductData()
            {
                ProductNumber = product.ProductNumber,
                Name = product.Name,
                ListPrice = product.ListPrice,
                Color = product.Color
            };
            callback.OnPriceChanged(productData);
        }
    }
}
```

8. Build the ProductsService project.

The next step is to implement the callback contract in the client application, but first you need to generate the proxy code for the client.

Generate the Client Proxy and Implement the Callback Contract

1. Generate a proxy class for the client application by using the following procedure:

  a. Open a Visual Studio Command Prompt window and move to the ProductsServiceV3\ProductsService\bin\Debug folder in the Microsoft Press\ WCF Step By Step\Chapter 16 folder.

  b. In the Visual Studio Command Prompt window, run the command:

```
svcutil ProductsService.dll
```

  c. Run the command (all on one line):

```
svcutil /namespace:*,ProductsClient.ProductsService *.wsdl *.xsd
    /out:ProductsServiceProxy.cs
```

2. Leave the Visual Studio Command Prompt window open, and then return to Visual Studio. In the ProductsClient project, delete the existing ProductsServiceProxy.cs file and add the new ProductsServiceProxy.cs file that you have just generated in the ProductsServiceV3\ProductsService\bin\Debug folder.

3. Edit the Program.cs file for the ProductsClient project in the Code And Text Editor window. Modify the *Client* class to implement the *ProductsServiceCallback* and *IDisposable* interfaces, as show in bold in the following:

```
class Client : ProductsServiceCallback, IDisposable
{
    ...
}
```

ProductsServiceCallback is the interface in the proxy that defines the callback contract.

> **Note** The name of this interface is governed by the logical *Name* property of the *Service Contract* attribute for the *ProductsService* service rather than the physical name of the interface implemented by this service. If you examine the *IProductsServiceV3* interface in the IProductsService.cs file for the ProductsService project, the *Name* property for the service is set to *ProductsService*, so the name of the interface for the callback contract generated by *svcutil* is *ProductsServiceCallback*.

4. Add the following *OnPriceChanged* method to the *Client* class, after the *TestProducts Service* method:

```
public void OnPriceChanged(ProductData product)
{
    Console.WriteLine("\nCallback from service:\nPrice of {0} changed to {1:C}",
        product.Name, product.ListPrice);
}
```

This method implements the operation in the *ProductsServiceCallback* interface defining the callback contract.

5. After the *OnPriceChanged* method, add the following *Dispose* method to the *Client* class:

```
public void Dispose()
{
    // Disconnect from the service
    proxy.Close();
}
```

This method is part of the *IDisposable* interface; it closes the connection to the service when the *Client* object is garbage collected.

6. In the *TestProductsService* method in the *Client* class, modify the statement that creates the *proxy* object, as shown in bold in the following code example:

```
public void TestProductsService()
{
    // Create a proxy object and connect to the service
    proxy = new ProductsServiceClient(new InstanceContext(this),
                              "WSDualHttpBinding_IProductsServiceV3");

    // Test the operations in the service
    ...
}
```

This code creates an *InstanceContext* object that references the *Client* object and passes it to the connection. Notice that the name of the endpoint for the connection has also changed (it was *WS2007HttpBinding_IProductsServiceV3*); you will add the definition of the *WSDuaHtpBinding_IProductsServiceV3* endpoint to the client configuration file shortly.

7. In the *TestProductsService* method, locate the *if/else* block of code that calls the *Change Price* method of the *proxy* object and reports the results. The *ChangePrice* operation is now one-way and does not return a value. Change this section of code to remove the *if/else* processing, as shown in bold below.

```
public void TestProductsService()
{
    ...
    // Test the operations in the service
    try
    {
        ...
        // Modify the price of this bicycle frame
        Console.WriteLine("Test 3: Modify the price of a bicycle frame");
        proxy.ChangePrice("FR-M21S-40", product.ListPrice + 10);
        Console.WriteLine();
    }

    catch (Exception e)
    {
        Console.WriteLine("Exception: {0}", e.Message);
    }
    ...
}
```

8. After the *catch* block, remove the statement that closes the proxy object; this is now handled by the *Dispose* method.

9. In the *Main* method of the *Program* class, refactor the statements that create the *Client* object, call the *TestProductsService* method, and wait for the user to press Enter when the application has finished into a *using* block, as shown in bold in the following code example:

```
static void Main(string[] args)
{
    Console.WriteLine("Press ENTER when the service has started");
    Console.ReadLine();

    using (Client client = new Client())
    {
        client.TestProductsService();

        Console.WriteLine("Press ENTER to finish");
        Console.ReadLine();
    }
}
```

The *Client* class now implements the *IDisposable* interface. The *using* block ensures that the *Dispose* method runs in a timely manner when the application finishes and closes the connection to the service. If you don't do this, you will notice that the service takes longer to shut down when you click Stop in the Products Service Host window while it waits to determine the status of the connection.

10. Build the solution.

Configure the WCF Service and Client Application to Use the *WSDualHttpBinding* Binding

1. Edit the App.config file for the ProductsServiceHost project by using the Service Configuration Editor.

2. In the Configuration pane, expand the Services folder, expand the *Products.Products ServiceImpl* service, expand the *Endpoints* folder, right-click the *WS2007HttpBinding_ IProductsService* endpoint, and then click Delete Endpoint. In the Microsoft Service Configuration Editor dialog box, click OK to confirm the deletion.

   The *WS2007HttpBinding_IProductsService* endpoint is no longer suitable for the *Products Service* service, and the service will not start if this endpoint is left in place.

3. In the Configuration pane, right-click the Endpoints folder, and then click New Service Endpoint. Add a new endpoint with the values specified in the following table:

Property	Value
Name	WSDualHttpEndpoint_IProductsService
Address	http://localhost:8010/ProductsService/Service.svc
Binding	wsDualHttpBinding
Contract	Products.IProductsServiceV3

 Note By default, the *wsDualHttpBinding* binding implements message-level security and uses Windows identities.

4. Save the configuration, and then exit the WCF Service Configuration Editor.

5. Edit the App.config file in the ProductsClient project by using the Service Configuration Editor.

6. In the Configuration pane, expand the Client folder, right-click the Endpoints folder, and then click New Client Endpoint to add a new endpoint. Set the properties of this endpoint using the values in this table:

Property	Value
Name	WSDualHttpBinding_IProductsServiceV3
Address	http://localhost:8010/ProductsService/Service.svc
Binding	wsDualHttpBinding
Contract	ProductsClient.ProductsService.ProductsService

   Note that—unlike the ProductsServiceHost application—you can leave the existing client endpoint definition in place in the application configuration file.

7. Save the configuration file, and then exit the Service Configuration Editor.

8. Start the solution without debugging. In the Products Service Host window, click Start. In the client application console window, press Enter.

   The client application displays a list of products, followed by the details for the bicycle frame with product number FR-M21S-40. The code then adds 10 to the price of the frame and invokes the *ChangePrice* operation with this new price. Notice that after Test 3 starts, the message "Callback from service: Price of LL Mountain Frame – Silver, 40 changed to $594.05" appears. This message was displayed by the *OnPriceChanged* operation that was invoked by the service, as shown in the following image:

> **Note** The price displayed might be different if you have previously modified the data in the *AdventureWorks* database. The important points are that this message appears, and that the price has increased by 10 from the value displayed in Test 2. Additionally, the text output by the callback may be displayed after the "Press ENTER to finish" message has appeared; again, this is not a problem but is due to the order in which the .NET Framework decides to schedule the callback to run compared to the main application thread.

9. Press Enter to close the client application console window. In the Products Service Host window, click Stop, and then close the window.

Using a Callback Contract to Implement an Eventing Mechanism

The callback contract enables the service to confirm to the client application that the product price has changed, but the client application instance that receives the confirmation probably already knew this because it initiated the change! It is arguably more useful for *other* concurrent instances of the client application to be informed of this update.

You can use callbacks to implement an eventing mechanism; the service can advertise events and provide operations to enable client applications to subscribe to these events or unsubscribe from them. The service can employ a callback contract to send a message to each subscribing client when an event occurs. To do this, the service must have a reference to each client application instance. In the following exercises, you will modify the *ProductsService* service to enable client application instances to register their interest in product price changes by adding a subscribe operation. The purpose of this operation is simply to cache a reference to the client application instance that the service can use later to invoke the *OnPriceChanged* operation. You will also add an unsubscribe operation so client application instances can remove themselves from notification list.

Add Subscribe and Unsubscribe Operations to the *ProductsService* Service

1. In Visual Studio, open the IProductsService.cs file for the ProductsService project in the Code And Text Editor window.

2. Add the following *SubscribeToPriceChangedEvent* and *UnsubscribeFromPriceChanged Event* methods (shown in bold) to the end of the IProductsServiceV3 service contract:

```
[ServiceContract(Namespace = "http://adventure-works.com/2010/07/22",
                 Name = "ProductsService",
                 CallbackContract = typeof(IProductsServiceV3Callback))]
public interface IProductsServiceV3
{
    ...
    // Subscribe to the "price changed" event
    [OperationContract]
    bool SubscribeToPriceChangedEvent();

    // Unsubscribe from the "price changed" event
    [OperationContract]
    bool UnsubscribeFromPriceChangedEvent();
}
```

Client applications will use the *SubscribeToPriceChangedEvent* operation to declare an interest in product price changes and the *UnsubscribeFromPriceChangedEvent* operation to indicate that they are no longer interested in product price changes.

3. Open the ProductsService.cs file in the Code And Text Editor window and add the following private variable to the *ProductsServiceImpl* class:

```
public class ProductsServiceImpl : IProductsServiceV3
{
    static List<IProductsServiceV3Callback> subscribers =
        new List<IProductsServiceV3Callback>();
    ...
}
```

The *ProductsServiceImpl* class will add references to client callbacks to this list for each client application instance that indicates its interest in product price changes.

4. Add the following *SubscribeToPriceChanged* method (shown in bold) to the *Products ServiceImpl* class:

```
public class ProductsServiceImpl : IProductsServiceV3
{
    ...
    public bool SubscribeToPriceChangedEvent()
    {
        try
        {
            IProductsServiceV3Callback callback =
                OperationContext.Current.GetCallbackChannel<
                IProductsServiceV3Callback>();
            if (!subscribers.Contains(callback))
            {
                subscribers.Add(callback);
            }
            return true;
        }
        catch (Exception)
        {
            return false;
        }
    }
}
```

This method obtains a reference to the callback contract for the client application instance invoking the operation and stores it in the subscribers list. If the callback contract reference is already in the list, this method does not add it again.

5. Add the *UnsubscribeFromPriceChangedEvent* method to the *ProductsServiceImpl* class, as follows:

```
public class ProductsServiceImpl : IProductsServiceV3
{
    ...
    public bool UnsubscribeFromPriceChangedEvent()
    {
        try
        {
            IProductsServiceV3Callback callback =
                OperationContext.Current.GetCallbackChannel<
                IProductsServiceV3Callback>();
            subscribers.Remove(callback);
            return true;
        }
        catch (Exception)
        {
            return false;
        }
    }
}
```

This method removes the callback reference for the client application instance invoking the operation from the subscribers list.

6. Add the private method (shown in bold) to the *ProductsServiceImpl* class:

```
public class ProductsServiceImpl : IProductsServiceV3
{
    ...
    private void raisePriceChangedEvent(ProductData product)
    {
        subscribers.AsParallel().ForAll(callback =>
        {
          if (((ICommunicationObject)callback).State == CommunicationState.Opened)
          {
            callback.OnPriceChanged(product);
          }
          else
          {
            subscribers.Remove(callback);
          }
        });
    }
}
```

This method iterates (in parallel) through all the callback references in the subscribers list. For each reference found, if it is still valid (the client application instance is still running), the method invokes the *OnPriceChanged* operation, passing in the specified product as the parameter. If the reference is not valid, the method removes it from the list of subscribers.

7. At the end of the *ChangePrice* method, remove the statements that obtain the callback reference to the client application and invoke the *OnPriceChanged* method. Replace them with code that creates a *ProductData* object to hold the details of the modified product and calls the *raisePriceChangedEvent* method instead, as shown in bold in the following code example:

```
public void ChangePrice(string productNumber, decimal price)
{
    ...
    // Notify registered clients that the price has been changed successfully
    ProductData productData = new ProductData()
       {
            ProductNumber = product.ProductNumber,
            Name = product.Name,
            ListPrice = product.ListPrice,
            Color = product.Color
       };
    raisePriceChangedEvent(productData);
}
```

When a client application instance changes the price of a product, all client application instances that have subscribed to the *"price changed"* event will be notified by running the *OnPriceChanged* method.

8. Rebuild the ProductsService project.

Update the WCF Client Application to Subscribe to the *"Price Changed"* Event

1. Regenerate the proxy class for the client application:

❑ In the Visual Studio Command Prompt window that you opened earlier, run the following commands:

```
svcutil ProductsService.dll
svcutil /namespace:*,ProductsClient.ProductsService *.wsdl *.xsd
    /out:ProductsServiceProxy.cs
```

2. Close the Visual Studio Command Prompt window, and then return to Visual Studio. Delete the ProductsServiceProxy.cs file from the ProductsClient project and add the new version of this file from the ProductsServiceV3\ProductsService\bin\Debug folder.

3. Open the Program.cs file for the ProductsClient project in the Code And Text Editor window. Invoke the *SubscribeToPriceChangedEvent* operation as the first action inside the *try* block in the *TestProductsService* method in the *Client* class:

```
public void TestProductsService()
{
    ...
    // Test the operations in the service
    try
    {
        proxy.SubscribeToPriceChangedEvent();

        // Obtain a list of products
        ...
    }
    ...
}
```

Whenever any instance of the client application updates the price of a product, the service will call the *OnPriceChanged* method in this instance (and any other instances that subscribe to the event) of the client application.

4. Rebuild the ProductsClient project.

Test the *"Price Changed"* Event in the *ProductsService* Service

1. In Solution Explorer, right-click the ProductsServiceHost project, select Debug, and then click Start new instance. In the Products Service Host window, click Start.

2. Using Windows Explorer, navigate to the Microsoft Press\WCF Step By Step\Chapter 16\ ProductsServiceV3\ProductsClient folder.

   Apart from the various code files, you should notice a command file called RunClients. cmd. This command file simply runs the ProductsClient application concurrently, three times, each time opening a new window, like this:

   ```
   start bin\Debug\ProductsClient
   start bin\Debug\ProductsClient
   start bin\Debug\ProductsClient
   ```

3. Double-click the RunClients.cmd file. Three console windows appear, one for each instance of the client application. In one console window, press Enter. Wait for the list of bicycle frames to appear, the details of frame FR-M21S-40 to be displayed, and the price of the frame to be changed. Verify that the message from the callback appears. Leave this command window open (*do not press Enter*).

4. In one of the other two console windows, press Enter. Again, wait while the list of frames and the details of frame FR-M21S-40 are displayed and the price of the frame is updated. Verify that the callback message appears in this client console window. Notice that a second callback message appears in the first client console window, also displaying the new price.

5. In the final console window, press Enter. Verify that when this instance of the client application updates the price of the bicycle frame and displays the callback message, the other two client console windows also output the callback message. The first client console window should now display three callback messages, as shown in the following image:

6. Press Enter in each of the client application console windows to close them. In the Products Service Host window, click Stop, and then close the window.

Delivery Models for Publishing and Subscribing

Using a callback contract makes it very easy to implement a basic publication and subscription service based on WCF. You should be aware that you have been using a somewhat artificial and idealized configuration for these exercises. If you are implementing such a system in a large enterprise, or across the Internet, you would need to consider security and scalability, and how they impact the operation of a WCF service calling back into a client application.

There are at least three well-known models that publication and subscription systems frequently implement, and you can use WCF to build systems based on any of them. Each model has its own advantages and disadvantages, as described in the following sections.

The Push Model

This is the model you have used in the exercises in this chapter. In this model, the publisher (the WCF service) sends messages directly to each subscriber (WCF client applications) through an operation in a callback contract. The service must have sufficient resources to be able to invoke operations in a potentially large number of subscribers simultaneously; the service could spawn a new thread for each subscriber if the callback operations return data or could make use of one-way operations if not. The primary disadvantage of this approach is security; the callback operations invoked by the service could be blocked by a firewall protecting client applications from unexpected incoming messages.

The Pull Model

In this model, the publisher updates a single, trusted third service with information about events as they occur. Each subscriber periodically queries this third service for updated information (they invoke an operation on the third service that returns the latest version of the data). This model is less prone to firewall blocking issues, but it requires more complexity on the part of the subscribers. There could also be scalability issues with the third service if a large number of subscribers query it too frequently. On the other hand, if a subscriber does not query the third site frequently enough, it might miss an event.

The Broker Model

This model is a hybrid of the first two schemes. The publisher updates a single, trusted third service with information about events as they occur. This third site is placed in a location, such as a perimeter network, that is trusted by both the publishing service and the subscribing clients. Subscribers register with this third site rather than with the site that originates events.

The third site handles calls back to the subscribers when an event occurs. As well as reducing the likelihood of messages being blocked by a firewall, this model also resolves some of the scalability issues associated with subscribers polling for updated information too quickly.

 Note You can also make use of Windows Network Load Balancing and clustering technologies to overcome some of the scalability concerns when using the Pull or Broker models.

The WS-Eventing Specification

The callback mechanism for implementing events described in this chapter depends primarily on features provided by WCF and the .NET Framework. Consequently, it works only with services and client applications built by using WCF. However, asynchronous notification is a universally useful pattern, and the World Wide Web Consortium has published several specifications over the last decade or so that propose a standardized approach to supporting eventing. This approach is based on Web services and SOAP messaging and is intended to be independent of and interoperable across different technologies. These are the WS-Eventing specifications.

The current draft (at the time of writing), dated August 5, 2010, lists the following requirements that the specification seeks to address (this list is taken from the W3C Web site, at *http://www.w3.org/TR/ws-eventing/*):

- Define a means to create and delete event subscriptions.

- Define expiration for subscriptions and allow them to be renewed.

- Define how one Web service can subscribe on behalf of another.

- Define how an event source delegates subscription management to another service.

- Allow subscribers to specify how notifications are to be delivered.

- Leverage other Web service specifications for secure, reliable, transacted message delivery.

- Support complex eventing topologies that allow the originating event source and the final event sink to be decoupled.

- Provide extensibility for more sophisticated and/or currently unanticipated subscription scenarios.

- Support a variety of encoding formats, including (but not limited to) SOAP 1.1 and SOAP 1.2 Envelopes.

In the current draft of the WS-Eventing specification, services that can raise events are referred to as Event Sources, and clients that can receive these events are called Event Sinks. The WS-Eventing specification also incorporates another actor, the Subscription Manager, which is responsible for receiving subscribe and unsubscribe requests from event sinks. The Subscription Manager typically stores subscription information in a data store, and the Event Source retrieves the details of subscriptions from this data store when an event is raised so it can send event messages (notifications) to the various subscribers.

You should note that the WS-Eventing specification is intended to be open and flexible and support a variety of scenarios over and above simple "publish/subscribe" interactions. For example, a client can subscribe to events on behalf of another client, and this second client will act as the event sink when the event source raises the event. Alternatively, a client subscribing to notifications could actually act as an event source itself and enable subscriptions from other clients; the first client effectively provides a forwarding mechanism, propagating notifications as it receives them to its own set of subscribers, implementing part of a tree-topology.

The WS-Eventing specification does not actually define how to build an eventing system; instead, it describes the message formats and protocols that a standard eventing solution should provide. For example, the terms Event Source, Subscription Manager, and Event Sink refer to roles rather than physical applications or services. It is possible for a single piece of software to fulfill any or all of these roles, as appropriate (in the event forwarding scenario described in the previous paragraph, it is probable that the same service acts in all three roles). As long as a service abides by the message formats and protocols documented by the WS-Eventing specification, it will be compatible with other services and client applications that follow the same specifications. The implementation details are left to the organizations that provide the technologies and frameworks that developers use to build interoperable services.

Sadly, WCF does not currently support the WS-Eventing specification out of the box (there are no bindings, binding elements, or service classes currently in the .NET Framework that conform to the WS-Eventing messaging formats and protocols), although several developers have built and published implementations based on WCF.

Summary

This chapter showed how to use a callback contract to define operations that a client application can expose to a service. Implementing a callback contract requires the client application and service to connect with each other over a bidirectional channel that supports duplex communications; this means using the *NetTcpBinding* binding, the *NetNamedPipeBinding* binding, and the *WSDualHttpBinding* binding.

You can use a callback contract to help implement a publish and subscribe eventing system so a service can register instances of client applications that wish to be notified when a particular event occurs, and then invoke an operation in the callback contract to inform the client application instances when the event actually happens.

Chapter 17
Managing Identity with Windows CardSpace

After completing this chapter, you will be able to:

■ Describe the purpose of Windows CardSpace.

■ Use Windows CardSpace with a WCF service to provide claims-based security.

■ Summarize how you can employ claims-based security to implement a federated security scheme.

Security is an important, if not vital, feature of most commercial Web services and applications. Throughout this book you have seen some of the mechanisms that WCF provides to help you protect Web services and client applications. At the heart of these mechanisms is a scheme by which a Web service identifies the user running the client application that is calling into the Web service. The means of identification is frequently a user name and password, a certificate, or possibly a Kerberos token. After a Web service has established the identity of the user running the client application, it can then authorize or deny access to the operation requested by the user, based on this identity. This use of identity to determine authorization has some interesting privacy implications—for example, if all a Web service needs to know is your age, do you really want to divulge your full identity? Consider the following real-world situations:

■ Being an avid cricket fan, I regularly visit the supporters club of my local county cricket team. On match days, you have to be a member of the club to be allowed in (at other times, anyone can enter). All members are issued with membership cards, and upon entering the club, I am obliged to show my card to the person on the door. As long as I have this card and can show it, I can get in. The door attendant is never actually interested in the details on the card (my name and membership number), just the fact that I actually have one.

■ If I pay for goods in a shop by using a credit card, the vendor does not need to know my full name, address, age, or even my inside leg measurement. She just needs to be confident that the credit card I am using is valid and that I have the necessary rights to use it (she will probably also do an initial visual check, just to make sure I am not using a credit card belonging to "Miss Jones" if I have a beard and a moustache, but on the Internet it is not yet possible to corroborate identity in this way). This scenario is actually a little more complicated than the previous one, as the vendor does not have access to the information needed to prove the validity of the card (strictly speaking, the door attendant at the cricket club cannot be totally sure that my membership card is not a forgery, but the quick examination performed by the door attendant usually provides an adequate level of security, given the circumstances). Instead, the vendor asks the credit card company to verify my claim that this is my credit card, usually by asking me to type my PIN number on a terminal connected to the credit card company's computers. The vendor then waits for the credit card company to respond that, 1) the card is genuine and valid, 2) I know the PIN for the credit card and therefore I am probably the real card holder rather than some imposter who found it lying in the street (we all know this is not foolproof, but it is the best mechanism that the credit card companies have at this point), and 3) I have sufficient credit available.

These are two examples of claims-based security. A claim is simply a facet of my identity that is relevant to the operation being performed. In the first case, the door attendant was able to verify my claim that I was a member of the club by seeing that I had a membership card; possession of the card was taken as sufficient proof of my identity. In the second case, the vendor required my claim as the valid holder of the credit card be verified by a trusted third party.

You can apply claims-based security to Web services as well as real-world situations. In contrast to a traditional identity-based system, in a claims-based system, the Web service does not necessarily need to know who I am, just that I should be allowed to use it. With WCF, you can integrate claims-based security into client applications by using Windows CardSpace. This is the subject of this chapter.

Using Windows CardSpace to Access a WCF Service

Windows CardSpace is an identity technology incorporated into Windows Vista and Windows 7. Windows CardSpace is based on a number of WS-* standards, in particular WS-Trust, WS-MetadataExchange, and WS-SecurityPolicy. Consequently, the security mechanism that it implements is interoperable with Web services and client applications built using other technologies but that conform to these specifications.

Implementing Claims-Based Security

The world of claims-based security refers to three roles describing the participants involved in accessing a protected service:

- The *subject* is the user or entity trying to access the service. The subject provides evidence of suitable rights (a claim) to gain access. This must be a claim that the service can accept. In the credit card scenario described earlier, it would be no good trying to use my cricket supporters' club membership card when trying to pay for goods—the membership card might well be valid, but the vendor will not accept it, because it does not confer the appropriate rights.

- The *identity provider* is the organization or entity that issues the rights to assert a particular claim (or set of claims) to the subject and verifies the authenticity of any claims to exercise these rights made by the subject. In the credit card example, the identity provider is the credit card company issuing the card.

- The *relying party* is the organization or entity representing the protected service. The relying party asks the identity provider to verify that the claim made by the subject to the specified rights is valid. Again, in the credit card example, the relying party is the vendor selling me the goods that I am attempting to purchase.

> **Note** From here on, I will refer to the information provided by a subject when attempting to prove its identity simply as a "claim." Identity providers are said to issue claims; services can demand verified claims; and subjects can submit claims when attempting to access a service.

Windows CardSpace comprises a Windows service, a set of components, and a framework for enabling identity providers to issue claims to users. This framework provides methods for those users to store and retrieve information about their claims in an accessible manner and provides assurance to a service that any claims asserted by a user are genuine. Windows CardSpace stores information about the set of claims (called a "claimset") issued by a provider as metadata in an *information card*. Information cards are issued by identity providers, who also take on responsibility for verifying the claims that these cards contain when requested by a service. Windows CardSpace also provides a graphical user interface that enables users to manage and control their information cards.

A service that uses claims-based security specifies the claims it demands as part of its security policy. Windows CardSpace includes an identity selector component that can query this policy and then determine which of the user's cards have claims that match the policy. In the real world, you could use several different forms of identity to prove a claim, such as your age—your driver's license or your passport, for example. Similarly, when a service demands proof of one particular aspect of a user's identity, the user might be able to select from among several information cards that contain a corresponding claim. When a WCF client application attempts to access a service, the WCF runtime can invoke the identity selector component to determine and display the matching cards, and the user can select which information card to use. The claims on the card then need to be verified by the identity provider before the client application can use them to access the service.

Here's the sequence of operations that occur when a client application calls a Web service that uses Windows CardSpace to validate a user:

1. The client application attempts to invoke an operation or access a resource in a Web service. The security policy for the Web service specifies the type of claims accepted by the service user (for example, an email address or a pin number). Note that the security policy for the service is published as part of the metadata for the service. If you use the

svcutil utility or the Add Service Reference command in Visual Studio, this policy information will be included in the information downloaded from the service and added to the client configuration file.

2. The WCF runtime on the client invokes the identity selector component of Windows CardSpace. The identity selector examines the user's information cards and displays a list of cards that contain claims of the types specified by the Web service.

3. The user selects the information card to use.

4. The identity selector contacts the identity provider that issued the information card, passing it the metadata describing the claim on the user's information card and the claims demanded by the service.

5. The identity provider examines the metadata describing the claim, authenticates the user's identity—and if authentication is successful—it generates a token verifying that the user's claim is valid. The identity provider sends this token back to the identity selector running on the client computer. Note that this token is signed to prevent tampering and to confirm its validity.

> **Note** The format for the token is important, because the Web service must be able to decode and understand it. The OASIS Security Services Technical Committee has attempted to standardize the representation of security tokens as serializable XML-based objects containing authentication and authorization data. The result is the Security Assertion Markup Language, or SAML. The SAML standards (there are currently three available—version 1.0, version 1.1, and version 2.0, although WCF does not yet support version 2.0) define an XML-based framework for communicating user authentication, entitlement, and attribute information. A service can use SAML to make assertions concerning the identity, properties, and privileges associated with a request from a client application (or other service), and make a decision as to whether to allow the requested operation to proceed.

6. The identity selector passes the token to the WCF runtime for the client application, which sends the token to the Web service as part of the original request made by the client application (the token is added to the SOAP header). The Web service examines the token to verify its validity. If the token is valid, the Web service can use the identity information in this token to determine whether the user is authorized to invoke the operation or access the resource.

All this sounds quite complicated. Fortunately, WCF and Windows CardSpace shield you from much of this complexity, and it is actually quite straightforward to incorporate claims-based security into a WCF service. You should note that the Web service no longer performs any form of user authentication; this task is left to the identity provider for the information card that the user selects (and that the Web service trusts). All the Web service needs to do is specify a policy that indicates the claims it will support and determine whether the authenticated user has sufficient rights to perform the operation being requested.

In the following set of exercises, you will configure the *ShoppingCartService* service to identify users by their email address. However, before delving into the world of Windows CardSpace, I need to explain one more thing. In a real-world environment, you will most likely use information cards issued by commercial, trusted, third-party identity providers (such as credit card companies, banks, governments, or other organizations). You can also use Windows CardSpace to create self-issued cards. A self-issued card is a one that you create by using the Windows CardSpace user interface, often for testing purposes (they have other uses as well). A self-issued card can contain a small but useful subset of claims, such as your name, home address, telephone number, and email address. In this case, the Windows CardSpace service running on your computer also acts as the identity provider. The exercises that follow use such self-issued information cards, so you don't need to obtain a commercial information card just for learning purposes. However, the technique is very similar when you use an information card issued by a trusted third party, as I will explain later.

> **Important** A production Web service should not rely on claims asserted by self-issued information cards for authorizing access to sensitive data. It is very easy for a user to create a self-issued card with whatever values they want for the claims it contains.

Configure the *ShoppingCartService* Service to Use Claims-based Security

1. Start Visual Studio as an Administrator and open the solution file ShoppingCart.sln located in the Microsoft Press\WCF Step By Step\Chapter 17\ShoppingCartService folder (within your Documents folder).

    This solution contains a completed version of the *ShoppingCartService* service, console host application, and test client application from Chapter 10, "Implementing Reliable Sessions."

> **Note** It is important that you run Visual Studio as Administrator because the *Shopping CartService* service will require access to a certificate only available to administrators.

2. Edit the App.config file in the ShoppingCartHost project by using the Service Configuration Editor.

3. In the Configuration pane, right-click the Bindings folder, and then click New Binding Configuration. Add a new binding configuration to the Bindings folder. Select the *ws2007FederationHttpBinding* binding type. Change the name of the binding configuration to **ShoppingCartServiceCardSpaceBindingConfig**. The *ShoppingCartService* service uses reliable sessions and transactions, so set the *TransactionFlow* property to **True** and set the *Enabled* property in the *ReliableSession Properties* section to **True**.

> **Note** You can also use claims-based security with the *ws2007HttpBinding* and *wsHttpBinding* bindings, but these bindings support only a limited set of claims. Using the *ws2007Federation HttpBinding* and *wsFederationHttpBinding* bindings, you can configure the service to specify a more extensive range.

4. In the Configuration pane, expand the *ShoppingCartServiceCardSpaceBindingConfig* node, expand the Security folder, and then click the *ClaimTypes* node. Click the New button at the bottom of the ClaimTypes pane on the right.

5. In the Claim Type Element Editor dialog box, in the *ClaimType* property field, type **http://schemas.xmlsoap.org/ws/2005/05/identity/claims/emailaddress**. Verify that the *IsOptional* property is set to **False**, and then click OK.

   The claims specified in the *ClaimTypes* property of the binding configuration constitute the claims security policy for the service. Each type of claim is identified by a well-known URI—the URI you have specified here indicates that the claim is an email address. You can add multiple claim types if you want to identify users based on more than one piece of information.

> **Note** Apart from an email address, Windows CardSpace provides support for a number of other built-in claim types, such as a user's name, address, telephone number, and date of birth. For a full list of the built-in claim types and the corresponding URIs that Windows CardSpace recognizes, see the properties of the *ClaimTypes* class in the Visual Studio documentation (also available online at *http://msdn.microsoft.com/en-us/library/system.identity model.claims.claimtypes.aspx*). However, you are not restricted to this set of claims. A key objective of the WCF claims-based security model was to make it extensible and interoperable with systems developed using other technologies. You can make use of claim types defined and supported by identity providers other than Windows CardSpace; you just need to know the URI that identifies the claim types you want to use.

6. In the Configuration pane, click the Security folder under the *ShoppingCartService CardSpaceBindingConfig* node. In the Security pane, in the *IssuedTokenType* property field, type **http://docs.oasis-open.org/wss/oasis-wss-saml-token-profile-1.1# SAMLV1.1**.

   A WCF service uses the *IssuedTokenType* property to specify the type of token it expects to receive from the identity provider containing the claim information (identity providers can send tokens conforming to a number of different standard formats). In this case, the *ShoppingCartService* service expects a SAML 1.1 token (SAML token types are identified by URIs, defined by the SAML standards).

   A fundamental requirement of solutions based on Windows CardSpace is that client applications must be able to verify the identity of the Web service requesting the claim, and the Web service must be able to trust the identity provider verifying the claim. This means that you should configure the requesting Web service with a certificate and provide the client application with a reference to this certificate. If you are using a third-party identity provider, it must also supply a certificate that the client application and Web service can use to confirm its identity (the identity provider signs tokens with its private key, so the Web service must have access to its public key in order to verify their signatures). Additionally, all messages must be encrypted, either at the message level or at the transport level.

> **More Info**   For more information about how you can use certificates to encrypt and sign messages and verify the authenticity of a service, refer back to Chapter 5, "Protecting a WCF Service over the Internet."

7. Open a Visual Studio Command Prompt as Administrator. Use the *makecert* utility to create a new certificate for the service, like this:

```
makecert -sr LocalMachine -ss My -n CN=ShoppingCartService -sky exchange
```

8. Leave the Visual Studio Command Prompt window open and return to the Service Configuration Editor. In the Configuration pane, expand the Advanced folder, right-click the Service Behaviors folder, and then click New Service Behavior Configuration to create a new service behavior. In the right pane, name this behavior **ShoppingCartService Behavior**.

9. In the lower part of the right pane, click Add and add a *<serviceCredentials>* element to the behavior. In the Configuration pane, expand the new *serviceCredentials* node, and then click the *serviceCertificate* node. In the right pane, in the *FindValue* property, type **ShoppingCartService** (this is the name of the certificate you have just created) and set the *X509FindType* property to **FindBySubjectName**.

   In this exercise, you are using an unverifiable self-issued information card rather than a card issued by a third-party identity provider. At run time, the Windows CardSpace service running on the client application computer provides the SAML token containing the claim token. Therefore, you need to configure the Web service to accept SAML tokens from an untrusted source (the user running the client application and who has issued the card to herself).

10. In the Configuration pane, click the *issuedTokenAuthentication* node under the *service Credentials* node. In the right pane, set the *AllowUntrustedRsaIssuers* property to **True**.

11. In the Configuration pane, expand the Services folder and select the *ShoppingCartService. ShoppingCartServiceImpl* service. In the right pane, set the *BehaviorConfiguration* property to **ShoppingCartServiceBehavior**.

12. In the Configuration pane, expand the *ShoppingCartService.ShoppingCartServiceImpl* service, right-click the Endpoints folder, and then click New Service Endpoint to create a new endpoint based on the *WS2007FederationHttpBinding* binding. Set the properties of this endpoint using the values in the following table:

Property	Value
Name	WS2007FederationHttpBinding_IShoppingCartService
Address	http://localhost:8010/ShoppingCartService/ShoppingCartService.svc
Binding	ws2007FederationHttpBinding
BindingConfiguration	ShoppingCartServiceCardSpaceBindingConfig
Contract	ShoppingCartService.IShoppingCartService

13. Save the configuration file, and then close the Service Configuration Editor.

The *ShoppingCartService* service now expects the client application to provide the user's email address to identify the user whenever it invokes an operation. You can use the email address to authorize users and grant or deny them access to specific operations. You can perform this task in a variety of ways. The most direct technique is to explicitly examine the value of the claim in the token passed to the service, which is what you will do in the next exercise.

Amend the *ShoppingCartService* Service to Authorize Users Based on Their Email Address

1. In Solution Explorer, add a reference to the *System.IdentityModel* assembly to the ShoppingCartService project.

2. Open the ShoppingCartService.cs file for the ShoppingCartService project in the Code And Text Editor window. Add the following *using* statements to the list at the top of the file:

```
using System.Security;
using System.IdentityModel.Claims;
using System.IdentityModel.Policy;
```

3. Add the following private array (shown in bold) to the start of the *ShoppingCartServiceImpl* class:

```
public class ShoppingCartServiceImpl : IShoppingCartService
{
    // The list of authorized users
    private string[] authorizedUsers = { "Fred@Adventure-Works.com",
                                         "Bert@Adventure-Works.com" };

    ...
}
```

This array contains the email addresses of the users to whom the service will allow access.

> **Note** This code is for testing purposes only. In a production environment, you should consider storing the details of authorized users in a database rather than using a hard-coded array of strings.

4. Add the following private method to the *ShoppingCartServiceImpl* class to determine whether the claimset in the token passed to the service contains an email claim with an email address that corresponds to one of the authorized users:

```
public class ShoppingCartServiceImpl : IShoppingCartService
{
    ...
    // Authorize the user if their email address is in the authorizedUsers list
    private bool authorizeUser()
    {
        bool authorized = false;

        AuthorizationContext authContext =
            OperationContext.Current.ServiceSecurityContext.AuthorizationContext;
        foreach (ClaimSet claimSet in authContext.ClaimSets)
        {
            foreach (Claim emailClaim in
                claimSet.FindClaims(ClaimTypes.Email, Rights.PossessProperty))
            {
                foreach (string validUser in authorizedUsers)
                {
                    if (String.Compare(emailClaim.Resource.ToString(), validUser,
                        true) == 0)
                    {
                        authorized = true;
                        break;
                    }
                }
            }
        }
        return authorized;
    }
    ...
}
```

When the WCF runtime for the service receives the tokenized claims from the client application, it matches the values for these claims against the security policy that it implements. The *AuthorizationContext* property of the service security context contains the results of this match. In this case, *AuthorizationContext* property should contain an email address claim with the email address sent by the client application (provided by a CardSpace information card).

> **Note** The *AuthorizationContext* property will also contain other claims resulting from the various WS-* protocols that Windows CardSpace uses, but the details are beyond the scope of this book.

The *AuthorizationContext* property comprises a collection of claimsets, and each claimset contains a collection of claims. This method iterates through each claimset looking for an email claim. If it finds one, it examines the value of the claim and compares it to each email address in the list of authorized users. Notice that the value of a claim is available through the *Resource* property. The type of this property is *Object,* and its contents are dependent on the type of the claim. An email claim is a string containing the authenticated email address of the user, so this method simply performs a case-insensitive string comparison. If the email address in the claim matches one of the authorized users, the *authorizeUser* method returns *true*, otherwise it returns *false*.

5. Locate the *AddItemToCart* method in the *ShoppingCartServiceImpl* class. At the start of the method, add a block of code that calls the *authorizeUser* method and throws a security exception if the user is not an authorized user, as shown in bold in the following code example:

```
public bool AddItemToCart(string productNumber)
{
    // Check that the user is authorized.
    // Throw a SecurityException if not.
    if (!authorizeUser())
    {
        throw new SecurityException("Access denied");
    }
    ...
}
```

6. Add the same statements to the start of the *RemoveItemFromCart, GetShoppingCart,* and *Checkout* methods.

7. Build the ShoppingCartService project.

You can now configure the client application to enable the user to select an information card and send the SAML token containing the user's email address to the *ShoppingCartService* service.

Implementing Custom Authorization

If you need to perform more extensive authorization checks than those shown in the exercise, the .NET Framework provides the *ServiceAuthorizationManager* class in the *System.ServiceModel* namespace. The WCF runtime on the service calls the methods of this class to perform authorization checks whenever it processes a client request.

However, this class is just a placeholder, which by default allows users to invoke all operations without restriction. To implement a more secure policy, extend this class by using inheritance and override its methods to perform your own custom authorization. You then register your implementation of the class with the WCF runtime by setting the *Authorization.ServiceAuthorizationManager* property of the service host object to an instance of your class, or by creating a service behavior in the service configuration file and specifying the name of your class in the *<serviceAuthorization>* element.

For a complete example, see the topic, "How To: Create a Custom AuthorizationManager for a Service," in the Visual Studio documentation (also available on the Microsoft Web site at *http://msdn.microsoft.com/en-us/library/ms731774.aspx*).

Configure the ShoppingCartClient Application to use Windows CardSpace to Send a Token Identifying the User

1. Open the App.config file for the ShoppingCartClient project by using the Service Configuration Editor.

2. In the Configuration pane, add a new binding configuration to the Bindings folder. Select the *ws2007FederationHttpBinding* binding type. Set the name of the binding configuration to **ShoppingCartClientCardSpaceBindingConfig**. Set the *Transaction Flow* property to **True** and set the *Enabled* property in the **ReliableSession** Properties section to **True**, to match the binding implemented by the *ShoppingCartService* service.

3. Add the claim type **http://schemas.xmlsoap.org/ws/2005/05/identity/claims/ emailaddress** to the *ClaimTypes* collection under the Security node in the Configuration pane. Verify that the *IsOptional* property is set to *False*.

4. Set the *IssuedTokenType* property of the Security node to **http://docs.oasis-open.org/ wss/oasis-wss-saml-token-profile-1.1#SAMLV1.1**.

5. Return to the Visual Studio Command Prompt window that you opened in an earlier exercise and type the following command:

```
certmgr –put –c –n ShoppingCartService –r LocalMachine –s My ShoppingCartService.cer
```

This command retrieves a copy of the *ShoppingCartService* certificate used by the WCF service to authenticate itself and creates a file called ShoppingCartService.cer. This file contains a copy of the certificate including its public key but *not* the private key.

Type the following command to import this certificate into the trusted people certificate store for the current user:

```
certmgr –add ShoppingCartService.cer –c –r CurrentUser –s TrustedPeople
```

6. Close the Visual Studio Command Prompt window and return to the Service Configuration Editor. In the Configuration pane, add a new endpoint behavior configuration to the Endpoint Behaviors folder under the Advanced folder. Name this behavior **ShoppingCartClientEndpointBehavior**.

7. In the lower part of the right pane, click Add, and add a *<clientCredentials>* element to the behavior. In the Configuration pane, expand the *clientCredentials* node, expand the *serviceCertificate* node, and then click the *authentication* node. In the right pane, set the *CertificateValidationMode* property to **PeerTrust** and the *RevocationMode* property to **NoCheck**.

> **Note** You are using a test certificate issued by the *certmgr* tool rather than a recognized certification authority. You placed the certificate in the *TrustedPeople* store; setting the validation mode to *PeerTrust* bypasses validation for certificates placed in this store.

8. In the Configuration pane, add a new client endpoint to the Endpoints folder under the Client folder. Set the properties of this endpoint using the values in the following table:

Property	Value
Name	WS2007FederationHttpBinding_IShoppingCartService
Address	http://localhost:8010/ShoppingCartService/ShoppingCartService.svc
BehaviorConfiguration	ShoppingCartClientEndpointBehavior
Binding	ws2007FederationHttpBinding
BindingConfiguration	ShoppingCartClientCardSpaceBindingConfig
Contract	ShoppingCartClient.ShoppingCartService.ShoppingCartService

9. In the Client Endpoint pane, click the Identity tab. In the *CertificateReference Properties* section, type **ShoppingCartService** in the *FindValue* property and set the *X509FindType* property to **FindBySubjectName**.

10. Save the configuration file, and then close the Service Configuration Editor.

11. In Solution Explorer, open the Program.cs file for the ShoppingCartClient project in the Code And Text Editor window. In the *Main* method in the *Program* class, change the statement that creates the proxy to use the *WS2007FederationHttpBinding_IShopping CartService* endpoint, as follows:

```
// Connect to the ShoppingCartService service
ShoppingCartServiceClient proxy =
    new ShoppingCartServiceClient("WS2007FederationHttpBinding_IShoppingCartService");
```

The next stage is to create some information cards that you can use to test the *Shopping CartService* service. You can do this with the Windows CardSpace application in the Control Panel.

Create Information Cards for Testing the *ShoppingCartService* Service

1. From the Windows Start menu, select Control Panel, click User Accounts And Family Safety, and then click Windows CardSpace.

   The Windows CardSpace console starts and displays the Windows CardSpace–Welcome dialog box. Click Don't Show Me This Page Again, and then click OK.

   If you have not yet created or installed any cards, the list of information cards will be empty, apart from the Add A Card icon.

2. Click the Add A Card icon, and then in the Add A Card window, click Create A Personal Card.

3. In the Edit A New Card window, type **Valid ShoppingCartService Test Card** for the *Card Name* property, type **Fred@Adventure-Works.com** in the *Email Address* property, and then click Save. The details for the information card are shown in the following image.

The new information card should appear in the list of cards in the Windows CardSpace console. The email address for this card represents a user that is authorized to access the operations in the *ShoppingCartService* service.

4.　Add another personal card. In the Edit A New Card window, specify **Invalid Shopping CartService Test Card** for the *Card Name* property, **Sid@Adventure-Works.com** for the *Email Address* property, and then click Save. The email address for this card represents a user that is not authorized to invoke the operations in the ShoppingCartService service.

5.　Close the Windows CardSpace console.

Test the *ShoppingCartService* Service

1.　In Visual Studio, start the solution without debugging. Wait for the service to start and display the message "Service running." In the client application console window displaying the message "Press ENTER when the service has started," press Enter.

> **Note** The ProductsServiceHost application assumes that you still have port 8010 reserved. If this is not the case, then open a Visual Studio Command Prompt window as Administrator and run the following command, replacing *UserName* with your Windows user name:
>
> ```
> netsh http add urlacl url=http://+:8010/ user=UserName
> ```

When the client application invokes the first operation in the *ShoppingCartService* service, the *Windows CardSpace* service intervenes and displays the Windows CardSpace console.

Note The Windows CardSpace identity selector runs in a separate desktop session from the user to prevent other applications from being able to interfere with it. For this reason, whenever the Windows CardSpace console appears, the user's desktop is dimmed and inaccessible.

Notice that Windows CardSpace recognizes that the certificate used by the *Shopping CartService* service is not fully verified and displays the following warning:

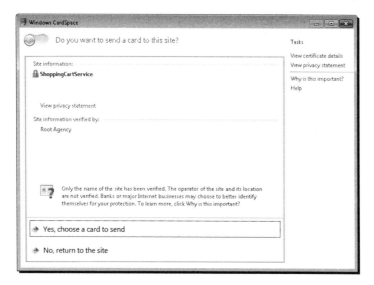

Click Yes, Choose A Card To Send.

Important If Windows CardSpace displays this message when you access a commercial Web service, you should be very careful because it indicates that the Web service's certificate might not have originated from a recognized certification authority. In this situation, you should probably click No and decline to send your credentials to the site.

2. Windows CardSpace displays a list of cards that contain email addresses and so match the claims required by the service. Select the Valid ShoppingCartService Test Card, and then click Send.

   The client application resumes and runs as it has done in previous chapters. The selected card contains an email address identifying a user that the *ShoppingCartService* service allows to invoke the various operations it implements. Notice that although the client application makes several calls to the service, Windows CardSpace intervenes only on the first call in the session.

> **Note** If you take more than one minute to select and send the card, the client application stops with the exception "The operation is not valid for the state of the transaction." This is because the *AddItemToCart* operation is part of a transaction initiated by the client application, and the transaction timeout specified by the client application is one minute. If this happens, stop the client application and service, restart the solution, and select the Valid ShoppingCartService Test Card when prompted by Windows CardSpace.
>
> Generally, it is not good practice to gather user input during a transaction. For situations such as this, you can programmatically request a token for a specific card in advance of the transaction starting and then supply this token when the first operation occurs. Note that the API that Windows CardSpace currently provides for performing these tasks is unmanaged and requires that you are familiar with C++.

3. Press Enter to close the client application console window, but leave the service running.

4. In Visual Studio, in Solution Explorer, right-click the ShoppingCartClient project, point to Debug, and then click Start new instance. This action starts a new instance of the client application.

5. In the client application console window, press Enter. The Windows CardSpace console appears again. This time, however, you don't get the warning that the Web service is using a suspect certificate—this warning only appears the first time you access the service. Windows CardSpace also organizes the list of matching cards and informs you which cards you have previously sent to the Web service:

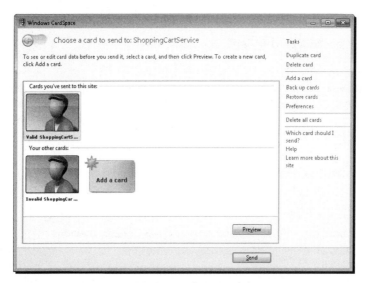

6. Select the Invalid ShoppingCartService Test Card, and then click Send.

This time the client application stops and reports the exception, "Access is denied." The email address in this card identifies a user (*Sid@Adventure-Works.com*) to which the *ShoppingCartService* service has not granted access.

7. Press Enter to close the client application console. Press Enter to close the service application console.

One important point that you should have learned from this exercise is that incorporating CardSpace into a client application reduces the need to provide custom code that gathers credentials from the user, authenticates them, and transmits them to the service. The binding configuration enables the WCF runtime and CardSpace to perform these tasks for you. This decoupling of the authentication mechanism from the application lets you concentrate on the business logic of the application. If a service decides it wants to identify users in a different way, you can update the security policy on the client accordingly and specify the details; the client application code should not need to change.

Using an Identity Provider

In the previous exercises, Windows CardSpace acted as its own identity provider, verifying the claim made by the user before sending a SAML token containing the claim information to the service. I mentioned earlier that you might not want to rely on the veracity of self-issued cards in a commercial environment. Instead, you should use information cards issued by trusted third-party identity providers, such as banks, credit card companies, government agencies, and so forth. It is important to realize that the claims on an information card are simply a representation of a set of rights. The rights themselves are retained by the identity provider, and the identity provider can withdraw these rights at any time, rendering the user's information card invalid. Additionally, the service must be prepared to trust the identity provider, as the identity provider authenticates requests on behalf of the service.

> **Note** The *System.IdentityModel.Claims.ClaimSet* class that you used in the *authorizeUser* method in the previous exercise contains a property called *Issuer*. You can examine this property to obtain information about the identity provider that issued the claims in the claimset and reject them if you do not wish to trust this particular provider. Additionally, rather than letting the WCF runtime determine which identity provider to use, a service can explicitly specify the address of an identity provider as part of its security policy; you can configure this information as part of the security settings for a binding.

A user can request an information card from a third party as an out-of-band operation. If the third party approves the request, it can create an information card file and send it to the user. This file is a signed XML file, containing data in a format that Windows CardSpace recognizes. The user can then install this file into Windows CardSpace using the "Install A Managed Card" feature of the Windows CardSpace console (this is on the same page in the Windows CardSpace console that you use to create self-issued cards). If the user tries to create a card with a forged set of claims, the third party will not be able to verify those claims. Consequently, it will not issue a token when the user attempts to use the card.

> **More Info**   Remember that Windows CardSpace is built on accepted WS-* protocols. Microsoft provides documentation on how Windows CardSpace uses these protocols and how to build non-WCF services that can interact with Windows CardSpace for issuing cards and verifying claims. For more information, see the document, "A Guide to Interoperating with the Information Card Profile V1.0," available online at *http://msdn.microsoft.com/en-us/library/bb298803.aspx*.
>
> The Microsoft Web site also provides an article called "Creating Managed Cards," which shows how to build an application that can create a signed XML file containing claims that a user can import into Windows CardSpace. This sample is available online at *http://msdn.microsoft.com/en-us/library/aa967567.aspx*.

Configuring a WCF Client Application and Service to Use an Identity Provider

You have seen that an identity provider actually needs to perform two related tasks: it issues claims, and it verifies that the claims submitted by a client application are genuine and issues a security token. The component of the identity provider that performs claims verification and issues tokens is usually referred to as a Security Token Service, or STS. In the exercises you performed earlier, Windows CardSpace provided the STS itself. For a production environment, you could consider deploying Active Directory Federation Services 2.0. This is a server role that runs on Windows Server 2008. It provides an STS that can issue, authenticate, and transform claims.

Alternatively, you can also build your own STS. The details are beyond the scope of this book, but the Visual Studio documentation includes a description of the process in the article, "How To: Create a Security Token Service" (also available on the Microsoft Web site at *http://msdn.microsoft.com/en-us/library/ms733095.aspx*).

When you use an STS other than that provided with Windows CardSpace, you must configure the client application with the address of this STS. The identity selector on the client computer uses this information to contact the STS and obtain a security token. You can provide this information programmatically or in the application configuration file. If you use the WCF Configuration Editor to edit the application configuration file, the key properties are in the *Issuer* page of the binding security configuration, as shown in Figure 17-1.

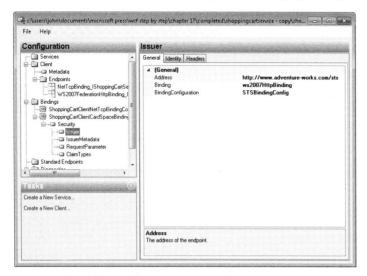

FIGURE 17-1 Configuring the *Issuer* properties for a WCF client application.

Specify the URI of the STS in the *Address* property. You can optionally provide a binding configuration if the STS has particular communications requirements, such as reliable sessions.
You can use the Identity tab to indicate a certificate in the local certificate store to use for validating the identity of the STS.

The token issued by an STS can be in one of several formats. By default, the client application
requests a token that conforms to the SAML 1.1 specification. However, if the WCF service
expects a token in a different format, you can specify the token type in the *IssuedTokenType*
property on the Security page. The STS should respond with a token of this type.

> **More Info** For more information about these properties and how to set them programmatically
> rather than using an application configuration file, see the topic "How To: Create a WSFederation
> HttpBinding," in the Visual Studio documentation (also available online at *http://msdn.microsoft.
> com/en-us/library/aa347982.aspx*).

Claims-Based Authentication in a Federated Environment

Claims-based authentication is an extremely powerful and flexible mechanism that you
can use in a variety of scenarios. For example, suppose the Fabrikam organization wants
to make one of its Web services available to users belonging to other partner companies,
such as AdventureWorks, but not to the general public. One way to authenticate users from

AdventureWorks who are attempting to access the Fabrikam service would be for Fabrikam to implement an STS and issue information cards for each employee of AdventureWorks. However, if AdventureWorks has a large number of employees, then maintaining a list of valid users in the Fabrikam system can quickly become an unmanageable task. If Fabrikam has several other partner organizations besides AdventureWorks, whose employees should also be able to access the Fabrikam service, then the scope of the problem multiplies. Furthermore, should Fabrikam really be concerned with the details of who works for AdventureWorks? All the Fabrikam service requires is that the user is a verified employee of AdventureWorks but not any other details.

To solve this problem, it can help to think of an STS as a service that converts claims of one type into claims of another. The WS-Trust specification on which the concept of an STS is based defines a "language" for requesting and issuing claims. An organization can implement an STS that verifies its employees' claims, and outputs tokens that can be used as claims for another STS belonging to another organization (the exact details of the WS-Trust specification are beyond the scope of this book). What does this mean, and how does it help? Look at the following possible solution to the problem of Fabrikam authenticating AdventureWorks employees.

- The Fabrikam organization has an STS that issues a single claim to AdventureWorks, effectively stating that it recognizes any employee that AdventureWorks authenticates as an employee as being a valid user of the Fabrikam Web service.

- AdventureWorks implements its own STS. Users inside AdventureWorks have information cards issued by the AdventureWorks STS containing a claim asserting that they are valid employees of AdventureWorks (the "employee claim").

- An application run by a user within AdventureWorks that requires access to the Fabrikam Web service actually sends the "employee claim" of the user to the AdventureWorks STS. This STS verifies that the user really is an employee and returns a token containing a verified "the user is an employee of AdventureWorks" claim.

- The application then sends this new claim to the STS inside the Fabrikam organization. The Fabrikam STS verifies the authenticity of this claim to establish that it is genuine and was issued by a recognized partner organization, and then issues another token containing an authenticated claim that the client application uses to access the Fabrikam Web service.

Figure 17-2 depicts the flow of claims and security tokens described by this scenario.

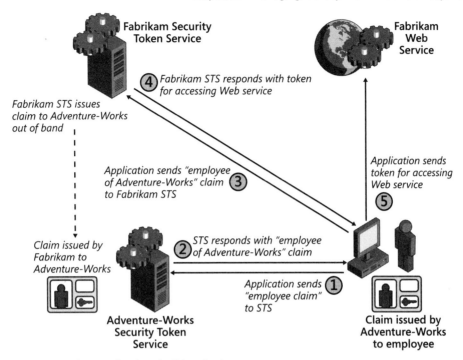

FIGURE 17-2 Cooperating Security Token Services.

> **Note** This is a somewhat simplified view of the process, and there are other security aspects that a scheme like this requires you to implement, such as authenticating and protecting the physical communications between organizations.

The Fabrikam organization can issue similar claims to other partner companies so that their employees can access the Fabrikam service as well. If Fabrikam wishes to withdraw the rights of a partner company, it needs to rescind only a single claim. Of course, Fabrikam can issue individual claims to its own employees as well.

This mechanism is generally referred to as *federated security*. Each user is authenticated, but the authentication is the responsibility of the individual organizations to which they belong. Internally, each organization operates in an autonomous manner, implementing its own security policies and authenticating users in its own way.

A key aspect of federated security is the confidence that different organizations have with each other's authentication mechanisms. As long as an organization implements a strong security policy, partner organizations can trust that if the organization maintains that "user x is valid," then that user is genuinely valid. Security is always a matter of confidence and trust. In the past, different organizations have tried to protect their systems from unauthorized access by using a wide variety of techniques, often based on proprietary protocols. This frequently becomes a problem as soon as organizations need to share information with each other, using ad hoc solutions that often open holes in the security infrastructure of these organizations. The increasing use of STSs and the adoption of the various WS-* protocols can help to standardize the way in which organizations protect their communications and their users, making their security mechanisms more interoperable.

Implementing federated security is a non-trivial exercise, but to assist you Microsoft has released Windows Identity Foundation (WIF). This is the new identity model framework for Windows, and it provides many of the features needed to build claims-based applications and services, configuring federated security, and supporting CardSpace information cards. WIF also includes a class called *SecurityTokenService* that you can extend to build your own custom STSs (WIF provides a Visual Studio template, "WCF Security Token Service," which generates a class and configuration based on the *SecurityTokenService* class).

WIF is a large framework in its own right, and the details of how to use it are beyond the bounds of this book, but for more information, visit the Microsoft Windows Identity Foundation page at *http://msdn.microsoft.com/en-us/security/aa570351.aspx*. Together with CardSpace and WCF, WIF provides an important set of tools for helping to implement identity management and federated security in a simple-to-use but robust manner.

Summary

In this chapter, you have seen how to use Windows CardSpace to implement claims-based security. You have learned how to configure a WCF client application and service to interact with Windows CardSpace and how to use a self-issued card to send a claim to a service. You have seen how a service can query the values of claims it receives to authorize access to operations. You have also looked at how to configure a client application and service to use an STS for authenticating claims. Finally, you have seen how organizations can use claims-based authentication and STSs to implement federated security.

Chapter 18
Integrating with ASP.NET Clients and Enterprise Services Components

After completing this chapter, you will be able to:

- Create a WCF service that can interoperate with an ASP.NET client application.

- Integrate a COM+ application into a WCF solution.

A key feature of WCF is the ability to use it to build heterogeneous solutions, protecting your existing investment in existing components and software. WCF is based on commonly accepted WS-* standards and protocols. This means that you can create services that can communicate with client applications running on platforms other than Microsoft Windows and developed using other technologies (such as Java), as long as they conform to the same WS-* standards and use the same protocols. If you publish the metadata for your WCF service, many Java tools vendors provide utilities that can query this metadata and generate Java proxy classes, in much the same way that *svcutil* does. The converse situation is also true. You can use WCF to build client applications that connect to Java Web services—again, as long as those Java Web services conform to the same WS-* standards and protocols as WCF. If these services publish their metadata, you can use the *svcutil* utility to generate proxy classes for these services.

You may also have a number of components, services, and applications created by using Microsoft technologies that predate WCF, such as COM+ and ASP.NET. Again, WCF protects your investment in these technologies by letting you to integrate these items into a WCF solution.

This chapter describes two common scenarios. First, you will see how to configure a WCF service to enable interoperability with a legacy ASP.NET Web client application. Then you will learn how to integrate a legacy COM+ application into a WCF solution by exposing it as a WCF service.

Creating a WCF Service That Supports an ASP.NET Client

Microsoft developed ASP.NET as a framework for building Web applications. It includes a large number of components that developers can incorporate into interactive Web pages, and a structure for processing requests and generating Web pages in response to those requests. Part of the ASP.NET framework is concerned with building Web services. However, the Web services model implemented by ASP.NET now seems quite primitive, as it does not provide support for many of the WS-* protocols that have emerged in recent years. Consequently, ASP.NET Web services and client applications cannot easily make use of the WS-* specifications that cover features such as reliable sessions, transactions, or even message-level security (ASP. NET provides its own implementation of some of these features, and you can use transport-level security over the HTTPS transport to protect messages).

Microsoft subsequently released the Web Services Enhancements (WSE) as an add-on to ASP. NET. WSE included support for some selected WS-* standards; however, WSE was just a temporary solution, and you should consider using WCF for all new Web service development. However, it is probably not feasible for your organization to suddenly stop using your existing ASP.NET services and applications while you build new versions with WCF. Furthermore, if your ASP.NET Web services and client applications are functioning perfectly, why should you replace them? You are far more likely to migrate Web services to WCF in a piecemeal fashion, either as you need to add new features to a specific Web service or as you retire a service and replace it with a Web service that implements new functionality. Additionally, it might not be feasible or desirable to migrate existing ASP.NET Web client applications to WCF. Consequently, you might have a large number of ASP.NET Web client applications in everyday use in your organization that need to be able to connect to ASP.NET and WCF Web services. It is therefore important to understand how to support existing ASP.NET Web client applications in a WCF service.

In the following exercise, you will see how to build a WCF service that an ASP.NET Web client application can access (WCF client applications can also access it, of course).

Examine an Existing ASP.NET Web Service and Client Application

1. Using Visual Studio, open the solution file ASPNETProductsService.sln located in the Microsoft Press\WCF Step By Step\Chapter 18\ASPNETService folder (within your Documents folder).

   This solution contains an ASP.NET Web service called *ASPNETProductsService* and a client application that connects to this service. Both applications are legacy applications that were constructed by using the .NET Framework version 2.0.

> **Note** In this exercise, assume that the *ASPNETProductsService* Web service is a copy of a production Web service deployed elsewhere in your organization by using IIS and implementing transport-level security. For ease of testing and configuration, this copy of the Web service executes using the ASP.NET Development Web Server supplied with Visual Studio and consequently does not support SSL and the HTTPS protocol. However, the Web client application can be configured to connect to the Web service over an HTTPS connection, and you *will* provide transport-level security when you implement the WCF version of the Web service.

2. Using Solution Explorer, open the ASPNETProductsService.cs file in the App_Code folder of the C:\...\ASPNETProductsService project and examine its contents in the Code And Text Editor window.

This Web service is a legacy ASP.NET version of the *ProductsService* service, providing the *ListProducts*, *GetProduct*, *CurrentStockLevel*, and *ChangeStockLevel* Web methods. However, the Web methods use ADO.NET rather than the Entity Framework to access the *AdventureWorks* database (the Web service was created before the Entity Framework was available). Also, because some of the Web methods construct raw SQL statements from the parameters passed in, they check that these parameters do not contain character sequences or strings that are indicative of a possible SQL injection attack.

The web.config file contains the connection string that the application uses to connect to the database.

> **Important** If you are not running a local instance of SQL Server Express, you will need to modify the *value* property of the configuration setting in this file to connect to the correct server.

The ASPNETProductsService.cs file provides an implementation of the *Product* class, tagged with the *Serializable* attribute to enable the ASP.NET runtime to transfer instances back to the ASP.NET client application.

Notice the namespace and name of the Web service (the *ASPNETProductsService* class). The namespace dates back to 2005, when the service was built; the WCF version of the Web service will use this same namespace to remain compatible with existing ASP.NET client applications, as shown in the following code example:

```
[WebService(Namespace = "http://adventure-works.com/2005/01/01",
            Name = "ProductsService")]
public class ASPNETProductsService : System.Web.Services.WebService,
                                     IProductsService
{
    ...
}
```

3. In the C:\...\ASPNETProductsService project, right-click the ASPNETProductsService.asmx file, and then select View In Browser.

Internet Explorer starts and displays the list of Web methods implemented by the service. Display the WSDL description of the Web service by clicking the Service Description link displayed on this page.

In the WSDL document displayed by Internet Explorer, note the following points:

❑ The return type of the *ListProducts* Web method (List<string>) is serialized as a sequence of strings in a type named *ArrayOfString* in the *http://adventure-works/2005/01/01* schema.

❑ The *Product* type is also in the *http://adventure-works/2005/01/01* schema. It has four elements named, in order: *Name*, *ProductNumber*, *Color*, and *ListPrice*.

❑ The SOAP action for the *ListProducts* Web method is *http://adventure-works/2005/01/01/ListProducts*.

❑ The SOAP action for the *GetProduct* Web method is *http://adventure-works/2005/01/01/GetProduct*.

❑ The SOAP action for the *CurrentStockLevel* Web method is *http://adventure-works/2005/01/01/CurrentStockLevel*.

❑ The SOAP action for the *ChangeStockLevel* Web method is *http://adventure-works/2005/01/01/ChangeStockLevel*.

Close Internet Explorer when you have finished browsing the WSDL document and return to Visual Studio.

4. In Solution Explorer, open the Program.cs file for the ASPNETProductsClient project in the Code And Text Editor window. You should recognize much of the code in this application. It connects to the ASP.NET Web service and tests each of the Web methods in turn.

The client application makes use of a Web service proxy generated by Visual Studio using the *Add Web Reference* command. You will use this same proxy to connect to the WCF service later.

> **Note** In the production environment, the Web service uses the *ASPNETProductsService* certificate to protect communications with the client application (this version of the Web service currently does not use this level of protection because it runs using the ASP.NET Development Server in this exercise). In a subsequent exercise, you will use a test certificate generated by using the *makecert* utility, so the client application contains code that invokes the *Enact* method of the *PermissiveCertificatePolicy* class to bypass certificate verification (you saw this class in Chapter 4, "Protecting an Enterprise WCF Service"). Once again, it is worth emphasizing that the *PermissiveCertificatePolicy* class is provided for testing purposes only because we do not have access to a genuine certificate; you should never include it in a production environment.

5. Open the app.config file in the ASPNETProductsClient project by using the Code And Text Editor. This configuration file contains the *ASPNETProductsClient_ProductsService_ProductsService* setting. This setting was generated by the *Add Web Reference* command in Visual Studio (the Add Web Reference command generates a proxy and configuration

file for accessing an ASP.NET Web service, in the same way that the Add Service Reference commands generates a proxy for a WCF service). It specifies the address of the ASP.NET Web service.

6. Start the solution without debugging. The ASP.NET Development Server starts, and the client application runs. The client application console generates a list of all product numbers, displays the details of a water bottle, displays the stock level of water bottles, and then updates this stock level.

Press Enter to close the client application console when the application has finished.

You have now seen the existing ASP.NET Web service and client application. Your next task is to implement a WCF service that provides the same functionality. Other than making minor modifications to the configuration file to refer to the new service, the ASP.NET client application must be able to connect to the WCF service and run unchanged using the .NET Framework 2.0.

Implement a WCF Service to Replace the ASP.NET Web Service

1. Add a new project to the solution by using the WCF Service Library template, which is located in the WCF folder, in the list of installed templates in the Add New Project dialog box. Name the project **WCFProductsService** and save it in the **Microsoft Press\ WCF Step By Step\Chapter 18\ASPNETService** folder (within your Documents folder).

2. In Solution Explorer, rename the file IService1.cs to **IProductsService.cs**. Allow Visual Studio to change references to the *IService1* types to *IProductsService*.

3. Open the IProductsService.cs file in the Code And Text Editor and remove all comments and code except for the *using* statements at the top of the file.

4. Copy the code for the *Product* class, and the *IProductsService* interface from the ASPNET ProductsService.cs file in the App_Code folder in the C:\...\ASPNETProductsService project to the IProductsService.cs file.

5. In the IProductsService.cs file, modify the definition of the *Product* class as follows:

   ❏ Replace the *Serializable* attribute for the *Product* class with the *DataContract* attribute.

   ❏ Set the *Namespace* property of the *DataContract* attribute to **http://adventure-works.com/2005/01/01**. This is the namespace expected by the legacy ASP.NET client application. If you specify a different namespace, the ASP.NET client application will not be able to connect to it without making changes to the code.

   ❏ Tag each member of the *Product* class with a *DataMember* attribute to ensure that the members are serialized in the same order in which they appear in the class, and that they have the correct names in the serialization stream.

The *Product* class should now look like this (the new additions are shown in bold):

```
// Data contract describing the details of a product
[DataContract (Namespace="http://adventure-works.com/2005/01/01")]
public class Product
{
    [DataMember(Order=0, Name="Name")]
    public string Name;

    [DataMember(Order=1, Name="ProductNumber")]
    public string ProductNumber;

    [DataMember(Order=2, Name="Color")]
    public string Color;

    [DataMember(Order=3, Name="ListPrice")]
    public decimal ListPrice;
}
```

6. By default, the WCF service will serialize the *List<string>* value returned by the *ListProducts* operation using a different type and schema from that expected by the ASP.NET client application, which expects an *ArrayOfString* type in the *http://adventure-works.com/ 2005/01/01* namespace. Add the following class to the IProductsService.cs file underneath the *Product* class:

```
// Data contract for seralizing a list of strings
// using the same schema as the ASP.NET Web service
[CollectionDataContract(Namespace = "http://adventure-works.com/2005/01/01")]
public class ArrayOfString : List<string>
{
}
```

The *CollectionDataContract* attribute indicates that the class is a collection and that it will be serialized appropriately as a series of elements.

7. Make the following modification to the *IProductsService* interface:

   ❑ Add the *ServiceContract* attribute shown in bold in the code that follows. In this attribute, specify the namespace (**http://adventure-works.com/2005/01/01**) and name (**ProductsService**) expected by the ASP.NET client application.

   ❑ Specify that the service should support sessions (*SessionMode.Allowed*).

   ❑ Mark each method with an *OperationContract* attribute that explicitly specifies the names of the *Action* and *ReplyAction* messages.

   ❑ Change the return type of the *ListProducts* operation to **ArrayOfString**.

   The *IProductsService* interface should look like this (the new additions are shown in bold):

```
// ASP.NET compatible version of the service contract
[ServiceContract(Namespace = "http://adventure-works.com/2005/01/01",
                 Name = "ProductsService",
                 SessionMode = SessionMode.Allowed)]
```

```
public interface IProductsService
{
    // Get the product number of selected products
    [OperationContract(
        Action = "http://adventure-works.com/2005/01/01/ListProducts",
        ReplyAction = "http://adventure-works.com/2005/01/01/ListProductsResponse")]
    [TransactionFlow(TransactionFlowOption.Allowed)]
    ArrayOfString ListProducts();

    // Get the details of a single product
    [OperationContract(
        Action = "http://adventure-works.com/2005/01/01/GetProduct",
        ReplyAction = "http://adventure-works.com/2005/01/01/GetProductResponse")]
    [TransactionFlow(TransactionFlowOption.Allowed)]
    Product GetProduct(string productNumber);

    // Get the current stock level for a product
    [OperationContract(
        Action = "http://adventure-works.com/2005/01/01/CurrentStockLevel",
        ReplyAction =
            "http://adventure-works.com/2005/01/01/CurrentStockLevelResponse")]
    [TransactionFlow(TransactionFlowOption.Allowed)]
    int CurrentStockLevel(string productNumber);

    // Change the stock level for a product
    [OperationContract(
        Action = "http://adventure-works.com/2005/01/01/ChangeStockLevel",
        ReplyAction =
            "http://adventure-works.com/2005/01/01/ChangeStockLevelResponse")]
    [TransactionFlow(TransactionFlowOption.Allowed)]
    bool ChangeStockLevel(string productNumber, int newStockLevel,
string shelf, int bin);
}
```

> **Note** WCF can automatically generate names for the *Action* and *ReplyAction* messages,
> based on the *namespace* and *name* properties of the service contract, but it is better to
> be explicit in this case. Additionally, WCF includes the name of the service contract when
> it generates message names, whereas the ASP.NET client application only expects the mes-
> sages to be named after the namespace. For example, the default message name gener-
> ated by WCF for the action for the *ListProducts* operation would be *http://adventure-works.
> com/2005/01/01/ProductsService/ListProducts*. However, the ASP.NET client application
> expects the action message to be named *http://adventure-works.com/2005/01/01/
> ListProducts*.

8. In Solution Explorer, delete the Service1.cs file from the WCFProductsService project
and add the ProductsService.cs file located in the Microsoft Press\WCF Step By Step\
Chapter 18 folder.

This file contains an implementation of the *ProductsService* service similar to that shown
in previous chapters. The code uses the Entity Framework to access the *AdventureWorks*

database rather than building SQL statements and executing them by using ADO.NET. The principal differences are:

- ❑ The *ListProducts* method returns an *ArrayOfString* object rather than a *List<string>* collection.

- ❑ The *newStockLevel* parameter to the *ChangeStockLevel* operation is an *int* rather than a *short*.

9. Add a reference to the *ProductsEntityModel* assembly to the WCFProductsService proj-ect. This assembly is located in the Microsoft Press\WCF Step By Step\Chapter 18 folder. Add a reference to the *System.Data.Entity* assembly as well.

10. In Solution Explorer, remove the C:\...\ASPNETProductsService project from the solution, and then build the WCFProductsService project.

You will use the familiar WPF application to host the WCF service. In doing so, you can imple-ment transport-level security for testing purposes.

Configure the WCF Host Application and Service

1. Add the ProductsServiceHost project located in the Microsoft Press\WCF Step By Step\Chapter 18\ProjectsServiceHost folder to the solution.

2. Add a reference to the WCFProductsService project to the ProductsServiceHost project.

3. Open the App.config file for the ProductsServiceHost project in the Code And Text Editor window.

   The configuration file defines a single service endpoint with an address of *https://localhost:8040/ProductsService/Service.svc*. The binding this endpoint uses is *basicHttpBinding*. The *basicHttpBinding* binding is designed for maximum interoperability with Web services and client applications that do not make use of any WS-* standards, such as ASP.NET client applications.

4. Build the solution.

5. Open a Visual Studio Command Prompt window as Administrator. Type the following command to create and install the certificate for the *ASPNETProductsService* service (refer back to Chapter 4 for a detailed explanation of using certificates to provide transport-level security):

```
makecert -sr LocalMachine -ss My -n CN=ASPNETProductsService -sky exchange
```

6. Using the Certificates snap-in in the Microsoft Management Console, retrieve the thumbprint for the *ASPNETProductsService* service from the Personal certificates store for the local computer (refer back to the exercise, "Configure the WCF HTTP Endpoint with an SSL Certificate" in Chapter 4 for a detailed description of how to do this).

7. In the Visual Studio Command Prompt window, type the following command to associate the certificate with port 8040 (the port used by the WCF service), replacing the
string of digits specified by the *certhash* argument with the thumbprint of your certificate (note that you should enter the command on a single line):

```
netsh http add sslcert ipport=0.0.0.0:8040
    certhash=cf60efed47ae63d73005c6cfa5807b3673176e98
    appid={00112233-4455-6677-8899-AABBCCDDEEFF}
```

8. Type the following command to add a new HTTPS reservation for port 8000 (replace
UserName with the name of your Windows account and make sure that you specify
https in the URL):

```
netsh http add urlacl url=https://+:8040/ user=UserName
```

9. Leave the Visual Studio Command Prompt window open and return to Visual Studio.

Test the ASP.NET Client Application

1. In Solution Explorer, open the app.config file ASPNETProductsClient project by using
the Code And Text Editor window. In the *<applicationSettings>* section of this file,
change the value of the ASPNETProductsClient_ProductsService_ProductsService setting
to **https://localhost:8040/ProductsService/Service.svc**. This is the URL of the WCF
service exposed by the ProductsServiceHost application. Save the file.

> **Important** Make sure that you specify the **https** scheme in this URL; otherwise, the client
> application will hang when it attempts to connect to the WCF service.

> **Note** In a production environment, an administrator would not have access to the source
> code and Visual Studio project files for the ASPNETProductsClient project. Consequently,
> the administrator would simply edit the ASPNETProductsClient.exe.config file deployed
> with the ASPNETProductsClient application and make this same change.

2. Set the ProductsServiceHost project as the startup project for the solution.

3. Rebuild the solution and start without debugging. In the Products Service Host window,
click Start.

4. Using Windows Explorer, move to the Microsoft Press\WCF Step By Step\Chapter 18
\ASPNETService\ASPNETProductsClient\bin\Debug folder within your Documents folder.
This folder contains the compiled executable for the ASP.NET client application.

5. In Windows Explorer, double-click the file ASPNETProductsClient.exe to start the ASP.NET
client application.

The client application runs exactly as before, except this time it connects to the WCF service rather than the ASP.NET Web service. You can verify this if you stop the WCF service and run the ASP.NET client application again; it should fail with the message "Exception: Unable to connect to the remote server."

6. When you have finished, in the Products Service Host window, click Stop, and then close the application.

7. Close Visual Studio.

The key to building a WCF service that can be accessed by applications created using other technologies is interoperability. You have seen throughout this book how WCF implements many of the standard WS-* standards and protocols, making it compatible with applications and services that adhere to these standards and protocols. To provide connectivity to older applications, like those created by using ASP.NET, you must ensure that you provide a binding that conforms to the limited functionality available to these applications. For maximum interoperability, you should supply a binding that is compatible with the WS-I Basic Profile. When you are building a WCF service, this essentially means using the *BasicHttpBinding* binding and not mandating the use of message-level security, transactions, or reliable messaging. However, there is nothing to stop you from adding further bindings that do enable these features for other capable client applications to use.

The WS-I Basic Profile and WCF Services

The WS-I Basic Profile constitutes a set of recommendations for building interoperable Web services. It was defined by the Web Services Interoperability Organization and describes how a Web service should apply many of the core Web services specifications that are not covered by the WS-* specifications, such as the SOAP messaging format, generating a WSDL description of a Web service, and defining the metadata to enable Web service discovery using Universal Description, Discovery, and Integration (UDDI). The WS-I Basic Profile essentially describes the lowest common denominator for features that a Web service must provide and remain useful. Web services that conform to the WS-I Basic Profile will be interoperable with client applications and other Web services that also conform to the WS-I Basic Profile. (Web services that implement the WS-* specifications are only interoperable with other Web services that implement the same WS-*specifications.)

You can use the WCF *BasicHttpBinding* binding to configure and expose endpoints that the service can use to communicate with client applications and services that conform to the WS-I Basic Profile 1.1, including ASP.NET Web client applications.

You can download the specification for the WS-I Basic Profile 1.1 from the WS-I Web site at *http://www.ws-i.org/Profiles/BasicProfile-1.1.html*.

Exposing a COM+ Application as a WCF Service

Any reasonably-sized organization that has been using the Microsoft Windows platform for any length of time as the basis for their applications will doubtless have systems that make use of COM+ services and components. Indeed, COM+ provides a fundamental underpinning of many parts of the .NET Framework. The good news is that with WCF, you can leverage this technology and reuse your existing COM+ components by building a WCF service wrapper around them. The .NET Framework 4.0 includes a useful tool called *ComSvcConfig*, which you can use to integrate COM+ applications into the WCF service model (you can find this tool in the C:\WINDOWS\Microsoft.NET\Framework\v4.0.30319 folder, although this location will change as new versions and updates to the .NET Framework are released). Additionally, the WCF Service Configuration Editor provides a graphical user interface to many of the features available in the *ComSvcConfig* utility.

In the final set of exercises, you will use the WCF Service Configuration Editor and the *Com SvcConfig* utility to configure a legacy COM+ application so client applications can access it in the same way as they access a WCF service. The COM+ application provides an interface that is very similar to the *ProductsService* service you examined in the previous exercise. You will start by examining the code for this component, then you will deploy it by using the COM+ Services Console.

Deploy the Products COM+ Application to the COM+ Catalog

1. Start Visual Studio as Administrator and open the solution file Products.sln located in the Microsoft Press\WCF Step By Step\Chapter 18\Products folder within your Documents folder.

   This solution contains a COM+ version of the *ProductsService* service. It was built by using the .NET Framework 2.0.

   Note If you are interested in how this COM+ application has been structured, follow steps 2–4 below. However, this understanding is not crucial to the exercise, and if you have never implemented a COM+ application you can safely skip to step 5.

2. In Solution Explorer, open the Products.cs file in the Code And Text Editor window. Examine the *Product* class in the *Products* namespace. Notice that this class is very similar to the *Product* data contract you implemented in the WCF service. As with the ASP.NET Web service implementation, this class has been tagged with the *Serializable* attribute, as shown in the following:

```
[Serializable]
public class Product
{
    public string Name;
    public string ProductNumber;
```

```
        public string Color;
        public decimal ListPrice;
    }
```

3. Inspect the *IProductsService* interface. This interface defines the methods that the service exposes through COM+, in a manner very similar to a WCF service contract:

```
[ComVisible(true)]
[Guid("A04ED9CA-D61C-984B-AE4D-A164BDC90FD5")]
public interface IProductsService
{
    // Get the product number of selected products
    ICollection ListProducts();

    // Get the details of a single product
    Product GetProduct(string productNumber);

    // Get the current stock level for a product
    int CurrentStockLevel(string productNumber);

    // Change the stock level for a product
    bool ChangeStockLevel(string productNumber, int newStockLevel,
                          string shelf, int bin);
}
```

Apart from the attributes required by COM+ to identify the component, the most important difference between this and the WCF version of the interface is the return type of the *ListProducts* method. In the WCF service contract, the corresponding operation returns a *List<string>* type. COM+ does not support generics, so this version of the method returns an untyped *ICollection* object.

4. Examine the *ProductsService* class.

This class implements the *IProductsService* interface and is the equivalent of the service class in the WCF service. Additionally, this class inherits from the *ServicedComponent* class—this is the base class for COM+ serviced components. Notice that this COM+ component does not expose a class interface (the only functionality available is that specified in the *IProductsService* interface), but it supports transactions (this is common practice for COM+ applications):

```
[ClassInterface(ClassInterfaceType.None)]
[Transaction(TransactionOption.Supported)]
public class ProductsService : ServicedComponent, IProductsService
{
    ...
}
```

5. Open the app.config file in the Code And Text Editor window.

Like the ASP.NET Web service in the previous set of exercises, the Products COM+ application uses ADO.NET rather than the Entity Framework for accessing the *Adventure Works* database. The app.config file contains the connection string that the application uses to connect to the database.

6. Build the solution.

The project compiles into an assembly called *Products.dll*. This assembly is signed because you will deploy it to the .NET Framework Global Assembly Cache. (The file holding the strong name key used for signing the assembly is called *ProductsService.snk*, visible in Solution Explorer.)

7. Open a Visual Studio Command Prompt window as Administrator and move to the Microsoft Press\WCF Step By Step\Chapter 18\Products\Products\bin\Debug folder within your Documents folder.

8. Type the following command to deploy the *Products.dll* assembly to the Global Assembly Cache:

```
gacutil /i Products.dll
```

9. On the Windows Start menu click Control Panel, click System And Security, click Administrative Tools, and then double-click Component Services to start the Component Services console.

10. In the Component Services Console, in the left pane, expand the Component Service node, expand the Computers folder, expand My Computer, right-click the COM+ Applications folder, point to New, and then click Application.

The COM+ Application Install Wizard starts.

11. On the Welcome To The COM+ Application Install Wizard page, click Next.

12. On the Install Or Create A New Application page, click Create An Empty Application.

13. On the Create An Empty Application page, type **ProductsService** for the name of the application, ensure that the Activation Type is set to *Server Application*, and then click Next.

14. On the Set Application Identity page, accept the default settings (Interactive User), and then click Next.

15. On the Add Application Roles page, click Next.

16. On the Add Users To Roles page, click Next.

17. On the Thank You For Using The COM+ Application Install Wizard page, click Finish.

The ProductsService application should appear in the list of COM+ applications, as shown in the image that follows.

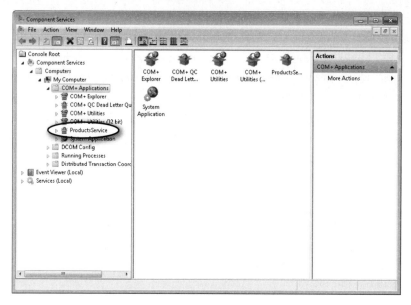

18. Expand the ProductsService application, right-click the Components folder, point to New, and then click Component.

    The COM+ Component Install Wizard starts.

19. On the Welcome To The COM+ Component Install Wizard page, click Next.

20. On the Import Or Install A Component page, click Install New Component(s).

21. In the Select Files To Install dialog box, move to the Microsoft Press\WCF Step By Step\ Chapter 18\Products\Products\bin\Debug folder within your Documents folder. Click the *Products.dll* assembly, and then click Open.

22. On the Install New Components page, verify that the *Products.ProductsService* component is correctly identified, as shown in the following image, and then click Next:

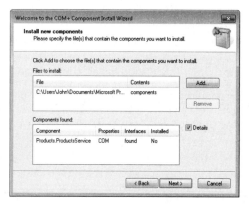

23. On the Thank You For Using The COM+ Component Install Wizard page, click Finish.

24. Refresh and expand the Components folder under the ProductsService application in the Component Services console. After a short delay, the *Products.ProductsService* component should appear:

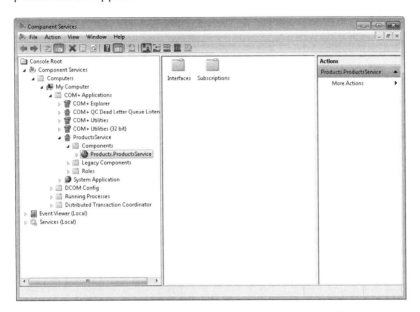

25. Leave the Component Services console open and return to Visual Studio.

You can now configure the COM+ application to make it available like a WCF service. The simplest way to do this is to create a new WCF application configuration file and use the *Integrate* command in the WCF Service Configuration Editor. This command provides similar functionality to using the *ComSvcConfig* utility from the command line.

Configure the Products COM+ Application as a WCF Service

1. In Visual Studio, on the Tools menu, click WCF Service Configuration Editor.

2. In the WCF Service Configuration Editor, on the File menu, point to Integrate, and then select COM+ Application.

The COM+ Integration Wizard starts.

3. On the Which Component Interface Would You Like To Integrate? page, expand the *ProductsService* node, expand the Components folder, expand the *Products.Products Service* component, expand the Interfaces folder, select the *IProductsService* interface, and then click Next.

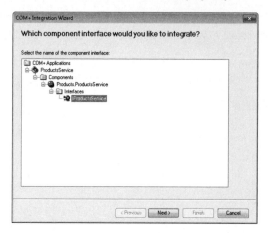

4. On the Which Methods Do You Want To Integrate? page, make sure that all four methods are selected, and then click Next.

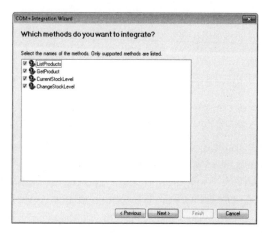

5. On the Which Hosting Mode Would You Like To Use? page, select COM+ Hosted, and then click Next.

   Note that by default, the wizard also creates an endpoint for metadata exchange. Leave this option enabled.

6. On the What Communication Mode Do You Want To Use? page, select HTTP, and then click Next.

7. On the What Is The Base Address Of Your Service? page, in the *Address* field, type **http://localhost:9090/COMProductsService**, and then click Next.

   Note that this is the base address of the service and not its URI. The wizard will generate an endpoint URI based on the name of the interface and append it to this base address. In this example, the URI of the service will actually be *http://localhost:9090/ COMProductsService/IProductsService*.

8. On the The Wizard Is Ready To Create A Service Configuration page, click Next.

9. Verify that the wizard completes without reporting any errors, and then click Finish.

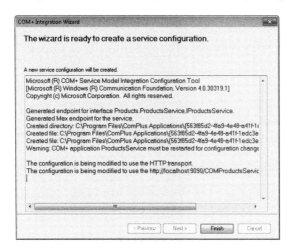

Note that when the wizard finishes, the configuration is *not* displayed in the WCF Service Configuration Editor.

10. In the WCF Service Configuration Editor, on the File menu, point to Open, and select COM+ Service.

A list of all COM+ applications configured as WCF services appears (just the Products Service application in this case).

Click the ProductsService application, and then click Select.

The configuration for this service is loaded and displayed in the WCF Service Configuration Editor.

The service is named using the same globally unique identifiers (GUIDs) that COM+ uses to identify the COM+ application and class. Make a note of the first GUID in the service name.

11. Expand the service and verify that it has two endpoints. One is based on the *wsHttp Binding* binding and is the endpoint that client applications connect to. The other is the metadata exchange endpoint.

   The COM+ component supports transactions, so the configuration file also includes transactional and nontransactional binding configurations for the *wsHttpBinding* and *netNamedPipeBinding* bindings. The binding configuration referenced by the HTTP endpoint refers to the binding that enables transactions by default.

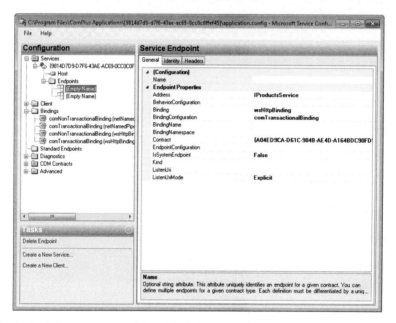

12. In the left pane, expand the COM Contracts folder. This folder appears only for COM+ applications configured as WCF services. Expand the child folder named after a GUID, and then click the *exposedMethods* node.

   The right pane displays the four methods available through this configuration. You can hide methods from client applications by clicking the Remove button in this pane. Do not change anything.

13. Close the WCF Service Configuration Editor. Do not save any changes if you are prompted (the configuration was saved earlier by the COM+ Integration Wizard).

14. Start Notepad as an Administrator. On the File menu click Open and move to the C:\ Program Files\ComPlus Applications folder. This folder contains folders for each config- ured COM+ application. Move to the folder with the same GUID as the application ID of the COM+ application (this is the GUID that you noted in step 10).

This folder contains two files: a manifest file, and an application configuration file. The application configuration file is the file you have just created using the COM+ Integration Wizard in the WCF Service Configuration Editor.

> **Note** You will need to select All Files (*.*) in the drop-down list adjacent to the File Name text box to see these files.

Select the application.config file, and then click Open.

15. Leave Notepad open and return to Visual Studio. In Solution Explorer, open the app.config file for the Products project in the Code And Text Editor window.

Copy the *<appSettings>* section of this file to the Windows clipboard. This section contains the connect string that the component requires to connect to the *AdventureWorks* database.

Return to Notepad and paste the contents of the Windows clipboard immediately after the opening *<configuration>* tag and before the *<system.ServiceModel>* tag, as shown in bold in the following:

```
<?xml version="1.0" encoding="utf-8"?>
<configuration>
  <appSettings>
    <add key="AdventureWorksConnection" value=
    "Database=AdventureWorks;Server=(local)\SQLEXPRESS;IntegratedSecurity=SSPI;"/>
  </appSettings>
  <system.serviceModel>
    ...
  </system.serviceModel>
</configuration>
```

16. Save the application.config file, and then close Notepad.

You should now be able to connect to this COM+ application from a client application, just like it was any other type of WCF service.

Test the Products COM+ Application

1. Return to the Visual Studio Command Prompt window running as Administrator and type the following command (replace *UserName* with your Windows user name):

```
netsh http add urlacl url=http://+:9000/ user=UserName
```

2. Switch to the Component Services console, right-click the ProductsService application in the COM+ Applications folder, and then click Start.

3. Start Internet Explorer and move to the URL *http://localhost:9090/COMProductsService*.

Internet Explorer displays the page describing how to create a client application for the WCF service:

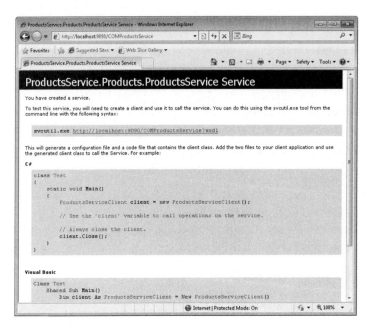

4. Click the link *http://localhost:9090/COMProductsService?wsdl*. The WSDL description of the service appears.

5. Close Internet Explorer.

6. In Visual Studio, open the solution file ProductsClient.sln located in the Microsoft Press\ WCF Step By Step\Chapter 18\ProductsClient folder.

This solution contains a copy of the client application for testing the *ProductsService* service. This code is not quite complete; you will add a statement to create the proxy object in a later step.

7. Open the Program.cs file. There is one small change to this code compared with the program you saw in previous chapters: the statement in the *Main* method that invokes the *ListProducts* operation returns the result into an *ICollection* object rather than a *List<string>*, for the reasons described earlier:

```
ICollection productNumbers = proxy.ListProducts();
```

8. In the Project menu, click Add Service Reference. In the Add Service Reference dialog box, enter **http://localhost:9090/COMProductsService?wsdl** for the service URI in the Address field, and then click Go. In the Namespace field enter **ProductsService** for the service reference name, and then click OK.

Note If the Add Service Reference Wizard fails to download the metadata for the service successfully, it is probably because the component has stopped running (it stops if it is inactive for a while). In this case, return to the Component Services console, right-click the Products Service application in the COM+ Applications folder, click Start, and then try again.

Visual Studio generates a proxy class for the service and adds it to the Services References folder in Solution Explorer. It also creates an application configuration file.

9. Open the app.config file by using the Service Configuration Editor. In the Configuration pane, expand the Client folder, expand the Endpoints folder, and then click the *WSHttp Binding_IProductsService* endpoint.

This is the endpoint that the client application uses for accessing the *COMProducts Service* service. It is based on the *wsHttpBinding* binding.

10. In the Configuration pane, expand the Bindings folder, and then click the *WSHttp Binding_IProductsService* binding configuration. The date format employed by the COM+ application is not as compact as that used by a native WCF service, so you must increase the *MaxReceivedMessageSize* property to prevent the *ListProducts* method from causing an exception in the WCF runtime for the client. Change the value of this property to **100000**.

11. Save the configuration file, and then close the Service Configuration Editor.

12. Add the following *using* statement to the list at the top of the Program.cs file:

```
using ProductsClient.ProductsService;
```

The proxy class you just generated is in this namespace.

13. In the *Main* method, add the following statement (shown in bold) before the *try* block to create the *proxy* object:

```
static void Main(string[] args)
{
    // Create a proxy object and connect to the service
    ProductsServiceClient proxy =
        new ProductsServiceClient("WSHttpBinding_IProductsService");

    // Test the operations in the service
    try
    {
        ...
    }
    ...
}
```

14. Start the solution without debugging.

The client application functions as it has done in previous chapters, generating a list of bicycle frames, displaying the details of a water bottle, and displaying the stock level of water bottles and then modifying this stock level.

> **Tip** If the client application console displays the error, "There was no endpoint listening at http://localhost:9090/COMProductsService/IProductsService that could accept the message," then the COM+ application has again probably shutdown due to inactivity. To restart the application, return to the Component Services console, right-click the Products Service application in the COM+ Applications folder, and then click Start.

15. Press Enter to close the client application console window.

As far as the client application is concerned, there is little discernable difference between this implementation of the service and previous versions constructed using WCF. The fact that it is a COM+ component is mostly transparent to the client application.

Summary

In this chapter, you have seen how to build WCF services that can interoperate with legacy ASP.NET Web client applications and how to integrate COM+ applications into a WCF solution. WCF also supports a number of other integration and interoperability scenarios. For example, you can register and configure a WCF service with a COM moniker, so you can access it from a COM environment such as Microsoft Office VBA, Visual Basic 6.0, or native Visual C++ COM components. You can also integrate WCF services with .NET Framework Remoting, and you can build WCF services that can interoperate with applications and services constructed using WSE. For more information, see the topic "Interoperability and Integration" in the Microsoft Windows SDK documentation. You can also find this topic online on the Microsoft Web site at *http://msdn.microsoft.com/en-us/library/ms730017.aspx*.

Index

About the Author

John Sharp is a Principal Technologist at Content Master Ltd, a technical authoring company based in the United Kingdom. There he researches and develops technical content for technical training courses, seminars, and white papers. Throughout his development career, John has been active in training, developing, and delivering courses. He has conducted training on subjects ranging from UNIX Systems Programming, to SQL Server Administration, to Enterprise Java Development.

John is deeply involved with .NET development, writing courses, building tutorials, and delivering conference presentations covering Visual C#, WCF, SQL Server, Visual J#, ASP.NET, and Windows Server AppFabric. Apart from *Windows Communication Foundation Step By Step*, John has also authored five editions of *Microsoft Visual C# Step By Step*, and *Microsoft Visual J# .NET*, all published by Microsoft Press.

What do you think of this book?

We want to hear from you!

To participate in a brief online survey, please visit:

microsoft.com/learning/booksurvey

Tell us how well this book meets your needs—what works effectively, and what we can do better. Your feedback will help us continually improve our books and learning resources for you.

Thank you in advance for your input!

Microsoft® *Press*

Stay in touch!

To subscribe to the *Microsoft Press® Book Connection Newsletter*—for news on upcoming books, events, and special offers—please visit:

microsoft.com/learning/books/newsletter